Scale 1: 500,000
or 8 miles to 1 inch
(5km to 1cm)

12th edition October 2009

© AA Media Limited 2009

Cartography:
All cartography in this atlas edited, designed and produced by the Mapping Services Department of AA Publishing (A04159).

 This product includes mapping data licensed from Ordnance Survey® with the permission of the Controller of Her Majesty's Stationery Office. © Crown copyright 2009. All rights reserved. Licence number 100021153.

 Land & Property Services. This is based upon Crown Copyright and is reproduced with the permission of the Land & Property Services under delegated authority from the Controller of Her Majesty's Stationery Office, © Crown Copyright and database rights 2009. Licence No 100,363. Permit No. 90022.

© Ordnance Survey Ireland/Government of Ireland Copyright Permit No. MP000109.

Publisher's notes:
Published by AA Publishing (a trading name of AA Media Limited, whose registered office is Fanum House, Basing View, Basingstoke, Hampshire RG21 4EA, UK. Registered number 06112600).

ISBN: 978 0 7495 6316 5

A CIP Catalogue record for this book is available from the British Library.

Disclaimer:
The contents of this atlas are believed to be correct at the time of the latest revision, it will not include any subsequent amended, new or temporary information including diversions and traffic control or enforcement systems. The publishers cannot be held responsible or liable for any loss or damage occasioned to any person acting or refraining from action as a result of any use or reliance on material in this atlas, nor for any errors, omissions or changes in such material. This does not affect your statutory rights.

The publishers would welcome information to correct any errors or omissions and to keep this atlas up to date. Please write to the Atlas Editor, AA Publishing, The Automobile Association, Fanum House, Basing View, Basingstoke, Hampshire RG21 4EA, UK.
Email: roadatlasfeedback@theaa.com

Printer:
Printed in China by Leo Paper Products.

GLOVEBOX ATLAS
BRITAIN
WITH 83 TOWN PLANS

Atlas contents

Map pages	II
Road map symbols	1
Road atlas Britain 1:500,000 scale	2–65
Index to places in Britain	66–81
County, administrative area map	66–67
Mileage charts	68 & 90
Britain	68
Ireland	90
Road atlas Ireland 1:1 million scale	82–89
Index to places in Ireland	91–94
Town plan section	95

GW00763828

Map pages

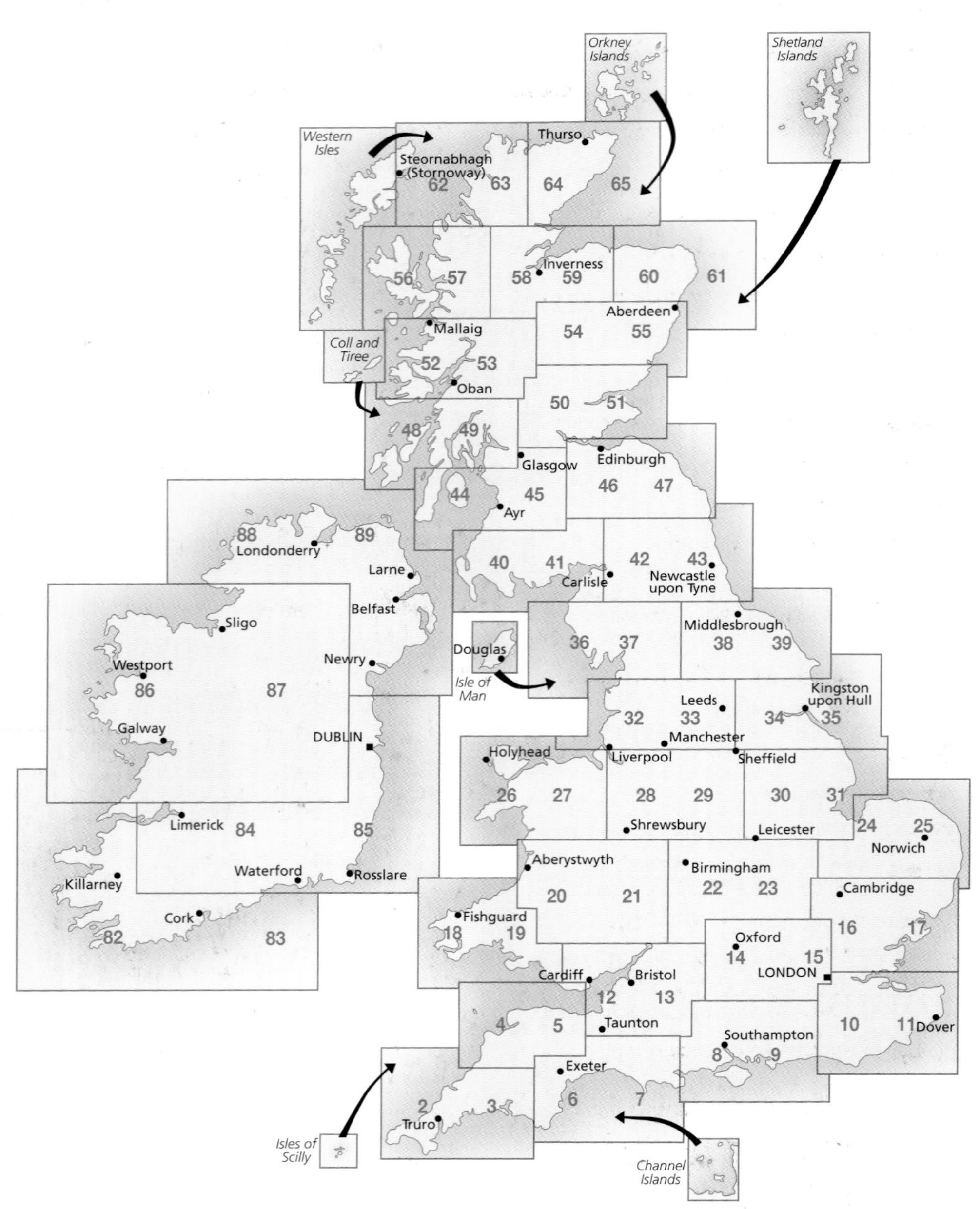

Orkney Islands

Shetland Islands

Western Isles

Thurso

Steornabhagh (Stornoway) 62   63   64   65

Inverness

56   57   58   59   60   61

Aberdeen

Mallaig   54   55

Coll and Tiree   52   53

Oban   50   51

48   49

Glasgow   Edinburgh

44   45   46   47

Ayr

88   89   Londonderry   Larne   40   41   42   43   Newcastle upon Tyne

Carlisle

Belfast   Sligo

Newry   Middlesbrough

36   37   38   39

Westport   Douglas

Isle of Man   Kingston upon Hull

86   87   Leeds   33   34   35

Galway   32   Manchester

DUBLIN   Holyhead   Liverpool   Sheffield

Limerick   84   85   26   27   28   29   30   31

Waterford   Rosslare   Shrewsbury   Leicester   24   25

Aberystwyth   Birmingham   Norwich

Killarney   Cork   20   21   22   23   Cambridge

82   83   Fishguard   16   17

18   19   Oxford   14   15   LONDON

Cardiff   Bristol   10   11   Dover

12   13

4   5   Taunton   Southampton

8   9

Exeter

2   3   6   7

Truro

Isles of Scilly

Channel Islands

Road map symbols

Britain

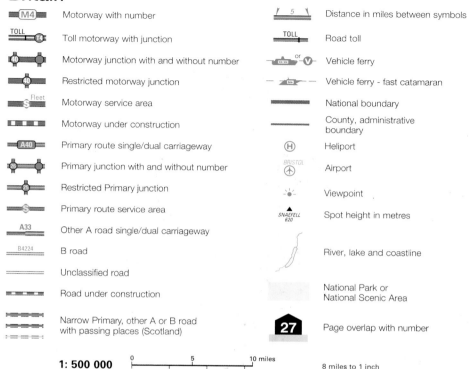

M4	Motorway with number
TOLL T4	Toll motorway with junction
40	Motorway junction with and without number
40	Restricted motorway junction
S Fleet	Motorway service area
	Motorway under construction
A40	Primary route single/dual carriageway
26	Primary junction with and without number
26	Restricted Primary junction
S	Primary route service area
A33	Other A road single/dual carriageway
B4224	B road
	Unclassified road
	Road under construction
	Narrow Primary, other A or B road with passing places (Scotland)

5	Distance in miles between symbols
TOLL	Road toll
or V	Vehicle ferry
	Vehicle ferry - fast catamaran
	National boundary
	County, administrative boundary
H	Heliport
BRISTOL	Airport
	Viewpoint
SNAEFELL 620	Spot height in metres
	River, lake and coastline
	National Park or National Scenic Area
27	Page overlap with number

1: 500 000   0 5 10 miles   0 5 10 15 kilometres   8 miles to 1 inch

Ireland

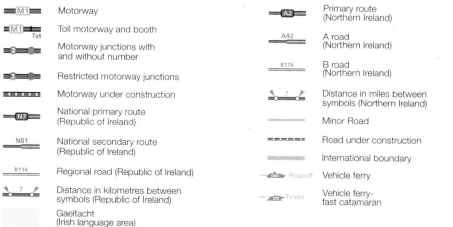

M1	Motorway
M1 Toll	Toll motorway and booth
8	Motorway junctions with and without number
3	Restricted motorway junctions
	Motorway under construction
N7	National primary route (Republic of Ireland)
N81	National secondary route (Republic of Ireland)
R116	Regional road (Republic of Ireland)
7	Distance in kilometres between symbols (Republic of Ireland)
	Gaeltacht (Irish language area)

A2	Primary route (Northern Ireland)
A42	A road (Northern Ireland)
B176	B road (Northern Ireland)
7	Distance in miles between symbols (Northern Ireland)
	Minor Road
	Road under construction
	International boundary
Roscoff	Vehicle ferry
Troon	Vehicle ferry-fast catamaran

1: 1 000 000   0 10 20 miles   0 10 20 30 kilometres   16 miles to 1 inch

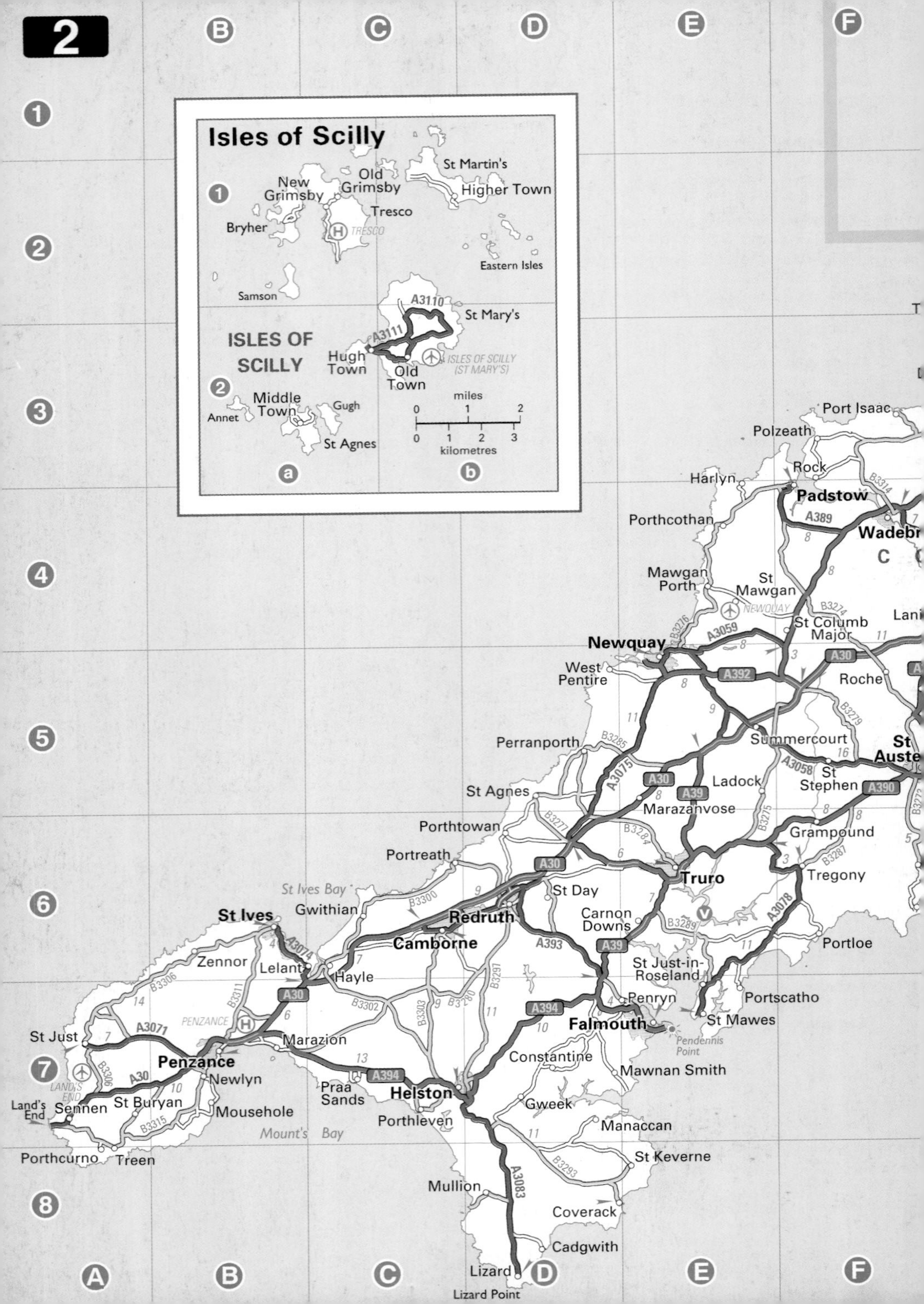

Isles of Scilly
St Martin's
Old Grimsby
New Grimsby
Higher Town
Tresco
Bryher
TRESCO
Eastern Isles
Samson
A3110
St Mary's
A3111
ISLES OF SCILLY
Hugh Town
ISLES OF SCILLY (ST MARY'S)
Old Town
Middle Town
Annet
Gugh
St Agnes
miles
kilometres
Port Isaac
Polzeath
Rock
Harlyn
Padstow
A389
Wadebr
Porthcothan
Mawgan Porth
St Mawgan
NEWQUAY
St Columb Major
A3059
Newquay
West Pentire
A30
A392
Roche
Perranporth
Summercourt
St Auste
A3075
A30
A39
Ladock
St Stephen
A3058
A390
St Agnes
Marazanvose
Porthtowan
Grampound
Portreath
A30
Truro
Tregony
St Ives Bay
St Day
Gwithian
Carnon Downs
St Ives
Redruth
A3078
Camborne
A393
A39
Portloe
Zennor
Lelant
Hayle
St Just-in-Roseland
Penryn
Portscatho
A30
A394
St Mawes
Falmouth
Pendennis Point
St Just
A3071
PENZANCE
Marazion
Constantine
Penzance
A30
Newlyn
A394
Mawnan Smith
LAND'S END
Land's End
Sennen
St Buryan
Praa Sands
Helston
Gweek
Mousehole
Porthleven
Manaccan
Mount's Bay
Porthcurno
Treen
St Keverne
A3083
Mullion
Coverack
Cadgwith
Lizard
Lizard Point

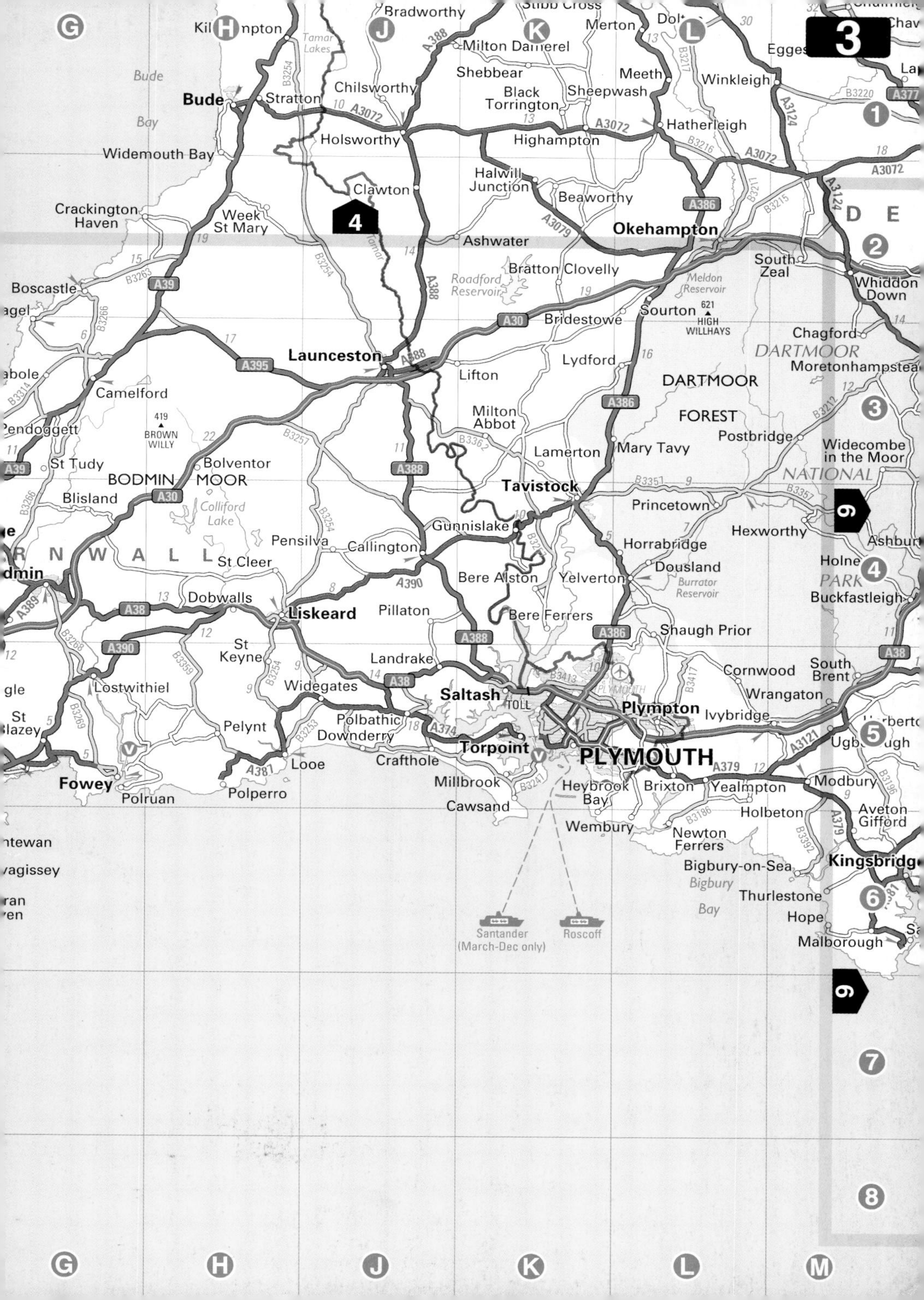

3
Bradworthy
Stibb Cross
Merton
Dolton
Chawleigh
Kilkhampton
Tamar Lakes
Milton Damerel
Eggesford
Bude
Shebbear
Meeth
Winkleigh
Stratton
Chilsworthy
Black Torrington
Sheepwash
Bude Bay
Holsworthy
Highampton
Hatherleigh
Widemouth Bay
Halwill Junction
Clawton
Beaworthy
Okehampton
Crackington Haven
Week St Mary
Ashwater
South Zeal
Boscastle
Bratton Clovelly
Whiddon Down
Roadford Reservoir
Meldon Reservoir
Tintagel
Bridestowe
Sourton
621 HIGH WILLHAYS
Chagford
Launceston
Lydford
DARTMOOR
Moretonhampstead
Lifton
DARTMOOR FOREST
Camelford
Milton Abbot
Postbridge
Widecombe in the Moor
Pendoggett
419 BROWN WILLY
Mary Tavy
Lamerton
NATIONAL
St Tudy
Bolventor
BODMIN MOOR
Tavistock
Princetown
Blisland
Colliford Lake
Hexworthy
Ashburton
Gunnislake
Pensilva
Callington
Horrabridge
CORNWALL
St Cleer
Dousland
Holne
Bodmin
Bere Alston
Yelverton
Burrator Reservoir
PARK
Buckfastleigh
Dobwalls
Liskeard
Pillaton
Bere Ferrers
Shaugh Prior
St Keyne
Landrake
Cornwood
South Brent
Lostwithiel
Widegates
Saltash
TOLL
PLYMOUTH
Wrangaton
Plympton
Ivybridge
St Blazey
Polbathic
Harbertonford
Pelynt
Downderry
Torpoint
Ugborough
Looe
Crafthole
PLYMOUTH
Fowey
Polruan
Polperro
Millbrook
Heybrook Bay
Brixton
Yealmpton
Modbury
Cawsand
Holbeton
Aveton Gifford
Wembury
Newton Ferrers
Pentewan
Mevagissey
Bigbury-on-Sea
Kingsbridge
Bigbury Bay
Thurlestone
Hope
Malborough
Santander (March-Dec only)
Roscoff
A388
A3072
A386
A3079
A39
A30
A395
A388
B3254
B3263
B3266
B3314
A388
B3257
B3362
A389
A38
A390
B3268
B3359
A374
A381
B3253
B3269
B3247
B3413
B3417
A379
A3121
B3186
B3392
B3196
A38
B3212
B3351
B3357
B3215
B3217
B3216
B3220
A3124
A377
DE
G
H
J
K
L
M
1
2
3
4
5
6
7
8
4
9
9

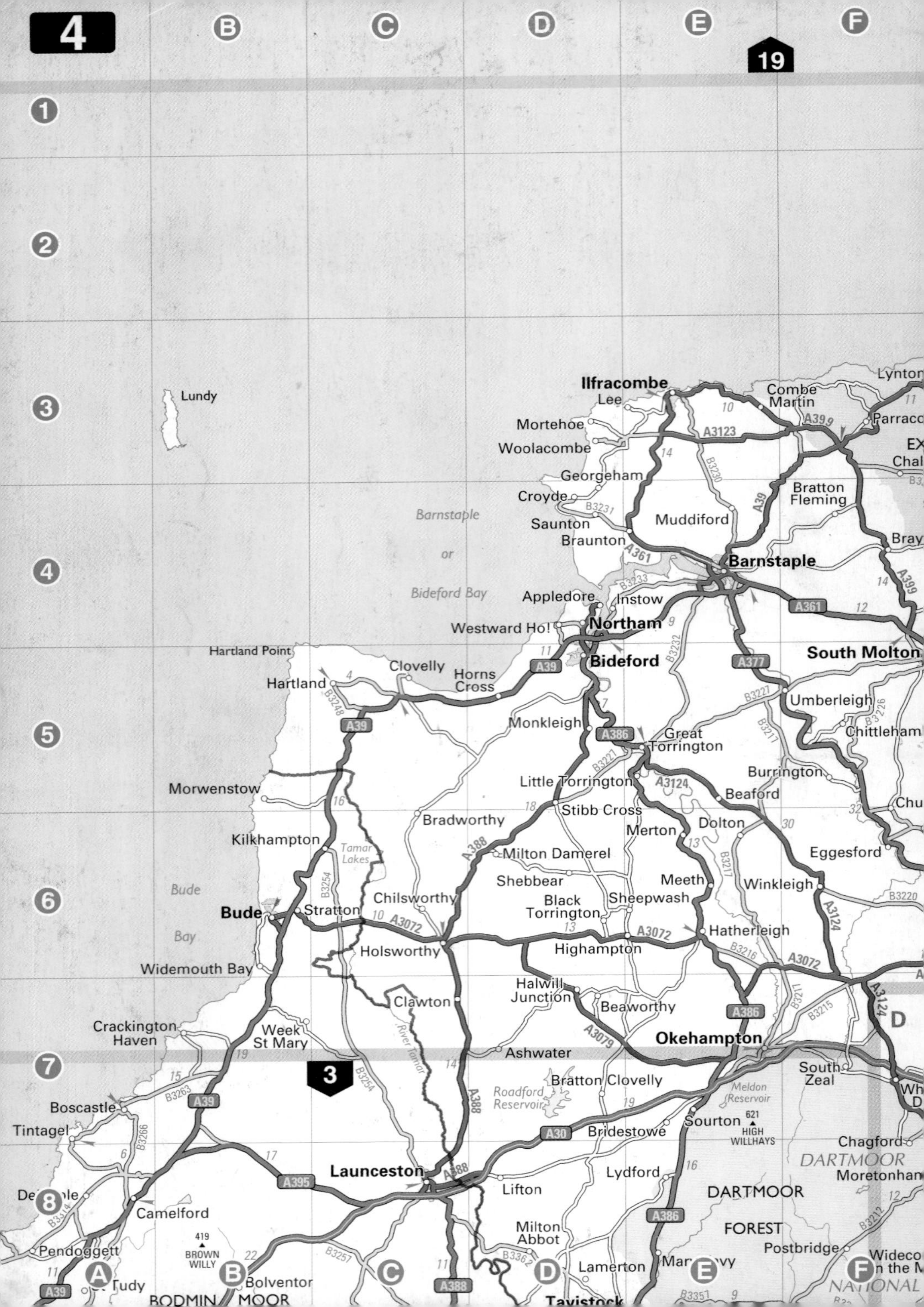
Lundy
Ilfracombe
Lee
Mortehoe
Woolacombe
Georgeham
Croyde
Saunton
Braunton
Combe Martin
Lynton
Parracombe
Bratton Fleming
Muddiford
Barnstaple
Bray
Barnstaple or Bideford Bay
Appledore
Instow
Westward Ho!
Northam
Bideford
Hartland Point
Hartland
Clovelly
Horns Cross
South Molton
Monkleigh
Umberleigh
Chittlehampton
Great Torrington
Little Torrington
Burrington
Beaford
Morwenstow
Bradworthy
Stibb Cross
Merton
Dolton
Kilkhampton
Tamar Lakes
Milton Damerel
Eggesford
Shebbear
Meeth
Winkleigh
Bude
Bude Bay
Stratton
Chilsworthy
Black Torrington
Sheepwash
Holsworthy
Highampton
Hatherleigh
Widemouth Bay
Halwill Junction
Beaworthy
Clawton
Crackington Haven
Week St Mary
Okehampton
Ashwater
River Tamar
South Zeal
Bratton Clovelly
Roadford Reservoir
Meldon Reservoir
Boscastle
Tintagel
Bridestowe
Sourton
621 HIGH WILLHAYS
Chagford
DARTMOOR
Moretonhampstead
Launceston
Lydford
Lifton
DARTMOOR FOREST
Camelford
Milton Abbot
Postbridge
Pendoggett
419 BROWN WILLY
Lamerton
Bolventor
BODMIN MOOR
Tavistock
Widecombe in the Moor
NATIONAL
A39
A3123
A399
B3230
B3231
A361
B3233
A377
B3232
B3248
A386
B3227
B3211
B3226
A3124
A388
B3254
B3217
B3220
A3072
B3216
A3079
B3215
B3263
A30
B3266
A395
B3314
B3257
B3362
B3351
B3212
19
3

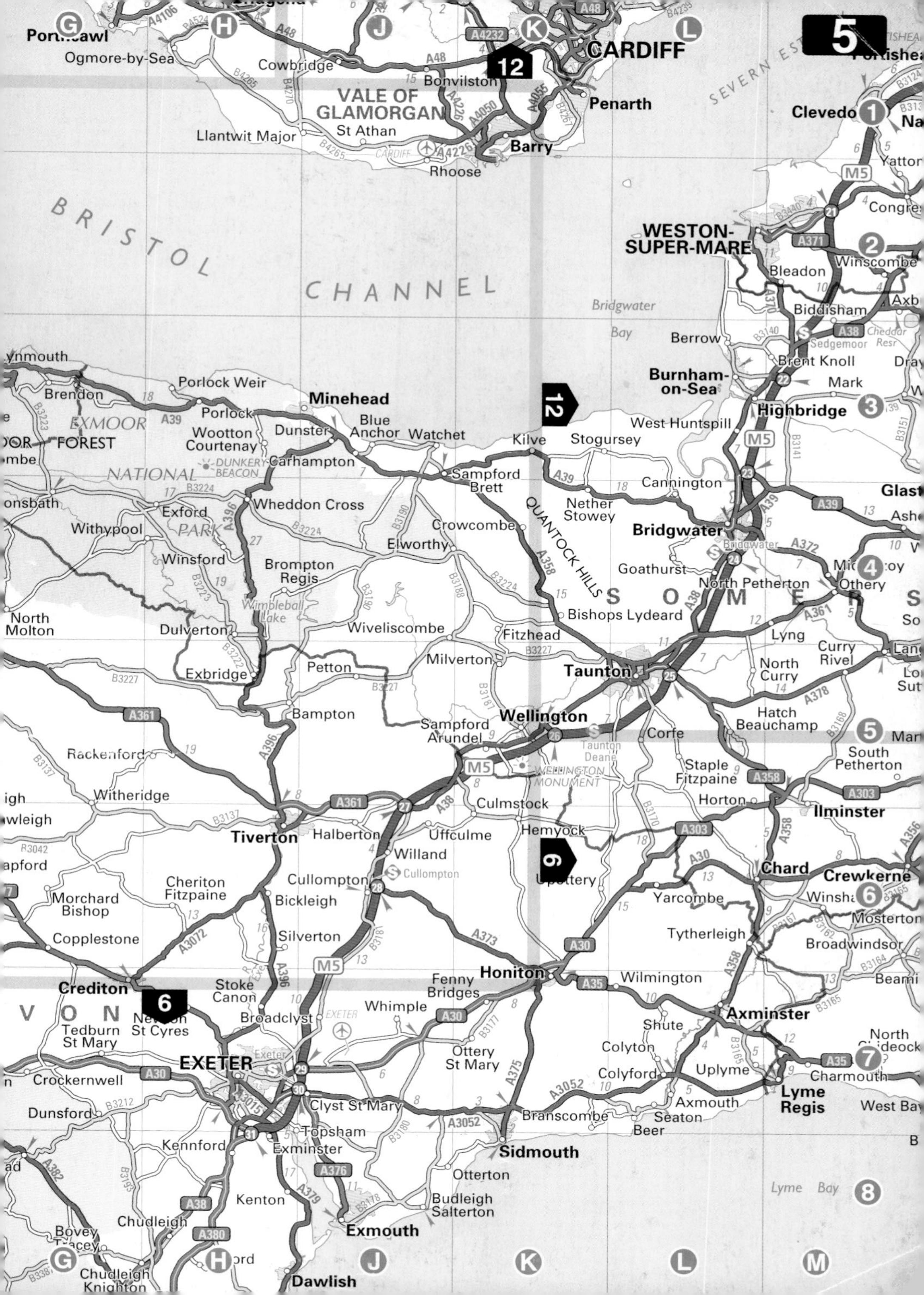
CARDIFF
Porthcawl
Ogmore-by-Sea
Cowbridge
Bonvilston
VALE OF GLAMORGAN
Llantwit Major
St Athan
Barry
Rhoose
Penarth
Portishead
Clevedon
Yatton
Congresbury
WESTON-SUPER-MARE
Winscombe
Bleadon
Axbridge
Biddisham
BRISTOL CHANNEL
SEVERN ESTUARY
Bridgwater Bay
Berrow
Sedgemoor
Cheddar Resr
Brent Knoll
Burnham-on-Sea
Mark
Highbridge
West Huntspill
Lynmouth
Porlock Weir
Brendon
Minehead
Porlock
EXMOOR FOREST
Wootton Courtenay
Dunster
Blue Anchor
Watchet
Kilve
Stogursey
DUNKERY BEACON
Carhampton
NATIONAL PARK
Sampford Brett
Cannington
Exford
Wheddon Cross
Nether Stowey
Withypool
Crowcombe
Bridgwater
Winsford
Elworthy
QUANTOCK HILLS
Goathurst
Brompton Regis
North Petherton
Othery
SOMERSET
North Molton
Wimbleball Lake
Bishops Lydeard
Dulverton
Wiveliscombe
Fitzhead
Lyng
Curry Rivel
Milverton
North Curry
Exbridge
Petton
Taunton
Bampton
Wellington
Hatch Beauchamp
Sampford Arundel
Corfe
Taunton Deane
South Petherton
Rackenford
WELLINGTON MONUMENT
Staple Fitzpaine
Witheridge
Culmstock
Horton
Ilminster
Tiverton
Halberton
Uffculme
Hemyock
Willand
Chard
Crewkerne
Cheriton Fitzpaine
Cullompton
Upottery
Yarcombe
Morchard Bishop
Bickleigh
Winsham
Mosterton
Tytherleigh
Copplestone
Silverton
Broadwindsor
Crediton
Honiton
Wilmington
Fenny Bridges
Stoke Canon
DEVON
Newton St Cyres
Broadclyst
Whimple
Axminster
Tedburn St Mary
Shute
North Chideock
Ottery St Mary
Colyton
EXETER
Colyford
Uplyme
Charmouth
Crockernwell
Lyme Regis
Clyst St Mary
Axmouth
Dunsford
Branscombe
Seaton
West Bay
Topsham
Beer
Kennford
Exminster
Sidmouth
Otterton
Lyme Bay
Kenton
Budleigh Salterton
Chudleigh
Exmouth
Bovey Tracey
Chudleigh Knighton
Dawlish
M5
A30
A35
A38
A39
A303
A358
A361
A373
A375
A376
A379
A380
A3052
A396
12
6

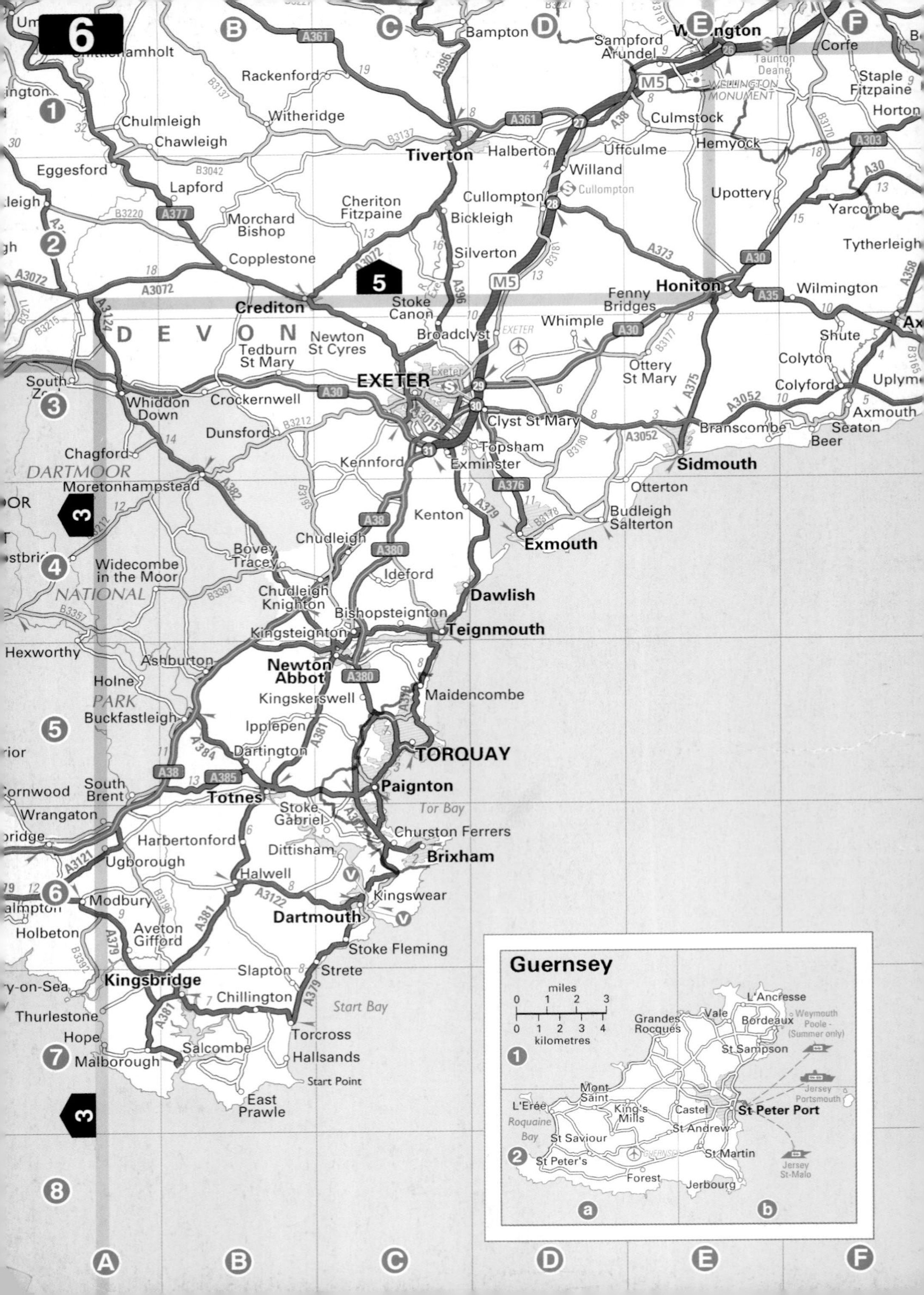
6
A
B
C
D
E
F
1
2
3
4
5
6
7
8
Bampton
Sampford Arundel
Wellington
Corfe
Taunton Deane
Wellington Monument
Staple Fitzpaine
Horton
Chittlehamholt
Rackenford
Chulmleigh
Witheridge
Chawleigh
Eggesford
Tiverton
Halberton
Uffculme
Culmstock
Hemyock
Willand
Cullompton
Upottery
Yarcombe
Lapford
Morchard Bishop
Cheriton Fitzpaine
Bickleigh
Silverton
Tytherleigh
Copplestone
Honiton
Wilmington
Fenny Bridges
Crediton
Stoke Canon
Whimple
Broadclyst
Exeter
Shute
Colyton
DEVON
Newton St Cyres
Tedburn St Mary
Ottery St Mary
Colyford
Uplyme
South Zeal
EXETER
Whiddon Down
Crockernwell
Clyst St Mary
Axmouth
Seaton
Beer
Branscombe
Dunsford
Topsham
Chagford
Exminster
Sidmouth
DARTMOOR
Kennford
Moretonhampstead
Otterton
Kenton
Budleigh Salterton
Chudleigh
Exmouth
Bovey Tracey
Widecombe in the Moor
Ideford
NATIONAL
Chudleigh Knighton
Dawlish
Bishopsteignton
Kingsteignton
Teignmouth
Hexworthy
Ashburton
Newton Abbot
Holne
PARK
Kingskerswell
Maidencombe
Buckfastleigh
Ipplepen
Dartington
TORQUAY
South Brent
Totnes
Paignton
Tor Bay
Cornwood
Wrangaton
Stoke Gabriel
Churston Ferrers
Harbertonford
Dittisham
Brixham
Ugborough
Halwell
Kingswear
Modbury
Dartmouth
Holbeton
Aveton Gifford
Stoke Fleming
Slapton
Strete
Kingsbridge
Chillington
Start Bay
Thurlestone
Hope
Torcross
Malborough
Salcombe
Hallsands
Start Point
East Prawle
M5
A361
A396
A38
A377
A3072
A373
A30
A303
A35
A358
A3124
A382
A3015
A375
A3052
A376
A379
A380
A381
A384
A385
A3122
A3121
B3137
B3042
B3220
B3215
B3212
B3193
B3387
B3357
B3181
B3177
B3180
B3178
B3170
B3165
B3196
B3392
Guernsey
miles
0
1
2
3
0
1
2
3
4
kilometres
L'Ancresse
Grandes Rocques
Vale
Bordeaux
Weymouth Poole - (Summer only)
St Sampson
Jersey Portsmouth
Mont Saint
L'Erée
King's Mills
Castel
St Peter Port
Roquaine Bay
St Saviour
St Andrew
St Peter's
St Martin
Jersey St-Malo
Forest
Jerbourg
a
b

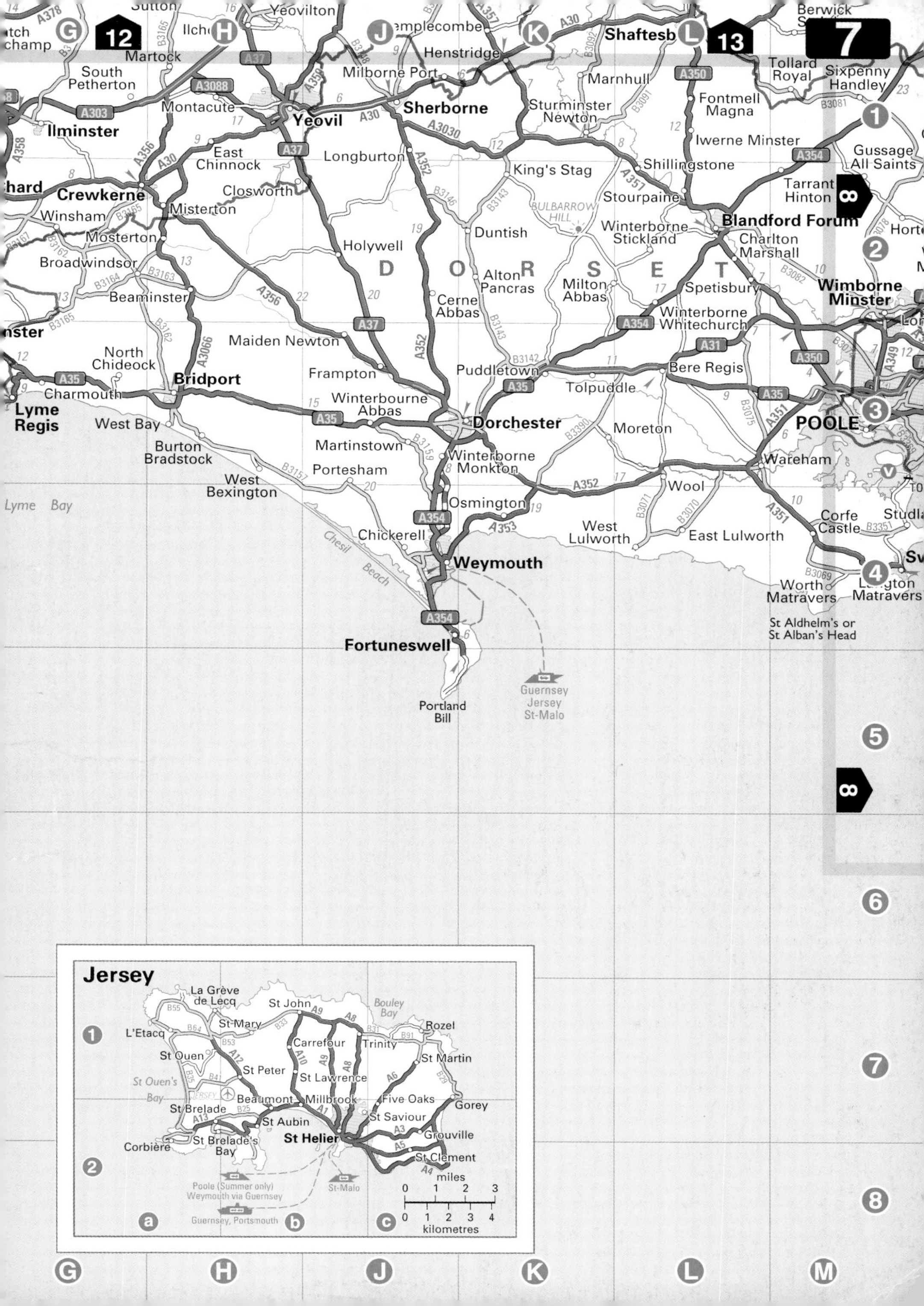
Yeovilton
Shaftesb
Martock
South Petherton
Milborne Port
Henstridge
Marnhull
Tollard Royal
Sixpenny Handley
Montacute
Yeovil
Sherborne
Sturminster Newton
Fontmell Magna
Ilminster
Iwerne Minster
Gussage All Saints
East Chinnock
Longburton
King's Stag
Shillingstone
Crewkerne
Closworth
Stourpaine
Tarrant Hinton
Misterton
Bulbarrow Hill
Winsham
Mosterton
Winterborne Stickland
Blandford Forum
Charlton Marshall
Duntish
Holywell
Broadwindsor
DORSET
Alton Pancras
Milton Abbas
Spetisbury
Wimborne Minster
Beaminster
Cerne Abbas
Winterborne Whitechurch
North Chideock
Maiden Newton
Puddletown
Bere Regis
Bridport
Frampton
Tolpuddle
Charmouth
Winterbourne Abbas
Lyme Regis
West Bay
Dorchester
Moreton
POOLE
Burton Bradstock
Martinstown
Winterborne Monkton
Wareham
West Bexington
Portesham
Wool
Lyme Bay
Osmington
Corfe Castle
West Lulworth
Chickerell
East Lulworth
Chesil Beach
Weymouth
Worth Matravers
Matravers
St Aldhelm's or St Alban's Head
Fortuneswell
Portland Bill
Guernsey
Jersey
St-Malo
Jersey
La Grève de Lecq
St John
Bouley Bay
St Mary
Rozel
L'Etacq
Carrefour
Trinity
St Ouen
St Martin
St Peter
St Lawrence
St Ouen's Bay
Beaumont
Millbrook
Five Oaks
Gorey
St Brelade
St Saviour
St Aubin
St Helier
Grouville
Corbière
St Brelade's Bay
St Clement
Poole (Summer only)
Weymouth via Guernsey
St-Malo
Guernsey, Portsmouth
miles
kilometres

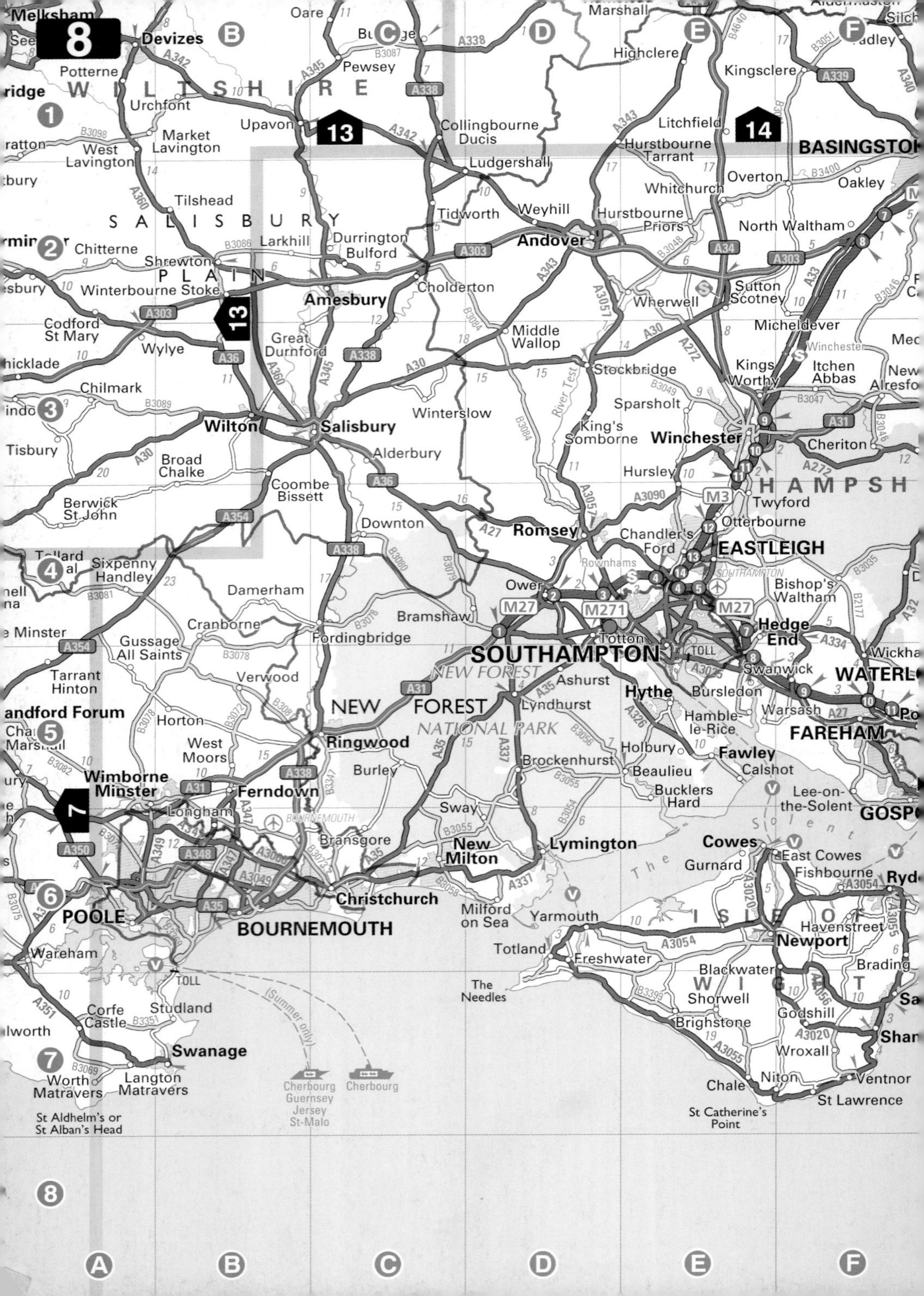
8
13
14
7
WILTSHIRE
SALISBURY PLAIN
HAMPSHIRE
ISLE OF WIGHT
NEW FOREST
NEW FOREST NATIONAL PARK
The Solent
Melksham
Devizes
Potterne
Urchfont
Market Lavington
West Lavington
Tilshead
Chitterne
Shrewton
Winterbourne Stoke
Codford St Mary
Wylye
Chilmark
Tisbury
Wilton
Broad Chalke
Berwick St John
Sixpenny Handley
Oare
Pewsey
Upavon
Collingbourne Ducis
Ludgershall
Tidworth
Larkhill
Durrington
Bulford
Amesbury
Cholderton
Great Durnford
Salisbury
Alderbury
Coombe Bissett
Downton
Winterslow
Middle Wallop
Weyhill
Andover
Marshall
Highclere
Kingsclere
Litchfield
Hurstbourne Tarrant
Whitchurch
Overton
Oakley
BASINGSTOKE
Hurstbourne Priors
North Waltham
Wherwell
Sutton Scotney
Micheldever
Kings Worthy
Itchen Abbas
Stockbridge
Sparsholt
King's Somborne
Winchester
Cheriton
Hursley
Twyford
Otterbourne
Romsey
Chandler's Ford
EASTLEIGH
Rownhams
Bishop's Waltham
Ower
Totton
SOUTHAMPTON
Hedge End
Swanwick
Bursledon
Warsash
Hamble-le-Rice
FAREHAM
Fawley
Calshot
Lee-on-the-Solent
Hythe
Ashurst
Lyndhurst
Brockenhurst
Beaulieu
Holbury
Bucklers Hard
Damerham
Cranborne
Gussage All Saints
Fordingbridge
Bramshaw
Verwood
Tarrant Hinton
Horton
West Moors
Ringwood
Burley
Wimborne Minster
Ferndown
Longham
Sway
New Milton
Lymington
Bransgore
Christchurch
POOLE
BOURNEMOUTH
Milford on Sea
Yarmouth
Totland
Freshwater
The Needles
Wareham
Corfe Castle
Studland
Swanage
Worth Matravers
Langton Matravers
St Aldhelm's or St Alban's Head
Cherbourg Guernsey Jersey St-Malo
Cherbourg
(Summer only)
Cowes
East Cowes
Gurnard
Fishbourne
Newport
Havenstreet
Blackwater
Shorwell
Brighstone
Godshill
Wroxall
Chale
Niton
Ventnor
St Lawrence
St Catherine's Point
Brading
A
B
C
D
E
F
1
2
3
4
5
6
7
8

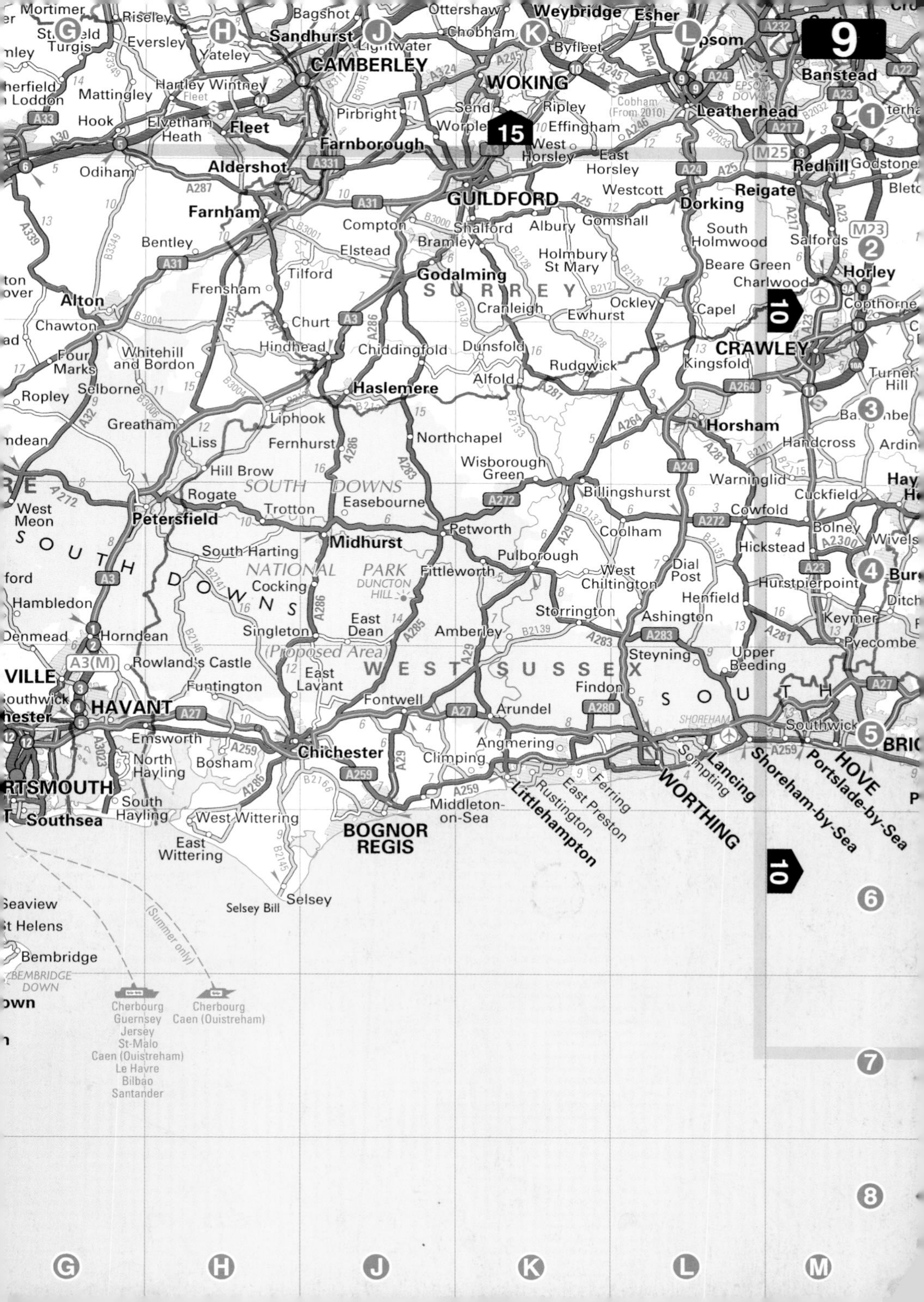

9
G
H
J
K
L
Mortimer
Riseley
Bagshot
Ottershaw
Weybridge
Esher
Turgis
Eversley
Yateley
Sandhurst
Lightwater
Chobham
Byfleet
Epsom
Banstead
CAMBERLEY
WOKING
Mattingley
Hartley Wintney
Fleet
Pirbright
Send
Ripley
Cobham (From 2010)
EPSOM DOWNS
Leatherhead
Hook
Elvetham Heath
Fleet
Worplesdon
15
Effingham
West Horsley
East Horsley
Farnborough
Odiham
Aldershot
Redhill
Godstone
Reigate
Farnham
GUILDFORD
Westcott
Dorking
Compton
Shalford
Albury
Gomshall
Bentley
Elstead
Bramley
South Holmwood
Salfords
Holmbury St Mary
Tilford
Godalming
Beare Green
Horley
Frensham
SURREY
Charlwood
Alton
Cranleigh
Ewhurst
Ockley
Capel
10
Copthorne
Chawton
Churt
Whitehill and Bordon
Hindhead
Chiddingfold
Dunsfold
Rudgwick
Kingsfold
CRAWLEY
Four Marks
Alfold
Turners Hill
Ropley
Selborne
Haslemere
Liphook
Greatham
Northchapel
Horsham
Liss
Fernhurst
Handcross
Ardingly
Hill Brow
Wisborough Green
Warninglid
SOUTH DOWNS
Billingshurst
Cuckfield
West Meon
Rogate
Trotton
Easebourne
Cowfold
Petersfield
Petworth
Coolham
Bolney
Midhurst
Hickstead
South Harting
Pulborough
SOUTH DOWNS
NATIONAL PARK
Fittleworth
West Chiltington
Dial Post
Cocking
DUNCTON HILL
Hurstpierpoint
Hambledon
Henfield
Storrington
Ashington
Keymer
Denmead
Horndean
East Dean
Singleton
Amberley
(Proposed Area)
Upper Beeding
Steyning
Pyecombe
Rowland's Castle
WEST SUSSEX
East Lavant
Findon
SOUTH
Funtington
HAVANT
Fontwell
Arundel
Southwick
Emsworth
Angmering
SHOREHAM
North Hayling
Bosham
Chichester
Climping
Sompting
Lancing
Shoreham-by-Sea
Portslade-by-Sea
HOVE
Middleton-on-Sea
Rustington
East Preston
Ferring
WORTHING
Littlehampton
PORTSMOUTH
South Hayling
Southsea
West Wittering
BOGNOR REGIS
East Wittering
Selsey
Selsey Bill
Seaview
St Helens
(Summer only)
Bembridge
BEMBRIDGE DOWN
Cherbourg
Guernsey
Jersey
St-Malo
Caen (Ouistreham)
Le Havre
Bilbao
Santander
Cherbourg
Caen (Ouistreham)
M

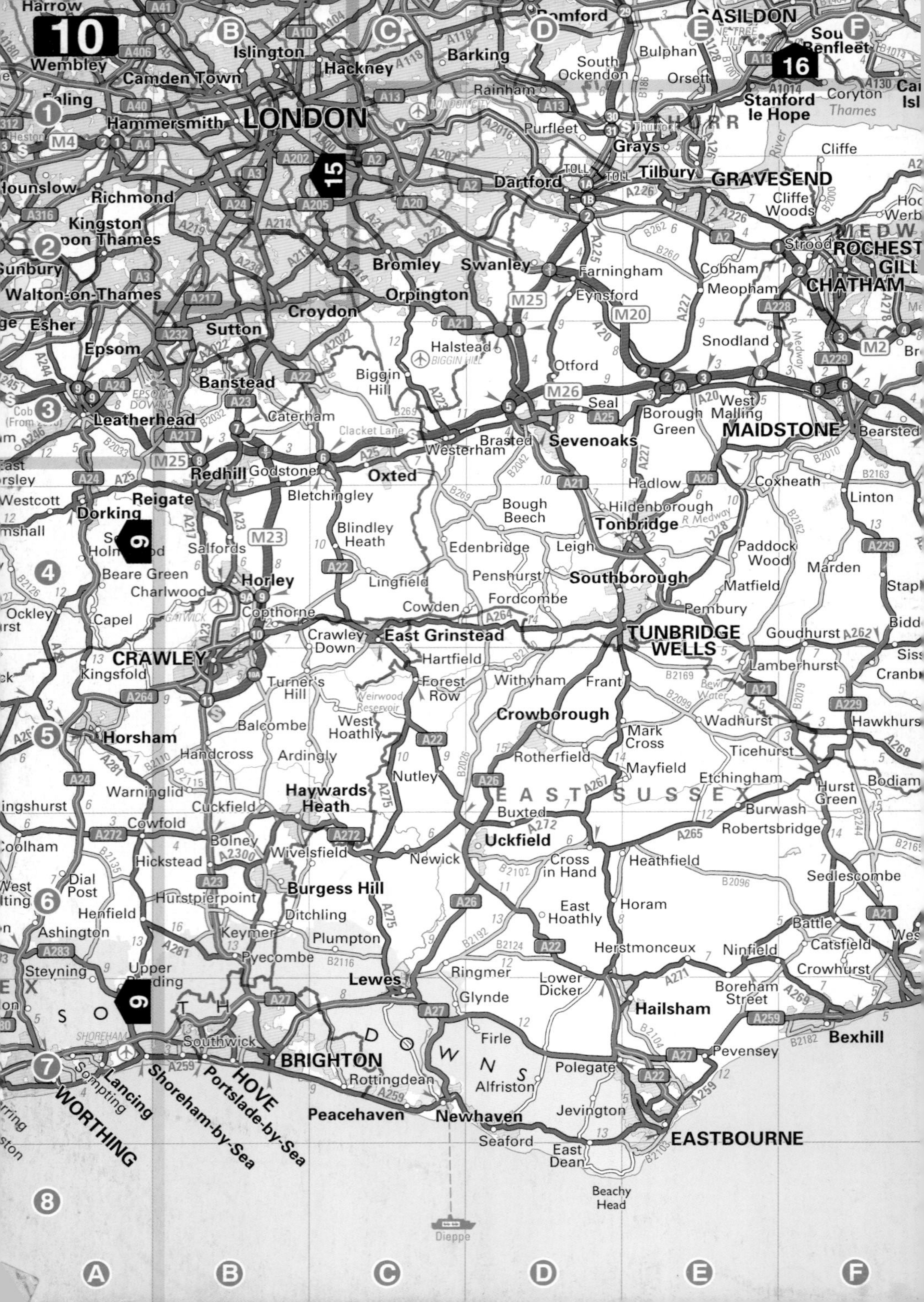

LONDON
Harrow
Wembley
Ealing
Islington
Camden Town
Hackney
Barking
Romford
Basildon
Bulphan
South Ockendon
Orsett
Rainham
Stanford le Hope
Coryton
Hammersmith
Purfleet
Grays
Tilbury
GRAVESEND
Cliffe
Hounslow
Richmond
Kingston upon Thames
Dartford
Cliffe Woods
Sunbury
Walton-on-Thames
Bromley
Swanley
Farningham
Cobham
Strood
ROCHESTER
CHATHAM
Esher
Croydon
Orpington
Eynsford
Meopham
Sutton
Epsom
Halstead
Snodland
Biggin Hill
Otford
Banstead
Leatherhead
Caterham
Seal
Borough Green
West Malling
MAIDSTONE
Bearsted
Brasted
Westerham
Sevenoaks
Redhill
Godstone
Oxted
Reigate
Dorking
Bletchingley
Hadlow
Coxheath
Linton
Bough Beech
Hildenborough
Tonbridge
Blindley Heath
Edenbridge
Leigh
Paddock Wood
Marden
Salfords
Horley
Beare Green
Charlwood
Lingfield
Penshurst
Southborough
Matfield
Capel
Ockley
Copthorne
Cowden
Fordcombe
Pembury
CRAWLEY
Crawley Down
East Grinstead
TUNBRIDGE WELLS
Goudhurst
Kingsfold
Hartfield
Turner's Hill
Forest Row
Withyham
Frant
Lamberhurst
Horsham
West Hoathly
Balcombe
Crowborough
Mark Cross
Wadhurst
Handcross
Ardingly
Rotherfield
Ticehurst
Mayfield
Warninglid
Nutley
Haywards Heath
EAST SUSSEX
Etchingham
Hurst Green
Bodiam
Cuckfield
Buxted
Burwash
Cowfold
Bolney
Uckfield
Robertsbridge
Coolham
Hickstead
Wivelsfield
Newick
Cross in Hand
Heathfield
Dial Post
Burgess Hill
Sedlescombe
Hurstpierpoint
Horam
Henfield
East Hoathly
Ashington
Ditchling
Keymer
Plumpton
Battle
Pyecombe
Herstmonceux
Ninfield
Catsfield
Steyning
Upper Beeding
Ringmer
Lower Dicker
Crowhurst
Lewes
Glynde
Hailsham
Boreham Street
Firle
Bexhill
Southwick
BRIGHTON
Polegate
Pevensey
Shoreham-by-Sea
Portslade-by-Sea
HOVE
Rottingdean
Alfriston
Lancing
Sompting
WORTHING
Peacehaven
Newhaven
Jevington
EASTBOURNE
Seaford
East Dean
Beachy Head
Dieppe
DOWNS

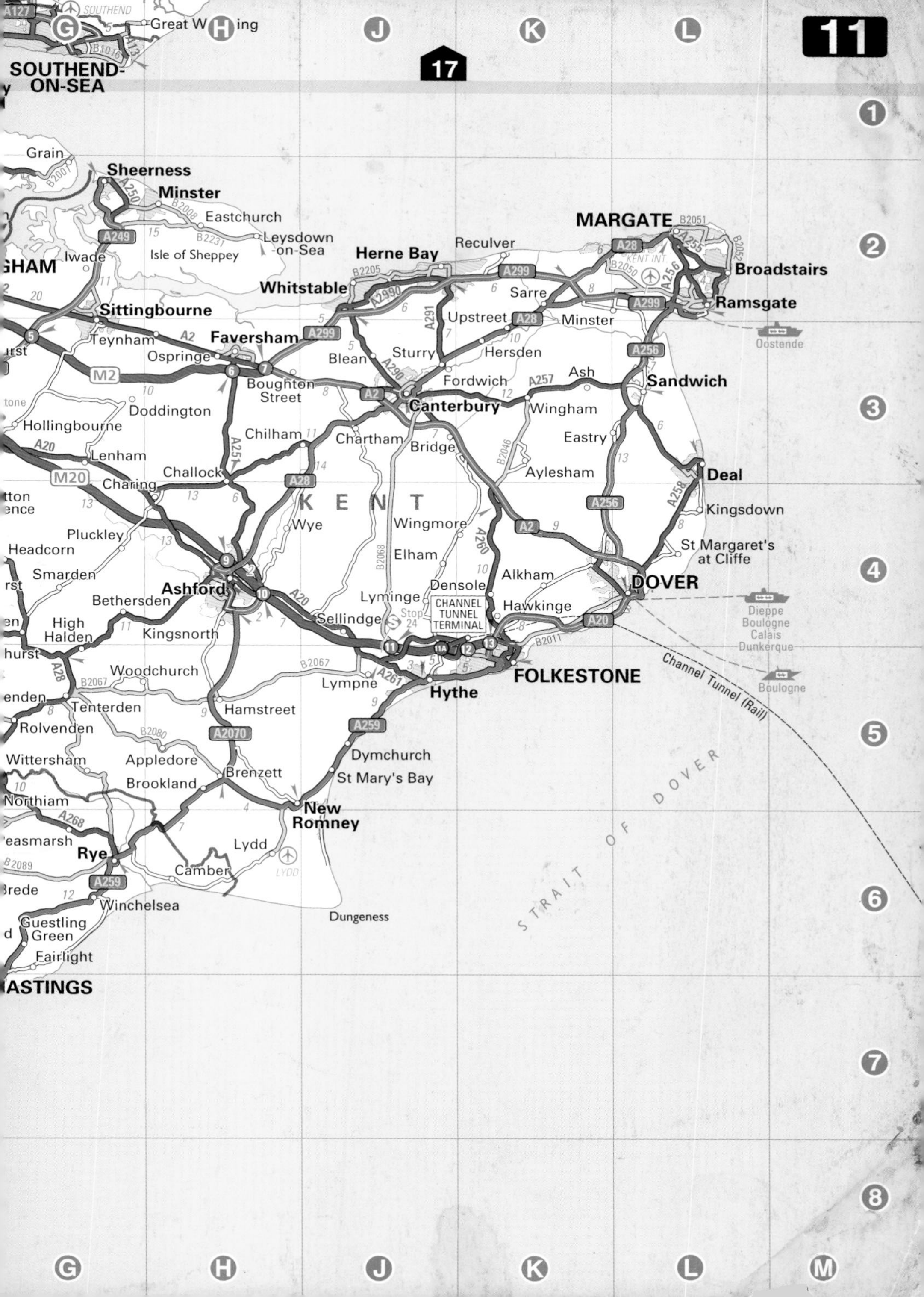
11
17
G
H
J
K
L
M
1
2
3
4
5
6
7
8
SOUTHEND-ON-SEA
Great Wakering
Grain
Sheerness
Minster
Eastchurch
Leysdown-on-Sea
Isle of Sheppey
Iwade
Sittingbourne
Teynham
Faversham
Ospringe
Boughton Street
Whitstable
Herne Bay
Reculver
MARGATE
Broadstairs
Ramsgate
Oostende
Sarre
Upstreet
Minster
Blean
Sturry
Hersden
Fordwich
Ash
Sandwich
Canterbury
Wingham
Eastry
Chartham
Bridge
Aylesham
Deal
Kingsdown
St Margaret's at Cliffe
DOVER
Dieppe
Boulogne
Calais
Dunkerque
Boulogne
Channel Tunnel (Rail)
Doddington
Hollingbourne
Lenham
Chilham
Challock
Charing
K E N T
Wye
Wingmore
Elham
Densole
Alkham
Hawkinge
Lyminge
CHANNEL TUNNEL TERMINAL
Pluckley
Headcorn
Smarden
Ashford
Bethersden
High Halden
Kingsnorth
Sellindge
Lympne
Hythe
FOLKESTONE
Woodchurch
Tenterden
Hamstreet
Rolvenden
Wittersham
Appledore
Brookland
Brenzett
Dymchurch
St Mary's Bay
New Romney
Northiam
Beasmarsh
Rye
Lydd
Camber
Brede
Winchelsea
Guestling Green
Fairlight
HASTINGS
Dungeness
STRAIT OF DOVER
M2
M20
A2
A20
A28
A249
A299
A256
A258
A260
A259
A2070
A268

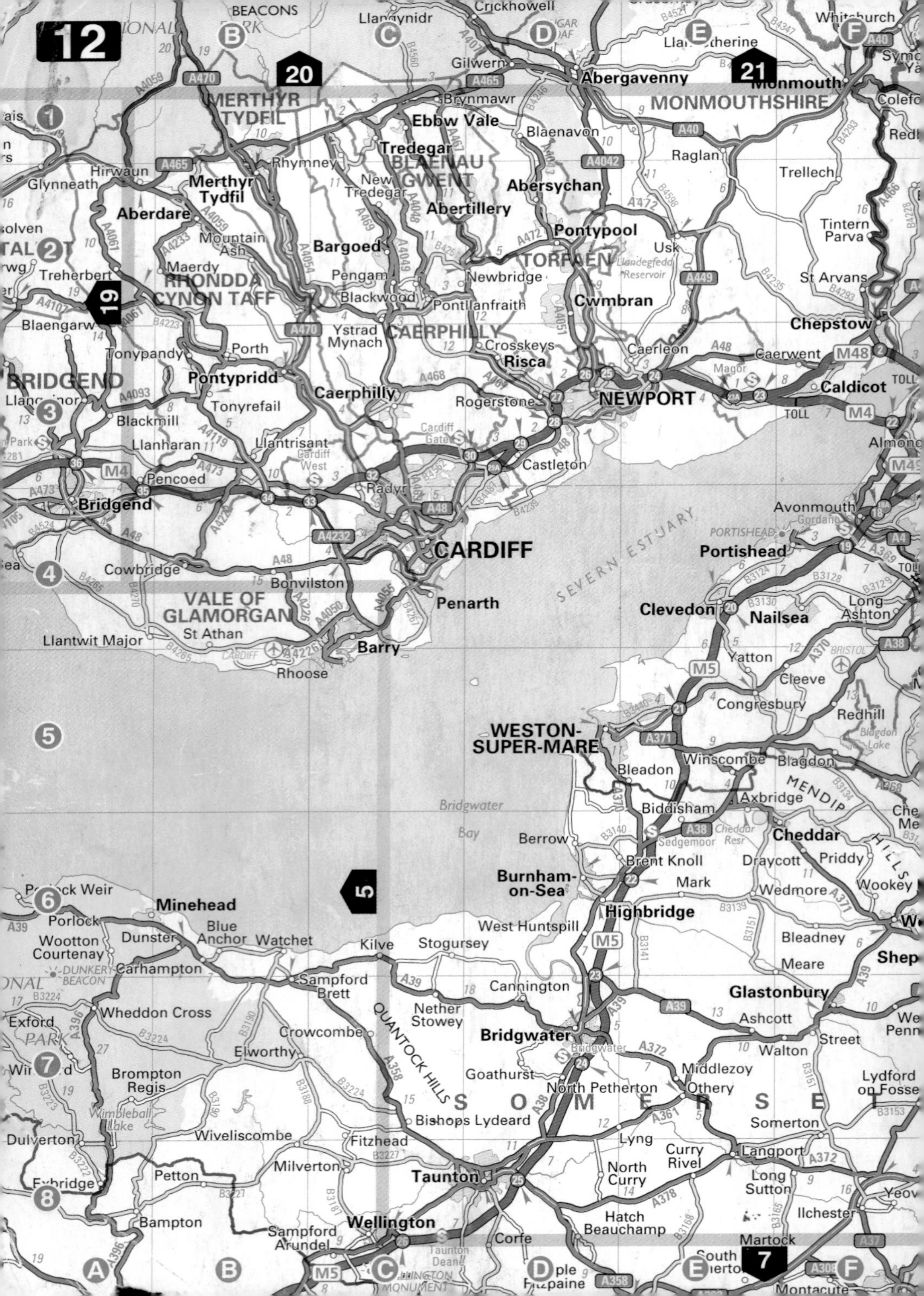
BEACONS
Crickhowell
Llangynidr
Whitchurch
Llanvetherine
20
21
Abergavenny
Monmouth
MONMOUTHSHIRE
Gilwern
Brynmawr
MERTHYR TYDFIL
Ebbw Vale
Tredegar
BLAENAU GWENT
Blaenavon
Raglan
Trellech
Coleford
Hirwaun
Glynneath
Rhymney
Merthyr Tydfil
New Tredegar
Abersychan
Aberdare
Abertillery
Pontypool
Tintern Parva
Mountain Ash
Bargoed
Usk
Maerdy
Treherbert
RHONDDA CYNON TAFF
Pengam
Blackwood
TORFAEN
Newbridge
Llandegfedd Reservoir
St Arvans
19
Pontllanfraith
Cwmbran
Blaengarw
Ystrad Mynach
CAERPHILLY
Crosskeys
Chepstow
Tonypandy
Porth
Risca
Caerleon
Caerwent
BRIDGEND
Pontypridd
Caerphilly
Rogerstone
NEWPORT
Magor
Caldicot
Tonyrefail
Blackmill
Cardiff Gate
Llantrisant
Llanharan
Cardiff West
Castleton
Almondsbury
Pencoed
Radyr
Bridgend
Avonmouth
SEVERN ESTUARY
Portishead
CARDIFF
Cowbridge
Bonvilston
Penarth
Clevedon
Nailsea
Long Ashton
VALE OF GLAMORGAN
Llantwit Major
St Athan
Barry
Yatton
Rhoose
Cleeve
Congresbury
Redhill
WESTON-SUPER-MARE
Blagdon Lake
Winscombe
Blagdon
Bleadon
MENDIP HILLS
Biddisham
Axbridge
Bridgwater Bay
Berrow
Sedgemoor
Cheddar Resr
Cheddar
Brent Knoll
Draycott
Priddy
Burnham-on-Sea
Mark
Wedmore
Wookey
5
Porlock Weir
Minehead
Highbridge
Porlock
Blue Anchor
Watchet
Dunster
West Huntspill
Bleadney
Wootton Courtenay
Kilve
Stogursey
Meare
Carhampton
DUNKERY BEACON
Sampford Brett
Cannington
Glastonbury
Nether Stowey
Wheddon Cross
Exford
Crowcombe
Bridgwater
Ashcott
QUANTOCK HILLS
Street
Elworthy
Walton
Brompton Regis
Goathurst
Middlezoy
North Petherton
Othery
Lydford on Fosse
Wimbleball Lake
SOMERSET
Bishops Lydeard
Somerton
Dulverton
Wiveliscombe
Fitzhead
Lyng
Curry Rivel
Langport
Milverton
North Curry
Petton
Taunton
Long Sutton
Exebridge
Bampton
Ilchester
Wellington
Hatch Beauchamp
Sampford Arundel
Taunton Deane
Corfe
Martock
South Petherton
Montacute
7
WELLINGTON MONUMENT
M4
M5
M48
A48
A470
A465
A40
A4042
A449
A39
A38
A371
A372
A358
A361
A378
A396

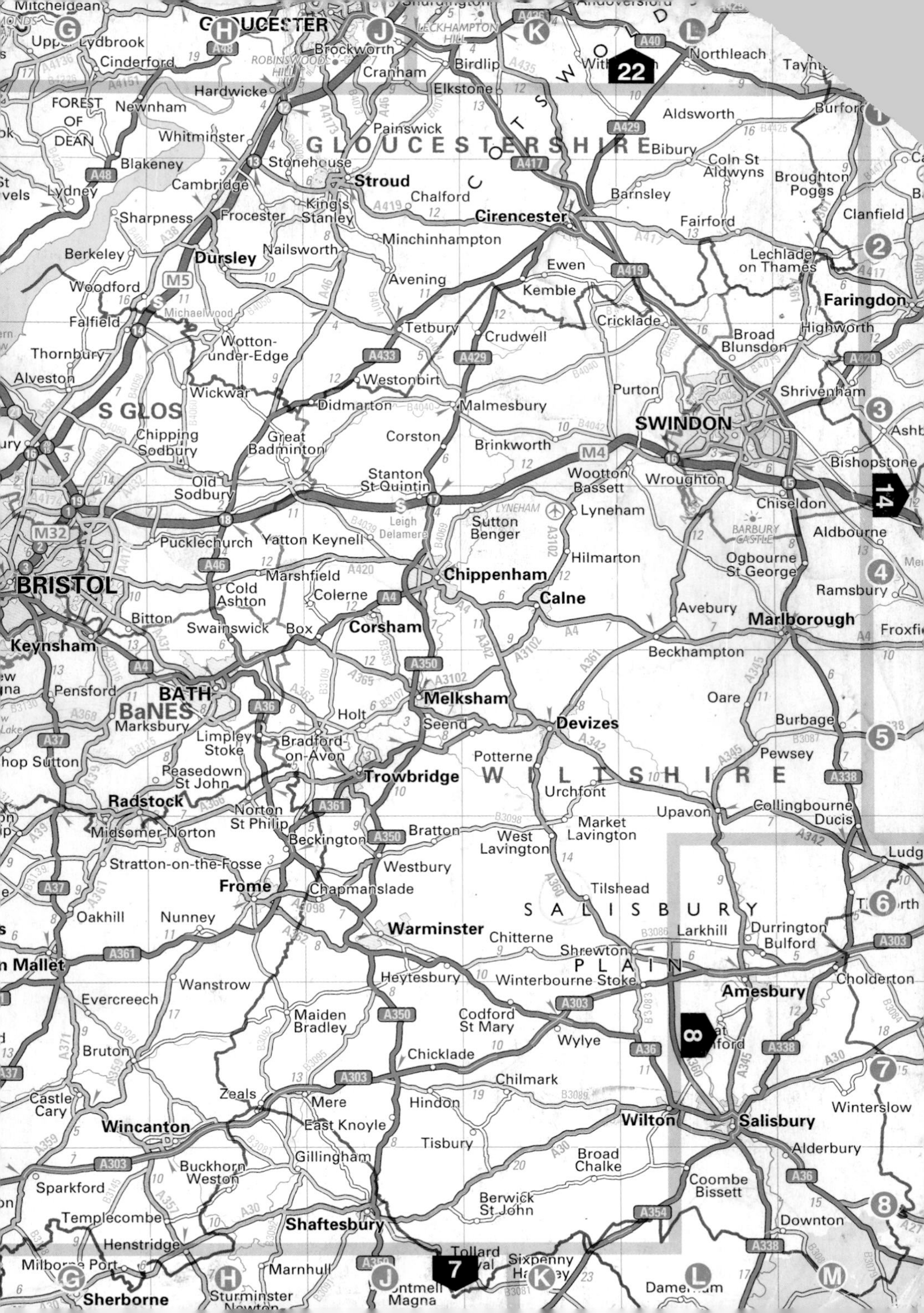

GLOUCESTER
Upper Lydbrook
Cinderford
Brockworth
ROBINSWOOD HILL
LECKHAMPTON HILL
Cranham
Birdlip
Elkstone
Northleach
22
Hardwicke
FOREST OF DEAN
Newnham
Painswick
Aldsworth
Burford
Whitminster
GLOUCESTERSHIRE
COTSWOLDS
Bibury
Coln St Aldwyns
Blakeney
Stonehouse
Stroud
Chalford
Barnsley
Broughton Poggs
Lydney
Cambridge
King's Stanley
Sharpness
Frocester
Cirencester
Fairford
Clanfield
Berkeley
Dursley
Nailsworth
Minchinhampton
Lechlade on Thames
Ewen
Woodford
Avening
Kemble
Faringdon
Michaelwood
Falfield
Tetbury
Crudwell
Cricklade
Broad Blunsdon
Highworth
Thornbury
Wotton-under-Edge
Westonbirt
Alveston
Wickwar
Didmarton
Malmesbury
Purton
Shrivenham
S GLOS
Chipping Sodbury
Great Badminton
Corston
Brinkworth
SWINDON
Ashbury
Bishopstone
Old Sodbury
Stanton St Quintin
Wootton Bassett
Wroughton
14
Leigh Delamere
LYNEHAM
Lyneham
Chiseldon
Pucklechurch
Yatton Keynell
Sutton Benger
BARBURY CASTLE
Aldbourne
Hilmarton
Ogbourne St George
BRISTOL
Marshfield
Cold Ashton
Colerne
Chippenham
Calne
Ramsbury
Bitton
Swainswick
Box
Corsham
Avebury
Marlborough
Froxfield
Keynsham
Beckhampton
Pensford
BATH
BaNES
Melksham
Oare
Marksbury
Holt
Seend
Devizes
Burbage
Limpley Stoke
Bradford-on-Avon
Pewsey
Peasedown St John
Trowbridge
Potterne
WILTSHIRE
Radstock
Urchfont
Upavon
Collingbourne Ducis
Midsomer Norton
Norton St Philip
Beckington
Bratton
West Lavington
Market Lavington
Ludgershall
Stratton-on-the-Fosse
Westbury
Frome
Chapmanslade
Tilshead
SALISBURY PLAIN
Oakhill
Nunney
Warminster
Chitterne
Larkhill
Durrington
Bulford
Shrewton
Cholderton
Wanstrow
Heytesbury
Winterbourne Stoke
Amesbury
Evercreech
Maiden Bradley
Codford St Mary
Wylye
8
Bruton
Chicklade
Chilmark
Zeals
Mere
Hindon
Castle Cary
Wincanton
East Knoyle
Wilton
Salisbury
Winterslow
Tisbury
Broad Chalke
Gillingham
Alderbury
Buckhorn Weston
Sparkford
Coombe Bissett
Berwick St John
Templecombe
Shaftesbury
Downton
Henstridge
Marnhull
7
Sixpenny Handley
Sherborne
Sturminster Newton
Magna

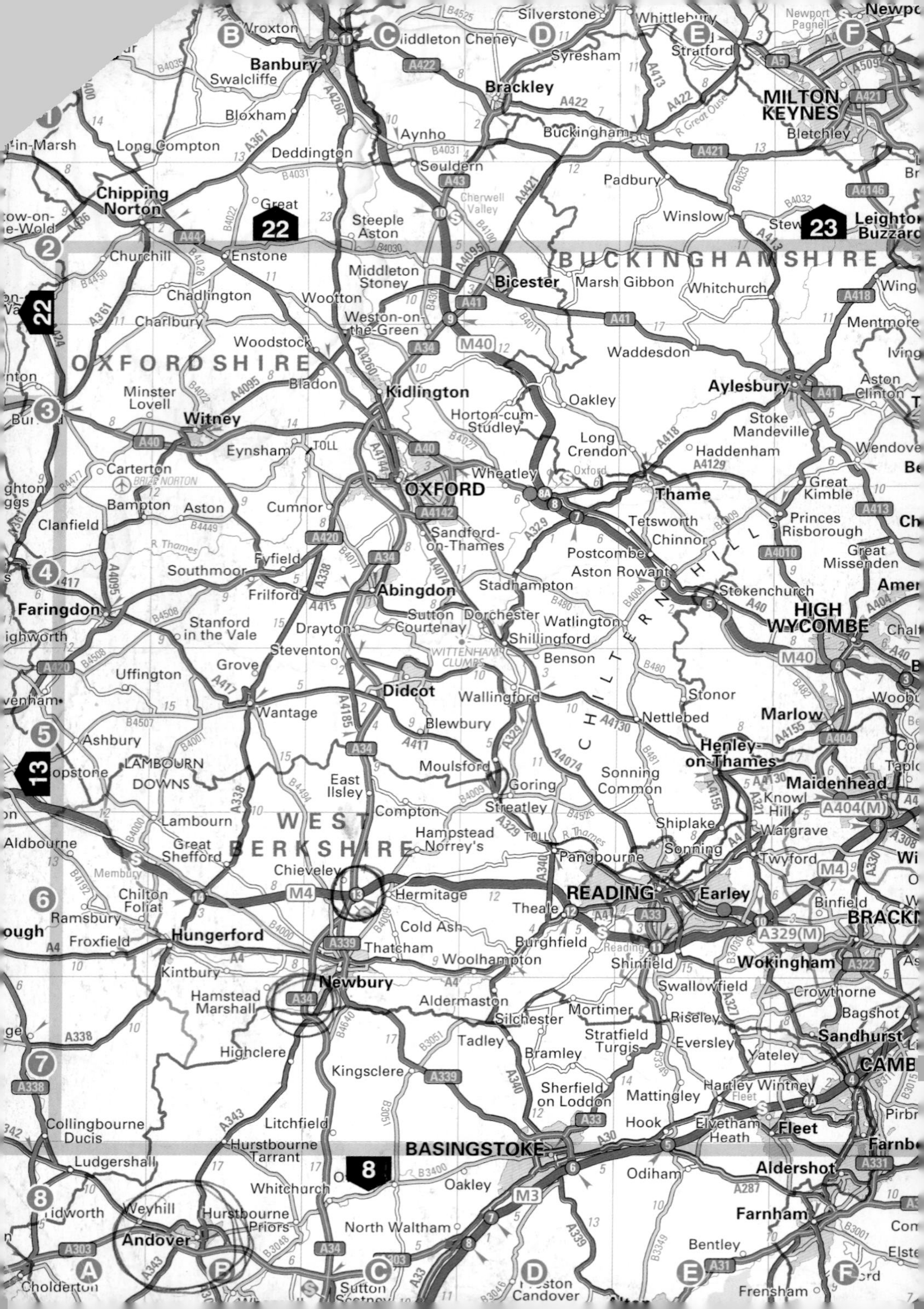

Wroxton
Middleton Cheney
Silverstone
Whittlebury
Syresham
Stratford
Banbury
Swalcliffe
Brackley
MILTON KEYNES
Bloxham
Aynho
Buckingham
Bletchley
Long Compton
Deddington
Souldern
Padbury
Chipping Norton
Great
22
Steeple Aston
Cherwell Valley
Winslow
23
Churchill
Enstone
BUCKINGHAMSHIRE
Middleton Stoney
Bicester
Marsh Gibbon
Whitchurch
Chadlington
Wootton
Charlbury
Weston-on-the-Green
Mentmore
Woodstock
Waddesdon
OXFORDSHIRE
Bladon
Minster Lovell
Kidlington
Oakley
Aylesbury
Aston Clinton
Witney
Horton-cum-Studley
Stoke Mandeville
Eynsham
TOLL
Long Crendon
Haddenham
Carterton
BRIZE NORTON
Wheatley
OXFORD
Thame
Great Kimble
Bampton
Aston
Cumnor
Clanfield
Sandford-on-Thames
Tetsworth
Chinnor
Princes Risborough
R Thames
Postcombe
Great Missenden
Southmoor
Fyfield
Aston Rowant
Frilford
Abingdon
Stadhampton
Stokenchurch
Faringdon
HIGH WYCOMBE
Stanford in the Vale
Drayton
Sutton Courtenay
Dorchester
Watlington
Shillingford
Steventon
WITTENHAM CLUMPS
Benson
Grove
Uffington
Didcot
Wallingford
Stonor
Wantage
Nettlebed
Marlow
CHILTERN HILLS
Ashbury
Blewbury
Henley-on-Thames
LAMBOURN DOWNS
Moulsford
Sonning Common
Maidenhead
East Ilsley
Goring
Knowl Hill
Compton
Streatley
Shiplake
Lambourn
WEST BERKSHIRE
Wargrave
Aldbourne
Great Shefford
Hampstead Norrey's
Pangbourne
Sonning
Twyford
Membury
Chieveley
Chilton Foliat
Hermitage
READING
Earley
Binfield
Ramsbury
Theale
Froxfield
Hungerford
Cold Ash
Burghfield
Thatcham
Woolhampton
Shinfield
Wokingham
Kintbury
Newbury
Swallowfield
Crowthorne
Hamstead Marshall
Aldermaston
Mortimer
Riseley
Bagshot
Silchester
Sandhurst
Tadley
Stratfield Turgis
Eversley
Highclere
Bramley
Yateley
Kingsclere
Sherfield on Loddon
Mattingley
Hartley Wintney
Fleet
Collingbourne Ducis
Litchfield
Hook
Elvetham Heath
Hurstbourne Tarrant
BASINGSTOKE
Ludgershall
8
Odiham
Aldershot
Whitchurch
Oakley
Tidworth
Weyhill
Hurstbourne Priors
North Waltham
Farnham
Andover
Bentley
Cholderton
Sutton Scotney
Preston Candover
Frensham
M40
M4
M3
A404(M)
A329(M)

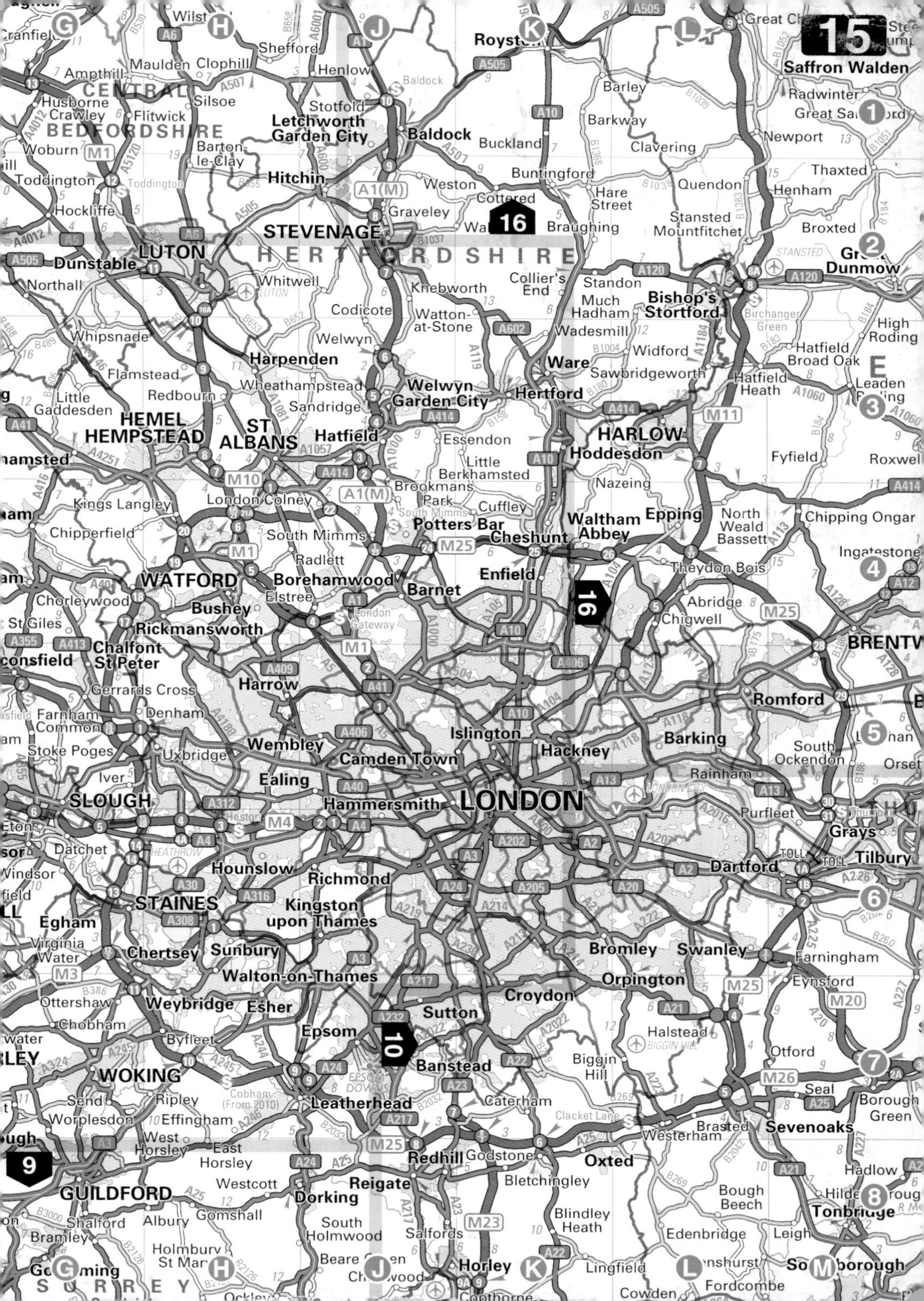
15
16
10
9
Saffron Walden
Royston
Baldock
Letchworth Garden City
Hitchin
STEVENAGE
LUTON
Dunstable
HERTFORDSHIRE
CENTRAL BEDFORDSHIRE
Bishop's Stortford
Great Dunmow
Harpenden
Welwyn Garden City
Hertford
Ware
HARLOW
HEMEL HEMPSTEAD
ST ALBANS
Hatfield
Hoddesdon
Potters Bar
Cheshunt
Waltham Abbey
Epping
Chipping Ongar
WATFORD
Borehamwood
Barnet
Enfield
Rickmansworth
Harrow
Romford
Wembley
Islington
Hackney
Barking
Camden Town
Ealing
SLOUGH
Hammersmith
LONDON
Hounslow
Richmond
STAINES
Kingston upon Thames
Dartford
Tilbury
Grays
Bromley
Swanley
Orpington
Croydon
Sutton
Epsom
WOKING
Leatherhead
Redhill
Reigate
Dorking
GUILDFORD
Sevenoaks
Tonbridge
Oxted
Horley
SURREY

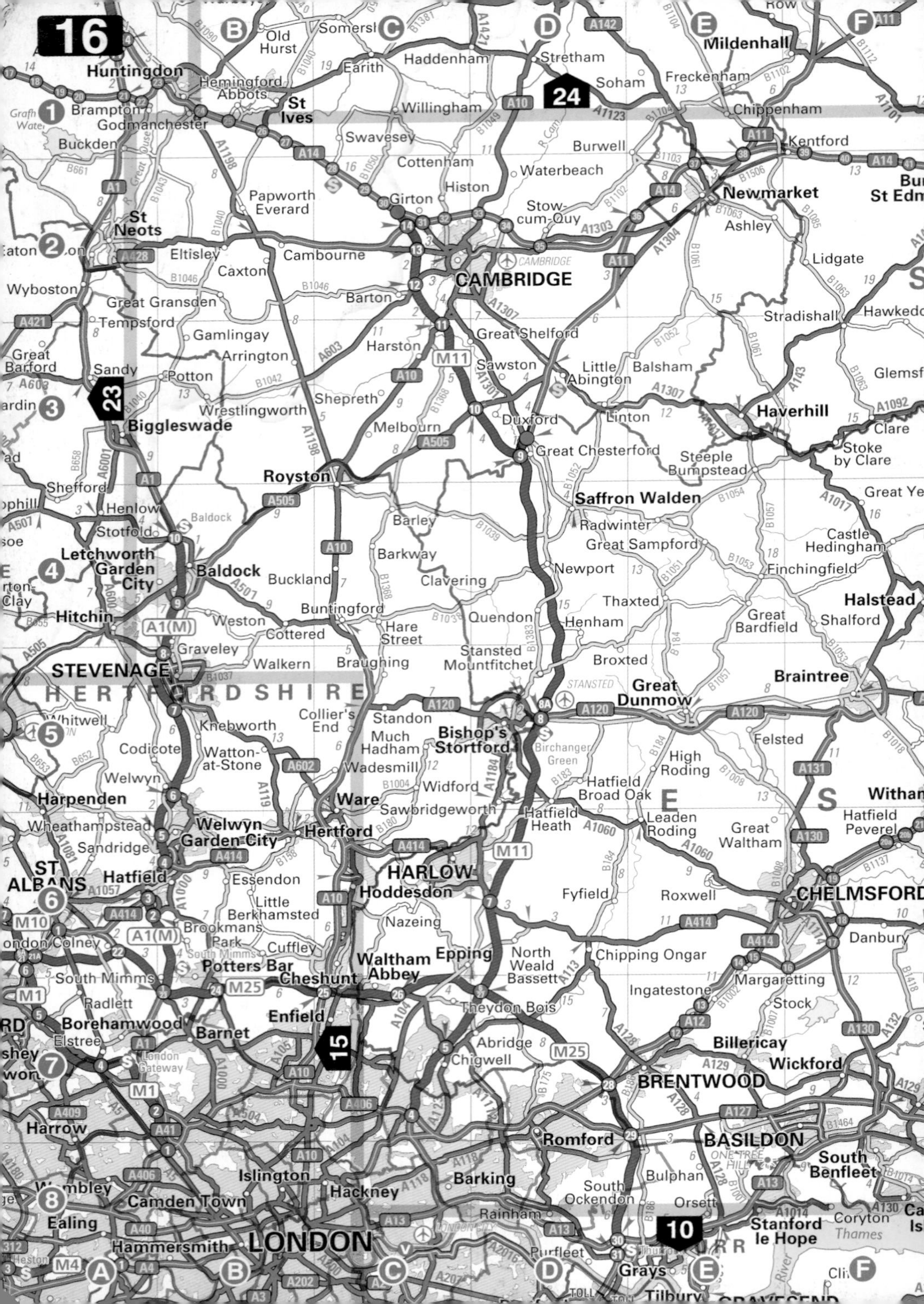

16
Huntingdon
Brampton
Godmanchester
Buckden
St Neots
Eltisley
Cambourne
Caxton
Wyboston
Great Gransden
Tempsford
Gamlingay
Great Barford
Sandy
Potton
Arrington
Biggleswade
Wrestlingworth
Shefford
Henlow
Stotfold
Letchworth Garden City
Baldock
Hitchin
Stevenage
Graveley
Walkern
Weston
Cottered
Buckland
Buntingford
Royston
Melbourn
Shepreth
Harston
Barton
Cambridge
Great Shelford
Sawston
Duxford
Great Chesterford
Saffron Walden
Linton
Little Abington
Balsham
Haverhill
Steeple Bumpstead
Stoke by Clare
Clare
Hemingford Abbots
St Ives
Old Hurst
Somersham
Earith
Haddenham
Stretham
Soham
Willingham
Swavesey
Cottenham
Histon
Girton
Waterbeach
Burwell
Stow-cum-Quy
Papworth Everard
Mildenhall
Freckenham
Chippenham
Kentford
Newmarket
Ashley
Lidgate
Stradishall
Hawkedon
Glemsford
Great Yeldham
Castle Hedingham
Radwinter
Great Sampford
Finchingfield
Newport
Barley
Barkway
Clavering
Quendon
Thaxted
Henham
Great Bardfield
Shalford
Halstead
Hare Street
Braughing
Stansted Mountfitchet
Broxted
Great Dunmow
Braintree
Felsted
Standon
Collier's End
Much Hadham
Bishop's Stortford
Birchanger Green
High Roding
Hatfield Broad Oak
Hertfordshire
Essex
Whitwell
Knebworth
Codicote
Watton-at-Stone
Welwyn
Harpenden
Wheathampstead
Welwyn Garden City
Sandridge
St Albans
Hatfield
Hertford
Ware
Wadesmill
Widford
Sawbridgeworth
Hatfield Heath
Leaden Roding
Great Waltham
Hatfield Peverel
Witham
Chelmsford
Harlow
Hoddesdon
Essendon
Little Berkhamsted
Brookmans Park
Nazeing
Fyfield
Roxwell
Danbury
London Colney
Cuffley
South Mimms
Potters Bar
Waltham Abbey
Cheshunt
Epping
North Weald Bassett
Chipping Ongar
Ingatestone
Margaretting
Stock
Radlett
Enfield
Theydon Bois
Borehamwood
Elstree
Barnet
Abridge
Chigwell
Billericay
Wickford
Brentwood
Harrow
Romford
Basildon
South Benfleet
Wembley
Islington
Hackney
Barking
South Ockendon
Bulphan
Orsett
Camden Town
Ealing
Rainham
Stanford le Hope
Coryton
Hammersmith
London
Purfleet
Grays
Tilbury
Gravesend
Thames
Cambridge (airport)
Stansted
London City
London Gateway
One Tree Hill
Baldock
A1 A1(M) A10 A11 A14 A120 A414 A505 A1198 M1 M10 M11 M25 A12 A13 A127 A130 A1307 A428 A603 A602
23
24
15
10

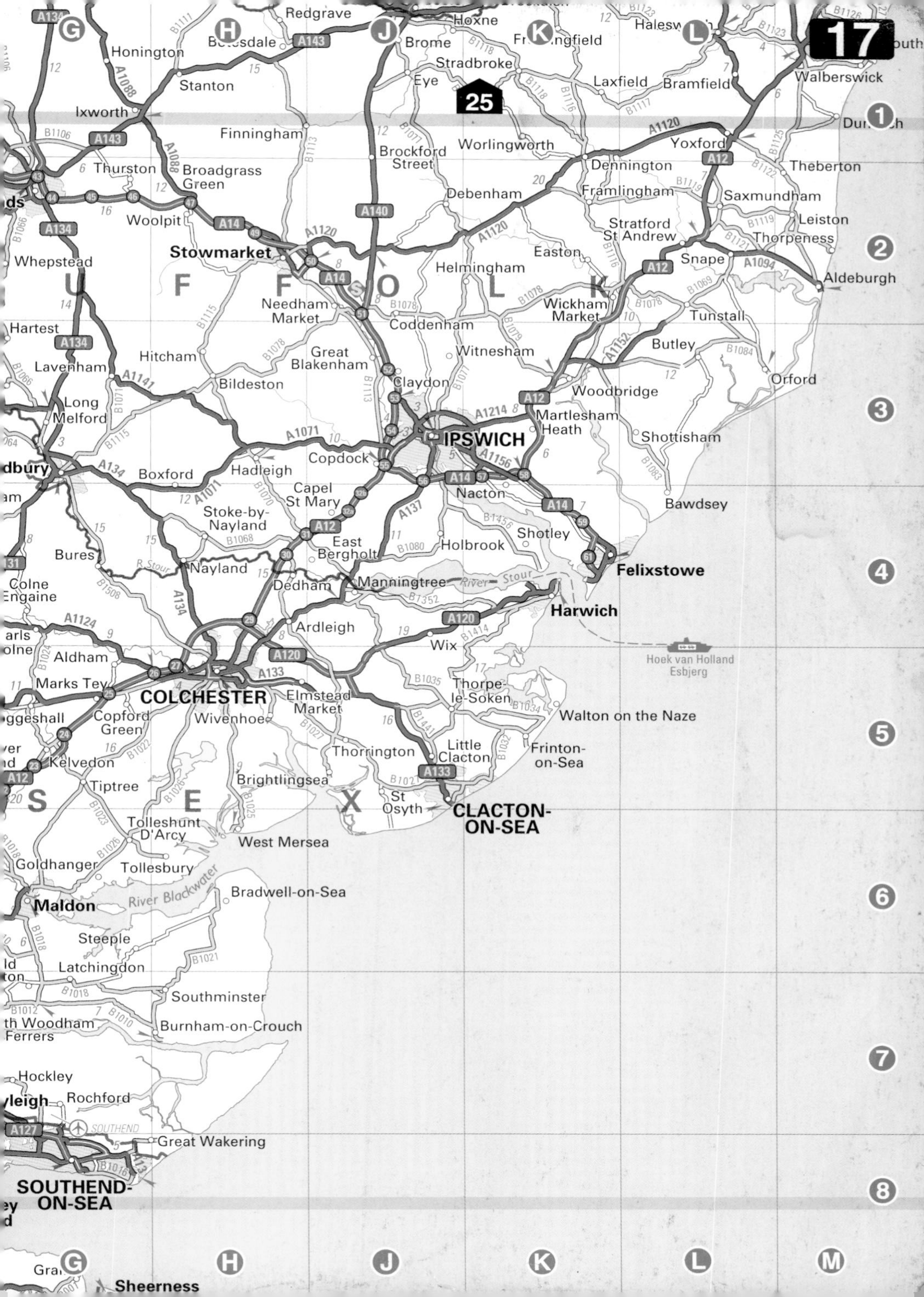

Redgrave
Hoxne
Halesworth
Brome
Stradbroke
Eye
25
Honington
Stanton
Ixworth
Laxfield
Bramfield
Walberswick
Finningham
Brockford Street
Worlingworth
Yoxford
Dennington
Theberton
Thurston
Broadgrass Green
Debenham
Framlingham
Saxmundham
Woolpit
Stratford St Andrew
Leiston
Thorpeness
Stowmarket
Easton
Snape
Aldeburgh
Whepstead
Helmingham
SUFFOLK
Needham Market
Wickham Market
Tunstall
Coddenham
Hartest
Great Blakenham
Witnesham
Butley
Hitcham
Lavenham
Claydon
Orford
Bildeston
Woodbridge
Long Melford
Martlesham Heath
IPSWICH
Shottisham
Copdock
Boxford
Hadleigh
Capel St Mary
Nacton
Bawdsey
Stoke-by-Nayland
Shotley
East Bergholt
Holbrook
Bures
Nayland
Felixstowe
Colne Engaine
Dedham
Manningtree
River Stour
Harwich
Ardleigh
Wix
Hoek van Holland
Esbjerg
Aldham
Marks Tey
COLCHESTER
Elmstead Market
Thorpe-le-Soken
Copford Green
Wivenhoe
Walton on the Naze
Kelvedon
Thorrington
Little Clacton
Frinton-on-Sea
Tiptree
Brightlingsea
ESSEX
St Osyth
CLACTON-ON-SEA
Tolleshunt D'Arcy
West Mersea
Goldhanger
Tollesbury
Bradwell-on-Sea
Maldon
River Blackwater
Steeple
Latchingdon
Southminster
Burnham-on-Crouch
Hockley
Rochford
SOUTHEND
Great Wakering
SOUTHEND-ON-SEA
Sheerness

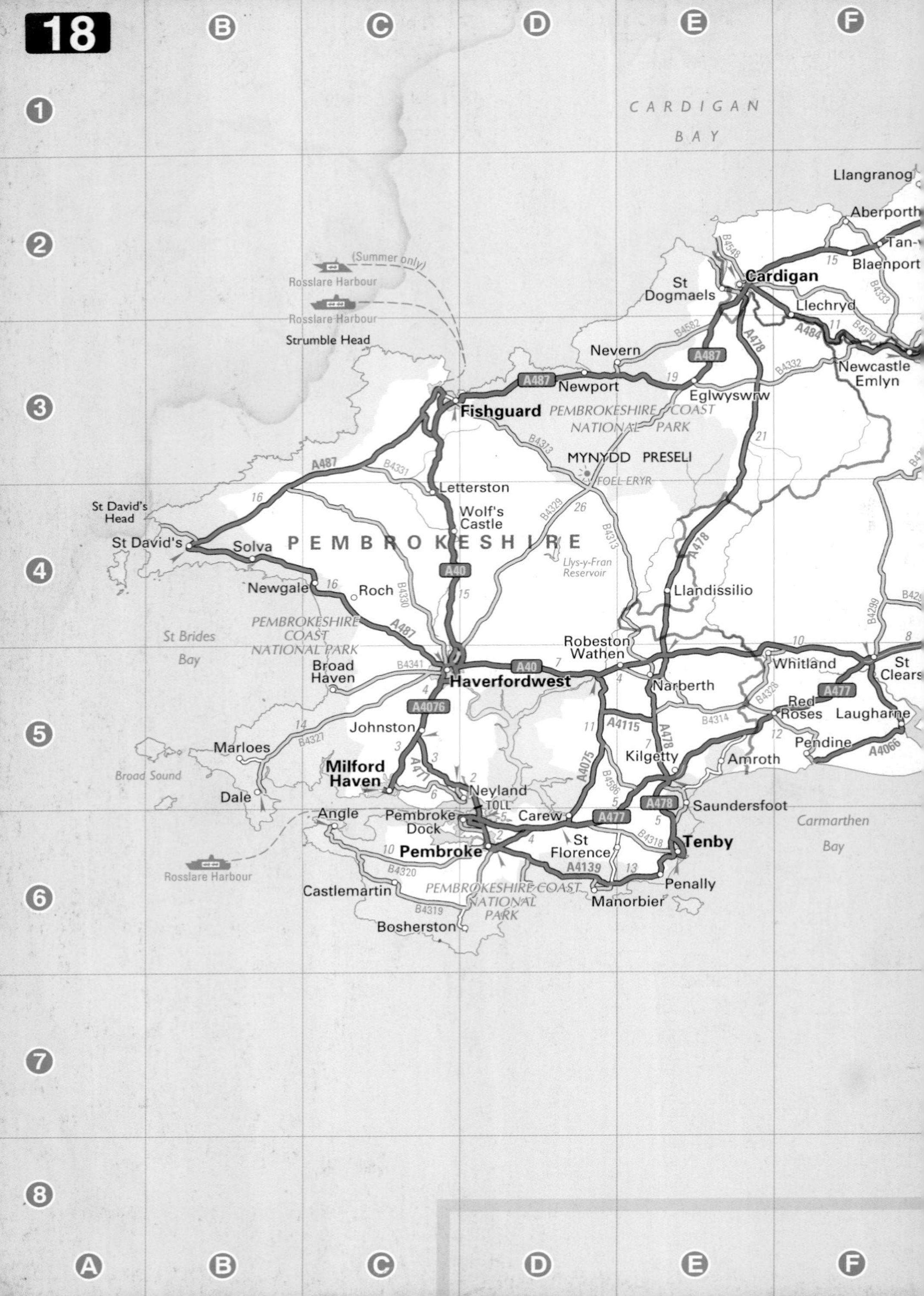
CARDIGAN BAY
Llangranog
Aberporth
Tan-y
Blaenport
Cardigan
St Dogmaels
Llechryd
Nevern
Newcastle Emlyn
Newport
Eglwyswrw
(Summer only)
Rosslare Harbour
Rosslare Harbour
Strumble Head
Fishguard
PEMBROKESHIRE COAST NATIONAL PARK
MYNYDD PRESELI
FOEL ERYR
Letterston
Wolf's Castle
St David's Head
St David's
Solva
PEMBROKESHIRE
Llys-y-Fran Reservoir
Newgale
Roch
Llandissilio
PEMBROKESHIRE COAST NATIONAL PARK
St Brides Bay
Robeston Wathen
Broad Haven
Haverfordwest
Whitland
St Clears
Narberth
Red Roses
Laugharne
Johnston
Marloes
Milford Haven
Kilgetty
Amroth
Pendine
Broad Sound
Dale
Neyland
TOLL
Saundersfoot
Angle
Pembroke Dock
Carew
Carmarthen Bay
St Florence
Tenby
Pembroke
Rosslare Harbour
Penally
Castlemartin
PEMBROKESHIRE COAST NATIONAL PARK
Manorbier
Bosherston
A487
A478
A484
A40
A4076
A477
A4115
A4075
A4139
A4066
A471
B4548
B4333
B4570
B4582
B4332
B4313
B4331
B4329
B4330
B4341
B4327
B4328
B4314
B4299
B4586
B4318
B4320
B4319

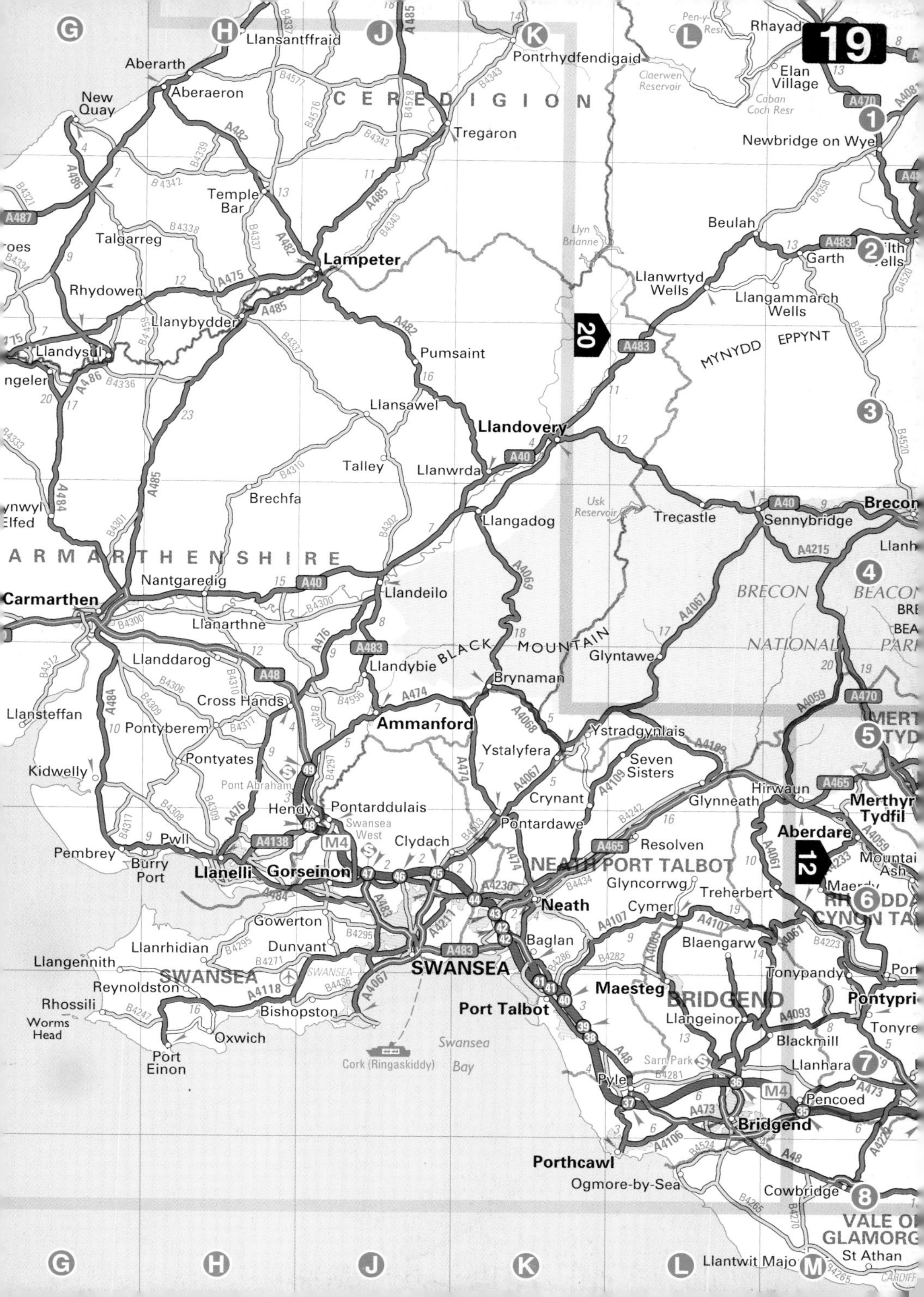
19
20
12
CEREDIGION
CARMARTHENSHIRE
NEATH PORT TALBOT
SWANSEA
BRIDGEND
VALE OF GLAMORG
BRECON BEACONS NATIONAL PARK
BLACK MOUNTAIN
MYNYDD EPPYNT
Llansantffraid
Aberarth
Aberaeron
New Quay
Pontrhydfendigaid
Rhayader
Pen-y-Garreg Resr
Claerwen Reservoir
Elan Village
Caban Coch Resr
Newbridge on Wye
Tregaron
Temple Bar
Talgarreg
Lampeter
Rhydowen
Llanybydder
Llandysul
Pumsaint
Llansawel
Llandovery
Talley
Llanwrda
Brechfa
Llangadog
Llyn Brianne
Beulah
Garth
Builth Wells
Llanwrtyd Wells
Llangammarch Wells
Usk Reservoir
Trecastle
Sennybridge
Brecon
Nantgaredig
Carmarthen
Llandeilo
Llanarthne
Llanddarog
Llandybie
Brynaman
Glyntawe
Cross Hands
Llansteffan
Pontyberem
Ammanford
Ystalyfera
Ystradgynlais
Seven Sisters
Kidwelly
Pontyates
Pont Abraham
Hendy
Pontarddulais
Swansea West
Crynant
Glynneath
Hirwaun
Merthyr Tydfil
Aberdare
Mountain Ash
Pembrey
Burry Port
Pwll
Llanelli
Gorseinon
Clydach
Pontardawe
Resolven
Neath
Glyncorrwg
Treherbert
Cymer
Gowerton
Llanrhidian
Dunvant
Llangennith
Baglan
Blaengarw
Tonypandy
Maerdy
Rhondda Cynon Taf
SWANSEA
Reynoldston
Rhossili
Worms Head
Bishopston
Oxwich
Port Einon
Port Talbot
Maesteg
Llangeinor
Pontypridd
Tonyrefail
Blackmill
Swansea Bay
Cork (Ringaskiddy)
Sarn Park
Llanharan
Pyle
Pencoed
Bridgend
Porthcawl
Ogmore-by-Sea
Cowbridge
Llantwit Major
St Athan
CARDIFF
M4
A40
A48
A470
A483
A485
A482
A486
A487
A484
A475
A476
A474
A4069
A4067
A4068
A4109
A465
A4059
A4061
A4107
A4063
A4093
A473
A4106
A4118
A4138
A4230
A4217
A4215
A4222
G
H
J
K
L
M
1
2
3
4
5
6
7
8

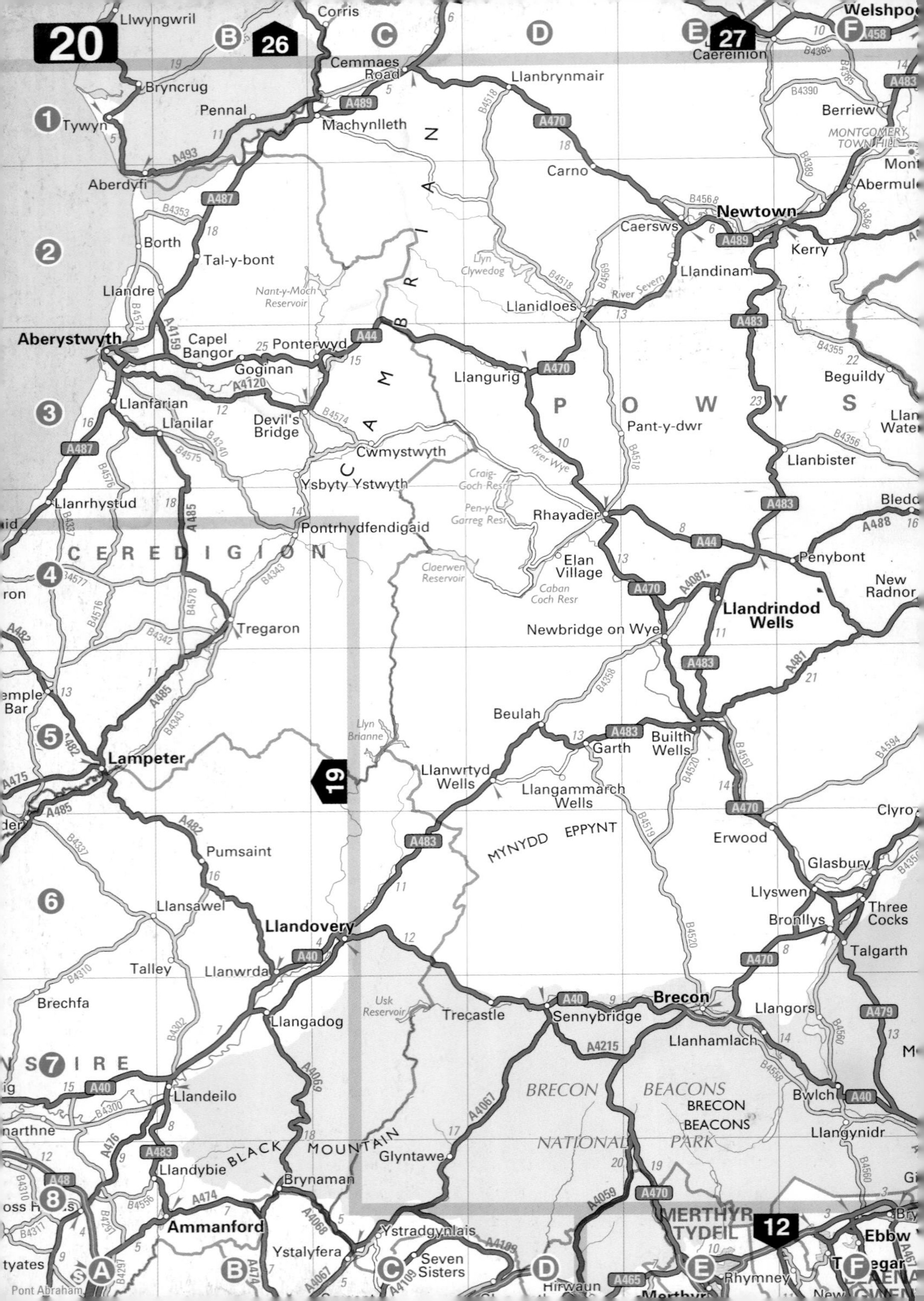
26
27
19
12
Corris
Llwyngwril
Welshpool
Caereinion
Cemmaes Road
Llanbrynmair
Bryncrug
Pennal
Machynlleth
Tywyn
Aberdyfi
Berriew
MONTGOMERY TOWN HILL
Carno
Abermule
Newtown
Caersws
Kerry
Borth
Tal-y-bont
Llandre
Nant-y-Moch Reservoir
Llyn Clywedog
River Severn
Llandinam
Llanidloes
Aberystwyth
Capel Bangor
Ponterwyd
Goginan
Llangurig
Beguildy
Llanfarian
Llanilar
Devil's Bridge
Cwmystwyth
Ysbyty Ystwyth
Pant-y-dwr
River Wye
Craig-Goch Resr
Pen-y-Garreg Resr
Llanbister
Llanrhystud
Rhayader
Pontrhydfendigaid
CAMBRIAN
POWYS
CEREDIGION
Elan Village
Claerwen Reservoir
Caban Coch Resr
Penybont
New Radnor
Tregaron
Llandrindod Wells
Newbridge on Wye
Lampeter
Beulah
Llyn Brianne
Garth
Builth Wells
Llanwrtyd Wells
Llangammarch Wells
Pumsaint
MYNYDD EPPYNT
Erwood
Clyro
Glasbury
Llansawel
Llyswen
Llandovery
Three Cocks
Bronllys
Talgarth
Talley
Llanwrda
Brechfa
Usk Reservoir
Trecastle
Sennybridge
Brecon
Llangors
Llangadog
Llanhamlach
Llandeilo
BRECON BEACONS NATIONAL PARK
BRECON BEACONS
Bwlch
Llangynidr
BLACK MOUNTAIN
Glyntawe
Llandybie
Brynaman
Ammanford
Ystradgynlais
Ystalyfera
Seven Sisters
MERTHYR TYDFIL
Hirwaun
Rhymney
Ebbw Vale
Tredegar
Pont Abraham
A487
A489
A493
A470
A44
A4120
A4159
A485
A482
A483
A488
A4081
A481
A40
A4069
A4067
A476
A48
A474
A4068
A4109
A4059
A465
A4215
A479

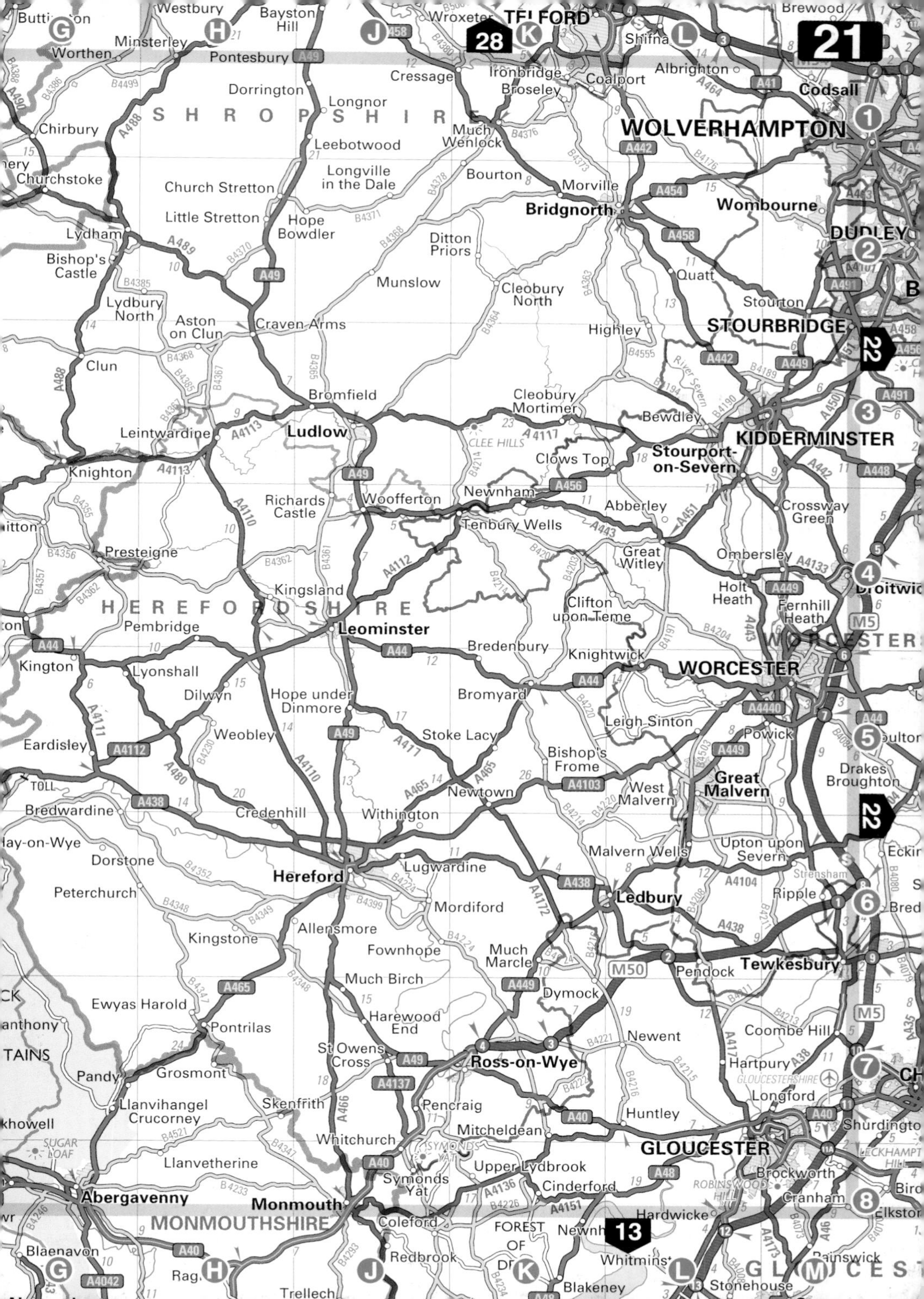
21
28
22
13
Westbury
Bayston Hill
Wroxeter
TELFORD
Shifnal
Brewood
Minsterley
Worthen
Pontesbury
Cressage
Ironbridge
Coalport
Albrighton
Codsall
Broseley
Dorrington
Longnor
SHROPSHIRE
Much Wenlock
WOLVERHAMPTON
Chirbury
Leebotwood
Churchstoke
Longville in the Dale
Bourton
Morville
Church Stretton
Wombourne
Little Stretton
Hope Bowdler
Bridgnorth
Lydham
Ditton Priors
DUDLEY
Bishop's Castle
Munslow
Cleobury North
Quatt
Lydbury North
Stourton
Aston on Clun
Craven Arms
Highley
STOURBRIDGE
Clun
River Severn
Bromfield
Cleobury Mortimer
Bewdley
Leintwardine
Ludlow
CLEE HILLS
KIDDERMINSTER
Knighton
Clows Top
Stourport-on-Severn
Richards Castle
Woofferton
Newnham
Abberley
Crossway Green
Tenbury Wells
Presteigne
Great Witley
Ombersley
Kingsland
Holt Heath
HEREFORDSHIRE
Clifton upon Teme
Fernhill Heath
Pembridge
Leominster
WORCESTER
Kington
Lyonshall
Bredenbury
Knightwick
Dilwyn
Hope under Dinmore
Bromyard
Leigh Sinton
Powick
Weobley
Stoke Lacy
Eardisley
Bishop's Frome
Drakes Broughton
TOLL
West Malvern
Great Malvern
Newtown
Bredwardine
Credenhill
Withington
Hay-on-Wye
Dorstone
Malvern Wells
Upton upon Severn
Lugwardine
Hereford
Strensham
Peterchurch
Ledbury
Ripple
Mordiford
Allensmore
Kingstone
Fownhope
Much Marcle
Pendock
Tewkesbury
Dymock
Much Birch
Ewyas Harold
Harewood End
Coombe Hill
Pontrilas
Newent
St Owens Cross
Ross-on-Wye
Hartpury
GLOUCESTERSHIRE
Pandy
Grosmont
Longford
Llanvihangel Crucorney
Skenfrith
Pencraig
Huntley
Mitcheldean
Shurdington
SUGAR LOAF
Whitchurch
SYMONDS YAT
GLOUCESTER
Llanvetherine
Upper Lydbrook
Symonds Yat
Brockworth
Abergavenny
Cinderford
ROBINSWOOD HILL
Cranham
Monmouth
Hardwicke
MONMOUTHSHIRE
Coleford
FOREST OF DEAN
Blaenavon
Redbrook
Painswick
Trellech
Blakeney
Stonehouse

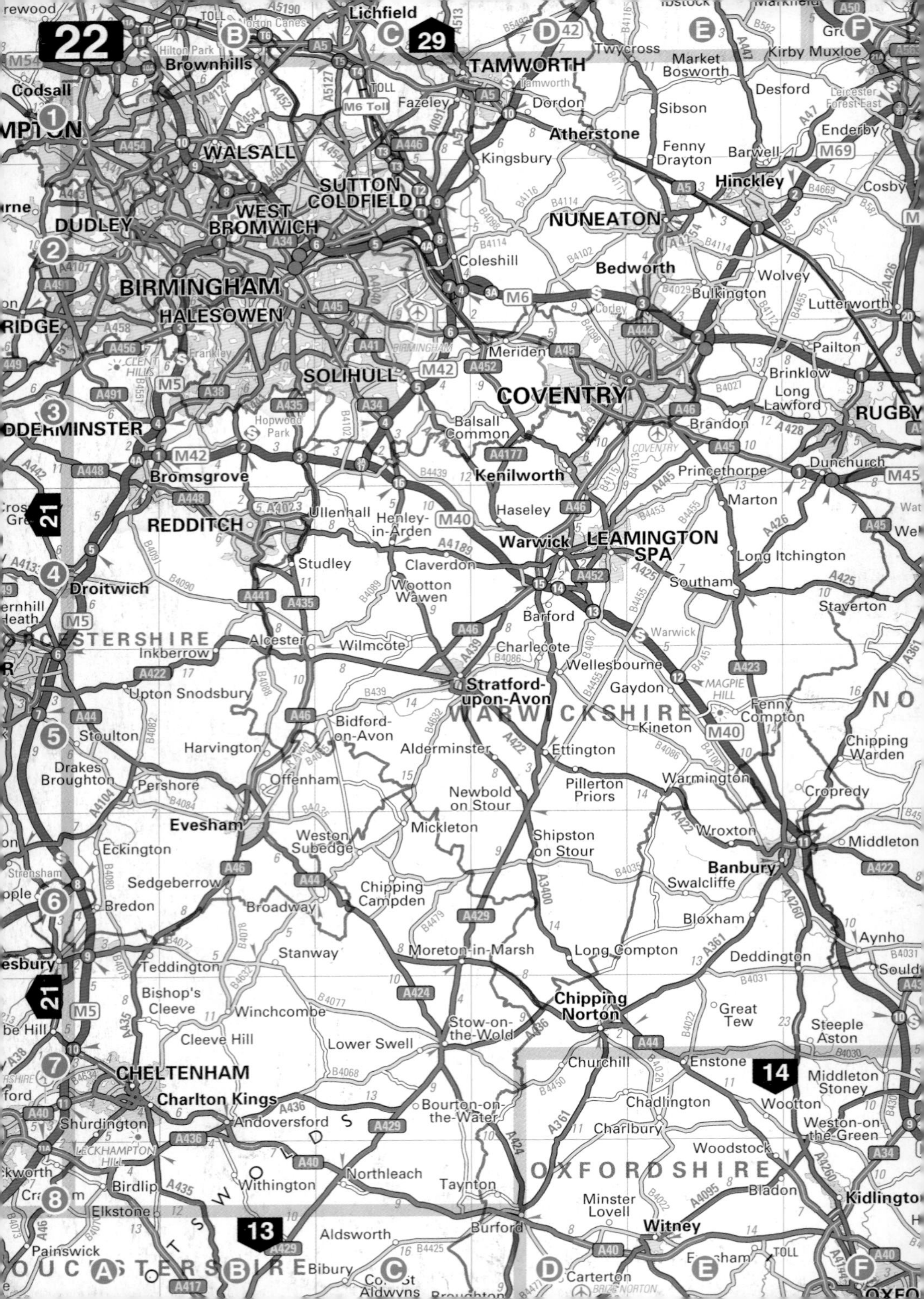

22
29
21
13
14
Lichfield
TAMWORTH
Twycross
Market Bosworth
Kirby Muxloe
Brownhills
Codsall
Fazeley
Dordon
Desford
Atherstone
Sibson
Enderby
WALSALL
Kingsbury
Fenny Drayton
Barwell
SUTTON COLDFIELD
Hinckley
Cosby
WEST BROMWICH
DUDLEY
NUNEATON
Coleshill
Bedworth
Wolvey
BIRMINGHAM
Bulkington
Lutterworth
HALESOWEN
Corley
Pailton
Meriden
SOLIHULL
Brinklow
COVENTRY
Long Lawford
RUGBY
Hopwood Park
Balsall Common
Brandon
Bromsgrove
Kenilworth
Princethorpe
Dunchurch
Marton
Haseley
REDDITCH
Ullenhall
Henley-in-Arden
Warwick
LEAMINGTON SPA
Long Itchington
Studley
Claverdon
Southam
Droitwich
Wootton Wawen
Staverton
Barford
ORCESTERSHIRE
Inkberrow
Alcester
Wilmcote
Charlecote
Wellesbourne
Upton Snodsbury
Stratford-upon-Avon
Gaydon
WARWICKSHIRE
Stoulton
Bidford-on-Avon
Kineton
Fenny Compton
Harvington
Alderminster
Ettington
Chipping Warden
Drakes Broughton
Offenham
Pershore
Newbold on Stour
Pillerton Priors
Warmington
Cropredy
Evesham
Mickleton
Eckington
Weston Subedge
Shipston on Stour
Wroxton
Middleton
Banbury
Sedgeberrow
Swalcliffe
Chipping Campden
Bredon
Broadway
Bloxham
Aynho
Stanway
Moreton-in-Marsh
Long Compton
Deddington
Teddington
Bishop's Cleeve
Winchcombe
Chipping Norton
Great Tew
Stow-on-the-Wold
Steeple Aston
Cleeve Hill
Lower Swell
Churchill
Enstone
CHELTENHAM
Middleton Stoney
Charlton Kings
Chadlington
Wootton
Bourton-on-the-Water
Shurdington
Andoversford
Charlbury
Weston-on-the-Green
Woodstock
OXFORDSHIRE
Northleach
Taynton
Birdlip
Withington
Bladon
Kidlington
Minster Lovell
Elkstone
Witney
Burford
Aldsworth
Painswick
Bibury
Carterton
COTSWOLDS
GLOUCESTERSHIRE

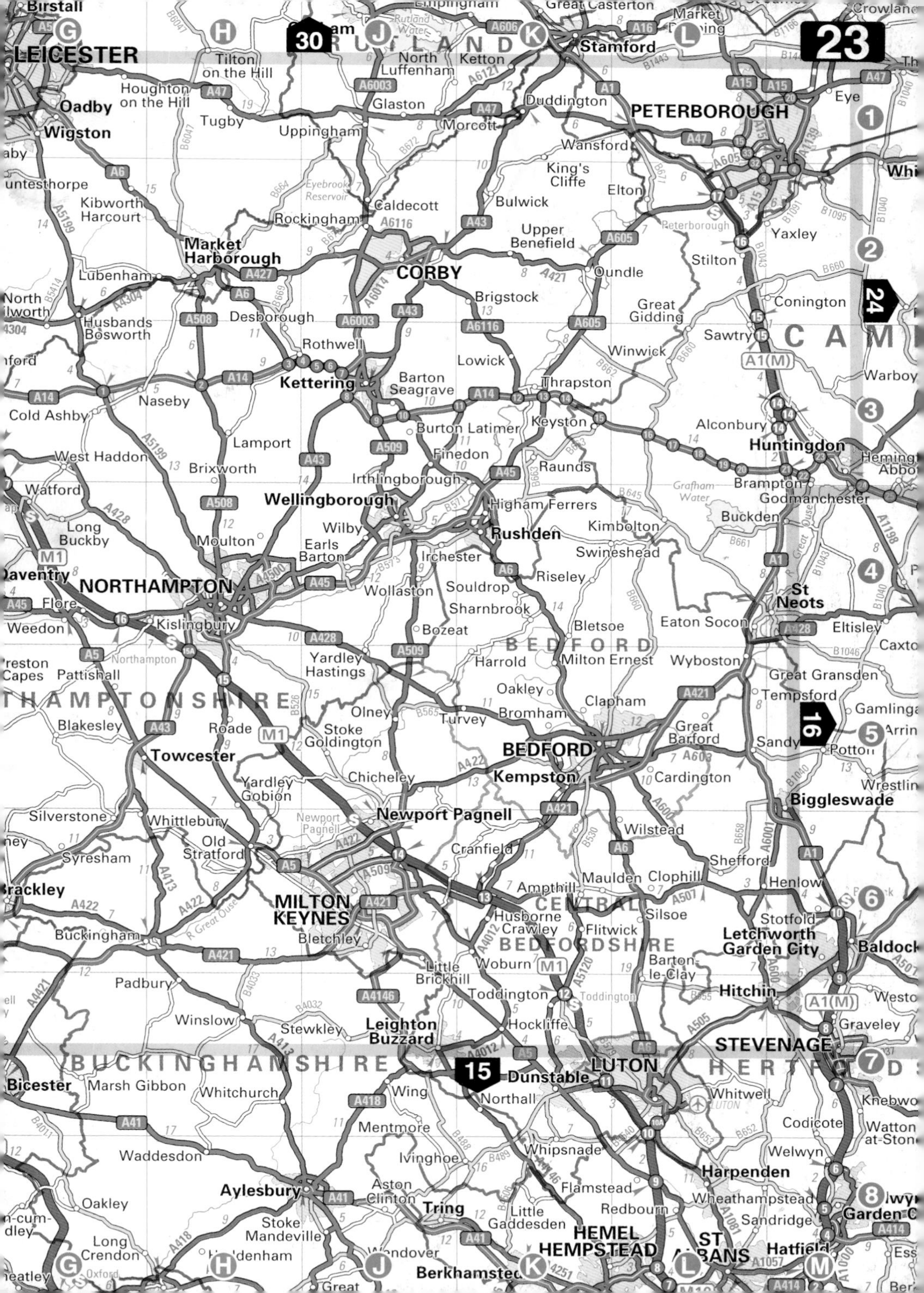

LEICESTER
Birstall
Oadby
Wigston
Tilton on the Hill
Houghton on the Hill
Tugby
RUTLAND
North Luffenham
Ketton
Stamford
Great Casterton
Market Deeping
Crowland
Glaston
Uppingham
Morcott
Duddington
PETERBOROUGH
Eye
Wansford
King's Cliffe
Elton
Bulwick
Eyebrook Reservoir
Caldecott
Rockingham
Kibworth Harcourt
Market Harborough
Lubenham
CORBY
Upper Benefield
Oundle
Stilton
Yaxley
Brigstock
Great Gidding
Conington
Sawtry
Desborough
Rothwell
Lowick
Winwick
Husbands Bosworth
Kettering
Barton Seagrave
Thrapston
Naseby
Cold Ashby
Burton Latimer
Keyston
Alconbury
Huntingdon
Lamport
Finedon
Raunds
West Haddon
Brixworth
Irthlingborough
Brampton
Godmanchester
Watford
Wellingborough
Higham Ferrers
Grafham Water
Buckden
Long Buckby
Wilby
Rushden
Kimbolton
Moulton
Earls Barton
Irchester
Swineshead
Daventry
NORTHAMPTON
Wollaston
Souldrop
Riseley
St Neots
Flore
Kislingbury
Sharnbrook
Weedon
Bozeat
Bletsoe
Eaton Socon
Eltisley
BEDFORD
Yardley Hastings
Harrold
Milton Ernest
Wyboston
Great Gransden
Pattishall
NORTHAMPTONSHIRE
Oakley
Tempsford
Clapham
Olney
Turvey
Bromham
Blakesley
Roade
Stoke Goldington
Great Barford
Sandy
Potton
Towcester
BEDFORD
Chicheley
Kempston
Cardington
Yardley Gobion
Biggleswade
Silverstone
Whittlebury
Newport Pagnell
Old Stratford
Syresham
Cranfield
Wilstead
Shefford
Brackley
MILTON KEYNES
Ampthill
Maulden
Clophill
Henlow
Husborne Crawley
CENTRAL BEDFORDSHIRE
Silsoe
Stotfold
Buckingham
Bletchley
Flitwick
Letchworth Garden City
Baldock
Woburn
Barton-le-Clay
Padbury
Little Brickhill
Hitchin
Toddington
Winslow
Stewkley
Leighton Buzzard
Hockliffe
Graveley
STEVENAGE
BUCKINGHAMSHIRE
Dunstable
LUTON
HERTFORDSHIRE
Bicester
Marsh Gibbon
Whitchurch
Wing
Northall
Whitwell
Knebworth
Mentmore
Codicote
Waddesdon
Ivinghoe
Whipsnade
Welwyn
Harpenden
Aylesbury
Aston Clinton
Flamstead
Oakley
Tring
Little Gaddesden
Redbourn
Wheathampstead
Stoke Mandeville
Sandridge
Long Crendon
HEMEL HEMPSTEAD
ST ALBANS
Hatfield
Wendover
Berkhamsted

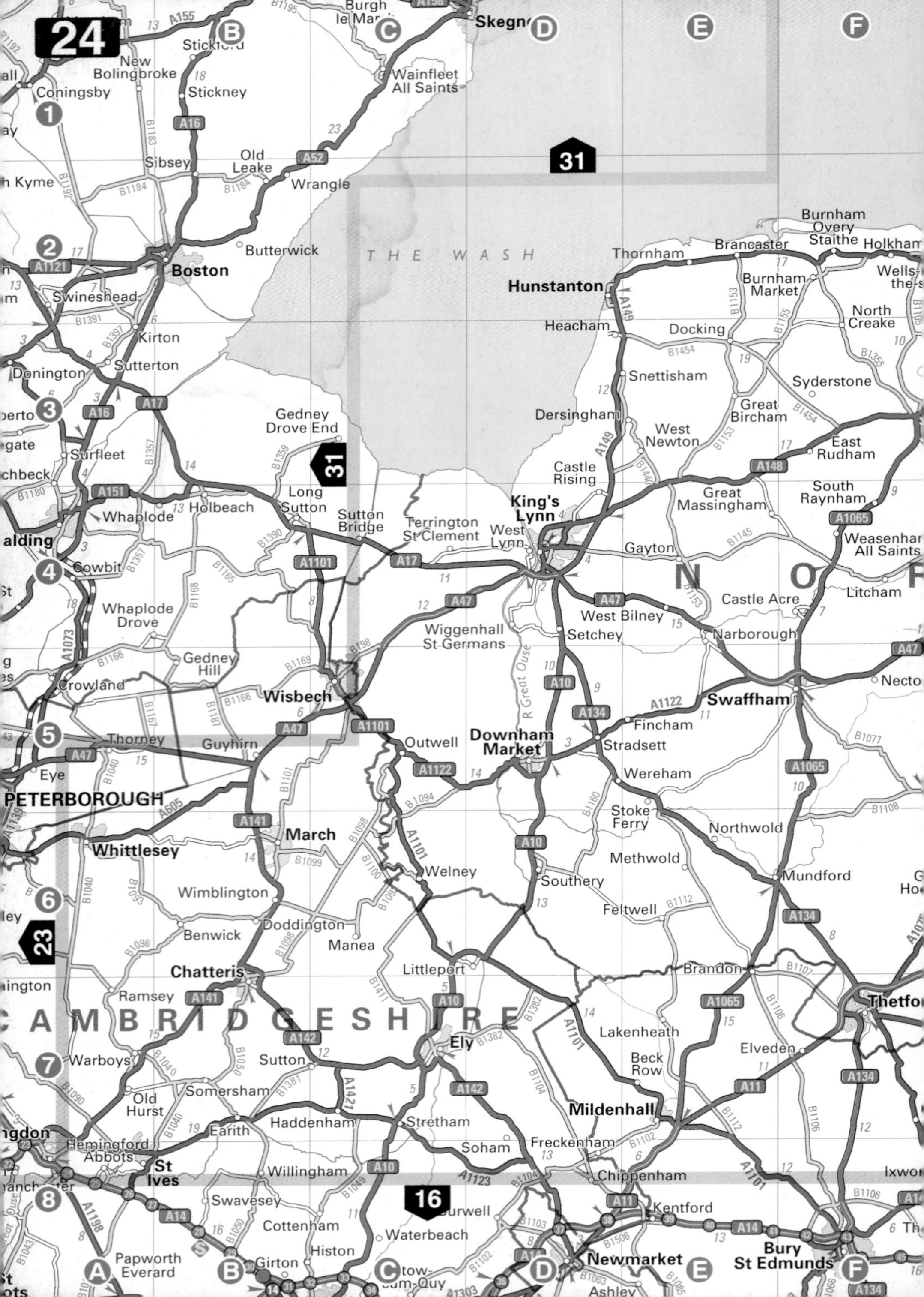

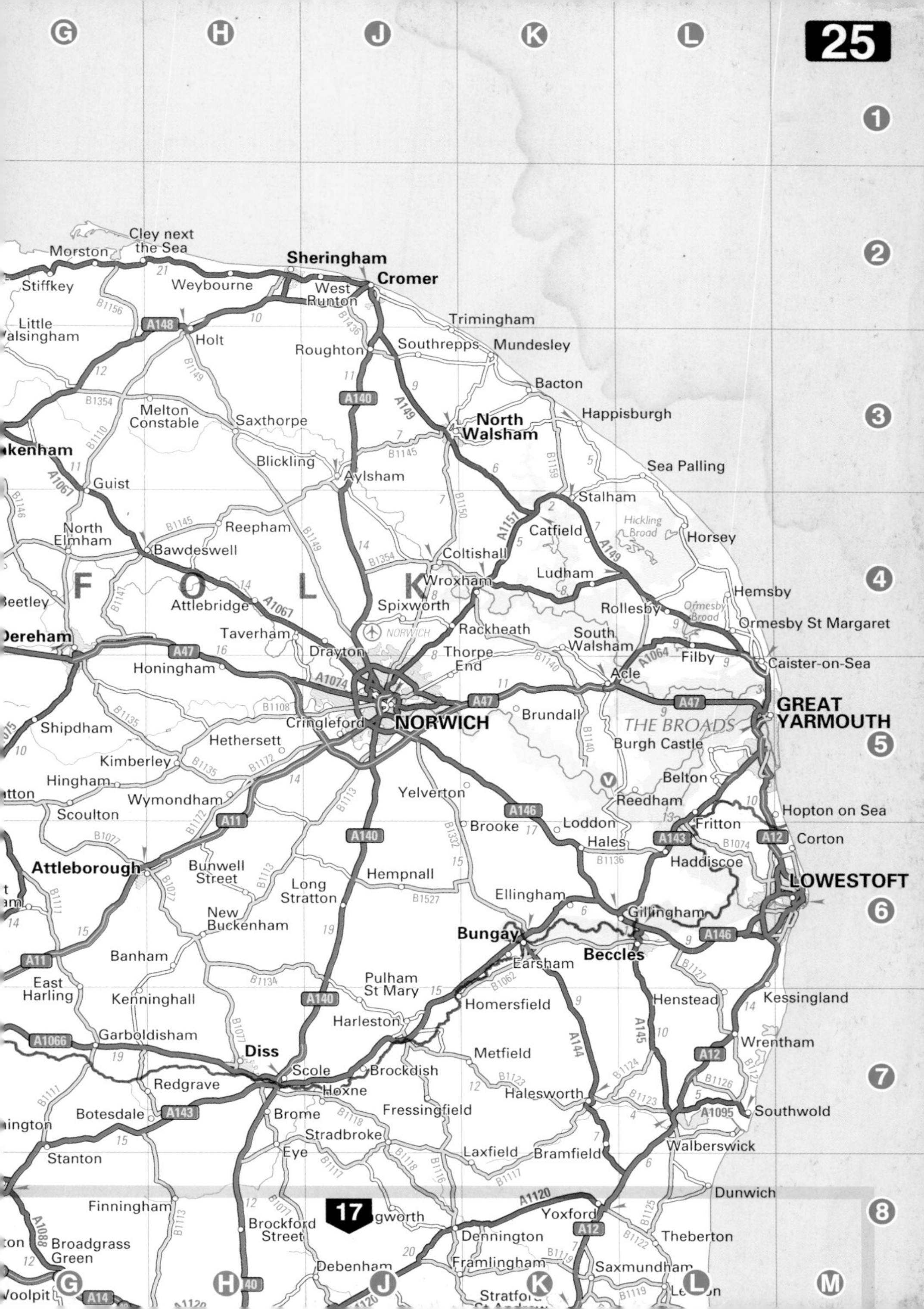

G
H
J
K
L
M
1
2
3
4
5
6
7
8
Cley next the Sea
Morston
Sheringham
Cromer
Stiffkey
Weybourne
West Runton
Little Walsingham
Holt
Trimingham
Roughton
Southrepps
Mundesley
Bacton
North Walsham
Happisburgh
Melton Constable
Saxthorpe
Blickling
Aylsham
Sea Palling
Guist
Stalham
Reepham
Catfield
Hickling Broad
Horsey
North Elmham
Bawdeswell
Coltishall
Ludham
Wroxham
F O L K
Attlebridge
Spixworth
Hemsby
Rollesby
Ormesby Broad
Ormesby St Margaret
Dereham
Taverham
Rackheath
South Walsham
Drayton
Thorpe End
Filby
Caister-on-Sea
Honingham
Acle
GREAT YARMOUTH
Shipdham
Cringleford
NORWICH
Brundall
THE BROADS
Hethersett
Burgh Castle
Kimberley
Belton
Hingham
Yelverton
Reedham
Wymondham
Hopton on Sea
Scoulton
Brooke
Loddon
Fritton
Hales
Corton
Haddiscoe
Attleborough
Bunwell Street
Long Stratton
Hempnall
LOWESTOFT
Ellingham
New Buckenham
Gillingham
Bungay
Beccles
Banham
Earsham
East Harling
Pulham St Mary
Kenninghall
Homersfield
Henstead
Kessingland
Harleston
Garboldisham
Wrentham
Diss
Metfield
Scole
Brockdish
Redgrave
Hoxne
Halesworth
Botesdale
Brome
Fressingfield
Southwold
Stradbroke
Walberswick
Stanton
Eye
Laxfield
Bramfield
Dunwich
Finningham
Yoxford
Brockford Street
Dennington
Theberton
Broadgrass Green
Debenham
Framlingham
Saxmundham
Woolpit
Stratford
17
A148
A140
A149
A1067
A1151
A47
A1074
A1064
A146
A11
A143
A12
A144
A145
A1066
A1095
A1120
A1088
A14
B1156
B1436
B1149
B1354
B1110
B1145
B1159
B1150
B1146
B1147
B1140
B1108
B1135
B1172
B1113
B1332
B1074
B1077
B1136
B1527
B1111
B1134
B1062
B1127
B1123
B1124
B1126
B1118
B1117
B1116
B1125
B1122
B1119
B1113
NORWICH

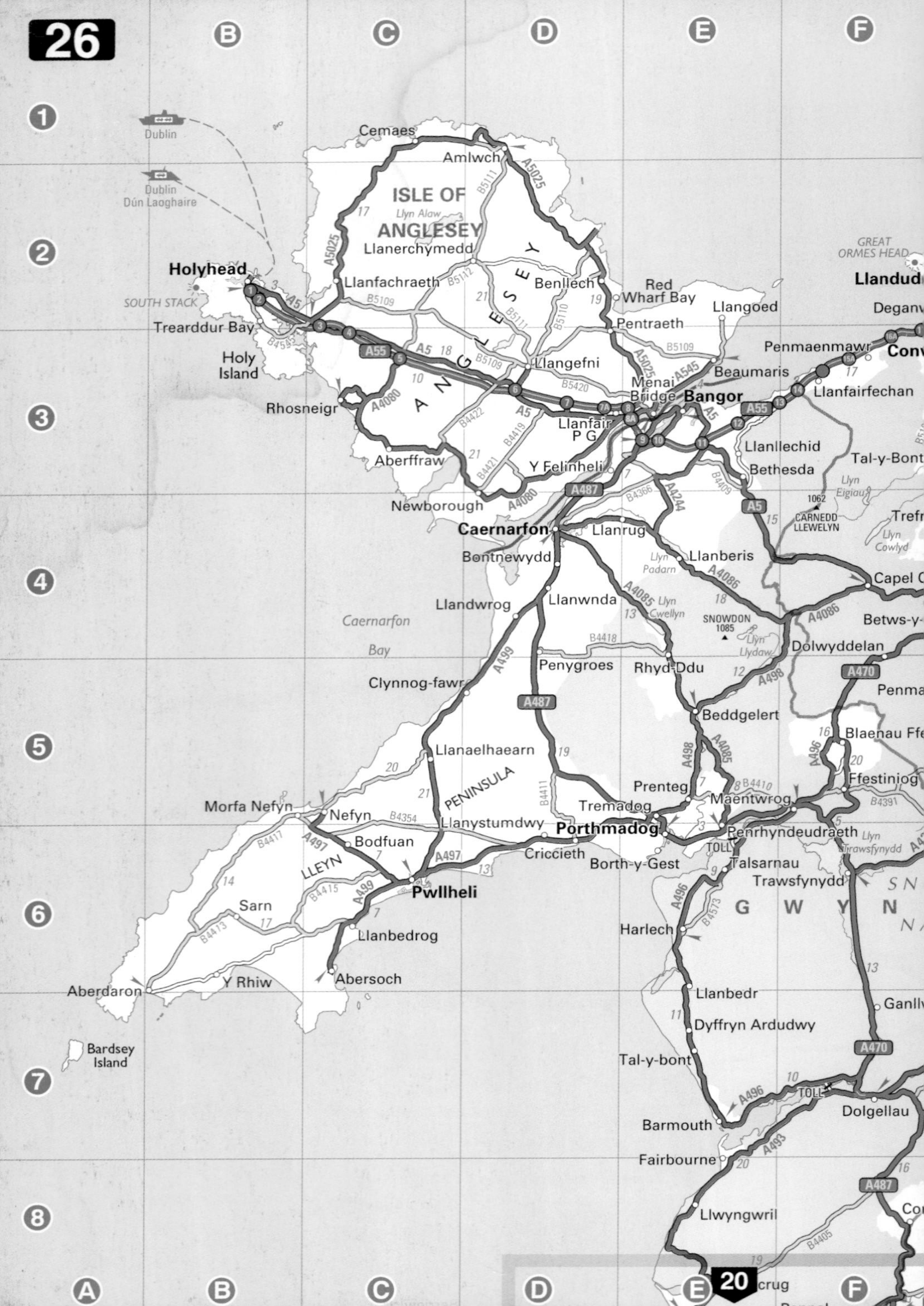

A   B   C   D   E   F

1
2
3
4
5
6
7
8

Dublin

Dublin
Dún Laoghaire

Cemaes
Amlwch
A5025
B5111

ISLE OF
17   Llyn Alaw
ANGLESEY
Llanerchymedd

Holyhead

A5025

Benllech
Red
Wharf Bay
Llangoed

SOUTH STACK

Llanfachraeth
B5109
B5112
21
B5110
19
Pentraeth

Trearddur Bay

B5109
Llangefni
B5420

**GREAT
ORMES HEAD**

Llandud

Degan

Penmaenmawr

Conw

Holy
Island

A55
A5
B4545

Menai
Bridge   **Bangor**

Beaumaris
17

18

Llanfairfechan

Rhosneigr

A4080
10
A5
Llanfair
P G

A55

A5

Llanllechid
Bethesda

Tal-y-Bont

Aberffraw

B4422
21
B4421
B4419
Y Felinheli

A4080

A487

B4366

A4244
A5405

A5

1062
CARNEDD
LLEWELYN
15

Llyn
Eigiau

Tref

Newborough

Caernarfon

Bontnewydd

Llanrug

Llanberis
A4086

Llyn
Padarn

Llyn
Cowlyd

Capel C

Betws-y-

Llandwrog

Llanwnda

A4085   Llyn
13   Cwellyn

18
SNOWDON
1085
Llyn
Llydaw

Dolwyddelan

A4086

Caernarfon

Bay

B4418

Penygroes

Rhyd-Ddu

12
A498
A470

Penma

Clynnog-fawr

A499

A487

Beddgelert

A498
A4085
A496
20

Blaenau Ffe

Ffestiniog

Llanaelhaearn

20

PENINSULA

19

B4411

Prenteg

Tremadog

7

8   B4410

Maentwrog

3
B4391

Morfa Nefyn

Nefyn

B4354

Llanystumdwy

Porthmadog

Penrhyndeudraeth

TOLL

Llyn
Trawsfynydd

Llyn
Crawsfynydd

SN

Bodfuan
7

A497
13

Criccieth

Borth-y-Gest

9

Talsarnau

Trawsfynydd

G W Y N

14

LLEYN

B4411
A497
B4415

A499

Sarn
17

Pwllheli

B4413

Llanbedrog

Harlech
B4573

Llanbedr

Dyffryn Ardudwy

11

A496

Aberdaron

Y Rhiw

Abersoch

Tal-y-bont

13

Ganll

A470

Bardsey
Island

A496
10
TOLL

Barmouth

Dolgellau

A493

Fairbourne

A487

Llwyngwril

B4405

Co

crug

Pennal

A   B   C   D   E   F

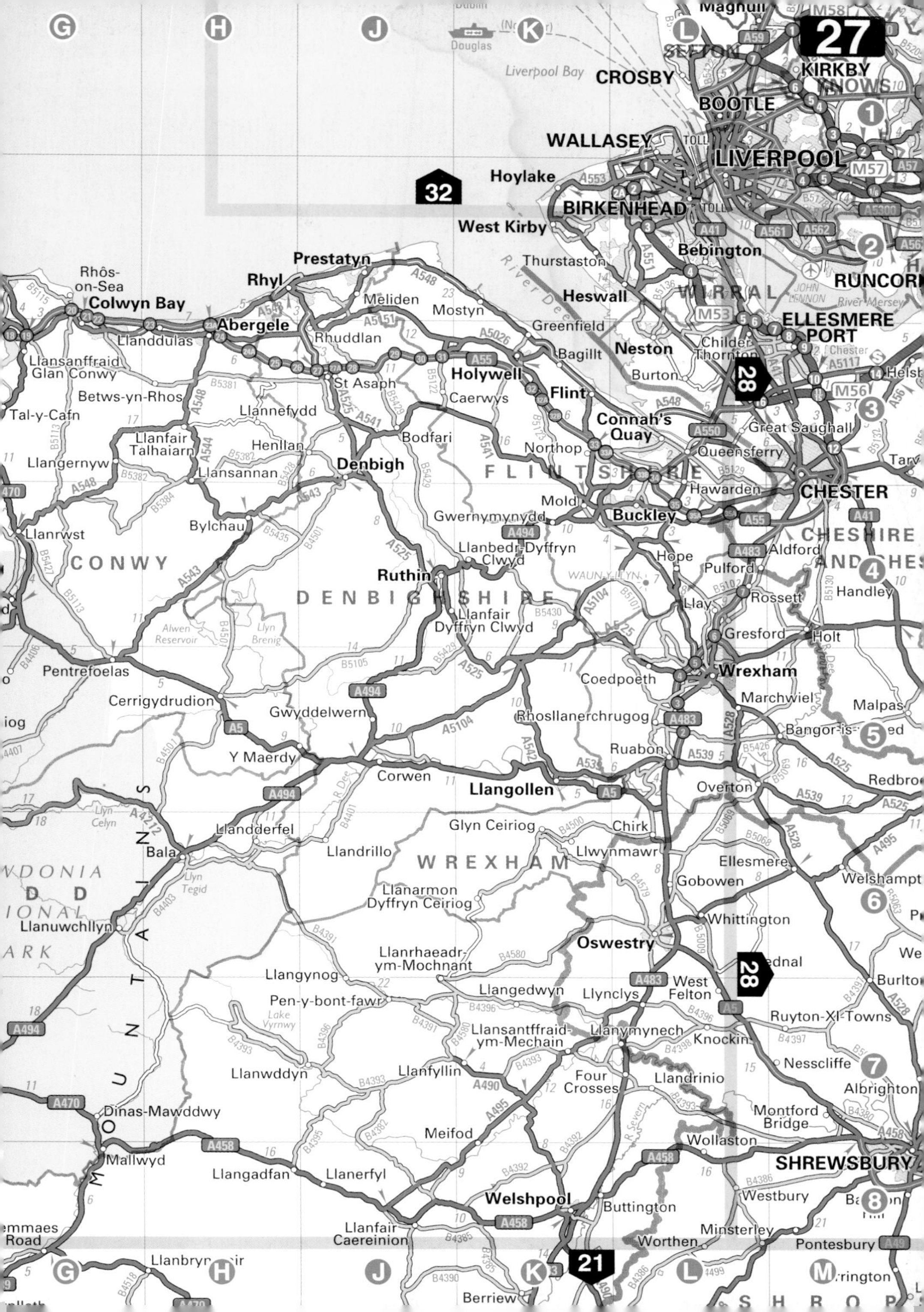
27
G
H
J
K
L
M
Douglas
Liverpool Bay
Maghull
SEFTON
CROSBY
KIRKBY
KNOWSLEY
BOOTLE
WALLASEY
LIVERPOOL
Hoylake
32
BIRKENHEAD
West Kirby
Bebington
Thurstaston
River Dee
WIRRAL
RUNCORN
JOHN LENNON
River Mersey
Heswall
ELLESMERE PORT
Prestatyn
Rhyl
Rhôs-on-Sea
Colwyn Bay
Meliden
Mostyn
Greenfield
Bagillt
Neston
Childer Thornton
Abergele
Llanddulas
Rhuddlan
Llansanffraid Glan Conwy
Holywell
Flint
Burton
28
Betws-yn-Rhos
St Asaph
Caerwys
Tal-y-Cafn
Llannefydd
Connah's Quay
Great Saughall
Llanfair Talhaiarn
Henllan
Bodfari
Northop
Queensferry
Llangernyw
Llansannan
Denbigh
FLINTSHIRE
Hawarden
CHESTER
Mold
Buckley
Bylchau
Gwernymynydd
CHESHIRE
Llanrwst
CONWY
Llanbedr-Dyffryn Clwyd
Hope
Aldford
Pulford
Ruthin
WAUN-Y-LLYN
DENBIGHSHIRE
Handley
Llay
Rossett
Llanfair Dyffryn Clwyd
Alwen Reservoir
Llyn Brenig
Gresford
Holt
Pentrefoelas
Wrexham
Coedpoeth
Cerrigydrudion
Marchwiel
Malpas
Gwyddelwern
Rhosllanerchrugog
Bangor-is-y-coed
Y Maerdy
Ruabon
Corwen
Llangollen
Overton
Redbrook
Llyn Celyn
Llandderfel
Glyn Ceiriog
Chirk
Bala
Llandrillo
Llwynmawr
WREXHAM
Ellesmere
Welshampton
Llyn Tegid
Llanarmon Dyffryn Ceiriog
Gobowen
Llanuwchllyn
Whittington
Oswestry
Llanrhaeadr-ym-Mochnant
Llangynog
West Felton
Llangedwyn
Llynclys
Burlton
Pen-y-bont-fawr
Lake Vyrnwy
Ruyton-XI-Towns
Llansantffraid-ym-Mechain
Llanymynech
Knockin
Nesscliffe
Llanwddyn
Llanfyllin
Four Crosses
Llandrinio
Albrighton
Dinas-Mawddwy
Montford Bridge
Meifod
R. Severn
Wollaston
SHREWSBURY
Mallwyd
Llangadfan
Llanerfyl
Welshpool
Buttington
Westbury
Minsterley
Llanfair Caereinion
Worthen
Pontesbury
21
Berriew
SNOWDONIA NATIONAL PARK
MOUNTAINS
A5
A55
A494
A458
A483
A41
A470
A548

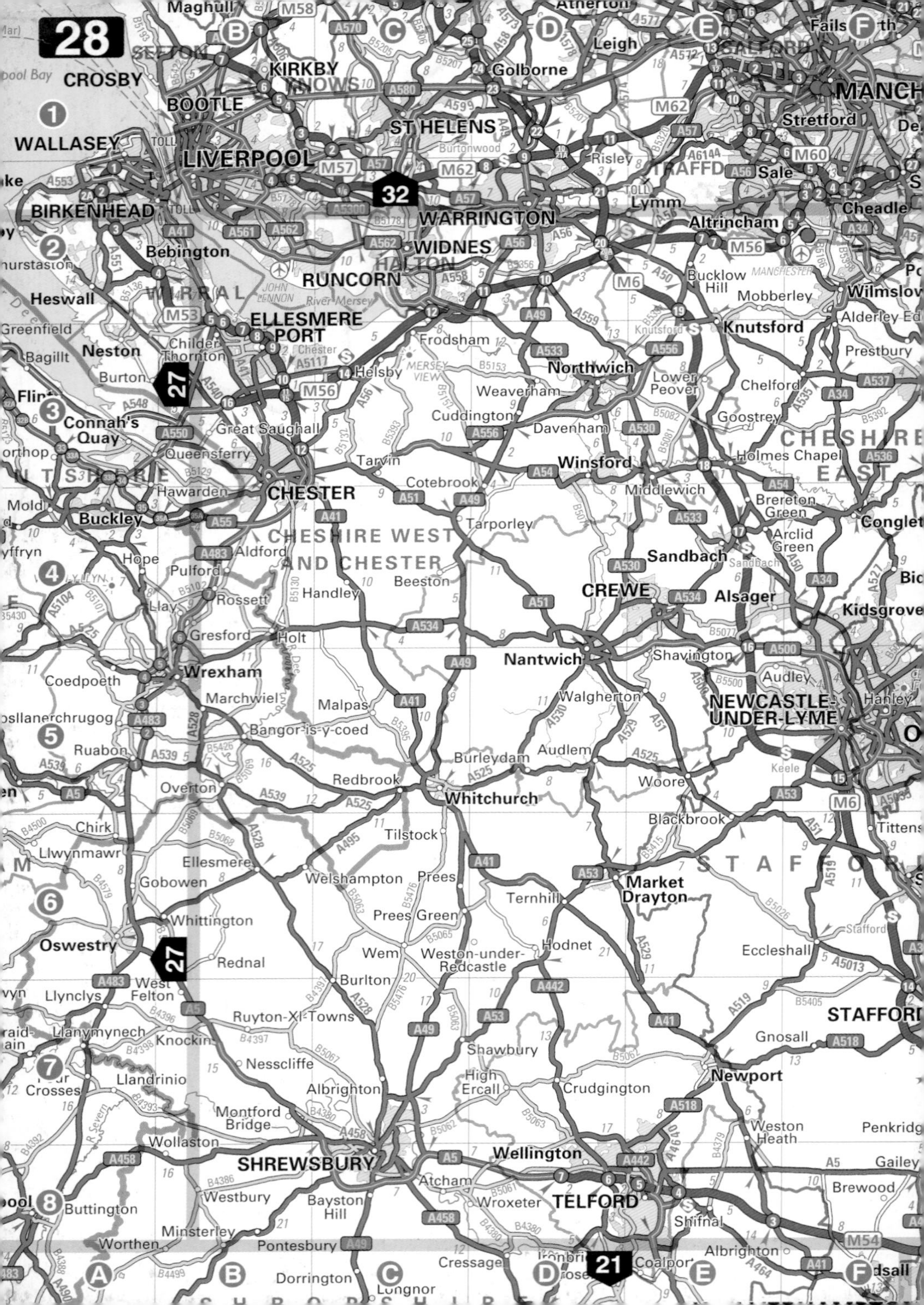

Maghull
M58
A570
Atherton
A577
Leigh
SALFORD
MANCH
Fails
Stretford
SEFTON
CROSBY
KIRKBY
KNOWSLEY
Golborne
A580
M62
BOOTLE
WALLASEY
LIVERPOOL
ST HELENS
A599
Burtonwood
Risley
TRAFFORD
A6144
M60
Sale
M57
A57
32
M62
A57
Lymm
Cheadle
A553
BIRKENHEAD
A5300
WARRINGTON
Altrincham
A41
A561
A562
Bebington
A562
WIDNES
A56
M56
Thurstaston
HALTON
A34
A551
RUNCORN
A558
Bucklow Hill
Mobberley
Wilmslow
Heswall
WIRRAL
JOHN LENNON
River Mersey
M6
A50
M53
ELLESMERE PORT
A49
Alderley Edge
Greenfield
Knutsford
Knutsford
Frodsham
A559
A533
A556
Childer Thornton
Neston
Chester
Bagillt
A5117
Helsby
MERSEY VIEW
Prestbury
Burton
27
B5153
Northwich
Lower Peover
Chelford
A537
Flint
A540
A548
M56
A56
Weaverham
A34
A535
Connah's Quay
A550
Great Saughall
Cuddington
Davenham
A530
Goostrey
Queensferry
A556
CHESHIRE EAST
Northop
Tarvin
Holmes Chapel
A536
FLINTSHIRE
Hawarden
A54
Winsford
Mold
CHESTER
Cotebrook
Middlewich
Buckley
A51
A49
A54
A55
A41
Brereton Green
A533
Congleton
Tarporley
CHESHIRE WEST AND CHESTER
Arclid Green
Ffrith
Hope
Aldford
A483
Sandbach
Sandbach
A50
Pulford
Beeston
A530
Handley
A534
Alsager
A34
A527
Llay
Rossett
CREWE
A51
A5104
B5130
Kidsgrove
A525
Gresford
Holt
A534
B5077
Nantwich
Shavington
A500
Wrexham
A49
Coedpoeth
Marchwiel
Audley
Hanley
A41
Walgherton
A528
Malpas
NEWCASTLE-UNDER-LYME
Rhosllanerchrugog
A483
Bangor-is-y-coed
A530
A529
A51
Ruabon
A539
Burleydam
Audlem
A525
Keele
A525
Woore
A5
Overton
Redbrook
A539
A525
Whitchurch
A53
M6
Chirk
Tilstock
Blackbrook
Tittensor
A495
A51
Llwynmawr
A528
Ellesmere
Welshampton
Prees
A41
A53
Market Drayton
STAFFORDSHIRE
Gobowen
Ternhill
Prees Green
A519
Whittington
Stafford
Oswestry
27
Wem
Weston-under-Redcastle
Hodnet
Eccleshall
A5013
Rednal
A483
West Felton
Burlton
A442
Llynclys
A5
A528
A49
A53
STAFFORD
Ruyton-XI-Towns
A41
A519
Llanymynech
Knockin
Gnosall
A518
Shawbury
Nesscliffe
Llandrinio
High Ercall
Newport
Four Crosses
Albrighton
Crudgington
A518
Montford Bridge
Weston Heath
Penkridge
A458
Wollaston
A4640
A458
A5
Wellington
A442
A5
Gailey
SHREWSBURY
Atcham
Brewood
Welshpool
Buttington
Westbury
Bayston Hill
Wroxeter
TELFORD
Shifnal
A458
M54
Minsterley
Worthen
Pontesbury
A49
Cressage
Ironbridge
21
Coalport
Albrighton
A41
Codsall
A464
Dorrington
Longnor
SHROPSHIRE

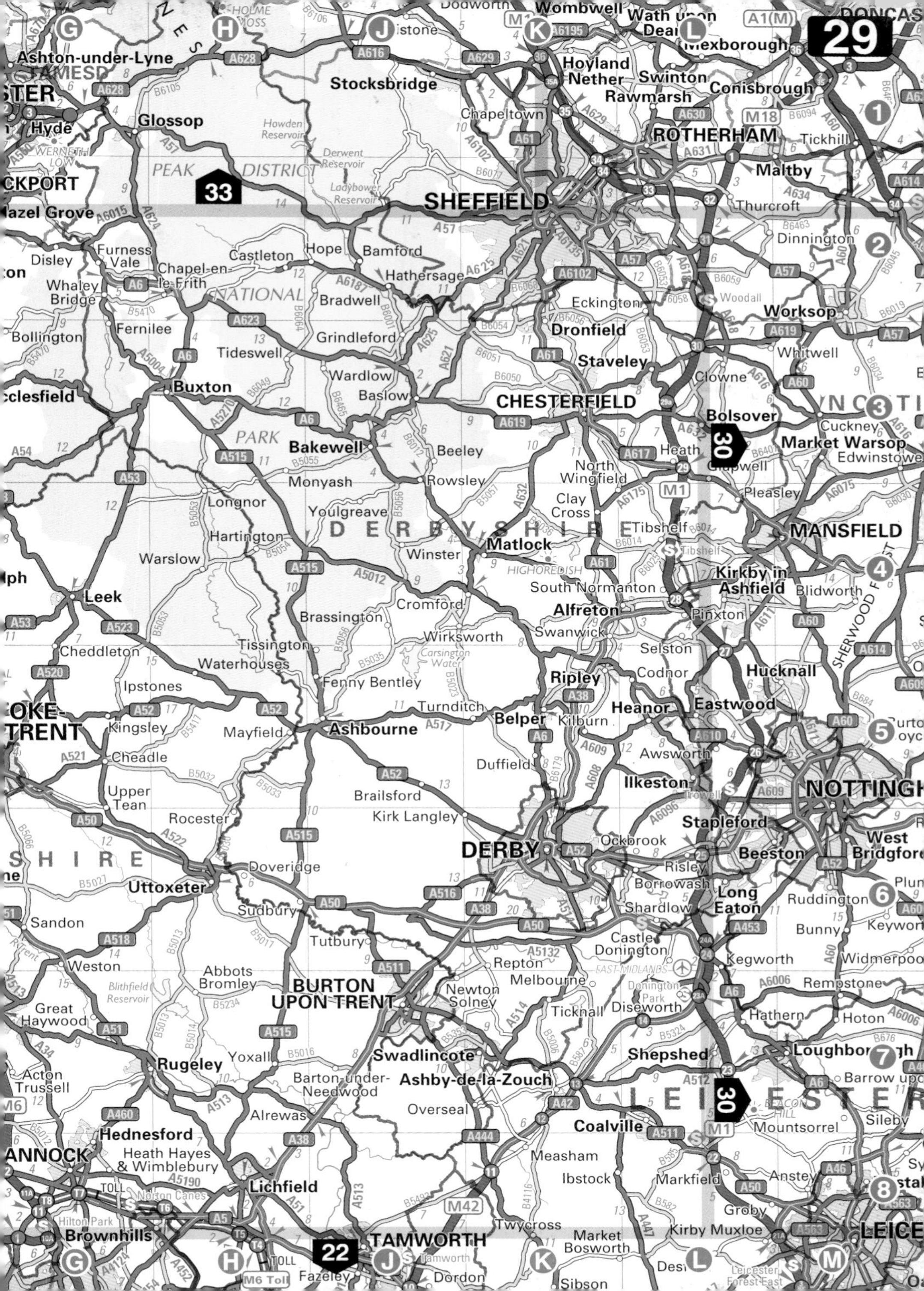
29
33
30
22
SHEFFIELD
ROTHERHAM
CHESTERFIELD
MANSFIELD
NOTTINGHAM
DERBY
BURTON UPON TRENT
TAMWORTH
LEICESTER
Ashton-under-Lyne
Hyde
Glossop
Stocksbridge
Chapeltown
Hoyland Nether
Swinton
Rawmarsh
Conisbrough
Mexborough
Wombwell
Tickhill
Maltby
Thurcroft
Dinnington
Worksop
Whitwell
Clowne
Bolsover
Market Warsop
Edwinstowe
Castleton
Hope
Bamford
Hathersage
Bradwell
Grindleford
Tideswell
Wardlow
Baslow
Buxton
Chapel-en-le-Frith
Furness Vale
Disley
Whaley Bridge
Fernilee
Bollington
Hazel Grove
Eckington
Dronfield
Staveley
Bakewell
Beeley
Rowsley
Monyash
Youlgreave
Longnor
Hartington
Warslow
Matlock
Winster
Cromford
Brassington
Wirksworth
Tissington
Waterhouses
Fenny Bentley
Turnditch
Belper
Ashbourne
Leek
Cheddleton
Ipstones
Kingsley
Mayfield
Cheadle
Upper Tean
Rocester
Uttoxeter
Doveridge
Sudbury
Tutbury
Sandon
Weston
Abbots Bromley
Great Haywood
Rugeley
Yoxall
Acton Trussell
Hednesford
Heath Hayes & Wimblebury
Lichfield
Alrewas
Barton-under-Needwood
Brownhills
Swadlincote
Ashby-de-la-Zouch
Overseal
Measham
Ibstock
Coalville
Twycross
Market Bosworth
Kirby Muxloe
Groby
Markfield
Anstey
Mountsorrel
Sileby
Loughborough
Barrow upon Soar
Shepshed
Hathern
Hoton
Rempstone
Kegworth
Castle Donington
Diseworth
Melbourne
Ticknall
Repton
Newton Solney
Shardlow
Long Eaton
Borrowash
Risley
Ockbrook
Stapleford
Beeston
West Bridgford
Ruddington
Bunny
Keyworth
Widmerpool
Ilkeston
Awsworth
Heanor
Eastwood
Kilburn
Duffield
Ripley
Codnor
Selston
Swanwick
Alfreton
Pinxton
Kirkby in Ashfield
Blidworth
Hucknall
South Normanton
Tibshelf
Clay Cross
North Wingfield
Heath
Glapwell
Pleasley
Brailsford
Kirk Langley
DERBYSHIRE
PEAK DISTRICT NATIONAL PARK
SHERWOOD FOREST
LEICESTERSHIRE
STOKE-ON-TRENT
Tamworth
Fazeley
Dordon
Sibson
Desford
Leicester Forest East
Hilton Park
Norton Canes
EAST MIDLANDS
Howden Reservoir
Derwent Reservoir
Ladybower Reservoir
Carsington Water
Blithfield Reservoir
HIGHOREDISH
BEACON HILL
Woodall
Trowell
M1
M18
M42
M6 Toll
A1(M)
TOLL

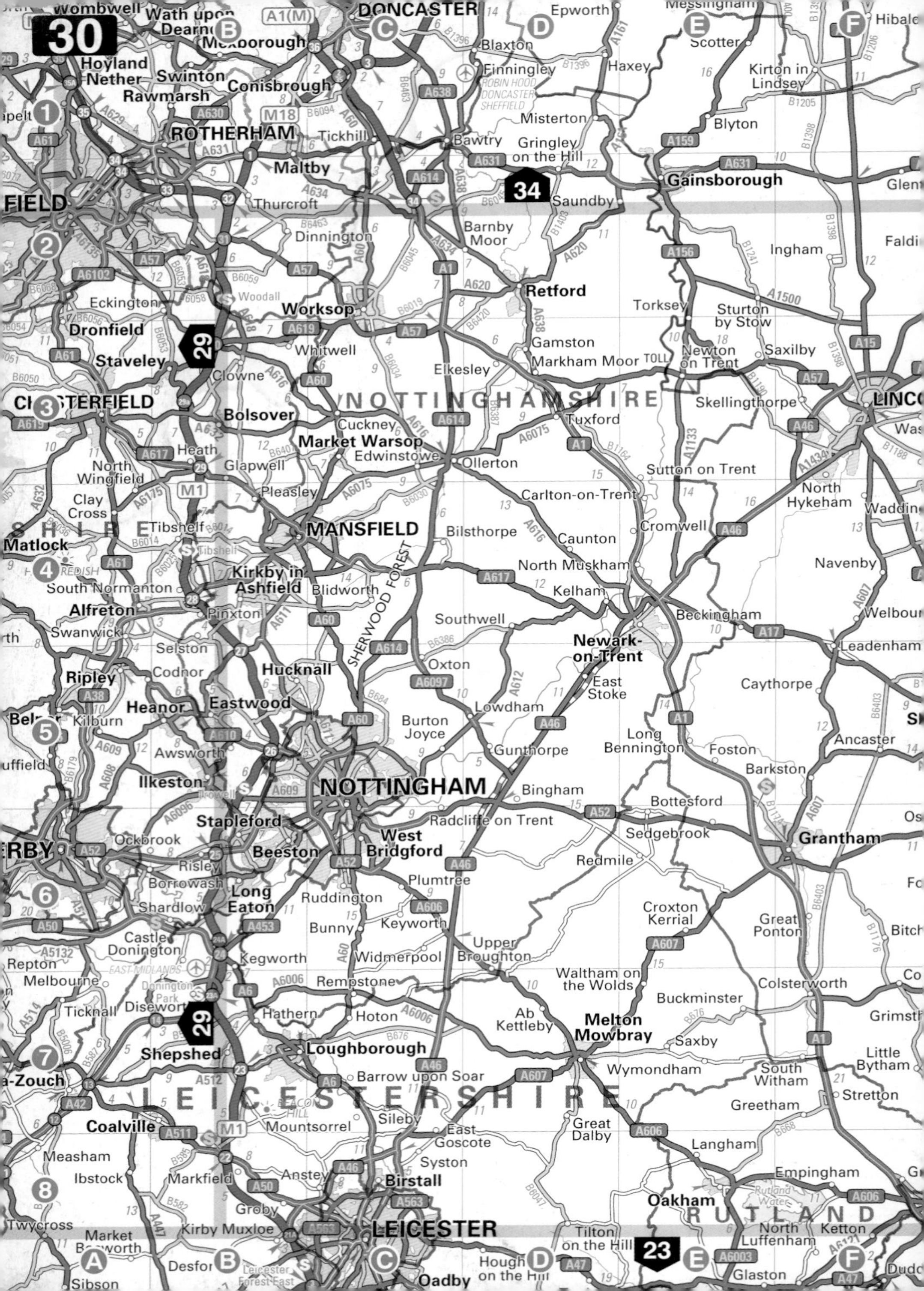

30
Wombwell
Wath upon Dearne
Mexborough
DONCASTER
Epworth
Messingham
Hibaldstow
Blaxton
Scotter
Hoyland Nether
Swinton
Conisbrough
Rawmarsh
Finningley
ROBIN HOOD DONCASTER SHEFFIELD
Haxey
Kirton in Lindsey
Misterton
Blyton
ROTHERHAM
Tickhill
Bawtry
Gringley on the Hill
Maltby
Gainsborough
34
Saundby
Thurcroft
SHEFFIELD
Dinnington
Barnby Moor
Ingham
Retford
Eckington
Woodall
Worksop
Torksey
Sturton by Stow
Dronfield
29
Whitwell
Gamston
Staveley
Markham Moor
TOLL
Newton on Trent
Saxilby
Elkesley
Clowne
NOTTINGHAMSHIRE
Skellingthorpe
CHESTERFIELD
Bolsover
Tuxford
LINCOLN
Cuckney
Market Warsop
Edwinstowe
Ollerton
Heath
North Wingfield
Glapwell
Sutton on Trent
North Hykeham
Pleasley
Carlton-on-Trent
Clay Cross
Tibshelf
MANSFIELD
Bilsthorpe
Cromwell
Caunton
Matlock
Navenby
Kirkby in Ashfield
North Muskham
South Normanton
Blidworth
SHERWOOD FOREST
Kelham
Alfreton
Pinxton
Southwell
Beckingham
Swanwick
Newark-on-Trent
Leadenham
Selston
Oxton
Ripley
Codnor
Hucknall
East Stoke
Caythorpe
Heanor
Eastwood
Lowdham
Kilburn
Burton Joyce
Long Bennington
Foston
Ancaster
Awsworth
Gunthorpe
Barkston
Ilkeston
NOTTINGHAM
Bingham
Bottesford
Stapleford
Radcliffe on Trent
Sedgebrook
Grantham
Ockbrook
West Bridgford
DERBY
Beeston
Risley
Redmile
Borrowash
Plumtree
Long Eaton
Ruddington
Shardlow
Croxton Kerrial
Great Ponton
Bunny
Keyworth
Castle Donington
Upper Broughton
Kegworth
Widmerpool
Repton
EAST MIDLANDS
Waltham on the Wolds
Colsterworth
Melbourne
Rempstone
Donington Park
Buckminster
Ticknall
Diseworth
Hathern
Hoton
Ab Kettleby
Melton Mowbray
Grimsthorpe
Shepshed
Loughborough
Saxby
Little Bytham
Ashby-de-la-Zouch
Barrow upon Soar
Wymondham
South Witham
Stretton
LEICESTERSHIRE
Greetham
Coalville
Mountsorrel
Sileby
Great Dalby
East Goscote
Langham
Measham
Syston
Empingham
Ibstock
Markfield
Anstey
Birstall
Oakham
Rutland Water
RUTLAND
Groby
Twycross
Market Bosworth
Kirby Muxloe
LEICESTER
Tilton on the Hill
North Luffenham
Ketton
Houghton on the Hill
23
Desford
Leicester Forest East
Oadby
Sibson
Glaston
M1
M18
A1(M)
A1
A46
A52
A60
A57
A614
A631
A17
A15
A607
A606
A6
A50

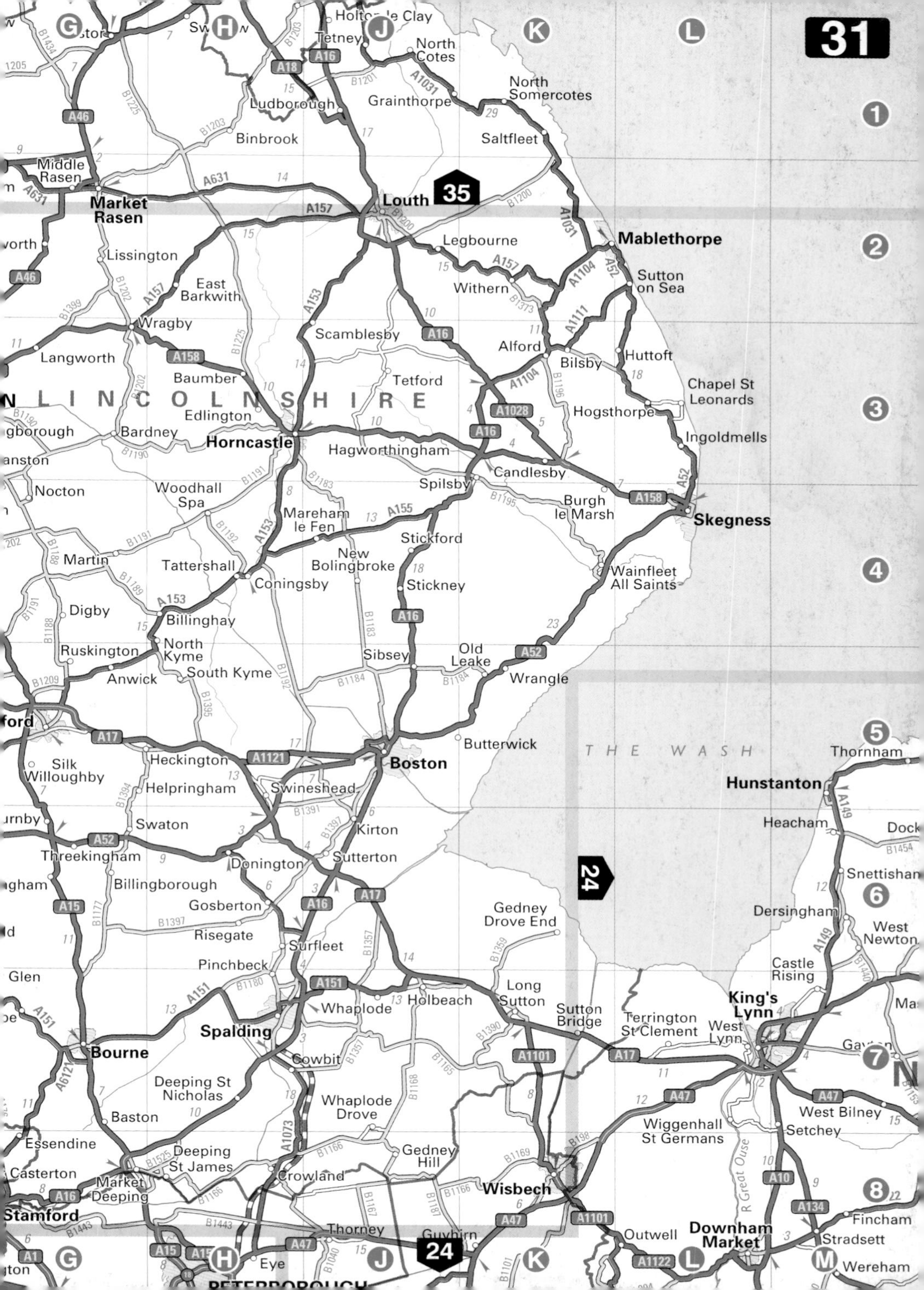

Holton le Clay
Tetney
North Cotes
North Somercotes
Ludborough
Grainthorpe
Saltfleet
Binbrook
Middle Rasen
Market Rasen
Louth
35
Mablethorpe
Legbourne
Sutton on Sea
Lissington
East Barkwith
Withern
Wragby
Scamblesby
Alford
Langworth
Bilsby
Huttoft
Baumber
Tetford
Chapel St Leonards
LINCOLNSHIRE
Edlington
Hogsthorpe
Bardney
Horncastle
Hagworthingham
Ingoldmells
Candlesby
Nocton
Woodhall Spa
Spilsby
Burgh le Marsh
Skegness
Mareham le Fen
Stickford
Martin
Tattershall
New Bolingbroke
Wainfleet All Saints
Coningsby
Stickney
Digby
Billinghay
Ruskington
North Kyme
Sibsey
Old Leake
Anwick
South Kyme
Wrangle
Butterwick
THE WASH
Thornham
Silk Willoughby
Heckington
Boston
Hunstanton
Helpringham
Swineshead
Heacham
Swaton
Kirton
Threekingham
Donington
Sutterton
Snettisham
Billingborough
24
Dersingham
Gosberton
Gedney Drove End
West Newton
Risegate
Surfleet
Pinchbeck
Castle Rising
Glen
Long Sutton
King's Lynn
Whaplode
Holbeach
Sutton Bridge
Terrington St Clement
West Lynn
Spalding
Bourne
Cowbit
Deeping St Nicholas
Whaplode Drove
West Bilney
Baston
Wiggenhall St Germans
Setchey
Essendine
Deeping St James
Gedney Hill
Casterton
Crowland
Market Deeping
Wisbech
Stamford
Thorney
Guyhirn
Outwell
Downham Market
Fincham
Stradsett
Eye
24
Wereham
R Great Ouse
PETERBOROUGH

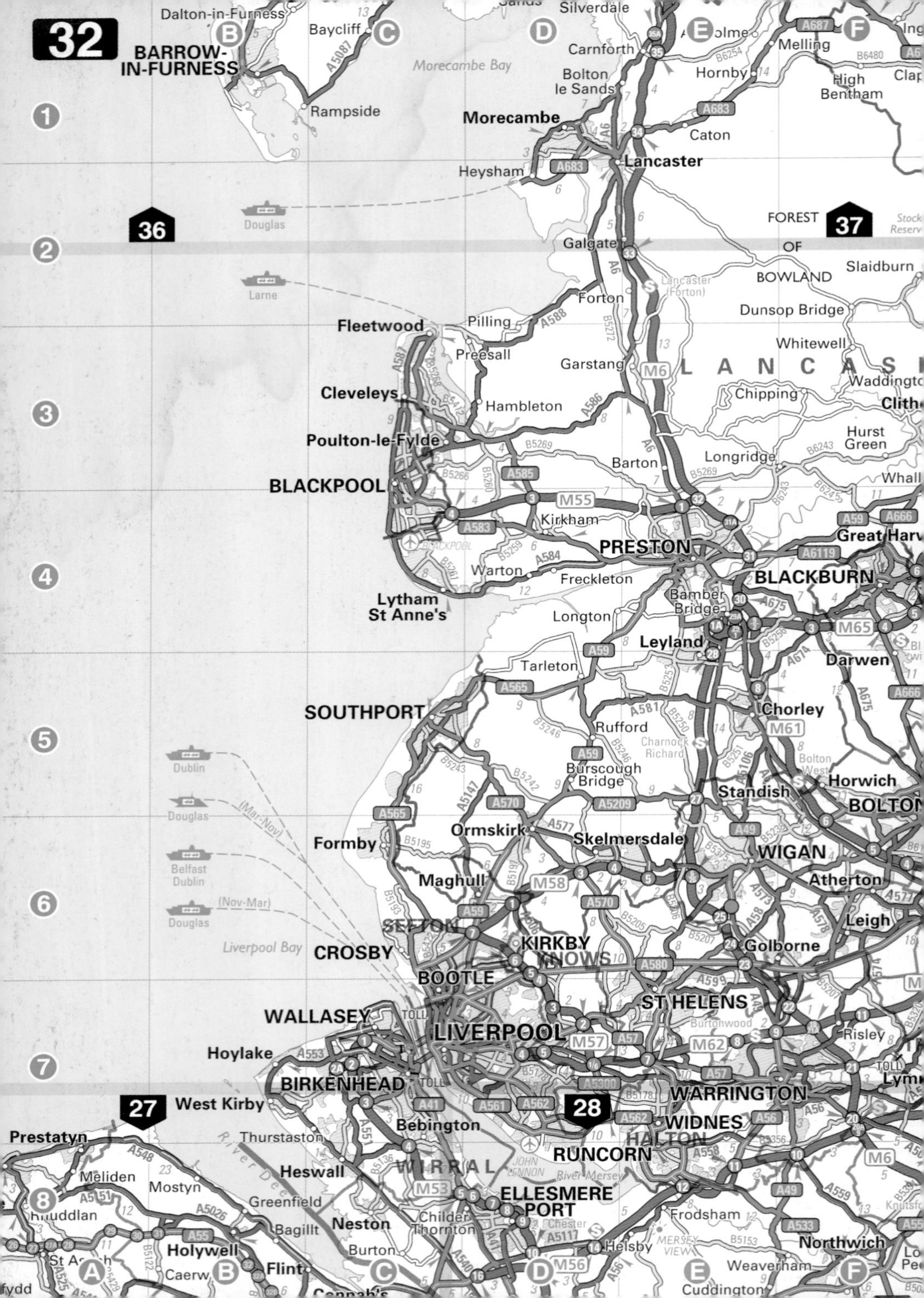
BARROW-IN-FURNESS
Dalton-in-Furness
Baycliff
Rampside
Morecambe Bay
Silverdale
Carnforth
Bolton le Sands
Morecambe
Heysham
Lancaster
Hornby
Melling
High Bentham
Caton
Galgate
Forton
Lancaster (Forton)
FOREST OF BOWLAND
Slaidburn
Dunsop Bridge
Whitewell
LANCASHIRE
Chipping
Waddington
Hurst Green
Longridge
Douglas
Larne
Fleetwood
Pilling
Preesall
Garstang
Cleveleys
Hambleton
Poulton-le-Fylde
BLACKPOOL
Barton
Kirkham
PRESTON
Great Harwood
Warton
Freckleton
Lytham St Anne's
BLACKBURN
Bamber Bridge
Longton
Leyland
Darwen
Tarleton
SOUTHPORT
Chorley
Rufford
Charnock Richard
Burscough Bridge
Bolton West
Horwich
Standish
BOLTON
Dublin
Douglas
(Mar-Nov)
Ormskirk
Skelmersdale
Formby
WIGAN
Belfast
Dublin
Maghull
Atherton
(Nov-Mar)
Douglas
Leigh
SEFTON
Liverpool Bay
CROSBY
KIRKBY
KNOWSLEY
Golborne
BOOTLE
WALLASEY
ST HELENS
Burtonwood
LIVERPOOL
Risley
Hoylake
BIRKENHEAD
WARRINGTON
West Kirby
Bebington
WIDNES
HALTON
Prestatyn
Thurstaston
River Dee
RUNCORN
JOHN LENNON
River Mersey
Meliden
Mostyn
Heswall
WIRRAL
Rhuddlan
Greenfield
ELLESMERE PORT
Childer Thornton
Neston
Bagillt
Chester
Frodsham
Holywell
Burton
Helsby
MERSEY VIEW
Northwich
St Asaph
Flint
Caerwys
Weaverham
Cuddington
M6
M55
M65
M61
M58
M57
M62
M53
M56
A6
A683
A687
A588
A586
A585
A583
A584
A59
A565
A570
A5209
A577
A49
A580
A599
A57
A5300
A561
A562
A56
A41
A551
A553
A5117
A548
A5151
A5026
A55
A533
A559
A6119
A666
A674
A675
A5147
A581
A587
A5087
36
37
27
28

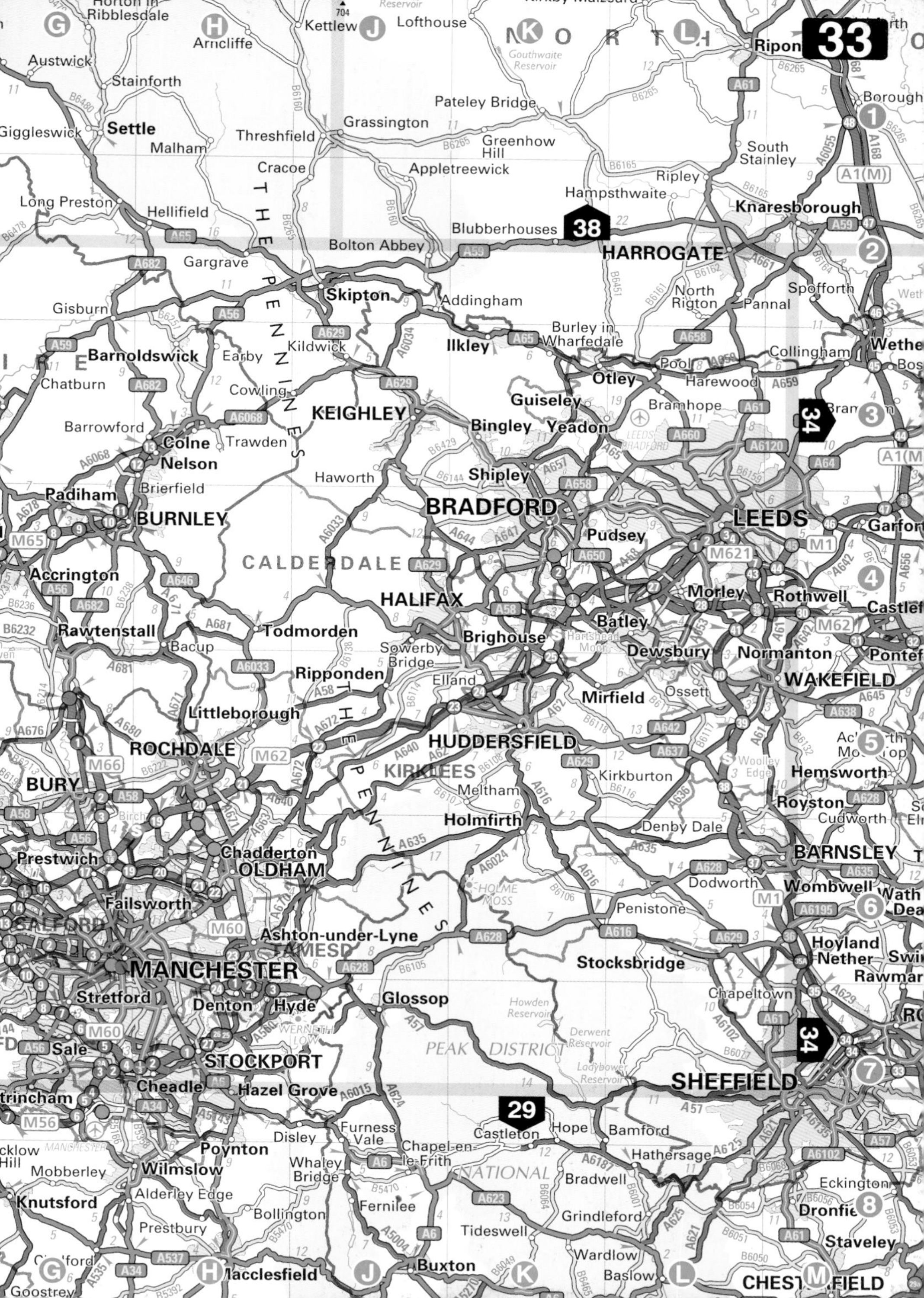
33
38
34
29
NORTH
Horton in Ribblesdale
Arncliffe
Kettlewell
Lofthouse
Ripon
Austwick
Stainforth
Gouthwaite Reservoir
Borough
Giggleswick
Settle
Malham
Threshfield
Grassington
Pateley Bridge
Greenhow Hill
South Stainley
Cracoe
Appletreewick
Ripley
Long Preston
Hellifield
Hampsthwaite
Knaresborough
Blubberhouses
Bolton Abbey
HARROGATE
Gargrave
Skipton
Addingham
North Rigton
Pannal
Spofforth
Gisburn
Kildwick
Ilkley
Burley in Wharfedale
Collingham
Barnoldswick
Earby
Otley
Pool
Harewood
Chatburn
Cowling
Guiseley
Bramhope
Barrowford
KEIGHLEY
Bingley
Yeadon
Colne
Trawden
Nelson
Haworth
Shipley
Leeds Bradford
Brierfield
Padiham
BURNLEY
BRADFORD
LEEDS
Pudsey
CALDERDALE
Accrington
HALIFAX
Morley
Rothwell
Rawtenstall
Bacup
Todmorden
Brighouse
Batley
Hartshead Moor
Dewsbury
Normanton
Sowerby Bridge
Ripponden
Elland
Mirfield
Ossett
WAKEFIELD
Littleborough
HUDDERSFIELD
ROCHDALE
KIRKLEES
Kirkburton
Woolley Edge
Hemsworth
BURY
Meltham
Royston
Cudworth
Holmfirth
Denby Dale
Prestwich
Chadderton
OLDHAM
BARNSLEY
Dodworth
Wombwell
Holme Moss
Penistone
Failsworth
SALFORD
Ashton-under-Lyne
TAMESIDE
Stocksbridge
Hoyland Nether
MANCHESTER
Stretford
Denton
Hyde
Glossop
Chapeltown
Howden Reservoir
Derwent Reservoir
Ladybower Reservoir
Sale
STOCKPORT
PEAK DISTRICT
Cheadle
Hazel Grove
SHEFFIELD
Altrincham
Castleton
Hope
Bamford
Disley
Furness Vale
Chapel-en-le-Frith
Hathersage
Poynton
Whaley Bridge
Wilmslow
Mobberley
NATIONAL
Bradwell
Eckington
Alderley Edge
Fernilee
Knutsford
Bollington
Grindleford
Dronfield
Prestbury
Tideswell
Wardlow
Staveley
Macclesfield
Buxton
Baslow
CHESTERFIELD
Goostrey
THE PENNINES
M62
M60
M66
M65
M56
M621
M1
A1(M)
A59
A65
A61
A629
A58
A628
A616
A635
A6
A57
A623

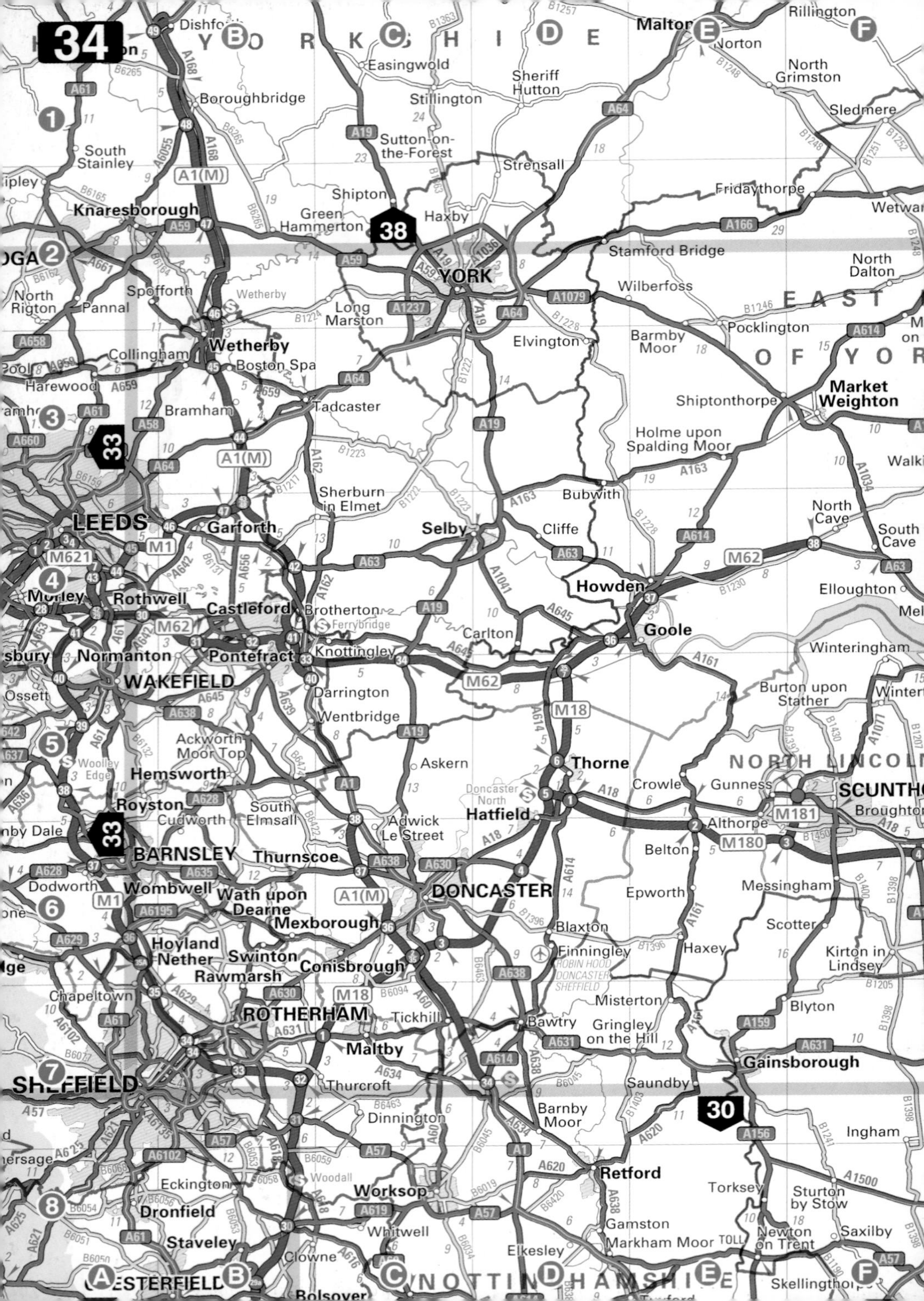
YORKSHIRE
EAST OF YORKSHIRE
NORTH LINCOLNSHIRE
NOTTINGHAMSHIRE
Malton
Norton
Rillington
North Grimston
Sledmere
Easingwold
Sheriff Hutton
Stillington
Boroughbridge
Sutton-on-the-Forest
South Stainley
Strensall
Fridaythorpe
Wetwang
Shipton
Haxby
Knaresborough
Green Hammerton
Stamford Bridge
North Dalton
YORK
Wilberfoss
Spofforth
North Rigton
Pannal
Wetherby
Long Marston
Pocklington
Barmby Moor
Elvington
Collingham
Harewood
Boston Spa
Bramham
Tadcaster
Shiptonthorpe
Market Weighton
Holme upon Spalding Moor
Sherburn in Elmet
Bubwith
North Cave
South Cave
LEEDS
Garforth
Selby
Cliffe
Howden
Elloughton
Morley
Rothwell
Castleford
Brotherton
Ferrybridge
Carlton
Goole
Normanton
Pontefract
Knottingley
Winteringham
WAKEFIELD
Ossett
Darrington
Burton upon Stather
Wentbridge
Ackworth Moor Top
Woolley Edge
Askern
Thorne
Hemsworth
Doncaster North
Crowle
Gunness
SCUNTHORPE
Royston
South Elmsall
Hatfield
Broughton
Cudworth
Adwick Le Street
Althorpe
Belton
BARNSLEY
Thurnscoe
Dodworth
Wombwell
Wath upon Dearne
DONCASTER
Epworth
Messingham
Mexborough
Blaxton
Scotter
Hoyland Nether
Swinton
Finningley
Haxey
Kirton in Lindsey
ROBIN HOOD DONCASTER SHEFFIELD
Rawmarsh
Conisbrough
Chapeltown
Misterton
Blyton
ROTHERHAM
Tickhill
Bawtry
Gringley on the Hill
Maltby
Gainsborough
SHEFFIELD
Thurcroft
Saundby
Dinnington
Barnby Moor
Ingham
Eckington
Woodall
Retford
Worksop
Torksey
Sturton by Stow
Dronfield
Whitwell
Gamston
Newton on Trent
Saxilby
Staveley
Markham Moor
Elkesley
CHESTERFIELD
Clowne
Bolsover
Skellingthorpe
A1(M)
M1
M62
M621
M18
M180
M181
A19
A64
A166
A1079
A59
A61
A168
A6055
A658
A659
A58
A660
A614
A163
A63
A1034
A645
A1041
A162
A656
A642
A639
A638
A628
A635
A6195
A629
A630
A631
A634
A6102
A57
A60
A1
A620
A619
A616
A156
A1500
A159
A161
A18
A6135
A621
A625
A1077
A1237
A1036
A661
A653
A636
A637
A6102
B6265
B6165
B1224
B1228
B1246
B1230
B1222
B1223
B1217
B1396
B6463
B6094
B6045
B6420
B6019
B6059
B6053
B6056
B6054
B6051
B6050
B6474
B6422
B6132
B6131
B1257
B1363
B1248
B1251
B1252
B1392
B1430
B1207
B1450
B1400
B1398
B1205
B1403
B1241
B1190
B1399
TOLL
30
33
38

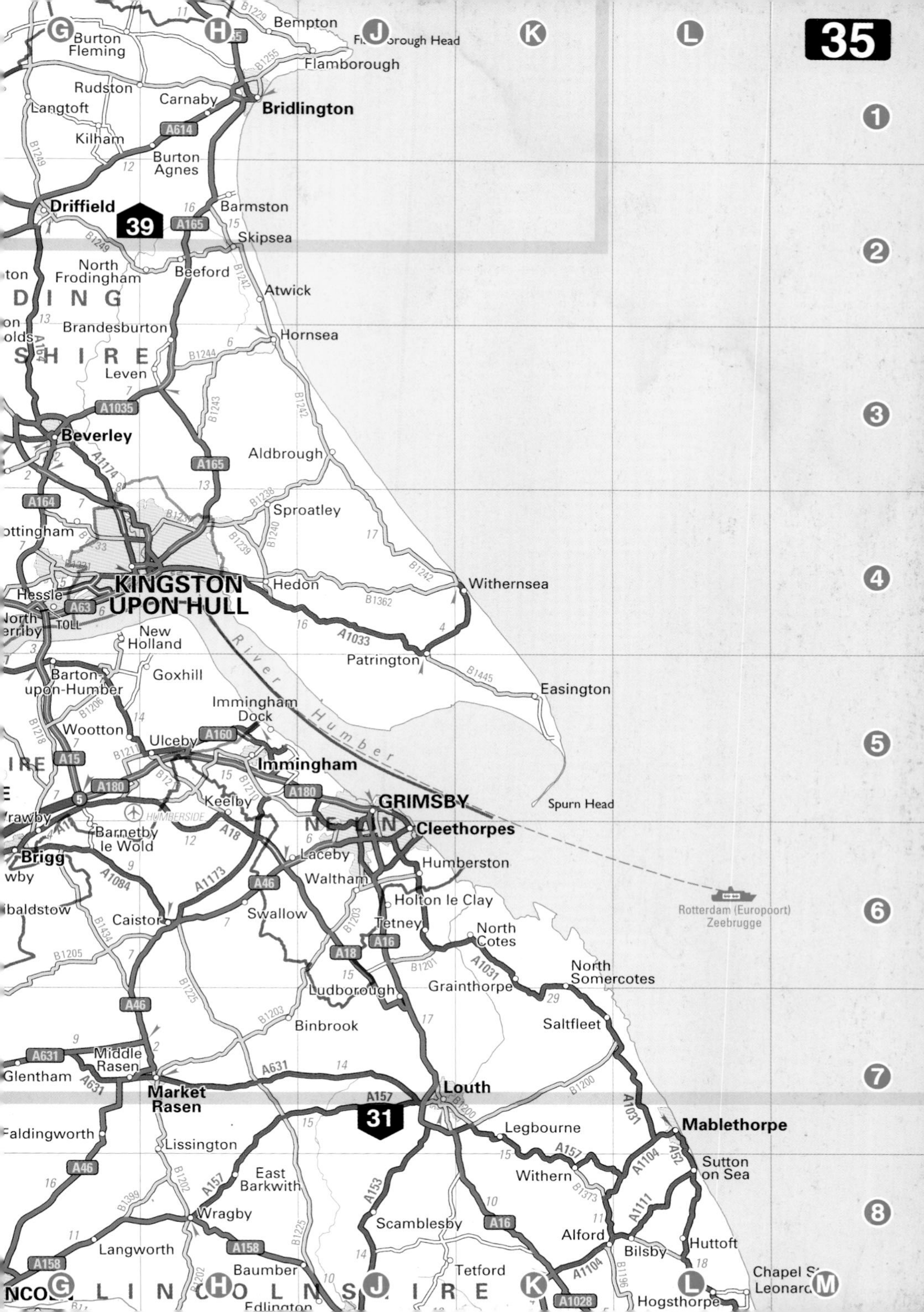

Bempton
Burton Fleming
Flamborough Head
Flamborough
Rudston
Carnaby
Bridlington
Langtoft
A614
Kilham
Burton Agnes
B1249
Driffield
39
A165
Barmston
Skipsea
North Frodingham
Beeford
B1242
Atwick
Brandesburton
Hornsea
B1244
Leven
A1035
B1243
Beverley
A1174
A165
Aldbrough
A164
B1238
Sproatley
B1240
B1239
B1242
Withernsea
KINGSTON UPON HULL
Hessle
A63
TOLL
Hedon
B1362
A1033
Patrington
B1445
Easington
New Holland
Barton-upon-Humber
Goxhill
B1206
River Humber
Immingham Dock
Wootton
B1218
A160
Ulceby
B1211
Immingham
A15
A180
A180
Keelby
HUMBERSIDE
A18
Spurn Head
GRIMSBY
NE LIN
Cleethorpes
Barnetby le Wold
Brigg
Laceby
Humberston
A1084
A1173
Waltham
A46
Holton le Clay
Rotterdam (Europoort)
Zeebrugge
Caistor
Swallow
B1203
Tetney
A16
North Cotes
B1434
B1205
A18
B1201
A1031
North Somercotes
Grainthorpe
B1225
Ludborough
A46
Saltfleet
B1203
Binbrook
A631
Middle Rasen
Glentham
A631
A631
Louth
B1200
Market Rasen
A157
31
B1200
A1031
Mablethorpe
Faldingworth
Lissington
Legbourne
A157
A1104
A52
Sutton on Sea
A46
East Barkwith
A157
Withern
B1373
B1202
B1399
A153
A1111
Wragby
Scamblesby
A16
Alford
Langworth
A158
B1225
Bilsby
Huttoft
A158
Baumber
B1202
Tetford
A1104
B1196
Chapel St Leonards
LINCOLNSHIRE
A1028
Hogsthorpe
Edlington

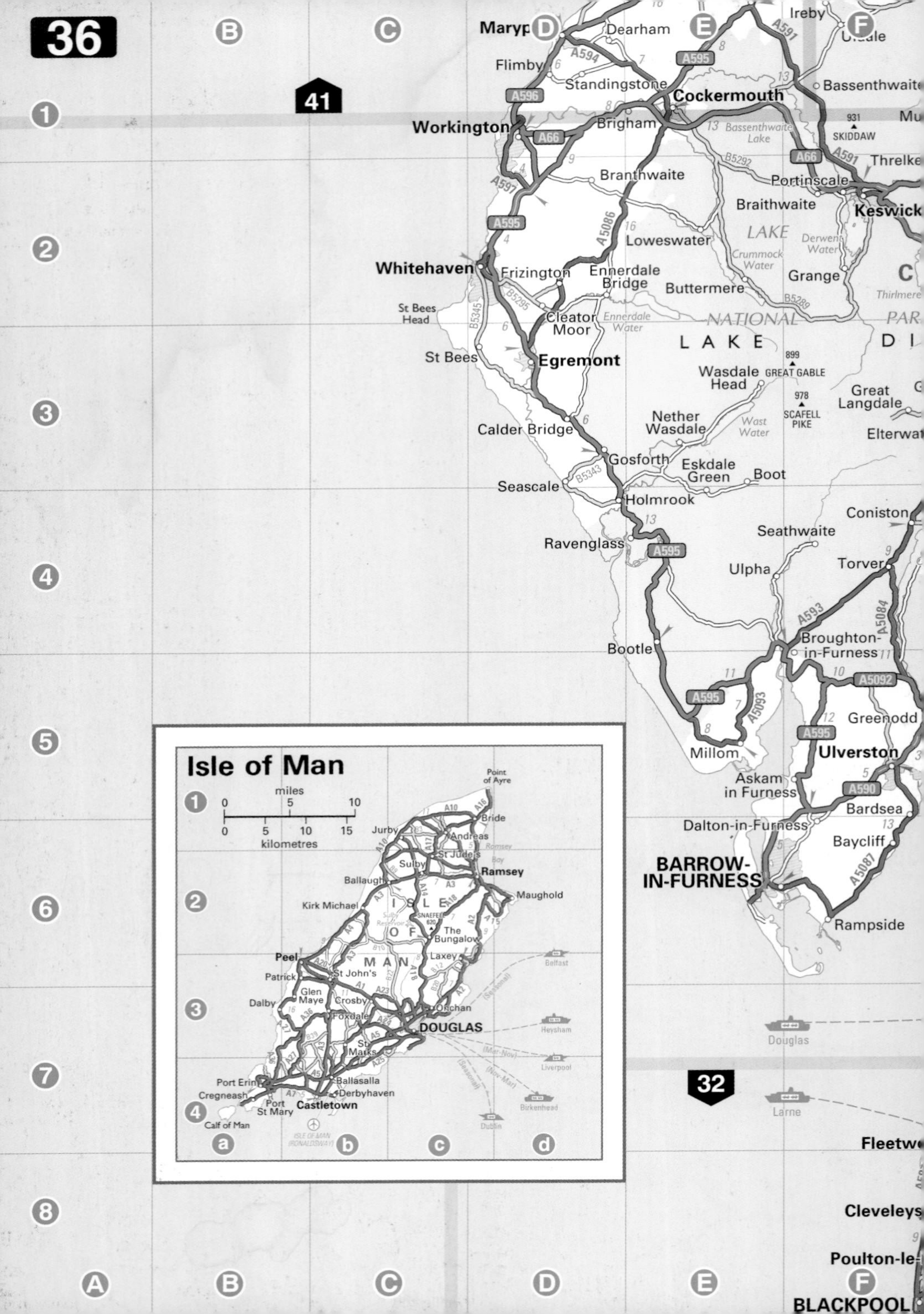
41
32
Maryport
Dearham
Ireby
Uldale
Flimby
Standingstone
Cockermouth
Bassenthwaite
Workington
Brigham
Bassenthwaite Lake
931
SKIDDAW
Threlkeld
Branthwaite
Portinscale
Braithwaite
Keswick
Loweswater
LAKE
Crummock Water
Derwent Water
Whitehaven
Frizington
Ennerdale Bridge
Buttermere
Grange
Thirlmere
St Bees Head
Cleator Moor
Ennerdale Water
NATIONAL
PARK
LAKE
DISTRICT
St Bees
Egremont
899
GREAT GABLE
Wasdale Head
978
SCAFELL PIKE
Great Langdale
Nether Wasdale
Wast Water
Elterwater
Calder Bridge
Gosforth
Eskdale Green
Boot
Seascale
Holmrook
Coniston
Seathwaite
Ravenglass
Ulpha
Torver
Bootle
Broughton-in-Furness
Greenodd
Millom
Ulverston
Askam in Furness
Bardsea
Dalton-in-Furness
Baycliff
BARROW-IN-FURNESS
Rampside
Douglas
Larne
Fleetwood
Cleveleys
Poulton-le-Fylde
BLACKPOOL
A591
A594
A595
A596
A66
A597
A5086
B5292
B5289
B5295
B5345
B5343
A593
A5084
A5092
A5093
A590
A5087
Isle of Man
miles
0
5
10
0
5
10
15
kilometres
Point of Ayre
Bride
Jurby
Andreas
Ramsey Bay
St Jude's
Sulby
Ramsey
Ballaugh
Maughold
Kirk Michael
ISLE
OF
MAN
Sulby Reservoir
SNAEFELL
620
The Bungalow
Peel
Laxey
St John's
Belfast
Patrick
Glen Maye
Crosby
Dalby
Onchan
Foxdale
DOUGLAS
Heysham
St Marks
(Seasonal)
(Mar-Nov)
(Nov-Mar)
Liverpool
Port Erin
Ballasalla
Derbyhaven
Cregneash
Port St Mary
Castletown
Birkenhead
Calf of Man
ISLE OF MAN (RONALDSWAY)
Dublin

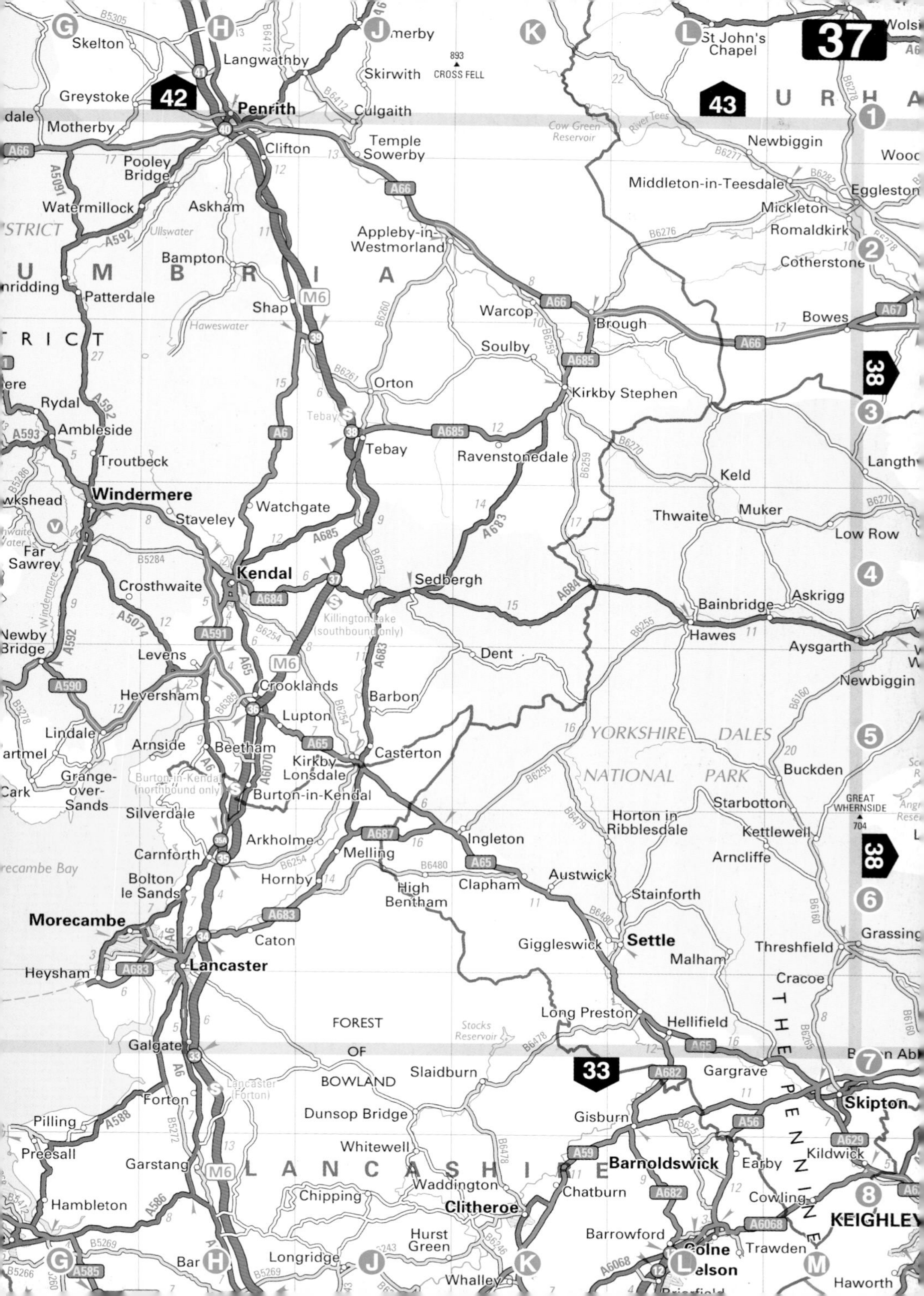
37
42
43
38
38
33
CROSS FELL
893
GREAT WHERNSIDE
704
Skelton
Langwathby
Skirwith
St John's Chapel
Greystoke
Penrith
Culgaith
Motherby
Clifton
Temple Sowerby
Pooley Bridge
Newbiggin
Middleton-in-Teesdale
Eggleston
Mickleton
Romaldkirk
Cotherstone
Watermillock
Askham
Appleby-in-Westmorland
Cow Green Reservoir
River Tees
Ullswater
Bampton
C U M B R I A
D U R H A M
Patterdale
Shap
Haweswater
Warcop
Brough
Bowes
Soulby
Kirkby Stephen
Orton
Rydal
Ambleside
Troutbeck
Tebay
Ravenstonedale
Windermere
Watchgate
Staveley
Keld
Thwaite
Muker
Low Row
Far Sawrey
Kendal
Crosthwaite
Sedbergh
Killington Lake (southbound only)
Bainbridge
Askrigg
Hawes
Aysgarth
Newby Bridge
Levens
Dent
Newbiggin
Heversham
Crooklands
Lupton
Barbon
Lindale
Arnside
Beetham
Kirkby Lonsdale
Casterton
YORKSHIRE DALES NATIONAL PARK
Grange-over-Sands
Burton-in-Kendal (northbound only)
Burton-in-Kendal
Buckden
Silverdale
Horton in Ribblesdale
Starbotton
Kettlewell
Arkholme
Ingleton
Arncliffe
Carnforth
Melling
Bolton le Sands
Hornby
High Bentham
Clapham
Austwick
Stainforth
Morecambe
Caton
Giggleswick
Settle
Malham
Threshfield
Grassington
Heysham
Lancaster
Cracoe
Long Preston
Hellifield
FOREST OF BOWLAND
Stocks Reservoir
Galgate
Slaidburn
Gargrave
Skipton
Forton
Lancaster (Forton)
Gisburn
Pilling
Dunsop Bridge
Whitewell
Preesall
Garstang
L A N C A S H I R E
Barnoldswick
Earby
Kildwick
THE PENNINES
Waddington
Chatburn
Chipping
Hambleton
Clitheroe
Cowling
KEIGHLEY
Hurst Green
Barrowford
Colne
Trawden
Bar
Longridge
Nelson
Whalley
Haworth
Morecambe Bay
M6
A66
A6
A685
A683
A684
A591
A65
A590
A592
A593
A5074
A687
A682
A59
A56
A629
A6068
A588
A586
A585
A67
A6070
B5305
B6412
B6413
B6278
B6277
B6282
B6276
B6259
B6260
B6261
B6270
B6255
B6257
B6254
B6385
B5284
B5286
B5278
B6479
B6480
B6160
B6265
B6478
B6251
B5272
B5269
B6243
B6246
B5266
B5412

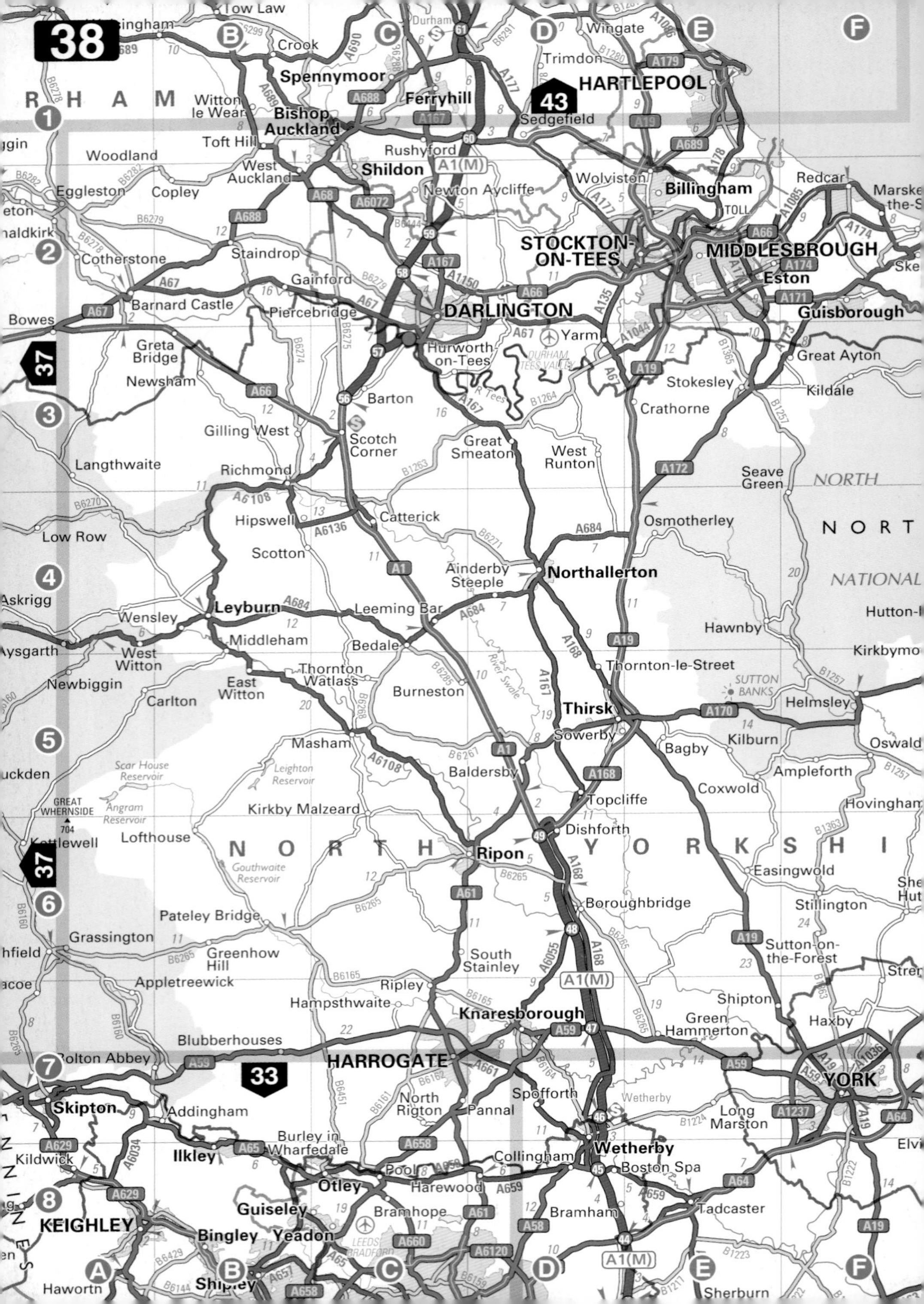

38
Crook
Spennymoor
Ferryhill
HARTLEPOOL
43
Trimdon
Wingate
Witton le Wear
Bishop Auckland
Sedgefield
Toft Hill
Woodland
Rushyford
West Auckland
Shildon
Eggleston
Copley
Newton Aycliffe
Wolviston
Billingham
Redcar
Staindrop
Cotherstone
STOCKTON-ON-TEES
MIDDLESBROUGH
Eston
Gainford
Barnard Castle
Piercebridge
DARLINGTON
Guisborough
Bowes
Greta Bridge
Hurworth-on-Tees
Yarm
Great Ayton
Newsham
Barton
Stokesley
Kildale
Crathorne
Durham Tees Valley
Gilling West
Scotch Corner
Great Smeaton
West Runton
Langthwaite
Richmond
Seave Green
Hipswell
Catterick
Osmotherley
Low Row
Scotton
Ainderby Steeple
Northallerton
NORTH
NORTH YORKSHIRE
NATIONAL
Askrigg
Leyburn
Leeming Bar
Wensley
Hawnby
Hutton-le-Hole
Aysgarth
West Witton
Middleham
Bedale
Thornton-le-Street
Kirkbymoorside
Newbiggin
East Witton
Thornton Watlass
Burneston
Sutton Banks
Helmsley
Carlton
Thirsk
Sowerby
Kilburn
Masham
Bagby
Baldersby
Ampleforth
Oswaldkirk
Scar House Reservoir
Leighton Reservoir
Coxwold
Topcliffe
Great Whernside
Angram Reservoir
Kirkby Malzeard
Hovingham
Kettlewell
Lofthouse
Dishforth
Ripon
Gouthwaite Reservoir
Easingwold
Boroughbridge
Stillington
Pateley Bridge
Grassington
Greenhow Hill
South Stainley
Sutton-on-the-Forest
Appletreewick
Ripley
Shipton
Hampsthwaite
Knaresborough
Green Hammerton
Haxby
Blubberhouses
Bolton Abbey
HARROGATE
33
YORK
Skipton
Addingham
North Rigton
Pannal
Spofforth
Wetherby
Long Marston
Burley in Wharfedale
Ilkley
Kildwick
Otley
Pool
Collingham
Boston Spa
Harewood
Guiseley
Bramhope
Bramham
Tadcaster
KEIGHLEY
Bingley
Yeadon
Leeds Bradford
Haworth
Shipley
Sherburn
A1(M)
A19
A59
A61
A66
A67
A168
A170
A172
A6108
A684

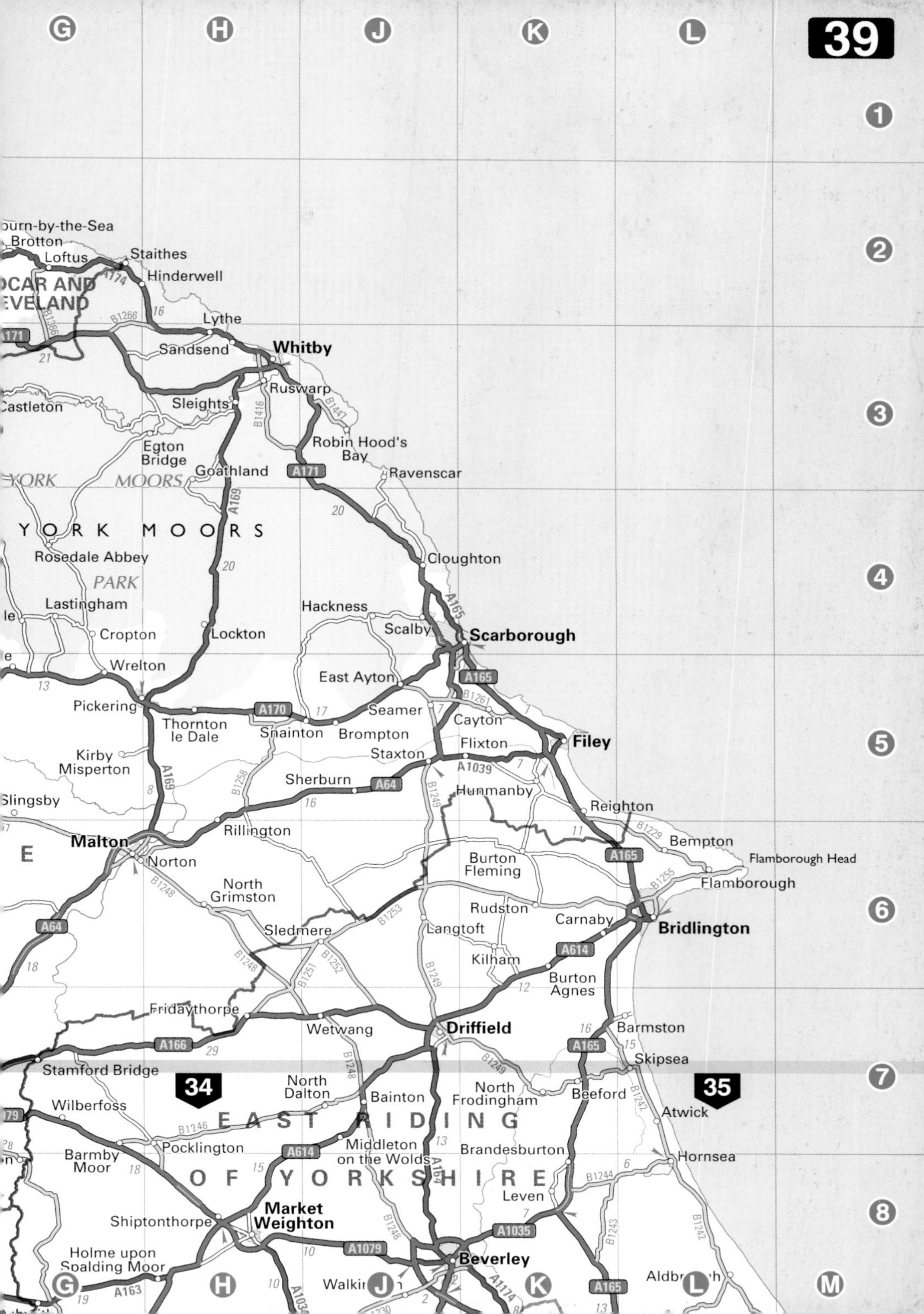
G
H
J
K
L
1
2
3
4
5
6
7
8
Brotton
Loftus
Staithes
Hinderwell
Lythe
Whitby
Sandsend
Ruswarp
Sleights
Castleton
Robin Hood's Bay
Egton Bridge
Goathland
Ravenscar
Rosedale Abbey
Cloughton
Lastingham
Hackness
Scalby
Scarborough
Cropton
Lockton
Wrelton
East Ayton
Pickering
Thornton le Dale
Snainton
Seamer
Brompton
Cayton
Filey
Flixton
Staxton
Kirby Misperton
Sherburn
Hunmanby
Slingsby
Reighton
Malton
Rillington
Bempton
Norton
Flamborough Head
Burton Fleming
Flamborough
North Grimston
Rudston
Carnaby
Bridlington
Sledmere
Langtoft
Kilham
Burton Agnes
Fridaythorpe
Wetwang
Driffield
Barmston
Skipsea
Stamford Bridge
North Dalton
Bainton
North Frodingham
Beeford
Atwick
Wilberfoss
EAST RIDING OF YORKSHIRE
Pocklington
Middleton on the Wolds
Brandesburton
Barmby Moor
Hornsea
Leven
Market Weighton
Shiptonthorpe
Holme upon Spalding Moor
Beverley
Walkington
Aldbrough
M
34
35

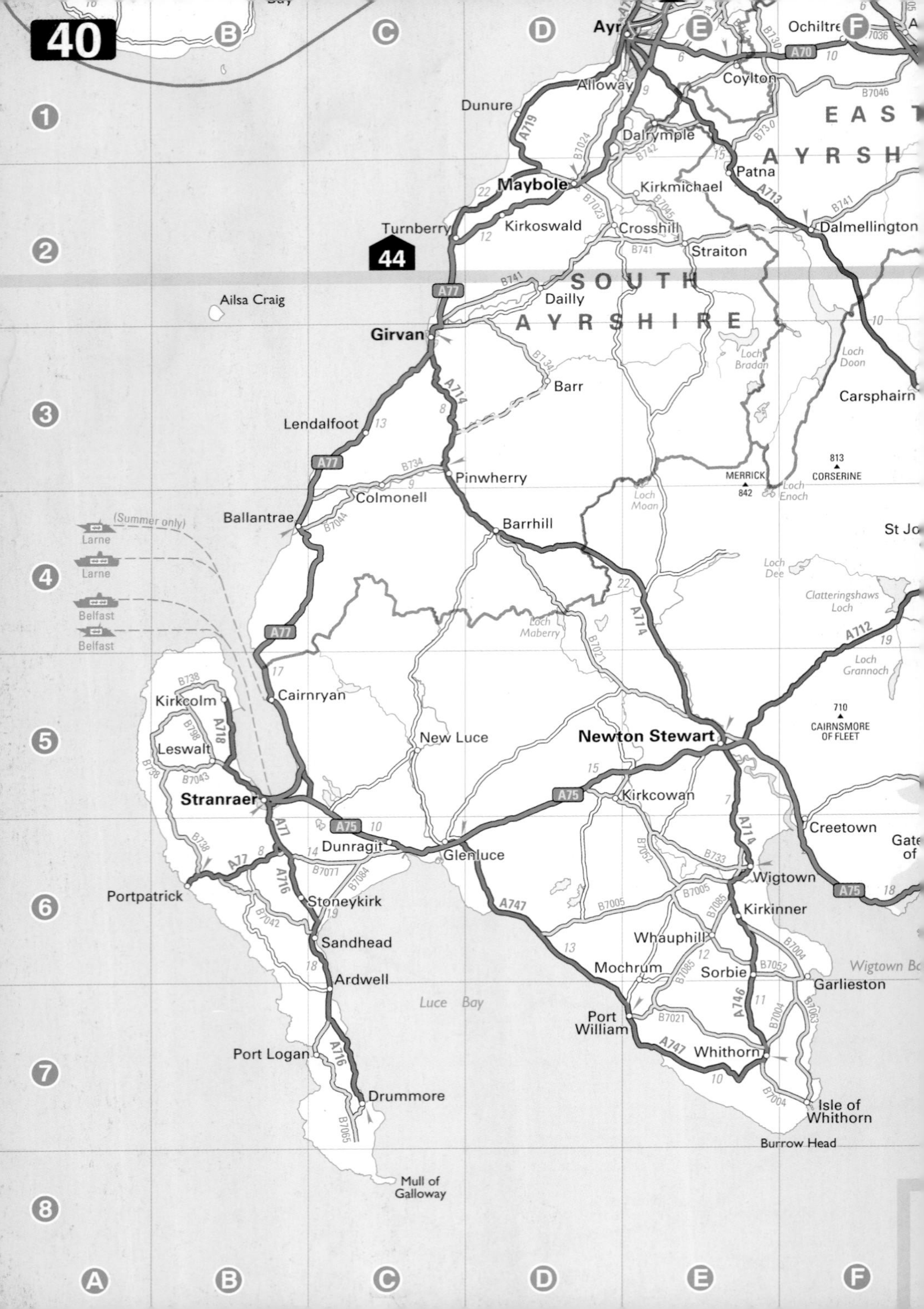
Ayr
Ochiltree
Alloway
Coylton
Dunure
Dalrymple
EAST AYRSHIRE
Patna
Maybole
Kirkmichael
Kirkoswald
Crosshill
Turnberry
Dalmellington
Straiton
44
SOUTH AYRSHIRE
Dailly
Ailsa Craig
Girvan
Loch Bradan
Loch Doon
Barr
Carsphairn
Lendalfoot
Pinwherry
MERRICK 842
813 CORSERINE
Loch Enoch
Loch Moan
Colmonell
(Summer only)
Larne
Larne
Belfast
Belfast
Ballantrae
Barrhill
St Jo
Loch Dee
Clatteringshaws Loch
Loch Maberry
Loch Grannoch
Cairnryan
Kirkcolm
710 CAIRNSMORE OF FLEET
Leswalt
New Luce
Newton Stewart
Stranraer
Kirkcowan
Creetown
Dunragit
Glenluce
Gate of
Portpatrick
Wigtown
Stoneykirk
Kirkinner
Whauphill
Sandhead
Mochrum
Sorbie
Wigtown Ba
Ardwell
Garlieston
Luce Bay
Port William
Port Logan
Whithorn
Drummore
Isle of Whithorn
Burrow Head
Mull of Galloway
A77
A70
A713
A719
A714
A75
A747
A746
A716
A718
A712
B741
B7024
B742
B7023
B7045
B7036
B7046
B7034
B734
B7044
B738
B798
B7043
B7077
B7084
B7042
B7021
B7052
B733
B7005
B7085
B7004
B7063
B7065
A B C D E F
1 2 3 4 5 6 7 8

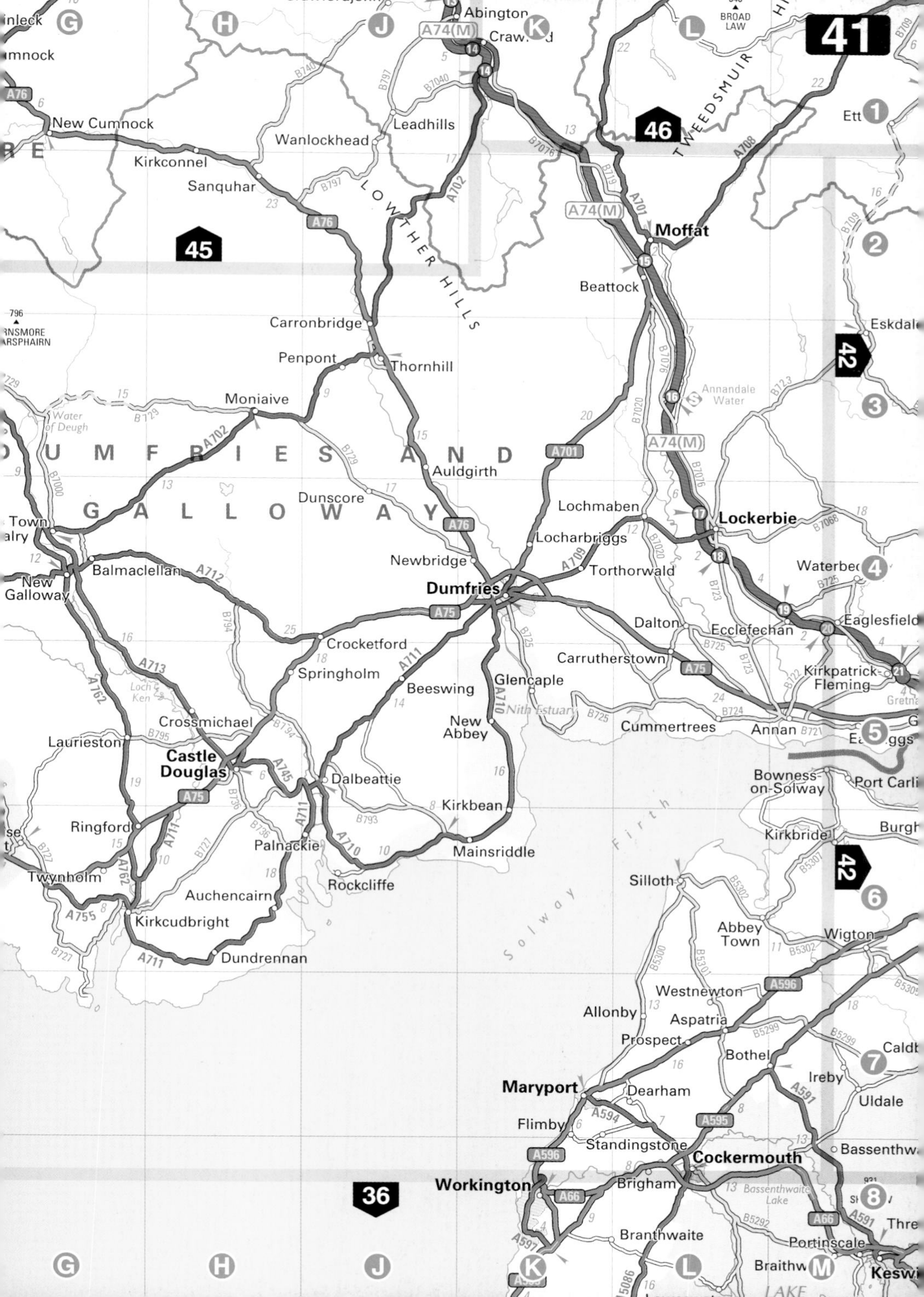
41
Abington
Crawford
Leadhills
Wanlockhead
New Cumnock
Kirkconnel
Sanquhar
LOWTHER HILLS
TWEEDSMUIR HILLS
BROAD LAW
Moffat
Beattock
Carronbridge
Penpont
Thornhill
Moniaive
Water of Deugh
DUMFRIES AND GALLOWAY
Auldgirth
Dunscore
Lochmaben
Lockerbie
Locharbriggs
Newbridge
Torthorwald
Dumfries
Balmaclellan
New Galloway
Annandale Water
Eskdale
Waterbeck
Eaglesfield
Ecclefechan
Dalton
Crocketford
Springholm
Carrutherstown
Kirkpatrick-Fleming
Gretna
Beeswing
Glencaple
Nith Estuary
Cummertrees
Annan
Crossmichael
Laurieston
Castle Douglas
New Abbey
Loch Ken
Dalbeattie
Kirkbean
Ringford
Palnackie
Mainsriddle
Twynholm
Rockcliffe
Auchencairn
Kirkcudbright
Dundrennan
Solway Firth
Bowness-on-Solway
Port Carlisle
Kirkbride
Burgh
Silloth
Abbey Town
Wigton
Westnewton
Allonby
Aspatria
Prospect
Bothel
Ireby
Uldale
Maryport
Dearham
Flimby
Standingstone
Cockermouth
Bassenthwaite
Workington
Brigham
Bassenthwaite Lake
Branthwaite
Portinscale
Braithwaite
Keswick
45
46
42
36
A74(M)
A76
A702
A701
A708
A75
A709
A712
A713
A711
A710
A745
A762
A755
A596
A595
A594
A591
A66
A597
G
H
J
K
L
M

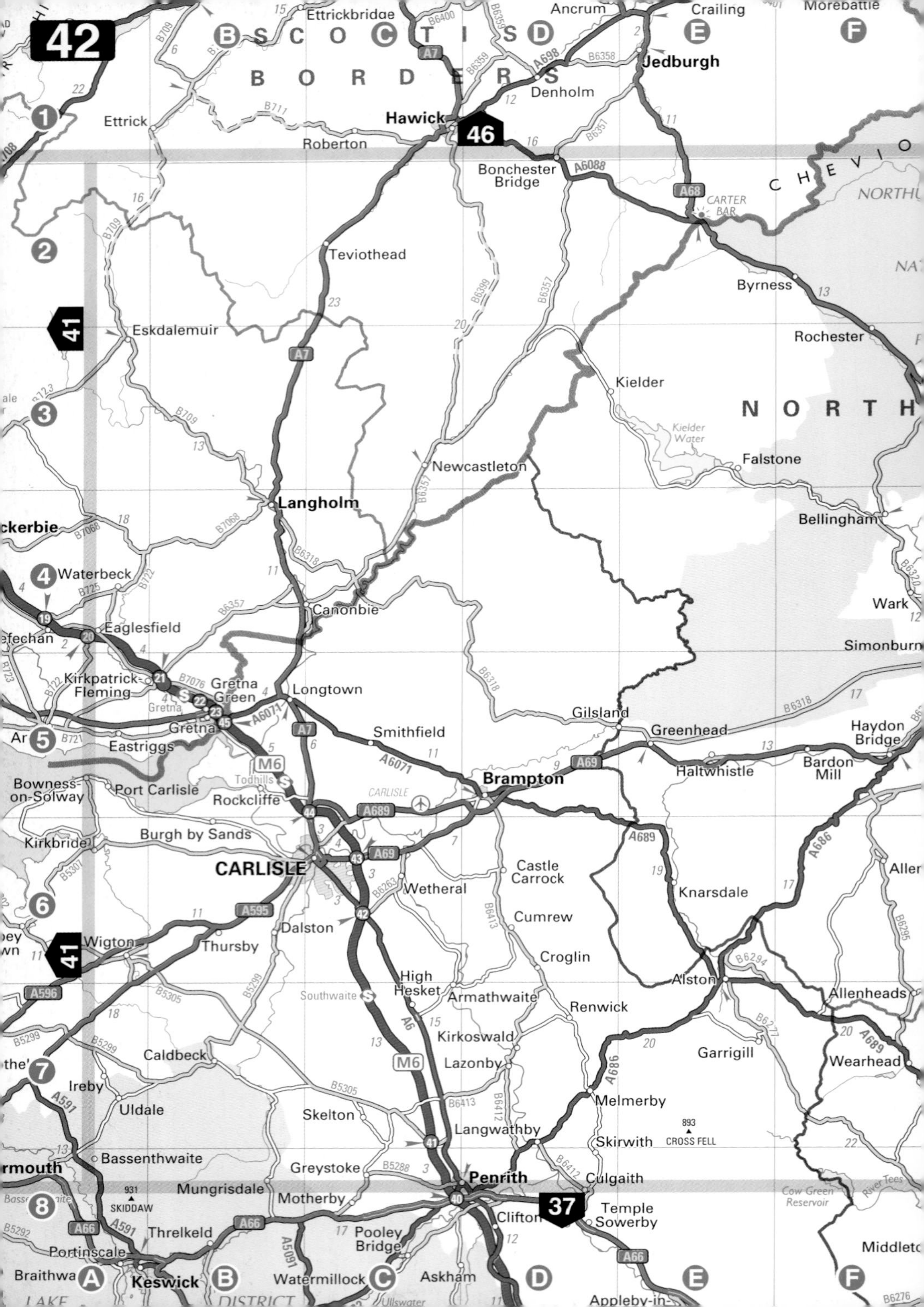
SCOTTISH BORDERS
NORTH
CHEVIO
Ettrickbridge
Ancrum
Crailing
Morebattle
Jedburgh
Denholm
Hawick
Ettrick
Roberton
Bonchester Bridge
CARTER BAR
Teviothead
Byrness
Eskdalemuir
Rochester
Kielder
Kielder Water
Falstone
Newcastleton
Langholm
Bellingham
Lockerbie
Waterbeck
Wark
Eaglesfield
Canonbie
Ecclefechan
Simonburn
Kirkpatrick-Fleming
Gretna Green
Gretna
Longtown
Gilsland
Greenhead
Haydon Bridge
Eastriggs
Smithfield
Haltwhistle
Bardon Mill
Bowness-on-Solway
Port Carlisle
Todhills
Rockcliffe
Brampton
Burgh by Sands
Kirkbride
CARLISLE
Castle Carrock
Wetheral
Knarsdale
Allen
Dalston
Cumrew
Wigton
Thursby
Croglin
Alston
Allenheads
Southwaite
High Hesket
Armathwaite
Renwick
Kirkoswald
Caldbeck
Lazonby
Garrigill
Wearhead
Ireby
Uldale
Melmerby
Skelton
Langwathby
Skirwith
893 CROSS FELL
Bassenthwaite
Greystoke
Penrith
Culgaith
931 SKIDDAW
Mungrisdale
Motherby
Cow Green Reservoir
River Tees
Threlkeld
Pooley Bridge
Clifton
Temple Sowerby
Portinscale
Middleton
Braithwaite
Keswick
Watermillock
Askham
Appleby-in-
LAKE DISTRICT
Ullswater
A7
A698
A68
A6088
A6071
A689
A69
A595
A596
A591
A66
A5091
A686
A6
M6
B6357
B6399
B709
B711
B7068
B6318
B6357
B722
B725
B7076
B721
B5301
B6263
B6413
B6412
B5299
B5305
B5288
B6294
B6277
B6295
B6320
B6276
B6359
B6358
B6400
B6351
CARLISLE
46
41
37

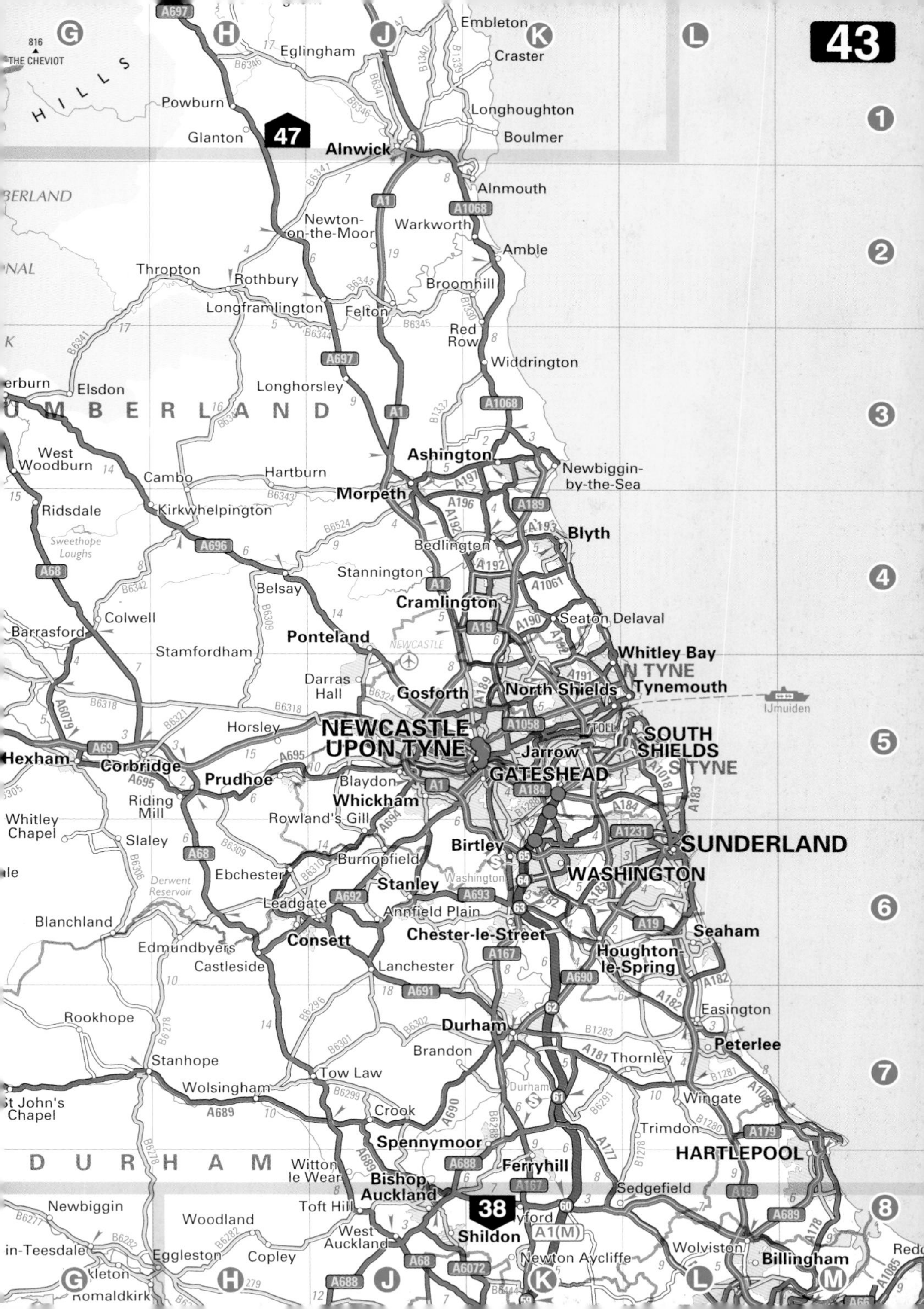
G
H
J
K
L
816
THE CHEVIOT
HILLS
Eglingham
Embleton
Craster
Powburn
Longhoughton
Glanton
47
Alnwick
Boulmer
Alnmouth
BERLAND
Newton-on-the-Moor
Warkworth
Amble
NAL
Thropton
Rothbury
Broomhill
Longframlington
Felton
Red Row
Widdrington
Elsdon
Longhorsley
UMBERLAND
Ashington
Newbiggin-by-the-Sea
West Woodburn
Cambo
Hartburn
Morpeth
Ridsdale
Kirkwhelpington
Blyth
Sweethope Loughs
Bedlington
Stannington
Belsay
Cramlington
Colwell
Seaton Delaval
Barrasford
Ponteland
Stamfordham
Whitley Bay
Darras Hall
Gosforth
North Shields
Tynemouth
IJmuiden
NEWCASTLE UPON TYNE
SOUTH SHIELDS
Horsley
Hexham
Corbridge
Prudhoe
Jarrow
GATESHEAD
Riding Mill
Blaydon
Whickham
Whitley Chapel
Rowland's Gill
Slaley
Birtley
SUNDERLAND
Burnopfield
Ebchester
WASHINGTON
Derwent Reservoir
Stanley
Leadgate
Annfield Plain
Blanchland
Consett
Chester-le-Street
Seaham
Edmundbyers
Castleside
Houghton-le-Spring
Lanchester
Rookhope
Durham
Easington
Peterlee
Brandon
Stanhope
Thornley
Tow Law
Wolsingham
Wingate
St John's Chapel
Crook
Trimdon
Spennymoor
DURHAM
Witton le Wear
Ferryhill
HARTLEPOOL
Bishop Auckland
Sedgefield
Newbiggin
Toft Hill
38
Woodland
West Auckland
Shildon
Wolviston
in-Teesdale
Eggleston
Copley
Newton Aycliffe
Billingham
Romaldkirk
M
1
2
3
4
5
6
7
8

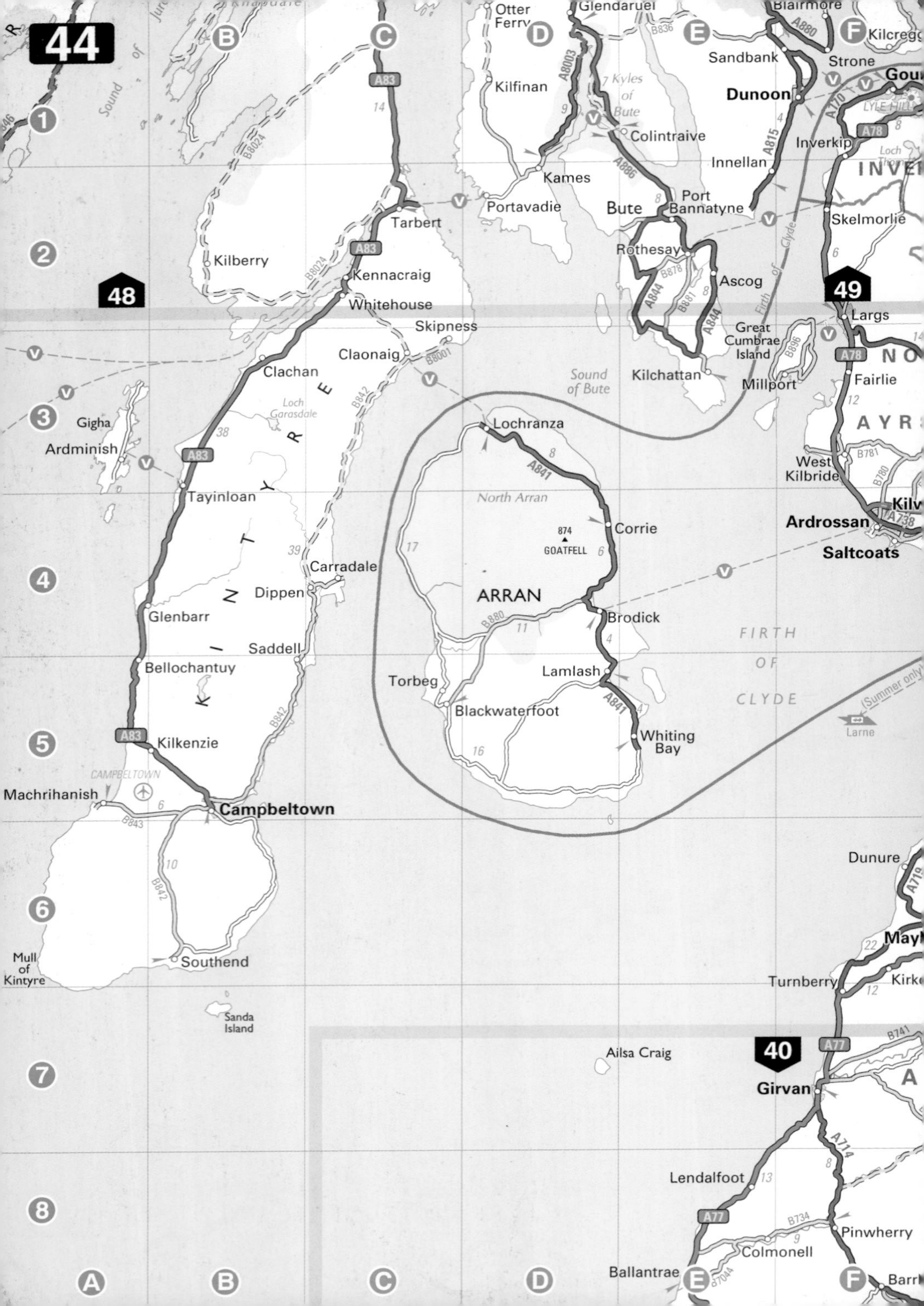
Otter Ferry
Glendaruel
Blairmore
Kilcregg
Sandbank
Strone
Dunoon
Kilfinan
Kyles of Bute
Colintraive
Inverkip
Innellan
Kames
Portavadie
Bute
Port Bannatyne
Tarbert
Skelmorlie
Kilberry
Rothesay
Ascog
Kennacraig
Whitehouse
48
49
Largs
Skipness
Claonaig
Great Cumbrae Island
Clachan
Sound of Bute
Kilchattan
Millport
Fairlie
Loch Garasdale
Gigha
Ardminish
Lochranza
KINTYRE
North Arran
West Kilbride
Tayinloan
Corrie
874 GOATFELL
Ardrossan
Saltcoats
Carradale
Dippen
ARRAN
Glenbarr
Brodick
FIRTH OF CLYDE
Saddell
Lamlash
Bellochantuy
Torbeg
Blackwaterfoot
(Summer only)
Larne
Whiting Bay
Kilkenzie
CAMPBELTOWN
Machrihanish
Campbeltown
Dunure
Mull of Kintyre
Southend
Turnberry
Sanda Island
Ailsa Craig
40
Girvan
Lendalfoot
Pinwherry
Colmonell
Ballantrae
Barr
A83
A841
A886
A8003
A815
A78
A844
A77
A714
B8024
B8001
B842
B880
B843
B878
B881
B896
B781
B780
B734
B741
B836
A880
A738
A719
A770
Sound of Jura
LYLE HILL
1 2 3 4 5 6 7 8
A B C D E F

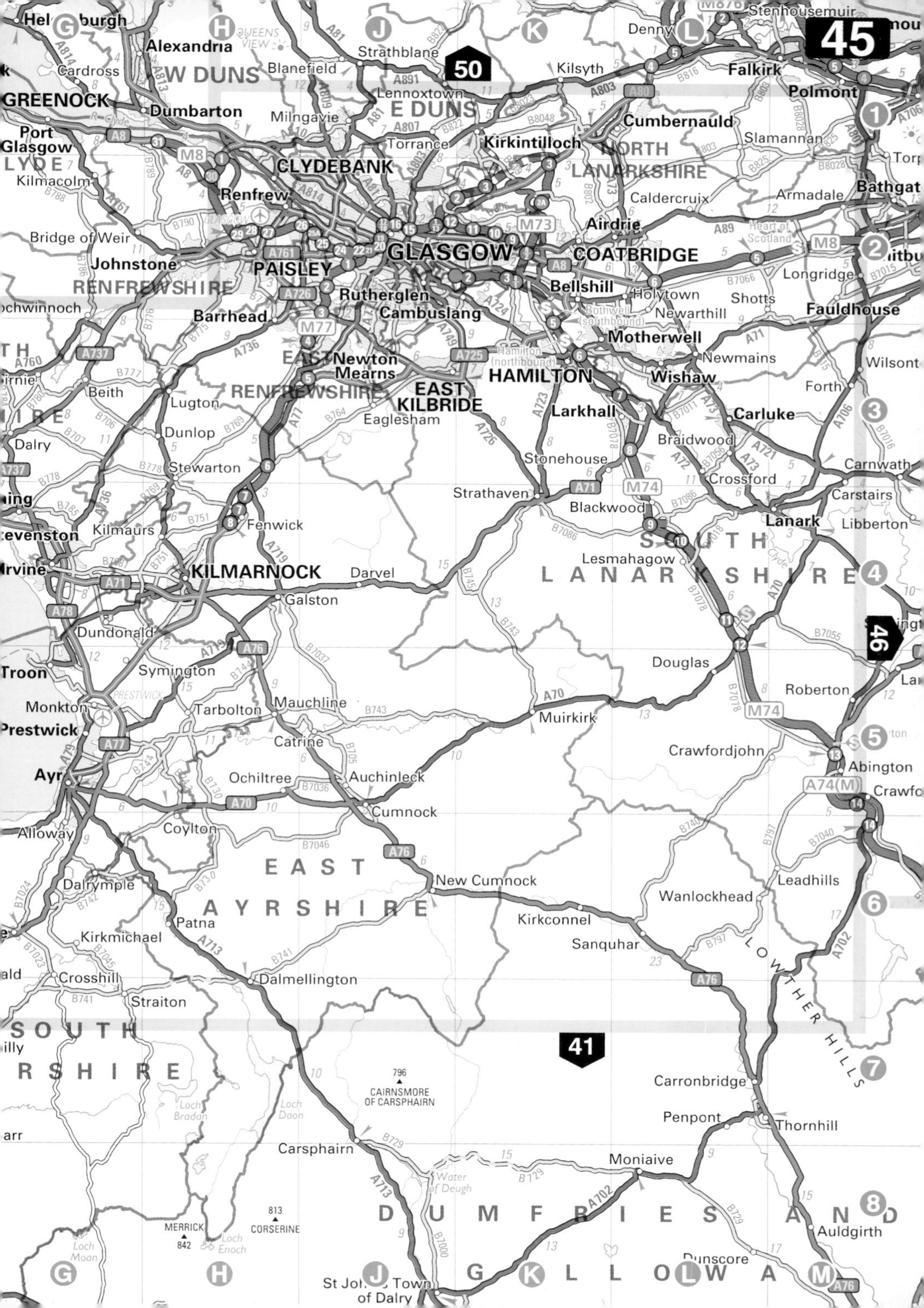

45
50
46
41
GREENOCK
Dumbarton
Alexandria
Cardross
Port Glasgow
Kilmacolm
Bridge of Weir
Johnstone
RENFREWSHIRE
PAISLEY
Renfrew
CLYDEBANK
Milngavie
Strathblane
Blanefield
Lennoxtown
E DUNS
Torrance
Kirkintilloch
Kilsyth
Denny
Stenhousemuir
Falkirk
Polmont
Cumbernauld
Slamannan
NORTH LANARKSHIRE
Caldercruix
Armadale
Bathgate
Airdrie
GLASGOW
COATBRIDGE
Longridge
Bellshill
Holytown
Shotts
Fauldhouse
Rutherglen
Cambuslang
Barrhead
Newarthill
Motherwell
EAST RENFREWSHIRE
Newton Mearns
HAMILTON
Wishaw
Newmains
Wilsontown
Forth
EAST KILBRIDE
Eaglesham
Larkhall
Carluke
Braidwood
Beith
Lugton
Dunlop
Dalry
Stewarton
Stonehouse
Crossford
Carnwath
Carstairs
Strathaven
Blackwood
Lanark
Libberton
Fenwick
Kilmaurs
Lesmahagow
SOUTH LANARKSHIRE
KILMARNOCK
Darvel
Galston
Dundonald
Troon
Symington
Douglas
Roberton
Monkton
Prestwick
Tarbolton
Mauchline
Muirkirk
Catrine
Crawfordjohn
Abington
Ayr
Ochiltree
Auchinleck
Cumnock
Alloway
Coylton
EAST AYRSHIRE
New Cumnock
Leadhills
Wanlockhead
Dalrymple
Patna
Kirkconnel
Sanquhar
Kirkmichael
LOWTHER HILLS
Crosshill
Dalmellington
Straiton
SOUTH AYRSHIRE
Carronbridge
CAIRNSMORE OF CARSPHAIRN
Loch Bradan
Loch Doon
Penpont
Thornhill
Carsphairn
Moniaive
Water of Deugh
DUMFRIES AND GALLOWAY
MERRICK
CORSERINE
Loch Moan
Loch Enoch
Auldgirth
Dunscore
St John's Town of Dalry

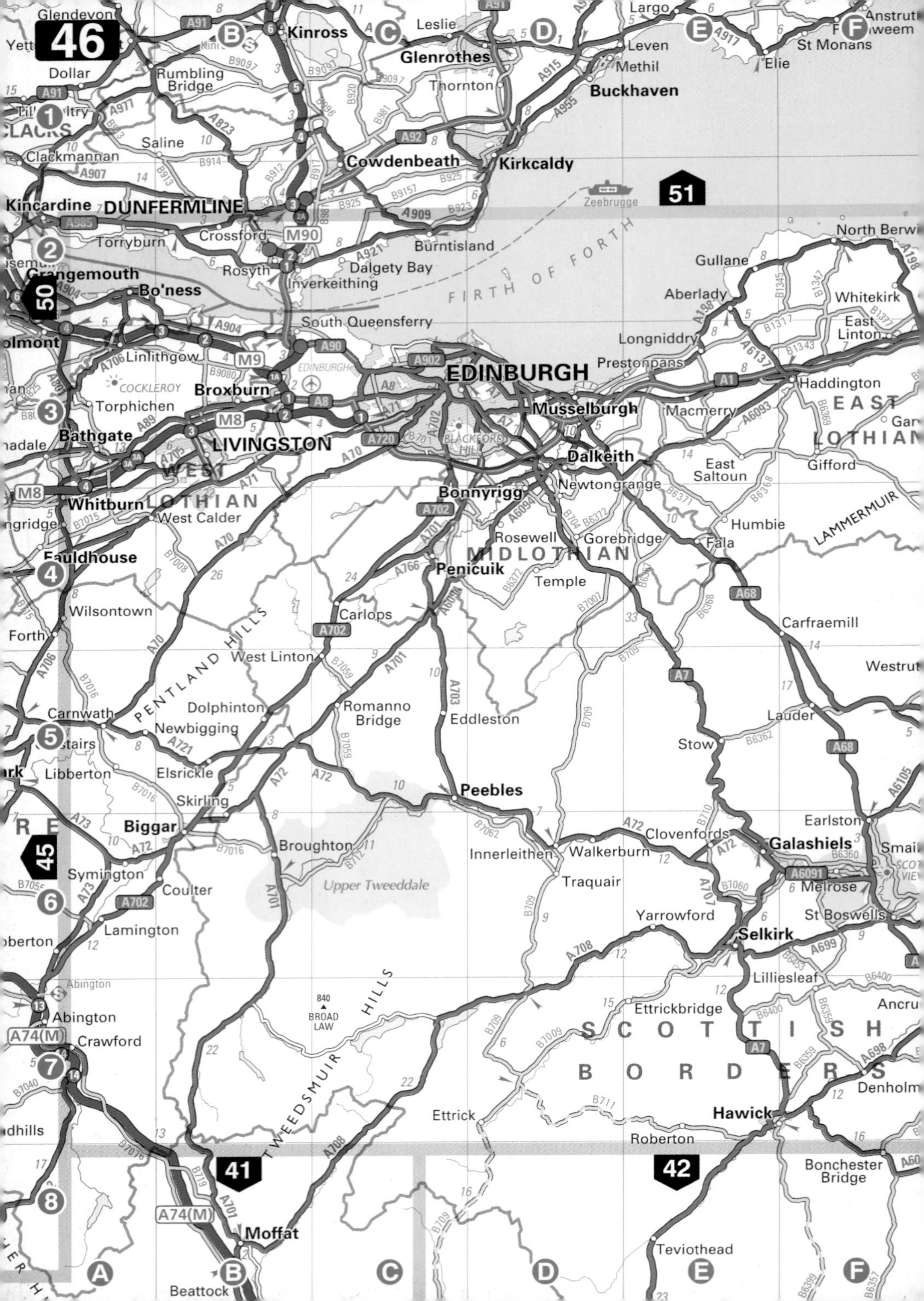
46
Glendevon
Kinross
Leslie
Largo
Anstruther
Pittenweem
St Monans
Elie
Leven
Methil
Glenrothes
Buckhaven
Thornton
Dollar
Rumbling Bridge
Saline
Clackmannan
Cowdenbeath
Kirkcaldy
51
Zeebrugge
Kincardine
DUNFERMLINE
Crossford
Torryburn
Burntisland
Rosyth
Dalgety Bay
Inverkeithing
Grangemouth
Bo'ness
50
FIRTH OF FORTH
North Berwick
Gullane
Aberlady
Whitekirk
East Linton
Longniddry
South Queensferry
Linlithgow
COCKLEROY
Broxburn
Torphichen
EDINBURGH
Prestonpans
Haddington
Musselburgh
Macmerry
EAST LOTHIAN
Bathgate
LIVINGSTON
BLACKFORD HILL
Dalkeith
East Saltoun
Gifford
WEST LOTHIAN
Whitburn
West Calder
Bonnyrigg
Newtongrange
Humbie
LAMMERMUIR
Rosewell
Gorebridge
Fala
Fauldhouse
MIDLOTHIAN
Penicuik
Temple
Wilsontown
Carlops
Carfraemill
Forth
West Linton
Westruther
PENTLAND HILLS
Carnwath
Dolphinton
Romanno Bridge
Eddleston
Lauder
Newbigging
Stow
Carstairs
Libberton
Elsrickle
Peebles
Skirling
Earlston
Biggar
Clovenfords
Galashiels
Broughton
Innerleithen
Walkerburn
Smailholm
45
Symington
Upper Tweeddale
Traquair
Melrose
Coulter
Yarrowford
St Boswells
Lamington
Selkirk
Roberton
Lilliesleaf
Abington
840
BROAD LAW
Ettrickbridge
Ancrum
Crawford
SCOTTISH BORDERS
Denholm
TWEEDSMUIR HILLS
Ettrick
Hawick
Leadhills
Roberton
41
42
Bonchester Bridge
Moffat
Teviothead
Beattock

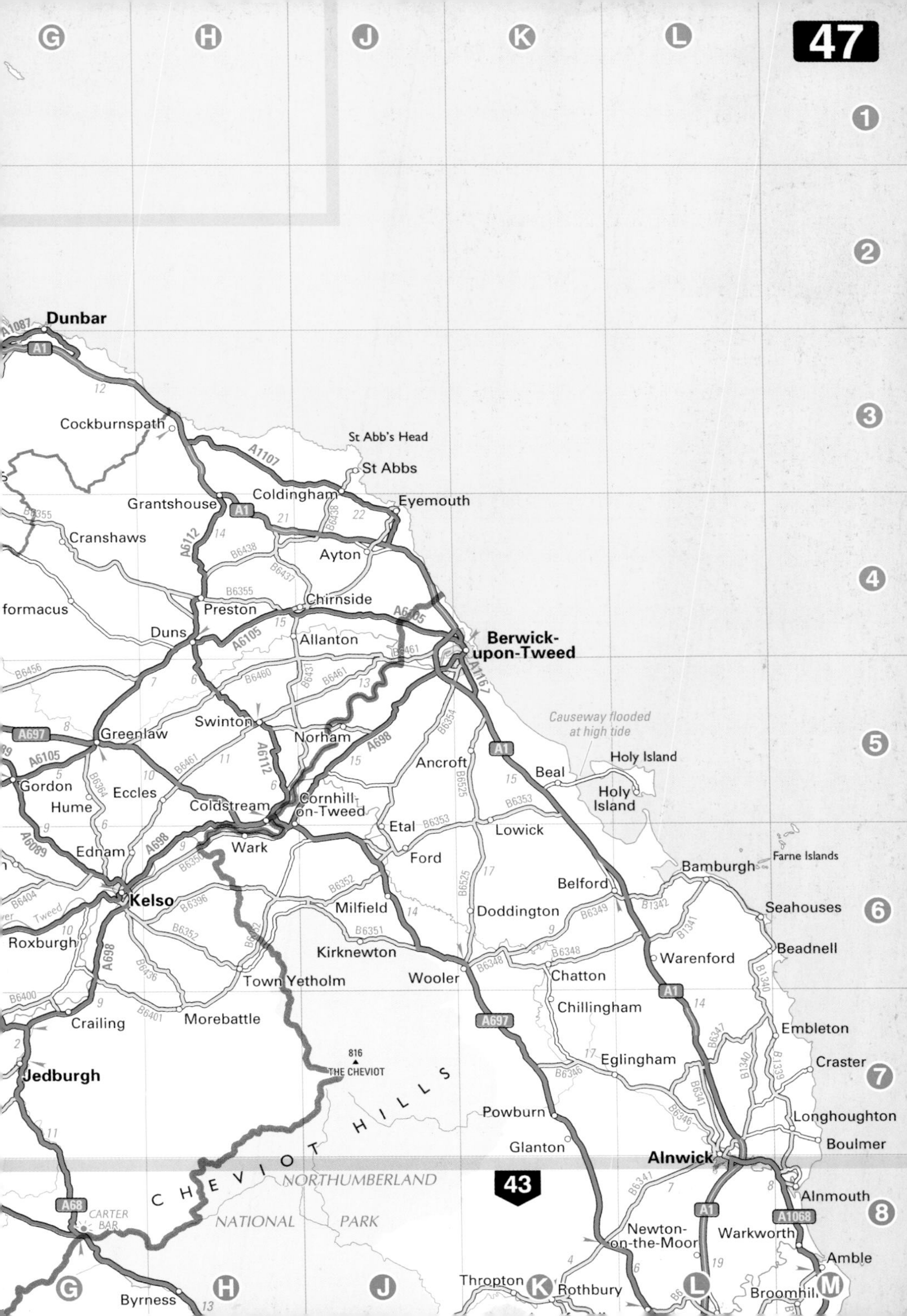
G
H
J
K
L
1
2
3
4
5
6
7
8
Dunbar
A1087
A1
12
Cockburnspath
St Abb's Head
St Abbs
A1107
Coldingham
Eyemouth
Grantshouse
B6355
Cranshaws
A6112
B6438
B6437
Ayton
B6355
Chirnside
Preston
formacus
Duns
A6105
Allanton
Berwick-upon-Tweed
A1167
B6461
B6456
B6460
B6461
B6431
Swinton
Norham
A698
B6354
Causeway flooded at high tide
Holy Island
A697
Greenlaw
A6105
A6112
Ancroft
A1
Beal
Holy Island
Gordon
B6364
Eccles
Hume
Coldstream
Cornhill-on-Tweed
B6525
Etal
B6353
Lowick
B6353
A6089
Ednam
A698
Wark
Ford
Farne Islands
Bamburgh
Belford
B6350
B6352
B6525
Tweed
Kelso
B6396
Milfield
Doddington
B6349
B1342
Seahouses
B6404
B6352
B6351
B1341
Beadnell
Roxburgh
A698
Kirknewton
B6348
Warenford
B6436
Town Yetholm
Wooler
B6348
Chatton
A1
B1340
B6400
B6401
Crailing
Morebattle
A697
Chillingham
Embleton
816
THE CHEVIOT
Eglingham
B6347
Craster
Jedburgh
CHEVIOT HILLS
B6346
B1340
B1339
B6341
Powburn
B6346
Longhoughton
Glanton
Boulmer
Alnwick
NORTHUMBERLAND NATIONAL PARK
A68
CARTER BAR
B6341
A1
Alnmouth
A1068
Newton-on-the-Moor
Warkworth
Amble
Byrness
Thropton
Rothbury
Broomhill
M

43

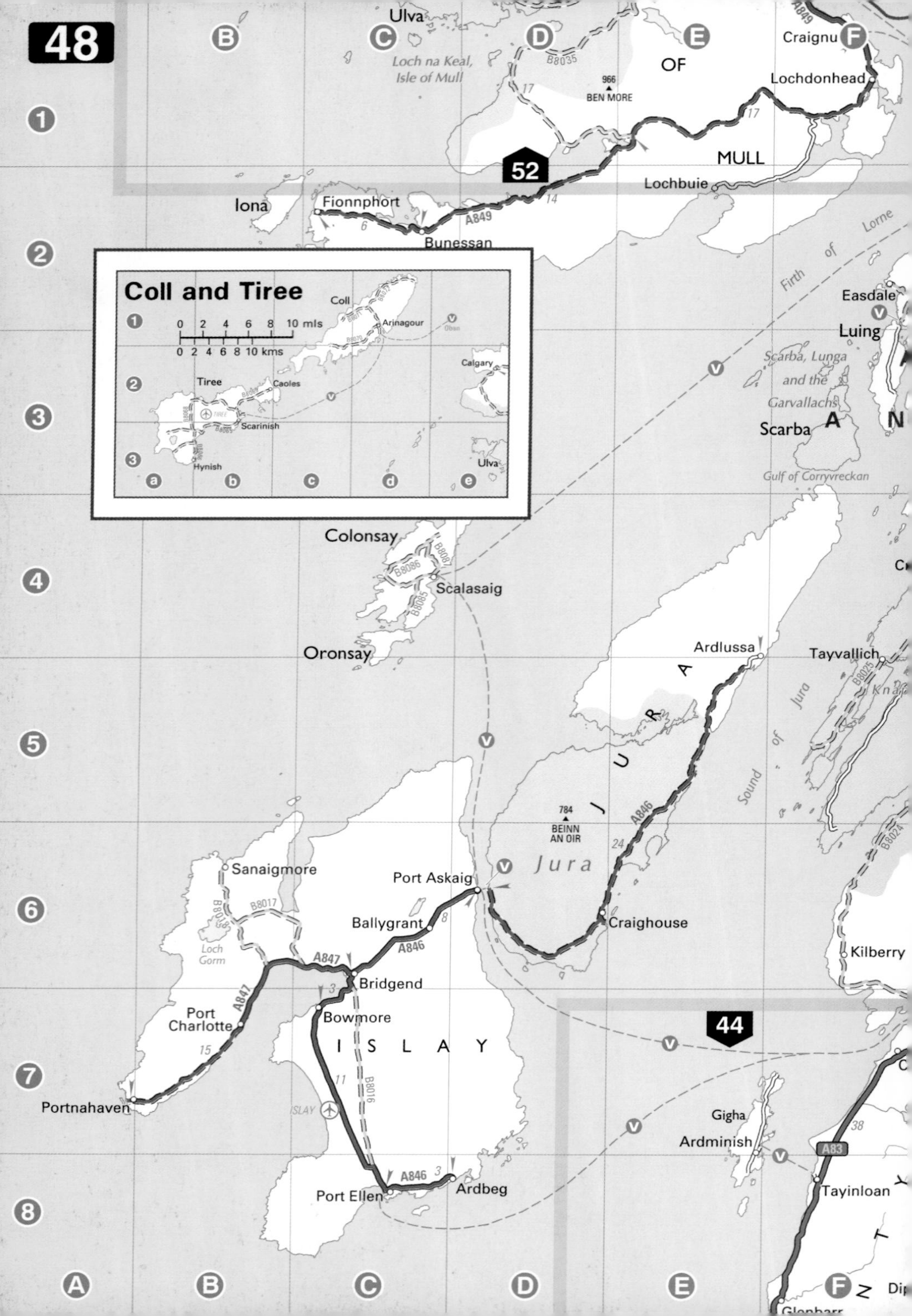

48

B   C   Ulva   D   E   Craignu   F

Loch na Keal,
Isle of Mull

❶   B8035   Lochdonhead

966 ▲   17
BEN MORE   OF

52   MULL

Iona   Fionnphort   Lochbuie

❷   A849

Bunessan   Firth   of   Lorne

Easdale

Luing

Scarba, Lunga
and the
Garvallachs

Scarba   A   N

Gulf of Corryvreckan

Coll and Tiree

❶   0 2 4 6 8   10 mls   Coll
     0 2 4 6 8 10 kms   Arinagour   V Gott

                                                      Calgary

❷   Tiree   Caoles   V

      Scarinish

❸   Hynish   a   b   c   d   Ulva   e

Colonsay
B8086
B8087
B8085   Scalasaig

❹   Ardlussa   Tayvallich   C

Oronsay   J   Kn

                              U
                              R
                              A   Sound   of   Jura   B8024

❺   V   B8025

                    784   A846   Jura
                    BEINN
                    AN OIR   24

Sanaigmore   Port Askaig   V   Jura
B8017
B8018   Ballygrant   8   Craighouse   Kilberry

❻   A847   A846

Loch   A847   Bridgend
Gorm   A847   Bowmore   **44**

Port   3
Charlotte   15   I S L A Y   V

❼   Portnahaven   11   B8016   Gigha
                    ISLAY   V   Ardminish   V
                              A846   3   A83
❽   Port Ellen   Ardbeg   Tayinloan

      A   B   C   D   E   F Z   Dip

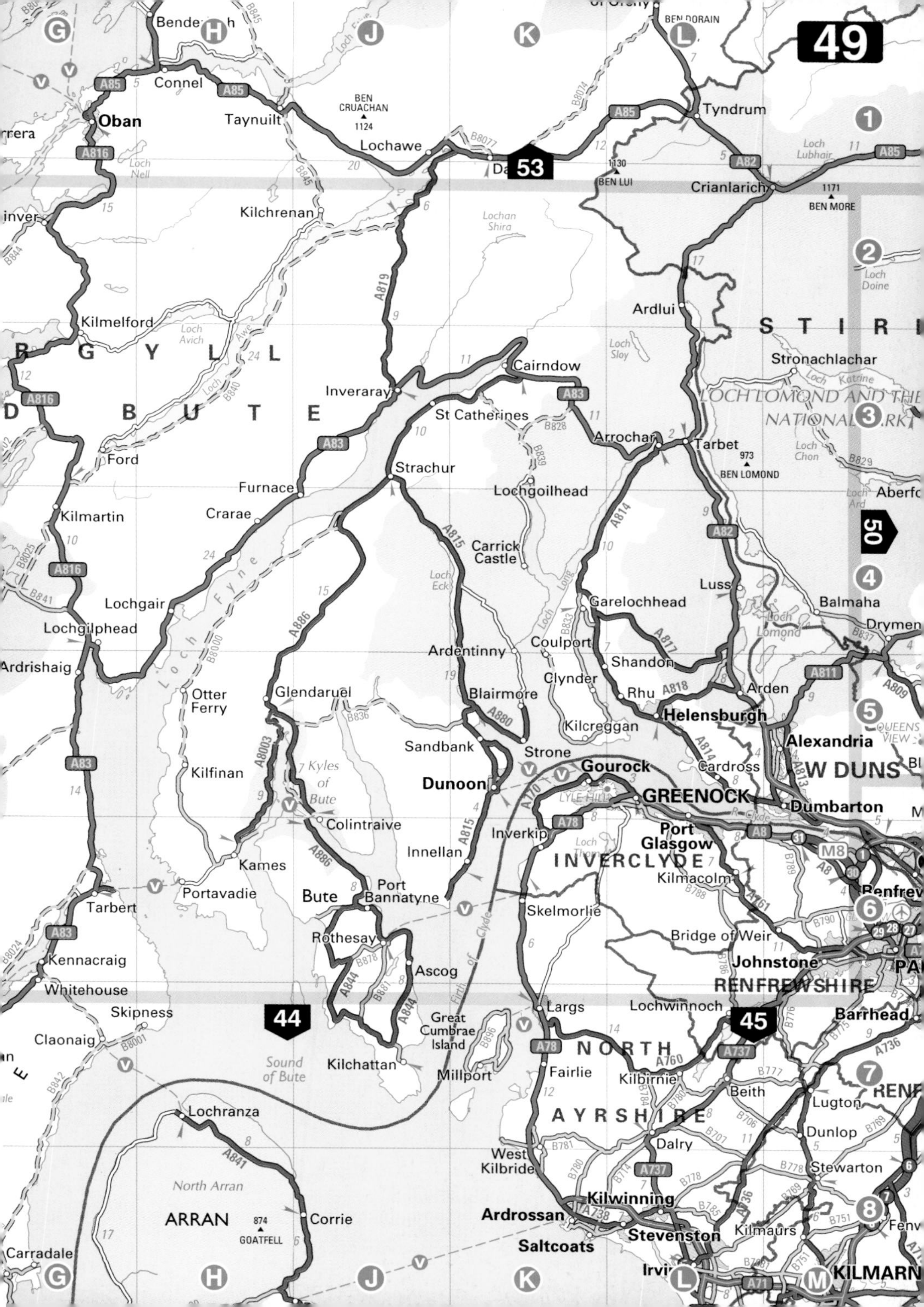

Oban
Connel
Taynuilt
BEN CRUACHAN 1124
Lochawe
Tyndrum
Crianlarich
BEN LUI 1130
BEN MORE 1171
BEN DORAIN
Loch Lubhair
Loch Nell
Kilchrenan
Lochan Shira
Loch Doine
Ardlui
Kilmelford
Loch Avich
ARGYLL & BUTE
STIRLING
Loch Sloy
Stronachlachar
Loch Katrine
LOCH LOMOND AND THE TROSSACHS NATIONAL PARK
Cairndow
Inveraray
St Catherines
Arrochar
Tarbet
BEN LOMOND 973
Loch Chon
Aberfoyle
Loch Ard
Ford
Strachur
Lochgoilhead
Furnace
Kilmartin
Crarae
Carrick Castle
Loch Eck
Loch Long
Luss
Balmaha
Lochgair
Garelochhead
Loch Lomond
Drymen
Lochgilphead
Loch Fyne
Ardentinny
Coulport
Ardrishaig
Shandon
Otter Ferry
Clynder
Glendaruel
Blairmore
Rhu
Arden
Helensburgh
Kilcreggan
Alexandria
QUEENS VIEW
Sandbank
Strone
Cardross
Kilfinan
Kyles of Bute
Gourock
Dunoon
LYLE HILL
GREENOCK
W DUNS
Dumbarton
Colintraive
Inverkip
Port Glasgow
Innellan
Loch Thom
INVERCLYDE
Kames
Kilmacolm
Renfrew
Portavadie
Port Bannatyne
Bute
Tarbert
Skelmorlie
Rothesay
Bridge of Weir
Kennacraig
Ascog
Johnstone
Whitehouse
RENFREWSHIRE
Firth of Clyde
Skipness
Largs
Lochwinnoch
Barrhead
Great Cumbrae Island
Claonaig
NORTH AYRSHIRE
Sound of Bute
Kilchattan
Millport
Fairlie
Kilbirnie
Beith
Lugton
Lochranza
Dalry
Dunlop
West Kilbride
Stewarton
North Arran
Kilwinning
ARRAN
GOATFELL 874
Corrie
Ardrossan
Stevenston
Kilmaurs
Saltcoats
Carradale
KILMARNOCK
A85
A816
A82
A819
A83
A815
A814
A886
A8003
A880
A817
A818
A811
A809
A813
A8
M8
A78
A770
A761
A760
A737
A736
A738
A71
A844
A841
B8074
B8077
B845
B844
B840
B828
B839
B833
B8000
B836
B8025
B841
B8024
B8001
B842
B829
B837
B789
B788
B790
B786
B776
B775
B777
B780
B784
B706
B707
B769
B781
B714
B778
B785
B751
B878
B881
B896
44
45
50
53

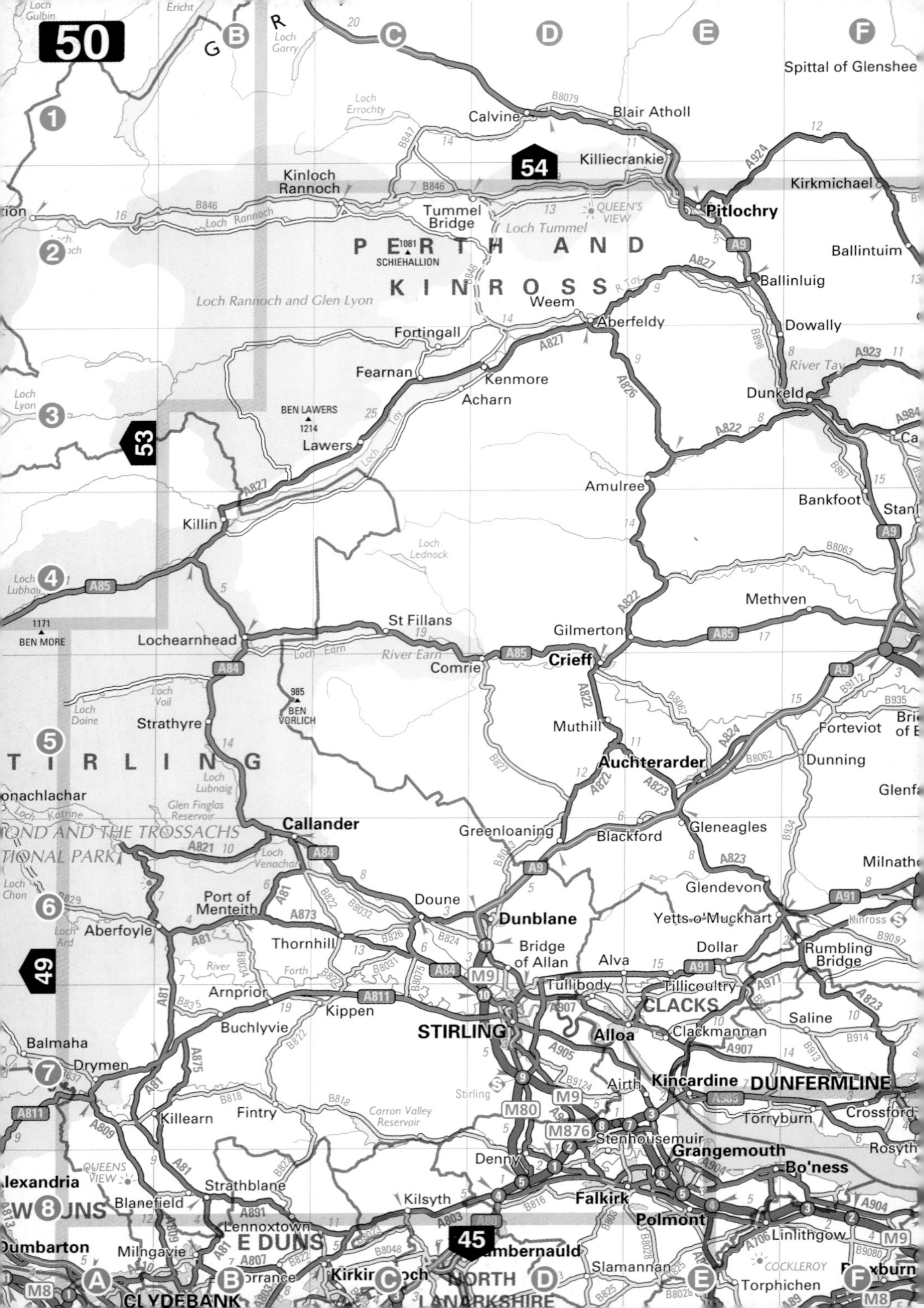
Loch Gulbin
Ericht
Loch Garry
Spittal of Glenshee
Loch Errochty
Calvine
Blair Atholl
54
Killiecrankie
Kinloch Rannoch
Kirkmichael
Tummel Bridge
QUEEN'S VIEW
Loch Tummel
Pitlochry
Loch Rannoch
PERTH AND KINROSS
1081
SCHIEHALLION
Ballintuim
Ballinluig
Loch Rannoch and Glen Lyon
Weem
Aberfeldy
Fortingall
Dowally
River Tay
Fearnan
Kenmore
Acharn
Dunkeld
Loch Lyon
BEN LAWERS
1214
Lawers
Loch Tay
53
Amulree
Bankfoot
Killin
Loch Lednock
Loch Lubhair
Methven
1171
BEN MORE
Lochearnhead
St Fillans
Gilmerton
Loch Earn
River Earn
Comrie
Crieff
Loch Voil
Loch Doine
Strathyre
985
BEN VORLICH
Muthill
Forteviot
STIRLING
Auchterarder
Dunning
Loch Lubnaig
Glen Finglas Reservoir
Loch Katrine
LOCH LOMOND AND THE TROSSACHS NATIONAL PARK
Callander
Greenloaning
Blackford
Gleneagles
Loch Venachar
Loch Chon
Port of Menteith
Doune
Glendevon
Loch Ard
Aberfoyle
Dunblane
Yetts o'Muckhart
Kinross
Thornhill
Bridge of Allan
Alva
Dollar
Rumbling Bridge
49
River Forth
Tullibody
Tillicoultry
Arnprior
Kippen
CLACKS
Saline
Buchlyvie
STIRLING
Alloa
Clackmannan
Balmaha
Drymen
Airth
Kincardine
DUNFERMLINE
Killearn
Fintry
Carron Valley Reservoir
Torryburn
Crossford
Stenhousemuir
Grangemouth
Rosyth
QUEENS VIEW
Denny
Bo'ness
Alexandria
Strathblane
Blanefield
Kilsyth
Falkirk
Polmont
Linlithgow
Lennoxtown
E DUNS
45
Dumbarton
Milngavie
Cumbernauld
COCKLEROY
Slamannan
Torrance
Kirkintilloch
NORTH LANARKSHIRE
Torphichen
Broxburn
CLYDEBANK

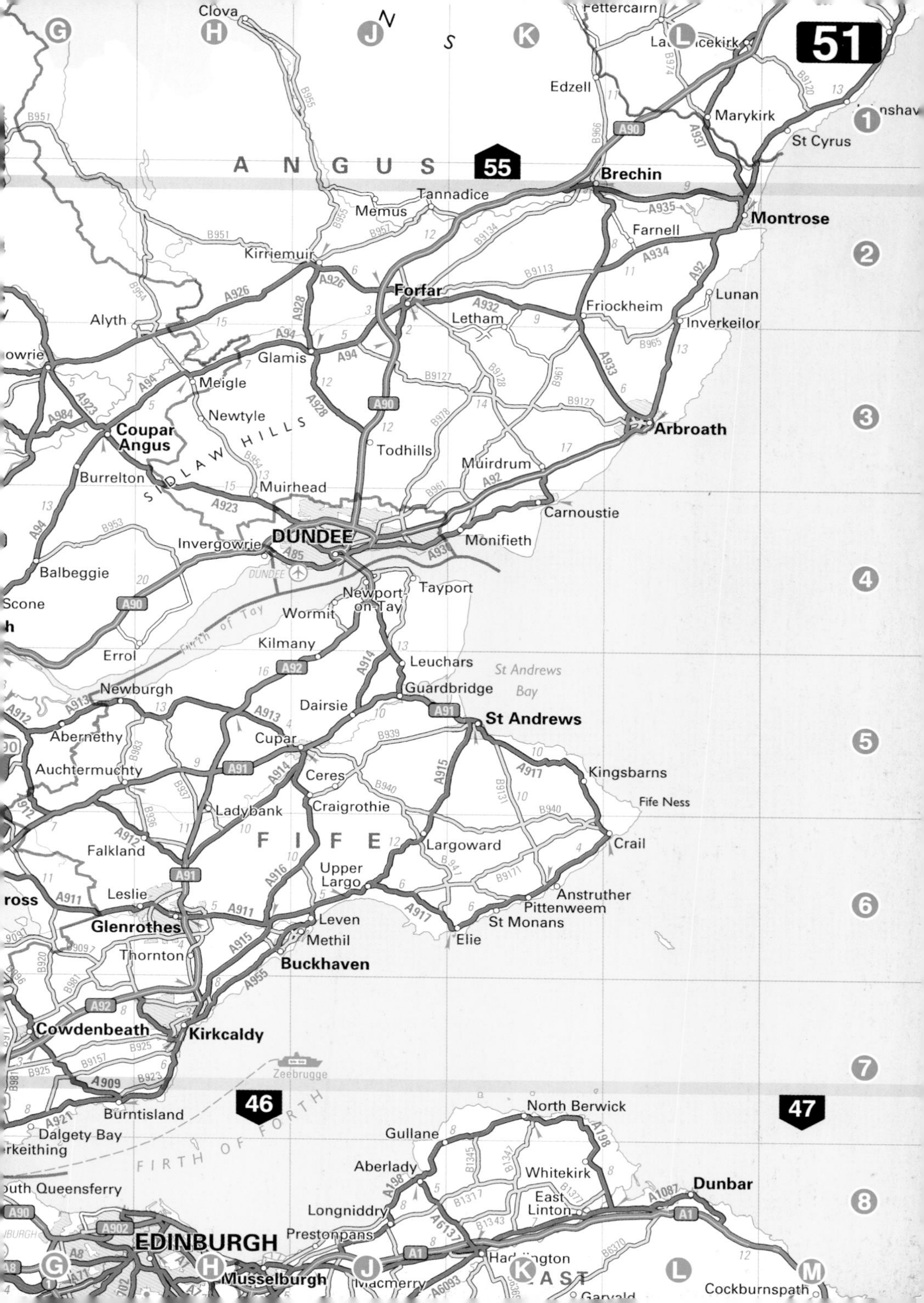

Clova
Fettercairn
Edzell
Marykirk
St Cyrus
ANGUS
55
Brechin
Tannadice
Memus
Montrose
Farnell
Kirriemuir
Forfar
Lunan
Friockheim
Inverkeilor
Letham
Alyth
Glamis
Meigle
Newtyle
SIDLAW HILLS
Coupar Angus
Arbroath
Todhills
Burrelton
Muirdrum
Muirhead
Carnoustie
DUNDEE
Invergowrie
Monifieth
Balbeggie
Tayport
Newport-on-Tay
Scone
Wormit
Firth of Tay
Kilmany
Errol
Leuchars
St Andrews Bay
Newburgh
Guardbridge
Dairsie
St Andrews
Abernethy
Cupar
Auchtermuchty
Ceres
Kingsbarns
Fife Ness
Ladybank
Craigrothie
FIFE
Crail
Falkland
Largoward
Upper Largo
Anstruther
Leslie
Pittenweem
St Monans
Leven
Glenrothes
Methil
Elie
Thornton
Buckhaven
Cowdenbeath
Kirkcaldy
Zeebrugge
46
47
North Berwick
Burntisland
FIRTH OF FORTH
Dalgety Bay
Gullane
Aberlady
Whitekirk
Dunbar
East Linton
Longniddry
Prestonpans
EDINBURGH
Musselburgh
Cockburnspath
A90
A935
A934
A92
A926
A928
A932
A94
A933
A923
A984
A85
A930
A914
A913
A912
A91
A915
A917
A916
A911
A955
A909
A921
A198
A1087
A1
A6137
A902
B951
B955
B957
B9134
B9113
B954
B9127
B9128
B961
B978
B965
B953
B983
B937
B936
B939
B940
B9131
B9171
B9097
B920
B981
B925
B9157
B923
B1345
B1347
B1377
B1343
B6370

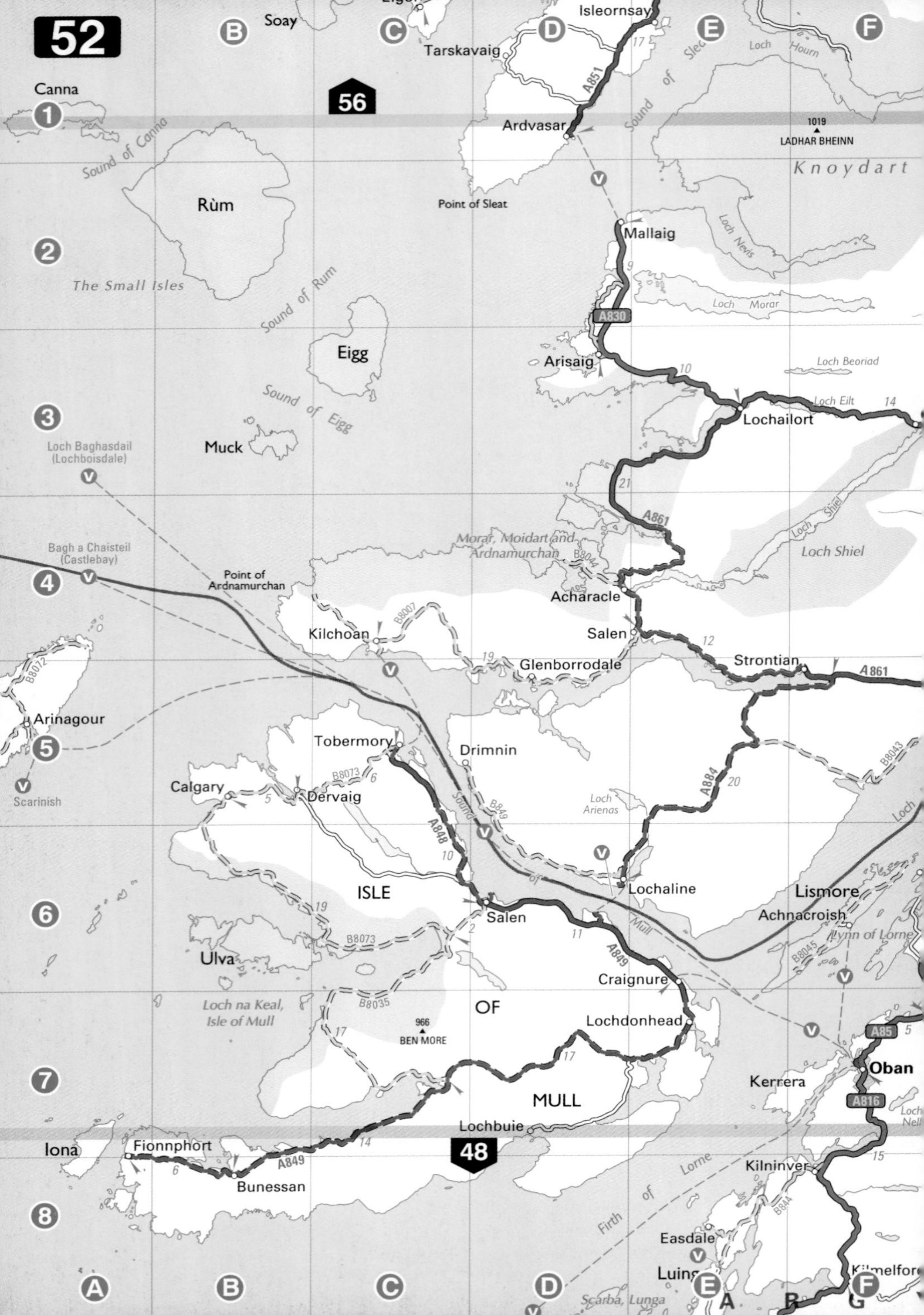

52
56
48
Canna
Soay
Isleornsay
Tarskavaig
Ardvasar
Point of Sleat
Sound of Canna
Sound of Sleat
Loch Hourn
1019
LADHAR BHEINN
Knoydart
Rùm
Mallaig
Loch Nevis
Loch Morar
The Small Isles
Sound of Rum
Eigg
A830
Arisaig
Loch Beoriad
Sound of Eigg
Lochailort
Loch Eilt
Muck
Loch Baghasdail
(Lochboisdale)
A861
Loch Shiel
Morar, Moidart and
Ardnamurchan
B8044
Bagh a Chaisteil
(Castlebay)
Point of
Ardnamurchan
Acharacle
B8007
Kilchoan
Salen
Strontian
Glenborrodale
B8072
Arinagour
Tobermory
Drimnin
B8043
Scarinish
Calgary
B8073
Dervaig
A884
A848
B849
Loch
Arienas
Sound of Mull
Lochaline
Lismore
ISLE
Salen
Achnacroish
Lynn of Lorne
B8045
Ulva
A849
Craignure
Loch na Keal,
Isle of Mull
B8035
OF
966
BEN MORE
Lochdonhead
A85
Oban
Kerrera
MULL
A816
Lochbuie
Iona
Fionnphort
Bunessan
Kilninver
Firth of Lorne
B844
Easdale
Luing
Kilmelford
Scarba, Lunga

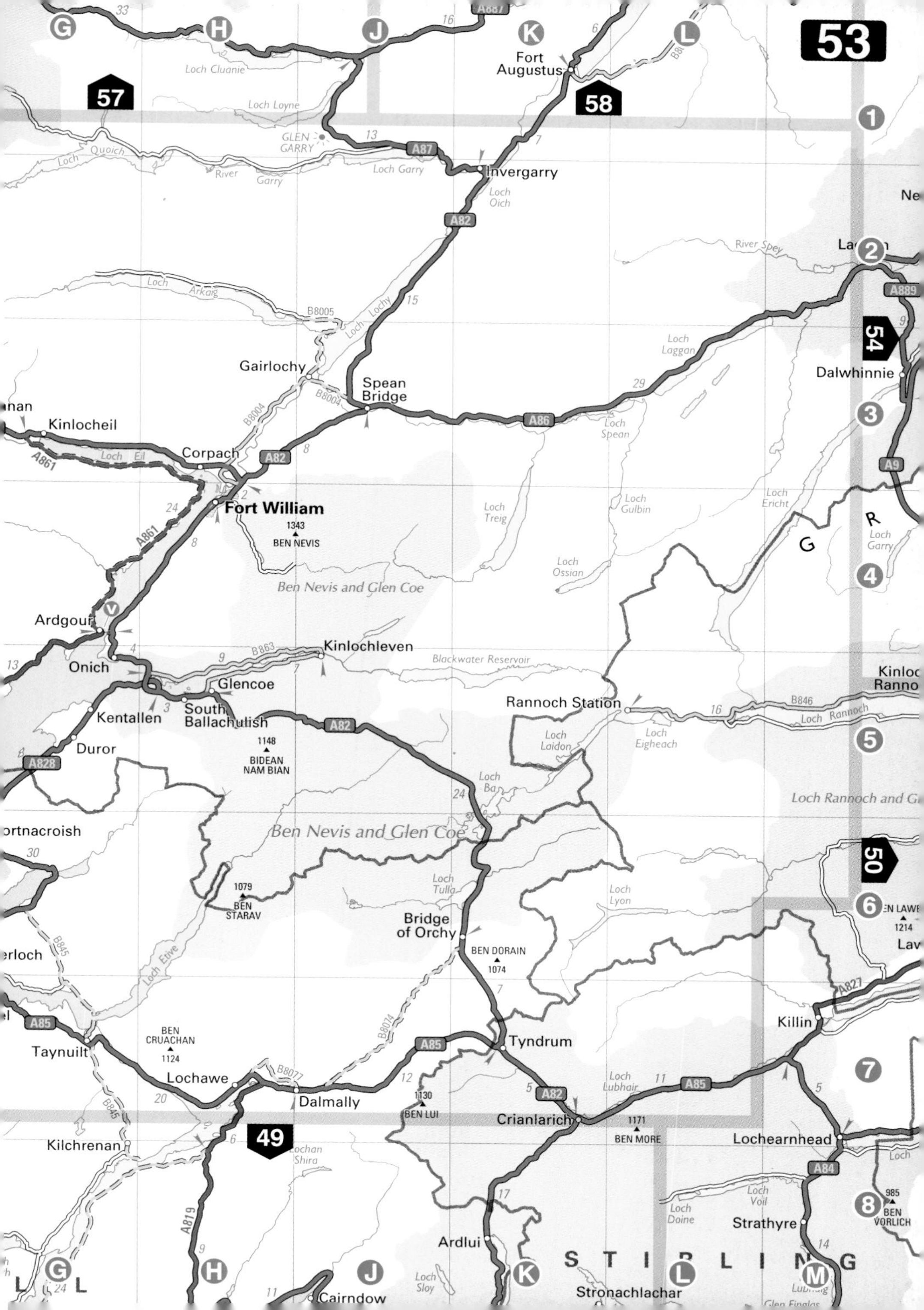

Fort Augustus
Loch Cluanie
Loch Loyne
GLEN GARRY
Loch Quoich
River Garry
Loch Garry
Invergarry
Loch Oich
River Spey
Loch Arkaig
Loch Lochy
Gairlochy
Spean Bridge
Loch Laggan
Dalwhinnie
Kinlocheil
Loch Eil
Corpach
Loch Spean
Fort William
1343
BEN NEVIS
Loch Treig
Loch Gulbin
Loch Ericht
Loch Garry
Loch Ossian
Ben Nevis and Glen Coe
Ardgour
Onich
Kinlochleven
Blackwater Reservoir
Glencoe
Kentallen
South Ballachulish
Rannoch Station
Loch Laidon
Loch Eigheach
Loch Rannoch
Duror
1148
BIDEAN NAM BIAN
Loch Ba
Loch Rannoch and G
Ben Nevis and Glen Coe
1079
BEN STARAV
Loch Tulla
Loch Lyon
Bridge of Orchy
BEN DORAIN
1074
Loch Etive
BEN LAWE
1214
Killin
BEN CRUACHAN
1124
Taynuilt
Tyndrum
Lochawe
Dalmally
1130
BEN LUI
Loch Lubhair
Crianlarich
1171
BEN MORE
Lochearnhead
Kilchrenan
Lochan Shira
Loch Voil
Loch Doine
Strathyre
985
BEN VORLICH
Ardlui
STIRLING
Loch Sloy
Cairndow
Stronachlachar

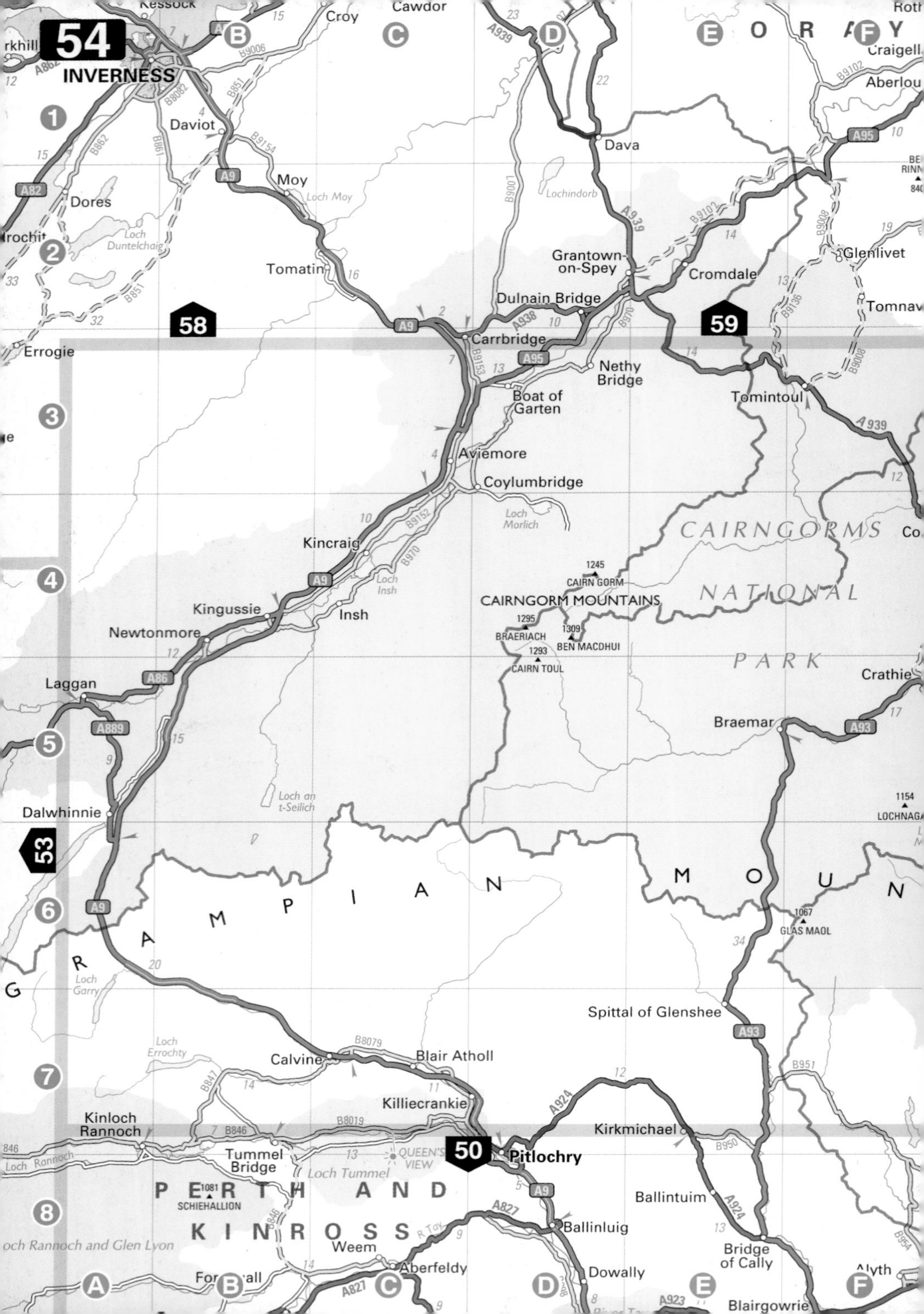
54
INVERNESS
Kessock
Croy
Cawdor
MORAY
Craigellachie
Aberlour
Daviot
Dava
Moy
Loch Moy
Lochindorb
Dores
Loch Duntelchaig
Tomatin
Grantown-on-Spey
Cromdale
Glenlivet
Tomnavoulin
Dulnain Bridge
58
59
Errogie
Carrbridge
Nethy Bridge
Boat of Garten
Tomintoul
Aviemore
Coylumbridge
Loch Morlich
Kincraig
Loch Insh
Insh
CAIRNGORMS NATIONAL PARK
1245 CAIRN GORM
CAIRNGORM MOUNTAINS
1295 BRAERIACH
1309 BEN MACDHUI
1293 CAIRN TOUL
Kingussie
Newtonmore
Laggan
Crathie
Braemar
Loch an t-Seilich
1154 LOCHNAGAR
Dalwhinnie
53
GRAMPIAN MOUNTAINS
1067 GLAS MAOL
Loch Garry
Spittal of Glenshee
Loch Errochty
Calvine
Blair Atholl
Killiecrankie
Kinloch Rannoch
Kirkmichael
Loch Rannoch
Tummel Bridge
Loch Tummel
QUEEN'S VIEW
50
Pitlochry
PERTH AND KINROSS
1081 SCHIEHALLION
Ballintuim
Ballinluig
Loch Rannoch and Glen Lyon
Weem
Aberfeldy
Bridge of Cally
Fortingall
Dowally
Alyth
Blairgowrie
A9
A82
A95
A938
A939
A86
A889
A93
A924
A827
A923
B9006
B851
B8082
B862
B861
B9154
B9007
B9102
B9008
B9136
B970
B9153
B9152
B8079
B847
B8019
B846
B950
B951
B954
A B C D E F
1 2 3 4 5 6 7 8

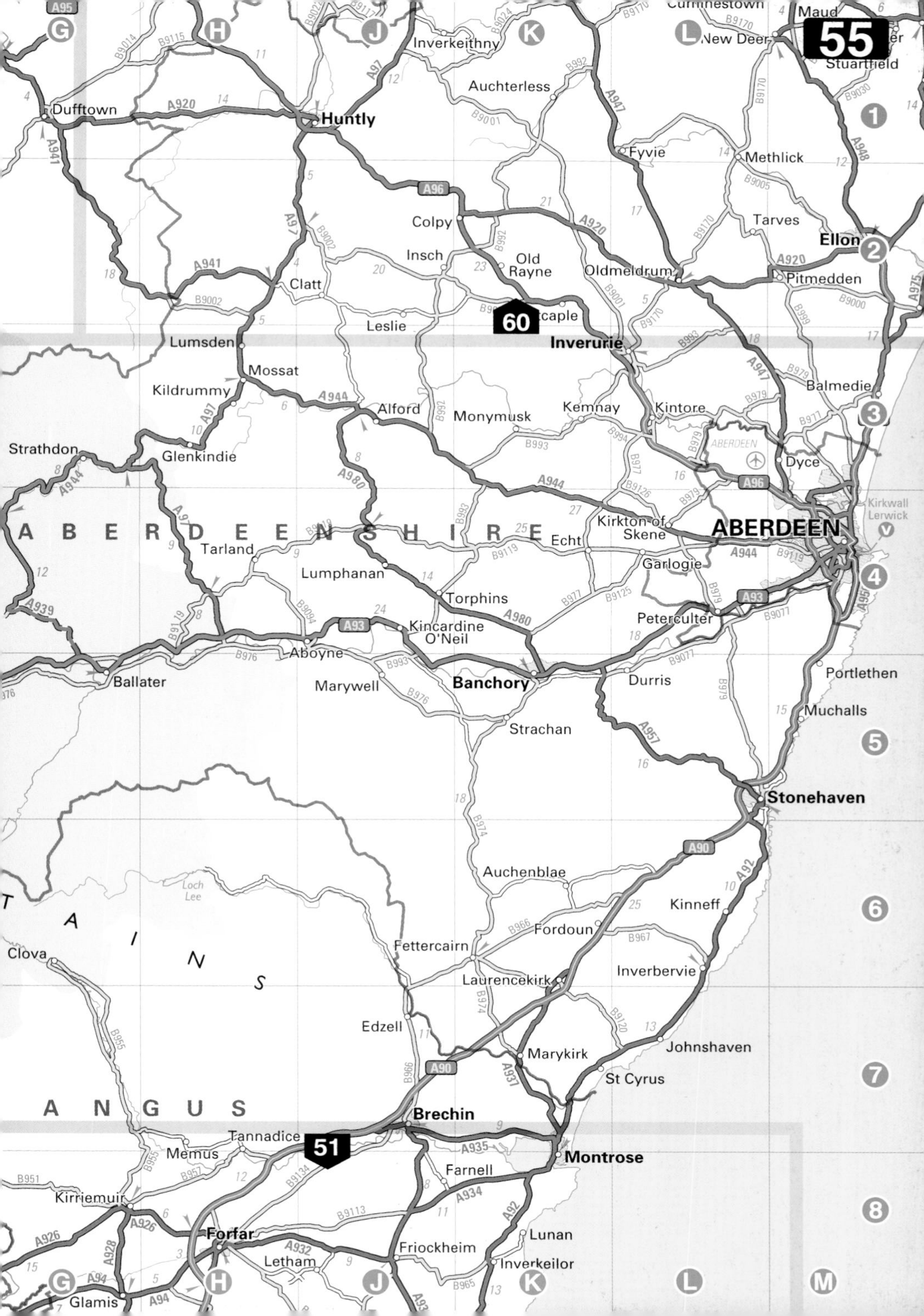
Huntly
Dufftown
Inverkeithny
Auchterless
Fyvie
Methlick
Tarves
Ellon
Pitmedden
Colpy
Insch
Old Rayne
Oldmeldrum
Clatt
Leslie
Inverurie
Lumsden
Mossat
Kildrummy
Alford
Monymusk
Kemnay
Kintore
Balmedie
Dyce
Strathdon
Glenkindie
ABERDEENSHIRE
ABERDEEN
Kirkton-of-Skene
Echt
Garlogie
Tarland
Lumphanan
Torphins
Peterculter
Kincardine O'Neil
Aboyne
Ballater
Marywell
Banchory
Durris
Portlethen
Strachan
Muchalls
Stonehaven
Auchenblae
Kinneff
Fordoun
Fettercairn
Laurencekirk
Inverbervie
Edzell
Marykirk
Johnshaven
St Cyrus
Clova
ANGUS
Brechin
Montrose
Tannadice
Memus
Farnell
Kirriemuir
Forfar
Lunan
Friockheim
Letham
Inverkeilor
Glamis
Maud
New Deer
Stuartfield
Kirkwall
Lerwick
Loch Lee
60
51

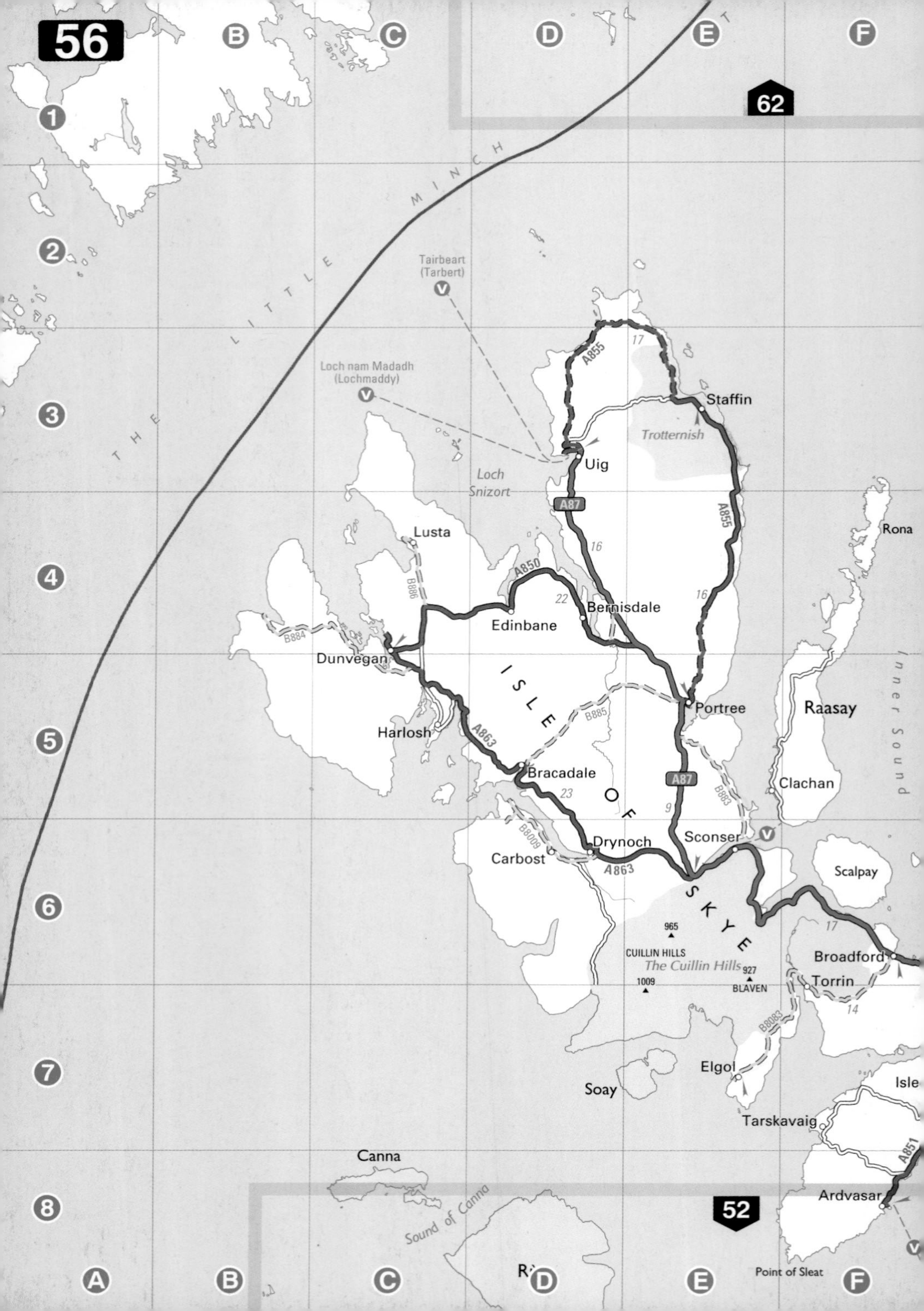
62
52
THE LITTLE MINCH
Tairbeart (Tarbert)
Loch nam Madadh (Lochmaddy)
Staffin
Trotternish
Uig
Loch Snizort
A855
A87
Lusta
Rona
A850
B886
Bernisdale
Edinbane
B884
Dunvegan
ISLE OF SKYE
Portree
Raasay
Inner Sound
B885
Harlosh
A863
Bracadale
Clachan
B883
B8009
Drynoch
Sconser
Carbost
Scalpay
965
CUILLIN HILLS
The Cuillin Hills
927
BLAVEN
1009
Broadford
Torrin
B8083
Elgol
Soay
Isle
Tarskavaig
A851
Canna
Ardvasar
Sound of Canna
Point of Sleat

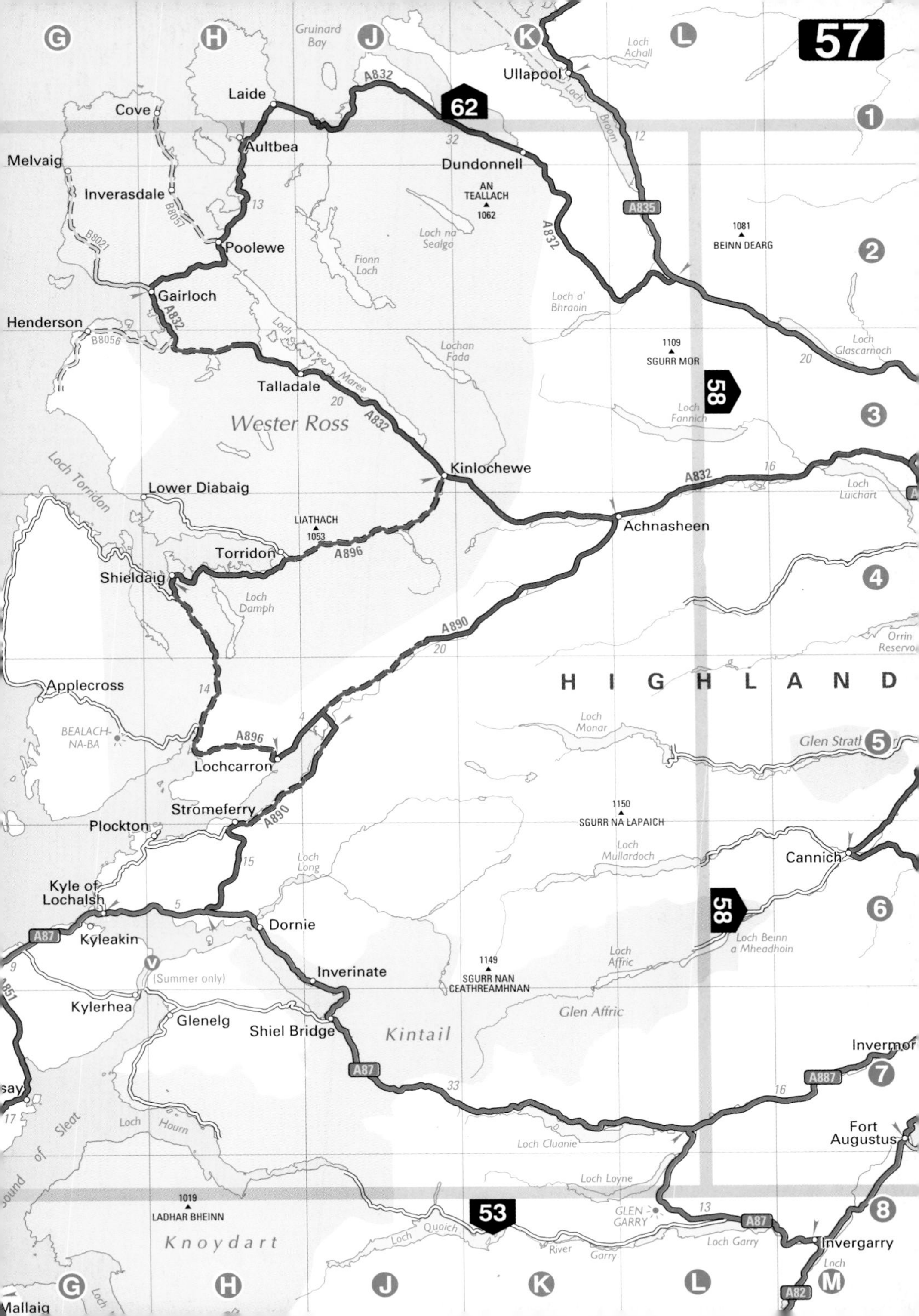
G
H
J
K
L
Gruinard Bay
Loch Achall
Ullapool
Loch Broom
A832
Laide
62
Cove
Aultbea
1
Melvaig
Dundonnell
Inverasdale
B8057
AN TEALLACH 1062
A835
B8021
Poolewe
Loch na Sealga
Fionn Loch
A832
1081 BEINN DEARG
2
Gairloch
A832
Loch a' Bhraoin
Henderson
B8056
Loch Maree
Lochan Fada
1109 SGURR MOR
Loch Glascarnoch
Talladale
A832
58
Loch Fannich
3
Wester Ross
Loch Torridon
Kinlochewe
A832
Loch Luichart
Lower Diabaig
LIATHACH 1053
Achnasheen
A896
Torridon
Shieldaig
Loch Damph
4
A890
Orrin Reservoir
Applecross
HIGHLAND
BEALACH-NA-BA
A896
Loch Monar
Glen Strath
5
Lochcarron
Stromeferry
A890
1150 SGURR NA LAPAICH
Plockton
Loch Mullardoch
Loch Long
Cannich
Kyle of Lochalsh
58
6
A87
Kyleakin
Dornie
Loch Beinn a Mheadhoin
Loch Affric
Inverinate
1149 SGURR NAN CEATHREAMHNAN
(Summer only)
Kylerhea
Glenelg
Shiel Bridge
Glen Affric
Kintail
Invermoriston
A87
A887
7
Sound of Sleat
Loch Hourn
Loch Cluanie
Fort Augustus
Loch Loyne
1019 LADHAR BHEINN
53
GLEN GARRY
A87
8
Loch Quoich
Knoydart
River Garry
Loch Garry
Invergarry
G
H
J
K
L
M
A82
Mallaig

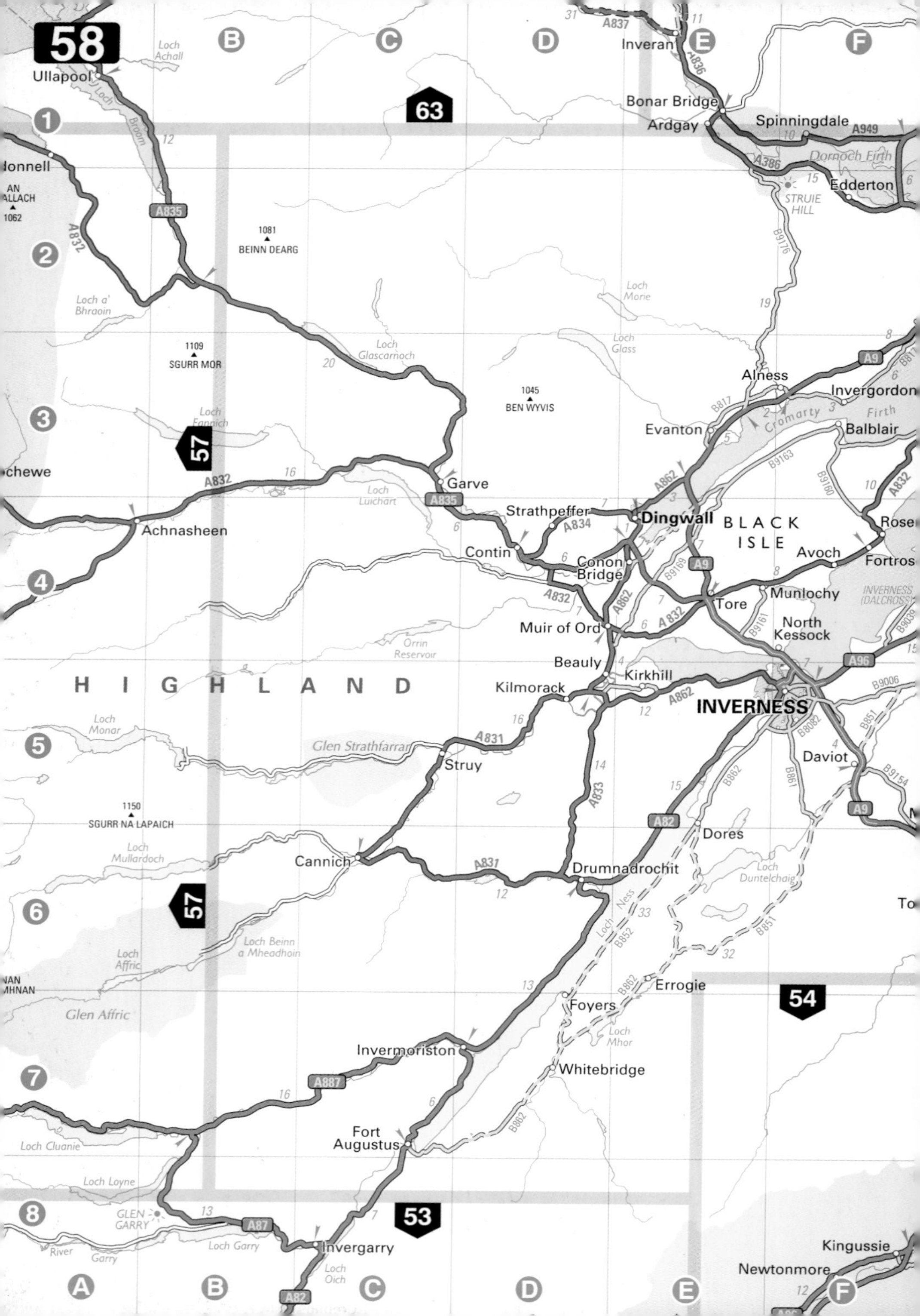

Ullapool
Loch Achall
Loch Broom
Inveran
Bonar Bridge
Ardgay
Spinningdale
Dornoch Firth
Edderton
STRUIE HILL
63
1081
BEINN DEARG
1109
SGURR MOR
Loch a' Bhraoin
Loch Glascarnoch
Loch Morie
Loch Glass
1045
BEN WYVIS
Loch Fannich
57
Garve
Loch Luichart
Alness
Invergordon
Cromarty Firth
Evanton
Balblair
Strathpeffer
Dingwall
BLACK ISLE
Achnasheen
Contin
Conon Bridge
Avoch
Fortrose
Tore
Munlochy
Muir of Ord
North Kessock
INVERNESS (DALCROSS)
Orrin Reservoir
Beauly
Kirkhill
Kilmorack
HIGHLAND
INVERNESS
Loch Monar
Glen Strathfarrar
Struy
Daviot
1150
SGURR NA LAPAICH
Loch Mullardoch
Cannich
Drumnadrochit
Dores
Loch Duntelchaig
Loch Ness
Loch Beinn a Mheadhoin
Loch Affric
Glen Affric
Errogie
Foyers
54
Loch Mhor
Invermoriston
Whitebridge
Loch Cluanie
Fort Augustus
Loch Loyne
GLEN GARRY
53
Loch Garry
River Garry
Invergarry
Loch Oich
Kingussie
Newtonmore
A835
A832
A837
A836
A949
A386
B9176
A9
B817
A862
A834
B9163
B9160
B9169
B9161
A96
B9006
A862
A831
A833
B862
B861
B8082
B851
B9154
A82
B852
A887
A87

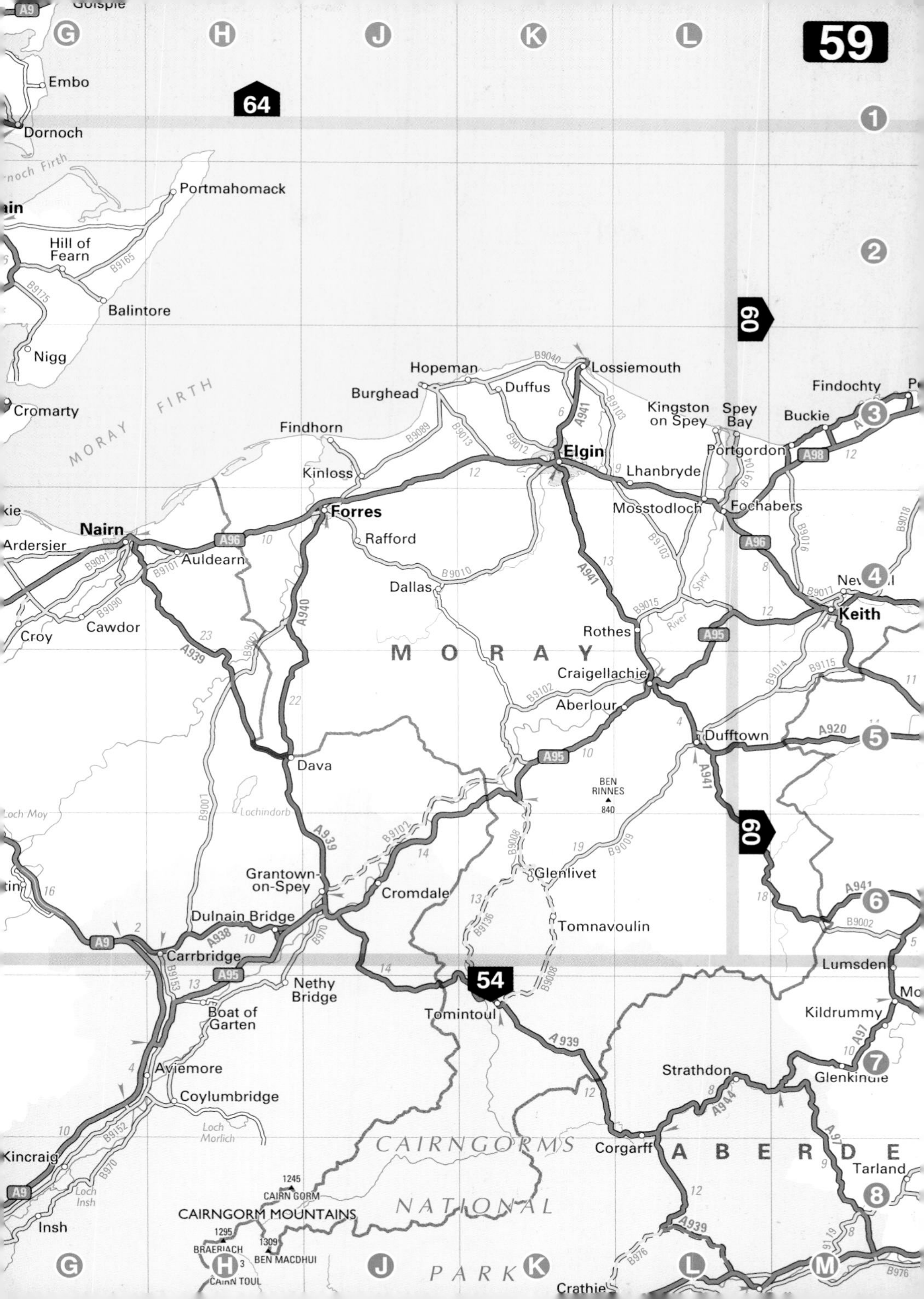
59
64
60
54
G
H
J
K
L
M
1
2
3
4
5
6
7
8
Golspie
Embo
Dornoch
Portmahomack
Hill of Fearn
Balintore
Nigg
Cromarty
MORAY FIRTH
Nairn
Ardersier
Auldearn
Croy
Cawdor
Findhorn
Kinloss
Forres
Rafford
Dallas
Burghead
Hopeman
Duffus
Lossiemouth
Elgin
Lhanbryde
Kingston on Spey
Spey Bay
Portgordon
Buckie
Findochty
Mosstodloch
Fochabers
Keith
Rothes
Craigellachie
Aberlour
Dufftown
MORAY
BEN RINNES
840
Dava
Lochindorb
Loch Moy
Grantown-on-Spey
Cromdale
Glenlivet
Tomnavoulin
Dulnain Bridge
Carrbridge
Nethy Bridge
Boat of Garten
Tomintoul
Aviemore
Coylumbridge
Loch Morlich
Kincraig
Loch Insh
Insh
CAIRNGORMS NATIONAL PARK
CAIRN GORM
1245
CAIRNGORM MOUNTAINS
BRAERIACH
1295
BEN MACDHUI
1309
CAIRN TOUL
Strathdon
Corgarff
Crathie
Lumsden
Kildrummy
Glenkindie
Tarland
ABERDE
A9
A96
A939
A940
A941
A95
A938
A98
A920
A97
A944
B9040
B9103
B9089
B9013
B9012
B9010
B9015
B9102
B9007
B9001
B9091
B9101
B9090
B9165
B9175
B9104
B9016
B9018
B9017
B9014
B9115
B9002
B9008
B9136
B9009
B970
B9153
B9152
B976

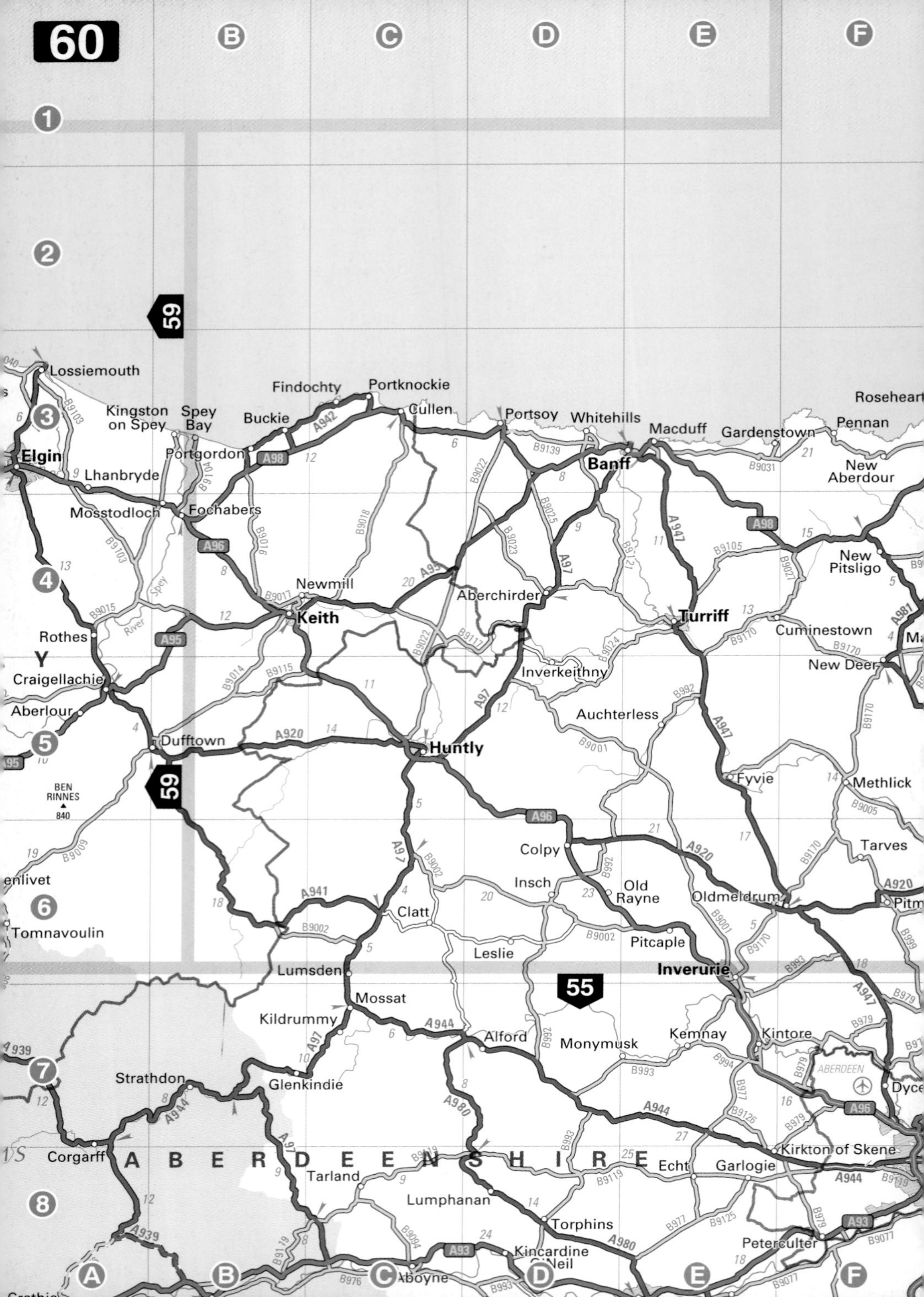

B
C
D
E
F
1
2
59
Lossiemouth
Findochty
Portknockie
Cullen
Portsoy
Whitehills
Macduff
Gardenstown
Pennan
Kingston on Spey
Spey Bay
Buckie
Portgordon
Elgin
Lhanbryde
Mosstodloch
Fochabers
Banff
New Aberdour
New Pitsligo
Newmill
Keith
Aberchirder
Turriff
Cuminestown
New Deer
Rothes
Craigellachie
Aberlour
Inverkeithny
Auchterless
Dufftown
Huntly
BEN RINNES
840
Fyvie
Methlick
Colpy
Tarves
Insch
Old Rayne
Oldmeldrum
Clatt
Tomnavoulin
Leslie
Pitcaple
Lumsden
Inverurie
Mossat
55
Kildrummy
Alford
Monymusk
Kemnay
Kintore
ABERDEEN
Strathdon
Glenkindie
Dyce
Corgarff
A B E R D E E N S H I R E
Echt
Garlogie
Kirkton of Skene
Tarland
Lumphanan
Torphins
Peterculter
Kincardine O'Neil
Aboyne
A98
A96
A95
A920
A97
A941
A944
A980
A93
A947
A942
A939
A981

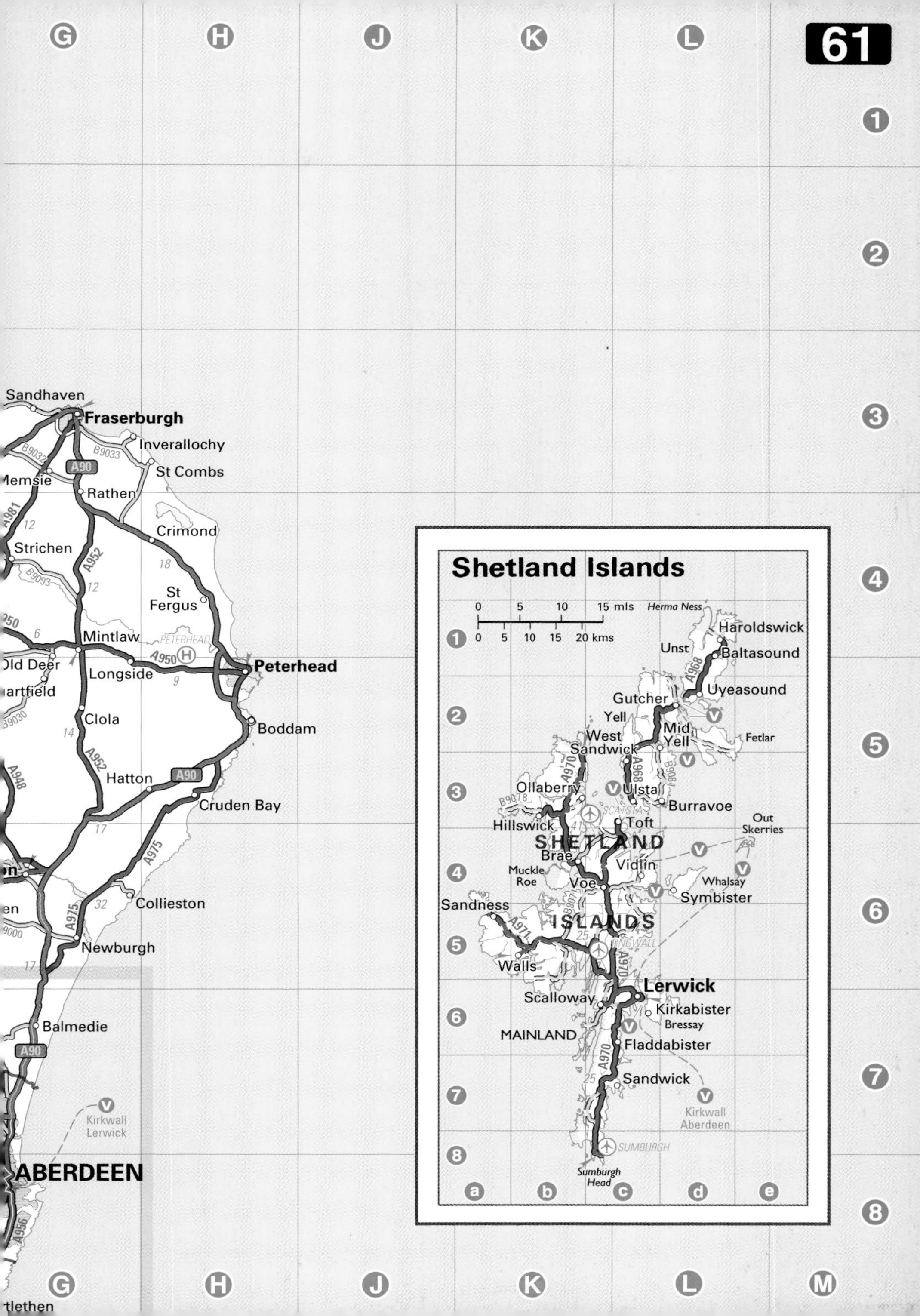

G H J K L

① ② ③ ④ ⑤ ⑥ ⑦ ⑧

Sandhaven
Fraserburgh
Inverallochy
B9033
A90
B9033
St Combs
Memsie
Rathen
A981
12
Crimond
Strichen
A952
18
B9093
12
St Fergus
950
6
Mintlaw
PETERHEAD
A950 H
Old Deer
Longside
9
Peterhead
artfield
B9030
Clola
A952
14
Boddam
Hatton
A90
A948
Cruden Bay
A975
17
n
A975
32
Collieston
B9000
Newburgh
A90
17
Balmedie
A90
V
Kirkwall
Lerwick
ABERDEEN

Shetland Islands

0 5 10 15 mls   *Herma Ness*
0 5 10 15 20 kms

①
Unst
Haroldswick
Baltasound
A968
Uyeasound
V

②
Gutcher
Yell
Mid Yell
V
Fetlar
West Sandwick
A968
B908
V

③
Ollaberry
V
Ulsta
Burravoe
B9078
SCARFSTA
Hillswick
SHETLAND
Toft
Out Skerries
V

④
Brae
Muckle Roe
Vidlin
Whalsay
V
Voe
V
Symbister
Sandness

⑤
ISLANDS
A971
Walls
NEW VIELL
A970

⑥
Scalloway
Lerwick
Kirkabister
Bressay
MAINLAND
V
Fladdabister

⑦
25
Sandwick
Kirkwall Aberdeen

⑧
SUMBURGH
Sumburgh Head

a b c d e

G H J K L M

tlethen

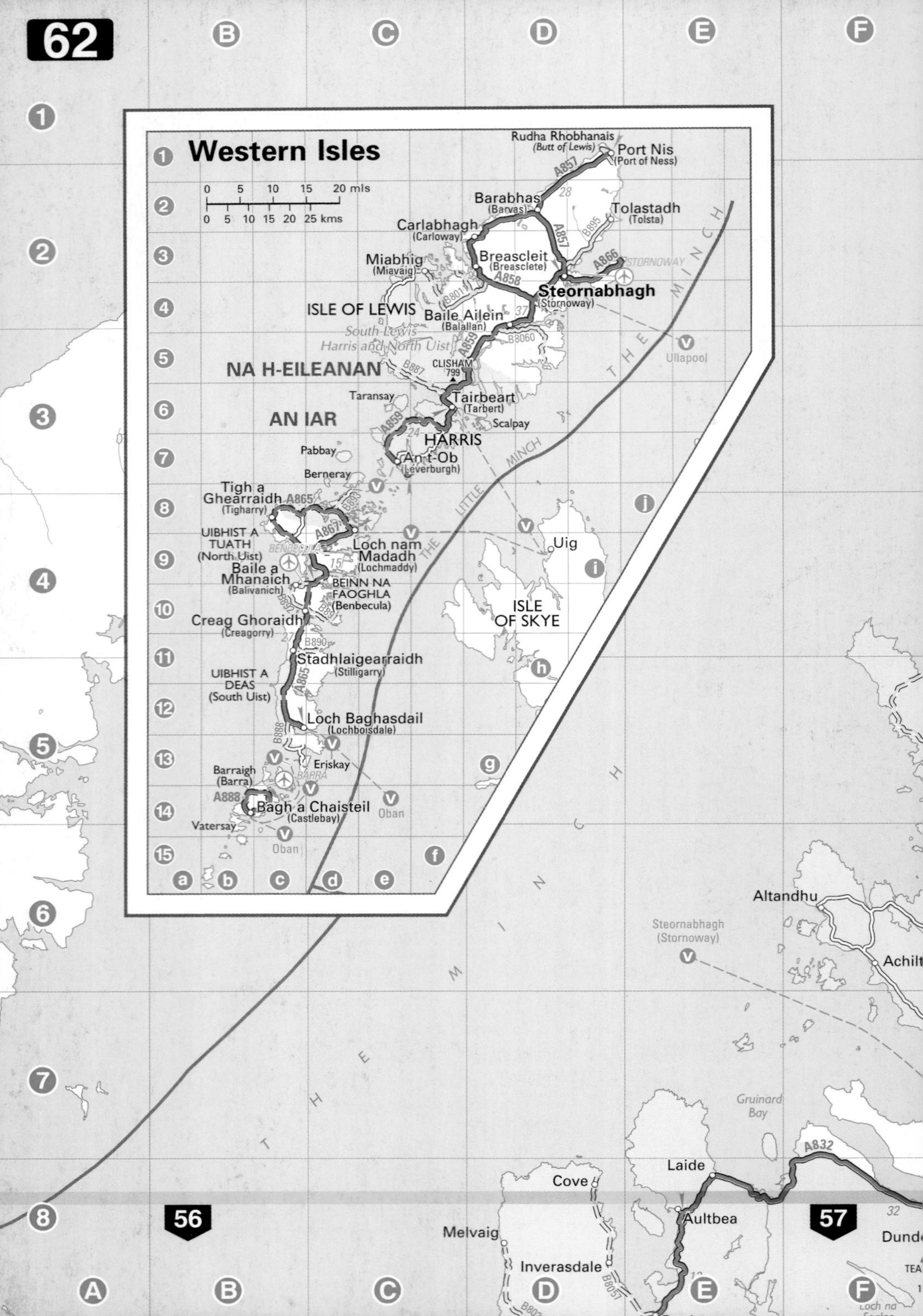

Western Isles

0 5 10 15 20 mls
0 5 10 15 20 25 kms

Rudha Rhobhanais
(Butt of Lewis)
Port Nis
(Port of Ness)
A857

28

Barabhas
(Barvas)

Tolastadh
(Tolsta)

Carlabhagh
(Carloway)
A857
B895

Miabhig
(Miavaig)
Breascleit
(Breasclete)
A858
A866
STORNOWAY

(B8011)
Steornabhagh
(Stornoway)

ISLE OF LEWIS
Baile Ailein
(Balallan)
37

South Lewis
Harris and North Uist
B8060

NA H-EILEANAN
CLISHAM
799
Ullapool

B887

Taransay
Tairbeart
(Tarbert)

AN IAR
Scalpay
B898

Pabbay
HARRIS
An t-Ob
(Leverburgh)

Berneray

Tigh a
Ghearraidh
(Tigharry)
A865

A867

BENBECULA

UIBHIST A
TUATH
(North Uist)
Loch nam
Madadh
(Lochmaddy)
Uig

i

Baile a
Mhanaich
(Balivanich)
BEINN NA
FAOGHLA
(Benbecula)
15

i

Creag Ghoraidh
(Creagorry)
**ISLE
OF SKYE**

B890

Stadhlaigearraidh
(Stilligarry)

h

A865

UIBHIST A
DEAS
(South Uist)

g

B888

Loch Baghasdail
(Lochboisdale)

Barraigh
(Barra)
Eriskay
BARRA

A888
Bagh a Chaisteil
(Castlebay)
Oban

Vatersay

Oban

f

a   b   c   d   e

THE MINCH

THE LITTLE MINCH

Altandhu

Steornabhagh
(Stornoway)

Achilt

V

Gruinard
Bay

A832

Laide
Cove

Aultbea
Dunde

Melvaig

Inverasdale
TEA

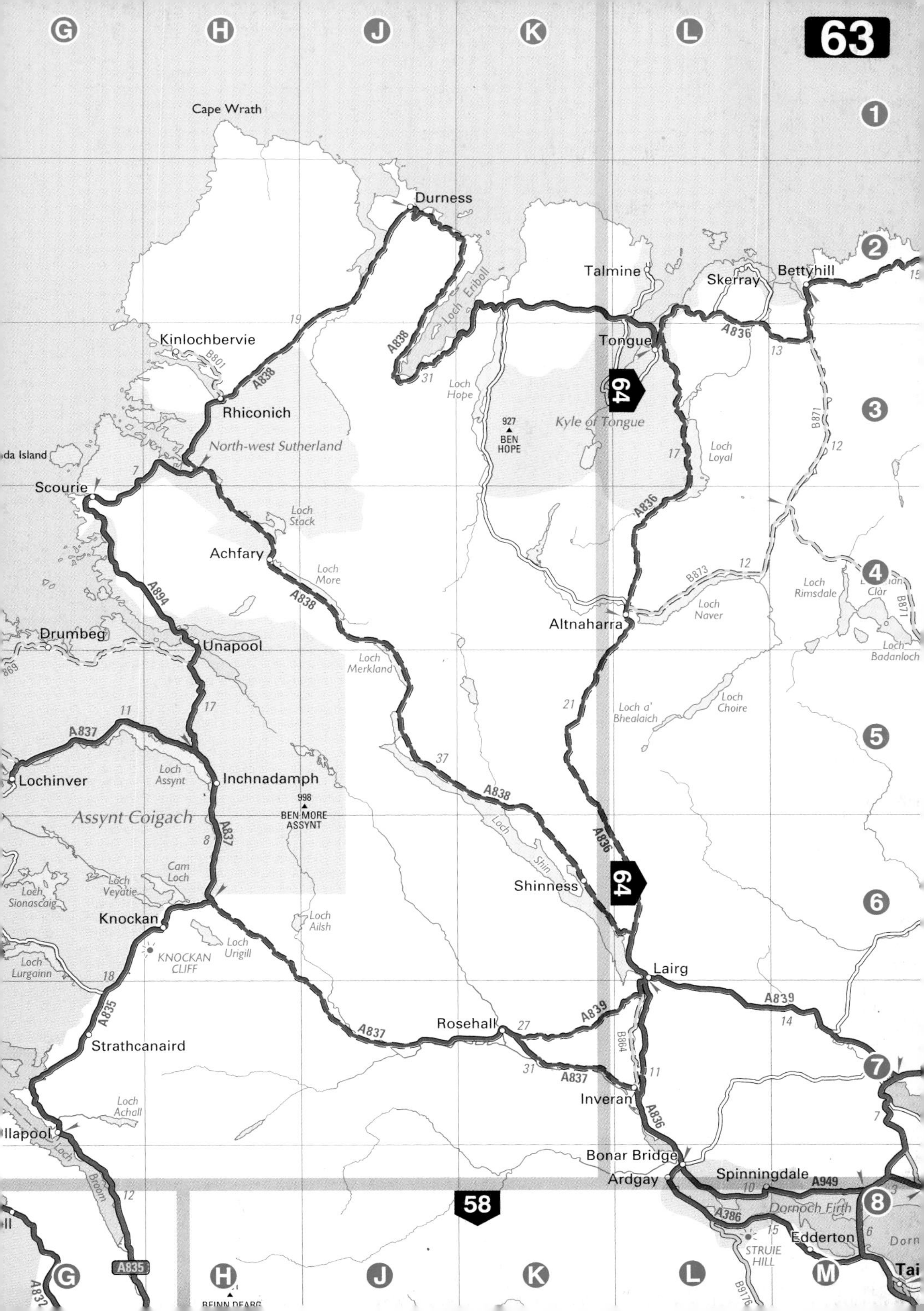
G
H
J
K
L
1
2
3
4
5
6
7
8
Cape Wrath
Durness
Talmine
Skerray
Bettyhill
Kinlochbervie
Tongue
Rhiconich
Loch Eriboll
Loch Hope
Kyle of Tongue
927 BEN HOPE
Loch Loyal
North-west Sutherland
Scourie
Loch Stack
Achfary
Loch More
Altnaharra
Loch Naver
Loch Rimsdale
Loch Badanloch
Drumbeg
Unapool
Loch Merkland
Loch a' Bhealaich
Loch Choire
Lochinver
Loch Assynt
Inchnadamph
998 BEN MORE ASSYNT
Assynt Coigach
Loch Shin
Shinness
Cam Loch
Loch Veyatie
Loch Sionascaig
Knockan
Loch Ailsh
Loch Urigill
KNOCKAN CLIFF
Loch Lurgainn
Lairg
Rosehall
Strathcanaird
Inveran
Loch Achall
Ullapool
Loch Broom
Bonar Bridge
Ardgay
Spinningdale
Dornoch Firth
Edderton
STRUIE HILL
BEINN DEARG
A838
A836
A894
A837
A835
A839
A949
A386
B801
B871
B873
B864
B869
B9176
64
58

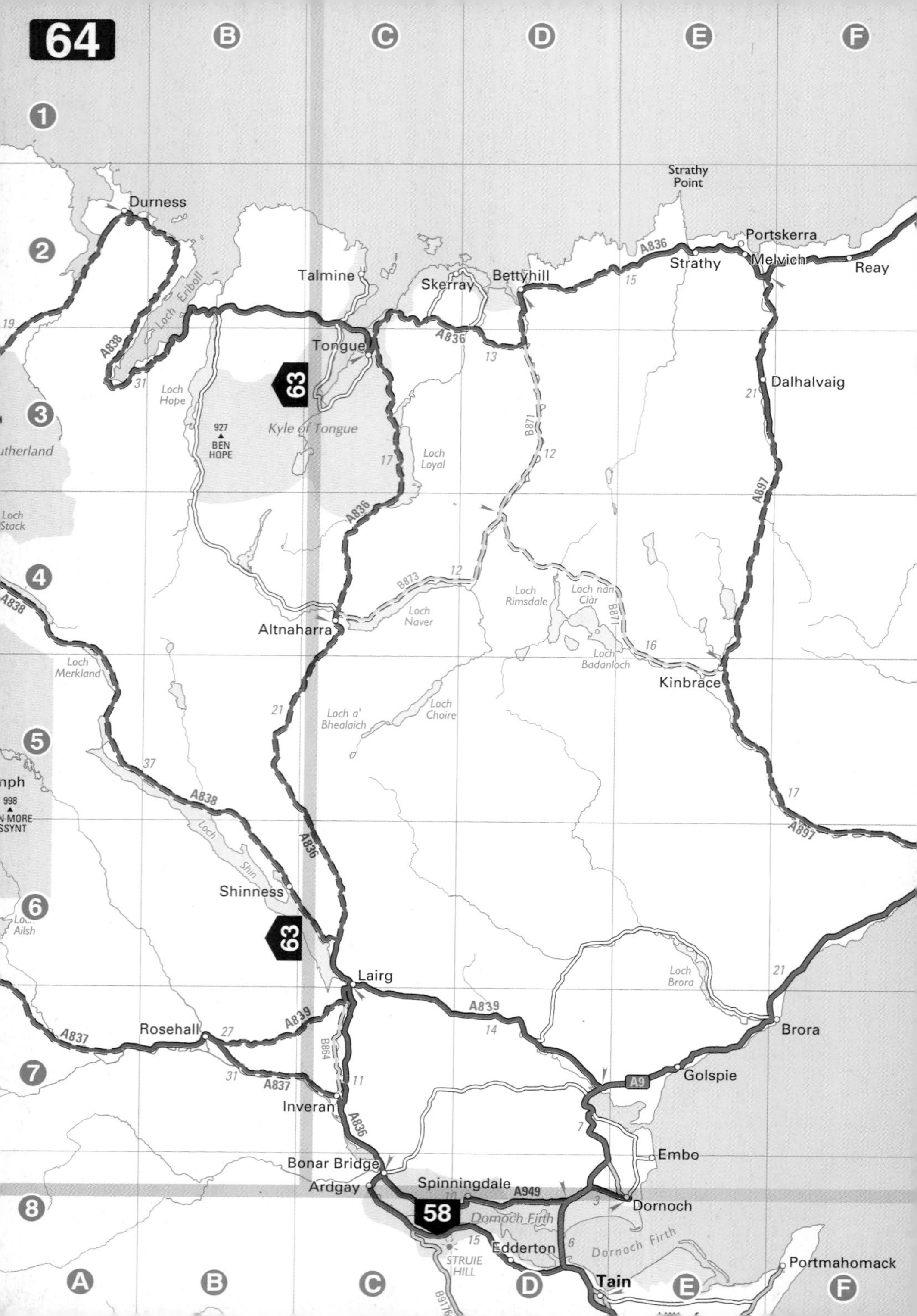
Durness
Loch Eriboll
A838
Talmine
Tongue
Skerray
Bettyhill
A836
Strathy Point
Strathy
Portskerra
Melvich
Reay
Loch Hope
BEN HOPE
927
Kyle of Tongue
63
Loch Loyal
B871
Dalhalvaig
A897
Loch Stack
A836
B873
Altnaharra
Loch Naver
Loch Rimsdale
Loch nan Clàr
Loch Badanloch
Kinbrace
Loch Merkland
Loch a' Bhealaich
Loch Choire
A838
Loch Shin
Shinness
63
Lairg
A839
Loch Brora
Brora
Rosehall
A837
B864
A9
Golspie
Inveran
Embo
Bonar Bridge
Ardgay
Spinningdale
A949
Dornoch
58
Dornoch Firth
Edderton
STRUIE HILL
Tain
Portmahomack
B9176

1

Stromness
V
Dunnet
Head
Island of
Stroma
St Margaret's Hope
V

2

Scrabster
Thurso
Dunnet
B855
15
Gills
A836
Duncansby
Head
John o' Groats
Castletown
5
Freswick

Loch
Calder
B874
A9
B876
16
B874
Halkirk
B870
Loch
Shurrery
A99
17
Keiss

3

Spittal
B874
B874
21
Watten
A882
WICK
Wick

4

A9
23
Thrumster
A99
17

Loch
More

Latheron
Lybster
A9
20

Dunbeath

5

Berriedale
A9
elmsdale

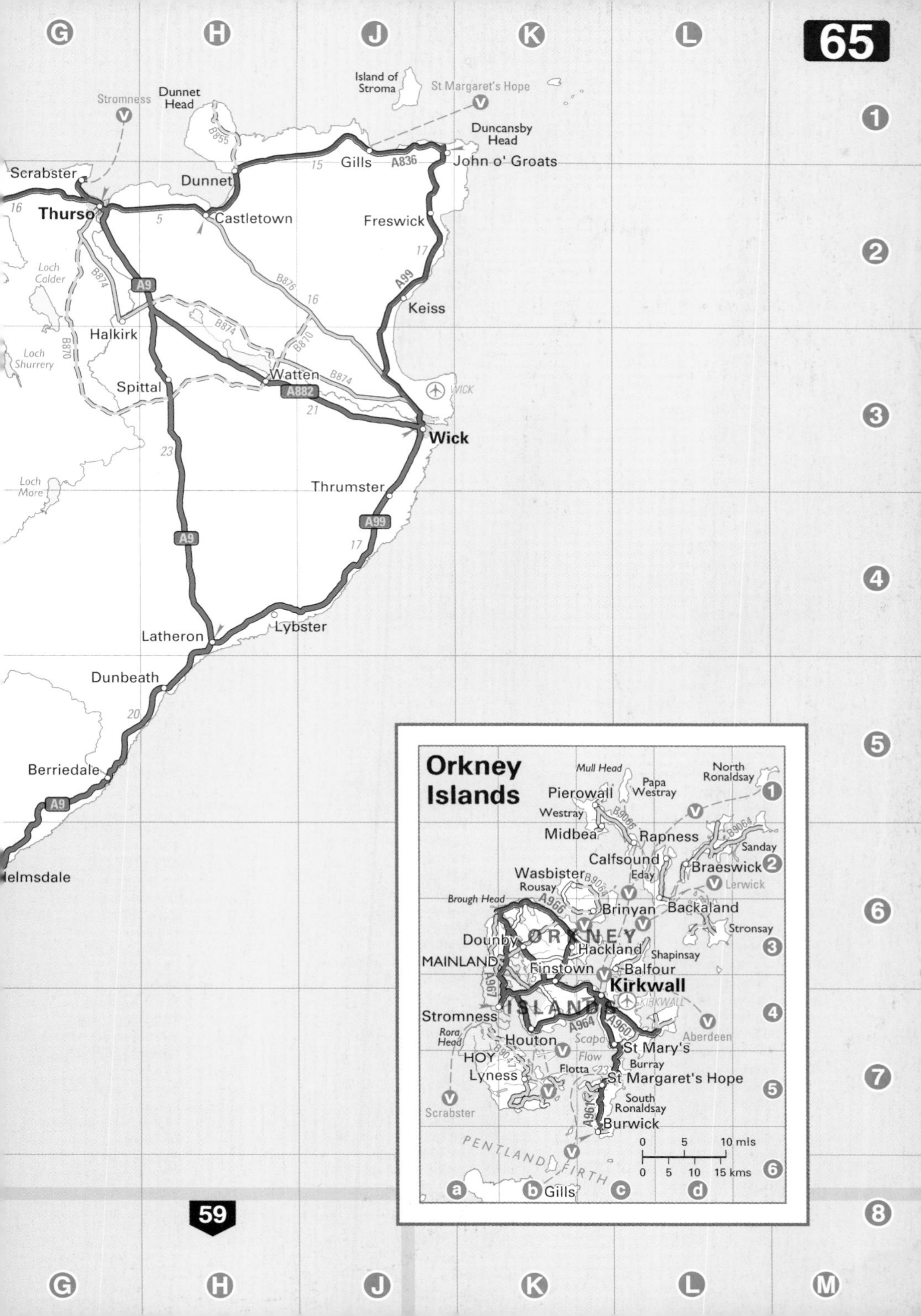

**Orkney
Islands**

Mull Head
North
Ronaldsay
Pierowall
Papa
Westray
V
1
Westray
B9066
Sanday
Midbea
Rapness
V
Braeswick
2
Calfsound
B9069
V
Larwick
Wasbister
Eday
V
Rousay
B9064
Backaland
Brough Head
A966
Brinyan
Stronsay
Dounby
ORKNEY
Hackland
3
MAINLAND
Finstown
Shapinsay
Balfour
Kirkwall
ISLANDS
A965
4
Stromness
Rora
Head
A964
A961
Aberdeen
V
Houton
St Mary's
HOY
Scapa
Flow
Burray
Lyness
V
Flotta
St Margaret's Hope
5
V
South
Ronaldsay
Scrabster
A961
Burwick
6
0   5   10 mls
PENTLAND FIRTH
0   5   10 15 kms
V
a
b Gills
c
d

5

6

7

8

Index to places in Britain

This index lists places appearing in the main-map section of the atlas in alphabetical order. The reference before each name gives the atlas page number and grid reference of the square in which the place appears. The map shows counties, unitary authorities and administrative areas, together with a list of the abbreviated name forms used in the index.

England

BaNES	**Bath & N E Somerset (18)**
Barns	**Barnsley (19)**
Bed	**Bedford**
Birm	**Birmingham**
Bl w D	**Blackburn with Darwen (20)**
Bmouth	**Bournemouth**
Bolton	**Bolton (21)**
Bpool	**Blackpool**
Br & H	**Brighton & Hove (22)**
Br For	**Bracknell Forest (23)**
Bristl	**City of Bristol**
Bucks	**Buckinghamshire**
Bury	**Bury (24)**
C Beds	**Central Bedfordshire**
C Brad	**City of Bradford**
C Derb	**City of Derby**
C KuH	**City of Kingston upon Hull**
C Leic	**City of Leicester**
C Nott	**City of Nottingham**
C Pete	**City of Peterborough**
C Plym	**City of Plymouth**
C Port	**City of Portsmouth**
C Sotn	**City of Southampton**
C Stke	**City of Stoke-on-Trent**
C York	**City of York**
Calder	**Calderdale (25)**
Cambs	**Cambridgeshire**
Ches E	**Cheshire East**
Ches W	**Cheshire West and Chester**
Cnwll	**Cornwall**
Covtry	**Coventry**
Cumb	**Cumbria**
Darltn	**Darlington (26)**
Derbys	**Derbyshire**
Devon	**Devon**
Donc	**Doncaster (27)**
Dorset	**Dorset**
Dudley	**Dudley (28)**
Dur	**Durham**
E R Yk	**East Riding of Yorkshire**
E Susx	**East Sussex**
Essex	**Essex**
Gatesd	**Gateshead (29)**
Gloucs	**Gloucestershire**
Gt Lon	**Greater London**
Halton	**Halton (30)**
Hants	**Hampshire**
Hartpl	**Hartlepool (31)**
Herefs	**Herefordshire**
Herts	**Hertfordshire**
IoS	**Isles of Scilly**
IoW	**Isle of Wight**
Kent	**Kent**
Kirk	**Kirklees (32)**
Knows	**Knowsley (33)**
Lancs	**Lancashire**
Leeds	**Leeds**
Leics	**Leicestershire**
Lincs	**Lincolnshire**
Lpool	**Liverpool**
Luton	**Luton**
M Keyn	**Milton Keynes**
Manch	**Manchester**

Medway	**Medway**
Middsb	**Middlesbrough**
NE Lin	**North East Lincolnshire**
N Linc	**North Lincolnshire**
N Som	**North Somerset (34)**
N Tyne	**North Tyneside (35)**
N u Ty	**Newcastle upon Tyne**
N York	**North Yorkshire**
Nhants	**Northamptonshire**
Norfk	**Norfolk**
Notts	**Nottinghamshire**
Nthumb	**Northumberland**
Oldham	**Oldham (36)**
Oxon	**Oxfordshire**
Poole	**Poole**
R & Cl	**Redcar & Cleveland**
Readg	**Reading**
Rochdl	**Rochdale (37)**
Rothm	**Rotherham (38)**
Rutlnd	**Rutland**
S Glos	**South Gloucestershire (39)**
S on T	**Stockton-on-Tees (40)**
S Tyne	**South Tyneside (41)**
Salfd	**Salford (42)**
Sandw	**Sandwell (43)**
Sefton	**Sefton (44)**
Sheff	**Sheffield**
Shrops	**Shropshire**
Slough	**Slough (45)**
Solhll	**Solihull (46)**
Somset	**Somerset**
St Hel	**St Helens (47)**
Staffs	**Staffordshire**
Sthend	**Southend-on-Sea**
Stockp	**Stockport (48)**
Suffk	**Suffolk**
Sundld	**Sunderland**
Surrey	**Surrey**
Swindn	**Swindon**
Tamesd	**Tameside (49)**
Thurr	**Thurrock (50)**
Torbay	**Torbay**
Traffd	**Trafford (51)**
W & M	**Windsor and Maidenhead (52)**
W Berk	**West Berkshire**
W Susx	**West Sussex**
Wakefd	**Wakefield (53)**
Warrtn	**Warrington (54)**
Warwks	**Warwickshire**
Wigan	**Wigan (55)**
Wilts	**Wiltshire**
Wirral	**Wirral (56)**
Wokham	**Wokingham (57)**
Wolves	**Wolverhampton (58)**
Worcs	**Worcestershire**
Wrekin	**Telford & Wrekin (59)**
Wsall	**Walsall (60)**

Channel Islands & Isle of Man

Guern	**Guernsey**
Jersey	**Jersey**
IoM	**Isle of Man**

Scotland

Abers	**Aberdeenshire**
Ag & B	**Argyll and Bute**
Angus	**Angus**
Border	**Scottish Borders**
C Aber	**City of Aberdeen**
C Dund	**City of Dundee**
C Edin	**City of Edinburgh**
C Glas	**City of Glasgow**
Clacks	**Clackmannanshire (1)**
D & G	**Dumfries & Galloway**
E Ayrs	**East Ayrshire**
E Duns	**East Dunbartonshire (2)**
E Loth	**East Lothian**
E Rens	**East Renfrewshire (3)**
Falk	**Falkirk**
Fife	**Fife**
Highld	**Highland**
Inver	**Inverclyde (4)**
Mdloth	**Midlothian (5)**
Moray	**Moray**
N Ayrs	**North Ayrshire**
N Lans	**North Lanarkshire (6)**
Ork	**Orkney Islands**
P & K	**Perth & Kinross**
Rens	**Renfrewshire (7)**
S Ayrs	**South Ayrshire**
Shet	**Shetland Islands**
S Lans	**South Lanarkshire**
Stirlg	**Stirling**
W Duns	**West Dunbartonshire (8)**
W Isls	**Western Isles (Na h-Eileanan an Iar)**
W Loth	**West Lothian**

Wales

Blae G	**Blaenau Gwent (9)**
Brdgnd	**Bridgend (10)**
Caerph	**Caerphilly (11)**
Cardif	**Cardiff**
Carmth	**Carmarthenshire**
Cerdgn	**Ceredigion**
Conwy	**Conwy**
Denbgs	**Denbighshire**
Flints	**Flintshire**
Gwynd	**Gwynedd**
IoA	**Isle of Anglesey**
Mons	**Monmouthshire**
Myr Td	**Merthyr Tydfil (12)**
Neath	**Neath Port Talbot (13)**
Newpt	**Newport (14)**
Pembks	**Pembrokeshire**
Powys	**Powys**
Rhondd	**Rhondda Cynon Taff (15)**
Swans	**Swansea**
Torfn	**Torfaen (16)**
V Glam	**Vale of Glamorgan (17)**
Wrexhm	**Wrexham**

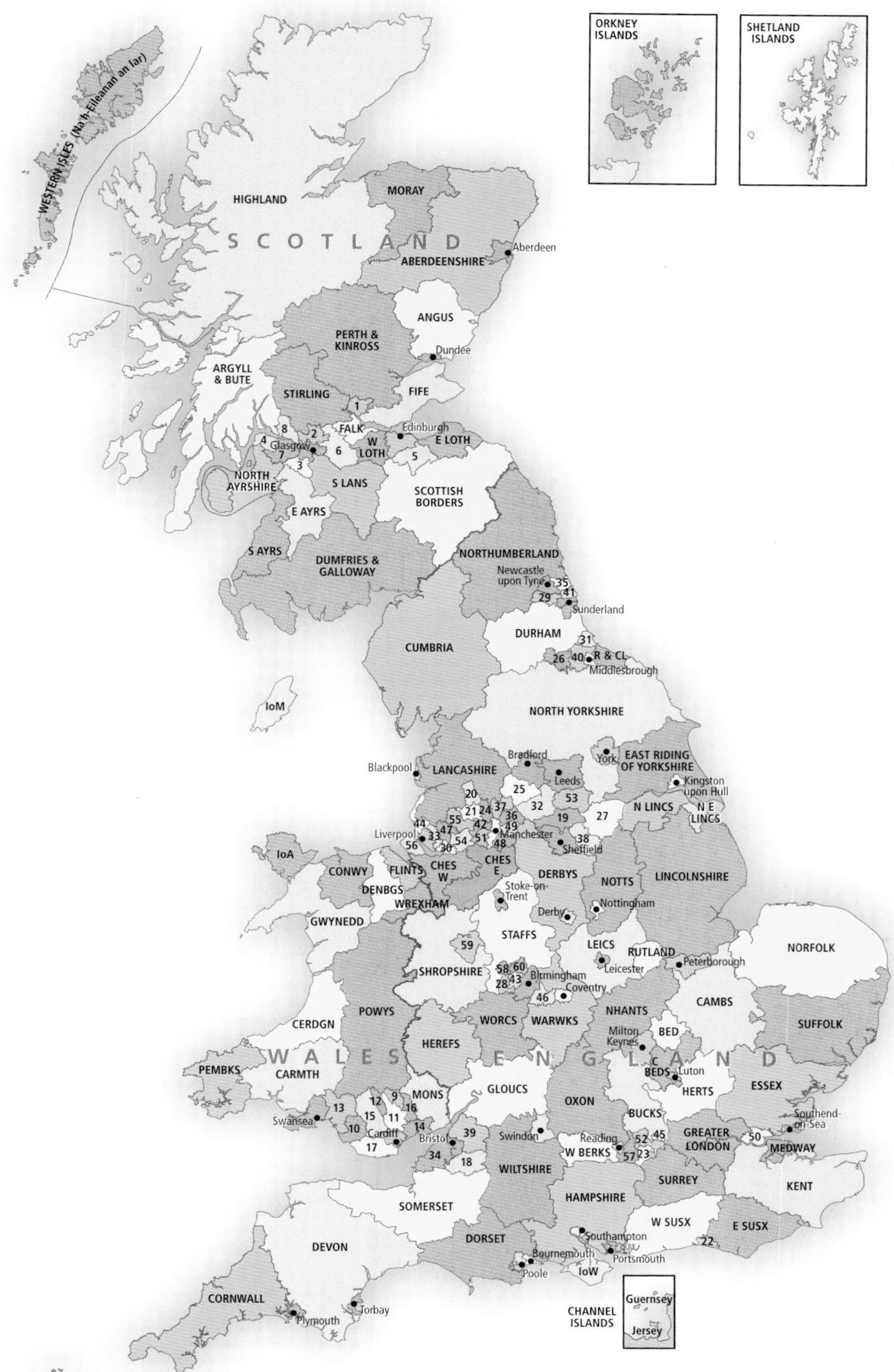
ORKNEY ISLANDS
SHETLAND ISLANDS
WESTERN ISLES (Na h-Eileanan an Iar)
HIGHLAND
MORAY
SCOTLAND
ABERDEENSHIRE
Aberdeen
ANGUS
PERTH & KINROSS
Dundee
ARGYLL & BUTE
STIRLING
FIFE
FALK
Edinburgh
E LOTH
Glasgow
W LOTH
NORTH AYRSHIRE
S LANS
SCOTTISH BORDERS
E AYRS
S AYRS
DUMFRIES & GALLOWAY
NORTHUMBERLAND
Newcastle upon Tyne
Sunderland
DURHAM
R & CL
Middlesbrough
CUMBRIA
IoM
NORTH YORKSHIRE
York
EAST RIDING OF YORKSHIRE
Bradford
Leeds
Kingston upon Hull
Blackpool
LANCASHIRE
N LINCS
N E LINCS
Liverpool
Manchester
Sheffield
IoA
CONWY
FLINTS
CHES W
CHES E
DERBYS
NOTTS
LINCOLNSHIRE
DENBGS
WREXHAM
Stoke-on-Trent
Nottingham
GWYNEDD
Derby
STAFFS
LEICS
RUTLAND
NORFOLK
Leicester
Peterborough
SHROPSHIRE
Birmingham
Coventry
CAMBS
POWYS
NHANTS
WORCS
WARWKS
SUFFOLK
CERDGN
Milton Keynes
BED
HEREFS
WALES
ENGLAND
PEMBKS
CARMTH
C BEDS
Luton
MONS
GLOUCS
HERTS
ESSEX
OXON
Swansea
BUCKS
Southend-on-Sea
Cardiff
Bristol
Swindon
Reading
GREATER LONDON
W BERKS
MEDWAY
WILTSHIRE
SURREY
KENT
SOMERSET
HAMPSHIRE
W SUSX
E SUSX
Southampton
DEVON
DORSET
Bournemouth
Portsmouth
Poole
IoW
CORNWALL
Torbay
Plymouth
CHANNEL ISLANDS
Guernsey
Jersey
IoS

Mileage chart - Britain

The mileage chart shows distances in miles between two towns along AA-recommended routes. Using motorways and other main roads this is normally the fastest route, though not necessarily the shortest.

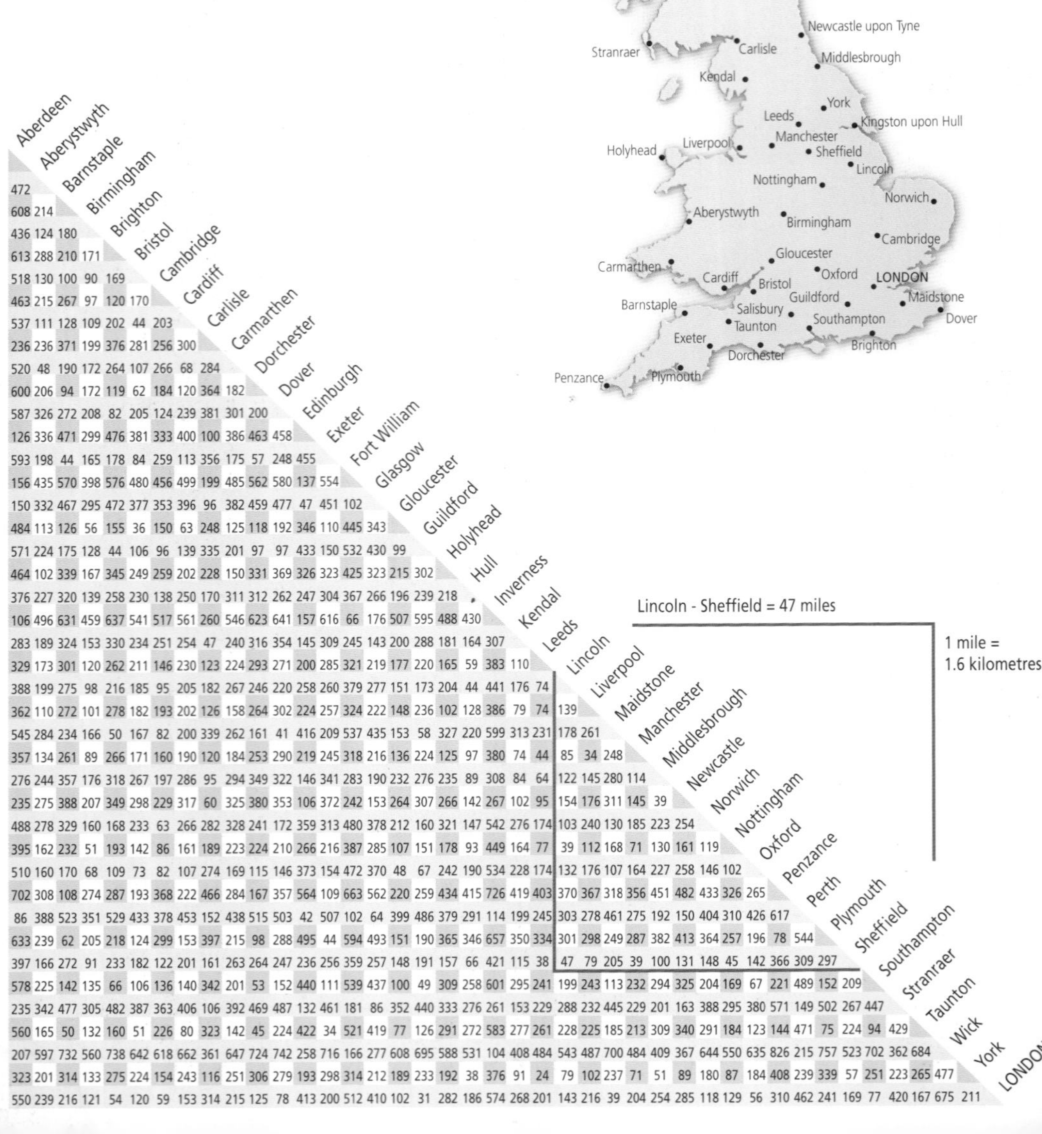

	Aberdeen	Aberystwyth	Barnstaple	Birmingham	Brighton	Bristol	Cambridge	Cardiff	Carlisle	Carmarthen	Dorchester	Dover	Edinburgh	Exeter	Fort William	Glasgow	Gloucester	Guildford	Holyhead	Hull	Inverness	Kendal	Leeds	Lincoln	Liverpool	Maidstone	Manchester	Middlesbrough	Newcastle	Norwich	Nottingham	Oxford	Penzance	Perth	Plymouth	Sheffield	Southampton	Stranraer	Taunton	Wick	York
Aberystwyth	472																																								
Barnstaple	608	214																																							
Birmingham	436	124	180																																						
Brighton	613	288	210	171																																					
Bristol	518	130	100	90	169																																				
Cambridge	463	215	267	97	120	170																																			
Cardiff	537	111	128	109	202	44	203																																		
Carlisle	236	236	371	199	376	281	256	300																																	
Carmarthen	520	48	190	172	264	107	266	68	284																																
Dorchester	600	206	94	172	119	62	184	120	364	182																															
Dover	587	326	272	208	82	205	124	239	381	301	200																														
Edinburgh	126	336	471	299	476	381	333	400	100	386	463	458																													
Exeter	593	198	44	165	178	84	259	113	356	175	57	248	455																												
Fort William	156	435	570	398	576	480	456	499	199	485	562	580	137	554																											
Glasgow	150	332	467	295	472	377	353	396	96	382	459	477	47	451	102																										
Gloucester	484	113	126	56	155	36	150	63	248	125	118	192	346	110	445	343																									
Guildford	571	224	175	128	44	106	96	139	335	201	97	97	433	150	532	430	99																								
Holyhead	464	102	339	167	345	249	259	202	228	150	331	369	326	323	425	323	215	302																							
Hull	376	227	320	139	258	230	138	250	170	311	312	262	247	304	367	266	196	239	218																						
Inverness	106	496	631	459	637	541	517	561	260	546	623	641	157	616	66	176	507	595	488	430																					
Kendal	283	189	324	153	330	234	251	254	47	240	316	354	145	309	245	143	200	288	181	164	307																				
Leeds	329	173	301	120	262	211	146	230	123	224	293	271	200	285	321	219	177	220	165	59	383	110																			
Lincoln	388	199	275	98	216	185	95	205	182	267	246	220	258	260	379	277	151	173	204	44	441	176	74																		
Liverpool	362	110	272	101	278	182	193	202	126	158	264	302	224	257	324	222	148	236	102	128	386	79	74	139																	
Maidstone	545	284	234	166	50	167	82	200	339	262	161	41	416	209	537	435	153	58	327	220	599	313	231	178	261																
Manchester	357	134	261	89	266	171	160	190	120	184	253	290	219	245	318	216	136	224	125	97	380	74	44	85	34	248															
Middlesbrough	276	244	357	176	318	267	197	286	95	294	349	322	146	341	283	190	232	276	235	89	308	84	64	122	145	280	114														
Newcastle	235	275	388	207	349	298	229	317	60	325	380	353	106	372	242	153	264	307	266	142	267	102	95	154	176	311	145	39													
Norwich	488	278	329	160	168	233	63	266	282	328	241	172	359	313	480	378	212	160	321	147	542	276	174	103	240	130	185	223	254												
Nottingham	395	162	232	51	193	142	86	161	189	223	224	210	266	216	387	285	107	151	178	93	449	164	77	39	112	168	71	130	161	119											
Oxford	510	160	170	68	109	73	82	107	274	169	115	146	373	154	472	370	48	67	242	190	534	228	174	132	176	107	164	227	258	146	102										
Penzance	702	308	108	274	287	193	368	222	466	284	167	357	564	109	663	562	220	259	434	415	726	419	403	370	367	318	356	451	482	433	326	265									
Perth	86	388	523	351	529	433	378	453	152	438	515	503	42	507	102	64	399	486	379	291	114	199	245	303	278	461	275	192	150	404	310	426	617								
Plymouth	633	239	62	205	218	124	299	153	397	215	98	288	495	44	594	493	151	190	365	346	657	350	334	301	298	249	287	382	413	364	257	196	78	544							
Sheffield	397	166	272	91	233	182	122	201	161	263	264	247	236	256	359	257	148	191	157	66	421	115	38	47	79	205	39	100	131	148	45	142	366	309	297						
Southampton	578	225	142	135	66	106	136	140	342	201	53	152	440	111	539	437	100	49	309	258	601	295	241	199	243	113	232	294	325	204	169	67	221	489	152	209					
Stranraer	235	342	477	305	482	387	363	406	106	392	469	487	132	461	181	86	352	440	333	276	261	153	229	288	232	445	229	201	163	388	295	380	571	149	502	267	447				
Taunton	560	165	50	132	160	51	226	80	323	142	45	224	422	34	521	419	77	126	291	272	583	277	261	228	225	185	213	309	340	291	184	123	144	471	75	224	94	429			
Wick	207	597	732	560	738	642	618	662	361	647	724	742	258	716	166	277	608	695	588	531	104	408	484	543	487	700	484	409	367	644	550	635	826	215	757	523	702	362	684		
York	323	201	314	133	275	224	154	243	116	251	306	279	193	298	314	212	189	233	192	38	376	91	24	79	102	237	71	51	89	180	87	184	408	239	339	57	251	223	265	477	
LONDON	550	239	216	121	54	120	59	153	314	215	125	78	413	200	512	410	102	31	282	186	574	268	201	143	216	39	204	254	285	118	129	56	310	462	241	169	77	420	167	675	211

A

21 L4 **Abberley** Worcs
41 L6 **Abbey Town** Cumb
29 H7 **Abbots Bromley** Staffs
19 H1 **Aberaeron** Cerdgn
19 H1 **Aberarth** Cerdgn
60 D4 **Aberchirder** Abers
12 B2 **Aberdare** Rhondd
26 B6 **Aberdaron** Gwynd
55 M4 **Aberdeen** C Aber
20 A2 **Aberdyfi** Gwynd
50 D2 **Aberfeldy** P & K
26 C3 **Aberffraw** IoA
50 B6 **Aberfoyle** Stirlg
21 G8 **Abergavenny** Mons
27 H3 **Abergele** Conwy
46 E2 **Aberlady** E Loth
59 L5 **Aberlour** Moray
20 F2 **Abermule** Powys
51 G5 **Abernethy** P & K
18 F2 **Aberporth** Cerdgn
26 C6 **Abersoch** Gwynd
12 D2 **Abersychan** Torfn
12 D2 **Abertillery** Blae G
20 A3 **Aberystwyth** Cerdgn
14 C4 **Abingdon** Oxon
45 M5 **Abington** S Lans
30 D7 **Ab Kettleby** Leics
55 J4 **Aboyne** Abers
16 D7 **Abridge** Essex
33 G4 **Accrington** Lancs
52 D4 **Acharacle** Highld
50 C3 **Acharn** P & K
63 H4 **Achfary** Highld
62 F6 **Achiltibuie** Highld
52 F6 **Achnacroish** Ag & B
57 L4 **Achnasheen** Highld
34 B5 **Ackworth Moor Top** Wakefd
25 K5 **Acle** Norfk
29 G7 **Acton Trussell** Staffs
33 J2 **Addingham** C Brad
34 C6 **Adwick Le Street** Donc
38 D4 **Ainderby Steeple** N York
45 L2 **Airdrie** N Lans
50 E7 **Airth** Falk
21 L1 **Albrighton** Shrops
28 C7 **Albrighton** Shrops
9 K2 **Albury** Surrey
22 B4 **Alcester** Warwks
23 M3 **Alconbury** Cambs
14 A6 **Aldbourne** Wilts
35 J3 **Aldbrough** E R Yk
17 M2 **Aldeburgh** Suffk
8 C3 **Alderbury** Wilts
28 F3 **Alderley Edge** Ches E
14 D7 **Aldermaston** W Berk
22 D5 **Alderminster** Warwks
9 H2 **Aldershot** Hants
28 B4 **Aldford** Ches W
17 G5 **Aldham** Essex
13 L1 **Aldsworth** Gloucs
49 M5 **Alexandria** W Duns
9 K3 **Alfold** Surrey
55 J3 **Alford** Abers
31 K3 **Alford** Lincs
29 L4 **Alfreton** Derbys
10 D7 **Alfriston** E Susx
11 K4 **Alkham** Kent
47 H4 **Allanton** Border
42 F6 **Allendale** Nthumb
42 F7 **Allenheads** Nthumb
21 J6 **Allensmore** Herefs
50 E7 **Alloa** Clacks
41 L7 **Allonby** Cumb
45 G6 **Alloway** S Ayrs
13 G3 **Almondsbury** S Glos
58 F3 **Alness** Highld
43 K2 **Alnmouth** Nthumb
47 L7 **Alnwick** Nthumb
29 J7 **Alrewas** Staffs
28 E4 **Alsager** Ches E
42 E6 **Alston** Cumb
62 F6 **Altandhu** Highld
34 E5 **Althorpe** N Linc
64 C4 **Altnaharra** Highld
9 G2 **Alton** Hants
7 K2 **Alton Pancras** Dorset
28 E2 **Altrincham** Traffd
50 E6 **Alva** Clacks
13 G3 **Alveston** S Glos
51 G3 **Alyth** P & K
9 K4 **Amberley** W Susx
43 K2 **Amble** Nthumb
37 G3 **Ambleside** Cumb
15 G4 **Amersham** Bucks
8 C2 **Amesbury** Wilts
26 D1 **Amlwch** IoA
19 J5 **Ammanford** Carmth
38 F5 **Ampleforth** N York
23 K6 **Ampthill** C Beds
18 E5 **Amroth** Pembks
50 E3 **Amulree** P & K
30 F5 **Ancaster** Lincs
47 K5 **Ancroft** Nthumb
47 G7 **Ancrum** Border
8 D2 **Andover** Hants
22 B7 **Andoversford** Gloucs
36 c1 **Andreas** IoM
18 C6 **Angle** Pembks
9 K5 **Angmering** W Susx
41 M5 **Annan** D & G
43 J6 **Annfield Plain** Dur
30 C8 **Anstey** Leics
51 K6 **Anstruther** Fife
62 e7 **An t-Ob** W Isls
31 G5 **Anwick** Lincs
37 J2 **Appleby-in-Westmorland** Cumb
57 G5 **Applecross** Highld
4 D4 **Appledore** Devon
11 H5 **Appledore** Kent
38 A7 **Appletreewick** N York
51 L3 **Arbroath** Angus
28 E4 **Arclid Green** Ches E
48 D8 **Ardbeg** Ag & B
49 L5 **Arden** Ag & B
49 K4 **Ardentinny** Ag & B
59 G4 **Ardersier** Highld
64 C8 **Ardgay** Highld
53 G4 **Ardgour** Highld
10 C5 **Ardingly** W Susx
17 H4 **Ardleigh** Essex
49 L2 **Ardlui** Ag & B
48 E4 **Ardlussa** Ag & B
44 A3 **Ardminish** Ag & B
49 G5 **Ardrishaig** Ag & B
44 F4 **Ardrossan** N Ayrs
52 D1 **Ardvasar** Highld
40 C7 **Ardwell** D & G
48 d1 **Arinagour** Ag & B
52 D3 **Arisaig** Highld
37 J6 **Arkholme** Lancs
45 M2 **Armadale** W Loth
42 C7 **Armathwaite** Cumb
37 M6 **Arncliffe** N York
50 B7 **Arnprior** Stirlg
37 H5 **Arnside** Cumb
16 B3 **Arrington** Cambs
49 L3 **Arrochar** Ag & B
9 K5 **Arundel** W Susx
49 J6 **Ascog** Ag & B
15 G6 **Ascot** W & M
11 K3 **Ash** Kent
29 J5 **Ashbourne** Derbys
6 B5 **Ashburton** Devon
14 A5 **Ashbury** Oxon
29 K7 **Ashby-de-la-Zouch** Leics
12 E7 **Ashcott** Somset
11 H4 **Ashford** Kent
43 K3 **Ashington** Nthumb
9 L4 **Ashington** W Susx
16 E2 **Ashley** Cambs
33 H6 **Ashton-under-Lyne** Tamesd
8 D5 **Ashurst** Hants
4 D7 **Ashwater** Devon
36 F5 **Askam in Furness** Cumb
34 C5 **Askern** Donc
37 H2 **Askham** Cumb
37 M4 **Askrigg** N York
41 L7 **Aspatria** Cumb
14 B4 **Aston** Oxon
14 F3 **Aston Clinton** Bucks
21 H3 **Aston on Clun** Shrops
14 E4 **Aston Rowant** Oxon
28 C8 **Atcham** Shrops
22 D1 **Atherstone** Warwks
32 F6 **Atherton** Wigan
25 H6 **Attleborough** Norfk
25 H4 **Attlebridge** Norfk
35 H2 **Atwick** E R Yk
55 K6 **Auchenblae** Abers
41 H6 **Auchencairn** D & G
45 J5 **Auchinleck** E Ayrs
50 E5 **Auchterarder** P & K
60 E5 **Auchterless** Abers
51 G5 **Auchtermuchty** Fife
28 D5 **Audlem** Ches E
28 E5 **Audley** Staffs
59 H4 **Auldearn** Highld
41 J3 **Auldgirth** D & G
57 H1 **Aultbea** Highld
37 K6 **Austwick** N York
13 L4 **Avebury** Wilts
13 J2 **Avening** Gloucs
6 A6 **Aveton Gifford** Devon
54 C3 **Aviemore** Highld
58 F4 **Avoch** Highld
12 F4 **Avonmouth** Bristl
30 B5 **Awsworth** Notts
12 E5 **Axbridge** Somset
6 F3 **Axminster** Devon
6 F3 **Axmouth** Devon
14 F3 **Aylesbury** Bucks
11 K3 **Aylesham** Kent
25 J3 **Aylsham** Norfk
22 F6 **Aynho** Nhants
45 G5 **Ayr** S Ayrs
38 A4 **Aysgarth** N York
47 J4 **Ayton** Border

B

65 d2 **Backaland** Ork
25 K3 **Bacton** Norfk
33 H4 **Bacup** Lancs
38 E5 **Bagby** N York
62 b14 **Bagh a Chaisteil** W Isls
27 K3 **Bagillt** Flints
19 K6 **Baglan** Neath
14 F7 **Bagshot** Surrey
62 g4 **Baile Ailein** W Isls
62 c10 **Baile a Mhanaich** W Isls
37 M4 **Bainbridge** N York
34 F2 **Bainton** E R Yk
29 J3 **Bakewell** Derbys
27 H6 **Bala** Gwynd
62 g4 **Balallan** W Isls
51 G4 **Balbeggie** P & K
58 F3 **Balblair** Highld
10 B5 **Balcombe** W Susx
38 D5 **Baldersby** N York
16 B4 **Baldock** Herts
65 c3 **Balfour** Ork
59 G2 **Balintore** Highld
62 c10 **Balivanich** W Isls
40 B4 **Ballantrae** S Ayrs
36 b4 **Ballasalla** IoM
55 G5 **Ballater** Abers
36 c2 **Ballaugh** IoM
50 E2 **Ballinluig** P & K
50 F2 **Ballintuim** P & K
48 C6 **Ballygrant** Ag & B
41 G4 **Balmaclellan** D & G
49 M4 **Balmaha** Stirlg
55 M3 **Balmedie** Abers
22 D3 **Balsall Common** Solhll
16 E3 **Balsham** Cambs
61 d1 **Baltasound** Shet
32 E4 **Bamber Bridge** Lancs
47 L6 **Bamburgh** Nthumb
29 J2 **Bamford** Derbys
37 H2 **Bampton** Cumb
5 H5 **Bampton** Devon
14 A4 **Bampton** Oxon
22 E6 **Banbury** Oxon
55 K5 **Banchory** Abers
60 E3 **Banff** Abers
26 E3 **Bangor** Gwynd
28 B5 **Bangor-is-y-coed** Wrexhm
25 H6 **Banham** Norfk
50 F4 **Bankfoot** P & K
10 B3 **Banstead** Surrey
62 h2 **Barabhas** W Isls
37 J5 **Barbon** Cumb
31 G3 **Bardney** Lincs
42 F5 **Bardon Mill** Nthumb
36 F5 **Bardsea** Cumb
22 D4 **Barford** Warwks
12 C2 **Bargoed** Caerph
16 C8 **Barking** Gt Lon
30 F5 **Barkston** Lincs
16 C4 **Barkway** Herts
16 C4 **Barley** Herts
34 E2 **Barmby Moor** E R Yk
26 E7 **Barmouth** Gwynd
39 L7 **Barmston** E R Yk
38 A2 **Barnard Castle** Dur
30 D2 **Barnby Moor** Notts
15 J4 **Barnet** Gt Lon
35 G6 **Barnetby le Wold** N Linc
33 H3 **Barnoldswick** Lancs
33 M6 **Barnsley** Barns
13 L2 **Barnsley** Gloucs
4 E4 **Barnstaple** Devon
40 D3 **Barr** S Ayrs
43 G4 **Barrasford** Nthumb
45 H3 **Barrhead** E Rens
40 D4 **Barrhill** S Ayrs
33 H3 **Barrowford** Lancs
36 E6 **Barrow-in-Furness** Cumb
30 C7 **Barrow upon Soar** Leics
5 K1 **Barry** V Glam
16 C2 **Barton** Cambs
32 E3 **Barton** Lancs
38 C3 **Barton** N York
23 L7 **Barton-le-Clay** C Beds
23 J3 **Barton Seagrave** Nhants
29 J7 **Barton-under-Needwood** Staffs
35 G5 **Barton-upon-Humber** N Linc
62 h2 **Barvas** W Isls
22 E2 **Barwell** Leics
16 F7 **Basildon** Essex
9 G1 **Basingstoke** Hants
29 J3 **Baslow** Derbys
42 A8 **Bassenthwaite** Cumb
31 G7 **Baston** Lincs
13 H5 **Bath** BaNES
46 A3 **Bathgate** W Loth
33 L4 **Batley** Kirk
10 F6 **Battle** E Susx
31 H3 **Baumber** Lincs
25 H4 **Bawdeswell** Norfk
17 L4 **Bawdsey** Suffk
34 D7 **Bawtry** Donc
36 F6 **Baycliff** Cumb
28 C8 **Bayston Hill** Shrops
15 G5 **Beaconsfield** Bucks
47 L6 **Beadnell** Nthumb
4 E5 **Beaford** Devon
47 K5 **Beal** Nthumb
7 H2 **Beaminster** Dorset
9 L2 **Beare Green** Surrey
10 F3 **Bearsted** Kent
41 L2 **Beattock** D & G
8 E5 **Beaulieu** Hants
58 D5 **Beauly** Highld
26 E3 **Beaumaris** IoA
7 b2 **Beaumont** Jersey
4 D7 **Beaworthy** Devon
27 L2 **Bebington** Wirral
25 L6 **Beccles** Suffk
13 L4 **Beckhampton** Wilts
30 E4 **Beckingham** Lincs
13 H6 **Beckington** Somset
24 E7 **Beck Row** Suffk
38 C4 **Bedale** N York
26 E5 **Beddgelert** Gwynd
23 K5 **Bedford** Bed
43 K4 **Bedlington** Nthumb
22 E2 **Bedworth** Warwks
35 H2 **Beeford** E R Yk
29 J3 **Beeley** Derbys
6 F3 **Beer** Devon
28 C4 **Beeston** Ches W
30 B6 **Beeston** Notts
41 J5 **Beeswing** D & G
37 H5 **Beetham** Cumb
25 G4 **Beetley** Norfk
20 F3 **Beguildy** Powys
45 G3 **Beith** N Ayrs
47 L6 **Belford** Nthumb
42 F4 **Bellingham** Nthumb
44 A5 **Bellochantuy** Ag & B
45 K2 **Bellshill** N Lans
29 K5 **Belper** Derbys
43 H4 **Belsay** Nthumb
34 E6 **Belton** N Linc
25 L5 **Belton** Norfk
9 G6 **Bembridge** IoW
39 L6 **Bempton** E R Yk
52 F6 **Benderloch** Ag & B
10 F5 **Benenden** Kent
26 D2 **Benllech** IoA
14 D5 **Benson** Oxon
9 H2 **Bentley** Hants
24 B6 **Benwick** Cambs
3 K4 **Bere Alston** Devon
3 K4 **Bere Ferrers** Devon
7 L3 **Bere Regis** Dorset
13 G2 **Berkeley** Gloucs
15 G3 **Berkhamsted** Herts
56 D4 **Bernisdale** Highld
65 G5 **Berriedale** Highld
20 F1 **Berriew** Powys
12 D6 **Berrow** Somset
13 K8 **Berwick St John** Wilts
47 K4 **Berwick-upon-Tweed** Nthumb
11 G4 **Bethersden** Kent
26 E3 **Bethesda** Gwynd

64 D2 **Bettyhill** Highld
27 G4 **Betws-y-Coed** Conwy
27 H3 **Betws-yn-Rhos** Conwy
20 D5 **Beulah** Powys
35 G3 **Beverley** E R Yk
21 L3 **Bewdley** Worcs
10 F7 **Bexhill** E Susx
13 L1 **Bibury** Gloucs
14 D2 **Bicester** Oxon
5 H6 **Bickleigh** Devon
11 G4 **Biddenden** Kent
12 E6 **Biddisham** Somset
28 F4 **Biddulph** Staffs
4 D5 **Bideford** Devon
22 C5 **Bidford-on-Avon** Warwks
3 M6 **Bigbury-on-Sea** Devon
46 B6 **Biggar** S Lans
10 C3 **Biggin Hill** Gt Lon
23 M5 **Biggleswade** C Beds
17 H3 **Bildeston** Suffk
16 E7 **Billericay** Essex
31 G6 **Billingborough** Lincs
38 E2 **Billingham** S on T
31 H4 **Billinghay** Lincs
9 K3 **Billingshurst** W Susx
31 K3 **Bilsby** Lincs
30 C4 **Bilsthorpe** Notts
35 H7 **Binbrook** Lincs
14 F6 **Binfield** Br For
30 D5 **Bingham** Notts
33 K3 **Bingley** C Brad
22 A8 **Birdlip** Gloucs
32 C7 **Birkenhead** Wirral
22 B2 **Birmingham** Birm
30 C8 **Birstall** Leics
43 K6 **Birtley** Gatesd
38 C1 **Bishop Auckland** Dur
21 G2 **Bishop's Castle** Shrops
22 A7 **Bishop's Cleeve** Gloucs
21 K5 **Bishop's Frome** Herefs
12 C7 **Bishops Lydeard** Somset
16 D5 **Bishop's Stortford** Herts
6 C4 **Bishopsteignton** Devon
19 J7 **Bishopston** Swans
13 M3 **Bishopstone** Swindn
13 G5 **Bishop Sutton** BaNES
8 F4 **Bishop's Waltham** Hants
30 F6 **Bitchfield** Lincs
13 G4 **Bitton** S Glos
22 F1 **Blaby** Leics
28 E6 **Blackbrook** Staffs
32 F4 **Blackburn** Bl w D
50 E6 **Blackford** P & K
19 M7 **Blackmill** Brdgnd
32 C3 **Blackpool** Bpool
4 D6 **Black Torrington** Devon
8 F6 **Blackwater** IoW
44 C5 **Blackwaterfoot** N Ayrs
12 C2 **Blackwood** Caerph
45 L4 **Blackwood** S Lans
14 C3 **Bladon** Oxon
26 F5 **Blaenau Ffestiniog** Gwynd
12 D1 **Blaenavon** Torfn
19 L6 **Blaengarw** Brdgnd
18 F2 **Blaenporth** Cerdgn
12 F5 **Blagdon** N Som
54 C7 **Blair Atholl** P & K
51 G3 **Blairgowrie** P & K
49 K5 **Blairmore** Ag & B
13 G1 **Blakeney** Gloucs
23 G5 **Blakesley** Nhants
43 G6 **Blanchland** Nthumb
7 L2 **Blandford Forum** Dorset
50 B8 **Blanefield** Stirlg
34 D6 **Blaxton** Donc
43 J5 **Blaydon** Gatesd
12 F6 **Bleadney** Somset
12 E5 **Bleadon** N Som
11 J3 **Blean** Kent
20 F4 **Bleddfa** Powys
10 B3 **Bletchingley** Surrey
23 J6 **Bletchley** M Keyn
23 K4 **Bletsoe** Bed
14 C5 **Blewbury** Oxon
25 J3 **Blickling** Norfk
30 C4 **Blidworth** Notts

10 C4 **Blindley Heath** Surrey
3 G4 **Blisland** Cnwll
22 E6 **Bloxham** Oxon
38 B7 **Blubberhouses** N York
5 J3 **Blue Anchor** Somset
43 K4 **Blyth** Nthumb
34 E7 **Blyton** Lincs
54 D3 **Boat of Garten** Highld
61 H5 **Boddam** Abers
27 J3 **Bodfari** Denbgs
26 C6 **Bodfuan** Gwynd
10 F5 **Bodiam** E Susx
3 G4 **Bodmin** Cnwll
9 J6 **Bognor Regis** W Susx
29 G3 **Bollington** Ches E
10 B6 **Bolney** W Susx
29 L3 **Bolsover** Derbys
32 F6 **Bolton** Bolton
33 J2 **Bolton Abbey** N York
37 H6 **Bolton le Sands** Lancs
3 H3 **Bolventor** Cnwll
64 C8 **Bonar Bridge** Highld
42 D1 **Bonchester Bridge** Border
46 A2 **Bo'ness** Falk
46 D4 **Bonnyrigg** Mdloth
26 D4 **Bontnewydd** Gwynd
12 B4 **Bonvilston** V Glam
36 E3 **Boot** Cumb
36 E4 **Bootle** Cumb
32 C7 **Bootle** Sefton
b b1 **Bordeaux** Guern
10 E6 **Boreham Street** E Susx
15 J4 **Borehamwood** Herts
38 D6 **Boroughbridge** N York
10 E3 **Borough Green** Kent
29 L6 **Borrowash** Derbys
20 A2 **Borth** Cerdgn
26 E6 **Borth-y-Gest** Gwynd
3 G2 **Boscastle** Cnwll
9 H5 **Bosham** W Susx
18 D6 **Bosherston** Pembks
31 J5 **Boston** Lincs
34 B3 **Boston Spa** Leeds
25 H7 **Botesdale** Suffk
41 M7 **Bothel** Cumb
30 E6 **Bottesford** Leics
10 D4 **Bough Beech** Kent
11 H3 **Boughton Street** Kent
47 M7 **Boulmer** Nthumb
31 G7 **Bourne** Lincs
8 B6 **Bournemouth** Bmouth
21 K2 **Bourton** Shrops
22 C7 **Bourton-on-the-Water** Gloucs
6 B4 **Bovey Tracey** Devon
37 M3 **Bowes** Dur
48 C7 **Bowmore** Ag & B
41 M5 **Bowness-on-Solway** Cumb
13 J4 **Box** Wilts
17 H4 **Boxford** Suffk
23 J4 **Bozeat** Nhants
56 D5 **Bracadale** Highld
23 G6 **Brackley** Nhants
14 F6 **Bracknell** Br For
33 K4 **Bradford** C Brad
13 J5 **Bradford-on-Avon** Wilts
8 F6 **Brading** IoW
29 J2 **Bradwell** Derbys
17 H6 **Bradwell-on-Sea** Essex
4 C6 **Bradworthy** Devon
61 b4 **Brae** Shet
54 E5 **Braemar** Abers
65 d2 **Braeswick** Ork
45 L3 **Braidwood** S Lans
29 J5 **Brailsford** Derbys
16 F5 **Braintree** Essex
36 F2 **Braithwaite** Cumb
8 F3 **Bramdean** Hants
25 K7 **Bramfield** Suffk
34 B3 **Bramham** Leeds
33 L3 **Bramhope** Leeds
14 D7 **Bramley** Hants
9 K2 **Bramley** Surrey
23 M3 **Brampton** Cambs
42 D5 **Brampton** Cumb
8 D4 **Bramshaw** Hants
24 E2 **Brancaster** Norfk
35 H3 **Brandesburton** E R Yk
43 J7 **Brandon** Dur
24 E6 **Brandon** Suffk
23 E3 **Brandon** Warwks

6 E3 **Branscombe** Devon
8 C6 **Bransgore** Hants
30 F3 **Branston** Lincs
36 D2 **Branthwaite** Cumb
29 J4 **Brassington** Derbys
10 D3 **Brasted** Kent
13 J6 **Bratton** Wilts
3 K2 **Bratton Clovelly** Devon
4 F4 **Bratton Fleming** Devon
16 C5 **Braughing** Herts
4 E4 **Braunton** Devon
8 D3 **Brayford** Devon
62 g3 **Breasclete** W Isls
62 g3 **Breaclete** W Isls
19 H4 **Brechfa** Carmth
55 J7 **Brechin** Angus
20 E7 **Brecon** Powys
11 G6 **Brede** E Susx
21 K5 **Bredenbury** Herefs
10 F3 **Bredhurst** Kent
22 A6 **Bredon** Worcs
21 H3 **Bredwardine** Herefs
5 G3 **Brendon** Devon
12 E6 **Brent Knoll** Somset
16 E7 **Brentwood** Essex
11 H5 **Brenzett** Kent
28 E4 **Brereton Green** Ches E
28 F8 **Brewood** Staffs
36 C1 **Bride** IoM
3 L2 **Bridestowe** Devon
11 J3 **Bridge** Kent
48 C6 **Bridgend** Ag & B
19 L7 **Bridgend** Brdgnd
50 D6 **Bridge of Allan** Stirlg
51 G2 **Bridge of Cally** P & K
51 G3 **Bridge of Earn** P & K
53 K6 **Bridge of Orchy** Ag & B
49 M6 **Bridge of Weir** Rens
21 L2 **Bridgnorth** Shrops
12 D7 **Bridgwater** Somset
39 L6 **Bridlington** E R Yk
7 H3 **Bridport** Dorset
13 H3 **Brierfield** Lancs
35 G6 **Brigg** N Linc
13 L8 **Brigham** Cumb
33 K4 **Brighouse** Calder
8 E7 **Brighstone** IoW
17 J5 **Brightlingsea** Essex
10 B7 **Brighton** Br & H
23 K2 **Brigstock** Nhants
22 E3 **Brinklow** Warwks
13 K3 **Brinkworth** Wilts
65 C3 **Brinyan** Ork
13 G4 **Bristol** Bristl
6 B7 **Brixham** Torbay
3 L5 **Brixton** Devon
23 H3 **Brixworth** Nhants
13 L3 **Broad Blunsdon** Swindn
13 K8 **Broad Chalke** Wilts
5 K7 **Broadclyst** Devon
56 F6 **Broadford** Highld
57 F6 **Broad Haven** Pembks
11 L2 **Broadstairs** Kent
22 C6 **Broadway** Worcs
7 G2 **Broadwindsor** Dorset
25 J7 **Brockdish** Norfk
21 L7 **Brockenhurst** Hants
17 J1 **Brockford Street** Suffk
21 M8 **Brockworth** Gloucs
44 D4 **Brodick** N Ayrs
25 H7 **Brome** Suffk
21 J3 **Bromfield** Shrops
23 K5 **Bromham** Bed
10 C2 **Bromley** Gt Lon
39 J5 **Brompton** N York
5 H4 **Brompton Regis** Somset
22 A3 **Bromsgrove** Worcs
21 K5 **Bromyard** Herefs
20 F6 **Bronllys** Powys
25 K6 **Brooke** Norfk
11 H5 **Brookland** Kent
15 J4 **Brookmans Park** Herts
43 K2 **Broomhill** Nthumb
64 F7 **Brora** Highld
21 K1 **Broseley** Shrops
34 B4 **Brotherton** N York
39 G2 **Brotton** R & Cl
37 K2 **Brough** Cumb
46 B6 **Broughton** Border
34 F6 **Broughton** N Linc
36 F5 **Broughton-in-Furness** Cumb

13 M2 **Broughton Poggs** Oxon
29 H5 **Brownhills** Wsall
46 B3 **Broxburn** W Loth
46 B5 **Broxted** Essex
25 K5 **Brundall** Norfk
13 G7 **Bruton** Somset
19 K5 **Brynamman** Carmth
20 A1 **Bryncrug** Gwynd
12 C1 **Brynmawr** Blae G
34 D3 **Bubwith** E R Yk
50 B7 **Buchlyvie** Stirlg
23 M4 **Buckden** Cambs
37 M5 **Buckden** N York
6 B5 **Buckfastleigh** Devon
51 H6 **Buckhaven** Fife
13 H8 **Buckhorn Weston** Dorset
60 B3 **Buckie** Moray
23 G6 **Buckingham** Bucks
16 C4 **Buckland** Herts
8 E5 **Bucklers Hard** Hants
27 L4 **Buckley** Flints
28 E2 **Bucklow Hill** Ches E
30 E7 **Buckminster** Leics
4 B6 **Bude** Cnwll
6 D4 **Budleigh Salterton** Devon
2 F5 **Bugle** Cnwll
20 E5 **Builth Wells** Powys
8 C2 **Bulford** Wilts
22 E2 **Bulkington** Warwks
16 E8 **Bulphan** Thurr
23 K2 **Bulwick** Nhants
48 C2 **Bunessan** Ag & B
25 K6 **Bungay** Suffk
30 C6 **Bunny** Notts
16 C4 **Buntingford** Herts
25 H6 **Bunwell** Norfk
13 M5 **Burbage** Wilts
17 G4 **Bures** Essex
13 M1 **Burford** Oxon
10 B6 **Burgess Hill** W Susx
42 B6 **Burgh by Sands** Cumb
25 L5 **Burgh Castle** Norfk
59 J3 **Burghead** Moray
14 D6 **Burghfield** W Berk
31 K4 **Burgh le Marsh** Lincs
8 C5 **Burley** Hants
28 D5 **Burleydam** Ches E
33 K3 **Burley in Wharfedale** C Brad
28 C7 **Burlton** Shrops
38 C5 **Burneston** N York
24 F2 **Burnham Market** Norfk
17 H7 **Burnham-on-Crouch** Essex
12 D6 **Burnham-on-Sea** Somset
24 F2 **Burnham Overy Staithe** Norfk
33 G4 **Burnley** Lancs
43 J6 **Burnopfield** Dur
46 C2 **Burntisland** Fife
61 d3 **Burravoe** Shet
51 G3 **Burrelton** P & K
4 F5 **Burrington** Devon
19 H6 **Burry Port** Carmth
32 D5 **Burscough Bridge** Lancs
8 E5 **Bursledon** Hants
27 L3 **Burton** Ches W
39 K6 **Burton Agnes** E R Yk
7 H3 **Burton Bradstock** Dorset
39 K6 **Burton Fleming** E R Yk
37 H5 **Burton-in-Kendal** Cumb
30 C5 **Burton Joyce** Notts
23 J3 **Burton Latimer** Nhants
34 F5 **Burton upon Stather** N Linc
29 J7 **Burton upon Trent** Staffs
10 E5 **Burwash** E Susx
16 E1 **Burwell** Cambs
65 c6 **Burwick** Ork
33 G5 **Bury** Bury
17 G2 **Bury St Edmunds** Suffk
15 H4 **Bushey** Herts
17 L3 **Butley** Suffk
36 E2 **Buttermere** Cumb
31 J5 **Butterwick** Lincs
27 K8 **Buttington** Powys
10 D6 **Buxted** E Susx

29 H3 **Buxton** Derbys
20 F7 **Bwlch** Powys
15 H7 **Byfleet** Surrey
27 H4 **Bylchau** Conwy
42 F2 **Byrness** Nthumb

C

2 D8 **Cadgwith** Cnwll
12 E3 **Caerleon** Newpt
26 D4 **Caernarfon** Gwynd
12 C3 **Caerphilly** Caerph
20 E2 **Caersws** Powys
12 F3 **Caerwent** Mons
27 J3 **Caerwys** Flints
49 K3 **Cairndow** Ag & B
40 B5 **Cairnryan** D & G
25 L5 **Caister-on-Sea** Norfk
35 H6 **Caistor** Lincs
42 B7 **Caldbeck** Cumb
23 J2 **Caldecott** Rutlnd
36 D3 **Calder Bridge** Cumb
45 L2 **Caldercruix** N Lans
12 F3 **Caldicot** Mons
65 d2 **Calfsound** Ork
52 B5 **Calgary** Ag & B
50 B6 **Callander** Stirlg
3 J4 **Callington** Cnwll
13 K4 **Calne** Wilts
8 E5 **Calshot** Hants
54 C7 **Calvine** P & K
11 H6 **Camber** E Susx
14 F7 **Camberley** Surrey
43 H4 **Cambo** Nthumb
2 C6 **Camborne** Cnwll
16 B2 **Cambourne** Cambs
16 C2 **Cambridge** Cambs
13 H2 **Cambridge** Gloucs
45 K2 **Cambuslang** S Lans
15 K5 **Camden Town** Gt Lon
3 G3 **Camelford** Cnwll
44 B5 **Campbeltown** Ag & B
31 K3 **Candlesby** Lincs
58 C6 **Cannich** Highld
12 D7 **Cannington** Somset
29 G8 **Cannock** Staffs
42 C4 **Canonbie** D & G
11 J3 **Canterbury** Kent
16 F8 **Canvey Island** Essex
48 b2 **Caoles** Ag & B
9 L2 **Capel** Surrey
20 B3 **Capel Bangor** Cerdgn
26 F4 **Capel Curig** Conwy
17 J4 **Capel St Mary** Suffk
50 F3 **Caputh** P & K
56 D6 **Carbost** Highld
12 C4 **Cardiff** Cardif
18 E2 **Cardigan** Cerdgn
23 L5 **Cardington** Bed
49 L5 **Cardross** Ag & B
18 D6 **Carew** Pembks
46 F4 **Carfraemill** Border
5 J3 **Carhampton** Somset
37 G5 **Cark** Cumb
62 g3 **Carlabhagh** W Isls
42 C6 **Carlisle** Cumb
46 C4 **Carlops** Border
62 g3 **Carloway** W Isls
34 D4 **Carlton** N York
38 A5 **Carlton** N York
30 E4 **Carlton-on-Trent** Notts
45 L3 **Carluke** S Lans
19 G4 **Carmarthen** Carmth
39 K6 **Carnaby** E R Yk
37 H6 **Carnforth** Lancs
20 D2 **Carno** Powys
2 E6 **Carnon Downs** Cnwll
51 K4 **Carnoustie** Angus
46 A5 **Carnwath** S Lans
44 C4 **Carradale** Ag & B
59 H6 **Carrbridge** Highld
7 b1 **Carrefour** Jersey
49 K4 **Carrick Castle** Ag & B
41 J3 **Carronbridge** D & G
41 L5 **Carrutherstown** D & G
40 F3 **Carsphairn** D & G
45 M3 **Carstairs** S Lans
14 A3 **Carterton** Oxon
37 G5 **Cartmel** Cumb
6 a2 **Castel** Guern
37 J5 **Casterton** Cumb
24 F4 **Castle Acre** Norfk
62 b14 **Castlebay** W Isls
42 D6 **Castle Carrock** Cumb
13 G7 **Castle Cary** Somset
29 L6 **Castle Donington** Leics
41 H5 **Castle Douglas** D & G
34 B4 **Castleford** Wakefd
16 F4 **Castle Hedingham** Essex
18 C6 **Castlemartin** Pembks
24 D4 **Castle Rising** Norfk
43 H6 **Castleside** Dur
29 H2 **Castleton** Derbys
39 G3 **Castleton** N York
12 D3 **Castleton** Newpt
65 H2 **Castletown** Highld
36 b4 **Castletown** IoM
10 C3 **Caterham** Surrey
25 K4 **Catfield** Norfk
37 H6 **Caton** Lancs
45 J5 **Catrine** E Ayrs
10 F6 **Catsfield** E Susx
38 C4 **Catterick** N York
30 D4 **Caunton** Notts
59 G4 **Cawdor** Highld
3 K5 **Cawsand** Cnwll
16 B2 **Caxton** Cambs
30 F5 **Caythorpe** Lincs
39 K5 **Cayton** N York
26 C1 **Cemaes** IoA
20 C1 **Cemmaes Road** Powys
51 J5 **Ceres** Fife
7 J2 **Cerne Abbas** Dorset
27 H5 **Cerrigydrudion** Conwy
33 H6 **Chadderton** Oldham
14 B2 **Chadlington** Oxon
6 A3 **Chagford** Devon
8 E7 **Chale** IoW
15 G4 **Chalfont St Giles** Bucks
15 G5 **Chalfont St Peter** Bucks
13 J2 **Chalford** Gloucs
4 F3 **Challacombe** Devon
11 H3 **Challock** Kent
8 E4 **Chandler's Ford** Hants
29 H2 **Chapel-en-le-Frith** Derbys
31 L3 **Chapel St Leonards** Lincs
34 A6 **Chapeltown** Sheff
13 J6 **Chapmanslade** Wilts
6 F2 **Chard** Somset
11 H4 **Charing** Kent
14 B2 **Charlbury** Oxon
22 D5 **Charlecote** Warwks
22 A7 **Charlton Kings** Gloucs
7 L2 **Charlton Marshall** Dorset
10 B4 **Charlwood** Surrey
7 G3 **Charmouth** Dorset
11 J3 **Chartham** Kent
33 G3 **Chatburn** Lancs
10 F2 **Chatham** Medway
24 B7 **Chatteris** Cambs
47 K6 **Chatton** Nthumb
4 F6 **Chawleigh** Devon
9 G3 **Chawton** Hants
29 G5 **Cheadle** Staffs
33 H7 **Cheadle** Stockp
12 F6 **Cheddar** Somset
29 G5 **Cheddleton** Staffs
28 F3 **Chelford** Ches E
16 F6 **Chelmsford** Essex
22 A7 **Cheltenham** Gloucs
12 F3 **Chepstow** Mons
8 F3 **Cheriton** Hants
5 H6 **Cheriton Fitzpaine** Devon
15 G6 **Chertsey** Surrey
15 G4 **Chesham** Bucks
15 K4 **Cheshunt** Herts
28 B3 **Chester** Ches W
29 K3 **Chesterfield** Derbys
43 K6 **Chester-le-Street** Dur
13 G5 **Chew Magna** BaNES
13 G6 **Chewton Mendip** Somset
23 J5 **Chicheley** M Keyn
9 H5 **Chichester** W Susx
7 J4 **Chickerell** Dorset
13 J7 **Chicklade** Wilts
9 J3 **Chiddingfold** Surrey
14 C6 **Chieveley** W Berk
16 C7 **Chigwell** Essex
28 B3 **Childer Thornton** Ches W
11 J3 **Chilham** Kent
47 K7 **Chillingham** Nthumb
6 B7 **Chillington** Devon
13 K7 **Chilmark** Wilts
4 C6 **Chilsworthy** Devon
14 A6 **Chilton Foliat** Wilts
14 E4 **Chinnor** Oxon
16 E1 **Chippenham** Cambs
13 J4 **Chippenham** Wilts
15 G4 **Chipperfield** Herts
32 F3 **Chipping** Lancs
22 C6 **Chipping Campden** Gloucs
22 D7 **Chipping Norton** Oxon
16 D6 **Chipping Ongar** Essex
13 H3 **Chipping Sodbury** S Glos
22 F5 **Chipping Warden** Nhants
21 G1 **Chirbury** Shrops
27 L6 **Chirk** Wrexhm
47 J4 **Chirnside** Border
13 M4 **Chiseldon** Swindn
13 K6 **Chitterne** Wilts
4 F5 **Chittlehamholt** Devon
15 G7 **Chobham** Surrey
8 C2 **Cholderton** Wilts
32 E5 **Chorley** Lancs
15 G4 **Chorleywood** Herts
8 C6 **Christchurch** Dorset
6 C4 **Chudleigh** Devon
6 C4 **Chudleigh Knighton** Devon
4 F6 **Chulmleigh** Devon
14 A2 **Churchill** Oxon
21 G2 **Churchstoke** Powys
21 H2 **Church Stretton** Shrops
6 C6 **Churston Ferrers** Torbay
9 H3 **Churt** Surrey
21 K8 **Cinderford** Gloucs
13 K2 **Cirencester** Gloucs
44 B3 **Clachan** Ag & B
56 E5 **Clachan** Highld
50 E7 **Clackmannan** Clacks
17 J5 **Clacton-on-Sea** Essex
14 A4 **Clanfield** Oxon
44 C3 **Claonaig** Ag & B
23 K5 **Clapham** Bed
37 K6 **Clapham** N York
16 F3 **Clare** Suffk
60 C6 **Clatt** Abers
22 C4 **Claverdon** Warwks
16 D4 **Clavering** Essex
4 C7 **Clawton** Devon
29 K4 **Clay Cross** Derbys
17 J3 **Claydon** Suffk
36 D2 **Cleator Moor** Cumb
35 J6 **Cleethorpes** NE Lin
12 F5 **Cleeve** N Som
22 B7 **Cleeve Hill** Gloucs
21 K3 **Cleobury Mortimer** Shrops
21 K2 **Cleobury North** Shrops
12 E4 **Clevedon** N Som
32 C3 **Cleveleys** Lancs
25 G2 **Cley next the Sea** Norfk
10 F2 **Cliffe** Medway
34 D4 **Cliffe** N York
10 F2 **Cliffe Woods** Medway
37 H2 **Clifton** Cumb
21 L4 **Clifton upon Teme** Worcs
9 K5 **Climping** W Susx
33 G3 **Clitheroe** Lancs
61 G5 **Clola** Abers
23 L6 **Clophill** C Beds
7 H2 **Closworth** Somset
39 J4 **Cloughton** N York
55 G6 **Clova** Angus
4 C5 **Clovelly** Devon
46 E6 **Clovenfords** Border
30 B3 **Clowne** Derbys
21 L3 **Clows Top** Worcs
21 G3 **Clun** Shrops
19 J6 **Clydach** Swans
45 H2 **Clydebank** W Duns
49 K5 **Clynder** Ag & B
26 D5 **Clynnog-fawr** Gwynd
20 F6 **Clyro** Powys
6 D3 **Clyst St Mary** Devon
21 K1 **Coalport** Wrekin
29 L7 **Coalville** Leics
45 K2 **Coatbridge** N Lans
10 E2 **Cobham** Kent
47 H3 **Cockburnspath** Border
41 L8 **Cockermouth** Cumb
9 J4 **Cocking** W Susx
17 J2 **Coddenham** Suffk
13 K7 **Codford St Mary** Wilts
15 J3 **Codicote** Herts
29 L5 **Codnor** Derbys
21 M1 **Codsall** Staffs
27 L5 **Coedpoeth** Wrexhm
17 G5 **Coggeshall** Essex
17 H5 **Colchester** Essex
14 C6 **Cold Ash** W Berk
23 G3 **Cold Ashby** Nhants
13 H4 **Cold Ashton** S Glos
47 J3 **Coldingham** Border
17 G7 **Cold Norton** Essex
47 H5 **Coldstream** Border
13 G1 **Coleford** Gloucs
13 J4 **Colerne** Wilts
22 C2 **Coleshill** Warwks
49 J6 **Colintraive** Ag & B
15 K2 **Collier's End** Herts
61 G6 **Collieston** Abers
13 M6 **Collingbourne Ducis** Wilts
34 B3 **Collingham** Leeds
40 C3 **Colmonell** S Ayrs
33 H3 **Colne** Lancs
17 G4 **Colne Engaine** Essex
13 L2 **Coln St Aldwyns** Gloucs
60 D6 **Colpy** Abers
30 F7 **Colsterworth** Lincs
25 J4 **Coltishall** Norfk
43 G4 **Colwell** Nthumb
27 G2 **Colwyn Bay** Conwy
6 F3 **Colyford** Devon
6 F3 **Colyton** Devon
4 E3 **Combe Martin** Devon
9 J2 **Compton** Surrey
14 C5 **Compton** W Berk
50 D5 **Comrie** P & K
28 F4 **Congleton** Ches E
12 E5 **Congresbury** N Som
31 H4 **Coningsby** Lincs
23 M2 **Conington** Cambs
34 C6 **Conisbrough** Donc
36 F4 **Coniston** Cumb
27 L3 **Connah's Quay** Flints
52 F7 **Connel** Ag & B
58 E4 **Conon Bridge** Highld
43 H6 **Consett** Dur
2 D7 **Constantine** Cnwll
58 D4 **Contin** Highld
27 G3 **Conwy** Conwy
14 F5 **Cookham** W & M
9 L4 **Coolham** W Susx
8 B3 **Coombe Bissett** Wilts
21 M7 **Coombe Hill** Gloucs
17 J3 **Copdock** Suffk
17 G5 **Copford Green** Essex
38 B2 **Copley** Dur
5 G6 **Copplestone** Devon
10 B4 **Copthorne** W Susx
7 a2 **Corbiere** Jersey
43 G5 **Corbridge** Nthumb
23 J2 **Corby** Nhants
30 F7 **Corby Glen** Lincs
6 F1 **Corfe** Somset
7 M4 **Corfe Castle** Dorset
55 G4 **Corgarff** Abers
47 H5 **Cornhill-on-Tweed** Nthumb
3 L5 **Cornwood** Devon
53 H3 **Corpach** Highld
44 D4 **Corrie** N Ayrs
26 F8 **Corris** Gwynd
13 J4 **Corsham** Wilts
13 J3 **Corston** Wilts
25 M6 **Corton** Suffk
27 J5 **Corwen** Denbgs
16 F8 **Coryton** Thurr
22 F2 **Cosby** Leics
28 D4 **Cotebrook** Ches W
38 A2 **Cotherstone** Dur
16 C1 **Cottenham** Cambs
16 B4 **Cottered** Herts
35 G4 **Cottingham** E R Yk
49 K5 **Coulport** Ag & B
46 B6 **Coulter** S Lans
23 G2 **Countesthorpe** Leics
51 G3 **Coupar Angus** P & K
62 D8 **Cove** Highld
22 E3 **Coventry** Covtry
2 D8 **Coverack** Cnwll
31 H7 **Cowbit** Lincs
12 B4 **Cowbridge** V Glam
10 D4 **Cowden** Kent
51 G7 **Cowdenbeath** Fife
8 E6 **Cowes** IoW
9 L4 **Cowfold** W Susx
33 J3 **Cowling** N York

10 F3 **Coxheath** Kent
38 E5 **Coxwold** N York
45 H6 **Coylton** S Ayrs
54 D3 **Coylumbridge** Highld
4 B7 **Crackington Haven** Cnwll
37 M7 **Cracoe** N York
3 J5 **Crafthole** Cnwll
59 L5 **Craigellachie** Moray
48 D6 **Craighouse** Ag & B
52 E6 **Craignure** Ag & B
51 J5 **Craigrothie** Fife
51 L6 **Crail** Fife
47 G7 **Crailing** Border
43 K4 **Cramlington** Nthumb
8 B4 **Cranborne** Dorset
10 F5 **Cranbrook** Kent
23 K6 **Cranfield** C Beds
21 M8 **Cranham** Gloucs
9 K2 **Cranleigh** Surrey
47 G4 **Cranshaws** Border
49 H4 **Crarae** Ag & B
47 M7 **Craster** Nthumb
54 F5 **Crathie** Abers
38 E3 **Crathorne** N York
21 H3 **Craven Arms** Shrops
46 A7 **Crawford** S Lans
45 M5 **Crawfordjohn** S Lans
10 B5 **Crawley** W Susx
10 B4 **Crawley Down** W Susx
62 c10 **Creag Ghoraidh** W Isls
62 c10 **Creagorry** W Isls
21 H6 **Credenhill** Herefs
5 G7 **Crediton** Devon
40 F6 **Creetown** D & G
36 a4 **Cregneash** IoM
21 K1 **Cressage** Shrops
28 E4 **Crewe** Ches E
7 G2 **Crewkerne** Somset
53 K7 **Crianlarich** Stirlg
26 D6 **Criccieth** Gwynd
20 F7 **Crickhowell** Powys
13 L3 **Cricklade** Wilts
50 D5 **Crieff** P & K
61 H4 **Crimond** Abers
49 G4 **Crinan** Ag & B
25 J5 **Cringleford** Norfk
6 B3 **Crockernwell** Devon
41 J4 **Crocketford** D & G
42 D6 **Croglin** Cumb
59 G3 **Cromarty** Highld
59 J6 **Cromdale** Highld
25 J2 **Cromer** Norfk
29 K4 **Cromford** Derbys
30 E4 **Cromwell** Notts
43 J7 **Crook** Dur
37 H5 **Crooklands** Cumb
22 F5 **Cropredy** Oxon
39 G4 **Cropton** N York
36 b3 **Crosby** IoM
32 C6 **Crosby** Sefton
46 B2 **Crossford** Fife
45 L3 **Crossford** S Lans
19 H5 **Cross Hands** Carmth
45 G6 **Crosshill** S Ayrs
10 D6 **Cross in Hand** E Susx
12 D3 **Crosskeys** Caerph
41 H5 **Crossmichael** D & G
21 M4 **Crossway Green** Worcs
37 G4 **Crosthwaite** Cumb
10 D5 **Crowborough** E Susx
5 K4 **Crowcombe** Somset
10 F6 **Crowhurst** E Susx
31 H8 **Crowland** Lincs
34 E5 **Crowle** N Linc
14 F7 **Crowthorne** Wokham
30 E6 **Croxton Kerrial** Leics
59 G4 **Croy** Highld
4 D4 **Croyde** Devon
15 K7 **Croydon** Gt Lon
61 H5 **Cruden Bay** Abers
28 D7 **Crudgington** Wrekin
13 K3 **Crudwell** Wilts
19 K5 **Crynant** Neath
10 B5 **Cuckfield** W Susx
30 C3 **Cuckney** Notts
28 D3 **Cuddington** Ches W
34 B6 **Cudworth** Barns
15 K4 **Cuffley** Herts
37 J1 **Culgaith** Cumb
60 C3 **Cullen** Moray
5 J6 **Cullompton** Devon
5 K6 **Culmstock** Devon
45 L1 **Cumbernauld** N Lans
60 E4 **Cuminestown** Abers
41 L5 **Cummertrees** D & G
45 J5 **Cumnock** E Ayrs
14 C4 **Cumnor** Oxon
42 D6 **Cumrew** Cumb
51 J5 **Cupar** Fife
12 E8 **Curry Rivel** Somset
12 D2 **Cwmbran** Torfn
20 C3 **Cwmystwyth** Cerdgn
19 L6 **Cymer** Neath
19 G4 **Cynwyl Elfed** Carmth

D

40 D2 **Dailly** S Ayrs
51 J5 **Dairsie** Fife
41 J5 **Dalbeattie** D & G
36 a3 **Dalby** IoM
18 B5 **Dale** Pembks
46 C2 **Dalgety Bay** Fife
64 E3 **Dalhalvaig** Highld
46 D3 **Dalkeith** Mdloth
59 J4 **Dallas** Moray
53 J7 **Dalmally** Ag & B
45 H7 **Dalmellington** E Ayrs
45 G3 **Dalry** N Ayrs
45 G6 **Dalrymple** E Ayrs
42 B6 **Dalston** Cumb
41 L4 **Dalton** D & G
36 F6 **Dalton-in-Furness** Cumb
54 A5 **Dalwhinnie** Highld
8 B4 **Damerham** Hants
16 F6 **Danbury** Essex
38 C2 **Darlington** Darltn
43 J5 **Darras Hall** Nthumb
34 B5 **Darrington** Wakefd
10 D2 **Dartford** Kent
6 B5 **Dartington** Devon
6 C6 **Dartmouth** Devon
45 J4 **Darvel** E Ayrs
32 F5 **Darwen** Bl w D
15 G6 **Datchet** W & M
59 H5 **Dava** Highld
28 D3 **Davenham** Ches W
23 G4 **Daventry** Nhants
58 F5 **Daviot** Highld
6 C4 **Dawlish** Devon
11 L3 **Deal** Kent
41 L7 **Dearham** Cumb
17 J2 **Debenham** Suffk
22 F6 **Deddington** Oxon
17 H4 **Dedham** Essex
31 H8 **Deeping St James** Lincs
31 H7 **Deeping St Nicholas** Lincs
27 G2 **Deganwy** Conwy
3 G3 **Delabole** Cnwll
27 J3 **Denbigh** Denbgs
33 L6 **Denby Dale** Kirk
15 G5 **Denham** Bucks
46 F7 **Denholm** Border
9 G5 **Denmead** Hants
17 K1 **Dennington** Suffk
50 D8 **Denny** Falk
11 K4 **Densole** Kent
37 K5 **Dent** Cumb
33 H7 **Denton** Tamesd
29 K6 **Derby** C Derb
36 b4 **Derbyhaven** IoM
25 G4 **Dereham** Norfk
24 E3 **Dersingham** Norfk
52 B5 **Dervaig** Ag & B
23 H3 **Desborough** Nhants
22 F1 **Desford** Leics
20 B3 **Devil's Bridge** Cerdgn
13 K5 **Devizes** Wilts
33 L5 **Dewsbury** Kirk
9 L4 **Dial Post** W Susx
14 C5 **Didcot** Oxon
13 J3 **Didmarton** Gloucs
31 G4 **Digby** Lincs
21 H5 **Dilwyn** Herefs
27 G7 **Dinas-Mawddwy** Gwynd
58 E4 **Dingwall** Highld
30 B2 **Dinnington** Rothm
44 C4 **Dippen** Ag & B
29 L7 **Diseworth** Leics
38 D6 **Dishforth** N York
29 G2 **Disley** Ches E
25 H7 **Diss** Norfk
10 B6 **Ditchling** E Susx
6 C6 **Dittisham** Devon
21 K2 **Ditton Priors** Shrops
3 H4 **Dobwalls** Cnwll
24 E3 **Docking** Norfk
24 B6 **Doddington** Cambs
11 G3 **Doddington** Kent
47 K6 **Doddington** Nthumb
33 L6 **Dodworth** Barns
26 F7 **Dolgellau** Gwynd
50 E6 **Dollar** Clacks
46 B5 **Dolphinton** S Lans
4 E6 **Dolton** Devon
26 F5 **Dolwyddelan** Conwy
34 C6 **Doncaster** Donc
31 H6 **Donington** Lincs
7 K3 **Dorchester** Dorset
14 D4 **Dorchester** Oxon
22 D1 **Dordon** Warwks
58 E5 **Dores** Highld
9 L2 **Dorking** Surrey
57 H6 **Dornie** Highld
59 G1 **Dornoch** Highld
21 J1 **Dorrington** Shrops
21 G6 **Dorstone** Herefs
36 c3 **Douglas** IoM
45 L5 **Douglas** S Lans
65 b3 **Dounby** Ork
50 C6 **Doune** Stirlg
3 L4 **Dousland** Devon
11 L4 **Dover** Kent
29 H6 **Doveridge** Derbys
50 E3 **Dowally** P & K
3 J5 **Downderry** Cnwll
24 D5 **Downham Market** Norfk
8 C4 **Downton** Wilts
22 A5 **Drakes Broughton** Worcs
12 F6 **Draycott** Somset
25 J4 **Drayton** Norfk
14 C4 **Drayton** Oxon
39 J7 **Driffield** E R Yk
52 C5 **Drimnin** Highld
22 A4 **Droitwich** Worcs
29 K3 **Dronfield** Derbys
8 F4 **Droxford** Hants
63 G4 **Drumbeg** Highld
40 C7 **Drummore** D & G
58 D6 **Drumnadrochit** Highld
50 A7 **Drymen** Stirlg
56 D6 **Drynoch** Highld
23 K1 **Duddington** Nhants
22 A2 **Dudley** Dudley
29 K5 **Duffield** Derbys
59 L5 **Dufftown** Moray
59 K3 **Duffus** Moray
59 H6 **Dulnain Bridge** Highld
5 H4 **Dulverton** Somset
49 M5 **Dumbarton** W Duns
41 K4 **Dumfries** D & G
47 G2 **Dunbar** E Loth
65 H5 **Dunbeath** Highld
50 D6 **Dunblane** Stirlg
22 F3 **Dunchurch** Warwks
51 J4 **Dundee** C Dund
45 G4 **Dundonald** S Ayrs
57 K1 **Dundonnell** Highld
41 H6 **Dundrennan** D & G
46 B2 **Dunfermline** Fife
50 F3 **Dunkeld** P & K
45 H3 **Dunlop** E Ayrs
65 H2 **Dunnet** Highld
50 F5 **Dunning** P & K
49 K5 **Dunoon** Ag & B
40 C6 **Dunragit** D & G
47 H4 **Duns** Border
41 J4 **Dunscore** D & G
9 K3 **Dunsfold** Surrey
6 B3 **Dunsford** Devon
32 F2 **Dunsop Bridge** Lancs
15 G2 **Dunstable** C Beds
5 J3 **Dunster** Somset
7 K2 **Duntish** Dorset
44 F6 **Dunure** S Ayrs
19 J6 **Dunvant** Swans
56 C4 **Dunvegan** Highld
25 L8 **Dunwich** Suffk
43 K7 **Durham** Dur
63 J2 **Durness** Highld
53 G5 **Duror** Highld
8 C2 **Durrington** Wilts
55 L5 **Durris** Abers
13 H2 **Dursley** Gloucs
16 D3 **Duxford** Cambs
55 M3 **Dyce** C Aber
26 E7 **Dyffryn Ardudwy** Gwynd
11 J5 **Dymchurch** Kent
21 K7 **Dymock** Gloucs

E

42 A4 **Eaglesfield** D & G
45 J3 **Eaglesham** E Rens
15 J5 **Ealing** Gt Lon
33 H3 **Earby** Lancs
21 G5 **Eardisley** Herefs
24 B7 **Earith** Cambs
14 E6 **Earley** Wokham
23 J4 **Earls Barton** Nhants
17 G4 **Earls Colne** Essex
46 F6 **Earlston** Border
25 K6 **Earsham** Norfk
48 F2 **Easdale** Ag & B
9 J4 **Easebourne** W Susx
43 L7 **Easington** Dur
35 K5 **Easington** E R Yk
38 E6 **Easingwold** N York
39 J5 **East Ayton** N York
31 H2 **East Barkwith** Lincs
17 J4 **East Bergholt** Suffk
10 E7 **Eastbourne** E Susx
7 H1 **East Chinnock** Somset
11 H2 **Eastchurch** Kent
8 E6 **East Cowes** IoW
10 D8 **East Dean** E Susx
9 J4 **East Dean** W Susx
30 C7 **East Goscote** Leics
10 C4 **East Grinstead** W Susx
25 G6 **East Harling** Norfk
10 D6 **East Hoathly** E Susx
15 H8 **East Horsley** Surrey
14 C5 **East Ilsley** W Berk
45 J3 **East Kilbride** S Lans
13 J7 **East Knoyle** Wilts
9 H5 **East Lavant** W Susx
8 E4 **Eastleigh** Hants
46 F3 **East Linton** E Loth
7 L4 **East Lulworth** Dorset
17 K2 **Easton** Suffk
6 B7 **East Prawle** Devon
9 K5 **East Preston** W Susx
42 A5 **Eastriggs** D & G
24 F3 **East Rudham** Norfk
11 L3 **Eastry** Kent
46 E3 **East Saltoun** E Loth
30 D5 **East Stoke** Notts
9 H6 **East Wittering** W Susx
38 B5 **East Witton** N York
29 L5 **Eastwood** Notts
23 L4 **Eaton Socon** Cambs
12 C1 **Ebbw Vale** Blae G
43 H6 **Ebchester** Dur
41 M4 **Ecclefechan** D & G
47 H5 **Eccles** Border
28 F6 **Eccleshall** Staffs
55 K4 **Echt** Abers
29 L2 **Eckington** Derbys
22 A6 **Eckington** Worcs
58 F2 **Edderton** Highld
46 C5 **Eddleston** Border
10 C4 **Edenbridge** Kent
56 D4 **Edinbane** Highld
46 C3 **Edinburgh** C Edin
31 H3 **Edlington** Lincs
43 H6 **Edmundbyers** Dur
47 G6 **Ednam** Border
30 C3 **Edwinstowe** Notts
55 J7 **Edzell** Angus
15 H7 **Effingham** Surrey
4 F6 **Eggesford** Devon
37 M2 **Eggleston** Dur
15 G6 **Egham** Surrey
47 K7 **Eglingham** Nthumb
18 E3 **Eglwyswrw** Pembks
36 D3 **Egremont** Cumb
39 H3 **Egton Bridge** N York
20 D4 **Elan Village** Powys
59 K3 **Elgin** Moray
56 E7 **Elgol** Highld
11 J4 **Elham** Kent
51 K6 **Elie** Fife
30 D3 **Elkesley** Notts
13 K1 **Elkstone** Gloucs
33 K5 **Elland** Calder
28 B6 **Ellesmere** Shrops
28 B3 **Ellesmere Port** Ches W
25 K6 **Ellingham** Norfk
61 G6 **Ellon** Abers
34 F4 **Elloughton** E R Yk
17 H5 **Elmstead Market** Essex
43 G3 **Elsdon** Nthumb
46 B5 **Elsrickle** S Lans
9 J2 **Elstead** Surrey
15 J4 **Elstree** Herts
37 G3 **Elterwater** Cumb
16 B2 **Eltisley** Cambs
23 L2 **Elton** Cambs
24 F7 **Elveden** Suffk
14 E7 **Elvetham Heath** Hants

34 D3	**Elvington** C York
5 J4	**Elworthy** Somset
24 C7	**Ely** Cambs
47 M7	**Embleton** Nthumb
64 E8	**Embo** Highld
30 F8	**Empingham** Rutlnd
9 H5	**Emsworth** Hants
22 F1	**Enderby** Leics
15 K4	**Enfield** Gt Lon
36 D2	**Ennerdale Bridge** Cumb
14 B2	**Enstone** Oxon
16 C6	**Epping** Essex
15 J7	**Epsom** Surrey
34 E6	**Epworth** N Linc
58 E6	**Errogie** Highld
51 H4	**Errol** P & K
20 E6	**Erwood** Powys
15 H7	**Esher** Surrey
36 E4	**Eskdale Green** Cumb
42 A3	**Eskdalemuir** D & G
31 G8	**Essendine** Rutlnd
15 J3	**Essendon** Herts
38 E2	**Eston** R & Cl
47 J6	**Etal** Nthumb
10 F5	**Etchingham** E Susx
15 G6	**Eton** W & M
22 D5	**Ettington** Warwks
46 D7	**Ettrick** Border
46 E7	**Ettrickbridge** Border
58 E3	**Evanton** Highld
13 G7	**Evercreech** Somset
14 E7	**Eversley** Hants
22 B6	**Evesham** Worcs
13 K2	**Ewen** Gloucs
9 K2	**Ewhurst** Surrey
21 H7	**Ewyas Harold** Herefs
5 H5	**Exbridge** Somset
6 C3	**Exeter** Devon
5 H4	**Exford** Somset
6 C3	**Exminster** Devon
6 D4	**Exmouth** Devon
23 M1	**Eye** C Pete
25 H7	**Eye** Suffk
47 J4	**Eyemouth** Border
10 D2	**Eynsford** Kent
14 B3	**Eynsham** Oxon

F

33 H6	**Failsworth** Oldham
26 E8	**Fairbourne** Gwynd
13 L2	**Fairford** Gloucs
44 F3	**Fairlie** N Ayrs
11 G6	**Fairlight** E Susx
24 F3	**Fakenham** Norfk
46 E4	**Fala** Mdloth
31 G2	**Faldingworth** Lincs
13 G3	**Falfield** S Glos
50 E8	**Falkirk** Falk
51 H6	**Falkland** Fife
2 E7	**Falmouth** Cnwll
42 E3	**Falstone** Nthumb
8 F5	**Fareham** Hants
14 A4	**Faringdon** Oxon
14 F7	**Farnborough** Hants
51 L2	**Farnell** Angus
9 H2	**Farnham** Surrey
15 G5	**Farnham Common** Bucks
10 D2	**Farningham** Kent
37 G4	**Far Sawrey** Cumb
45 M2	**Fauldhouse** W Loth
11 H3	**Faversham** Kent
8 E5	**Fawley** Hants
22 C1	**Fazeley** Staffs
50 C3	**Fearnan** P & K
17 K4	**Felixstowe** Suffk
16 E5	**Felsted** Essex
43 J2	**Felton** Nthumb
24 E6	**Feltwell** Norfk
29 J5	**Fenny Bentley** Derbys
6 E3	**Fenny Bridges** Devon
22 E5	**Fenny Compton** Warwks
22 E1	**Fenny Drayton** Leics
45 H4	**Fenwick** E Ayrs
8 B5	**Ferndown** Dorset
21 M4	**Fernhill Heath** Worcs
9 J3	**Fernhurst** W Susx
29 G3	**Fernilee** Derbys
9 K5	**Ferring** W Susx
43 K8	**Ferryhill** Dur
55 K6	**Fettercairn** Abers
26 F5	**Ffestiniog** Gwynd
25 L4	**Filby** Norfk
39 K5	**Filey** N York
24 E5	**Fincham** Norfk

16 E4	**Finchingfield** Essex
59 J3	**Findhorn** Moray
60 C3	**Findochty** Moray
9 L5	**Findon** W Susx
23 J3	**Finedon** Nhants
17 H1	**Finningham** Suffk
34 D6	**Finningley** Donc
65 b4	**Finstown** Ork
50 B7	**Fintry** Stirlg
48 C2	**Fionnphort** Ag & B
10 D7	**Firle** E Susx
8 F6	**Fishbourne** IoW
18 C3	**Fishguard** Pembks
9 K4	**Fittleworth** W Susx
5 K4	**Fitzhead** Somset
7 c2	**Five Oaks** Jersey
61 c6	**Fladdabister** Shet
39 L6	**Flamborough** E R Yk
15 H3	**Flamstead** Herts
14 F7	**Fleet** Hants
32 C3	**Fleetwood** Lancs
41 K7	**Flimby** Cumb
27 K3	**Flint** Flints
23 K6	**Flitwick** C Beds
39 K5	**Flixton** N York
23 G4	**Flore** Nhants
59 L4	**Fochabers** Moray
11 K5	**Folkestone** Kent
31 G6	**Folkingham** Lincs
7 L1	**Fontmell Magna** Dorset
9 J5	**Fontwell** W Susx
49 G3	**Ford** Ag & B
47 J6	**Ford** Nthumb
10 D4	**Fordcombe** Kent
8 C4	**Fordingbridge** Hants
55 K6	**Fordoun** Abers
11 J3	**Fordwich** Kent
6 a2	**Forest** Guern
10 C5	**Forest Row** E Susx
51 J2	**Forfar** Angus
32 C6	**Formby** Sefton
59 J4	**Forres** Moray
58 C7	**Fort Augustus** Highld
50 F5	**Forteviot** P & K
45 M3	**Forth** S Lans
32 E2	**Forton** Lancs
58 F4	**Fortrose** Highld
7 J4	**Fortuneswell** Dorset
53 H4	**Fort William** Highld
30 E5	**Foston** Lincs
27 L7	**Four Crosses** Powys
9 G3	**Four Marks** Hants
3 G5	**Fowey** Cnwll
21 J6	**Fownhope** Herefs
36 b3	**Foxdale** IoM
58 D7	**Foyers** Highld
17 K2	**Framlingham** Suffk
7 J3	**Frampton** Dorset
10 E5	**Frant** E Susx
61 G3	**Fraserburgh** Abers
24 D8	**Freckenham** Suffk
32 D4	**Freckleton** Lancs
9 H2	**Frensham** Surrey
8 D6	**Freshwater** IoW
25 J7	**Fressingfield** Suffk
65 J2	**Freswick** Highld
39 H7	**Fridaythorpe** E R Yk
14 B4	**Frilford** Oxon
17 K5	**Frinton-on-Sea** Essex
51 K2	**Friockheim** Angus
25 L5	**Fritton** Norfk
36 D2	**Frizington** Cumb
13 H2	**Frocester** Gloucs
28 C3	**Frodsham** Ches W
13 H6	**Frome** Somset
14 A6	**Froxfield** Wilts
9 H5	**Funtington** W Susx
49 J4	**Furnace** Ag & B
29 G2	**Furness Vale** Derbys
16 D6	**Fyfield** Essex
14 B4	**Fyfield** Oxon
60 E5	**Fyvie** Abers

G

28 F8	**Gailey** Staffs
38 B2	**Gainford** Dur
34 E7	**Gainsborough** Lincs
57 H2	**Gairloch** Highld
53 J3	**Gairlochy** Highld
46 E6	**Galashiels** Border
37 H7	**Galgate** Lancs
45 H4	**Galston** E Ayrs
16 B3	**Gamlingay** Cambs
30 D3	**Gamston** Notts
26 F7	**Ganllwyd** Gwynd

25 G7	**Garboldisham** Norfk
60 E3	**Gardenstown** Abers
49 K4	**Garelochhead** Ag & B
34 B4	**Garforth** Leeds
33 H2	**Gargrave** N York
40 F6	**Garlieston** D & G
55 L4	**Garlogie** Abers
42 E7	**Garrigill** Cumb
32 E3	**Garstang** Lancs
20 D5	**Garth** Powys
46 F3	**Garvald** E Loth
58 C3	**Garve** Highld
41 G6	**Gatehouse of Fleet** D & G
43 K5	**Gateshead** Gatesd
22 E5	**Gaydon** Warwks
24 E4	**Gayton** Norfk
31 K6	**Gedney Drove End** Lincs
31 J8	**Gedney Hill** Lincs
4 D4	**Georgeham** Devon
15 G5	**Gerrards Cross** Bucks
46 F3	**Gifford** E Loth
37 L6	**Giggleswick** N York
13 H8	**Gillingham** Dorset
10 F2	**Gillingham** Medway
25 L6	**Gillingham** Norfk
38 B3	**Gilling West** N York
65 J1	**Gills** Highld
50 E4	**Gilmerton** P & K
42 E5	**Gilsland** Nthumb
21 G8	**Gilwern** Mons
16 C2	**Girton** Cambs
40 C3	**Girvan** S Ayrs
33 G2	**Gisburn** Lancs
51 J3	**Glamis** Angus
47 K7	**Glanton** Nthumb
30 B3	**Glapwell** Derbys
20 F6	**Glasbury** Powys
45 J2	**Glasgow** C Glas
23 J1	**Glaston** Rutlnd
12 F7	**Glastonbury** Somset
17 G3	**Glemsford** Suffk
44 A4	**Glenbarr** Ag & B
52 D5	**Glenborrodale** Highld
41 K5	**Glencaple** D & G
53 H5	**Glencoe** Highld
49 H5	**Glendaruel** Ag & B
50 E6	**Glendevon** P & K
50 E6	**Gleneagles** P & K
57 H7	**Glenelg** Highld
51 G5	**Glenfarg** P & K
52 F3	**Glenfinnan** Highld
55 H3	**Glenkindie** Abers
59 K6	**Glenlivet** Moray
40 C6	**Glenluce** D & G
36 b3	**Glen Maye** IoM
57 G2	**Glenridding** Cumb
51 H6	**Glenrothes** Fife
35 G7	**Glentham** Lincs
33 J7	**Glossop** Derbys
21 M7	**Gloucester** Gloucs
27 K6	**Glyn Ceiriog** Wrexhm
19 L6	**Glyncorrwg** Neath
10 C7	**Glynde** E Susx
19 L5	**Glynneath** Neath
20 C8	**Glyntawe** Powys
28 F7	**Gnosall** Staffs
39 H3	**Goathland** N York
12 D7	**Goathurst** Somset
27 L6	**Gobowen** Shrops
9 J2	**Godalming** Surrey
23 M4	**Godmanchester** Cambs
8 F7	**Godshill** IoW
10 C3	**Godstone** Surrey
20 B3	**Goginan** Cerdgn
32 F6	**Golborne** Wigan
17 G6	**Goldhanger** Essex
64 E7	**Golspie** Highld
9 K2	**Gomshall** Surrey
34 E4	**Goole** E R Yk
28 E3	**Goostrey** Ches E
47 G5	**Gordon** Border
46 D4	**Gorebridge** Mdloth
7 C1	**Gorey** Jersey
14 D5	**Goring** Oxon
2 F6	**Gorran Haven** Cnwll
19 J6	**Gorseinon** Swans
31 H6	**Gosberton** Lincs
36 D3	**Gosforth** Cumb
43 J5	**Gosforth** N u Ty
8 F5	**Gosport** Hants
10 F4	**Goudhurst** Kent
49 K5	**Gourock** Inver
19 J6	**Gowerton** Swans
35 H5	**Goxhill** N Linc
11 G2	**Grain** Medway
35 K6	**Grainthorpe** Lincs
2 F6	**Grampound** Cnwll

62 d9	**Gramsdal** W Isls
62 d9	**Gramsdale** W Isls
6 a1	**Grandes Rocques** Guern
36 F2	**Grange** Cumb
50 E8	**Grangemouth** Falk
37 G5	**Grange-over-Sands** Cumb
30 F6	**Grantham** Lincs
59 J6	**Grantown-on-Spey** Highld
47 H4	**Grantshouse** Border
37 G3	**Grasmere** Cumb
38 A6	**Grassington** N York
16 B4	**Graveley** Herts
10 E2	**Gravesend** Kent
10 E1	**Grays** Thurr
38 F3	**Great Ayton** N York
13 H3	**Great Badminton** S Glos
16 E4	**Great Bardfield** Essex
23 L5	**Great Barford** Bed
24 E3	**Great Bircham** Norfk
17 J3	**Great Blakenham** Suffk
30 F8	**Great Casterton** Rutlnd
16 D3	**Great Chesterford** Essex
30 D7	**Great Dalby** Leics
16 E5	**Great Dunmow** Essex
8 B3	**Great Durnford** Wilts
23 L3	**Great Gidding** Cambs
16 B2	**Great Gransden** Cambs
9 H3	**Greatham** Hants
33 G4	**Great Harwood** Lancs
29 G2	**Great Haywood** Staffs
25 G6	**Great Hockham** Norfk
14 F3	**Great Kimble** Bucks
36 F3	**Great Langdale** Cumb
21 L5	**Great Malvern** Worcs
24 E4	**Great Massingham** Norfk
14 F4	**Great Missenden** Bucks
30 F6	**Great Ponton** Lincs
16 E4	**Great Sampford** Essex
28 B3	**Great Saughall** Ches W
14 B6	**Great Shefford** W Berk
16 C3	**Great Shelford** Cambs
38 D3	**Great Smeaton** N York
22 E7	**Great Tew** Oxon
4 E5	**Great Torrington** Devon
17 G8	**Great Wakering** Essex
16 E4	**Great Waltham** Essex
21 L4	**Great Witley** Worcs
25 L5	**Great Yarmouth** Norfk
16 F4	**Great Yeldham** Essex
27 K3	**Greenfield** Flints
38 E7	**Green Hammerton** N York
42 E5	**Greenhead** Nthumb
38 B6	**Greenhow Hill** N York
47 G5	**Greenlaw** Border
50 D6	**Greenloaning** P & K
49 L5	**Greenock** Inver
36 F5	**Greenodd** Cumb
30 F7	**Greetham** Rutlnd
27 L4	**Gresford** Wrexhm
38 B3	**Greta Bridge** Dur
42 B5	**Gretna** D & G
42 B5	**Gretna Green** D & G
42 C8	**Greystoke** Cumb
35 J5	**Grimsby** NE Lin
31 G7	**Grimsthorpe** Lincs
29 J3	**Grindleford** Derbys
34 E7	**Gringley on the Hill** Notts
30 B8	**Groby** Leics
21 H7	**Grosmont** Mons
7 C2	**Grouville** Jersey
14 B5	**Grove** Oxon
51 J5	**Guardbridge** Fife
11 G6	**Guestling Green** E Susx
9 K2	**Guildford** Surrey
38 F2	**Guisborough** R & Cl
33 K3	**Guiseley** Leeds
25 G4	**Guist** Norfk
46 E2	**Gullane** E Loth
34 E5	**Gunness** N Linc
3 K4	**Gunnislake** Cnwll
30 D5	**Gunthorpe** Notts

8 E6 **Gurnard** IoW
8 A5 **Gussage All Saints** Dorset
61 d2 **Gutcher** Shet
24 B5 **Guyhirn** Cambs
2 D7 **Gweek** Cnwll
27 K4 **Gwernymynydd** Flints
2 C6 **Gwithian** Cnwll
27 J5 **Gwyddelwern** Denbgs

H

65 b3 **Hackland** Ork
39 J4 **Hackness** N York
15 K5 **Hackney** Gt Lon
14 E3 **Haddenham** Bucks
24 C7 **Haddenham** Cambs
46 F3 **Haddington** E Loth
25 L6 **Haddiscoe** Norfk
17 H3 **Hadleigh** Suffk
10 E4 **Hadlow** Kent
31 J3 **Hagworthingham** Lincs
10 E7 **Hailsham** E Susx
5 J6 **Halberton** Devon
25 K6 **Hales** Norfk
22 A3 **Halesowen** Dudley
25 K7 **Halesworth** Suffk
33 K4 **Halifax** Calder
65 G2 **Halkirk** Highld
6 B7 **Hallsands** Devon
16 F4 **Halstead** Essex
10 D3 **Halstead** Kent
42 E5 **Haltwhistle** Nthumb
6 B6 **Halwell** Devon
4 D7 **Halwill Junction** Devon
9 G4 **Hambledon** Hants
8 E5 **Hamble-le-Rice** Hants
32 D3 **Hambleton** Lancs
45 K3 **Hamilton** S Lans
15 J6 **Hammersmith** Gt Lon
14 C6 **Hampstead Norrey's** W Berk
38 C7 **Hampsthwaite** N York
14 B7 **Hamstead Marshall** W Berk
11 H5 **Hamstreet** Kent
10 B5 **Handcross** W Susx
28 C4 **Handley** Ches W
28 F5 **Hanley** C Stke
28 F5 **Hanley** C Stke
25 K3 **Happisburgh** Norfk
6 B6 **Harbertonford** Devon
13 H1 **Hardwicke** Gloucs
16 C4 **Hare Street** Herts
33 L3 **Harewood** Leeds
21 J7 **Harewood End** Herefs
26 E6 **Harlech** Gwynd
25 J7 **Harleston** Norfk
56 C5 **Harlosh** Highld
16 C6 **Harlow** Essex
2 E4 **Harlyn** Cnwll
61 d1 **Haroldswick** Shet
15 H3 **Harpenden** Herts
33 L2 **Harrogate** N York
23 K5 **Harrold** Bed
15 H5 **Harrow** Gt Lon
16 C3 **Harston** Cambs
43 H3 **Hartburn** Nthumb
17 G3 **Hartest** Suffk
10 D5 **Hartfield** E Susx
29 H4 **Hartington** Derbys
4 C5 **Hartland** Devon
43 M8 **Hartlepool** Hartpl
14 E7 **Hartley Wintney** Hants
21 L7 **Hartpury** Gloucs
22 B5 **Harvington** Worcs
17 K4 **Harwich** Essex
22 D4 **Haseley** Warwks
9 J3 **Haslemere** Surrey
10 F7 **Hastings** E Susx
12 D8 **Hatch Beauchamp** Somset
34 D5 **Hatfield** Donc
15 J3 **Hatfield** Herts
16 D5 **Hatfield Broad Oak** Essex
16 D5 **Hatfield Heath** Essex
16 F6 **Hatfield Peverel** Essex
4 E6 **Hatherleigh** Devon
30 B7 **Hathern** Leics
29 J2 **Hathersage** Derbys
61 H5 **Hatton** Abers
9 G5 **Havant** Hants
8 F6 **Havenstreet** IoW
18 C5 **Haverfordwest** Pembks
16 E3 **Haverhill** Suffk
27 L3 **Hawarden** Flints
37 L4 **Hawes** N York
46 F7 **Hawick** Border
16 F3 **Hawkedon** Suffk
10 F5 **Hawkhurst** Kent
11 K4 **Hawkinge** Kent
37 G4 **Hawkshead** Cumb
38 E4 **Hawnby** N York
33 J3 **Haworth** C Brad
38 F7 **Haxby** C York
34 E6 **Haxey** N Linc
42 F5 **Haydon Bridge** Nthumb
2 C6 **Hayle** Cnwll
21 G6 **Hay-on-Wye** Powys
10 B6 **Haywards Heath** W Susx
28 F2 **Hazel Grove** Stockp
24 D3 **Heacham** Norfk
11 G4 **Headcorn** Kent
29 L5 **Heanor** Derbys
29 L3 **Heath** Derbys
10 E6 **Heathfield** E Susx
29 G8 **Heath Hayes & Wimblebury** Staffs
31 G5 **Heckington** Lincs
8 E4 **Hedge End** Hants
29 G8 **Hednesford** Staffs
35 H4 **Hedon** E R Yk
49 L5 **Helensburgh** Ag & B
37 L7 **Hellifield** N York
17 K2 **Helmingham** Suffk
65 G6 **Helmsdale** Highld
38 F5 **Helmsley** N York
31 G5 **Helpringham** Lincs
28 C3 **Helsby** Ches W
2 C7 **Helston** Cnwll
15 H3 **Hemel Hempstead** Herts
24 A8 **Hemingford Abbots** Cambs
25 J6 **Hempnall** Norfk
25 L4 **Hemsby** Norfk
34 B5 **Hemsworth** Wakefd
5 K6 **Hemyock** Devon
19 J6 **Hendy** Carmth
9 L4 **Henfield** W Susx
16 D4 **Henham** Essex
22 C4 **Henley-in-Arden** Warwks
14 E5 **Henley-on-Thames** Oxon
27 J3 **Henllan** Denbgs
23 L6 **Henlow** C Beds
25 L7 **Henstead** Suffk
7 K1 **Henstridge** Somset
21 J6 **Hereford** Herefs
14 C6 **Hermitage** W Berk
11 J2 **Herne Bay** Kent
11 K3 **Hersden** Kent
10 E6 **Herstmonceux** E Susx
15 K3 **Hertford** Herts
35 G4 **Hessle** E R Yk
27 L2 **Heswall** Wirral
25 H5 **Hethersett** Norfk
37 H5 **Heversham** Cumb
43 G5 **Hexham** Nthumb
3 M4 **Hexworthy** Devon
3 K6 **Heybrook Bay** Devon
37 G7 **Heysham** Lancs
13 J6 **Heytesbury** Wilts
35 G6 **Hibaldstow** N Linc
10 B6 **Hickstead** W Susx
23 K4 **Higham Ferrers** Nhants
4 E6 **Highampton** Devon
37 J6 **High Bentham** N York
12 D6 **Highbridge** Somset
14 B7 **Highclere** Hants
28 D7 **High Ercall** Wrekin
2 b1 **Higher Town** IoS
11 G5 **High Halden** Kent
42 C7 **High Hesket** Cumb
21 L3 **Highley** Shrops
16 E5 **High Roding** Essex
13 M3 **Highworth** Swindn
14 F4 **High Wycombe** Bucks
10 D4 **Hildenborough** Kent
9 H3 **Hill Brow** Hants
59 G2 **Hill of Fearn** Highld
61 b3 **Hillswick** Shet
13 K4 **Hilmarton** Wilts
22 E2 **Hinckley** Leics
39 G2 **Hinderwell** N York
9 J3 **Hindhead** Surrey
13 J7 **Hindon** Wilts
25 G5 **Hingham** Norfk
38 B4 **Hipswell** N York
12 A2 **Hirwaun** Rhondd
16 C2 **Histon** Cambs
17 H3 **Hitcham** Suffk
23 M7 **Hitchin** Herts
17 G7 **Hockley** Essex
23 K7 **Hockliffe** C Beds
15 K3 **Hoddesdon** Herts
28 D6 **Hodnet** Shrops
31 L3 **Hogsthorpe** Lincs
31 J7 **Holbeach** Lincs
3 L5 **Holbeton** Devon
17 J4 **Holbrook** Suffk
8 E5 **Holbury** Hants
24 F2 **Holkham** Norfk
11 G3 **Hollingbourne** Kent
9 L2 **Holmbury St Mary** Surrey
28 E3 **Holmes Chapel** Ches E
34 E3 **Holme upon Spalding Moor** E R Yk
33 K6 **Holmfirth** Kirk
36 D4 **Holmrook** Cumb
6 A5 **Holne** Devon
4 C6 **Holsworthy** Devon
25 H3 **Holt** Norfk
13 J5 **Holt** Wilts
28 B4 **Holt** Wrexhm
21 L4 **Holt Heath** Worcs
35 J6 **Holton le Clay** Lincs
26 B2 **Holyhead** IoA
47 L5 **Holy Island** Nthumb
45 L2 **Holytown** N Lans
7 J2 **Holywell** Dorset
27 K3 **Holywell** Flints
25 J7 **Homersfield** Suffk
25 H5 **Honingham** Norfk
24 F7 **Honington** Suffk
6 E2 **Honiton** Devon
14 E7 **Hook** Hants
10 F2 **Hoo St Werburgh** Medway
29 J2 **Hope** Derbys
6 A7 **Hope** Devon
27 L4 **Hope** Flints
21 J2 **Hope Bowdler** Shrops
59 K3 **Hopeman** Moray
21 J5 **Hope under Dinmore** Herefs
25 M5 **Hopton on Sea** Norfk
10 D6 **Horam** E Susx
10 B4 **Horley** Surrey
37 J6 **Hornby** Lancs
31 H3 **Horncastle** Lincs
9 G4 **Horndean** Hants
4 D5 **Horns Cross** Devon
35 H3 **Hornsea** E R Yk
3 L4 **Horrabridge** Devon
25 L4 **Horsey** Norfk
9 L3 **Horsham** W Susx
43 H5 **Horsley** Nthumb
8 B5 **Horton** Dorset
6 F1 **Horton** Somset
14 D3 **Horton-cum-Studley** Oxon
37 L6 **Horton in Ribblesdale** N York
32 F5 **Horwich** Bolton
30 C7 **Hoton** Leics
43 K6 **Houghton-le-Spring** Sundld
23 G1 **Houghton on the Hill** Leics
15 H6 **Hounslow** Gt Lon
65 b4 **Houton** Ork
10 B7 **Hove** Br & H
38 F5 **Hovingham** N York
34 E4 **Howden** E R Yk
25 J7 **Hoxne** Suffk
32 B7 **Hoylake** Wirral
34 B6 **Hoyland Nether** Barns
30 B5 **Hucknall** Notts
33 K5 **Huddersfield** Kirk
2 a2 **Hugh Town** IoS
35 J6 **Humberston** NE Lin
46 E4 **Humbie** E Loth
47 G5 **Hume** Border
14 B6 **Hungerford** W Berk
39 K5 **Hunmanby** N York
24 D2 **Hunstanton** Norfk
23 M3 **Huntingdon** Cambs
21 L7 **Huntley** Gloucs
60 C5 **Huntly** Abers
8 E4 **Hursley** Hants
8 E2 **Hurstbourne Priors** Hants
14 B7 **Hurstbourne Tarrant** Hants
10 F5 **Hurst Green** E Susx
32 F3 **Hurst Green** Lancs
10 B6 **Hurstpierpoint** W Susx
38 C3 **Hurworth-on-Tees** Darltn
23 G2 **Husbands Bosworth** Leics
23 K6 **Husborne Crawley** C Beds
31 L3 **Huttoft** Lincs
39 G4 **Hutton-le-Hole** N York
33 H7 **Hyde** Tamesd
48 b3 **Hynish** Ag & B
8 E5 **Hythe** Hants
11 J5 **Hythe** Kent

I

29 K8 **Ibstock** Leics
6 C4 **Ideford** Devon
12 F8 **Ilchester** Somset
4 E3 **Ilfracombe** Devon
29 L5 **Ilkeston** Derbys
33 K3 **Ilkley** C Brad
7 G1 **Ilminster** Somset
35 H5 **Immingham** NE Lin
35 H5 **Immingham Dock** NE Lin
63 H5 **Inchnadamph** Highld
16 E7 **Ingatestone** Essex
30 F2 **Ingham** Lincs
37 K6 **Ingleton** N York
31 L3 **Ingoldmells** Lincs
22 B5 **Inkberrow** Worcs
49 K6 **Innellan** Ag & B
46 D6 **Innerleithen** Border
60 D6 **Insch** Abers
54 C4 **Insh** Highld
4 D4 **Instow** Devon
61 G3 **Inverallochy** Abers
64 C7 **Inveran** Highld
49 J3 **Inveraray** Ag & B
57 H2 **Inverasdale** Highld
55 L6 **Inverbervie** Abers
53 K2 **Invergarry** Highld
58 F3 **Invergordon** Highld
51 H4 **Invergowrie** P & K
57 J6 **Inverinate** Highld
51 L2 **Inverkeilor** Angus
46 B2 **Inverkeithing** Fife
60 D5 **Inverkeithny** Abers
49 K6 **Inverkip** Inver
58 D7 **Invermoriston** Highld
58 F5 **Inverness** Highld
55 L3 **Inverurie** Abers
6 B5 **Ipplepen** Devon
29 G5 **Ipstones** Staffs
17 J3 **Ipswich** Suffk
23 J4 **Irchester** Nhants
42 A7 **Ireby** Cumb
21 K1 **Ironbridge** Wrekin
23 K3 **Irthlingborough** Nhants
45 G4 **Irvine** N Ayrs
40 F7 **Isle of Whithorn** D & G
57 G7 **Isleornsay** Highld
15 K5 **Islington** Gt Lon
8 F3 **Itchen Abbas** Hants
15 G5 **Iver** Bucks
15 G3 **Ivinghoe** Bucks
3 M5 **Ivybridge** Devon
11 G2 **Iwade** Kent
7 L1 **Iwerne Minster** Dorset
25 G8 **Ixworth** Suffk

J

43 K5 **Jarrow** S Tyne
47 G7 **Jedburgh** Border
6 b2 **Jerbourg** Guern
10 D7 **Jevington** E Susx
65 J1 **John o' Groats** Highld
55 L7 **Johnshaven** Abers
18 C5 **Johnston** Pembks
49 M6 **Johnstone** Rens
36 c1 **Jurby** IoM

K

49 H6 Kames Ag & B
35 H5 Keelby Lincs
30 B6 Kegworth Leics
33 J3 Keighley C Brad
65 J2 Keiss Highld
60 B4 Keith Moray
37 L3 Keld N York
30 D4 Kelham Notts
47 G6 Kelso Border
17 G5 Kelvedon Essex
K2 Kemble Gloucs
55 K3 Kemnay Abers
23 K5 Kempston Bed
37 H4 Kendal Cumb
22 D3 Kenilworth Warwks
50 D3 Kenmore P & K
49 G6 Kennacraig Ag & B
6 C3 Kennford Devon
25 G7 Kenninghall Norfk
53 G5 Kentallen Highld
16 F2 Kentford Suffk
6 C4 Kenton Devon
20 F2 Kerry Powys
25 L6 Kessingland Suffk
36 F2 Keswick Cumb
23 J3 Kettering Nhants
37 M6 Kettlewell N York
23 K1 Ketton Rutlnd
10 B6 Keymer W Susx
13 G4 Keynsham BaNES
23 K3 Keyston Cambs
30 C6 Keyworth Notts
23 G2 Kibworth Harcourt Leics
21 M3 Kidderminster Worcs
14 C3 Kidlington Oxon
28 F4 Kidsgrove Staffs
19 G5 Kidwelly Carmth
42 D3 Kielder Nthumb
48 F6 Kilberry Ag & B
45 G3 Kilbirnie N Ayrs
29 K5 Kilburn Derbys
38 E5 Kilburn N York
44 E3 Kilchattan Ag & B
52 C4 Kilchoan Highld
49 J2 Kilchrenan Ag & B
49 K5 Kilcreggan Ag & B
38 F3 Kildale N York
55 H3 Kildrummy Abers
33 J3 Kildwick N York
49 H5 Kilfinan Ag & B
18 E5 Kilgetty Pembks
39 K6 Kilham E R Yk
44 B5 Kilkenzie Ag & B
4 C6 Kilkhampton Cnwll
50 B7 Killearn Stirlg
54 D7 Killiecrankie P & K
50 B4 Killin Stirlg
49 L6 Kilmacolm Inver
51 J5 Kilmany Fife
45 H4 Kilmarnock E Ayrs
49 G4 Kilmartin Ag & B
45 H4 Kilmaurs E Ayrs
49 G3 Kilmelford Ag & B
58 D5 Kilmorack Highld
49 G2 Kilninver Ag & B
50 C8 Kilsyth N Lans
5 K3 Kilve Somset
45 G4 Kilwinning N Ayrs
25 H5 Kimberley Norfk
23 L4 Kimbolton Cambs
64 E5 Kinbrace Highld
50 E7 Kincardine Fife
55 J4 Kincardine O'Neil Abers
54 C4 Kincraig Highld
22 K5 Kineton Warwks
51 K5 Kingsbarns Fife
6 B7 Kingsbridge Devon
22 D2 Kingsbury Warwks
14 C7 Kingsclere Hants
23 K1 King's Cliffe Nhants
11 L4 Kingsdown Kent
9 L3 Kingsfold W Susx
6 C5 Kingskerswell Devon
21 H4 Kingsland Herefs
15 H4 Kings Langley Herts
29 G5 Kingsley Staffs
24 D4 King's Lynn Norfk
6 a2 King's Mills Guern
11 H4 Kingsnorth Kent
8 D3 King's Somborne Hants
7 K2 King's Stag Dorset
13 H2 King's Stanley Gloucs
6 C4 Kingsteignton Devon
21 H6 Kingstone Herefs

59 L3 Kingston on Spey Moray
35 G4 Kingston upon Hull C KuH
15 J6 Kingston upon Thames Gt Lon
6 C6 Kingswear Devon
8 E3 Kings Worthy Hants
21 G5 Kington Herefs
54 B4 Kingussie Highld
63 H3 Kinlochbervie Highld
53 G3 Kinlocheil Highld
57 J3 Kinlochewe Highld
53 J5 Kinlochleven Highld
50 C2 Kinloch Rannoch P & K
59 J3 Kinloss Moray
55 L6 Kinneff Abers
50 F6 Kinross P & K
14 B6 Kintbury W Berk
55 L3 Kintore Abers
50 C7 Kippen Stirlg
39 G5 Kirby Misperton N York
22 F1 Kirby Muxloe Leics
61 c6 Kirkabister Shet
41 K6 Kirkbean D & G
42 A6 Kirkbride Cumb
33 K5 Kirkburton Kirk
32 D6 Kirkby Knows
30 B4 Kirkby in Ashfield Notts
37 J5 Kirkby Lonsdale Cumb
38 C5 Kirkby Malzeard N York
39 G5 Kirkbymoorside N York
37 K3 Kirkby Stephen Cumb
51 H7 Kirkcaldy Fife
40 B5 Kirkcolm D & G
45 K6 Kirkconnel D & G
40 D5 Kirkcowan D & G
41 G6 Kirkcudbright D & G
32 D4 Kirkham Lancs
58 E5 Kirkhill Highld
40 E6 Kirkinner D & G
45 K1 Kirkintilloch E Duns
29 K6 Kirk Langley Derbys
36 b2 Kirk Michael IoM
50 F2 Kirkmichael P & K
45 G6 Kirkmichael S Ayrs
47 J6 Kirknewton Nthumb
42 D7 Kirkoswald Cumb
44 F6 Kirkoswald S Ayrs
42 B5 Kirkpatrick-Fleming D & G
55 L4 Kirkton of Skene Abers
65 c4 Kirkwall Ork
43 H4 Kirkwhelpington Nthumb
51 J2 Kirriemuir Angus
31 J6 Kirton Lincs
34 F6 Kirton in Lindsey N Linc
23 H4 Kislingbury Nhants
38 D7 Knaresborough N York
42 E6 Knarsdale Nthumb
15 J2 Knebworth Herts
21 G3 Knighton Powys
21 L5 Knightwick Worcs
63 H6 Knockan Highld
27 L7 Knockin Shrops
34 C4 Knottingley Wakefd
14 F5 Knowl Hill W & M
28 E3 Knutsford Ches E
57 G6 Kyleakin Highld
57 G6 Kyle of Lochalsh Highld
57 G7 Kylerhea Highld

L

35 H6 Laceby NE Lin
2 E5 Ladock Cnwll
51 H5 Ladybank Fife
54 A5 Laggan Highld
7 a1 La Greve de Lecq Jersey
62 E8 Laide Highld
64 C6 Lairg Highld
24 E7 Lakenheath Suffk
10 E5 Lamberhurst Kent
14 B6 Lambourn W Berk
3 K3 Lamerton Devon

46 A6 Lamington S Lans
44 D5 Lamlash N Ayrs
19 J2 Lampeter Cerdgn
23 H3 Lamport Nhants
45 M4 Lanark S Lans
37 H6 Lancaster Lancs
43 J6 Lanchester Dur
9 L5 Lancing W Susx
6 b1 L'Ancresse Guern
3 J5 Landrake Cnwll
30 E8 Langham Rutlnd
42 B4 Langholm D & G
12 E8 Langport Somset
38 A3 Langthwaite N York
39 J6 Langtoft E R Yk
8 A7 Langton Matravers Dorset
42 D7 Langwathby Cumb
31 G3 Langworth Lincs
3 G4 Lanivet Cnwll
5 G6 Lapford Devon
51 J6 Largoward Fife
44 F2 Largs N Ayrs
45 L3 Larkhall S Lans
8 B2 Larkhill Wilts
39 G4 Lastingham N York
17 G7 Latchingdon Essex
65 H4 Latheron Highld
46 F5 Lauder Border
18 F5 Laugharne Carmth
3 J3 Launceston Cnwll
55 K6 Laurencekirk Abers
41 G5 Laurieston D & G
17 G3 Lavenham Suffk
50 C3 Lawers P & K
36 c3 Laxey IoM
25 K8 Laxfield Suffk
42 D7 Lazonby Cumb
50 F5 Leadenham Lincs
16 E6 Leaden Roding Essex
43 J6 Leadgate Dur
45 M6 Leadhills S Lans
22 D4 Leamington Spa Warwks
15 J7 Leatherhead Surrey
13 M2 Lechlade on Thames Gloucs
21 L6 Ledbury Herefs
4 E3 Lee Devon
21 J1 Leebotwood Shrops
33 L4 Leeds Leeds
29 G4 Leek Staffs
38 C4 Leeming Bar N York
8 F5 Lee-on-the-Solent Hants
31 J2 Legbourne Lincs
23 G1 Leicester C Leic
10 D4 Leigh Kent
32 F6 Leigh Wigan
21 L5 Leigh Sinton Worcs
23 J7 Leighton Buzzard C Beds
21 H3 Leintwardine Herefs
17 M2 Leiston Suffk
2 C6 Lelant Cnwll
40 C3 Lendalfoot S Ayrs
11 G3 Lenham Kent
50 B8 Lennoxtown E Duns
21 J4 Leominster Herefs
6 a2 L'Eree Guern
61 c6 Lerwick Shet
60 D6 Leslie Abers
51 H6 Leslie Fife
44 L4 Lesmahagow S Lans
40 B5 Leswalt D & G
7 a1 L'Etacq Jersey
16 B4 Letchworth Garden City Herts
51 K3 Letham Angus
18 C4 Letterston Pembks
51 J5 Leuchars Fife
35 H3 Leven E R Yk
51 J6 Leven Fife
37 H5 Levens Cumb
62 e7 Leverburgh W Isls
10 C7 Lewes E Susx
38 B4 Leyburn N York
32 E5 Leyland Lancs
11 H2 Leysdown-on-Sea Kent
59 L3 Lhanbryde Moray
46 A5 Libberton S Lans
29 H8 Lichfield Staffs
16 F2 Lidgate Suffk
3 J3 Lifton Devon
15 G7 Lightwater Surrey
46 F7 Lilliesleaf Border
15 H5 Limpley Stoke Wilts
30 F3 Lincoln Lincs
37 G5 Lindale Cumb

10 C4 Lingfield Surrey
46 A3 Linlithgow W Loth
16 D3 Linton Cambs
10 F4 Linton Kent
9 H3 Liphook Hants
3 H4 Liskeard Cnwll
9 H3 Liss Hants
31 G2 Lissington Lincs
24 F4 Litcham Norfk
14 C7 Litchfield Hants
16 D3 Little Abington Cambs
15 K3 Little Berkhamsted Herts
33 H5 Littleborough Rochdl
23 J6 Little Brickhill M Keyn
30 F7 Little Bytham Lincs
17 J5 Little Clacton Essex
15 G3 Little Gaddesden Herts
9 K5 Littlehampton W Susx
24 D6 Littleport Cambs
21 H2 Little Stretton Shrops
4 E5 Little Torrington Devon
25 G3 Little Walsingham Norfk
32 C7 Liverpool Lpool
46 B3 Livingston W Loth
2 D8 Lizard Cnwll
26 C5 Llanaelhaearn Gwynd
27 K6 Llanarmon Dyffryn Ceiriog Wrexhm
19 H4 Llanarthne Carmth
26 E6 Llanbedr Gwynd
27 K4 Llanbedr-Dyffryn-Clwyd Denbgs
26 C6 Llanbedrog Gwynd
26 E4 Llanberis Gwynd
20 F3 Llanbister Powys
20 D1 Llanbrynmair Powys
19 H5 Llanddarog Carmth
27 H3 Llandderfel Gwynd
27 H3 Llanddulas Conwy
19 J4 Llandeilo Carmth
20 E2 Llandinam Powys
18 E4 Llandissilio Pembks
19 K3 Llandovery Carmth
27 J6 Llandre Cerdgn
20 E4 Llandrindod Wells Powys
27 L7 Llandrinio Powys
27 G2 Llandudno Conwy
26 D4 Llandwrog Gwynd
19 J5 Llandybie Carmth
19 J5 Llandysul Cerdgn
19 H6 Llanelli Carmth
26 D2 Llanerchymedd IoA
27 J8 Llanerfyl Powys
27 J8 Llanfachraeth IoA
27 J8 Llanfair Caereinion Powys
27 J4 Llanfair Dyffryn Clwyd Denbgs
26 F3 Llanfairfechan Conwy
26 D2 Llanfair P G IoA
27 H3 Llanfair Talhaiarn Conwy
21 G3 Llanfair Waterdine Shrops
20 A3 Llanfarian Cerdgn
27 K7 Llanfyllin Powys
27 H8 Llangadfan Powys
19 K4 Llangadog Carmth
20 D5 Llangammarch Wells Powys
27 K7 Llangedwyn Powys
26 D3 Llangefni IoA
19 L7 Llangeinor Brdgnd
19 J7 Llangeler Carmth
19 G6 Llangennith Swans
27 H3 Llangernyw Conwy
26 E2 Llangoed IoA
27 K5 Llangollen Denbgs
19 F2 Llangors Powys
18 F2 Llangranog Cerdgn
20 D3 Llangurig Powys
20 F7 Llangynidr Powys
27 J7 Llangynog Powys
19 H6 Llanhamlach Powys
12 B3 Llanharan Rhondd
20 B3 Llanidloes Powys
26 E3 Llanilar Cerdgn
27 H3 Llannefydd Conwy
27 J7 Llanrhaeadr-ym-Mochnant Powys
19 H6 Llanrhidian Swans
20 A4 Llanrhystud Cerdgn

Llanrug - Much Marcle

26 E4 **Llanrug** Gwynd
27 G4 **Llanrwst** Conwy
27 G3 **Llansanffraid Glan Conwy** Conwy
27 H3 **Llansannan** Conwy
19 H1 **Llansantffraid** Cerdgn
27 K7 **Llansantffraid-ym-Mechain** Powys
19 J3 **Llansawel** Carmth
19 G5 **Llansteffan** Carmth
21 G7 **Llanthony** Mons
12 B3 **Llantrisant** Rhondd
5 J1 **Llantwit Major** V Glam
27 G6 **Llanuwchllyn** Gwynd
21 H8 **Llanvetherine** Mons
21 G7 **Llanvihangel Crucorney** Mons
27 J7 **Llanwddyn** Powys
26 D4 **Llanwnda** Gwynd
19 K3 **Llanwrda** Carmth
20 D5 **Llanwrtyd Wells** Powys
19 H2 **Llanybydder** Carmth
27 L7 **Llanymynech** Powys
26 D6 **Llanystumdwy** Gwynd
27 L4 **Llay** Wrexhm
18 F3 **Llechryd** Cerdgn
26 E8 **Llwyngwril** Gwynd
27 K6 **Llwynmawr** Wrexhm
27 L7 **Llynclys** Shrops
20 F6 **Llyswen** Powys
52 E3 **Lochailort** Highld
52 D6 **Lochaline** Highld
41 K4 **Locharbriggs** D & G
53 H7 **Lochawe** Ag & B
62 c12 **Loch Baghasdail** W Isls
62 c12 **Lochboisdale** W Isls
52 D7 **Lochbuie** Ag & B
57 H5 **Lochcarron** Highld
52 E7 **Lochdonhead** Ag & B
50 B4 **Lochearnhead** Stirlg
49 H4 **Lochgair** Ag & B
49 G4 **Lochgilphead** Ag & B
49 K3 **Lochgoilhead** Ag & B
63 G5 **Lochinver** Highld
41 L4 **Lochmaben** D & G
62 d8 **Lochmaddy** W Isls
62 d8 **Loch nam Madadh** W Isls
44 D3 **Lochranza** N Ayrs
45 G2 **Lochwinnoch** Rens
41 L4 **Lockerbie** D & G
39 H4 **Lockton** N York
25 K6 **Loddon** Norfk
38 B6 **Lofthouse** N York
39 G2 **Loftus** R & Cl
15 J5 **London** Gt Lon
15 J4 **London Colney** Herts
12 F4 **Long Ashton** N Som
30 E5 **Long Bennington** Lincs
23 G4 **Long Buckby** Nhants
7 J1 **Longburton** Dorset
22 D6 **Long Compton** Warwks
14 E3 **Long Crendon** Bucks
30 B6 **Long Eaton** Derbys
21 M7 **Longford** Gloucs
47 G4 **Longformacus** Border
43 J2 **Longframlington** Nthumb
8 B6 **Longham** Dorset
43 J3 **Longhorsley** Nthumb
47 M7 **Longhoughton** Nthumb
22 E4 **Long Itchington** Warwks
22 F3 **Long Lawford** Warwks
34 C2 **Long Marston** N York
17 G3 **Long Melford** Suffk
46 E3 **Longniddry** E Loth
21 J1 **Longnor** Shrops
29 H4 **Longnor** Staffs
37 L7 **Long Preston** N York
32 F3 **Longridge** Lancs
45 M2 **Longridge** W Loth
61 G5 **Longside** Abers
25 J6 **Long Stratton** Norfk
31 K7 **Long Sutton** Lincs
12 F8 **Long Sutton** Somset
32 D4 **Longton** Lancs
42 B5 **Longtown** Cumb
21 J2 **Longville in the Dale** Shrops
3 H5 **Looe** Cnwll
59 K3 **Lossiemouth** Moray
3 G5 **Lostwithiel** Cnwll
30 B7 **Loughborough** Leics
31 J2 **Louth** Lincs
30 D5 **Lowdham** Notts
57 H4 **Lower Diabaig** Highld
10 D6 **Lower Dicker** E Susx
28 E3 **Lower Peover** Ches E
22 C7 **Lower Swell** Gloucs
25 M6 **Lowestoft** Suffk
36 E2 **Loweswater** Cumb
23 K3 **Lowick** Nhants
47 K5 **Lowick** Nthumb
37 M4 **Low Row** N York
23 H2 **Lubenham** Leics
35 J7 **Ludborough** Lincs
8 D2 **Ludgershall** Wilts
25 K4 **Ludham** Norfk
21 J3 **Ludlow** Shrops
45 H3 **Lugton** E Ayrs
21 J6 **Lugwardine** Herefs
55 J4 **Lumphanan** Abers
55 H3 **Lumsden** Abers
51 L2 **Lunan** Angus
37 H5 **Lupton** Cumb
49 L4 **Luss** Ag & B
56 C4 **Lusta** Highld
15 H2 **Luton** Luton
22 F2 **Lutterworth** Leics
65 H4 **Lybster** Highld
21 H2 **Lydbury North** Shrops
11 H6 **Lydd** Kent
3 L3 **Lydford** Devon
12 F7 **Lydford on Fosse** Somset
21 G2 **Lydham** Shrops
13 G2 **Lydney** Gloucs
7 G3 **Lyme Regis** Dorset
11 J4 **Lyminge** Kent
8 D6 **Lymington** Hants
28 E2 **Lymm** Warrtn
11 J5 **Lympne** Kent
8 D5 **Lyndhurst** Hants
13 K4 **Lyneham** Wilts
65 b5 **Lyness** Ork
12 E7 **Lyng** Somset
5 G3 **Lynmouth** Devon
4 F3 **Lynton** Devon
21 G5 **Lyonshall** Herefs
32 C4 **Lytham St Anne's** Lancs
39 H3 **Lythe** N York

M

31 K2 **Mablethorpe** Lincs
28 F3 **Macclesfield** Ches E
60 E3 **Macduff** Abers
44 A5 **Machrihanish** Ag & B
20 C1 **Machynlleth** Powys
46 E3 **Macmerry** E Loth
26 F5 **Maentwrog** Gwynd
12 B2 **Maerdy** Rhondd
19 L7 **Maesteg** Brdgnd
32 D6 **Maghull** Sefton
13 H7 **Maiden Bradley** Wilts
6 C5 **Maidencombe** Torbay
14 F5 **Maidenhead** W & M
7 J3 **Maiden Newton** Dorset
10 F3 **Maidstone** Kent
41 K6 **Mainsriddle** D & G
6 A7 **Malborough** Devon
17 G6 **Maldon** Essex
37 L6 **Malham** N York
52 D2 **Mallaig** Highld
27 G8 **Mallwyd** Gwynd
13 J3 **Malmesbury** Wilts
28 C5 **Malpas** Ches W
34 C7 **Maltby** Rothm
39 G6 **Malton** N York
21 L6 **Malvern Wells** Worcs
2 D7 **Manaccan** Cnwll
33 G6 **Manchester** Manch
24 C6 **Manea** Cambs
17 J4 **Manningtree** Essex
18 D6 **Manorbier** Pembks
30 B4 **Mansfield** Notts
2 E5 **Marazanvose** Cnwll
2 B7 **Marazion** Cnwll
24 B6 **March** Cambs
28 B5 **Marchwiel** Wrexhm
10 F4 **Marden** Kent
31 J4 **Mareham le Fen** Lincs
16 E6 **Margaretting** Essex
11 L2 **Margate** Kent
12 E6 **Mark** Somset
10 E5 **Mark Cross** E Susx
22 E1 **Market Bosworth** Leics
31 G8 **Market Deeping** Lincs
28 D6 **Market Drayton** Shrops
23 H2 **Market Harborough** Leics
13 K6 **Market Lavington** Wilts
35 H7 **Market Rasen** Lincs
30 C3 **Market Warsop** Notts
34 F3 **Market Weighton** E R Yk
30 B8 **Markfield** Leics
30 D3 **Markham Moor** Notts
13 G5 **Marksbury** BaNES
17 G5 **Marks Tey** Essex
13 M4 **Marlborough** Wilts
18 B5 **Marloes** Pembks
14 F5 **Marlow** Bucks
7 K1 **Marnhull** Dorset
13 H4 **Marshfield** S Glos
14 D2 **Marsh Gibbon** Bucks
38 F2 **Marske-by-the-Sea** R & Cl
31 G4 **Martin** Lincs
7 J3 **Martinstown** Dorset
17 K3 **Martlesham Heath** Suffk
7 H1 **Martock** Somset
22 E4 **Marton** Warwks
55 K7 **Marykirk** Abers
41 K7 **Maryport** Cumb
3 L3 **Mary Tavy** Devon
55 J5 **Marywell** Abers
38 C5 **Masham** N York
10 E4 **Matfield** Kent
29 K4 **Matlock** Derbys
14 E7 **Mattingley** Hants
45 H5 **Mauchline** E Ayrs
60 F4 **Maud** Abers
36 d2 **Maughold** IoM
23 K6 **Maulden** C Beds
2 E4 **Mawgan Porth** Cnwll
2 D7 **Mawnan Smith** Cnwll
45 G6 **Maybole** S Ayrs
10 E5 **Mayfield** E Susx
29 H5 **Mayfield** Staffs
12 F6 **Meare** Somset
29 K8 **Measham** Leics
9 G3 **Medstead** Hants
4 E6 **Meeth** Devon
27 K8 **Meifod** Powys
51 H3 **Meigle** P & K
16 C3 **Melbourn** Cambs
29 K7 **Melbourne** Derbys
27 J2 **Meliden** Denbgs
13 J5 **Melksham** Wilts
37 J6 **Melling** Lancs
42 D7 **Melmerby** Cumb
46 F6 **Melrose** Border
33 K5 **Meltham** Kirk
34 F4 **Melton** E R Yk
25 H3 **Melton Constable** Norfk
30 D7 **Melton Mowbray** Leics
57 G2 **Melvaig** Highld
64 E2 **Melvich** Highld
61 G3 **Memsie** Abers
51 J2 **Memus** Angus
26 E3 **Menai Bridge** IoA
14 F2 **Mentmore** Bucks
10 E2 **Meopham** Kent
13 H7 **Mere** Wilts
22 D3 **Meriden** Solhll
12 B2 **Merthyr Tydfil** Myr Td
4 E6 **Merton** Devon
34 F6 **Messingham** N Linc
25 K7 **Metfield** Suffk
51 J6 **Methil** Fife
60 F5 **Methlick** Abers
50 F4 **Methven** P & K
24 E6 **Methwold** Norfk
2 F6 **Mevagissey** Cnwll
34 B6 **Mexborough** Donc
62 f3 **Miabhig** W Isls
62 f3 **Miavaig** W Isls
8 F2 **Micheldever** Hants
37 M2 **Mickleton** Dur
22 C6 **Mickleton** Gloucs
65 c2 **Midbea** Ork
38 B4 **Middleham** N York
35 G7 **Middle Rasen** Lincs
38 E2 **Middlesbrough** Middsb
22 F6 **Middleton Cheney** Nhants
37 M2 **Middleton-in-Teesdale** Dur
9 J5 **Middleton-on-Sea** W Susx
34 F2 **Middleton on the Wolds** E R Yk
14 C2 **Middleton Stoney** Oxon
2 a2 **Middle Town** IoS
8 D3 **Middle Wallop** Hants
28 E3 **Middlewich** Ches E
12 E7 **Middlezoy** Somset
9 J4 **Midhurst** W Susx
13 G6 **Midsomer Norton** BaNES
61 d2 **Mid Yell** Shet
7 J1 **Milborne Port** Somset
24 E7 **Mildenhall** Suffk
47 J6 **Milfield** Nthumb
18 C5 **Milford Haven** Pembks
8 D6 **Milford on Sea** Hants
3 K5 **Millbrook** Cnwll
7 b2 **Millbrook** Jersey
36 E5 **Millom** Cumb
44 F3 **Millport** N Ayrs
50 F6 **Milnathort** P & K
45 J1 **Milngavie** E Duns
7 K2 **Milton Abbas** Dorset
3 K3 **Milton Abbot** Devon
4 D6 **Milton Damerel** Devon
23 K5 **Milton Ernest** Bed
23 J6 **Milton Keynes** M Keyn
5 K5 **Milverton** Somset
13 J2 **Minchinhampton** Gloucs
5 J3 **Minehead** Somset
11 H2 **Minster** Kent
11 L2 **Minster** Kent
28 B8 **Minsterley** Shrops
14 A3 **Minster Lovell** Oxon
61 G4 **Mintlaw** Abers
33 K5 **Mirfield** Kirk
34 E7 **Misterton** Notts
7 H2 **Misterton** Somset
21 K7 **Mitcheldean** Gloucs
28 E2 **Mobberley** Ches E
40 E6 **Mochrum** D & G
3 M5 **Modbury** Devon
41 L2 **Moffat** D & G
27 K4 **Mold** Flints
41 H3 **Moniaive** D & G
51 K4 **Monifieth** Angus
4 D5 **Monkleigh** Devon
45 G5 **Monkton** S Ayrs
21 J8 **Monmouth** Mons
7 H1 **Montacute** Somset
28 B7 **Montford Bridge** Shrops
20 F1 **Montgomery** Powys
51 L2 **Montrose** Angus
6 a2 **Mont Saint** Guern
29 H3 **Monyash** Derbys
55 K3 **Monymusk** Abers
5 G6 **Morchard Bishop** Devon
23 J1 **Morcott** Rutlnd
21 J6 **Mordiford** Herefs
47 H7 **Morebattle** Border
37 G6 **Morecambe** Lancs
7 K3 **Moreton** Dorset
6 B3 **Moretonhampstead** Devon
22 C6 **Moreton-in-Marsh** Gloucs
26 B5 **Morfa Nefyn** Gwynd
33 L4 **Morley** Leeds
43 J3 **Morpeth** Nthumb
25 G2 **Morston** Norfk
4 D3 **Mortehoe** Devon
14 D7 **Mortimer** W Berk
21 K2 **Morville** Shrops
4 B5 **Morwenstow** Cnwll
55 H3 **Mossat** Abers
59 L4 **Mosstodloch** Moray
7 H2 **Mosterton** Dorset
27 K2 **Mostyn** Flints
37 G1 **Motherby** Cumb
45 K3 **Motherwell** N Lans
14 D5 **Moulsford** Oxon
23 H4 **Moulton** Nhants
12 B2 **Mountain Ash** Rhondd
30 C7 **Mountsorrel** Leics
2 B7 **Mousehole** Cnwll
58 F5 **Moy** Highld
55 M5 **Muchalls** Abers
21 J7 **Much Birch** Herefs
16 C5 **Much Hadham** Herts
21 K6 **Much Marcle** Herefs

21 K1 **Much Wenlock** Shrops
4 E4 **Muddiford** Devon
51 K3 **Muirdrum** Angus
51 H4 **Muirhead** Angus
45 K5 **Muirkirk** E Ayrs
58 D4 **Muir of Ord** Highld
37 L4 **Muker** N York
2 D8 **Mullion** Cnwll
25 K3 **Mundesley** Norfk
24 E6 **Mundford** Norfk
42 B8 **Mungrisdale** Cumb
58 E4 **Munlochy** Highld
21 J2 **Munslow** Shrops
46 D3 **Musselburgh** E Loth
50 D5 **Muthill** P & K

N

17 K4 **Nacton** Suffk
12 F4 **Nailsea** N Som
13 J2 **Nailsworth** Gloucs
59 G4 **Nairn** Highld
19 H4 **Nantgaredig** Carmth
28 D5 **Nantwich** Ches E
18 E5 **Narberth** Pembks
24 E4 **Narborough** Norfk
23 G3 **Naseby** Nhants
30 F4 **Navenby** Lincs
17 H4 **Nayland** Suffk
16 C6 **Nazeing** Essex
19 K6 **Neath** Neath
24 F5 **Necton** Norfk
17 J2 **Needham Market** Suffk
26 C5 **Nefyn** Gwynd
33 H3 **Nelson** Lancs
28 B7 **Nesscliffe** Shrops
27 L3 **Neston** Ches W
12 C7 **Nether Stowey** Somset
36 E3 **Nether Wasdale** Cumb
54 D3 **Nethy Bridge** Highld
14 E5 **Nettlebed** Oxon
18 E3 **Nevern** Pembks
41 K5 **New Abbey** D & G
60 F3 **New Aberdour** Abers
8 F3 **New Alresford** Hants
30 E4 **Newark-on-Trent** Notts
45 L2 **Newarthill** N Lans
37 L1 **Newbiggin** Dur
38 A5 **Newbiggin** N York
43 K3 **Newbiggin-by-the-Sea** Nthumb
46 A5 **Newbigging** S Lans
22 D5 **Newbold on Stour** Warwks
31 J4 **New Bolingbroke** Lincs
26 D4 **Newborough** IoA
12 C2 **Newbridge** Caerph
41 K4 **Newbridge** D & G
20 E4 **Newbridge on Wye** Powys
25 H6 **New Buckenham** Norfk
61 G6 **Newburgh** Abers
51 G5 **Newburgh** Fife
14 C6 **Newbury** W Berk
37 G5 **Newby Bridge** Cumb
18 F3 **Newcastle Emlyn** Carmth
42 C3 **Newcastleton** Border
28 F5 **Newcastle-under-Lyme** Staffs
43 K5 **Newcastle upon Tyne** N u Ty
45 J6 **New Cumnock** E Ayrs
60 F5 **New Deer** Abers
21 L7 **Newent** Gloucs
18 C4 **Newgale** Pembks
41 G4 **New Galloway** D & G
2 a1 **New Grimsby** IoS
10 C7 **Newhaven** E Susx
35 G4 **New Holland** N Linc
10 C6 **Newick** E Susx
40 C5 **New Luce** D & G
2 B7 **Newlyn** Cnwll
45 L3 **Newmains** N Lans
16 E2 **Newmarket** Suffk
60 B4 **Newmill** Moray
8 C6 **New Milton** Hants
13 G1 **Newnham** Gloucs
21 K4 **Newnham** Worcs
60 F4 **New Pitsligo** Abers
16 D4 **Newport** Essex

8 E6 **Newport** IoW
12 D3 **Newport** Newpt
18 D3 **Newport** Pembks
28 E7 **Newport** Wrekin
51 J4 **Newport-on-Tay** Fife
23 J6 **Newport Pagnell** M Keyn
19 G1 **New Quay** Cerdgn
2 E5 **Newquay** Cnwll
20 F4 **New Radnor** Powys
11 H5 **New Romney** Kent
38 B3 **Newsham** N York
6 C5 **Newton Abbot** Devon
38 C2 **Newton Aycliffe** Dur
3 L6 **Newton Ferrers** Devon
62 d8 **Newton Ferry** W Isls
46 D4 **Newtongrange** Mdloth
45 J3 **Newton Mearns** E Rens
54 B4 **Newtonmore** Highld
43 J2 **Newton-on-the-Moor** Nthumb
30 E3 **Newton on Trent** Lincs
6 C3 **Newton St Cyres** Devon
29 J7 **Newton Solney** Derbys
40 E5 **Newton Stewart** D & G
21 K5 **Newtown** Herefs
20 F2 **Newtown** Powys
12 C2 **New Tredegar** Caerph
51 H3 **Newtyle** Angus
18 D5 **Neyland** Pembks
59 G3 **Nigg** Highld
10 E6 **Ninfield** E Susx
8 F7 **Niton** IoW
31 G4 **Nocton** Lincs
47 J5 **Norham** Nthumb
34 B4 **Normanton** Wakefd
15 G2 **Northall** Bucks
38 D4 **Northallerton** N York
4 D4 **Northam** Devon
23 H4 **Northampton** Nhants
46 F2 **North Berwick** E Loth
34 F4 **North Cave** E R Yk
9 J3 **Northchapel** W Susx
7 G3 **North Chideock** Dorset
35 K6 **North Cotes** Lincs
24 F3 **North Creake** Norfk
12 D8 **North Curry** Somset
34 F2 **North Dalton** E R Yk
25 G4 **North Elmham** Norfk
35 G4 **North Ferriby** E R Yk
35 H2 **North Frodingham** E R Yk
39 H6 **North Grimston** N York
9 G5 **North Hayling** Hants
30 F3 **North Hykeham** Lincs
11 G6 **Northiam** E Susx
58 F4 **North Kessock** Highld
23 G3 **North Kilworth** Leics
31 H4 **North Kyme** Lincs
22 C8 **Northleach** Gloucs
23 J1 **North Luffenham** Rutlnd
5 G4 **North Molton** Devon
30 E4 **North Muskham** Notts
27 K3 **Northop** Flints
12 D7 **North Petherton** Somset
33 L2 **North Rigton** N York
43 K5 **North Shields** N York
35 K6 **North Somercotes** Lincs
25 J3 **North Walsham** Norfk
8 F2 **North Waltham** Hants
16 D6 **North Weald Bassett** Essex
28 D3 **Northwich** Ches W
29 K4 **North Wingfield** Derbys
24 E6 **Northwold** Norfk
39 G6 **Norton** N York
15 H5 **Norton St Philip** Somset
25 J5 **Norwich** Norfk
30 C5 **Nottingham** C Nott
22 E2 **Nuneaton** Warwks
13 H6 **Nunney** Somset
10 C5 **Nutley** E Susx

O

23 G1 **Oadby** Leics
30 E8 **Oakham** Rutlnd
13 G6 **Oakhill** Somset
23 K5 **Oakley** Bed
14 D3 **Oakley** Bucks
8 F2 **Oakley** Hants
13 L5 **Oare** Wilts
52 F7 **Oban** Ag & B
45 H5 **Ochiltree** E Ayrs
29 L6 **Ockbrook** Derbys
9 L2 **Ockley** Surrey
9 G2 **Odiham** Hants
22 B5 **Offenham** Worcs
13 M4 **Ogbourne St George** Wilts
19 L8 **Ogmore-by-Sea** V Glam
4 E7 **Okehampton** Devon
61 G4 **Old Deer** Abers
2 a1 **Old Grimsby** IoS
33 H6 **Oldham** Oldham
24 A7 **Old Hurst** Cambs
31 K5 **Old Leake** Lincs
60 F6 **Oldmeldrum** Abers
60 D6 **Old Rayne** Abers
13 H3 **Old Sodbury** S Glos
23 H6 **Old Stratford** Nhants
2 b2 **Old Town** IoS
15 G6 **Old Windsor** W & M
61 b3 **Ollaberry** Shet
30 C3 **Ollerton** Notts
23 J5 **Olney** M Keyn
21 M4 **Ombersley** Worcs
36 C3 **Onchan** IoM
53 G5 **Onich** Highld
17 L3 **Orford** Suffk
25 L4 **Ormesby St Margaret** Norfk
32 D6 **Ormskirk** Lancs
10 D2 **Orpington** Gt Lon
10 E1 **Orsett** Thurr
37 J3 **Orton** Cumb
31 G6 **Osbournby** Lincs
7 K4 **Osmington** Dorset
38 E4 **Osmotherley** N York
11 H3 **Ospringe** Kent
33 L5 **Ossett** Wakefd
38 F5 **Oswaldkirk** N York
27 L6 **Oswestry** Shrops
10 D3 **Otford** Kent
12 E7 **Othery** Somset
33 K3 **Otley** Leeds
8 E4 **Otterbourne** Hants
43 G3 **Otterburn** Nthumb
49 H5 **Otter Ferry** Ag & B
15 G7 **Ottershaw** Surrey
6 E4 **Otterton** Devon
6 E3 **Ottery St Mary** Devon
23 K2 **Oundle** Nhants
24 C5 **Outwell** Norfk
29 K7 **Overseal** Derbys
8 F2 **Overton** Hants
28 B5 **Overton** Wrexhm
8 D4 **Ower** Hants
14 C3 **Oxford** Oxon
10 C3 **Oxted** Surrey
30 C5 **Oxton** Notts
19 H7 **Oxwich** Swans

P

23 H7 **Padbury** Bucks
10 E4 **Paddock Wood** Kent
33 G4 **Padiham** Lancs
2 F4 **Padstow** Cnwll
6 C5 **Paignton** Torbay
22 F3 **Pailton** Warwks
13 J1 **Painswick** Gloucs
45 H2 **Paisley** Rens
41 J6 **Palnackie** D & G
21 G7 **Pandy** Mons
14 D6 **Pangbourne** W Berk
33 L2 **Pannal** N York
20 E3 **Pant-y-dwr** Powys
16 B2 **Papworth Everard** Cambs
4 F3 **Parracombe** Devon
38 B6 **Pateley Bridge** N York
45 H6 **Patna** E Ayrs
36 b3 **Patrick** IoM
35 J4 **Patrington** E R Yk
37 G2 **Patterdale** Cumb
23 G5 **Pattishall** Nhants
10 C7 **Peacehaven** E Susx

13 H5 **Peasedown St John** BaNES
11 G6 **Peasmarsh** E Susx
46 C5 **Peebles** Border
36 b3 **Peel** IoM
3 H5 **Pelynt** Cnwll
19 G6 **Pembrey** Carmth
21 H4 **Pembridge** Herefs
18 D6 **Pembroke** Pembks
18 D6 **Pembroke Dock** Pembks
10 E4 **Pembury** Kent
18 E6 **Penally** Pembks
12 C4 **Penarth** V Glam
12 A3 **Pencoed** Brdgnd
21 J7 **Pencraig** Herefs
18 F5 **Pendine** Carmth
21 L6 **Pendock** Worcs
3 G3 **Pendoggett** Cnwll
12 C2 **Pengam** Caerph
46 C4 **Penicuik** Mdloth
33 L6 **Penistone** Barns
29 G7 **Penkridge** Staffs
27 G5 **Penmachno** Conwy
26 F3 **Penmaenmawr** Conwy
20 B1 **Pennal** Gwynd
60 F3 **Pennan** Abers
41 J3 **Penpont** D & G
26 E6 **Penrhyndeudraeth** Gwynd
42 D8 **Penrith** Cumb
2 E7 **Penryn** Cnwll
13 G5 **Pensford** BaNES
10 D4 **Penshurst** Kent
3 J4 **Pensilva** Cnwll
2 F6 **Pentewan** Cnwll
26 D3 **Pentraeth** IoA
27 G5 **Pentrefoelas** Conwy
20 F4 **Penybont** Powys
27 J7 **Pen-y-bont-fawr** Powys
26 D4 **Penygroes** Gwynd
2 B7 **Penzance** Cnwll
2 D5 **Perranporth** Cnwll
22 A5 **Pershore** Worcs
50 F4 **Perth** P & K
23 M1 **Peterborough** C Pete
21 H6 **Peterchurch** Herefs
55 L4 **Peterculter** C Aber
61 H5 **Peterhead** Abers
43 L7 **Peterlee** Dur
9 H4 **Petersfield** Hants
5 J4 **Petton** Devon
10 E7 **Petworth** W Susx
10 E7 **Pevensey** E Susx
13 L5 **Pewsey** Wilts
39 G5 **Pickering** N York
38 C2 **Piercebridge** Darltn
65 c1 **Pierowall** Ork
3 J4 **Pillaton** Cnwll
22 D5 **Pillerton Priors** Warwks
32 D3 **Pilling** Lancs
31 H7 **Pinchbeck** Lincs
40 C3 **Pinwherry** S Ayrs
29 L4 **Pinxton** Derbys
15 G7 **Pirbright** Surrey
60 E6 **Pitcaple** Abers
50 E2 **Pitlochry** P & K
60 F6 **Pitmedden** Abers
51 K6 **Pittenweem** Fife
30 B4 **Pleasley** Derbys
57 H6 **Plockton** Highld
11 G4 **Pluckley** Kent
10 C6 **Plumpton** E Susx
30 C6 **Plumtree** Notts
3 K5 **Plymouth** C Plym
3 L5 **Plympton** C Plym
34 E2 **Pocklington** E R Yk
3 J5 **Polbathic** Cnwll
10 D7 **Polegate** E Susx
50 E8 **Polmont** Falk
3 H5 **Polperro** Cnwll
3 G5 **Polruan** Cnwll
2 F3 **Polzeath** Cnwll
19 K6 **Pontardawe** Neath
19 J6 **Pontarddulais** Swans
34 B5 **Pontefract** Wakefd
43 J4 **Ponteland** Nthumb
20 C3 **Ponterwyd** Cerdgn
28 B8 **Pontesbury** Shrops
12 C2 **Pontllanfraith** Caerph
19 K1 **Pontrhydfendigaid** Cerdgn
21 H7 **Pontrilas** Herefs
19 H5 **Pontyates** Carmth
19 H5 **Pontyberem** Carmth
12 D2 **Pontypool** Torfn
12 B3 **Pontypridd** Rhondd

33 L3 **Pool** Leeds
8 A6 **Poole** Poole
57 H2 **Poolewe** Highld
37 H2 **Pooley Bridge** Cumb
5 H3 **Porlock** Somset
5 H3 **Porlock Weir** Somset
52 F6 **Port Appin** Ag & B
48 D6 **Port Askaig** Ag & B
49 H6 **Portavadie** Ag & B
49 J6 **Port Bannatyne** Ag & B
42 A5 **Port Carlisle** Cumb
48 B7 **Port Charlotte** Ag & B
8 F5 **Portchester** Hants
19 H7 **Port Einon** Swans
48 C8 **Port Ellen** Ag & B
36 a4 **Port Erin** IoM
7 J3 **Portesham** Dorset
49 L5 **Port Glasgow** Inver
60 B3 **Portgordon** Moray
12 B3 **Porth** Rhondd
19 L8 **Porthcawl** Brdgnd
2 E4 **Porthcothan** Cnwll
2 A8 **Porthcurno** Cnwll
57 G3 **Port Henderson** Highld
2 C7 **Porthleven** Cnwll
26 E6 **Porthmadog** Gwynd
2 D6 **Porthtowan** Cnwll
36 F2 **Portinscale** Cumb
2 F3 **Port Isaac** Cnwll
12 F4 **Portishead** N Som
60 C3 **Portknockie** Moray
55 M5 **Portlethen** Abers
2 F6 **Portloe** Cnwll
40 C7 **Port Logan** D & G
59 H2 **Portmahomack** Highld
53 G6 **Portnacroish** Ag & B
48 A7 **Portnahaven** Ag & B
62 d8 **Port nan Long** W Isls
62 i1 **Port Nis** W Isls
50 B6 **Port of Menteith** Stirlg
62 i1 **Port of Ness** W Isls
40 B6 **Portpatrick** D & G
2 C6 **Portreath** Cnwll
56 E5 **Portree** Highld
36 a4 **Port St Mary** IoM
2 E7 **Portscatho** Cnwll
64 E2 **Portskerra** Highld
10 B7 **Portslade-by-Sea** Br & H
9 G5 **Portsmouth** C Port
60 D3 **Portsoy** Abers
19 K7 **Port Talbot** Neath
40 E7 **Port William** D & G
3 M3 **Postbridge** Devon
14 E4 **Postcombe** Oxon
13 K5 **Potterne** Wilts
15 J4 **Potters Bar** Herts
16 B3 **Potton** C Beds
32 C3 **Poulton-le-Fylde** Lancs
47 K7 **Powburn** Nthumb
21 M5 **Powick** Worcs
28 F2 **Poynton** Ches E
2 C7 **Praa Sands** Cnwll
28 C6 **Prees** Shrops
32 D3 **Preesall** Lancs
28 C6 **Prees Green** Shrops
26 E5 **Prenteg** Gwynd
27 J2 **Prestatyn** Denbgs
28 F3 **Prestbury** Ches E
21 G4 **Presteigne** Powys
47 H4 **Preston** Border
32 E4 **Preston** Lancs
8 F2 **Preston Candover** Hants
22 F5 **Preston Capes** Nhants
46 E3 **Prestonpans** E Loth
33 G6 **Prestwich** Bury
45 G5 **Prestwick** S Ayrs
12 F6 **Priddy** Somset
14 F4 **Princes Risborough** Bucks
22 E3 **Princethorpe** Warwks
3 L4 **Princetown** Devon
41 L7 **Prospect** Cumb
43 H5 **Prudhoe** Nthumb
13 H4 **Pucklechurch** S Glos
7 K3 **Puddletown** Dorset
33 L4 **Pudsey** Leeds
9 K4 **Pulborough** W Susx
28 B4 **Pulford** Ches W
25 J7 **Pulham St Mary** Norfk
19 J3 **Pumsaint** Carmth
10 D1 **Purfleet** Thurr
13 L3 **Purton** Wilts
19 H6 **Pwll** Carmth
26 C6 **Pwllheli** Gwynd
10 B6 **Pyecombe** W Susx
19 L7 **Pyle** Brdgnd

Q

21 L2 **Quatt** Shrops
27 L3 **Queensferry** Flints
16 D4 **Quendon** Essex

R

5 H5 **Rackenford** Devon
25 J4 **Rackheath** Norfk
30 C6 **Radcliffe on Trent** Notts
15 H4 **Radlett** Herts
13 G5 **Radstock** BaNES
16 E4 **Radwinter** Essex
12 C4 **Radyr** Cardif
59 J4 **Rafford** Moray
12 E1 **Raglan** Mons
10 D1 **Rainham** Gt Lon
36 F6 **Rampside** Cumb
14 A6 **Ramsbury** Wilts
24 A7 **Ramsey** Cambs
36 c2 **Ramsey** IoM
11 L2 **Ramsgate** Kent
53 L5 **Rannoch Station** P & K
65 c2 **Rapness** Ork
61 G3 **Rathen** Abers
23 K3 **Raunds** Nhants
36 E4 **Ravenglass** Cumb
39 J3 **Ravenscar** N York
37 K3 **Ravenstonedale** Cumb
34 B7 **Rawmarsh** Rothm
33 G4 **Rawtenstall** Lancs
16 F7 **Rayleigh** Essex
14 E6 **Reading** Readg
64 F2 **Reay** Highld
11 K2 **Reculver** Kent
15 H3 **Redbourn** Herts
12 F1 **Redbrook** Gloucs
28 C5 **Redbrook** Wrexhm
38 F2 **Redcar** R & Cl
22 B4 **Redditch** Worcs
25 G7 **Redgrave** Suffk
12 F5 **Redhill** N Som
10 B4 **Redhill** Surrey
30 E6 **Redmile** Leics
28 B6 **Rednal** Shrops
18 F5 **Red Roses** Carmth
43 K2 **Red Row** Nthumb
2 D6 **Redruth** Cnwll
26 D2 **Red Wharf Bay** IoA
25 L5 **Reedham** Norfk
25 H4 **Reepham** Norfk
10 B4 **Reigate** Surrey
39 K5 **Reighton** N York
30 C7 **Rempstone** Notts
45 H2 **Renfrew** Rens
42 D7 **Renwick** Cumb
29 K6 **Repton** Derbys
19 L6 **Resolven** Neath
30 D2 **Retford** Notts
19 H7 **Reynoldston** Swans
20 D4 **Rhayader** Powys
63 H3 **Rhiconich** Highld
5 J2 **Rhoose** V Glam
27 L5 **Rhosllanerchrugog** Wrexhm
26 C3 **Rhosneigr** IoA
27 G2 **Rhôs-on-Sea** Conwy
19 G7 **Rhossili** Swans
49 L5 **Rhu** Ag & B
27 J3 **Rhuddlan** Denbgs
26 E4 **Rhyd-Ddu** Gwynd
19 G2 **Rhydowen** Cerdgn
27 H2 **Rhyl** Denbgs
12 C1 **Rhymney** Caerph
21 J4 **Richards Castle** Herefs
15 J6 **Richmond** Gt Lon
38 B3 **Richmond** N York
15 H4 **Rickmansworth** Herts
43 H5 **Riding Mill** Nthumb
43 G4 **Ridsdale** Nthumb
39 H5 **Rillington** N York
41 G6 **Ringford** D & G
10 C6 **Ringmer** E Susx
8 C5 **Ringwood** Hants
29 K5 **Ripley** Derbys
38 C7 **Ripley** N York
15 H7 **Ripley** Surrey
38 D6 **Ripon** N York
21 M6 **Ripple** Worcs
33 J5 **Ripponden** Calder
12 D3 **Risca** Caerph
31 H6 **Risegate** Lincs
23 K4 **Riseley** Bed
14 E7 **Riseley** Wokham
29 L6 **Risley** Derbys
32 F7 **Risley** Warrtn
23 H5 **Roade** Nhants
46 E7 **Roberton** Border
45 M5 **Roberton** S Lans
10 F6 **Robertsbridge** E Susx
18 E5 **Robeston Wathen** Pembks
39 J3 **Robin Hood's Bay** N York
29 H6 **Rocester** Staffs
18 C4 **Roch** Pembks
33 H5 **Rochdale** Rochdl
2 F5 **Roche** Cnwll
10 F2 **Rochester** Medway
42 F3 **Rochester** Nthumb
17 G7 **Rochford** Essex
2 F3 **Rock** Cnwll
42 B5 **Rockcliffe** Cumb
41 J6 **Rockcliffe** D & G
23 J2 **Rockingham** Nhants
9 H4 **Rogate** W Susx
12 D3 **Rogerstone** Newpt
25 L4 **Rollesby** Norfk
11 G5 **Rolvenden** Kent
37 M2 **Romaldkirk** Dur
46 C5 **Romanno Bridge** Border
16 D7 **Romford** Gt Lon
8 D4 **Romsey** Hants
43 G7 **Rookhope** Dur
9 G3 **Ropley** Hants
39 G4 **Rosedale Abbey** N York
63 K7 **Rosehall** Highld
61 G3 **Rosehearty** Abers
58 F4 **Rosemarkie** Highld
46 D4 **Rosewell** Mdloth
28 B4 **Rossett** Wrexhm
21 K7 **Ross-on-Wye** Herefs
46 B2 **Rosyth** Fife
43 H2 **Rothbury** Nthumb
10 D5 **Rotherfield** E Susx
34 B7 **Rotherham** Rothm
59 L4 **Rothes** Moray
49 J6 **Rothesay** Ag & B
33 M4 **Rothwell** Leeds
23 H3 **Rothwell** Nhants
10 C7 **Rottingdean** Br & H
25 J3 **Roughton** Norfk
9 G5 **Rowland's Castle** Hants
43 J6 **Rowland's Gill** Gatesd
29 J3 **Rowsley** Derbys
47 G6 **Roxburgh** Border
16 E6 **Roxwell** Essex
34 A5 **Royston** Barns
16 C4 **Royston** Herts
7 c1 **Rozel** Jersey
27 L5 **Ruabon** Wrexhm
30 C6 **Ruddington** Notts
9 K3 **Rudgwick** W Susx
39 K6 **Rudston** E R Yk
32 D5 **Rufford** Lancs
22 F3 **Rugby** Warwks
29 G7 **Rugeley** Staffs
50 F6 **Rumbling Bridge** P & K
28 C2 **Runcorn** Halton
23 K4 **Rushden** Nhants
38 C1 **Rushyford** Dur
31 G5 **Ruskington** Lincs
9 K5 **Rustington** W Susx
39 H3 **Ruswarp** N York
45 J2 **Rutherglen** S Lans
27 J4 **Ruthin** Denbgs
28 B7 **Ruyton-XI-Towns** Shrops
37 G3 **Rydal** Cumb
8 F6 **Ryde** IoW
11 G6 **Rye** E Susx

S

44 B5 **Saddell** Ag & B
16 D4 **Saffron Walden** Essex
47 J3 **St Abbs** Border
2 D5 **St Agnes** Cnwll
15 H3 **St Albans** Herts
6 a2 **St Andrew** Guern
51 K5 **St Andrews** Fife
12 F2 **St Arvans** Mons
27 J3 **St Asaph** Denbgs
5 J1 **St Athan** V Glam
7 b2 **St Aubin** Jersey
2 F5 **St Austell** Cnwll
36 D3 **St Bees** Cumb
3 G5 **St Blazey** Cnwll
46 F6 **St Boswells** Border
7 a2 **St Brelade** Jersey
7 a2 **St Brelade's Bay** Jersey
12 F2 **St Briavels** Gloucs
2 A7 **St Buryan** Cnwll
49 J3 **St Catherines** Ag & B
18 F5 **St Clears** Carmth
3 H4 **St Cleer** Cnwll
7 c2 **St Clement** Jersey
2 F4 **St Columb Major** Cnwll
61 H3 **St Combs** Abers
55 K7 **St Cyrus** Abers
18 B4 **St David's** Pembks
2 D6 **St Day** Cnwll
18 E2 **St Dogmaels** Pembks
61 H4 **St Fergus** Abers
50 C4 **St Fillans** P & K
18 E6 **St Florence** Pembks
9 G6 **St Helens** IoW
32 E7 **St Helens** St Hel
7 b2 **St Helier** Jersey
24 A8 **St Ives** Cambs
2 B6 **St Ives** Cnwll
7 b1 **St John** Jersey
36 b3 **St John's** IoM
43 G7 **St John's Chapel** Dur
41 G4 **St John's Town of Dalry** D & G
36 c2 **St Jude's** IoM
2 A7 **St Just** Cnwll
2 E7 **St Just-in-Roseland** Cnwll
2 E8 **St Keverne** Cnwll
3 H5 **St Keyne** Cnwll
8 F7 **St Lawrence** IoW
7 b1 **St Lawrence** Jersey
11 L4 **St Margaret's at Cliffe** Kent
65 c5 **St Margaret's Hope** Ork
36 b3 **St Marks** IoM
6 b2 **St Martin** Guern
7 c1 **St Martin** Jersey
7 b1 **St Mary** Jersey
65 c4 **St Mary's** Ork
11 J5 **St Mary's Bay** Kent
2 E7 **St Mawes** Cnwll
2 E4 **St Mawgan** Cnwll
51 K6 **St Monans** Fife
23 M4 **St Neots** Cambs
17 J5 **St Osyth** Essex
7 a1 **St Ouen** Jersey
21 J7 **St Owens Cross** Herefs
7 b1 **St Peter** Jersey
6 b2 **St Peter Port** Guern
6 a2 **St Peter's** Guern
6 b1 **St Sampson** Guern
6 a2 **St Saviour** Guern
7 b2 **St Saviour** Jersey
2 F5 **St Stephen** Cnwll
3 G3 **St Tudy** Cnwll
6 B7 **Salcombe** Devon
33 G7 **Sale** Traffd
52 D6 **Salen** Ag & B
52 E4 **Salen** Highld
10 B4 **Salfords** Surrey
50 F7 **Saline** Fife
8 C3 **Salisbury** Wilts
3 K5 **Saltash** Cnwll
38 F2 **Saltburn-by-the-Sea** R & Cl
44 F4 **Saltcoats** N Ayrs
35 K7 **Saltfleet** Lincs
5 K5 **Sampford Arundel** Somset
5 J3 **Sampford Brett** Somset
48 B6 **Sanaigmore** Ag & B
28 E4 **Sandbach** Ches E
49 K5 **Sandbank** Ag & B
14 C4 **Sandford-on-Thames** Oxon
61 G3 **Sandhaven** Abers
40 C6 **Sandhead** D & G
14 F7 **Sandhurst** Br For
61 a5 **Sandness** Shet
29 G6 **Sandon** Staffs
8 F7 **Sandown** IoW

15 J3 **Sandridge** Herts
39 H3 **Sandsend** N York
11 L3 **Sandwich** Kent
61 c7 **Sandwick** Shet
23 L5 **Sandy** C Beds
45 L6 **Sanquhar** D & G
26 B6 **Sarn** Gwynd
11 K2 **Sarre** Kent
34 E7 **Saundby** Notts
18 E5 **Saundersfoot** Pembks
4 D4 **Saunton** Devon
16 D5 **Sawbridgeworth** Herts
16 D3 **Sawston** Cambs
23 L3 **Sawtry** Cambs
30 E7 **Saxby** Leics
30 E3 **Saxilby** Lincs
17 L2 **Saxmundham** Suffk
25 H3 **Saxthorpe** Norfk
48 C4 **Scalasaig** Ag & B
39 J4 **Scalby** N York
61 c6 **Scalloway** Shet
31 J3 **Scamblesby** Lincs
39 K4 **Scarborough** N York
48 b2 **Scarinish** Ag & B
34 F6 **Scawby** N Linc
25 H7 **Scole** Norfk
51 G4 **Scone** P & K
56 E6 **Sconser** Highld
38 C3 **Scotch Corner** N York
34 F6 **Scotter** Lincs
38 B4 **Scotton** N York
25 G5 **Scoulton** Norfk
63 G4 **Scourie** Highld
65 G2 **Scrabster** Highld
34 F5 **Scunthorpe** N Linc
10 D7 **Seaford** E Susx
43 L6 **Seaham** Dur
47 L6 **Seahouses** Nthumb
10 D3 **Seal** Kent
39 J5 **Seamer** N York
25 L3 **Sea Palling** Norfk
36 D3 **Seascale** Cumb
36 F4 **Seathwaite** Cumb
6 F3 **Seaton** Devon
43 K4 **Seaton Delaval** Nthumb
38 F4 **Seave Green** N York
9 G6 **Seaview** IoW
37 J4 **Sedbergh** Cumb
22 B6 **Sedgeberrow** Worcs
30 E6 **Sedgebrook** Lincs
38 D1 **Sedgefield** Dur
10 F6 **Sedlescombe** E Susx
13 K5 **Seend** Wilts
9 G3 **Selborne** Hants
34 D4 **Selby** N York
46 E6 **Selkirk** Border
11 J4 **Sellindge** Kent
9 H6 **Selsey** W Susx
29 L4 **Selston** Notts
15 G7 **Send** Surrey
2 A7 **Sennen** Cnwll
20 D7 **Sennybridge** Powys
24 D4 **Setchey** Norfk
37 L6 **Settle** N York
10 D3 **Sevenoaks** Kent
19 L5 **Seven Sisters** Neath
13 J8 **Shaftesbury** Dorset
16 F4 **Shalford** Essex
9 K2 **Shalford** Surrey
49 K5 **Shandon** Ag & B
8 F7 **Shanklin** IoW
37 H2 **Shap** Cumb
29 L6 **Shardlow** Derbys
23 K4 **Sharnbrook** Bed
13 G2 **Sharpness** Gloucs
3 L4 **Shaugh Prior** Devon
28 C7 **Shavington** Ches E
28 C7 **Shawbury** Shrops
4 D6 **Shebbear** Devon
4 E6 **Sheepwash** Devon
11 G2 **Sheerness** Kent
29 K2 **Sheffield** Sheff
23 L6 **Shefford** C Beds
16 C3 **Shepreth** Cambs
30 B7 **Shepshed** Leics
13 G6 **Shepton Mallet** Somset
7 J1 **Sherborne** Dorset
39 J5 **Sherburn** N York
34 C4 **Sherburn in Elmet** N York
14 D7 **Sherfield on Loddon** Hants
38 F6 **Sheriff Hutton** N York
25 H2 **Sheringham** Norfk
57 J7 **Shiel Bridge** Highld
57 H4 **Shieldaig** Highld

28 E8 **Shifnal** Shrops
38 C2 **Shildon** Dur
14 D4 **Shillingford** Oxon
7 L2 **Shillingstone** Dorset
14 E6 **Shinfield** Wokham
63 K6 **Shinness** Highld
25 G5 **Shipdham** Norfk
14 E6 **Shiplake** Oxon
33 K3 **Shipley** C Brad
22 D6 **Shipston on Stour** Warwks
38 E7 **Shipton** N York
34 E3 **Shiptonthorpe** E R Yk
9 L5 **Shoreham-by-Sea** W Susx
8 E7 **Shorwell** IoW
17 K4 **Shotley** Suffk
17 L3 **Shottisham** Suffk
45 L2 **Shotts** N Lans
28 C8 **Shrewsbury** Shrops
13 L6 **Shrewton** Wilts
21 M3 **Shrivenham** Oxon
22 A7 **Shurdington** Gloucs
6 F3 **Shute** Devon
31 J5 **Sibsey** Lincs
22 E1 **Sibson** Leics
6 E3 **Sidmouth** Devon
14 D7 **Silchester** Hants
30 C7 **Sileby** Leics
31 G5 **Silk Willoughby** Lincs
41 L6 **Silloth** Cumb
23 L6 **Silsoe** C Beds
37 H5 **Silverdale** Lancs
16 F5 **Silver End** Essex
23 G6 **Silverstone** Nhants
5 H6 **Silverton** Devon
42 F4 **Simonburn** Nthumb
5 G4 **Simonsbath** Somset
9 J4 **Singleton** W Susx
10 F4 **Sissinghurst** Kent
11 G3 **Sittingbourne** Kent
8 A4 **Sixpenny Handley** Dorset
31 L4 **Skegness** Lincs
30 F3 **Skellingthorpe** Lincs
32 D6 **Skelmersdale** Lancs
49 K6 **Skelmorlie** N Ayrs
42 C7 **Skelton** Cumb
38 F2 **Skelton** R & Cl
21 H7 **Skenfrith** Mons
64 C2 **Skerray** Highld
44 C3 **Skipness** Ag & B
35 H2 **Skipsea** E R Yk
33 J2 **Skipton** N York
46 B6 **Skirling** Border
42 D8 **Skirwith** Cumb
32 F7 **Slaidburn** Lancs
43 G6 **Slaley** Nthumb
45 L1 **Slamannan** Falk
6 B7 **Slapton** Devon
31 G5 **Sleaford** Lincs
39 J6 **Sledmere** E R Yk
39 H3 **Sleights** N York
39 G5 **Slingsby** N York
15 G5 **Slough** Slough
47 G6 **Smailholm** Border
11 G4 **Smarden** Kent
42 C5 **Smithfield** Cumb
39 J5 **Snainton** N York
17 L2 **Snape** Suffk
24 E3 **Snettisham** Norfk
10 E3 **Snodland** Kent
24 D7 **Soham** Cambs
22 C3 **Solihull** Solhll
18 B4 **Solva** Pembks
24 B7 **Somersham** Cambs
12 F7 **Somerton** Somset
9 L5 **Sompting** W Susx
14 E6 **Sonning** Wokham
14 E5 **Sonning Common** Oxon
40 E6 **Sorbie** D & G
37 K3 **Soulby** Cumb
22 F6 **Souldern** Oxon
23 K4 **Souldrop** Bed
3 L2 **Sourton** Devon
22 E4 **Southam** Warwks
8 E5 **Southampton** C Sotn
53 H5 **South Ballachulish** Highld
16 F8 **South Benfleet** Essex
10 D4 **Southborough** Kent
6 A5 **South Brent** Devon
34 F4 **South Cave** E R Yk
34 B5 **South Elmsall** Wakefd
44 B6 **Southend** Ag & B
17 G8 **Southend-on-Sea** Sthend
24 D6 **Southery** Norfk
9 H4 **South Harting** W Susx

9 G5 **South Hayling** Hants
9 L2 **South Holmwood** Surrey
31 H5 **South Kyme** Lincs
15 J4 **South Mimms** Herts
17 H7 **Southminster** Essex
4 F5 **South Molton** Devon
14 B4 **Southmoor** Oxon
29 L4 **South Normanton** Derbys
16 E8 **South Ockendon** Thurr
7 G1 **South Petherton** Somset
32 C5 **Southport** Sefton
46 B3 **South Queensferry** C Edin
24 F4 **South Raynham** Norfk
25 J3 **Southrepps** Norfk
9 G6 **Southsea** C Port
43 L5 **South Shields** S Tyne
58 C6 **South Stainley** N York
25 K4 **South Walsham** Norfk
30 D4 **Southwell** Notts
9 G5 **Southwick** Hants
10 B7 **Southwick** W Susx
30 F7 **South Witham** Lincs
25 L7 **Southwold** Suffk
16 F7 **South Woodham Ferrers** Essex
3 M2 **South Zeal** Devon
38 D5 **Sowerby** N York
33 J4 **Sowerby Bridge** Calder
31 H7 **Spalding** Lincs
13 G8 **Sparkford** Somset
8 E3 **Sparsholt** Hants
53 J3 **Spean Bridge** Highld
43 K7 **Spennymoor** Dur
7 L2 **Spetisbury** Dorset
60 B3 **Spey Bay** Moray
31 K3 **Spilsby** Lincs
58 F1 **Spinningdale** Highld
65 H3 **Spittal** Highld
54 E7 **Spittal of Glenshee** P & K
25 J4 **Spixworth** Norfk
34 A2 **Spofforth** N York
41 H5 **Springholm** D & G
35 H4 **Sproatley** E R Yk
14 D4 **Stadhampton** Oxon
62 c11 **Stadhlaigearraidh** W Isls
56 E3 **Staffin** Highld
38 B2 **Stafford** Staffs
38 B2 **Staindrop** Dur
15 G6 **Staines** Surrey
37 L6 **Stainforth** N York
39 G2 **Staithes** N York
25 K4 **Stalham** Norfk
31 G8 **Stamford** Lincs
39 G7 **Stamford Bridge** E R Yk
43 H5 **Stamfordham** Nthumb
41 K7 **Standingstone** Cumb
32 E5 **Standish** Wigan
16 C5 **Standon** Herts
14 B4 **Stanford in the Vale** Oxon
10 E1 **Stanford le Hope** Thurr
43 G7 **Stanhope** Dur
43 J6 **Stanley** Dur
50 F4 **Stanley** P & K
43 J4 **Stannington** Nthumb
16 D5 **Stansted Mountfitchet** Essex
25 G7 **Stanton** Suffk
13 J4 **Stanton St Quintin** Wilts
22 B6 **Stanway** Gloucs
6 F1 **Staple Fitzpaine** Somset
30 B6 **Stapleford** Notts
10 F4 **Staplehurst** Kent
37 M5 **Starbotton** N York
37 H4 **Staveley** Cumb
29 L3 **Staveley** Derbys
22 F4 **Staverton** Nhants
39 J5 **Staxton** N York
17 G6 **Steeple** Essex
22 F7 **Steeple Aston** Oxon
16 E3 **Steeple Bumpstead** Essex
50 D8 **Stenhousemuir** Falk
62 h3 **Stenabhagh** W Isls
16 B5 **Stevenage** Herts
44 F4 **Stevenston** N Ayrs

14 C5 **Steventon** Oxon
45 H3 **Stewarton** E Ayrs
23 J7 **Stewkley** Bucks
9 L5 **Steyning** W Susx
4 D5 **Stibb Cross** Devon
31 J4 **Stickford** Lincs
31 J4 **Stickney** Lincs
25 G2 **Stiffkey** Norfk
62 c11 **Stilligarry** W Isls
38 F6 **Stillington** N York
23 L2 **Stilton** Cambs
50 D7 **Stirling** Stirlg
16 E7 **Stock** Essex
8 D3 **Stockbridge** Hants
33 H7 **Stockport** Stockp
33 L6 **Stocksbridge** Sheff
38 E2 **Stockton-on-Tees** S on T
12 C6 **Stogursey** Somset
16 F3 **Stoke by Clare** Suffk
17 H4 **Stoke-by-Nayland** Suffk
6 C3 **Stoke Canon** Devon
24 E5 **Stoke Ferry** Norfk
6 C6 **Stoke Fleming** Devon
6 C6 **Stoke Gabriel** Devon
23 J5 **Stoke Goldington** M Keyn
21 K5 **Stoke Lacy** Herefs
14 F3 **Stoke Mandeville** Bucks
14 E4 **Stokenchurch** Bucks
28 F5 **Stoke-on-Trent** C Stke
15 G5 **Stoke Poges** Bucks
38 E3 **Stokesley** N York
28 F6 **Stone** Staffs
55 L5 **Stonehaven** Abers
13 H2 **Stonehouse** Gloucs
45 K3 **Stonehouse** S Lans
40 B6 **Stoneykirk** D & G
14 E5 **Stonor** Oxon
62 h3 **Stornoway** W Isls
9 K4 **Storrington** W Susx
16 A4 **Stotfold** C Beds
22 A5 **Stoulton** Worcs
21 M3 **Stourbridge** Dudley
7 L2 **Stourpaine** Dorset
21 L3 **Stourport-on-Severn** Worcs
21 M2 **Stourton** Staffs
46 E5 **Stow** Border
16 D2 **Stow-cum-Quy** Cambs
17 H2 **Stowmarket** Suffk
22 C7 **Stow-on-the-Wold** Gloucs
55 K5 **Strachan** Abers
49 J3 **Strachur** Ag & B
25 J7 **Stradbroke** Suffk
16 F3 **Stradishall** Suffk
24 D5 **Stradsett** Norfk
45 G7 **Straiton** S Ayrs
40 B5 **Stranraer** D & G
14 E7 **Stratfield Turgis** Hants
17 L2 **Stratford St Andrew** Suffk
22 C5 **Stratford-upon-Avon** Warwks
44 K4 **Strathaven** S Lans
50 B8 **Strathblane** Stirlg
63 G7 **Strathcanaird** Highld
55 G3 **Strathdon** Abers
58 D4 **Strathpeffer** Highld
64 E2 **Strathy** Highld
50 B5 **Strathyre** Stirlg
4 B6 **Stratton** Cnwll
13 G6 **Stratton-on-the-Fosse** Somset
14 D5 **Streatley** W Berk
12 F7 **Street** Somset
38 F7 **Strensall** C York
6 C6 **Strete** Devon
33 G7 **Stretford** Traffd
24 C7 **Stretham** Cambs
30 F7 **Stretton** Rutlnd
61 G4 **Strichen** Abers
57 H5 **Stromeferry** Highld
65 b4 **Stromness** Ork
49 M3 **Stronachlachar** Stirlg
49 K5 **Strone** Ag & B
52 F5 **Strontian** Highld
10 F2 **Strood** Medway
13 G6 **Stroud** Gloucs
58 C5 **Struy** Highld
61 G5 **Stuartfield** Abers
8 B7 **Studland** Dorset
22 B4 **Studley** Warwks
7 K1 **Sturminster Newton** Dorset

11 J3 **Sturry** Kent
30 E2 **Sturton by Stow** Lincs
29 H6 **Sudbury** Derbys
17 G3 **Sudbury** Suffk
36 c2 **Sulby** IoM
2 E5 **Summercourt** Cnwll
15 H6 **Sunbury** Surrey
43 L6 **Sunderland** Sundld
31 H6 **Surfleet** Lincs
31 J6 **Sutterton** Lincs
24 C7 **Sutton** Cambs
10 B2 **Sutton** Gt Lon
13 K4 **Sutton Benger** Wilts
24 C4 **Sutton Bridge** Lincs
22 C2 **Sutton Coldfield** Birm
14 C4 **Sutton Courtenay** Oxon
31 L2 **Sutton on Sea** Lincs
38 F6 **Sutton-on-the-Forest** N York
30 E3 **Sutton on Trent** Notts
8 E2 **Sutton Scotney** Hants
10 F4 **Sutton Valence** Kent
29 K7 **Swadlincote** Derbys
24 F5 **Swaffham** Norfk
13 H4 **Swainswick** BaNES
22 E6 **Swalcliffe** Oxon
35 H6 **Swallow** Lincs
14 E7 **Swallowfield** Wokham
8 B7 **Swanage** Dorset
10 D2 **Swanley** Kent
19 J6 **Swansea** Swans
29 K4 **Swanwick** Derbys
8 F5 **Swanwick** Hants
31 G6 **Swaton** Lincs
16 C1 **Swavesey** Cambs
8 D6 **Sway** Hants
13 L3 **Swindon** Swindn
23 K4 **Swineshead** Bed
31 H5 **Swineshead** Lincs
22 F3 **Swinford** Leics
47 H5 **Swinton** Border
34 B6 **Swinton** Rothm
24 F3 **Syderstone** Norfk
61 d4 **Symbister** Shet
45 G5 **Symington** S Ayrs
46 A6 **Symington** S Lans
21 J8 **Symonds Yat** Herefs
23 G6 **Syresham** Nhants
30 C8 **Syston** Leics

T

34 B3 **Tadcaster** N York
14 D7 **Tadley** Hants
59 G2 **Tain** Highld
62 f6 **Tairbeart** W Isls
19 G2 **Talgarreg** Cerdgn
20 F6 **Talgarth** Powys
57 J3 **Talladale** Highld
19 J3 **Talley** Carmth
64 C2 **Talmine** Highld
26 E6 **Talsarnau** Gwynd
20 B2 **Tal-y-bont** Cerdgn
26 F3 **Tal-y-Bont** Conwy
26 E7 **Tal-y-bont** Gwynd
27 G3 **Tal-y-Cafn** Conwy
22 C1 **Tamworth** Staffs
51 J2 **Tannadice** Angus
18 F2 **Tan-y-groes** Cerdgn
14 F5 **Taplow** Bucks
49 G6 **Tarbert** Ag & B
62 f6 **Tarbert** W Isls
49 L3 **Tarbet** Ag & B
45 H5 **Tarbolton** S Ayrs
55 H4 **Tarland** Abers
32 D5 **Tarleton** Lancs
28 C4 **Tarporley** Ches W
7 M2 **Tarrant Hinton** Dorset
56 F7 **Tarskavaig** Highld
60 F6 **Tarves** Abers
28 C3 **Tarvin** Ches W
31 H4 **Tattershall** Lincs
12 D8 **Taunton** Somset
25 H4 **Taverham** Norfk
3 K4 **Tavistock** Devon
44 B3 **Tayinloan** Ag & B
22 D8 **Taynton** Oxon
53 G7 **Taynuilt** Ag & B
51 J4 **Tayport** Fife
48 F5 **Tayvallich** Ag & B
37 J3 **Tebay** Cumb
6 B3 **Tedburn St Mary** Devon
22 A6 **Teddington** Gloucs
6 C4 **Teignmouth** Devon
28 E8 **Telford** Wrekin
46 D4 **Temple** Mdloth
19 H2 **Temple Bar** Cerdgn
13 H8 **Templecombe** Somset
37 J1 **Temple Sowerby** Cumb
23 L5 **Tempsford** C Beds
21 K4 **Tenbury Wells** Worcs
18 E6 **Tenby** Pembks
11 G5 **Tenterden** Kent
28 D6 **Ternhill** Shrops
24 C4 **Terrington St Clement** Norfk
13 J3 **Tetbury** Gloucs
31 J3 **Tetford** Lincs
35 J6 **Tetney** Lincs
14 E4 **Tetsworth** Oxon
42 C2 **Teviothead** Border
21 M6 **Tewkesbury** Gloucs
11 H3 **Teynham** Kent
14 E3 **Thame** Oxon
14 C6 **Thatcham** W Berk
16 E4 **Thaxted** Essex
14 D6 **Theale** W Berk
17 M2 **Theberton** Suffk
36 c2 **The Bungalow** IoM
24 F7 **Thetford** Norfk
16 C7 **Theydon Bois** Essex
38 D5 **Thirsk** N York
13 G3 **Thornbury** S Glos
34 D5 **Thorne** Donc
24 A5 **Thorney** C Pete
24 E2 **Thornham** Norfk
41 J3 **Thornhill** D & G
50 C6 **Thornhill** Stirlg
43 L7 **Thornley** Dur
51 H6 **Thornton** Fife
39 H5 **Thornton le Dale** N York
38 D5 **Thornton-le-Street** N York
38 C5 **Thornton Watlass** N York
25 J5 **Thorpe End** Norfk
17 J5 **Thorpe-le-Soken** Essex
17 M2 **Thorpeness** Suffk
17 J5 **Thorrington** Essex
23 K3 **Thrapston** Nhants
20 F6 **Three Cocks** Powys
31 G6 **Threekingham** Lincs
36 F2 **Threlkeld** Cumb
37 M6 **Threshfield** N York
43 H2 **Thropton** Nthumb
65 J4 **Thrumster** Highld
34 C7 **Thurcroft** Rothm
6 A7 **Thurlestone** Devon
34 B6 **Thurnscoe** Barns
42 B6 **Thursby** Cumb
65 G2 **Thurso** Highld
27 K2 **Thurstaston** Wirral
17 G2 **Thurston** Suffk
37 L4 **Thwaite** N York
29 L4 **Tibshelf** Derbys
10 E5 **Ticehurst** E Susx
34 C7 **Tickhill** Donc
29 K7 **Ticknall** Derbys
29 H3 **Tideswell** Derbys
8 C2 **Tidworth** Wilts
62 c8 **Tigh a Ghearraidh** W Isls
62 c8 **Tigharry** W Isls
10 E2 **Tilbury** Thurr
9 J2 **Tilford** Surrey
50 E6 **Tillicoultry** Clacks
13 K6 **Tilshead** Wilts
28 C6 **Tilstock** Shrops
30 D8 **Tilton on the Hill** Leics
3 G3 **Tintagel** Cnwll
12 F2 **Tintern Parva** Mons
17 G5 **Tiptree** Essex
13 K7 **Tisbury** Wilts
29 J5 **Tissington** Derbys
28 F6 **Tittensor** Staffs
5 H6 **Tiverton** Devon
52 C5 **Tobermory** Ag & B
23 K7 **Toddington** C Beds
51 J3 **Todhills** Angus
33 H4 **Todmorden** Calder
61 c3 **Toft** Shet
38 B1 **Toft Hill** Dur
62 i2 **Tolastadh** W Isls
7 M1 **Tollard Royal** Wilts
17 H6 **Tollesbury** Essex
17 G6 **Tolleshunt D'Arcy** Essex
7 K3 **Tolpuddle** Dorset
62 i2 **Tolsta** W Isls
59 G6 **Tomatin** Highld
54 F3 **Tomintoul** Moray
59 K6 **Tomnavoulin** Moray
10 E4 **Tonbridge** Kent
64 C3 **Tongue** Highld
12 B3 **Tonypandy** Rhondd
12 B3 **Tonyrefail** Rhondd
38 D5 **Topcliffe** N York
6 D3 **Topsham** Devon
44 C5 **Torbeg** N Ayrs
6 B7 **Torcross** Devon
58 E4 **Tore** Highld
30 E3 **Torksey** Lincs
46 A3 **Torphichen** W Loth
55 J4 **Torphins** Abers
3 K5 **Torpoint** Cnwll
6 C5 **Torquay** Torbay
45 J1 **Torrance** E Duns
57 H4 **Torridon** Highld
56 F7 **Torrin** Highld
46 B2 **Torryburn** Fife
41 K4 **Torthorwald** D & G
36 F4 **Torver** Cumb
8 D6 **Totland** IoW
6 B5 **Totnes** Devon
8 D4 **Totton** Hants
23 G5 **Towcester** Nhants
43 J7 **Tow Law** Dur
47 H6 **Town Yetholm** Border
46 D6 **Traquair** Border
33 H3 **Trawden** Lancs
26 F6 **Trawsfynydd** Gwynd
26 B2 **Trearddur Bay** IoA
20 D7 **Trecastle** Powys
12 C1 **Tredegar** Blae G
2 A8 **Treen** Cnwll
27 G4 **Trefriw** Conwy
19 J1 **Tregaron** Cerdgn
2 F6 **Tregony** Cnwll
19 M6 **Treherbert** Rhondd
12 F2 **Trellech** Mons
26 E5 **Tremadog** Gwynd
43 L7 **Trimdon** Dur
25 J3 **Trimingham** Norfk
14 F3 **Tring** Herts
7 b1 **Trinity** Jersey
45 G5 **Troon** S Ayrs
9 H4 **Trotton** W Susx
37 G3 **Troutbeck** Cumb
13 J5 **Trowbridge** Wilts
2 E6 **Truro** Cnwll
23 H1 **Tugby** Leics
50 D7 **Tullibody** Clacks
50 D2 **Tummel Bridge** P & K
10 E4 **Tunbridge Wells** Kent
17 L2 **Tunstall** Suffk
44 F7 **Turnberry** S Ayrs
29 K5 **Turnditch** Derbys
10 B5 **Turner's Hill** W Susx
60 E4 **Turriff** Abers
23 K5 **Turvey** Bed
29 J6 **Tutbury** Staffs
30 D3 **Tuxford** Notts
22 E1 **Twycross** Leics
8 E4 **Twyford** Hants
14 E6 **Twyford** Wokham
41 G6 **Twynholm** D & G
53 K7 **Tyndrum** Stirlg
43 L5 **Tynemouth** N Tyne
6 F2 **Tytherleigh** Devon
20 A1 **Tywyn** Gwynd

U

10 D6 **Uckfield** E Susx
5 J6 **Uffculme** Devon
14 A5 **Uffington** Oxon
6 A6 **Ugborough** Devon
56 D3 **Uig** Highld
35 H5 **Ulceby** N Linc
42 A7 **Uldale** Cumb
63 G7 **Ullapool** Highld
22 C4 **Ullenhall** Warwks
36 E4 **Ulpha** Cumb
61 c3 **Ulsta** Shet
36 F5 **Ulverston** Cumb
4 F5 **Umberleigh** Devon
63 H4 **Unapool** Highld
13 L5 **Upavon** Wilts
6 F3 **Uplyme** Devon
6 E2 **Upottery** Devon
9 L5 **Upper Beeding** W Susx
23 K2 **Upper Benefield** Nhants
30 D7 **Upper Broughton** Notts
51 J6 **Upper Largo** Fife
21 K8 **Upper Lydbrook** Gloucs
29 G5 **Upper Tean** Staffs
23 J1 **Uppingham** Rutlnd
11 K3 **Upstreet** Kent
22 A5 **Upton Snodsbury** Worcs
21 M6 **Upton upon Severn** Worcs
13 K5 **Urchfont** Wilts
12 E2 **Usk** Mons
29 H6 **Uttoxeter** Staffs
15 H5 **Uxbridge** Gt Lon
61 d2 **Uyeasound** Shet

V

6 b1 **Vale** Guern
8 F7 **Ventnor** IoW
8 B5 **Verwood** Dorset
61 c4 **Vidlin** Shet
15 G6 **Virginia Water** Surrey
61 c4 **Voe** Shet

W

14 E3 **Waddesdon** Bucks
33 G3 **Waddington** Lancs
30 F4 **Waddington** Lincs
2 F4 **Wadebridge** Cnwll
15 K3 **Wadesmill** Herts
10 E5 **Wadhurst** E Susx
31 K4 **Wainfleet All Saints** Lincs
33 M5 **Wakefield** Wakefd
25 L7 **Walberswick** Suffk
28 E5 **Walgherton** Ches E
46 D6 **Walkerburn** Border
16 B5 **Walkern** Herts
35 G3 **Walkington** E R Yk
32 C7 **Wallasey** Wirral
14 D5 **Wallingford** Oxon
61 b5 **Walls** Shet
22 B1 **Walsall** Wsall
35 J6 **Waltham** NE Lin
16 C7 **Waltham Abbey** Essex
30 E7 **Waltham on the Wolds** Leics
21 G4 **Walton** Powys
12 F7 **Walton** Somset
15 H6 **Walton-on-Thames** Surrey
17 K5 **Walton on the Naze** Essex
45 L6 **Wanlockhead** D & G
23 L1 **Wansford** C Pete
13 H6 **Wanstrow** Somset
14 B5 **Wantage** Oxon
24 A7 **Warboys** Cambs
37 K2 **Warcop** Cumb
29 J3 **Wardlow** Derbys
15 K3 **Ware** Herts
7 L3 **Wareham** Dorset
47 L6 **Warenford** Nthumb
14 E6 **Wargrave** Wokham
42 F4 **Wark** Nthumb
47 H6 **Wark** Nthumb
43 K2 **Warkworth** Nthumb
22 E5 **Warmington** Warwks
13 J6 **Warminster** Wilts
10 B5 **Warninglid** W Susx
32 F7 **Warrington** Warrtn
8 E5 **Warsash** Hants
29 H4 **Warslow** Staffs
32 D4 **Warton** Lancs
22 D4 **Warwick** Warwks
65 b2 **Wasbister** Ork
36 E3 **Wasdale Head** Cumb
30 F3 **Washingborough** Lincs
43 K6 **Washington** Sundld
5 J3 **Watchet** Somset
37 H4 **Watchgate** Cumb
16 D2 **Waterbeach** Cambs
42 A4 **Waterbeck** D & G
29 H5 **Waterhouses** Staffs
9 G5 **Waterlooville** Hants
37 G2 **Watermillock** Cumb
15 H4 **Watford** Herts
23 G4 **Watford** Nhants
34 B6 **Wath upon Dearne** Rothm
14 E4 **Watlington** Oxon
65 H3 **Watten** Highld
24 F5 **Watton** Norfk

15 K2 **Watton-at-Stone** Herts
42 F7 **Wearhead** Dur
24 F4 **Weasenham All Saints** Norfk
28 D3 **Weaverham** Ches W
12 E6 **Wedmore** Somset
23 G4 **Weedon** Nhants
4 B7 **Week St Mary** Cnwll
50 D2 **Weem** P & K
30 F4 **Welbourn** Lincs
22 D5 **Wellesbourne** Warwks
23 J4 **Wellingborough** Nhants
5 K5 **Wellington** Somset
28 D8 **Wellington** Wrekin
12 F6 **Wells** Somset
24 F2 **Wells-next-the-sea** Norfk
24 C6 **Welney** Norfk
28 B6 **Welshampton** Shrops
27 K8 **Welshpool** Powys
23 G4 **Welton** Nhants
15 J3 **Welwyn** Herts
15 J3 **Welwyn Garden City** Herts
28 C6 **Wem** Shrops
15 J5 **Wembley** Gt Lon
3 L6 **Wembury** Devon
14 F3 **Wendover** Bucks
38 B4 **Wensley** N York
34 B5 **Wentbridge** Wakefd
21 H5 **Weobley** Herefs
24 D5 **Wereham** Norfk
38 B2 **West Auckland** Dur
7 H3 **West Bay** Dorset
7 H3 **West Bexington** Dorset
24 E4 **West Bilney** Norfk
30 C6 **West Bridgford** Notts
22 B2 **West Bromwich** Sandw
28 B8 **Westbury** Shrops
13 J6 **Westbury** Wilts
46 A4 **West Calder** W Loth
9 K4 **West Chiltington** W Susx
9 L2 **Westcott** Surrey
10 C3 **Westerham** Kent
27 L7 **West Felton** Shrops
10 F6 **Westfield** E Susx
23 G3 **West Haddon** Nhants
10 C5 **West Hoathly** W Susx
15 H8 **West Horsley** Surrey
12 D6 **West Huntspill** Somset
44 F3 **West Kilbride** N Ayrs
27 K2 **West Kirby** Wirral
13 K6 **West Lavington** Wilts
46 C5 **West Linton** Border
7 L4 **West Lulworth** Dorset
24 D4 **West Lynn** Norfk
10 E3 **West Malling** Kent
21 L5 **West Malvern** Worcs
9 G4 **West Meon** Hants
17 H6 **West Mersea** Essex
8 B5 **West Moors** Dorset
41 L7 **Westnewton** Cumb
24 E3 **West Newton** Norfk
16 B4 **Weston** Herts
29 G6 **Weston** Staffs
13 J3 **Westonbirt** Gloucs
28 E7 **Weston Heath** Shrops
14 C3 **Weston-on-the-Green** Oxon
22 C6 **Weston Subedge** Gloucs
12 D5 **Weston-Super-Mare** N Som
28 D6 **Weston-under-Redcastle** Shrops
12 F7 **West Pennard** Somset
2 D5 **West Pentire** Cnwll
38 D3 **West Rounton** N York
25 J2 **West Runton** Norfk
47 G5 **Westruther** Border
61 C3 **West Sandwick** Shet
4 D4 **Westward Ho!** Devon
9 H6 **West Wittering** W Susx
38 A4 **West Witton** N York
43 G3 **West Woodburn** Nthumb
42 C6 **Wetheral** Cumb
34 B3 **Wetherby** Leeds
39 J7 **Wetwang** E R Yk
25 H2 **Weybourne** Norfk
15 H7 **Weybridge** Surrey
8 D2 **Weyhill** Hants
7 J4 **Weymouth** Dorset
29 G2 **Whaley Bridge** Derbys
33 G3 **Whalley** Lancs
31 J7 **Whaplode** Lincs
31 J7 **Whaplode Drove** Lincs
40 E6 **Whauphill** D & G
15 J3 **Wheathampstead** Herts
14 D3 **Wheatley** Oxon
5 H4 **Wheddon Cross** Somset
17 G2 **Whepstead** Suffk
8 E2 **Wherwell** Hants
43 J5 **Whickham** Gatesd
6 A3 **Whiddon Down** Devon
6 D3 **Whimple** Devon
15 G3 **Whipsnade** C Beds
46 A4 **Whitburn** W Loth
39 H3 **Whitby** N York
14 E2 **Whitchurch** Bucks
8 E2 **Whitchurch** Hants
21 J8 **Whitchurch** Herefs
28 C5 **Whitchurch** Shrops
58 D7 **Whitebridge** Highld
36 D2 **Whitehaven** Cumb
9 H3 **Whitehill and Bordon** Hants
60 D3 **Whitehills** Abers
49 G6 **Whitehouse** Ag & B
46 F2 **Whitekirk** E Loth
32 F3 **Whitewell** Lancs
40 E7 **Whithorn** D & G
44 E5 **Whiting Bay** N Ayrs
18 E5 **Whitland** Carmth
43 K5 **Whitley Bay** N Tyne
43 G6 **Whitley Chapel** Nthumb
13 H1 **Whitminster** Gloucs
11 J2 **Whitstable** Kent
27 L6 **Whittington** Shrops
23 G6 **Whittlebury** Nhants
24 A6 **Whittlesey** Cambs
21 G4 **Whitton** Powys
30 B3 **Whitwell** Derbys
15 J2 **Whitwell** Herts
65 J3 **Wick** Highld
16 F7 **Wickford** Essex
8 F5 **Wickham** Hants
17 K2 **Wickham Market** Suffk
13 H3 **Wickwar** S Glos
43 K3 **Widdrington** Nthumb
6 A4 **Widecombe in the Moor** Devon
3 J5 **Widegates** Cnwll
4 B6 **Widemouth Bay** Cnwll
16 C5 **Widford** Herts
30 C6 **Widmerpool** Notts
28 C2 **Widnes** Halton
32 E6 **Wigan** Wigan
24 D4 **Wiggenhall St Germans** Norfk
23 G1 **Wigston** Leics
42 A6 **Wigton** Cumb
40 E6 **Wigtown** D & G
34 D2 **Wilberfoss** E R Yk
23 J4 **Wilby** Nhants
5 J6 **Willand** Devon
24 B8 **Willingham** Cambs
22 C4 **Wilmcote** Warwks
6 F2 **Wilmington** Devon
28 F2 **Wilmslow** Ches E
46 A4 **Wilsontown** S Lans
23 L6 **Wilstead** Bed
13 L7 **Wilton** Wilts
24 B6 **Wimblington** Cambs
8 A5 **Wimborne Minster** Dorset
13 H7 **Wincanton** Somset
22 B7 **Winchcombe** Gloucs
11 G6 **Winchelsea** E Susx
8 E3 **Winchester** Hants
37 G4 **Windermere** Cumb
15 G6 **Windsor** W & M
14 F2 **Wing** Bucks
43 L7 **Wingate** Dur
11 K3 **Wingham** Kent
11 K4 **Wingmore** Kent
14 F6 **Winkfield** Br For
4 F6 **Winkleigh** Devon
12 E5 **Winscombe** N Som
28 D3 **Winsford** Ches W
5 H4 **Winsford** Somset
7 G2 **Winsham** Somset
23 H7 **Winslow** Bucks
29 J4 **Winster** Derbys
7 J3 **Winterborne Monkton** Dorset
7 L2 **Winterborne Stickland** Dorset
7 L2 **Winterborne Whitechurch** Dorset
7 J3 **Winterbourne Abbas** Dorset
13 L7 **Winterbourne Stoke** Wilts
34 F5 **Winteringham** N Linc
8 C3 **Winterslow** Wilts
34 F5 **Winterton** N Linc
23 L3 **Winwick** Cambs
29 J4 **Wirksworth** Derbys
31 K8 **Wisbech** Cambs
9 K3 **Wisborough Green** W Susx
45 L3 **Wishaw** N Lans
16 F5 **Witham** Essex
5 G6 **Witheridge** Devon
31 K2 **Withern** Lincs
35 K4 **Withernsea** E R Yk
22 B8 **Withington** Gloucs
21 J6 **Withington** Herefs
10 D5 **Withyham** E Susx
5 H4 **Withypool** Somset
17 J3 **Witnesham** Suffk
14 B3 **Witney** Oxon
11 G5 **Wittersham** Kent
43 J8 **Witton le Wear** Dur
5 J4 **Wiveliscombe** Somset
10 C6 **Wivelsfield** E Susx
17 H5 **Wivenhoe** Essex
17 J4 **Wix** Essex
23 K6 **Woburn** C Beds
15 G7 **Woking** Surrey
14 F6 **Wokingham** Wokham
18 C4 **Wolf's Castle** Pembks
23 J4 **Wollaston** Nhants
27 L8 **Wollaston** Shrops
43 H7 **Wolsingham** Dur
21 M1 **Wolverhampton** Wolves
22 E2 **Wolvey** Warwks
38 E2 **Wolviston** S on T
21 M2 **Wombourne** Staffs
34 B6 **Wombwell** Barns
14 F5 **Wooburn** Bucks
17 K3 **Woodbridge** Suffk
11 G5 **Woodchurch** Kent
13 G2 **Woodford** Gloucs
31 H4 **Woodhall Spa** Lincs
38 B2 **Woodland** Dur
14 C3 **Woodstock** Oxon
21 J4 **Woofferton** Shrops
12 F6 **Wookey Hole** Somset
7 L3 **Wool** Dorset
4 D3 **Woolacombe** Devon
47 K6 **Wooler** Nthumb
14 D6 **Woolhampton** W Berk
17 H2 **Woolpit** Suffk
28 E5 **Woore** Shrops
35 G5 **Wootton** N Linc
14 B2 **Wootton** Oxon
13 L3 **Wootton Bassett** Wilts
5 H3 **Wootton Courtenay** Somset
22 C4 **Wootton Wawen** Warwks
21 M5 **Worcester** Worcs
36 D1 **Workington** Cumb
30 C2 **Worksop** Notts
17 K1 **Worlingworth** Suffk
51 J4 **Wormit** Fife
15 G7 **Worplesdon** Surrey
21 G1 **Worthen** Shrops
9 L5 **Worthing** W Susx
7 M4 **Worth Matravers** Dorset
13 H3 **Wotton-under-Edge** Gloucs
31 G3 **Wragby** Lincs
6 A6 **Wrangaton** Devon
31 K5 **Wrangle** Lincs
35 G6 **Wrawby** N Linc
39 G5 **Wrelton** N York
25 L7 **Wrentham** Suffk
16 B3 **Wrestlingworth** C Beds
27 L5 **Wrexham** Wrexhm
13 L4 **Wroughton** Swindn
8 F7 **Wroxall** IoW
28 D8 **Wroxeter** Shrops
25 K4 **Wroxham** Norfk
22 E6 **Wroxton** Oxon
23 L5 **Wyboston** Bed
11 H4 **Wye** Kent
13 K7 **Wylye** Wilts
30 E7 **Wymondham** Leics
25 H5 **Wymondham** Norfk

Y

6 F2 **Yarcombe** Devon
23 H5 **Yardley Gobion** Nhants
23 J5 **Yardley Hastings** Nhants
38 D3 **Yarm** S on T
8 D6 **Yarmouth** IoW
46 E6 **Yarrowford** Border
14 F7 **Yateley** Hants
12 E5 **Yatton** N Som
13 J4 **Yatton Keynell** Wilts
23 M2 **Yaxley** Cambs
33 K3 **Yeadon** Leeds
3 L5 **Yealmpton** Devon
3 L4 **Yelverton** Devon
25 K5 **Yelverton** Norfk
7 H1 **Yeovil** Somset
12 F8 **Yeovilton** Somset
50 E6 **Yetts o'Muckhart** Clacks
26 D3 **Y Felinheli** Gwynd
27 J5 **Y Maerdy** Conwy
34 C2 **York** C York
29 J4 **Youlgreave** Derbys
29 H7 **Yoxall** Staffs
17 L1 **Yoxford** Suffk
26 B6 **Y Rhiw** Gwynd
20 B3 **Ysbyty Ystwyth** Cerdgn
19 K5 **Ystalyfera** Neath
19 K5 **Ystradgynlais** Powys
12 C2 **Ystrad Mynach** Caerph

Z

13 H7 **Zeals** Wilts
2 B6 **Zennor** Cnwll

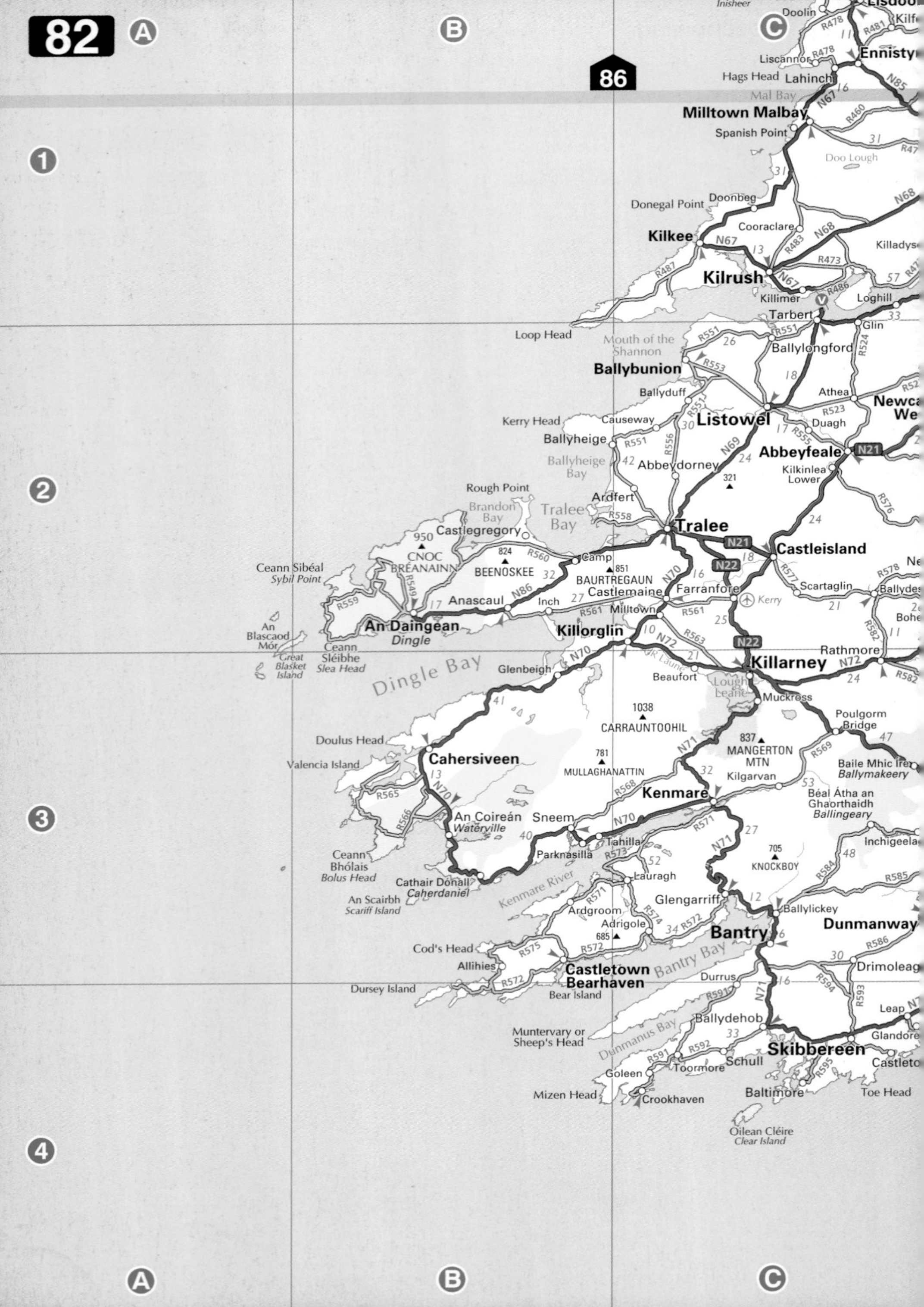
A
B
C
86
1
2
3
4
Inisheer
Doolin
Lisdoonvarna
Ennistymon
Liscannor
Hags Head
Lahinch
Mal Bay
Milltown Malbay
Spanish Point
Doo Lough
Donegal Point
Doonbeg
Cooraclare
Kilkee
Killadysert
Kilrush
Killimer
Loghill
Tarbert
Glin
Loop Head
Mouth of the Shannon
Ballybunion
Ballylongford
Ballyduff
Athea
Kerry Head
Causeway
Listowel
Duagh
Ballyheige
Abbeyfeale
Ballyheige Bay
Abbeydorney
Kilkinlea Lower
Rough Point
Ardfert
Brandon Bay
Tralee Bay
Tralee
Castlegregory
950
CNOC BRÉANAINN
824
BEENOSKEE
Camp
851
BAURTREGAUN
Castleisland
Ceann Sibéal
Sybil Point
Anascaul
Inch
Castlemaine
Farranfore
Kerry
Scartaglin
Milltown
An Daingean
Dingle
Killorglin
An Blascaod Mór
Great Blasket Island
Ceann Sléibhe
Slea Head
Dingle Bay
Glenbeigh
Beaufort
Lough Leane
Killarney
Rathmore
Muckross
1038
CARRAUNTOOHIL
Poulgorm Bridge
Doulus Head
Valencia Island
Cahersiveen
781
MULLAGHANATTIN
837
MANGERTON MTN
Kilgarvan
Baile Mhic Ire
Ballymakeery
Kenmare
Béal Átha an Ghaorthaidh
Ballingeary
An Coireán
Waterville
Sneem
Tahilla
Parknasilla
Inchigeelagh
705
KNOCKBOY
Ceann Bhólais
Bolus Head
Cathair Dónall
Caherdaniel
Lauragh
Kenmare River
An Scairbh
Scariff Island
Glengarriff
Ballylickey
Ardgroom
Adrigole
685
Dunmanway
Bantry
Cod's Head
Bantry Bay
Allihies
Castletown Bearhaven
Drimoleague
Dursey Island
Bear Island
Durrus
Leap
Ballydehob
Muntervary or Sheep's Head
Dunmanus Bay
Glandore
Skibbereen
Schull
Toormore
Castletownshend
Goleen
Mizen Head
Crookhaven
Baltimore
Toe Head
Oilean Cléire
Clear Island

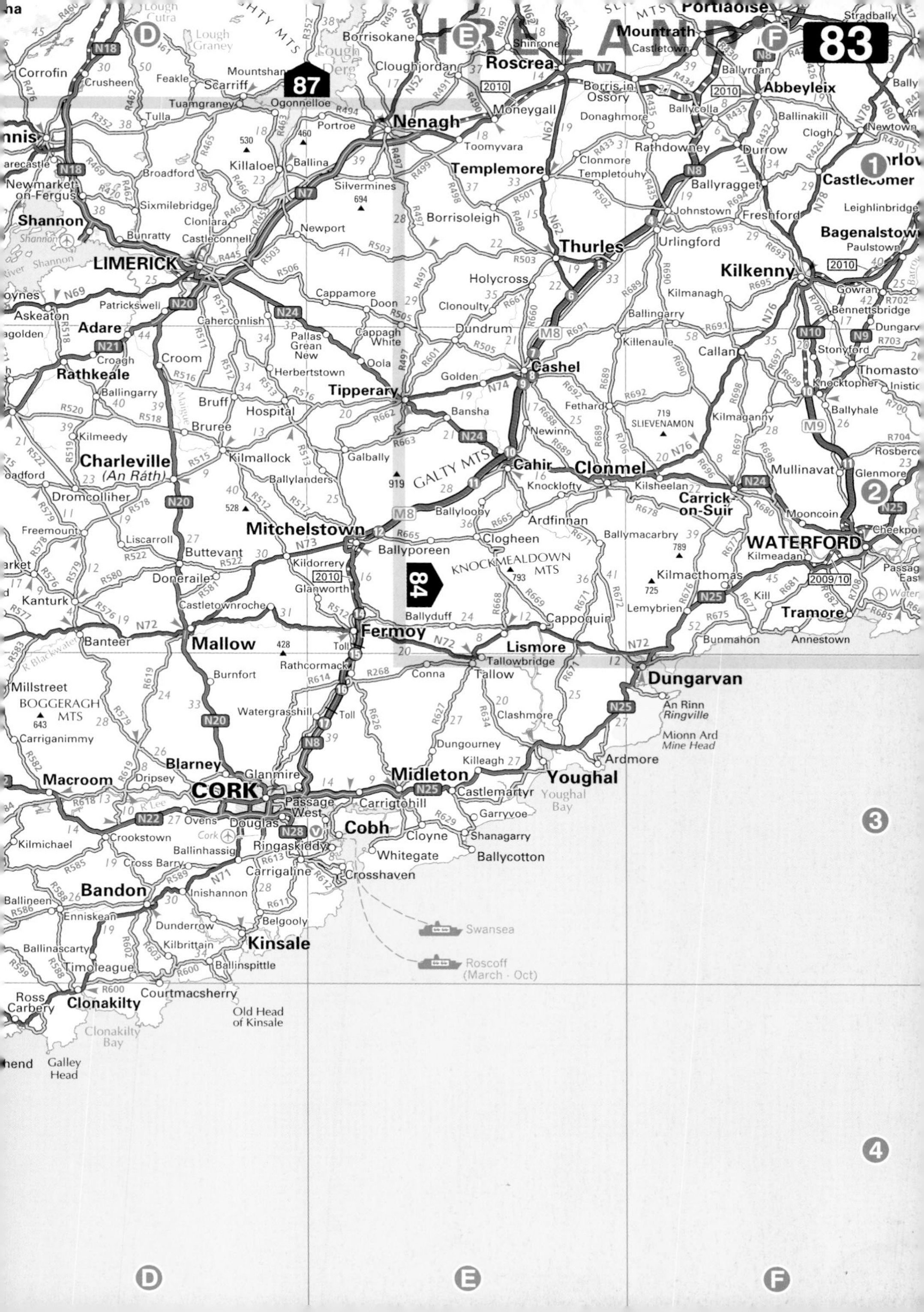
83
IRELAND
Portlaoise
Mountrath
Castletown
Stradbally
Borrisokane
Shinrone
Roscrea
Cloughjordan
Lough Derg
Lough Graney
Corrofin
Crusheen
Feakle
Mountshannon
Scarriff
87
Tuamgraney
Ogonnelloe
Tulla
Portroe
Nenagh
Moneygall
Borris in Ossory
Ballyroan
Abbeyleix
Ballinakill
Donaghmore
Ballycolla
Toomyvarra
Killaloe
Ballina
Broadford
Newmarket-on-Fergus
Sixmilebridge
Clonlara
Shannon
Bunratty
Castleconnell
Newport
Silvermines
Templemore
Clonmore
Templetouhy
Rathdowney
Durrow
Newtown
Clogh
Ballyragget
Castlecomer
Leighlinbridge
Johnstown
Freshford
Bagenalstown
Paulstown
Borrisoleigh
Thurles
Urlingford
LIMERICK
Kilkenny
Holycross
Clonoulty
Kilmanagh
Gowran
Bennettsbridge
Patrickswell
Cappamore
Doon
Askeaton
Adare
Caherconlish
Pallas Grean New
Cappagh White
Oola
Dundrum
Ballingarry
Killenaule
Callan
Dungarvan
Stonyford
Thomastown
Inistioge
Croagh
Croom
Rathkeale
Herbertstown
Tipperary
Golden
Cashel
Knocktopher
Ballyhale
Fethard
Kilmaganny
SLIEVENAMON
Ballingarry
Bruff
Hospital
Bruree
Bansha
Newinn
Kilmeedy
Charleville
(An Ráth)
Kilmallock
Galbally
Ballylanders
GALTY MTS
Cahir
Clonmel
Kilsheelan
Mullinavat
Glenmore
Rosbercon
Dromcolliher
Knocklofty
Carrick-on-Suir
Mooncoin
Freemount
Liscarroll
Mitchelstown
Ballylooby
Ardfinnan
Ballymacarbry
WATERFORD
Cheekpoint
Kilmeadan
Passage East
Buttevant
Kildorrery
Ballyporeen
Clogheen
KNOCKMEALDOWN MTS
Kilmacthomas
Doneraile
Glanworth
Kanturk
Castletownroche
84
Lemybrien
Kill
Tramore
Waterford
Ballyduff
Cappoquin
Banteer
Mallow
Fermoy
Lismore
Bunmahon
Annestown
Rathcormack
Tallowbridge
Millstreet
Burnfort
Conna
Tallow
Dungarvan
BOGGERAGH MTS
Watergrasshill
Clashmore
An Rinn
Ringville
Carriganimmy
Dungourney
Mionn Ard
Mine Head
Killeagh
Ardmore
Blarney
Glanmire
Midleton
Youghal
Macroom
Dripsey
CORK
Passage West
Castlemartyr
Youghal Bay
Carrigtohill
Ovens
Douglas
Garryvoe
Cobh
Kilmichael
Crookstown
Cork
Ringaskiddy
Cloyne
Shanagarry
Ballinhassig
Whitegate
Ballycotton
Cross Barry
Carrigaline
Crosshaven
Bandon
Inishannon
Ballineen
Enniskean
Dunderrow
Belgooly
Swansea
Kilbrittain
Kinsale
Ballinascarty
Timoleague
Ballinspittle
Roscoff
(March - Oct)
Courtmacsherry
Ross Carbery
Clonakilty
Old Head of Kinsale
Clonakilty Bay
Galley Head
D
E
F
1
2
3
4

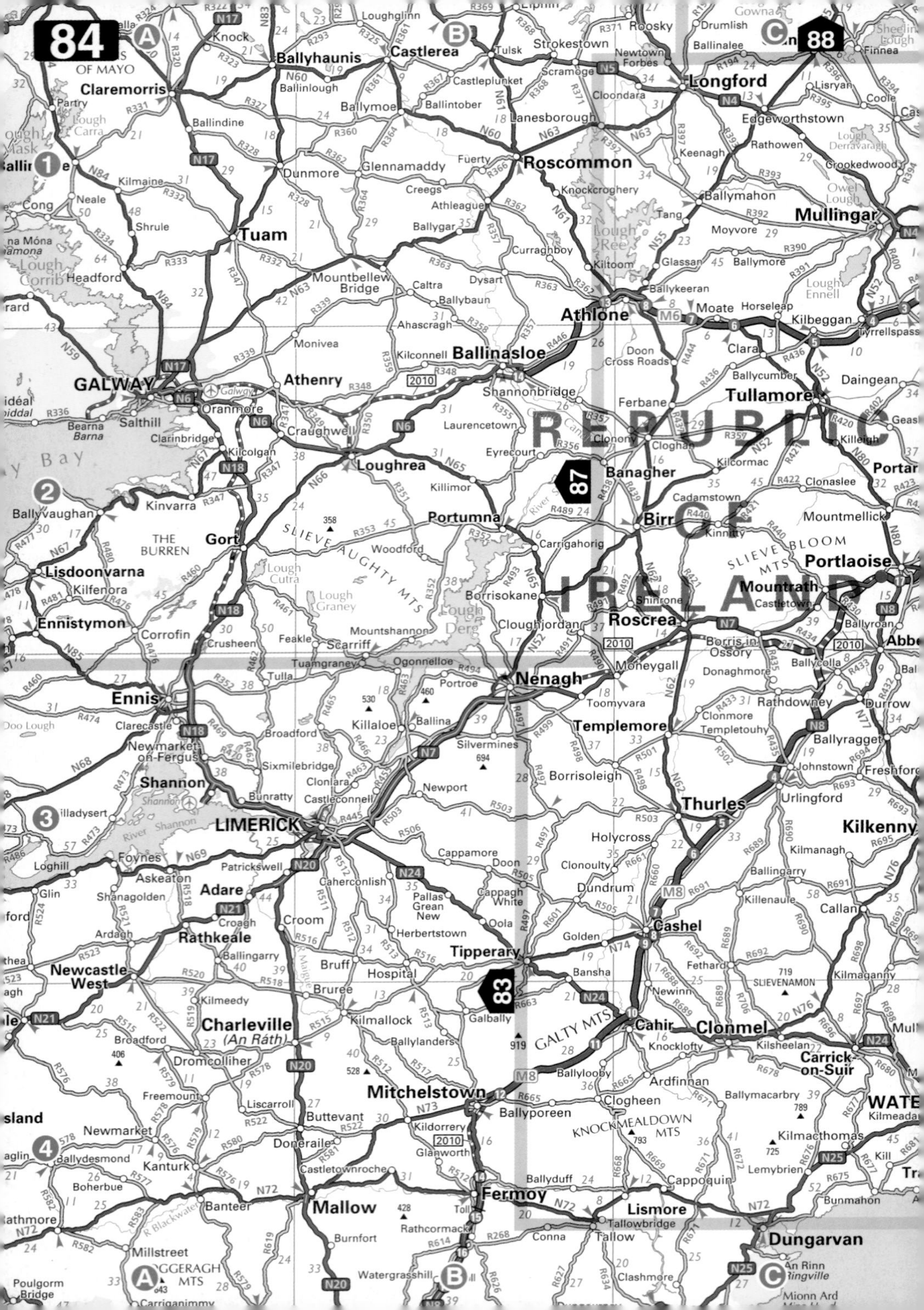

84
88
87
83
REPUBLIC OF IRELAND
Knock
Loughglinn
Ballyhaunis
Castlerea
Tulsk
Strokestown
Roosky
Drumlish
Ballinalee
Finnea
Claremorris
Partry
Lough Carra
Ballindine
Ballinlough
Ballymoe
Castleplunket
Ballintober
Scramoge
Newtown Forbes
Longford
Lisryan
Coole
Edgeworthstown
Lanesborough
Cloondara
Keenagh
Rathowen
Lough Derravaragh
Crookedwood
Roscommon
Fuerty
Dunmore
Glennamaddy
Creegs
Athleague
Knockcroghery
Ballymahon
Owel Lough
Mullingar
Kilmaine
Cong
Neale
Shrule
Tuam
Ballygar
Tang
Moyvore
Lough Ree
Curraghboy
Kiltoom
Glassan
Ballymore
Lough Corrib
Headford
Mountbellew Bridge
Caltra
Dysart
Ballykeeran
Lough Ennell
Ballybaun
Athlone
Moate
Horseleap
Kilbeggan
Tyrrellspass
Ahascragh
Monivea
Kilconnell
Ballinasloe
Doon Cross Roads
Clara
Galway
Athenry
Shannonbridge
Ferbane
Ballycumber
Daingean
Tullamore
Oranmore
Salthill
Bearna
Barna
Clarinbridge
Craughwell
Laurencetown
Clonony
Cloghan
Killeigh
Kilcolgan
Loughrea
Eyrecourt
Banagher
Kilcormac
Portarlington
Kinvarra
Killimor
Cadamstown
Clonaslee
Ballyvaughan
Portumna
Birr
Kinnitty
Mountmellick
The Burren
Gort
Slieve Aughty Mts
Woodford
Carrigahorig
Slieve Bloom Mts
Portlaoise
Lisdoonvarna
Kilfenora
Lough Cutra
Lough Graney
Borrisokane
Shinrone
Mountrath
Castletown
Ennistymon
Corrofin
Crusheen
Feakle
Mountshannon
Lough Derg
Cloughjordan
Roscrea
Ballyroan
Scarriff
Borris in Ossory
Abbeyleix
Tuamgraney
Ogonnelloe
Portroe
Nenagh
Moneygall
Donaghmore
Ballycolla
Tulla
Toomyvara
Ennis
Killaloe
Ballina
Rathdowney
Durrow
Clarecastle
Broadford
Templemore
Clonmore
Templetouhy
Doo Lough
Silvermines
Ballyragget
Newmarket-on-Fergus
Sixmilebridge
Johnstown
Freshford
Clonlara
Borrisoleigh
Shannon
Castleconnell
Newport
Urlingford
Bunratty
Thurles
Killadysert
Limerick
River Shannon
Kilkenny
Holycross
Kilmanagh
Foynes
Cappamore
Doon
Loghill
Askeaton
Patrickswell
Clonoulty
Ballingarry
Glin
Shanagolden
Adare
Caherconlish
Pallas Grean New
Cappagh White
Dundrum
Killenaule
Callan
Croom
Oola
Croagh
Herbertstown
Cashel
Ardagh
Rathkeale
Golden
Ballingarry
Tipperary
Fethard
Newcastle West
Bruff
Hospital
Bansha
Slievenamon
Kilmaganny
Bruree
Newinn
Kilmeedy
Galbally
Charleville
(An Ráth)
Kilmallock
Cahir
Clonmel
Broadford
Ballylanders
Galty Mts
Knocklofty
Kilsheelan
Carrick-on-Suir
Dromcolliher
Ardfinnan
Freemount
Mitchelstown
Ballylooby
Ballymacarbry
Waterford
Kilmeadan
Liscarroll
Buttevant
Clogheen
Ballyporeen
Knockmealdown Mts
Newmarket
Kildorrery
Kilmacthomas
Doneraile
Lemybrien
Kanturk
Glanworth
Ballydesmond
Castletownroche
Kill
Boherbue
Ballyduff
Cappoquin
Banteer
Mallow
Fermoy
Lismore
Bunmahon
Rathmore
Rathcormack
Tallowbridge
Tallow
Dungarvan
R Blackwater
Millstreet
Burnfort
Conna
An Rinn
Ringville
Boggeragh Mts
Watergrasshill
Clashmore
Poulgorm Bridge
Carriganimmy
Mionn Ard

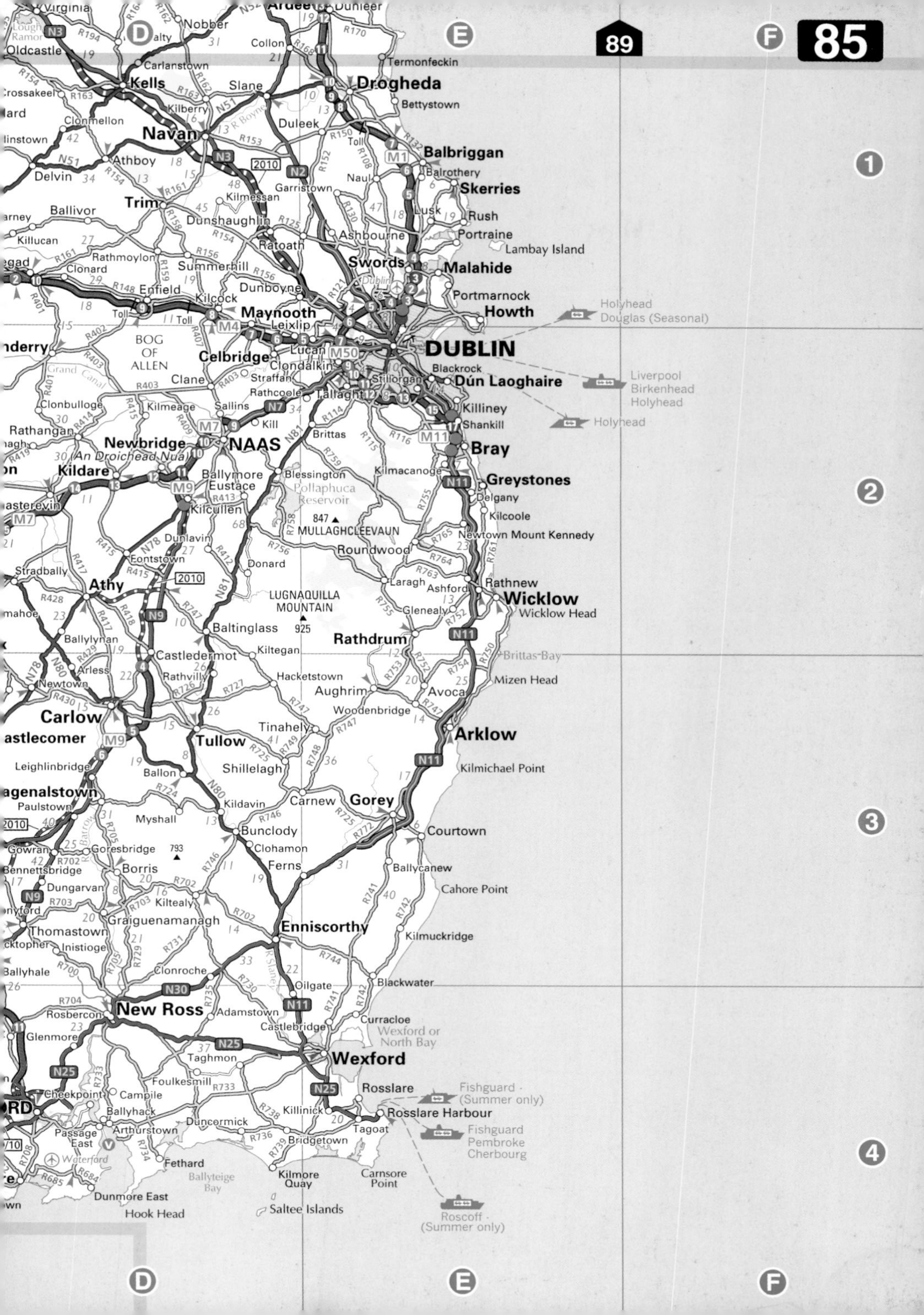

DUBLIN
Drogheda
Balbriggan
Skerries
Rush
Lambay Island
Swords
Malahide
Portmarnock
Howth
Dún Laoghaire
Bray
Greystones
Wicklow
Wicklow Head
Arklow
Gorey
Courtown
Enniscorthy
Wexford
Rosslare
Rosslare Harbour
New Ross
Carlow
Athy
Naas
Newbridge
Kildare
Navan
Kells
Trim
Maynooth
Celbridge
Tullow
Baltinglass
Rathdrum
Holyhead
Douglas (Seasonal)
Liverpool
Birkenhead
Fishguard
Pembroke
Cherbourg
Roscoff (Summer only)
Saltee Islands
Hook Head
LUGNAQUILLA MOUNTAIN
MULLAGHCLEEVAUN
BOG OF ALLEN

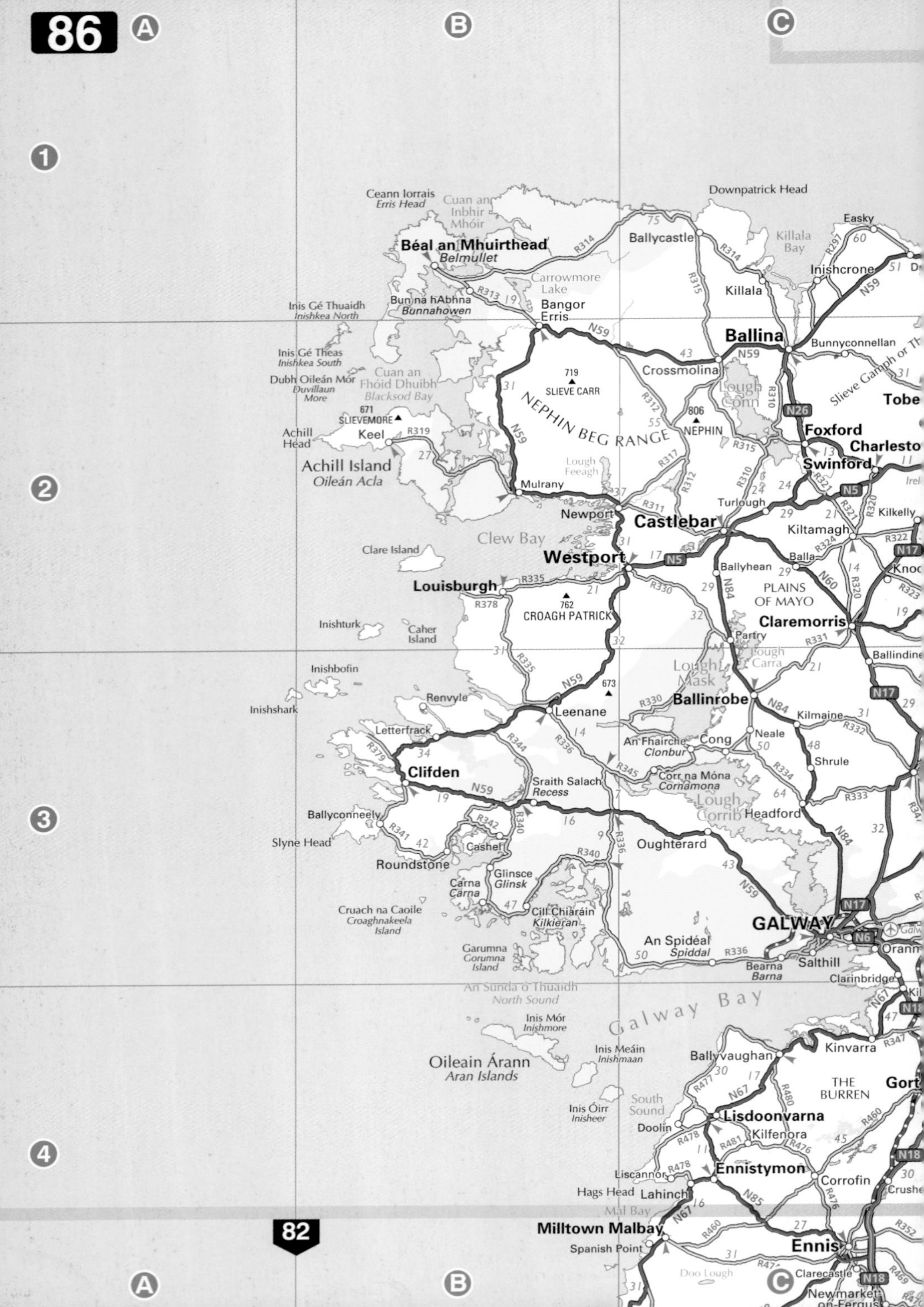
Ceann Iorrais
Erris Head
Cuan an Inbhir Mhóir
Downpatrick Head
Béal an Mhuirthead
Belmullet
Ballycastle
Killala Bay
Easky
Inishcrone
Carrowmore Lake
Killala
Bun na hAbhna
Bunnahowen
Bangor Erris
Inis Gé Thuaidh
Inishkea North
Inis Gé Theas
Inishkea South
Ballina
Bunnyconnellan
Slieve Gamph or The Ox Mts
Crossmolina
Dubh Oileán Mór
Duvillaun More
Cuan an Fhóid Dhuibh
Blacksod Bay
SLIEVE CARR
NEPHIN BEG RANGE
Lough Conn
NEPHIN
SLIEVEMORE
Achill Head
Keel
Achill Island
Oileán Acla
Lough Feeagh
Foxford
Charlestown
Swinford
Mulrany
Turlough
Kilkelly
Newport
Castlebar
Kiltamagh
Clew Bay
Westport
Balla
Clare Island
Louisburgh
Ballyhean
PLAINS OF MAYO
CROAGH PATRICK
Claremorris
Inishturk
Caher Island
Partry
Lough Carra
Ballindine
Inishbofin
Lough Mask
Renvyle
Ballinrobe
Inishshark
Leenane
Kilmaine
Letterfrack
An Fhairche
Clonbur
Cong
Neale
Shrule
Clifden
Sraith Salach
Recess
Corr na Móna
Cornamona
Lough Corrib
Headford
Ballyconneely
Slyne Head
Cashel
Oughterard
Roundstone
Carna
Glinsce
Glinsk
Cruach na Caoile
Croaghnakeela Island
Cill Chiaráin
Kilkieran
GALWAY
Garumna
Gorumna Island
An Spidéal
Spiddal
Salthill
Bearna
Barna
Oranmore
Clarinbridge
An Sunda ó Thuaidh
North Sound
Galway Bay
Inis Mór
Inishmore
Oileain Árann
Aran Islands
Inis Meáin
Inishmaan
Ballyvaughan
Kinvarra
THE BURREN
Gort
Inis Óirr
Inisheer
South Sound
Doolin
Lisdoonvarna
Kilfenora
Liscannor
Ennistymon
Corrofin
Hags Head
Lahinch
Mal Bay
Milltown Malbay
Spanish Point
Ennis
Doo Lough
Clarecastle
Newmarket-on-Fergus
82

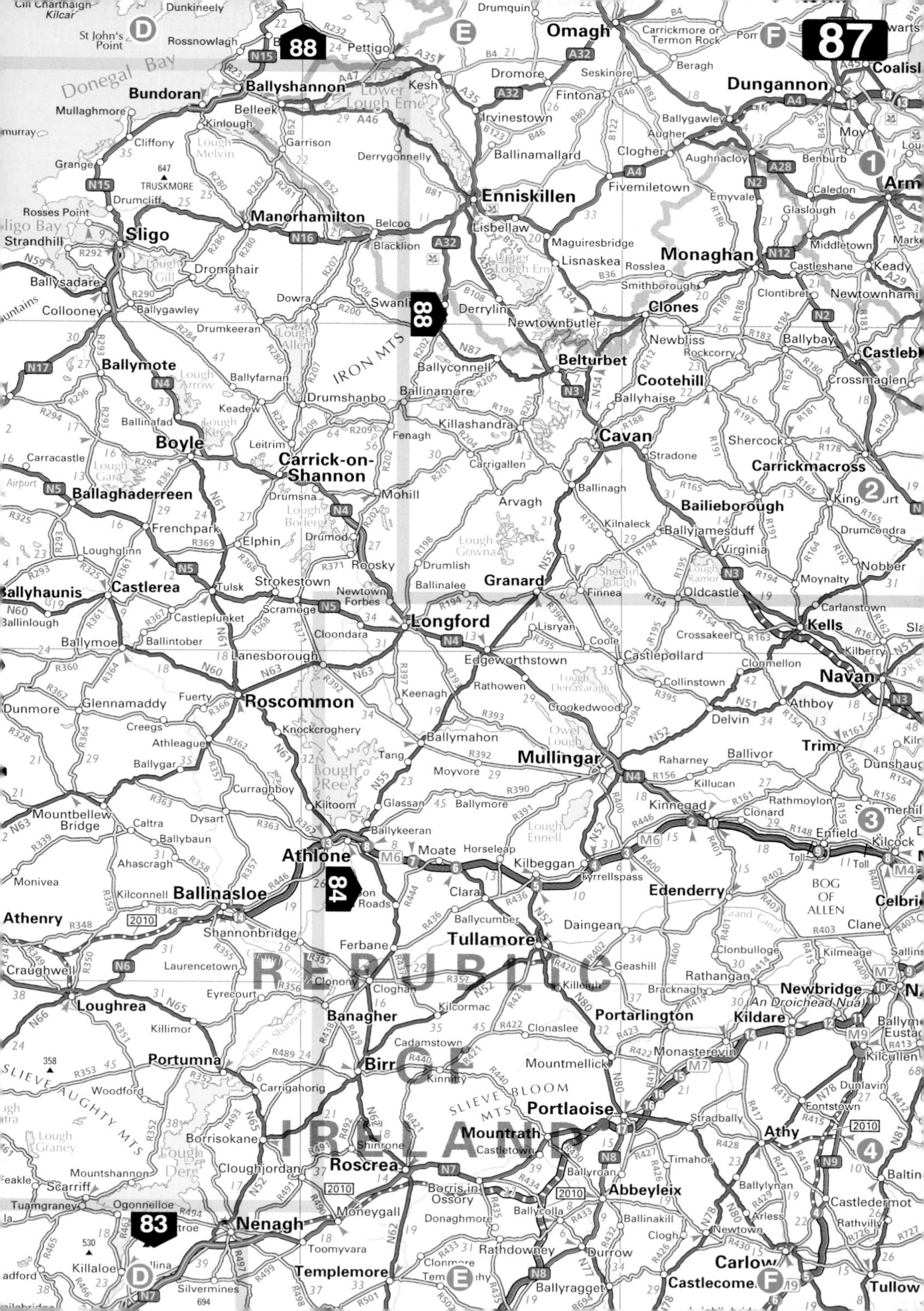

87
88
84
83
Donegal Bay
Dunkineely
Kilcar
St John's Point
Rossnowlagh
Pettigo
Omagh
Carrickmore or Termon Rock
Coalisland
Bundoran
Ballyshannon
Lower Lough Erne
Kesh
Dromore
Seskinore
Beragh
Dungannon
Mullaghmore
Belleek
Fintona
Kinlough
Irvinestown
Ballygawley
Moy
Cliffony
Lough Melvin
Garrison
Augher
Grange
Ballinamallard
Clogher
Aughnacloy
Benburb
Derrygonnelly
Truskmore
Fivemiletown
Drumcliff
Enniskillen
Caledon
Emyvale
Armagh
Rosses Point
Manorhamilton
Glaslough
Sligo Bay
Belcoo
Lisbellaw
Sligo
Strandhill
Blacklion
Maguiresbridge
Middletown
Monaghan
Lisnaskea
Rosslea
Castleshane
Keady
Upper Lough Erne
Lough Gill
Dromahair
Ballysadare
Smithborough
Clontibret
Newtownhamilton
Dowra
Swanlinbar
Derrylin
Clones
Collooney
Ballygawley
Newtownbutler
Drumkeeran
Lough Allen
Iron Mts
Newbliss
Ballybay
Rockcorry
Castleblayney
Ballymote
Lough Arrow
Ballyfarnan
Ballyconnell
Belturbet
Cootehill
Crossmaglen
Drumshanbo
Ballinamore
Ballyhaise
Keadew
Lough Key
Ballinafad
Killashandra
Boyle
Leitrim
Fenagh
Cavan
Shercock
Carrick-on-Shannon
Carrigallen
Stradone
Carrickmacross
Carracastle
Lough Gara
Airport
Ballaghaderreen
Mohill
Ballinagh
Drumsna
Arvagh
Lough Boderg
Bailieborough
Kingscourt
Frenchpark
Drumod
Kilnaleck
Ballyjamesduff
Drumcondra
Elphin
Lough Gowna
Virginia
Loughglinn
Roosky
Drumlish
Sheelin Lough
Lough Ramor
Nobber
Strokestown
Granard
Moynalty
Ballyhaunis
Castlerea
Tulsk
Ballinalee
Finnea
Oldcastle
Newtown Forbes
Carlanstown
Ballinlough
Scramoge
Castleplunket
Longford
Lisryan
Kells
Ballymoe
Ballintober
Cloondara
Crossakeel
Coole
Lanesborough
Edgeworthstown
Castlepollard
Kilberry
Clonmellon
Navan
Collinstown
Rathowen
Lough Derravaragh
Fuerty
Dunmore
Glennamaddy
Roscommon
Keenagh
Athboy
Crookedwood
Delvin
Creggs
Knockcroghery
Owel Lough
Athleague
Ballymahon
Trim
Ballygar
Tang
Mullingar
Raharney
Ballivor
Dunshaughlin
Moyvore
Killucan
Curraghboy
Lough Ree
Glassan
Ballymore
Rathmoylon
Kiltoom
Mountbellew Bridge
Caltra
Dysart
Kinnegad
Clonard
Summerhill
Ballykeeran
Lough Ennell
Enfield
Kilcock
Ballybaun
Athlone
Moate
Horseleap
Kilbeggan
Toll
Ahascragh
Tyrrellspass
Monivea
Clara
Edenderry
Bog of Allen
Celbridge
Kilconnell
Ballinasloe
Halfway Roads
Athenry
Ballycumber
Daingean
Clane
Grand Canal
Shannonbridge
Ferbane
Tullamore
Clonbullogue
Kilmeage
Sallins
Craughwell
Laurencetown
Geashill
Rathangan
Republic of Ireland
Clonony
Cloghan
Killeigh
Bracknagh
Newbridge
(An Droichead Nua)
Eyrecourt
Loughrea
Banagher
Kilcormac
Portarlington
Kildare
Killimor
Clonaslee
Ballymore Eustace
Cadamstown
Monasterevin
Kilcullen
Portumna
Birr
Mountmellick
River Shannon
Slieve Aughty Mts
Woodford
Kinnitty
Carrigahorig
Slieve Bloom Mts
Dunlavin
Portlaoise
Eontstown
Stradbally
Lough Graney
Mountrath
Athy
Castletown
Borrisokane
Shinrone
Roscrea
Timahoe
Ballyroan
Mountshannon
Cloughjordan
Lough Derg
Ballylynan
Baltinglass
Scarriff
Borris-in-Ossory
Abbeyleix
Castledermot
Tuamgraney
Ogonnelloe
Moneygall
Arless
Donaghmore
Ballycolla
Ballinakill
Rathvilly
Newtown
Nenagh
Toomyvarra
Cloghan
Killaloe
Rathdowney
Durrow
Carlow
Ballina
Clonmore
Templemore
Castlecomer
Tullow
Silvermines
Templetuohy
Ballyragget

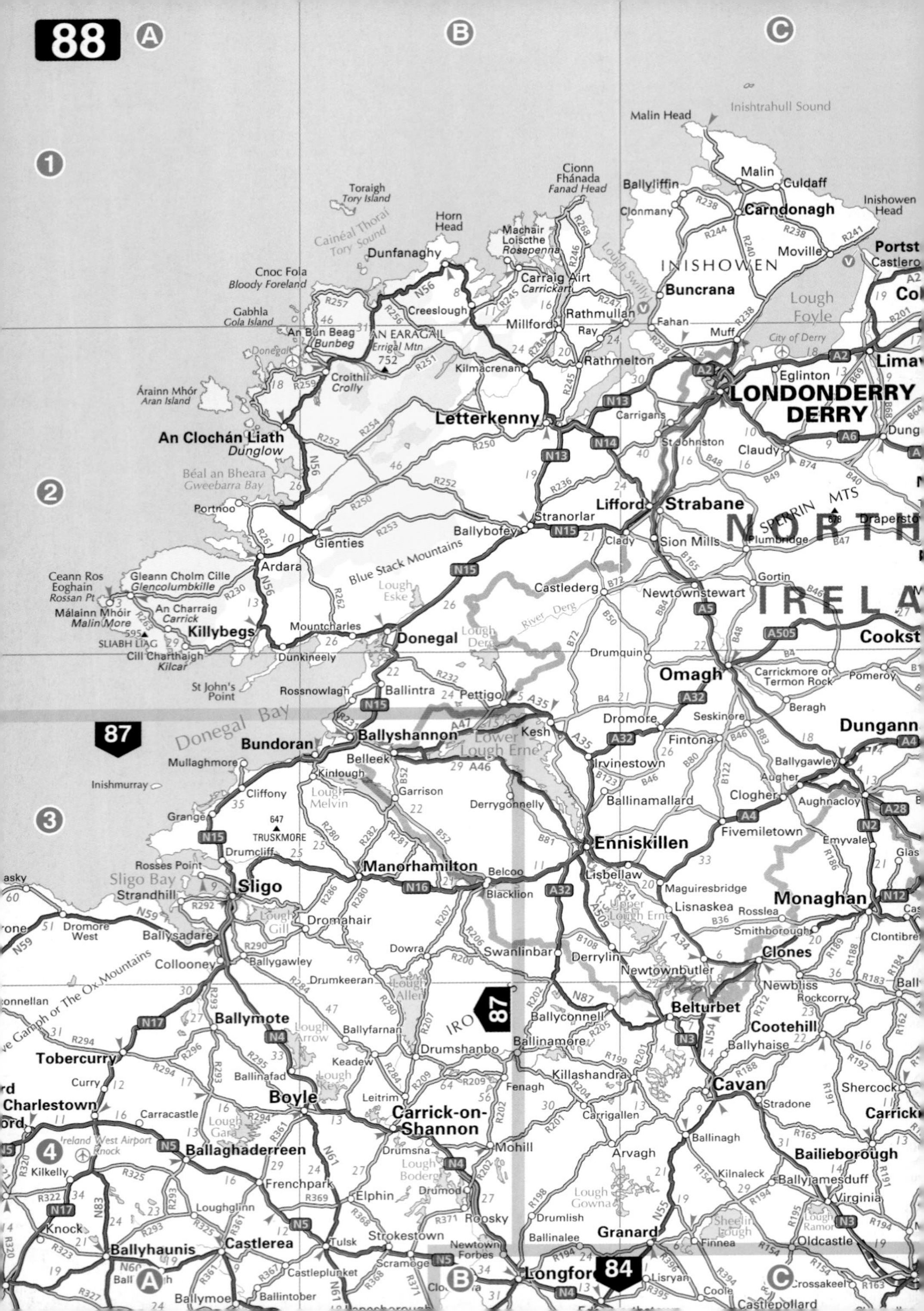
Malin Head
Inishtrahull Sound
Toraigh
Tory Island
Horn Head
Cionn Fhánada
Fanad Head
Ballyliffin
Malin
Culdaff
Carndonagh
Clonmany
Inishowen Head
Moville
INISHOWEN
Portstewart
Castlerock
Coleraine
Dunfanaghy
Cnoc Fola
Bloody Foreland
Gabhla
Gola Island
An Bun Beag
Bunbeg
Creeslough
AN EARAGAIL
Errigal Mtn
752
Carraig Airt
Carrickart
Machair Loiscthe
Rosepenna
Rathmullan
Buncrana
Lough Foyle
Millford
Fahan
Muff
Ray
City of Derry
Limavady
Eglinton
Kilmacrenan
Rathmelton
Croithlí
Crolly
Árainn Mhór
Aran Island
LONDONDERRY
DERRY
Letterkenny
Carrigans
An Clochán Liath
Dunglow
St Johnston
Claudy
Dungiven
Béal an Bheara
Gweebarra Bay
SPERRIN MTS
Portnoo
Lifford
Strabane
Stranorlar
Ballybofey
Glenties
Clady
Sion Mills
Plumbridge
Draperstown
NORTHERN IRELAND
Blue Stack Mountains
Ardara
Ceann Ros Eoghain
Rossan Pt
Gleann Cholm Cille
Glencolumbkille
Lough Eske
Castlederg
Newtownstewart
Gortin
An Charraig
Carrick
Málainn Mhóir
Malin More
Killybegs
Mountcharles
Donegal
River Derg
Lough Derg
Cookstown
595
SLIABH LIAG
Cill Charthaigh
Kilcar
Dunkineely
Drumquin
Omagh
Carrickmore or Termon Rock
Pomeroy
St John's Point
Rossnowlagh
Ballintra
Pettigo
Beragh
Donegal Bay
Kesh
Dromore
Seskinore
Dungannon
Bundoran
Ballyshannon
Lower Lough Erne
Fintona
Mullaghmore
Belleek
Irvinestown
Ballygawley
Inishmurray
Kinlough
Augher
Cliffony
Lough Melvin
Garrison
Derrygonnelly
Ballinamallard
Clogher
Aughnacloy
Grange
647
TRUSKMORE
Enniskillen
Fivemiletown
Emyvale
Drumcliff
Rosses Point
Manorhamilton
Belcoo
Lisbellaw
Glaslough
Sligo Bay
Sligo
Blacklion
Maguiresbridge
Strandhill
Upper Lough Erne
Monaghan
Lisnaskea
Rosslea
Dromore West
Dromahair
Lough Gill
Smithborough
Ballysadare
Clontibret
Collooney
Ballygawley
Dowra
Swanlinbar
Derrylin
Clones
Ox Mountains
Newtownbutler
Newbliss
Drumkeeran
Lough Allen
Rockcorry
Ballyconnell
Belturbet
Ballymote
Lough Arrow
Ballyfarnan
Cootehill
Tobercurry
Drumshanbo
Ballinamore
Ballyhaise
Keadew
Killashandra
Curry
Ballinafad
Lough Key
Fenagh
Cavan
Shercock
Charlestown
Boyle
Leitrim
Stradone
Carracastle
Lough Gara
Carrick-on-Shannon
Carrigallen
Carrickmacross
Ireland West Airport Knock
Ballaghaderreen
Drumsna
Mohill
Ballinagh
Bailieborough
Kilkelly
Arvagh
Frenchpark
Lough Boderg
Kilnaleck
Ballyjamesduff
Elphin
Drumod
Virginia
Loughglinn
Lough Gowna
Drumlish
Knock
Rooskey
Sheelin Lough
Lough Ramor
Strokestown
Granard
Ballyhaunis
Castlerea
Tulsk
Ballinalee
Finnea
Oldcastle
Newtown Forbes
Scramoge
Castleplunket
Longford
Lisryan
Crossakeel
Ballymoe
Ballintober
Coole
Castlepollard
87
84

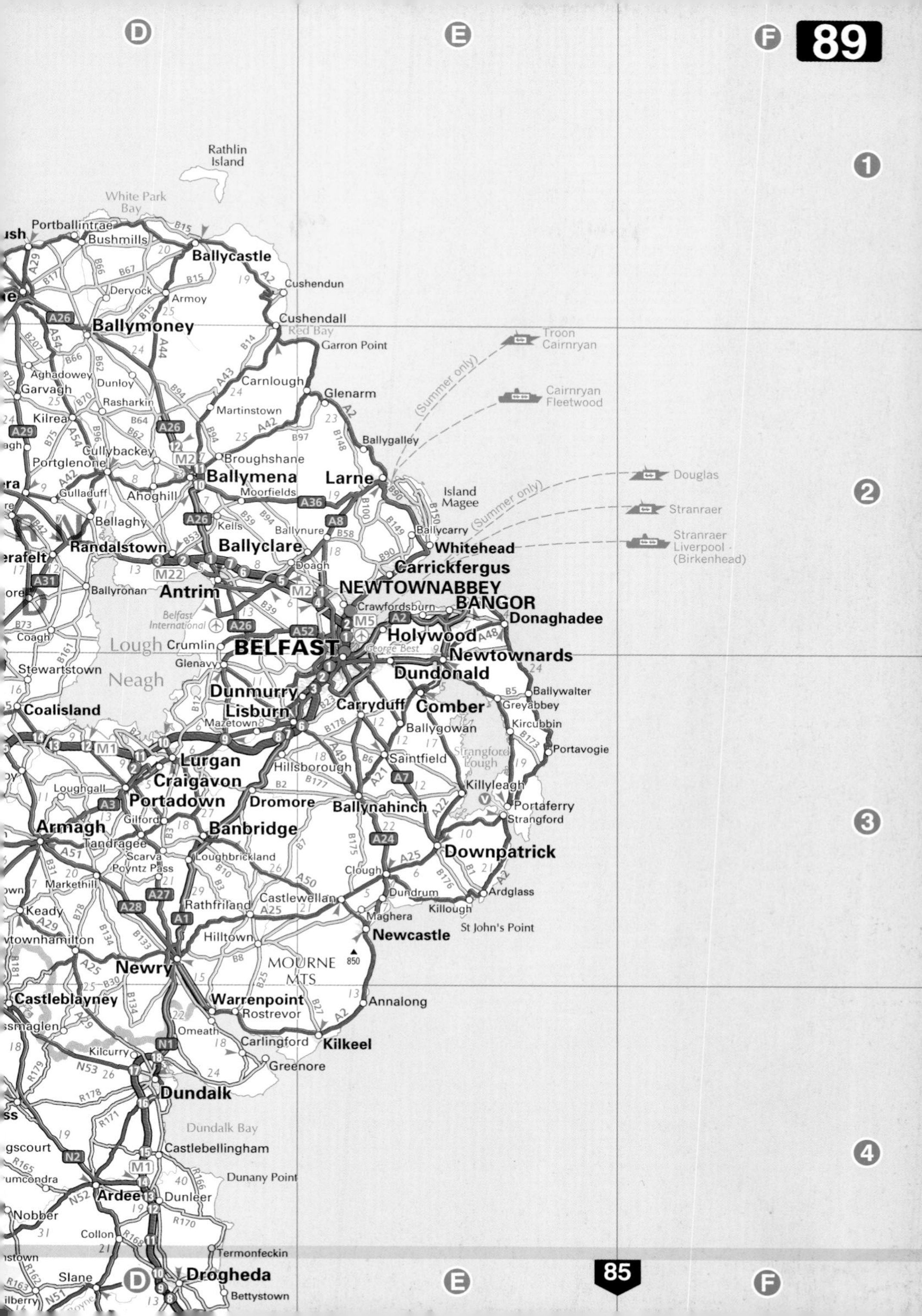
D
E
F
1
2
3
4
Rathlin Island
White Park Bay
Portballintrae
Bushmills
Ballycastle
Cushendun
Dervock
Armoy
Cushendall
Red Bay
Garron Point
Ballymoney
Aghadowey
Dunloy
Garvagh
Rasharkin
Kilrea
Carnlough
Glenarm
Martinstown
Cullybackey
Portglenone
Broughshane
Ballygalley
Ballymena
Larne
Moorfields
Gulladuff
Ahoghill
Island Magee
Bellaghy
Kells
Ballynure
Ballycarry
Randalstown
Ballyclare
Whitehead
Doagh
Carrickfergus
Ballyronan
Antrim
NEWTOWNABBEY
Crawfordsburn
BANGOR
Belfast International
Donaghadee
Coagh
Holywood
Lough Neagh
Crumlin
BELFAST
George Best
Newtownards
Glenavy
Stewartstown
Dundonald
Ballywalter
Dunmurry
Greyabbey
Coalisland
Carryduff
Comber
Lisburn
Kircubbin
Mazetown
Ballygowan
Portavogie
Lurgan
Hillsborough
Saintfield
Strangford Lough
Craigavon
Loughgall
Killyleagh
Portadown
Dromore
Ballynahinch
Portaferry
Strangford
Gilford
Armagh
Banbridge
Tandragee
Downpatrick
Scarva
Loughbrickland
Poyntz Pass
Markethill
Clough
Ardglass
Dundrum
Castlewellan
Keady
Rathfriland
Killough
Maghera
St John's Point
Newcastle
Hilltown
Newtownhamilton
Newry
MOURNE MTS
850
Castleblayney
Warrenpoint
Annalong
Rostrevor
Crossmaglen
Omeath
Carlingford
Kilkeel
Kilcurry
Greenore
Dundalk
Dundalk Bay
Castlebellingham
Dunany Point
Ardee
Dunleer
Nobber
Collon
Termonfeckin
Slane
Drogheda
Bettystown
Troon
Cairnryan
(Summer only)
Cairnryan
Fleetwood
Douglas
Stranraer
(Summer only)
Stranraer
Liverpool
(Birkenhead)

85

Mileage chart - Ireland

The mileage chart shows distances in miles between two towns along AA-recommended routes. Using motorways and other main roads this is normally the fastest route, though not necessarily the shortest.

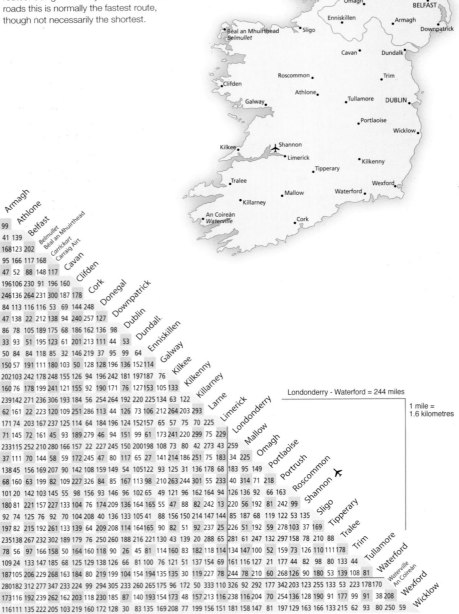

Londonderry - Waterford = 244 miles

1 mile = 1.6 kilometres

Mileage chart (distances in miles). Town labels run along the diagonal: Armagh, Athlone, Belfast, Belmullet / Béal an Mhuirthead, Carrickart / Carraig Airt, Cavan, Clifden, Cork, Donegal, Downpatrick, Dublin, Dundalk, Enniskillen, Galway, Kilkee, Kilkenny, Killarney, Larne, Limerick, Londonderry, Mallow, Omagh, Portlaoise, Portrush, Roscommon, Shannon, Sligo, Tipperary, Tralee, Trim, Tullamore, Waterford, Waterville / An Coireán, Wexford, Wicklow.

```
Armagh
99    Athlone
41   139   Belfast
168  123  202   Béal an Mhuirthead / Belmullet
95   166  117  168   Carraig Airt / Carrickart
47    52   88  148  117   Cavan
196  106  230   91  196  160   Clifden
246  136  264  231  300  187  178   Cork
84   113  116  116   53   69  144  248   Donegal
47   138   22  212  138   94  240  257  127   Downpatrick
86    78  105  189  175   68  186  162  136   98   Dublin
33    93   51  195  123   61  201  213  111   44   53   Dundalk
50    84   84  118   85   32  146  219   37   95   99   64   Enniskillen
150   57  191  111  180  103   50  128  128  196  136  152  114   Galway
202  103  242  178  248  155  126   94  196  242  181  197  187   76   Kilkee
160   76  178  199  241  121  155   92  190  171   76  127  153  105  133   Kilkenny
239  142  271  236  306  193  184   56  254  264  192  220  225  134   63  122   Killarney
62   161   22  223  120  109  251  286  113   44  126   73  106  212  264  203  293   Larne
171   74  203  167  237  125  114   64  184  196  124  152  157   65   57   75   70  225   Limerick
71   145   72  161   45   93  189  279   46   94  151   99   61  173  241  220  299   75  229   Londonderry
233  115  252  210  280  166  157   22  227  245  150  200  198  108   73   80   42  273   43  259   Mallow
37   111   70  144   58   59  172  245   47   80  117   65   27  141  214  186  251   75  183   34  225   Omagh
138   45  156  169  207   90  142  108  159  149   54  105  122   93  125   31  136  178   68  183   95  149   Portlaoise
68   160   63  199   82  109  227  326   84   85  167  113   98  210  263  244  301   55  233   40  314   71  218   Portrush
101   20  142  103  145   55   98  156   93  146   96  102   65   49  121   96  162  164   94  126  136   92   66  163   Roscommon
180   81  221  157  227  133  104   76  174  209  136  164  165   55   47   88   82  242   13  220   56  192   81  242   99   Shannon
92    74  125   76   92   70  104  208   40  136  133  105   41   88  156  150  214  147  144   85  187   68  119  122   53  135   Sligo
197   82  215  192  261  133  139   64  209  208  114  164  165   90   82   51   92  237   25  226   51  192   59  278  103   37  169   Tipperary
235  138  267  232  302  189  179   76  250  260  188  216  221  130   43  139   20  288   65  281   61  247  132  297  158   78  210   88   Tralee
78    56   97  166  158   50  164  160  118   90   26   45   81  114  160   83  182  118  114  134  147  100   52  159   73  126  110  111  178   Trim
109   24  133  147  185   68  125  129  138  126   66   81  100   76  121   51  137  154   69  161  116  127   21  177   44   82   98   80  133   44   Tullamore
187  105  206  229  268  163  184   80  219  199  104  154  194  135  135   30  119  227   78  244   78  210   60  268  126   90  180   53  139  108   81   Waterford
280  182  312  277  347  233  224   99  294  305  233  260  265  175   96  172   50  333  110  326   92  292  177  342  203  123  255  133   53  223  178  170   An Coireán / Waterville
173  116  192  239  262  162  203  118  230  185   87  140  193  154  173   48  157  213  116  238  116  204   70  254  136  128  190   91  177   99   91   38  208   Wexford
116  111  135  222  205  103  219  160  172  128   30   83  135  169  208   77  199  156  151  181  158  147   81  197  129  163  166  133  215   62   93   80  250   59   Wicklow
```

A

82 C2 **Abbeydorney** Kerry
82 C2 **Abbeyfeale** Limrck
84 C3 **Abbeyleix** Laois
85 D4 **Adamstown** Wexfd
83 D2 **Adare** Limrck
82 C3 **Adrigole** Cork
89 D2 **Aghadowey** Lderry
87 D3 **Ahascragh** Galway
89 D2 **Ahoghill** Antrim
82 B3 **Allihies** Cork
82 B2 **Anascaul** Kerry
88 B2 **An Bun Beag** Donegl
88 A2 **An Charraig** Donegl
88 A2 **An Clochán Liath** Donegl
82 B3 **An Coireán** Kerry
82 B2 **An Daingean** Kerry
86 C3 **An Fhairche** Galway
89 E4 **Annalong** Down
84 C4 **Annestown** Watfd
83 F3 **An Rinn** Watfd
86 C3 **An Spidéal** Galway
89 D2 **Antrim** Antrim
83 D2 **Ardagh** Limrck
88 A2 **Ardara** Donegl
89 D4 **Ardee** Louth
82 C2 **Ardfert** Kerry
84 C4 **Ardfinnan** Tippry
89 E3 **Ardglass** Down
82 B3 **Ardgroom** Cork
83 E3 **Ardmore** Watfd
85 E3 **Arklow** Wicklw
85 D3 **Arless** Laois
89 D3 **Armagh** Armagh
89 D1 **Armoy** Antrim
85 D4 **Arthurstown** Wexfd
88 B4 **Arvagh** Cavan
85 E1 **Ashbourne** Meath
85 E2 **Ashford** Wicklw
83 D1 **Askeaton** Limrck
85 D1 **Athboy** Meath
82 C2 **Athea** Limrck
87 D3 **Athenry** Galway
87 D3 **Athleague** Roscom
84 C1 **Athlone** Wmeath
85 D2 **Athy** Kildre
88 C3 **Augher** Tyrone
88 C3 **Aughnacloy** Tyrone
85 E3 **Aughrim** Wicklw
85 E3 **Avoca** Wicklw

B

85 D3 **Bagenalstown** Carlow
82 C3 **Baile Mhic Íre** Cork
88 C4 **Bailieborough** Cavan
85 E1 **Balbriggan** Dublin
86 C2 **Balla** Mayo
87 D2 **Ballaghaderreen** Roscom
86 C2 **Ballina** Mayo
83 D1 **Ballina** Tippry
87 D2 **Ballinafad** Sligo
84 C3 **Ballinakill** Laois
88 B4 **Ballinalee** Longfd
88 B3 **Ballinamallard** Ferman
88 B4 **Ballinamore** Leitrm
83 D3 **Ballinascarty** Cork
84 B2 **Ballinasloe** Galway
86 C3 **Ballindine** Mayo
83 D3 **Ballineen** Cork
83 D2 **Ballingarry** Limrck
84 C3 **Ballingarry** Tippry
82 C3 **Ballingeary** Cork
83 D3 **Ballinhassig** Cork
87 D2 **Ballinlough** Roscom
86 C3 **Ballinrobe** Mayo
83 D3 **Ballinspittle** Cork
87 D2 **Ballintober** Roscom
88 B3 **Ballintra** Donegl
85 D1 **Ballivor** Meath
85 D3 **Ballon** Carlow
87 D3 **Ballybay** Galway
88 C4 **Ballybay** Monhan
88 B2 **Ballybofey** Donegl
82 C2 **Ballybunion** Kerry
85 E3 **Ballycanew** Wexfd
89 E2 **Ballycarry** Antrim
89 D1 **Ballycastle** Antrim
86 C1 **Ballycastle** Mayo
89 E2 **Ballyclare** Antrim
84 C3 **Ballycolla** Laois
86 B3 **Ballyconneely** Galway
88 B4 **Ballyconnell** Cavan
83 E3 **Ballycotton** Cork
84 C2 **Ballycumber** Offaly
82 C4 **Ballydehob** Cork
82 C2 **Ballydesmond** Cork
82 C2 **Ballyduff** Kerry
84 B4 **Ballyduff** Watfd
87 D2 **Ballyfarnan** Roscom
89 E2 **Ballygalley** Antrim
87 D3 **Ballygar** Galway
87 D1 **Ballygawley** Sligo
88 C3 **Ballygawley** Tyrone
89 E3 **Ballygowan** Down
85 D4 **Ballyhack** Wexfd
88 C4 **Ballyhaise** Cavan
85 D3 **Ballyhale** Kilken
87 D2 **Ballyhaunis** Mayo
86 C2 **Ballyhean** Mayo
82 B2 **Ballyheige** Kerry
88 C4 **Ballyjamesduff** Cavan
84 C1 **Ballykeeran** Wmeath
83 E2 **Ballylanders** Limrck
82 C3 **Ballylickey** Cork
88 C1 **Ballyliffin** Donegl
82 C2 **Ballylongford** Kerry
84 B4 **Ballylooby** Tippry
85 D2 **Ballylynan** Laois
84 C4 **Ballymacarbry** Watfd
84 C1 **Ballymahon** Longfd
82 C3 **Ballymakeery** Cork
89 D2 **Ballymena** Antrim
87 D2 **Ballymoe** Galway
89 D2 **Ballymoney** Antrim
84 C1 **Ballymore** Wmeath
85 D2 **Ballymore Eustace** Kildre
87 D2 **Ballymote** Sligo
89 E3 **Ballynahinch** Down
89 E2 **Ballynure** Antrim
84 B4 **Ballyporeen** Tippry
84 C3 **Ballyragget** Kilken
84 C2 **Ballyroan** Laois
89 D2 **Ballyronan** Lderry
87 D1 **Ballysadare** Sligo
87 D1 **Ballyshannon** Donegl
86 C4 **Ballyvaughan** Clare
89 E3 **Ballywalter** Down
85 E1 **Balrothery** Dublin
82 C4 **Baltimore** Cork
85 D2 **Baltinglass** Wicklw
84 B2 **Banagher** Offaly

89 D3 **Banbridge** Down
83 D3 **Bandon** Cork
89 E2 **Bangor** Down
86 B2 **Bangor Erris** Mayo
84 B3 **Bansha** Tippry
83 D2 **Banteer** Cork
82 C3 **Bantry** Cork
86 C3 **Barna** Galway
86 B1 **Béal an Mhuirthead** Mayo
82 C3 **Béal Átha an Ghaorthaidh** Cork
86 C3 **Bearna** Galway
82 C3 **Beaufort** Kerry
87 E1 **Belcoo** Ferman
89 E3 **Belfast** Belfst
83 D3 **Belgooly** Cork
89 D2 **Bellaghy** Lderry
88 C4 **Bellananagh** Cavan
87 D1 **Belleek** Ferman
86 B1 **Belmullet** Mayo
88 C4 **Belturbet** Cavan
89 D3 **Benburb** Tyrone
85 D3 **Bennettsbridge** Kilken
88 C3 **Beragh** Tyrone
85 E1 **Bettystown** Meath
84 C2 **Birr** Offaly
87 E1 **Blacklion** Cavan
85 E2 **Blackrock** Dublin
85 E3 **Blackwater** Wexfd
83 D3 **Blarney** Cork
85 D2 **Blessington** Wicklw
83 D3 **Boherbue** Cork
85 D3 **Borris** Carlow
84 C2 **Borris in Ossory** Laois
84 B3 **Borrisokane** Tippry
84 C3 **Borrisoleigh** Tippry
87 D2 **Boyle** Roscom
84 B2 **Bracknagh** Offaly
85 E2 **Bray** Wicklw
85 D4 **Bridgetown** Wexfd
85 E2 **Brittas** Dublin
83 D1 **Broadford** Clare
83 D2 **Broadford** Limrck
89 D2 **Broughshane** Antrim
83 D2 **Bruff** Limrck
83 D2 **Bruree** Limrck
88 B2 **Bunbeg** Donegl
85 D3 **Bunclody** Wexfd
88 C1 **Buncrana** Donegl
87 D1 **Bundoran** Donegl
84 C4 **Bunmahon** Watfd
86 B1 **Bun na hAbhna** Mayo
86 B1 **Bunnahowen** Mayo
86 C2 **Bunnyconnellan** Mayo
83 D1 **Bunratty** Clare
83 D3 **Burnfort** Cork
89 D1 **Bushmills** Antrim
83 D2 **Buttevant** Cork

C

84 C2 **Cadamstown** Offaly
83 D1 **Caherconlish** Limrck
82 B3 **Caherdaniel** Kerry
82 B3 **Cahersiveen** Kerry
84 C4 **Cahir** Tippry
88 C3 **Caledon** Tyrone
84 C3 **Callan** Kilken
87 D3 **Caltra** Galway
82 B2 **Camp** Kerry

85 D4 **Campile** Wexfd
84 B3 **Cappagh White** Tippry
83 E1 **Cappamore** Limrck
84 C4 **Cappoquin** Watfd
85 D1 **Carlanstown** Meath
89 D4 **Carlingford** Louth
85 D3 **Carlow** Carlow
86 B3 **Carna** Galway
88 C1 **Carndonagh** Donegl
85 E3 **Carnew** Wicklw
89 E2 **Carnlough** Antrim
87 D2 **Carracastle** Mayo
88 B1 **Carraig Airt** Donegl
88 A2 **Carrick** Donegl
88 B1 **Carrickart** Donegl
89 E2 **Carrickfergus** Antrim
89 D4 **Carrickmacross** Monhan
88 C3 **Carrickmore or Termon Rock** Tyrone
87 D2 **Carrick-on-Shannon** Leitrm
84 C4 **Carrick-on-Suir** Tippry
87 D4 **Carrigahorig** Tippry
83 D3 **Carrigaline** Cork
88 B4 **Carrigallen** Leitrm
83 D3 **Carriganimmy** Cork
88 C2 **Carrigans** Donegl
83 E3 **Carrigtohill** Cork
89 E3 **Carryduff** Down
86 B3 **Cashel** Galway
84 C3 **Cashel** Tippry
86 C2 **Castlebar** Mayo
89 D4 **Castlebellingham** Louth
89 D4 **Castleblayney** Monhan
85 E4 **Castlebridge** Wexfd
85 D3 **Castlecomer** Kilken
83 D1 **Castleconnell** Limrck
88 B2 **Castlederg** Tyrone
85 D2 **Castledermot** Kildre
82 B2 **Castlegregory** Kerry
82 C2 **Castleisland** Kerry
82 C2 **Castlemaine** Kerry
83 E3 **Castlemartyr** Cork
87 D2 **Castleplunket** Roscom
84 C1 **Castlepollard** Wmeath
87 D2 **Castlerea** Roscom
88 C1 **Castlerock** Lderry
88 C3 **Castleshane** Monhan
84 C2 **Castletown** Laois
82 B3 **Castletown Bearhaven** Cork
83 D2 **Castletownroche** Cork
82 C4 **Castletownshend** Cork
89 E3 **Castlewellan** Down
82 B3 **Cathair Dónall** Kerry
82 C2 **Causeway** Kerry
88 C4 **Cavan** Cavan
85 D2 **Celbridge** Kildre
86 C2 **Charlestown** Mayo
83 D2 **Charleville** Cork
85 D4 **Cheekpoint** Watfd
88 A2 **Cill Charthaigh** Donegl
86 B3 **Cill Chiaráin** Galway
88 C2 **Clady** Tyrone
85 D2 **Clane** Kildre
84 C2 **Clara** Offaly

83 D1	**Clarecastle** Clare	
86 C2	**Claremorris** Mayo	
86 C3	**Clarinbridge** Galway	
83 E3	**Clashmore** Watfd	
88 C2	**Claudy** Lderry	
86 B3	**Clifden** Galway	
87 D1	**Cliffony** Sligo	
85 D3	**Clogh** Kilken	
84 C2	**Cloghan** Offaly	
84 B4	**Clogheen** Tippry	
88 C3	**Clogher** Tyrone	
85 D3	**Clohamon** Wexfd	
83 D4	**Clonakilty** Cork	
85 D1	**Clonard** Meath	
84 C2	**Clonaslee** Laois	
85 D2	**Clonbulloge** Offaly	
86 C3	**Clonbur** Galway	
85 E2	**Clondalkin** Dublin	
88 C3	**Clones** Monhan	
83 D1	**Clonlara** Clare	
88 C1	**Clonmany** Donegl	
84 C4	**Clonmel** Tippry	
85 D1	**Clonmellon** Wmeath	
84 C3	**Clonmore** Tippry	
84 C2	**Clonony** Offaly	
84 C3	**Clonoulty** Tippry	
85 D3	**Clonroche** Wexfd	
88 C3	**Clontibret** Monhan	
84 C1	**Cloondara** Longfd	
89 E3	**Clough** Down	
87 E4	**Cloughjordan** Tippry	
83 E3	**Cloyne** Cork	
89 D2	**Coagh** Tyrone	
89 D3	**Coalisland** Tyrone	
83 E3	**Cobh** Cork	
89 D1	**Coleraine** Lderry	
85 D1	**Collinstown** Wmeath	
89 D4	**Collon** Louth	
87 D1	**Collooney** Sligo	
89 E3	**Comber** Down	
86 C3	**Cong** Mayo	
83 E3	**Conna** Cork	
89 D2	**Cookstown** Tyrone	
84 C1	**Coole** Wmeath	
82 C1	**Cooraclare** Clare	
88 C4	**Cootehill** Cavan	
83 D3	**Cork** Cork	
86 C3	**Cornamona** Galway	
86 C3	**Corr na Móna** Galway	
86 C4	**Corrofin** Clare	
83 D3	**Courtmacsherry** Cork	
85 E3	**Courtown** Wexfd	
89 D3	**Craigavon** Armagh	
87 D3	**Craughwell** Galway	
89 E2	**Crawfordsburn** Down	
87 D3	**Creegs** Galway	
88 B1	**Creeslough** Donegl	
83 D2	**Croagh** Limrck	
88 B2	**Croithlí** Donegl	
88 B2	**Crolly** Donegl	
84 C1	**Crookedwood** Wmeath	
82 C4	**Crookhaven** Cork	
83 D3	**Crookstown** Cork	
83 D2	**Croom** Limrck	
85 D1	**Crossakeel** Meath	
83 D3	**Cross Barry** Cork	
83 E3	**Crosshaven** Cork	
89 D4	**Crossmaglen** Armagh	
86 C2	**Crossmolina** Mayo	
89 D2	**Crumlin** Antrim	
86 C4	**Crusheen** Clare	
88 C1	**Culdaff** Donegl	
89 D2	**Cullybackey** Antrim	
85 E4	**Curracloe** Wexfd	
87 D3	**Curraghboy** Roscom	
87 D2	**Curry** Sligo	
89 D2	**Cushendall** Antrim	
89 D1	**Cushendun** Antrim	

D

84 C2	**Daingean** Offaly	
85 E2	**Delgany** Wicklw	
85 D1	**Delvin** Wmeath	
88 C2	**Derry** Lderry	
87 E1	**Derrygonnelly** Ferman	
88 B3	**Derrylin** Ferman	
89 D1	**Dervock** Antrim	
82 B2	**Dingle** Kerry	
89 D2	**Doagh** Antrim	
89 E2	**Donaghadee** Down	
84 C3	**Donaghmore** Laois	
85 D2	**Donard** Wicklw	
88 B2	**Donegal** Donegl	
83 D2	**Doneraile** Cork	
86 C4	**Doolin** Clare	
83 E1	**Doon** Limrck	
82 C1	**Doonbeg** Clare	
84 C2	**Doon Cross Roads** Offaly	
83 D3	**Douglas** Cork	
89 E3	**Downpatrick** Down	
87 E1	**Dowra** Cavan	
89 D2	**Draperstown** Lderry	
82 C3	**Drimoleague** Cork	
83 D3	**Dripsey** Cork	
85 E1	**Drogheda** Louth	
87 D1	**Dromahair** Leitrm	
83 D2	**Dromcolliher** Limrck	
89 D3	**Dromore** Down	
88 C3	**Dromore** Tyrone	
86 C1	**Dromore West** Sligo	
87 D1	**Drumcliff** Sligo	
89 D4	**Drumcondra** Meath	
87 D1	**Drumkeeran** Leitrm	
88 B4	**Drumlish** Longfd	
87 E2	**Drumod** Leitrm	
88 C3	**Drumquin** Tyrone	
87 E2	**Drumshanbo** Leitrm	
87 E2	**Drumsna** Leitrm	
82 C2	**Duagh** Kerry	
85 E2	**Dublin** Dublin	
85 E1	**Duleek** Meath	
85 E1	**Dunboyne** Meath	
85 D4	**Duncormick** Wexfd	
89 D4	**Dundalk** Louth	
83 D3	**Dunderrow** Cork	
89 E3	**Dundonald** Down	
89 E3	**Dundrum** Down	
84 B3	**Dundrum** Tippry	
88 B1	**Dunfanaghy** Donegl	
89 D3	**Dungannon** Tyrone	
85 D3	**Dungarvan** Kilken	
83 F3	**Dungarvan** Watfd	
88 C2	**Dungiven** Lderry	
88 A2	**Dunglow** Donegl	
85 E3	**Dungourney** Cork	
88 A2	**Dunkineely** Donegl	
85 E2	**Dún Laoghaire** Dublin	
85 D2	**Dunlavin** Wicklw	
89 D4	**Dunleer** Louth	
89 D2	**Dunloy** Antrim	
82 C3	**Dunmanway** Cork	
87 D3	**Dunmore** Galway	
83 D4	**Dunmore East** Watfd	
89 E3	**Dunmurry** Antrim	

E

85 D1	**Dunshaughlin** Meath	
84 C3	**Durrow** Laois	
82 C4	**Durrus** Cork	
87 D3	**Dysart** Roscom	

86 C1	**Easky** Sligo	
85 D2	**Edenderry** Offaly	
84 C1	**Edgeworthstown** Longfd	
88 C2	**Eglinton** Lderry	
87 D2	**Elphin** Roscom	
88 C3	**Emyvale** Monhan	
85 D1	**Enfield** Meath	
83 D1	**Ennis** Clare	
85 D3	**Enniscorthy** Wexfd	
83 D3	**Enniskean** Cork	
88 B3	**Enniskillen** Ferman	
86 C4	**Ennistymon** Clare	
87 D4	**Eyrecourt** Galway	

F

88 C2	**Fahan** Donegl	
82 C2	**Farranfore** Kerry	
87 D4	**Feakle** Clare	
87 E2	**Fenagh** Leitrm	
84 C2	**Ferbane** Offaly	
83 E2	**Fermoy** Cork	
85 E3	**Ferns** Wexfd	
84 C3	**Fethard** Tippry	
85 D4	**Fethard** Wexfd	
88 C4	**Finnea** Wmeath	
88 C3	**Fintona** Tyrone	
88 C3	**Fivemiletown** Tyrone	
85 D2	**Fontstown** Kildre	
85 D4	**Foulkesmill** Wexfd	
86 C2	**Foxford** Mayo	
83 D1	**Foynes** Limrck	
83 D2	**Freemount** Cork	
87 D2	**Frenchpark** Roscom	
85 D3	**Freshford** Kilken	
87 D3	**Fuerty** Roscom	

G

83 E2	**Galbally** Limrck	
86 C3	**Galway** Galway	
87 D1	**Garrison** Ferman	
85 E1	**Garristown** Dublin	
83 E3	**Garryvoe** Cork	
89 D2	**Garvagh** Lderry	
84 C2	**Geashill** Offaly	
89 D3	**Gilford** Down	
82 C4	**Glandore** Cork	
83 E2	**Glanmire** Cork	
83 E2	**Glanworth** Cork	
88 C3	**Glaslough** Monhan	
84 C1	**Glassan** Wmeath	
88 A2	**Gleann Cholm Cille** Donegl	
89 E2	**Glenarm** Antrim	
89 D3	**Glenavy** Antrim	
82 B3	**Glenbeigh** Kerry	
88 A2	**Glencolumbkille** Donegl	
85 E2	**Glenealy** Wicklw	
82 C3	**Glengarriff** Cork	

85 D4	**Glenmore** Kilken	
87 D3	**Glennamaddy** Galway	
88 B2	**Glenties** Donegl	
82 C2	**Glin** Limrck	
86 B3	**Glinsce** Galway	
86 B3	**Glinsk** Galway	
84 B3	**Golden** Tippry	
82 C4	**Goleen** Cork	
85 D3	**Goresbridge** Kilken	
85 E3	**Gorey** Wexfd	
86 C4	**Gort** Galway	
88 C2	**Gortin** Tyrone	
85 D3	**Gowran** Kilken	
85 D3	**Graiguenamanagh** Kilken	
88 C4	**Granard** Longfd	
87 D1	**Grange** Sligo	
89 D4	**Greenore** Louth	
89 E3	**Greyabbey** Down	
85 E2	**Greystones** Wicklw	
89 D2	**Gulladuff** Lderry	

H

85 D3	**Hacketstown** Carlow	
86 C3	**Headford** Galway	
83 D2	**Herbertstown** Limrck	
89 D3	**Hillsborough** Down	
89 D3	**Hilltown** Down	
84 C3	**Holycross** Tippry	
89 E2	**Holywood** Down	
84 C1	**Horseleap** Wmeath	
83 D2	**Hospital** Limrck	
85 E1	**Howth** Dublin	

I

82 B2	**Inch** Kerry	
82 C3	**Inchigeelagh** Cork	
83 D3	**Inishannon** Cork	
86 C1	**Inishcrone** Sligo	
85 D3	**Inistioge** Kilken	
88 B3	**Irvinestown** Ferman	

J

84 C3	**Johnstown** Kilken	

K

83 D2	**Kanturk** Cork	
87 D2	**Keadew** Roscom	
89 D3	**Keady** Armagh	
86 B2	**Keel** Mayo	
84 C1	**Keenagh** Longfd	
89 D2	**Kells** Antrim	
85 D1	**Kells** Meath	
82 C3	**Kenmare** Kerry	
88 B3	**Kesh** Ferman	
84 C2	**Kilbeggan** Wmeath	
85 D1	**Kilberry** Meath	
83 D3	**Kilbrittain** Cork	
88 A2	**Kilcar** Donegl	
85 D1	**Kilcock** Kildre	
86 C4	**Kilcolgan** Galway	
87 D3	**Kilconnell** Galway	
85 E2	**Kilcoole** Wicklw	

84 C2 **Kilcormac** Offaly
85 D2 **Kilcullen** Kildre
89 D4 **Kilcurry** Louth
85 D2 **Kildare** Kildre
85 D3 **Kildavin** Carlow
83 D2 **Kildorrery** Cork
86 C4 **Kilfenora** Clare
82 C3 **Kilgarvan** Kerry
82 C1 **Kilkee** Clare
89 E4 **Kilkeel** Down
86 C2 **Kilkelly** Mayo
84 C3 **Kilkenny** Kilken
86 B3 **Kilkieran** Galway
82 C2 **Kilkinlea Lower** Limrck
85 D2 **Kill** Kildre
84 C4 **Kill** Watfd
83 D1 **Killadysert** Clare
86 C1 **Killala** Mayo
83 D1 **Killaloe** Clare
82 C3 **Killarney** Kerry
88 C4 **Killashandra** Cavan
83 E3 **Killeagh** Cork
84 C2 **Killeigh** Offaly
84 C3 **Killenaule** Tippry
82 C1 **Killimer** Clare
87 D4 **Killimor** Galway
85 E2 **Killiney** Dublin
85 E4 **Killinick** Wexfd
82 C2 **Killorglin** Kerry
89 E3 **Killough** Down
85 D1 **Killucan** Wmeath
88 A2 **Killybegs** Donegl
89 E3 **Killyleagh** Down
85 E2 **Kilmacanoge** Wicklw
88 B2 **Kilmacrenan** Donegl
84 C4 **Kilmacthomas** Watfd
84 C3 **Kilmaganny** Kilken
86 C3 **Kilmaine** Mayo
83 D2 **Kilmallock** Limrck
84 C3 **Kilmanagh** Kilken
84 C4 **Kilmeadan** Watfd
85 D2 **Kilmeage** Kildre
83 D2 **Kilmeedy** Limrck
85 D1 **Kilmessan** Meath
83 D3 **Kilmichael** Cork
85 D4 **Kilmore Quay** Wexfd
85 E3 **Kilmuckridge** Wexfd
88 C4 **Kilnaleck** Cavan
89 D2 **Kilrea** Lderry
82 C1 **Kilrush** Clare
84 C4 **Kilsheelan** Tippry
86 C2 **Kiltamagh** Mayo
85 D3 **Kiltealy** Wexfd
85 D3 **Kiltegan** Wicklw
87 E3 **Kiltoom** Roscom
89 D4 **Kingscourt** Cavan
87 D1 **Kinlough** Leitrm
85 D1 **Kinnegad** Wmeath
84 C2 **Kinnitty** Offaly
83 D3 **Kinsale** Cork
86 C4 **Kinvarra** Galway
89 E3 **Kircubbin** Down
86 C2 **Knock** Mayo
87 D3 **Knockcroghery** Roscom
84 C4 **Knocklofty** Tippry
85 D3 **Knocktopher** Kilken

86 C4 **Lahinch** Clare

84 B1 **Lanesborough** Roscom
85 E2 **Laragh** Wicklw
89 E2 **Larne** Antrim
82 C3 **Lauragh** Kerry
87 D3 **Laurencetown** Galway
82 C4 **Leap** Cork
86 B3 **Leenane** Galway
85 D3 **Leighlinbridge** Carlow
87 D2 **Leitrim** Leitrm
85 D2 **Leixlip** Kildre
84 C4 **Lemybrien** Watfd
86 B3 **Letterfrack** Galway
88 B2 **Letterkenny** Donegl
88 C2 **Lifford** Donegl
88 C2 **Limavady** Lderry
83 D1 **Limerick** Limrck
88 C3 **Lisbellaw** Ferman
89 D3 **Lisburn** Antrim
86 C4 **Liscannor** Clare
83 D2 **Liscarroll** Cork
86 C4 **Lisdoonvarna** Clare
84 C4 **Lismore** Watfd
88 C3 **Lisnaskea** Ferman
84 C1 **Lisryan** Longfd
82 C2 **Listowel** Kerry
82 C1 **Loghill** Limrck
88 C2 **Londonderry** Lderry
84 C1 **Longford** Longfd
89 D3 **Loughbrickland** Down
89 D3 **Loughgall** Armagh
87 D2 **Loughglinn** Roscom
87 D4 **Loughrea** Galway
86 B2 **Louisburgh** Mayo
85 E2 **Lucan** Dublin
89 D3 **Lurgan** Armagh
85 E1 **Lusk** Dublin

88 B1 **Machair Loiscthe** Donegl
83 D2 **Macroom** Cork
89 E3 **Maghera** Down
89 D2 **Maghera** Lderry
89 D2 **Magherafelt** Lderry
88 C3 **Maguiresbridge** Ferman
85 E1 **Malahide** Dublin
88 A2 **Málainn Mhóir** Donegl
88 C1 **Malin** Donegl
88 A2 **Malin More** Donegl
83 D2 **Mallow** Cork
87 D1 **Manorhamilton** Leitrm
89 D3 **Markethill** Armagh
89 D2 **Martinstown** Antrim
85 D1 **Maynooth** Kildre
89 D3 **Mazetown** Antrim
88 C3 **Middletown** Armagh
83 E3 **Midleton** Cork
88 B2 **Milford** Donegl
83 D3 **Millstreet** Cork
82 C2 **Milltown** Kerry
82 C1 **Milltown Malbay** Clare
83 E2 **Mitchelstown** Cork
84 C1 **Moate** Wmeath
87 E2 **Mohill** Leitrm
88 C3 **Monaghan** Monhan
85 D2 **Monasterevin** Kildre
84 C3 **Moneygall** Offaly

89 D2 **Moneymore** Lderry
87 D3 **Monivea** Galway
84 C4 **Mooncoin** Kilken
89 D2 **Moorfields** Antrim
87 D3 **Mountbellew Bridge** Galway
88 B2 **Mountcharles** Donegl
84 C2 **Mountmellick** Laois
84 C2 **Mountrath** Laois
87 D4 **Mountshannon** Clare
88 C1 **Moville** Donegl
89 D3 **Moy** Tyrone
88 C4 **Moynalty** Meath
84 C1 **Moyvore** Wmeath
82 C3 **Muckross** Kerry
88 C2 **Muff** Donegl
87 D1 **Mullaghmore** Sligo
85 D4 **Mullinavat** Kilken
84 C1 **Mullingar** Wmeath
86 B2 **Mulrany** Mayo
85 D3 **Myshall** Carlow

85 D2 **Naas** Kildre
85 D1 **Naul** Dublin
85 D1 **Navan** Meath
86 C3 **Neale** Mayo
83 E1 **Nenagh** Tippry
88 C3 **Newbliss** Monhan
85 D2 **Newbridge** Kildre
89 E3 **Newcastle** Down
83 D2 **Newcastle West** Limrck
84 C4 **Newinn** Tippry
83 D2 **Newmarket** Cork
83 D1 **Newmarket-on-Fergus** Clare
86 B2 **Newport** Mayo
83 D1 **Newport** Tippry
85 D4 **New Ross** Wexfd
89 D3 **Newry** Lderry
84 C2 **Newtown** Laois
89 E2 **Newtownabbey** Antrim
89 E3 **Newtownards** Down
88 C3 **Newtownbutler** Ferman
84 C1 **Newtown Forbes** Longfd
89 D3 **Newtownhamilton** Armagh
85 E2 **Newtown Mount Kennedy** Wicklw
88 C2 **Newtownstewart** Tyrone
89 D4 **Nobber** Meath

83 D1 **Ogonnelloe** Clare
85 D4 **Oilgate** Wexfd
88 C4 **Oldcastle** Meath
88 C3 **Omagh** Tyrone
89 D4 **Omeath** Louth
83 E2 **Oola** Limrck
86 C3 **Oranmore** Galway
86 C3 **Oughterard** Galway

83 D3 **Ovens** Cork

83 E2 **Pallas Grean New** Limrck
82 B3 **Parknasilla** Kerry
86 C2 **Partry** Mayo
85 D4 **Passage East** Watfd
83 E3 **Passage West** Cork
83 D1 **Patrickswell** Limrck
85 D3 **Paulstown** Kilken
88 B3 **Pettigo** Donegl
88 C2 **Plumbridge** Tyrone
88 C3 **Pomeroy** Tyrone
89 D3 **Portadown** Armagh
89 E3 **Portaferry** Down
85 D2 **Portarlington** Laois
89 E3 **Portavogie** Down
89 D1 **Portballintrae** Antrim
89 D2 **Portglenone** Antrim
84 C2 **Portlaoise** Laois
85 E1 **Portmarnock** Dublin
88 A2 **Portnoo** Donegl
85 E1 **Portraine** Dublin
83 E1 **Portroe** Tippry
89 D1 **Portrush** Antrim
89 D1 **Portstewart** Lderry
87 D4 **Portumna** Galway
82 C3 **Poulgorm Bridge** Kerry
89 D3 **Poyntz Pass** Armagh

85 D1 **Raharney** Wmeath
89 D2 **Randalstown** Antrim
89 D2 **Rasharkin** Antrim
85 D2 **Rathangan** Kildre
85 E2 **Rathcoole** Dublin
83 E3 **Rathcormack** Cork
84 C3 **Rathdowney** Laois
85 E2 **Rathdrum** Wicklw
89 D3 **Rathfriland** Down
83 D2 **Rathkeale** Limrck
88 B2 **Rathmelton** Donegl
82 C3 **Rathmore** Kerry
85 D1 **Rathmoylon** Meath
88 C1 **Rathmullan** Donegl
85 E2 **Rathnew** Wicklw
84 C1 **Rathowen** Wmeath
85 D3 **Rathvilly** Carlow
85 E1 **Ratoath** Meath
88 B2 **Ray** Donegl
86 B3 **Recess** Galway
86 B3 **Renvyle** Galway
83 E3 **Ringaskiddy** Cork
83 F3 **Ringville** Watfd
88 C4 **Rockcorry** Monhan
87 E2 **Roosky** Roscom
85 D4 **Rosbercon** Wexfd
87 D3 **Roscommon** Roscom
84 C2 **Roscrea** Tippry
88 B1 **Rosepenna** Donegl
83 D4 **Ross Carbery** Cork
87 D1 **Rosses Point** Sligo
85 E4 **Rosslare** Wexfd
85 E4 **Rosslare Harbour** Wexfd
88 C3 **Rosslea** Ferman
88 B3 **Rossnowlagh** Donegl

89	D4	**Rostrevor** Down
86	B3	**Roundstone** Galway
85	E2	**Roundwood** Wicklw
85	E1	**Rush** Dublin

S

89	E3	**Saintfield** Down
88	C2	**St Johnston** Donegl
85	D2	**Sallins** Kildre
86	C3	**Salthill** Galway
87	D4	**Scarriff** Clare
82	C2	**Scartaglin** Kerry
89	D3	**Scarva** Down
82	C4	**Schull** Cork
87	D2	**Scramoge** Roscom
88	C3	**Seskinore** Tyrone
83	E3	**Shanagarry** Cork
83	D1	**Shanagolden** Limrck
85	E2	**Shankill** Dublin
83	D1	**Shannon** Clare
87	D3	**Shannonbridge** Offaly
88	C4	**Shercock** Cavan
85	D3	**Shillelagh** Wicklw
84	C2	**Shinrone** Offaly
86	C3	**Shrule** Mayo
83	E1	**Silvermines** Tippry
88	C2	**Sion Mills** Tyrone
83	D1	**Sixmilebridge** Clare
85	E1	**Skerries** Dublin
82	C4	**Skibbereen** Cork
85	D1	**Slane** Meath
87	D1	**Sligo** Sligo
88	C3	**Smithborough** Monhan
82	B3	**Sneem** Kerry

82	C1	**Spanish Point** Clare
86	C3	**Spiddal** Galway
86	B3	**Sraith Salach** Galway
89	D3	**Stewartstown** Tyrone
85	E2	**Stillorgan** Dublin
85	D3	**Stonyford** Kilken
88	C2	**Strabane** Tyrone
85	D2	**Stradbally** Laois
88	C4	**Stradone** Cavan
85	D2	**Straffan** Kildre
87	D1	**Strandhill** Sligo
89	E3	**Strangford** Down
88	B2	**Stranorlar** Donegl
87	D2	**Strokestown** Roscom
85	D1	**Summerhill** Meath
88	B3	**Swanlinbar** Cavan
89	D2	**Swatragh** Lderry
86	C2	**Swinford** Mayo
85	E1	**Swords** Dublin

T

85	D4	**Taghmon** Wexfd
85	E4	**Tagoat** Wexfd
82	B3	**Tahilla** Kerry
85	E2	**Tallaght** Dublin
83	E3	**Tallow** Watfd
84	B4	**Tallowbridge** Watfd
89	D3	**Tandragee** Armagh
84	C1	**Tang** Wmeath
82	C1	**Tarbert** Kerry
84	C3	**Templemore** Tippry
84	C3	**Templetouhy** Tippry
89	D4	**Termonfeckin** Louth
85	D3	**Thomastown** Kilken
84	C3	**Thurles** Tippry

85	D2	**Timahoe** Laois
83	D3	**Timoleague** Cork
85	E3	**Tinahely** Wicklw
84	B3	**Tipperary** Tippry
87	D2	**Tobercurry** Sligo
89	D2	**Tobermore** Lderry
84	B3	**Toomyvara** Tippry
82	C4	**Toormore** Cork
82	C2	**Tralee** Kerry
85	D4	**Tramore** Watfd
85	D1	**Trim** Meath
86	C3	**Tuam** Galway
83	D1	**Tuamgraney** Clare
83	D1	**Tulla** Clare
84	C2	**Tullamore** Offaly
85	D3	**Tullow** Carlow
87	D2	**Tulsk** Roscom
86	C2	**Turlough** Mayo
84	C1	**Tyrrellspass** Wmeath

U

| 84 | C3 | **Urlingford** Kilken |

V

| 88 | C4 | **Virginia** Cavan |

W

| 89 | D4 | **Warrenpoint** Down |
| 85 | D4 | **Waterford** Watfd |

83	E3	**Watergrasshill** Cork
82	B3	**Waterville** Kerry
86	C2	**Westport** Mayo
85	E4	**Wexford** Wexfd
83	E3	**Whitegate** Cork
89	E2	**Whitehead** Antrim
85	E2	**Wicklow** Wicklw
85	E3	**Woodenbridge** Wicklw
87	D4	**Woodford** Galway

Y

| 83 | E3 | **Youghal** Cork |

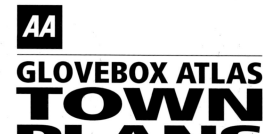

GLOVEBOX ATLAS
TOWN
PLANS

Atlas contents

Key to town plans	96
Town plans	97–183
Major airports	184–189
Channel Tunnel	190
Index to town plans	inside back cover

Key to town plans

Town plan legend

M8	Motorway with number
	Primary Road
	A Road
	B Road
	Other road
6 3	Numbered junction
	Restricted road / pedestrians only
COLLEGE ■	Building of interest
†	Church
	Park and open space
P	Car park
	Toilet
←	One-way street
	Shopmobility
P+	Park and Ride
★	World Heritage Site (UNESCO)
H	24-hour Accident & Emergency hospital
i	Tourist Information Centre
	Light rapid transit system

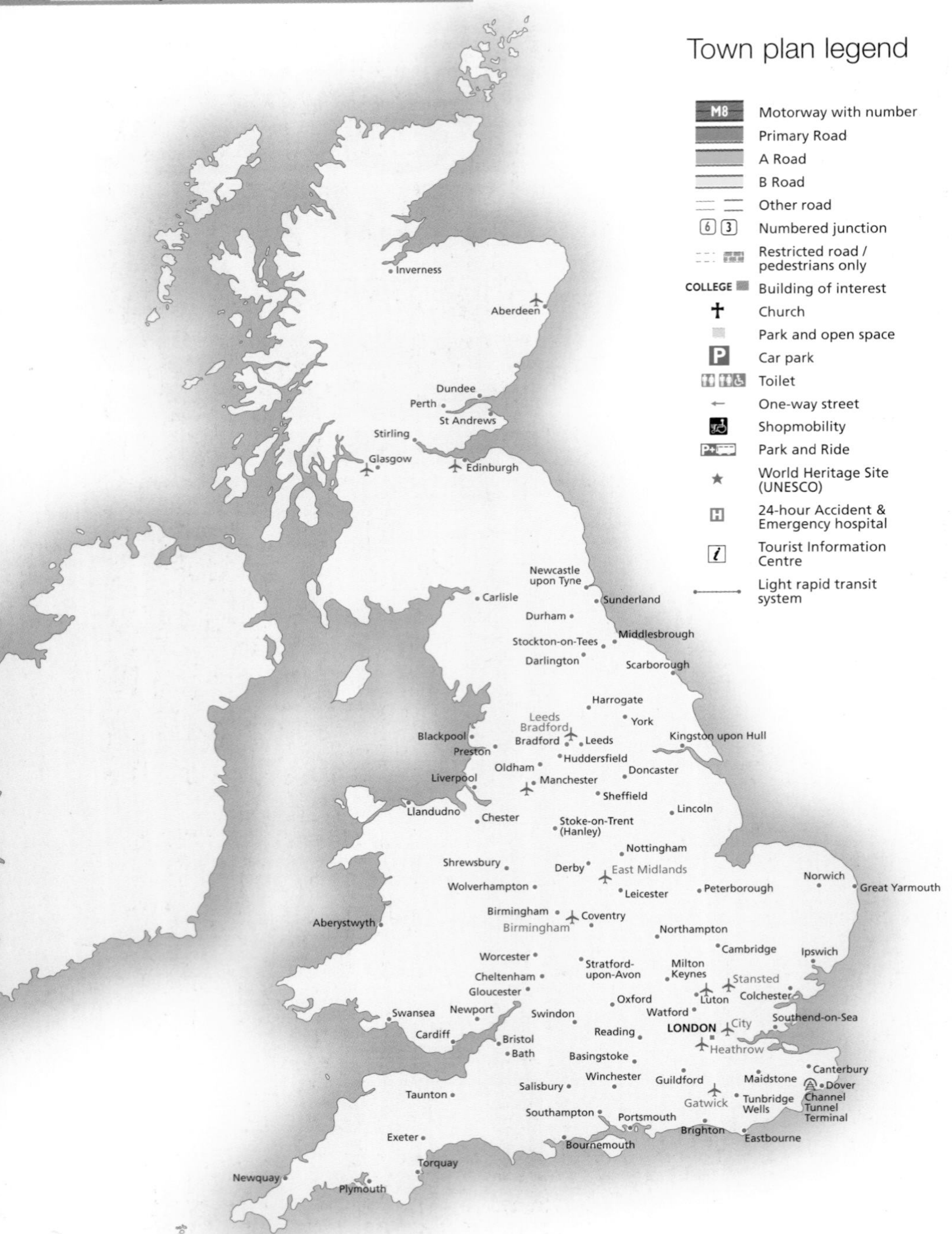

Inverness

Aberdeen

Dundee
Perth
St Andrews
Stirling
Glasgow
Edinburgh

Newcastle upon Tyne
Carlisle
Durham
Sunderland
Stockton-on-Tees
Middlesbrough
Darlington
Scarborough

Harrogate
Leeds
Bradford
York
Blackpool
Bradford
Leeds
Kingston upon Hull
Preston
Oldham
Huddersfield
Liverpool
Manchester
Doncaster
Llandudno
Chester
Sheffield
Stoke-on-Trent
(Hanley)
Lincoln
Nottingham
Shrewsbury
Derby
East Midlands
Wolverhampton
Leicester
Peterborough
Norwich
Great Yarmouth
Birmingham
Coventry
Aberystwyth
Birmingham
Northampton
Worcester
Stratford-upon-Avon
Milton Keynes
Cambridge
Ipswich
Cheltenham
Stansted
Gloucester
Luton
Colchester
Swansea
Newport
Oxford
Watford
Newquay
Swindon
Reading
LONDON
City
Southend-on-Sea
Cardiff
Bristol
Heathrow
Bath
Basingstoke
Taunton
Salisbury
Winchester
Guildford
Maidstone
Canterbury
Dover
Gatwick
Tunbridge Wells
Channel Tunnel Terminal
Southampton
Portsmouth
Brighton
Eastbourne
Exeter
Bournemouth
Torquay
Newquay
Plymouth

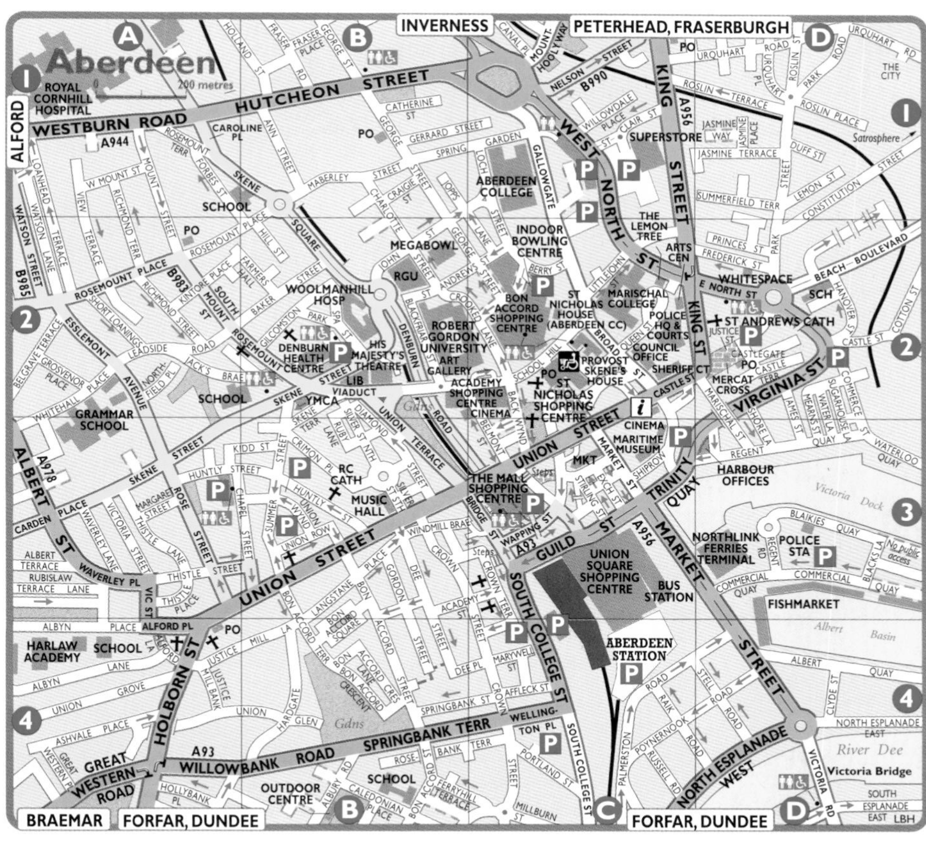

B3	Academy Street	D4	Clyde Street	A4	Holborn Street	D1	Park Road	B4	Springbank Street
C4	Affleck Street	D2	Commerce Street	A1	Holland Street	D2	Park Street	B4	Springbank Terrace
D4	Albert Quay	D3	Commercial Quay	A4	Hollybank Place	C4	Portland Street	D4	Stell Road
A3	Albert Street	D1	Constitution Street	A3	Huntly Street	C4	Poynernook Road	C3	Stirling Street
A3	Albert Terrace	D2	Cotton Street	B1	Hutcheon Street	D2	Princes Street	D2	Sugarhouse Lane
B4	Albury Road	B1	Craigie Street	A2	Jack's Brae	C2	Queen Street	B3	Summer Street
A4	Albyn Lane	B3	Crimon Place	D2	James Street	C4	Raik Road	D1	Summerfield Terrace
A4	Albyn Place	B2	Crooked Lane	D1	Jasmine Place	D3	Regent Road	A3	Thistle Lane
A4	Alford Place	B3	Crown Street	D1	Jasmine Terrace	D3	Regent Quay	A3	Thistle Street
B1	Ann Street	C3	Crown Terrace	B2	John Street	A2	Richmond Street	C3	Trinity Quay
A4	Ashvale Place	B4	Dee Place	B1	Jopps Lane	A1	Richmond Terrace	A4	Union Glen
C2	Back Wynd	B3	Dee Street	A4	Justice Mill Bank	A3	Rose Street	A4	Union Grove
B2	Baker Street	B2	Denburn Road	A4	Justice Mill Lane	B4	Rosebank Terrace	B3	Union Row
D2	Beach Boulevard	B3	Diamond Street	B3	Kidd Street	A2	Rosemount Place	B3	Union Street
A2	Belgrave Terrace	D1	Duff Street	C1	King Street	A1	Rosemount Terrace	B2	Union Terrace
C3	Belmont Street	D2	East North Street	A2	Kintore Place	B2	Rosemount Viaduct	B3	Union Wynd
C2	Berry Street	A2	Esslemont Avenue	B3	Langstane Place	D1	Roslin Place	D1	Urquhart Place
B2	Blackfriar Street	C3	Exchange Street	A2	Leadside Road	D1	Roslin Street	D1	Urquhart Road
D3	Blacks Lane	B2	Farmers Hall	D1	Lemon Street	C1	Roslin Terrace	D4	Victoria Road
D3	Blaikies Quay	B4	Ferryhill Terrace	C2	Little John Street	A3	Runislaw Terrace Lane	A3	Victoria Street
B4	Bon Accord Crescent	A1	Forbes Street	A1	Loanhead Terrace	C4	Russell Road	A1	View Terrace
B4	Bon Accord Square	B1	Fraser Place	C1	Loch Street	B2	St Andrews Street	D2	Virginia Street
B3	Bon Accord Street	B1	Fraser Road	B1	Maberley Street	C1	St Clair Street	C1	Wapping Street
B3	Bon Accord Terrace	D2	Frederick Street	A3	Margaret Street	C1	School Hill	D2	Water Lane
C3	Bridge Street	C1	Gallowgate	D2	Marischal Street	D2	Shore Lane	D3	Waterloo Quay
C2	Broad Street	B1	George Street	C3	Market Street	A2	Short Loanings	A1	Watson Lane
B4	Caledonian Place	B2	Gilcomston Park	C4	Marywell Street	B2	Silver Street North	A2	Watson Street
C1	Canal Place	B3	Gordon Street	D2	Mearns Street	B3	Silver Street South	A3	Waverley Place
A3	Carden Place	A4	Great Western Place	C4	Millburn Street	B1	Skene Square	C4	Wellington Place
C2	Caroline Place	A4	Great Western Road	C1	Mount Hooly Way	A3	Skene Street	A1	West Mount Street
D2	Castle Street	A2	Grosvenor Place	C1	Mount Street	B2	Skene Terrace	C1	West North Street
D2	Castle Terrace	C3	Guild Street	C1	Nelson Street	C3	South College Street	A1	Westburn Road
D2	Castlegate	D2	Hanover Street	D4	North Esplanade East	D4	South Esplanade East	A2	Whitehall Place
B1	Catherine Street	B4	Hardgate	D4	North Esplanade West	A2	South Mount Street	A4	Willowbank Road
B3	Chapel Street	B2	Hill Street	A2	Northfield Place	B2	Spa Street	C1	Willowdale Place
B1	Charlotte Street			C4	Palmerston Road	B1	Spring Garden	B3	Windmill Brae

Aberystwyth

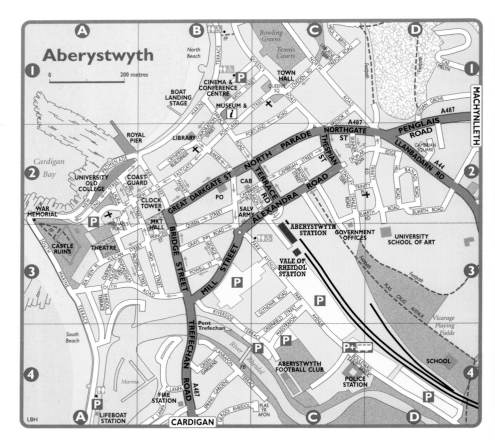

C2	Alexandra Road	B2	Laura Place	B2	St Michael's Place
B2	Baker Street	C1	Lisburne Terrace	A3	Sea View Place
D2	Banadl Road	D2	Llanbadarn Road	D2	Skinner Street
C1	Bath Street	C1	Loveden Road	A3	South Marine Terrace
D4	Boulevard Saint Brieuc	C4	Maesyrafon	A3	South Road
C2	Brewer Street	B1	Marine Terrace	B4	Spring Gardens
B3	Bridge Street	B2	Market Street	D2	Stanley Road
D2	Buarth Road	B3	Mill Street	D2	Stanley Terrace
D1	Cae Melyn	A2	New Promenade	B1	Terrace Road
C2	Cambrian Place	B2	New Street	C2	Thespian Street
D2	Cambrian Square	C2	North Parade	B4	Trefechan Road
C2	Cambrian Street	C1	North Road	C1	Trefor Road
B2	Castle Street	C2	Northgate Street	D2	Trinity Place
B2	Corporation Street	C3	Park Avenue	D2	Trinity Road
B2	Crynfryn Buildings	D2	Penglais Road	C2	Union Street
A3	Custom House Street	B3	Penmaesglas Road	C1	Vaynor Street
B2	Eastgate	B2	Pier Street	A3	Vulcan Street
D2	Edge Hill Road	D3	Plas Crug Avenue	B4	Y Lanfa
D1	Elysian Grove	C4	Plas Yr Afon		
B3	George Street	D2	Poplar Row		
B4	Gerddi Rheidol	C2	Portland Road		
B4	Glanrafon Terrace	B2	Portland Street		
C3	Glyndwr Road	B3	Powell Street		
B3	Grays Inn Road	B3	Princess Street		
B2	Great Darkgate Street	B3	Prospect Street		
B4	Green Gardens	B2	Queen Street		
C4	Greenfield Street	C1	Queen's Road		
C1	Heol Y Bryn	C1	Queen's Square		
B3	High Street	A3	Rheidol Terrace		
A2	King Street	B3	Riverside Terrace		

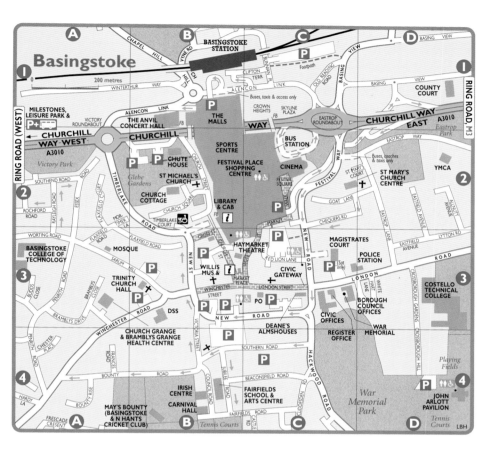

Basingstoke

B1 Alencon Link
D2 Allnutt Avenue
C1 Basing View
C4 Beaconsfield Road
A4 Bounty Rise
A4 Bounty Road
A3 Bramblys Close
A3 Bramblys Drive
A3 Budds Close
C1 Bunnian Place
B1 Chapel Hill
C3 Chequers Road
A4 Chester Place
B1 Church Hill
B2 Church Square
B2 Church Street
B2 Churchill Way
D1 Churchill Way East
A2 Churchill Way West
C4 Cliddesden Road
B4 Council Road
B3 Cross Street
D3 Crossborough Gardens
D4 Crossborough Hill
C1 Crown Heights
D2 Eastfield Avenue
D2 Eastrop Lane
D2 Eastrop Way

A2 Essex Road
B4 Fairfields Road
C2 Festival Way
A2 Flaxfield Court
A3 Flaxfield Road
A4 Frances Road
A4 Frescade Crescent
C2 Goat Lane
C4 Hackwood Road
A4 Hardy Lane
B4 Jubilee Road
D3 London Road
C3 London Street
D3 Lytton Road
B3 Market Place
C2 Market Walk
A2 Mortimer Lane
B3 New Road
B3 New Street
C1 Old Reading Road
A4 Penrith Road
A2 Rayleigh Road
C3 Red Lion Lane
A2 Rochford Road
C2 St Mary's Court
A3 Sarum Hill
A2 Southend Road
C4 Southern Road
B2 Timberlake Court
A2 Timberlake Road

B3 Victoria Street
B1 Vyne Road
D3 White Hart Lane
A4 Winchester Road
B3 Winchester Street
B1 Winterthur Way
A3 Worting Road
C3 Wote Street

C3	Abbey Square	D2	Edward Street	C3	Manvers Street	B1	Russell Street	A4	Westmoreland Station Road
B1	Alfred Street	D4	Excelsior Street	A1	Marlborough Buildings	B1	St Andrew's Terrace	A4	Westmoreland Street
B4	Ambury	D3	Ferry Lane	A3	Midland Bridge Road	C1	St John's Road	D4	Widcombe Hill
C3	Amery Lane	B1	Gay Street	B1	Miles Buildings	C4	St Mark's Gardens	D2	William Street
D4	Archway Street	B1	George Street	B3	Mill Street	C4	St Mark's Road	B2	Wood Street
C2	Argyle Street	C2	Grand Parade	B2	Milsom Street	B1	Saville Row	C3	York Street
B3	Avon Street	C2	Grange Grove	A2	Monmouth Place	B2	Saw Close		
B1	Bartlett Street	D2	Great Pulteney Street	B2	Monmouth Street	C4	Somerset Street		
B2	Barton Buildings	A2	Great Stanhope Street	A2	New King Street	C3	South Parade		
B2	Barton Street	A3	Green Park	B2	New Bond Street	C4	Southgate Street		
B3	Bath Street	B3	Green Park Road	C3	New Orchard Street	D3	Spring Crescent		
D1	Bathwick Street	B2	Green Street	A2	Nile Street	D3	Spring Gardens		
C3	Beau Street	C2	Grove Street	A3	Norfolk Buildings	C2	Spring Gardens Road		
B1	Bennett Street	D4	Hatfield Buildings	A2	Norfolk Crescent	B2	Squires Yard		
C1	Bladud Buildings	D1	Henrietta Gardens	C3	North Parade Pass	C3	Stall Street		
B2	Bridewell Lane	D1	Henrietta Mews	D3	North Parade Road	D4	Sussex Place		
C2	Bridge Street	C1	Henrietta Place	B4	Oak Street	D1	Sutton Street		
C2	Broad Quay	C1	Henrietta Road	B2	Old King Street	D1	Sydney Place		
C2	Broad Street	C1	Henrietta Street	C3	Old Orchard Street	B1	The Circus		
D3	Broadway	C3	Henry Street	C3	Pierrepont Street	C1	The Vineyards		
A1	Brock Street	A3	Ivo Peters Road	D4	Prince's Buildings	A4	Thornbank Place		
A1	Cathedral Place	A2	James Street West	B2	Princes Street	B2	Trim Street		
A4	Cedar Way	B2	John Street	D2	Pulteney Mews	B3	Trinity Street		
B2	Chapel Row	C2	Johnstone Street	D2	Pulteney Road	C2	Union Passage		
B3	Charles Street	B3	Kingsmead North	B2	Queen Square	C2	Union Street		
A2	Charlotte Street	B3	Kingsmead Street	B2	Queen Square Place	B2	Upper Borough Walls		
C3	Cheap Street	B3	Kingsmead West	B2	Queen Street	A2	Upper Bristol Road		
A4	Cheltenham Street	C3	Kingstone Road	B2	Queens Parade	A1	Upper Church Street		
B1	Circus Mews	B1	Lansdown Road	B2	Queens Parade Place				
B1	Circus Place	C2	Laura Place	B2	Quiet Street	D2	Vane Street		
C4	Claverton Street	A2	Little Stanhope Street	C4	Railway Place	C1	Walcot Street		
A2	Cumb Row	B3	Lower Borough Walls	B1	River Street Mews	B4	Wells Road		
B3	Corn Street	A3	Lower Bristol Road	B1	Rivers Street	B3	Westgate Buildings		
D1	Daniel Street	A4	Lower Oldfield Park	A4	Riverside Road	B3	Westgate Street		
C4	Dorchester Street	B4	Magdalen Avenue	A1	Royal Avenue	A4	Westmoreland Road		
C3	Duke Street			A1	Royal Crescent				

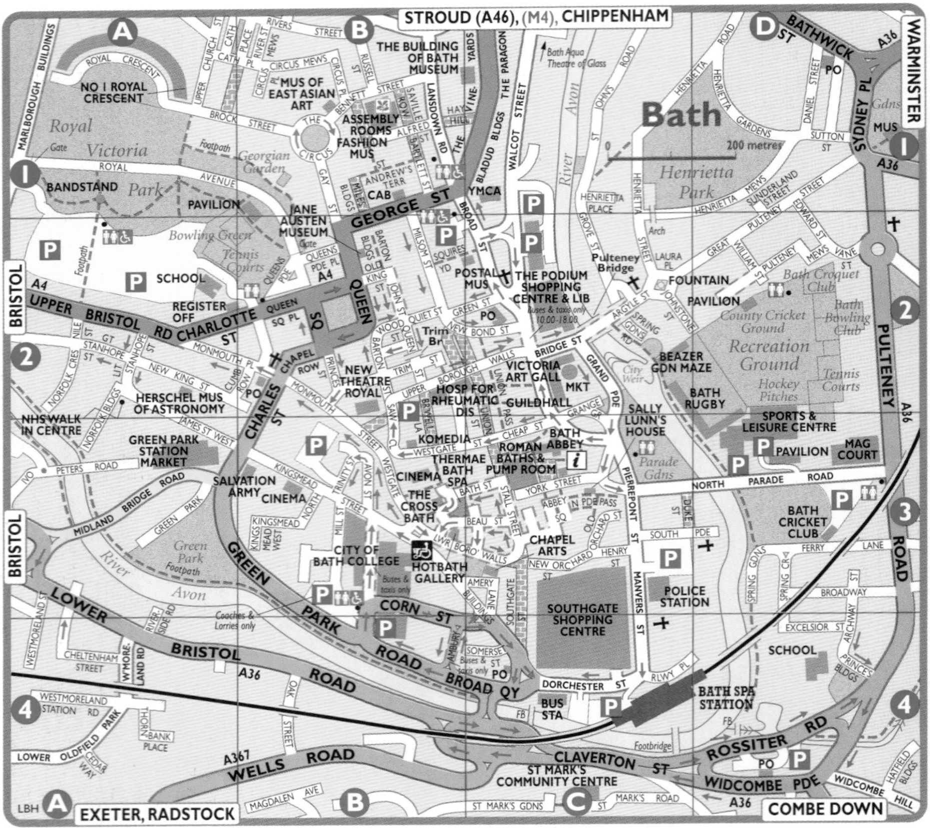

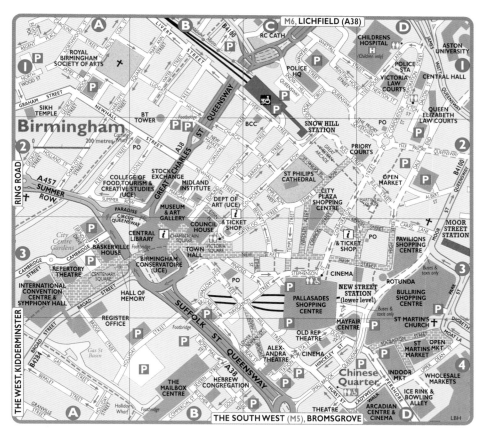

D2	Albert Street	B2	Eden Place	B1	Mary Ann Street	A2	Summer Row
C2	Barwick Street	D4	Edgbaston Street	D3	Moor Street	B3	Swallow Street
C4	Beak Street	B2	Edmund Street		Queensway	C2	Temple Row
C2	Bennetts Hill	B4	Ellis Street	B3	Navigation Street	C2	Temple Row West
A4	Berkley Street	C3	Ethel Street	C3	Needless Alley	C3	Temple Street
B4	Blucher Street	A2	Fleet Street	B2	New Market Street	D2	The Priory Queensway
A4	Bridge Street	A4	Gas Street	C3	New Street	D3	Union Street
A3	Brindley Drive	A2	George Street	A1	Newhall Street	D4	Upper Dean Street
A4	Broad Street	B4	Gough Street	D1	Newton Street	B3	Victoria Square
A1	Brook Street	A1	Graham Street	A1	Northwood Street	B1	Water Street
B3	Brunel Street	A4	Granville Street	D2	Old Square	C3	Waterloo Street
C2	Bull Street	B2	Great Charles Street	A2	Paradise Circus	C1	Weaman Street
A3	Cambridge Street		Queensway		Queensway	C1	Whittall Street
C3	Cannon Street	C2	Great Western Arcade	D3	Park Street		
A1	Caroline Street	D3	High Street	D4	Pershore Street		
D3	Carrs Lane	B3	Hill Street	B3	Pinfold Street		
A3	Centenary Square	C4	Hinckley Street	C1	Printing House Street		
B3	Chamberlain Square	A2	Holland Street	A1	Regent Parade		
A2	Charlotte Street	A4	Holliday Street	A1	Regent Place		
B2	Church Street	C4	Hurst Street	B4	Royal Mail Street		
C1	Colmore Circus	A1	James Street	A1	St Paul's Square		
	Queensway	D1	James Watt Queensway	C2	St Philips Place		
C2	Colmore Row	C1	John Bright Street	B4	Severn Street		
B4	Commercial Street	D4	Ladywell Walk	C4	Smallbrook Queensway		
B2	Cornwall Street	B2	Lionel Street	C1	Snow Hill Queensway		
C3	Corporation Street	B1	Livery Street	C4	Station Street		
A1	Cox Street	C4	Lower Severn Street	D1	Steelhouse Lane		
D2	Dale End	B1	Ludgate Hill	C3	Stephenson Street		
D1	Dalton Street	B2	Margaret Street	B3	Suffolk Street		
C4	Dudley Street	D2	Martineau Square		Queensway		

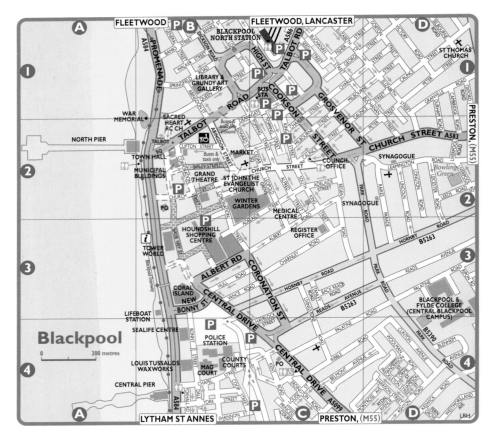

Blackpool

0 ___ 200 metres

B2	Abingdon Street	B1	Dickson Road	C3	Livingstone Road	B3	Vance Road

B2 Abingdon Street
C2 Adelaide Street
B3 Albert Road
C2 Alfred Street
D4 Anderson Street
D4 Ashton Road
C3 Back Reads Road
B3 Bank Hey Street
B1 Banks Street
C4 Belmont Avenue
B2 Birley Street
D4 Blenheim Avenue
B4 Bonny Street
C1 Buchanan Street
D1 Cambridge Road
D1 Caunce Street
C2 Cedar Square
B3 Central Drive
B4 Chapel Street
C1 Charles Street
C3 Charnley Road
C2 Church Street
B2 Clifton Street
D4 Clinton Avenue
C1 Cookson Street
B4 Coop Street
C3 Coronation Street
B2 Corporation Street
B4 Dale Street
B2 Deansgate

B1 Dickson Road
D1 Durham Road
C2 East Topping Street
B2 Edward Street
C1 Elizabeth Street
C4 Erdington Road
D4 Fern Grove
C1 Fisher Street
B4 Foxhall Road
D4 Freckleton Street
B1 General Street
C1 George Street
D1 Gorton Street
D1 Granville Road
C1 Grosvenor Street
D4 Harrison Street
C4 Havelock Street
C1 High Street
C3 Hornby Road
B3 Hull Road
D4 Jameson Street
C4 Kent Road
D4 Keswick Road
C2 King Street
D2 Leamington Road
D2 Leeds Road
D2 Leicester Road
C2 Leopold Grove
D2 Lincoln Road
D2 Liverpool Road

C3 Livingstone Road
D2 Longton Road
B1 Lord Street
C4 Louise Street
C1 Milbourne Street
D4 Montrose Avenue
B3 New Bonny Street
D4 Orme Street
D1 Oxford Road
C4 Palatine Road
D3 Park Road
D1 Peter Street
C4 Princess Court
B1 Promenade
B1 Queen Street
D2 Raikes Parade
C3 Reads Avenue
C2 Regent Road
C4 Ribble Road
D3 Ripon Road
D4 Rydal Avenue
C1 Seed Street
D1 Selbourne Road
B4 Shannon Street
C2 South King Street
B1 Springfield Road
C3 Stanley Road
B2 Talbot Road
B2 Talbot Square
C2 Topping Street

B3 Vance Road
D1 Victory Road
B1 Walker Street
D4 Westmoreland Avenue
D4 Woolman Road
B4 York Street

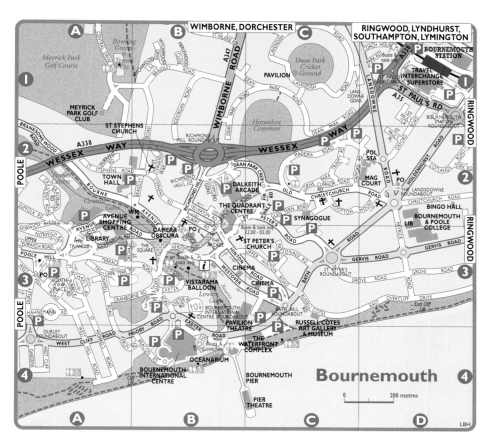

B2	Albert Road	D3	Gervis Road	D1	St Paul's Lane	D2	York Road
A3	Avenue Lane	C2	Glen Fern Road	D2	St Paul's Place		
A3	Avenue Road	D3	Grove Road	D1	St Paul's Road		
C3	Bath Road	A3	Hahnemann Road	C2	St Peter's Road		
B4	Beacon Road	B3	Hinton Road	A2	St Stephens Road		
B1	Bodorgan Road	D2	Holdenhurst Road	B2	St Stephens Way		
A2	Bourne Avenue	A4	Kerley Road	B1	St Valerie Road		
A2	Bradburne Road	C1	Lansdowne Gardens	B4	South Cliff Road		
B2	Braidley Road	D1	Lansdowne Road	A3	South View Place		
A2	Branksome Wood	C2	Lorne Park Road	C2	Stafford Road		
	Road	C2	Madeira Road	A2	Suffolk Road		
C1	Cavendish Road	B1	Merlewood Close	A3	Terrace Road		
A1	Central Drive	D3	Meyrick Road	B3	The Arcade		
D2	Christchurch Road	A3	Norwich Avenue	B3	The Square		
D1	Coach House Place	A3	Norwich Road	A3	The Triangle		
A3	Commercial Road	B3	Old Christchurch	A3	Tregonwell Road		
C2	Cumnor Road		Road	C2	Trinity Road		
D2	Cotlands Road	A3	Orchard Street	C3	Upper Hinton Road		
A3	Cranborne Road	D2	Oxford Road	A3	Upper Norwich Road		
A2	Crescent Road	D1	Park Road	A3	Upper Terrace Road		
B2	Dean Park Crescent	C3	Parsonage Road	A2	Wessex Way		
C1	Dean Park Road	A3	Poole Hill	A4	West Cliff Gardens		
A3	Durley Road	B3	Post Office Road	A4	West Cliff Road		
A2	Durrant Road	B4	Priory Road	A3	West Hill Road		
D3	East Overcliff Drive	A3	Purbeck Road	B3	Westover Road		
B3	Exeter Crescent	B2	Richmond Gardens	B1	Wimborne Road		
B3	Exeter Park Road	B2	Richmond Hill	C2	Wootton Mount		
B3	Exeter Road	B2	Richmond Hill Drive	B1	Wychwood Close		
C2	Fir Vale Road	C3	Russell Cotes Road	B1	Wychwood Drive		
B3	Gervis Place	A3	St Michael's Road	B2	Yelverton Road		

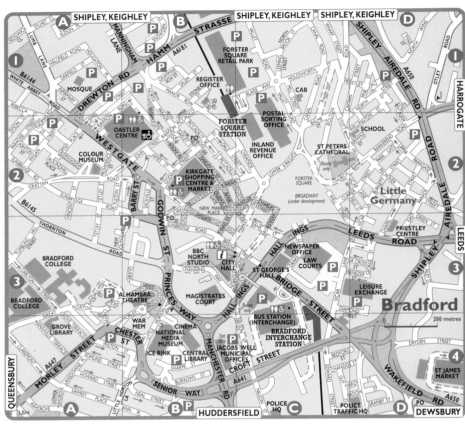

B4	Ann Place	D4	Dryden Street	A4	Lansdowne Place	A2	Rawson Road	
D2	Anne Gate	B2	Duke Street	D3	Leeds Road	B2	Rawson Square	
A4	Ashgrove	A2	Dyson Street	C1	Leeming Street	A1	Rebecca Street	
A2	Ashton Street	D3	East Parade	B4	Little Horton Lane	A2	Roundhill Place	
C2	Balme Street	D3	Ebenezer Street	A4	Lower Ashgrove	B2	Sackville Street	
B2	Bank Street	A4	Edmund Street	C2	Lower Kirkgate	C1	St Blaise Way	
A2	Baptist Place	C4	Edward Street	A1	Lumb Lane	A2	St Thomas Road	
D2	Barkerend Road	A1	Eldon Place	B4	Manchester Road	B1	Salem Street	
B2	Barry Street	D2	Field Street	B1	Manningham Lane	A4	Sawrey Place	
C4	Bedford Street	D3	Filey Street	A4	Mannville Terrace	B4	Senior Way	
C2	Bolton Road	C2	Forster Square	B1	Manor Row	B4	Sharpe Street	
B3	Bridge Street	A2	Fulton Street	C3	Market Street	D3	Shipley Airedale Road	
B1	Broad Street	D3	George Street	C1	Mill Street	A2	Simes Street	
C3	Broadway	B2	Godwin Street	A4	Morley Street	B1	Snowden Street	
D2	Broom Street	B1	Grammer School Street	B4	Neal Street	B1	Stone Street	
D2	Burnett Street	D4	Granby Street	C4	Nelson Street	C2	Stott Hill	
B4	Burrows Street	A2	Grattan Road	B3	Norfolk Gardens	A2	Sunbridge Road	
C2	Canal Road	D3	Great Cross Street	C1	North Brook Street	A1	Sylhet Close	
D1	Captain Street	A3	Great Horton Road	B1	North Parade	A3	Tetley Street	
A3	Carlton Street	D3	Green Street	D1	North Street	A3	Thornton Road	
C4	Chandos Street	A4	Grove Terrace	D1	North Wing	A3	Tumbling Hill Street	
B3	Channing Way	C4	Guy Street	B1	Northgate	D1	Tyne Street	
D3	Chapel Street	C3	Hall Ings	D1	Otley Road	B3	Tyrrel Street	
C2	Charles Street	A1	Hallfield Road	A2	Paradise Street	D2	Upper Parkgate	
C2	Cheapside	B1	Hamm Strasse	D2	Park Gate	B2	Upper Piccadilly	
A4	Chester Street	D4	Hardy Street	D2	Peckover Street	C1	Valley Road	
C2	Church Bank	C1	Holdsworth Street	C2	Petergate	C3	Vicar Lane	
A4	Claremont	A1	Houghton Place	D1	Pine Street	D4	Wakefield Road	
C4	Croft Street	A4	Howard Street	B2	Piccadilly	A2	Vincent Street	
C2	Currer Street	C2	Hustler Gate	C1	Priestley Street	C2	Well Street	
B2	Dale Street	A1	Infirmary Street	B3	Princes Way	D2	Wellington Street	
A1	Darfield Street	B3	Ivegate	B3	Providence Street	A2	Westgate	
B2	Darley Street	D2	Jermyn Street	B3	Quebec Street	C1	Wharf Street	
C3	Diamond Street	B2	James Street	B2	Queens Gate	A1	White Abbey Road	
C3	Drake Street	B2	John Street	A3	Randall Well Street	A2	Wigan Street	
A1	Drewton Road	B2	Kirkgate	B2	Rawson Place	A4	Wilton Street	

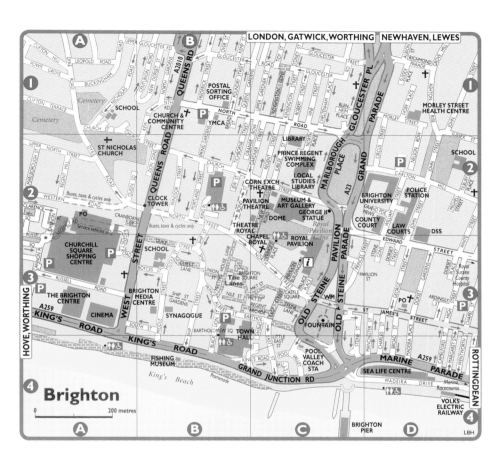

LONDON, GATWICK, WORTHING | NEWHAVEN, LEWES

Brighton

0   200 metres

BRIGHTON PIER

D1	Albion Street	B1	Foundry Street	D2	Nelson Row	A3	South Street
D3	Ardingly Street	B1	Frederick Street	B1	New Dorset Street	B2	Spring Gardens
D1	Ashton Rise	C2	Gardner Street	C2	New Road	C3	Steine Lane
B3	Bartholomew Square	D3	George Street	B3	Nile Street	C4	Steine Street
B3	Bartholomews	C1	Gloucester Place	B1	North Gardens	D1	Sussex Place
B4	Black Lion Street	B1	Gloucester Road	C2	North Place	D2	Sussex Street
C1	Blenheim Place	C1	Gloucester Street	B1	North Road	C1	Sydney Street
B2	Bond Street	B4	Grand Junction Road	B2	North Street	B2	Tichborne Street
B3	Boyces Street	C2	Grand Parade	C3	Old Steine	C1	Tidy Street
B1	Bread Street	D2	Grand Parade Mews	B2	Orange Row	D2	Tilbury Place
B3	Brighton Square	D1	Grove Hill	B1	Over Street	B3	Union Street
C4	Brill's Lane	D3	High Street	C3	Palace Place	C1	Upper Gardner Street
D4	Broad Street	D1	Ivory Place	C3	Pavilion Buildings	A1	Upper Gloucester Road
A1	Buckingham Road	B2	Jew Street	C3	Pavilion Parade	A2	Upper North Street
D4	Camelford Street	D2	John Street	C3	Pavilion Street	C1	Vine Street
A3	Cannon Place	C2	Jubilee Street	C4	Pool Valley	D4	Wentworth Street
D2	Carlton Hill	B1	Kemp Street	B2	Portland Street	A3	West Street
C3	Castle Square	C1	Kensington Gardens	A1	Powis Grove	A2	Western Road
B1	Centurion Road	C1	Kensington Street	B3	Prince Albert Street	D3	White Street
D3	Chapel Street	B1	Kew Street	C3	Prince's Place	D2	William Street
D4	Charles Street	B2	King Place	C3	Princes Street	B2	Windsor Street
C1	Cheltenham Place	A3	King's Road	A2	Queen Square	B2	Zion Gardens
A1	Church Street	A1	Leopold Road	B1	Queens Gardens		
D2	Circus Street	C4	Little East Street	B2	Queens Road		
A2	Clarence Square	D4	Madeira Drive	A2	Regency Road		
A1	Clifton Hill	D4	Madeira Place	C3	Regent Arcade		
A1	Clifton Terrace	D4	Manchester Street	A2	Regent Hill		
A2	Cranborne Street	D4	Margaret Street	C2	Regent Street		
D3	Dorset Gardens	D4	Marine Parade	D1	Richmond Parade		
D3	Dorset Place	C3	Market Street	C1	Robert Street		
D3	Dorset Street	C2	Marlborough Place	A3	Russell Road		
B3	Duke Street	A2	Marlborough Street	A3	Russell Square		
B3	Duke's Lane	B3	Meeting House Lane	D3	St James's Street		
A1	Dyke Road	B3	Middle Street	A1	St Nicholas Road		
C4	East Street	D2	Mighell Street	B3	Ship Street		
D3	Edward Street	D1	Morley Street	B3	Ship Street Gardens		

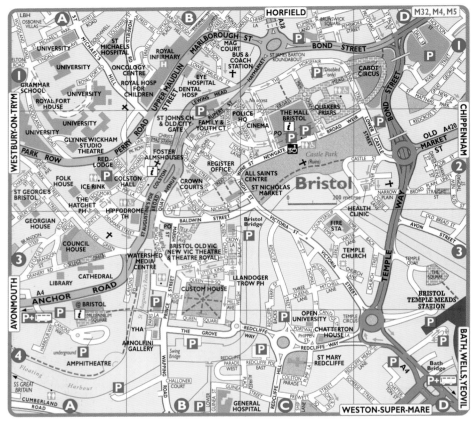

B1	Alfred Hill	C3	Countership	B2	Lower Park Row	B3	Queen Charlotte	B1	Terrell Street
C4	Alfred Place	B3	Crow Lane	B1	Marlborough Hill		Street	B4	The Grove
A3	Anchor Road	A4	Cumberland Road	B1	Marlborough Street	B4	Queen Square	C1	The Horsefair
D3	Avon Street	C1	Cumberland Street	B3	Marsh Street	C2	Queen Street	C2	The Pithay
B3	Baldwin Street	D1	Dale Street	C1	Merchant Street	C3	Redcliff Street	C3	Three Queens Lane
B2	Bell Lane	D2	David Street	B3	Middle Avenue	C4	Redcliffe Backs	D2	Tower Hill
C1	Bond Street	A3	Deanery Road	B3	Mill Avenue	C4	Redcliffe Hill	B2	Tower Lane
A3	Brandon Steep	A3	Denmark Street	A4	Millennium Square	C4	Redcliffe Mead Lane	B2	Trenchard Street
A3	Brandon Street	B1	Dighton Street	C3	Mitchell Court	C4	Redcliffe Parade East	A1	Tyndall Avenue
B2	Bridewell Street	B1	Earl Street	C3	Mitchell Lane	B4	Redcliffe Parade West	C1	Union Street
C1	Broad Mead	A1	Elton Road	B1	Montague Street	C4	Redcliffe Way	A3	Unity Street
D2	Broad Plain	B1	Eugene Street	A1	Myrtle Road	D2	Redcross Street	D2	Unity Street
B2	Broad Quay	C2	Fairfax Street	B2	Nelson Street	D1	River Street	B1	Upper Maudlin Street
B2	Broad Street	B4	Farrs Lane	D1	New Street	A1	Royal Fort Road	C3	Victoria Street
C2	Broad Weir	C3	Ferry Street	D2	New Thomas Street	B2	Rupert Street	B4	Wapping Road
C1	Brunswick Square	A3	Frog Lane	D1	Newfoundland Street	D2	Russ Street	C3	Water Lane
B3	Canons Road	A2	Frogmore Street	C2	Newgate	B3	St Augustine's Parade	C3	Welsh Back
A4	Canons Way	A3	Great George Street	D3	Old Bread Street	A3	St George's Road	B1	Whitson Street
C4	Canynge Street	D1	Great George Street	D2	Old Market Street	D1	St Matthias Park	C3	Wine Street
D2	Castle Street	B4	Guinea Street	A1	Osborne Villas	A1	St Michael's Hill	A1	Woodland Road
B4	Challoner Court	A4	Harbour Way	A2	Park Row	A1	St Michael's Park	C1	York Street
C1	Charles Street	D2	Hawkins Street	A2	Park Street	B2	St Nicholas Street		
A2	Charlotte Street	C1	Haymarket	A2	Park Street Avenue	D1	St Paul's Street		
D4	Chatterton Street	C2	High Street	C1	Pembroke Street	B2	St Stephen's Street		
D2	Cheese Lane	A2	Hill Street	C1	Penn Street	C3	St Thomas Street		
C1	Cherry Lane	B1	Horfield Road	A2	Perry Road	C4	Ship Lane		
B2	Christmas Steps	D1	Houlton Street	C4	Phippen Street	C1	Silver Street		
C3	Church Lane	D2	Jacob Street	A2	Pipe Lane	B2	Small Street		
D3	Church Street	B2	John Street	C4	Portwall Lane	C4	Somerset Square		
B2	Clare Street	B3	King Street	C4	Prewett Street	C4	Somerset Street		
A3	College Green	B1	Lewins Mead	B4	Prince Street	A1	Southwell Street		
C4	Colston Avenue	B3	Little King Street	D1	Pritchard Street	D2	Straight Street		
C4	Colston Parade	A2	Lodge Street	C4	Pump Lane	B3	Telephone Avenue		
B2	Colston Street	D2	Lower Castle Street	C1	Quakers Friars	C3	Temple Back		
C2	Corn Street	B4	Lower Guinea Street	B2	Quay Street	C3	Temple Street		
B1	Cottage Place	B1	Lower Maudlin Street			D3	Temple Way		

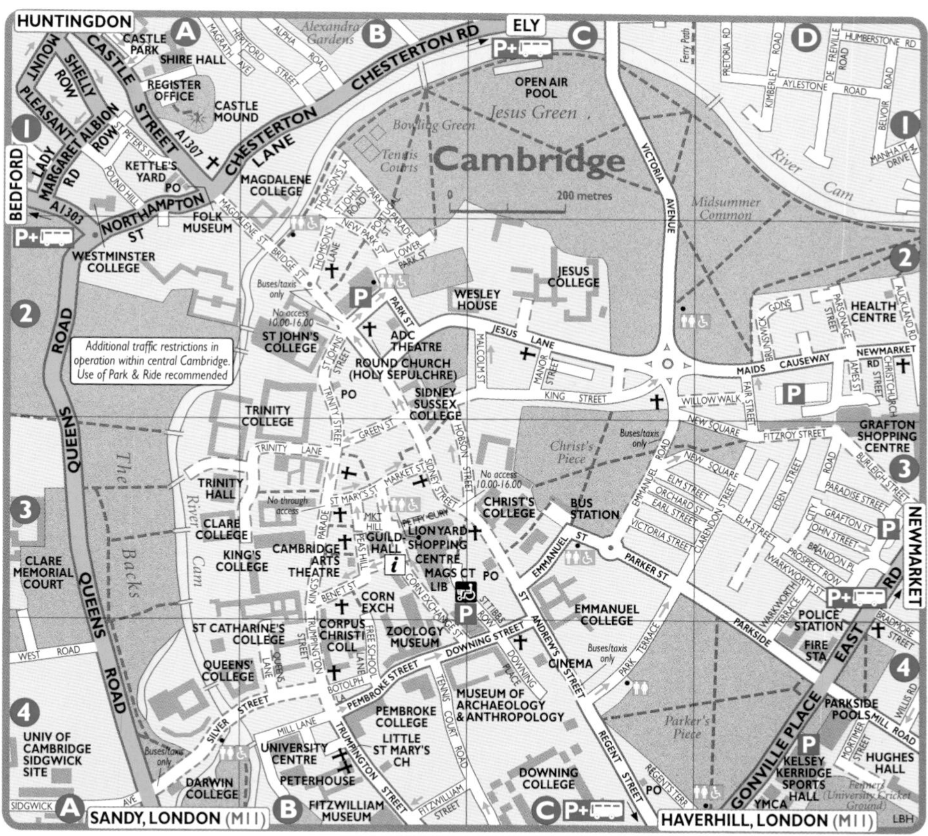

A1	Albion Row	D4	Gonville Place	B1	Park Parade	C1	Victoria Avenue
B1	Alpha Road	D3	Grafton Street	B2	Park Street	C3	Victoria Street
D2	Auckland Road	B3	Green Street	C4	Park Terrace	D3	Warkworth Street
D1	Aylestone Road	B1	Hertford Street	C3	Parker Street	D3	Warkworth Terrace
D1	Belvoir Road	B3	Hobson Street	D4	Parkside	A4	West Road
B3	Bene't Street	D1	Humberstone Road	D2	Parsonage Street	D4	Willis Road
B4	Botolph Lane	D2	James Street	B3	Peas Hill	D2	Willow Walk
D3	Bradmore Street	C2	Jesus Lane	B4	Pembroke Street		
D3	Brandon Place	D3	John Street	B3	Petty Cury		**University Colleges**
B2	Bridge Street	D1	Kimberley Road	B2	Portugal Street	C3	Christ's College
D2	Brunswick Gardens	C2	King Street	A1	Pound Hill	A3	Clare College
D3	Burleigh Street	B3	King's Parade	D1	Pretoria Road	B4	Corpus Christi College
A1	Castle Street	A1	Lady Margaret Road	D3	Prospect Row	A4	Darwin College
B1	Chesterton Lane	B2	Lower Park Street	B4	Queens Lane	C4	Downing College
B1	Chesterton Road	A1	Magdalene Street	A3	Queens Road	C3	Emmanuel College
D2	Christchurch Street	A1	Magrath Avenue	C4	Regent Street	D4	Hughes Hall
D3	City Road	D2	Maids Causeway	C4	Regents Terrace	C2	Jesus College
C3	Clarendon Street	D1	Malcolm Street	C3	St Andrew's Street	B3	King's College
B3	Corn Exchange Street	C2	Manor Street	B1	St Johns Road	B1	Magdalene College
D1	De Freiville Road	B3	Market Hill	B2	St Johns Street	B4	Pembroke College
C4	Downing Place	B3	Market Street	B3	St Mary's Street	B4	Peterhouse
C4	Downing Street	B4	Mill Lane	A1	St Peter's Street	A4	Queen's College
C3	Earl Street	D4	Mill Road	C3	St Tibbs Row	B4	St Catherine's College
D4	East Road	D4	Mortimer Street	A1	Shelly Row	B2	St John's College
D3	Eden Street	A1	Mount Pleasant	A4	Sidgwick Avenue	B2	Sidney Sussex College
C3	Elm Street	B2	New Park Street	B3	Sidney Street	B2	Trinity College
C3	Emmanuel Road	C3	New Square	A4	Silver Street	A3	Trinity Hall
C3	Emmanuel Street	D2	Newmarket Road	C4	Tennis Court Road	B2	Wesley House
D2	Fair Street	A2	Northampton Street	B1	Thomson's Lane	A2	Westminster College
D3	Fitzroy Street	C3	Orchard Street	B3	Trinity Lane		
B3	Fitzwilliam Street	D3	Paradise Street	C3	Trinity Street		
B4	Free School Lane			B4	Trumpington Street		

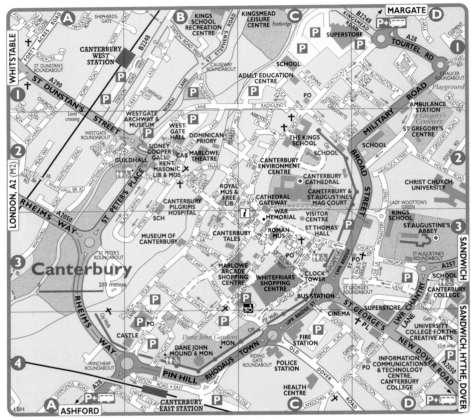

C2	Abbots Place	B3	Hawks Lane	C1	Northgate	A2	St Peter's Place
D3	Albert Road	B4	Henry Court	D1	Notley Street	B2	St Peter's Street
C2	Albion Place	B2	High Street	C4	Oaten Hill	C1	St Radigund's Street
B2	All Saints Lane	B3	Hospital Lane	C4	Old Dover Road	B1	St Stephen's Road
D1	Artillery Street	C3	Iron Bar Lane	B2	Orange Street	A4	Simmonds Road
B3	Beer Cart Lane	D3	Ivy Lane	A2	Orchard Street	D1	Starle Close
B2	Best Lane	B3	Jewry Lane	B1	Orient Place	B4	Station Road East
B2	Black Griffin Way	B2	King Street	C2	Palace Street	A1	Station Road West
B2	Blackfriars Street	C1	Kingsmead Road	C3	Parade	B3	Stour Street
D2	Broad Street	B1	Kirby's Lane	B4	Pin Hill	C2	Sun Street
C3	Burgate	C2	Knotts Lane	B2	Pound Lane	B1	The Causeway
C3	Burgate Lane	C4	Lansdown Road	A3	Rheims Way	C2	The Borough
C3	Butchery Lane	A2	Linden Grove	B4	Rhodaus Close	B2	The Friars
C3	Canterbury Lane	C3	Link Lane	B4	Rhodaus Town	D1	Tourtel Road
B1	Carriage Mews	D3	Longport	A1	Roper Road	B2	Tower Way
B4	Castle Row	D3	Love Lane	B3	Rose Lane	D1	Union Place
B4	Castle Street	C3	Lower Bridge Street	A1	Roseacre Close	D1	Union Street
A4	Church Lane	D4	Lower Chantry Lane	B3	Rosemary Lane	C4	Upper Bridge Street
D3	Church Street	A1	Mandeville Road	C2	St Alphege Street	D4	Upper Chantry Lane
D4	Cossington Road	B4	Marlowe Avenue	A1	St Dunstan's Street	C4	Vernon Place
A2	Cross Street	A2	Mead Way	C3	St George's Lane	C1	Victoria Row
C4	Dover Street	C3	Mercery Lane	C3	St George's Street	B3	Watling Street
C1	Duck Lane	D2	Military Road	D2	St Gregory's Road	A2	Westgate Grove
D4	Edward Road	B2	Mill Lane	B3	St John's Lane	B2	Westgate Hall Road
D4	Ersham Road	D3	Monastery Street	C1	St John's Place	B3	White Horse Lane
A1	Forty Acres Road	D4	New Dover Road	B3	St Margaret's Street	A2	Whitehall Bridge Road
A4	Gordon Road	D1	New Ruttington Lane	B4	St Mary's Street	A3	Whitehall Close
C3	Gravel Walk	A2	New Street	D3	St Paul's Terrace	A2	Whitehall Gardens
B3	Guildhall Street	D2	North Holmes Road	B3	St Peter's Grove	A2	Whitehall Road
D2	Havelock Street	B1	North Lane	B2	St Peter's Lane	B4	Worthgate Place

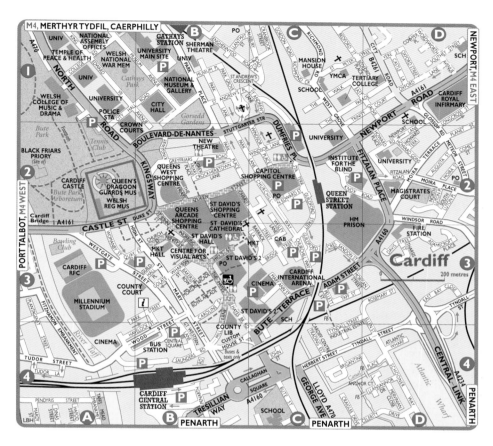

D3	Adam Street	D3	Ellen Street	D2	Moira Street	D2	South Luton Place
D3	Adamscroft Place	D2	Fitzalan Place	D2	Moira Terrace	D1	Southey Street
D4	Atlantic Wharf	D2	Fitzalan Road	B3	Morgan Arcade	C2	Station Terrace
D2	Augusta Street	A3	Fitzhamon Embankment	B1	Museum Avenue	B2	Stuttgarter Strasse
B3	Bakers Row	B3	Frederick Street	B1	Museum Place	A4	Taff's Mead Embankment
C3	Barrack Lane	D1	Glossop Road	B1	Newport Road	C3	Taff Street
C1	Bedford Street	B3	Golate	C2	North Edward Street	B2	The Friary
B2	Boulevard de Nantes	C1	Gordon Road	D2	North Luton Place	B3	The Hayes
C3	Bridge Street	B4	Great Western Lane	A1	North Road	C1	The Parade
C4	Brigantine Place	B2	Greyfriars Place	D1	Oxford Lane	C1	The Walk
C4	Bute Street	B2	Greyfriars Road	D1	Oxford Street	B4	Tresillian Way
C3	Bute Terrace	C3	Guildford Crescent	B1	Park Grove	B3	Trinity Street
B4	Callaghan Square	C2	Guildford Street	B1	Park Lane	A4	Tudor Street
B3	Caroline Street	B3	Guildhall Place	B1	Park Place	D3	Tyndall Street
A3	Castle Street	A4	Hafod Street	B3	Park Street	C4	Tyndall Street Industrial
D4	Celerity Drive	B4	Havelock Street	B4	Penarth Road		Estate
D4	Central Link	B3	Hayes Bridge Road	A4	Pendyris Street		
B4	Central Square	C4	Herbert Street	D2	Planet Street	D1	Vere Street
B2	Charles Street	B3	High Street	A3	Plantagenet Street	C2	Wesley Lane
B3	Church Street	B3	Hill's Street	A3	Quay Street	C1	West Grove
C2	Churchill Way	D2	Howard Gardens	B2	Queen Street	A3	Westgate Street
A1	City Hall Road	D2	Howard Place	C1	Richmond Crescent	B3	Wharton Street
D1	City Road	D2	Howard Terrace	C1	Richmond Road	C2	Windsor Lane
A1	College Road	A1	King Edward VII Avenue	D3	Rosemary Street	C2	Windsor Place
D2	Comet Street	B2	Kingsway	B3	Royal Arcade	D2	Windsor Road
D1	Cowper Place	C2	Knox Road	B1	St Andrew's Crescent	A3	Womanby Street
C4	Craiglee Drive	D4	Llansannor Drive	C1	St Andrew's Lane	B4	Wood Street
C1	Cranbrook Street	B1	Llantwit Street	B1	St Andrew's Place	D1	Wordsworth Avenue
B2	Crockherbtown Lane	C4	Lloyd George Avenue	B2	St John Street	B3	Working Street
B4	Custom House Street	D1	Longcross Street	B3	St Mary Street		
D3	Davis Street	A4	Mardy Street	C1	St Peter's Street		
A4	Dinas Street	C3	Mary Ann Street	C1	Salisbury Road		
B2	Duke Street	D4	Mervinian Close	C3	Sandon Street		
D3	Dumfries Place	D2	Meteor Street	B4	Saunders Road		
D3	East Bay Close	B4	Mill Lane	D4	Schooner Way		
C1	East Grove	D2	Moira Place	B1	Senghennydd Road		

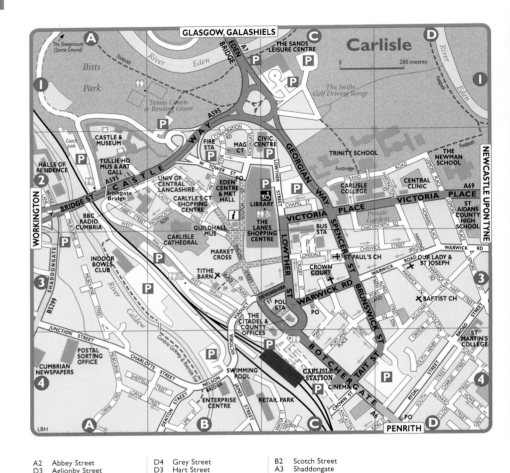

A2	Abbey Street	D4	Grey Street	B2	Scotch Street
D3	Aglionby Street	D3	Hart Street	A3	Shaddongate
D3	Alfred Street North	D3	Hartington Place	B4	Sheffield Street
D3	Alfred Street South	D2	Hartington Street	D4	South Henry Street
B3	Blackfriars Street	D2	Howard Place	D4	South Street
C4	Botchergate	D4	Howe Street	C3	Spencer Street
A2	Bridge Lane	B4	James Street	C2	Strand Road
A2	Bridge Street	A4	Junction Street	C4	Tait Street
D3	Broad Street	D4	King Street	C2	Victoria Place
C3	Brunswick Street	C4	Lancaster Street	B4	Victoria Viaduct
B2	Castle Street	B4	Lime Street	C3	Warwick Road
A2	Castle Way	D2	Lismore Place	D3	Warwick Square
C3	Cecil Street	D3	Lismore Street	C4	Water Street
C2	Chapel Street	C3	Lonsdale Street	B2	West Tower Street
D4	Charles Street	A4	Lorne Crescent	A2	West Walls
A4	Charlotte Street	A4	Lorne Street		
C2	Chatsworth Square	C2	Lowther Street		
C3	Chiswick Street	B2	Market Street		
D4	Close Street	C3	Mary Street		
B2	Corporation Road	A3	Milbourne Street		
C3	Crosby Street	D3	Myddleton Street		
C4	Crown Street	B4	Nelson Bridge		
B4	Denton Street	D4	Orfeur Street		
C3	Devonshire Street	B2	Paternoster Row		
B1	Eden Bridge	B2	Peter Street		
D4	Edward Street	C4	Portland Place		
B3	English Street	D3	Portland Square		
B2	Fisher Street	B2	Rickergate		
D4	Fusehill Street	C4	Robert Street		
C2	Georgian Way	D4	Rydal Street		

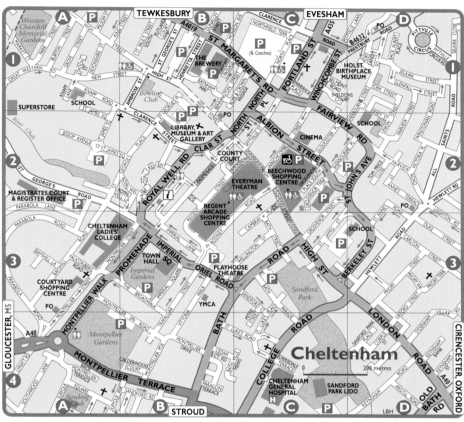

C2	Albion Street	C2	Grosvenor Place South	C1	North Place	B2	St George's Place
D2	All Saints Road	C3	Grosvenor Street	C2	North Street	A2	St George's Road
B1	Ambrose Street	C2	Grosvenor Terrace	C1	Northfield Terrace	B1	St George's Street
D4	Argyll Road	A1	Grove Street	D4	Old Bath Road	A2	St James Square
D1	Back Albert Place	B1	Henrietta Street	B3	Oriel Road	C3	St James Street
C3	Bath Parade	D3	Hewlett Road	C4	Orrisdale Terrace	D2	St John's Avenue
B4	Bath Road	A1	High Street	D3	Oxford Street	C4	St Luke's Place
C3	Bath Street	B3	Imperial Lane	A2	Parabola Lane	C4	St Luke's Road
B1	Baynham Way	B3	Imperial Square	A3	Parabola Road	B1	St Margaret's Road
A3	Bayshill Lane	D2	Jersey Street	A1	Park Street	B1	St Paul's Street South
A3	Bayshill Road	A2	Jessop Avenue	D1	Pittville Circus	B4	Sandford Road
B1	Bennington Street	D4	Keynsham Bank	D1	Pittville Circus Road	C3	Sandford Street
D3	Berkeley Street	D4	Keynsham Road	D1	Pittville Lawn	D1	Selkirk Close
A1	Burton Street	D4	Keynsham Street	C2	Pittville Street	D1	Selkirk Street
C3	Cambray Place	A1	King Street	D1	Portland Square	C2	Sherborne Place
D3	Carlton Street	A1	Knapp Lane	C1	Portland Street	D1	Sherbourne Street
B4	Cedar Court Road	A1	Knapp Road	D1	Prestbury Road	A4	Southwood Lane
C1	Clarence Road	D2	Leighton Road	D3	Priory Street	A1	Station Street
B2	Clarence Street	D4	London Road	D3	Priory Terrace	A4	Suffolk Parade
C4	College Road	A4	Lypiatt Road	D3	Priory Walk	A4	Suffolk Square
D4	Corpus Street	A1	Market Street	B3	Promenade	D4	Sydenham Villas Road
A1	Devonshire Street	A1	Milsom Street	B3	Regent Street	B3	The Broadwalk
D3	Duke Street	B1	Monson Avenue	B3	Rodney Road	B3	Trafalgar Street
B1	Dunalley Street	B4	Montpellier Drive	C1	Rose and Crown Passage	D2	Union Street
C2	Fairview Road	B4	Montpellier Parade	B2	Royal Crescent	D2	Victoria Place
D2	Fairview Street	A3	Montpellier Spa Road	A2	Royal Well Lane	B4	Vittoria Walk
A3	Fauconberg Road	A3	Montpellier Street	B2	Royal Well Place	C3	Wellington Street
D1	Glenfall Street	A4	Montpellier Terrace	B2	Royal Well Road	C1	Winchcombe Street
C2	Gloucester Place	A4	Montpellier Walk	D3	St Anne's Road	D2	Winstonian Road
A1	Great Western Road	A1	New Street	D2	St Anne's Terrace	D1	York Street

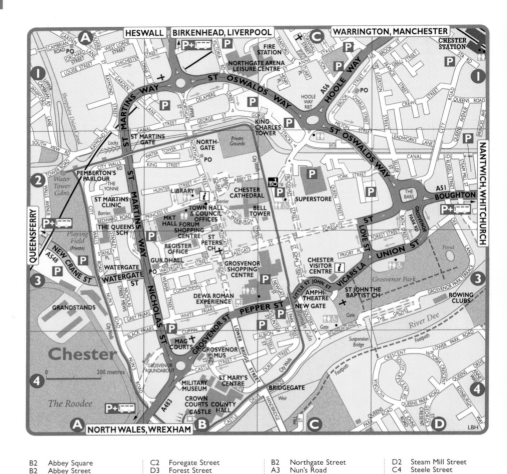

Chester

B2 Abbey Square
B2 Abbey Street
C4 Albion Street
D4 Anne's Way
D2 Bath Street
A2 Bedward Road
A4 Black Friars
D2 Boughton
B3 Bridge Street
C1 Brook Street
B4 Bunce Street
A1 Cambrian Road
D2 Canal Side
B1 Canal Street
B4 Castle Drive
B4 Castle Street
C1 Charles Street
A1 Chichester Street
D1 City Road
A2 City Walls Road
B3 Commonhall Street
C1 Cornwall Street
D1 Crewe Street
B3 Cuppin Street
D2 Dee Lane
B1 Delamere Street
C4 Duke Street
B3 Eastgate Street
D4 Edinburgh Way
D1 Egerton Street
C2 Foregate Street
D3 Forest Street
D1 Francis Street
C2 Frodsham Street
A1 Garden Lane
B1 George Street
C1 Gorse Stacks
A3 Grey Friars
D2 Grosvenor Park Road
D3 Grosvenor Park Terrace
B4 Grosvenor Street
C4 Handbridge
C1 Henry Place
C1 Hoole Way
B2 Hunter Street
B2 King Street
D2 Leadworks Lane
C3 Little St John Street
B1 Lorne Street
A1 Louise Street
C3 Love Street
B4 Lower Bridge Street
D4 Lower Park Road
C1 Lyon Street
C4 Mill Street
C1 Milton Street
A3 New Crane Street
C3 Newgate Street
B3 Nicholas Street
A3 Nicholas Street Mews
B2 Northgate Street
A3 Nun's Road
A1 Orchard Street
C3 Park Street
B3 Pepper Street
D2 Princes Avenue
B2 Princess Street
C3 Priory Place
C2 Queen Street
D2 Queens Avenue
D4 Queens Drive
D4 Queens Park Road
D1 Queens Road
A1 Raymond Street
D2 Russell Street
C1 St Anne Street
D4 St George's Crescent
C3 St John Street
D4 St Johns Road
A2 St Martins Way
B1 St Oswalds Way
B2 St Werburgh Street
D2 Seller Street
D1 Sibell Street
C3 Souters Lane
D4 South Crescent Road
A2 South View Road
A3 Stanley Place
A3 Stanley Street
D1 Station Road
D2 Steam Mill Street
C4 Steele Street
C1 Stuart Place
D2 The Bars
D3 The Groves
A2 The Yonne
A2 Tower Road
C1 Trafford Street
D3 Union Street
A1 Upper Cambrian Road
B1 Upper Northgate Street
C3 Vicars Lane
D4 Victoria Crescent
B1 Victoria Road
C3 Volunteer Street
A2 Walls Avenue
B2 Water Tower Street
A3 Watergate Street
B3 Weaver Street
A1 West Lorne Street
A1 Whipcord Lane
B3 White Friars
C2 York Street

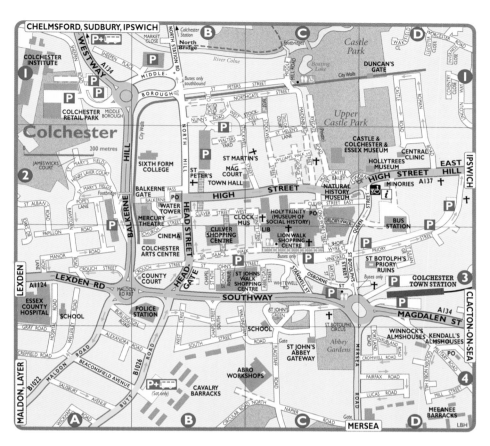

C3	Abbeygate Street	A2	Henry Laver Court	D4	Portland Road	D1	Wakefield Close
A4	Alexandra Road	B2	High Street	D3	Priory Street	B3	Walsingham Road
C3	Arthur Street	A3	Hospital Lane	C2	Priory Walk	B2	Walters Yard
A2	Balkerne Hill	A4	Hospital Road	C3	Queen Street	A4	Wellesley Road
B2	Balkerne Passage	D1	Inverness Close	A2	Rawstorn Road	B1	West Stockwell Street
A4	Beaconsfield Avenue	A2	James Wicks Court	D1	Roman Road	B4	West Street
A3	Burlington Road	D1	Leicester Close	C2	Ryegate Road	A1	Westway
A4	Butt Road	A3	Lexden Road	A2	St Alban's Road	C3	Whitewell Road
C2	Castle Bailey	D1	Lincoln Way	C3	St Botolph's Street	A4	Wickham Road
D1	Castle Road	C2	Long Wyre Street	C2	St Helen's Lane	C2	William's Walk
B3	Chapel Street North	D4	Lucas Road	B3	St John's Avenue	D1	Worcester Road
B3	Chapel Street South	D3	Magdalen Street	C3	St John's Green		
B3	Church Street	C1	Maidenburgh Street	B3	St John's Street		
B4	Circular Road North	A4	Maldon Road	D3	St Julian Grove		
D1	Coventry Close	A3	Manor Road	A2	St Mary's Fields		
C2	Cowdray Crescent	B1	Market Close	B1	St Peters Street		
A4	Creffield Road	C4	Mersea Road	A4	Salisbury Avenue		
D4	Cromwell Road	C1	Middle Mill Road	A1	Sheepen Place		
B3	Crouch Street	B1	Middleborough	A1	Sheepen Road		
C2	Culver Street East	D4	Military Road	B1	Short Cut Road		
B2	Culver Street West	D4	Mill Road	C3	Short Wyre Street		
D2	East Hill	C2	Museum Street	D4	Shrubland Road		
C2	East Stockwell Street	C4	Napier Road	B3	Sir Isaac's Walk		
D4	Fairfax Road	B2	North Hill	B4	South Street		
C4	Flagstaff Road	B1	North Station Road	B3	Southway		
B3	George Street	B1	Northgate Street	C3	Stanwell Street		
D4	Golden Noble Hill	B1	Nunn's Road	C1	Stockwell Street		
A4	Gray Road	C3	Osborne Street	C1	Taylor Court		
B2	Head Street	A3	Papillon Road	C2	Trinity Street		
B3	Headgate	A2	Pope's Lane	C3	Vineyard Street		

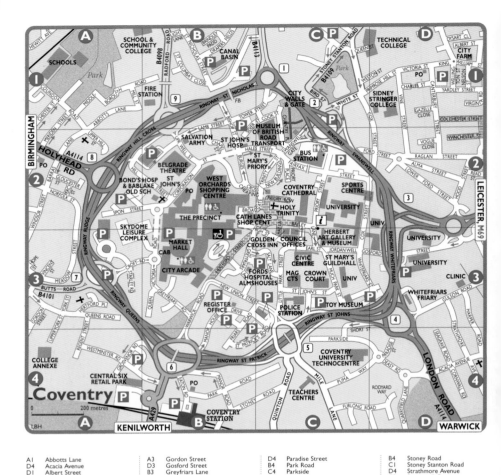

A1	Abbotts Lane	A3	Gordon Street	D4	Paradise Street	B4	Stoney Road
D4	Acacia Avenue	D3	Gosford Street	B4	Park Road	C1	Stoney Stanton Road
D1	Albert Street	B3	Greyfriars Lane	C4	Parkside	D4	Strathmore Avenue
D2	Alma Street	B3	Greyfriars Road	A2	Percy Street	C2	Swanswell Gate
A2	Barras Lane	A4	Grosvenor Road	D1	Primrose Hill Street	B1	Tower Street
C2	Bayley Lane	D3	Gulson Road	C2	Priory Row	C2	Trinity Street
C1	Bird Street	B2	Hales Street	C2	Priory Street	A2	Upper Hill Street
B1	Bishop Street	D3	Harper Road	C4	Puma Way	B2	Upper Well Street
B1	Brindley Padd	C3	Hay Lane	D4	Quarryfield Lane	A4	Upper York Street
B2	Broadgate	A3	Hertford Place	C1	Queen Street	D1	Victoria Street
B2	Burges	B3	Hertford Street	B3	Queen Victoria Road	A3	Vincent Street
A3	Butts Road	A1	Hewitt Avenue	A3	Queens Road	D1	Vine Street
D1	Canterbury Street	C3	High Street	C4	Quinton Road	D1	Virginia Road
C2	Chantry Place	A2	Holyhead Road	B1	Radford Road	D2	Vogue Close
B2	Chapel Street	D2	Hood Street	D2	Raglan Street	B3	Warwick Road
D1	Charles Street	A3	Hope Street	A4	Regent Street	D1	Wellington Street
A1	Chester Street	C3	Jordan Well	A2	Ringway Hill Cross	A4	Westminster Road
D1	Colchester Street	D1	King William Street	A3	Ringway Queens	C1	Weston Street
C1	Cook Street	B1	Lamb Street	A3	Ringway Rudge	C1	White Street
D4	Cornwall Road	B1	Light Lane	C3	Ringway St Johns	C3	Whitefriars Street
B2	Corporation Street	C3	Little Park Street	B1	Ringway St Nicholas	D2	Winchester Street
A1	Coundon Road	D4	London Road	B4	Ringway St Patrick	A2	Windsor Street
D1	Cox Street	D2	Lower Ford Street	C2	Ringway Swanswell	D1	Yardley Street
A3	Croft Road	B3	Manor House Drive	D3	Ringway Whitefriars	A3	York Street
B2	Cross Cheaping	B4	Manor Road	D4	Rodyard Way		
D4	Deasy Road	A3	Meadow Street	B1	St Columba's Close		
B1	Drapers Fields	A2	Meriden Street	C3	St John's Street		
D1	Dysart Close	A1	Middleborough Road	B1	St Nicholas Street		
C3	Earl Street	C4	Mile Lane	B4	St Patrick's Road		
B4	Eaton Road	A1	Mill Street	C3	Salt Lane		
C2	Fairfax Street	C3	Much Park Street	D4	Seagrave Road		
D2	Ford Street	D1	Nelson Street	C4	Short Street		
B4	Friars Road	C2	New Buildings	B1	Silver Street		
C4	Furlong Road	B3	New Union Street	A2	Spon Street		
D1	Gazelle Close	A2	Norfolk Street	A3	Starley Road		
A2	Gloucester Street						

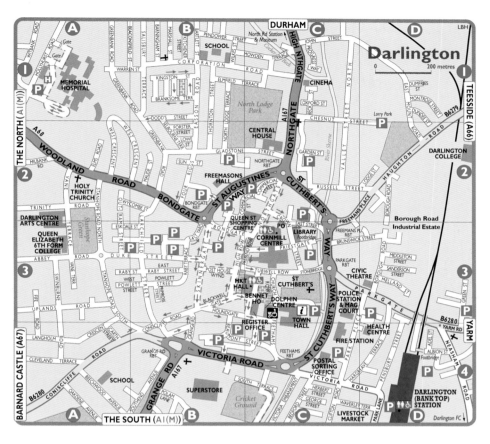

A3	Abbey Road	C3	East Street	B2	Maude Street	B3	Salt Yard
D4	Adel Street	B1	Elmfield Terrace	D3	Melland Street	D3	Sanderson Street
D4	Albion Street	A2	Elms Road	D3	Middleton Street	A4	Scarth Street
B1	Barningham Street	A3	Eskdale Street	A2	Milbank Road	B2	Selbourne Terrace
B1	Bartlett Street	C4	Feethams	D1	Montrose Street	B3	Skinnergate
A1	Beaconsfield Street	A3	Fife Road	C1	Mowden Terrace	C4	South Terrace
B4	Beaumont Street	B2	Forster Street	D4	Neasham Road	B4	Southend Avenue
C1	Beck Street	B2	Four Riggs	B1	North Lodge Terrace	A2	Stanhope Road North
C4	Bedford Street	C2	Freemans Place	C2	Northgate	A3	Stanhope Road South
A4	Beechwood Avenue	C2	Garden Street	A4	Oakdene Avenue	C3	Stonebridge
B3	Blackwell Gate	C4	George Street	A2	Outram Street	B2	Sun Street
B2	Bondgate	B2	Gladstone Street	C1	Oxford Street	A3	Swinburne Road
D3	Borough Road	B4	Grange Road	D4	Park Lane	B1	Thornton Street
B1	Branksome Terrace	D3	Green Street	C4	Park Place	A2	Trinity Road
C3	Brunswick Street	A1	Greenbank Road	D3	Parkgate	C3	Tubwell Row
C1	Chesnut Street	D4	Hargreave Terrace	B1	Pendower Street	A3	Uplands Road
C3	Church Row	D2	Haughton Road	D4	Pensbury Street	C2	Valley Street North
A4	Cleveland Terrace	C4	Herbert Street	B4	Polam Lane	A2	Vane Terrace
C4	Clifton Road	C1	High Northgate	B3	Post House Wynd	C4	Victoria Embankment
B2	Commercial Street	B3	High Row	B3	Powlett Street	B4	Victoria Road
A4	Coniscliffe Road	A1	Hollyhurst Road	C3	Prebend Row	A1	Warren Street
B1	Corporation Road	B3	Houndgate	C3	Priestgate	C4	Waverley Terrace
C2	Crown Street	C1	John Street	B3	Primrose Street	A2	West Crescent
B1	Dodd's Street	B1	Kingston Street	C1	Progress Way	A3	West Powlett Street
A3	Duke Street	B1	Kitchener Street	A3	Raby Street	B1	Wilkes Street
D1	Dumfries Street	A4	Langholm Crescent	B3	Raby Terrace	A1	Witbank Road
D1	Dundee Street	B3	Larchfield Street	C2	Russell Street	A2	Woodland Road
B1	Easson Road	D2	Lodge Street	B2	St Augustines Way	A2	Wycombe Street
D1	East Mount Road	B2	Lowe Street	C4	St Cuthbert's Way	D4	Yarm Road
B3	East Raby Street	B1	Marshall Street	B1	Salisbury Terrace		

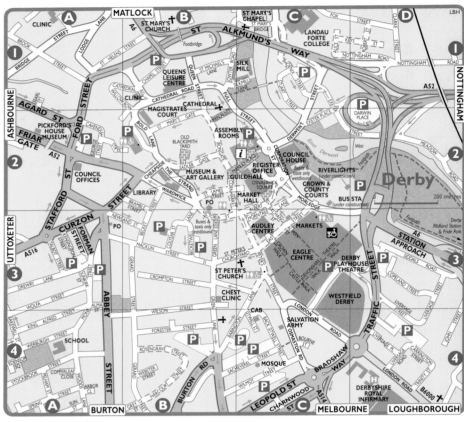

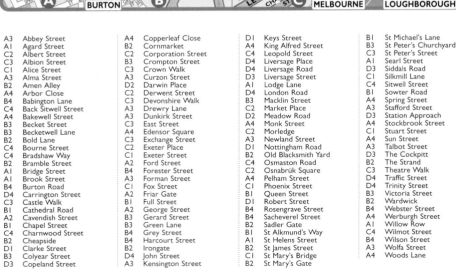

A3	Abbey Street	A4	Copperleaf Close	D1	Keys Street	B1	St Michael's Lane
A1	Agard Street	B2	Cornmarket	A4	King Alfred Street	B3	St Peter's Churchyard
C2	Albert Street	C2	Corporation Street	C4	Leopold Street	C3	St Peter's Street
C3	Albion Street	B3	Crompton Street	D4	Liversage Place	A1	Searl Street
C1	Alice Street	C3	Crown Walk	D4	Liversage Road	D3	Siddals Road
A3	Alma Street	A3	Curzon Street	D3	Liversage Street	C1	Silkmill Lane
B2	Amen Alley	D2	Darwin Place	A1	Lodge Lane	C4	Sitwell Street
A4	Arbor Close	C2	Derwent Street	D4	London Road	B1	Sowter Road
B4	Babington Lane	C3	Devonshire Walk	B3	Macklin Street	A4	Spring Street
C4	Back Sitwell Street	A3	Drewry Lane	C2	Market Place	A3	Stafford Street
A4	Bakewell Street	A3	Dunkirk Street	D2	Meadow Road	D3	Station Approach
B3	Becket Street	C3	East Street	A4	Monk Street	A4	Stockbrook Street
B3	Becketwell Lane	A4	Edensor Square	C2	Morledge	C1	Stuart Street
B2	Bold Lane	C3	Exchange Street	A3	Newland Street	A4	Sun Street
C4	Bourne Street	C2	Exeter Place	D1	Nottingham Road	A3	Talbot Street
C4	Bradshaw Way	C1	Exeter Street	B2	Old Blacksmith Yard	D3	The Cockpitt
B2	Bramble Street	A2	Ford Street	C4	Osmaston Road	B2	The Strand
A1	Bridge Street	B4	Forester Street	C2	Osnabrük Square	C3	Theatre Walk
A1	Brook Street	A3	Forman Street	A4	Pelham Street	D4	Traffic Street
B4	Burton Road	C1	Fox Street	C1	Phoenix Street	D4	Trinity Street
D4	Carrington Street	A2	Friar Gate	B1	Queen Street	B3	Victoria Street
C3	Castle Walk	B1	Full Street	D1	Robert Street	B2	Wardwick
B1	Cathedral Road	A2	George Street	B4	Rosengrave Street	B4	Webster Street
A2	Cavendish Street	B3	Gerard Street	B4	Sacheverel Street	A4	Werburgh Street
B1	Chapel Street	B3	Green Lane	B2	Sadler Gate	A1	Willow Row
C4	Charnwood Street	B4	Grey Street	B1	St Alkmund's Way	C4	Wilmot Street
B2	Cheapside	B4	Harcourt Street	A1	St Helens Street	B4	Wilson Street
D1	Clarke Street	B2	Irongate	B2	St James Street	A3	Wolfa Street
B3	Colyear Street	D4	John Street	C1	St Mary's Bridge	A4	Woods Lane
D3	Copeland Street	A3	Kensington Street	B2	St Mary's Gate		

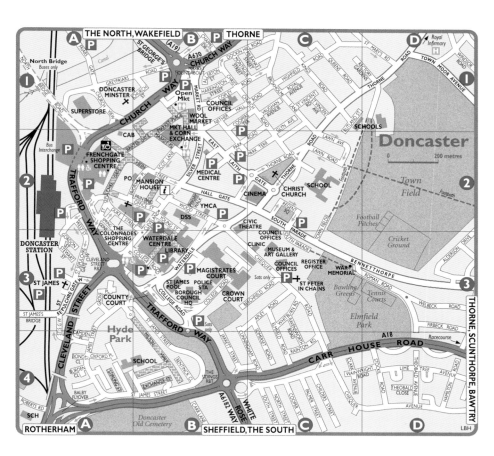

D3	Alderson Drive	C3	Elmfield Road	B2	Printing Office Street	D4	Theobald Close

D3 Alderson Drive
B1 Allerton Street
C3 Apley Road
A2 Baxter Gate
C3 Beechfield Road
C3 Bennetthorpe
B4 Bentinck Close
A4 Bond Close
C1 Broxholme Lane
A4 Burden Close
A4 Camden Place
C4 Carr House Road
B1 Chappel Drive
C4 Chequer Avenue
C3 Chequer Road
C4 Childers Street
B1 Christ Church Road
B1 Church Street
A1 Church View
B1 Church Way
C4 Clark Avenue
A4 Cleveland Street
B3 College Road
C4 Cooper Street
B1 Coopers Terrace
B1 Copley Road
B4 Cunningham Road
A2 Duke Street
B1 Dockin Hill Road
B2 East Laith Gate

C3 Elmfield Road
B4 Exchange Street
D3 Firbeck Road
A1 Friars Gate
C1 Glyn Avenue
A3 Gordon Street
A1 Greyfriars Road
A3 Grove Place
B2 Hall Gate
D4 Hamilton Road
B1 Harrington Street
B2 High Street
C1 Highfield Road
B4 Jarrett Street
C1 Kings Road
C2 Lawn Avenue
C2 Lawn Road
D4 Lime Tree Avenue
B1 Market Place
B1 Market Road
C1 Milbanke Street
B4 Milton Walk
B1 Montague Street
B1 Nether Hall Road
A1 North Bridge Road
C4 North Street
A4 Oxford Place
C4 Palmer Street
B2 Park Road
B2 Park Terrace

B2 Printing Office Street
B2 Priory Place
B2 Priory Walk
C1 Queens Road
C4 Rainton Road
C3 Ravensworth Road
D1 Rectory Gardens
C2 Regent Square
A4 Roberts Road
D3 Roman Road
C1 Royal Avenue
C1 Rutland Street
B1 St George's Bridge
A4 St James Street
A3 St James's Bridge
D1 St Mary's Road
A2 St Sepulchre Gate
A3 St Sepulchre Gate West
C1 St Vincent Avenue
C1 St Vincent Road
B2 Scot Lane
B2 Silver Street
C4 Somerset Road
C2 South Parade
C4 South Street
A2 Spring Gardens
A4 Stirling Street
A3 Stewart Street
D4 Stockil Road
D4 Theobald Avenue

D4 Theobald Close
C2 Thorne Road
C3 Town Fields
D1 Town Moor Avenue
A2 Trafford Way
C1 Vaughan Avenue
C4 Wainwright Road
B3 Waterdale
D3 Welbeck Road
A2 West Street
C3 Whitburn Road
B4 White Rose Way
D1 Windsor Road
B2 Wood Street
B2 Young Street

Dover

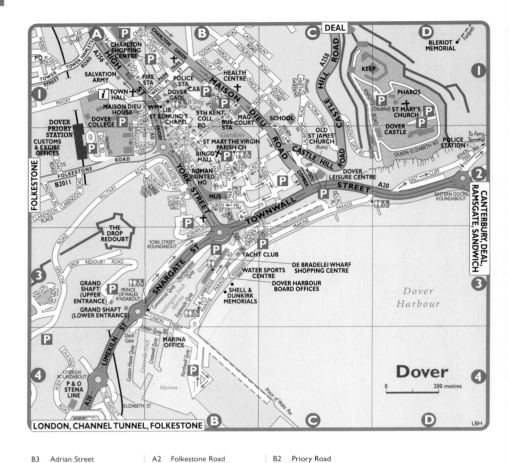

B3	Adrian Street	A2	Folkestone Road	B2	Priory Road
C2	Ashen Tree Lane	B1	Godwyne Close	B2	Priory Street
D2	Athol Terrace	B1	Godwyne Road	D2	Queen Elizabeth Road
B2	Bench Street	B1	Harold Street	B2	Queen Street
B2	Biggin Street	C1	Heritage Gardens	B2	Queens Gardens
B2	Bowling Green Terrace	B1	Hewitt Road	C2	Russell Street
B3	Cambridge Road	A1	High Street	A2	St John's Road
B3	Camden Crescent	B2	King Street	A2	Saxon Street
B2	Cannon Street	C1	Knights Road	B3	Snargate Street
C2	Canon's Gate Road	A3	Knights Templars	B2	Stem Brook
C2	Castle Hill Road	B1	Ladywell	C1	Taswell Close
B1	Castle Mount Road	B2	Lancaster Road	C1	Taswell Street
B2	Castle Street	C2	Laureston Place	A1	Templar Street
A4	Channel View Road	B1	Leyburne Road	B1	The Paddock
B1	Charlton Green	A4	Limekiln Street	A4	The Viaduct
B2	Church Street	B1	Maison Dieu Road	A1	Tower Hamlets Road
A2	Clarendon Place	A2	Malvern Road	A1	Tower Street
A2	Clarendon Road	B3	Marine Parade	C2	Townwall Street
B2	Cowgate Hill	B2	Market Square	B3	Union Street
A1	Crafford Street	A3	Military Road	C1	Victoria Park
B1	Dour Street	B2	Mill Lane	C2	Wellesley Road
C2	Douro Place	B3	New Bridge	A1	Widred Road
A3	Drop Redoubt Road	B2	New Street	A1	Wood Street
B2	Durham Close	A2	Norman Street	C2	Woolcomber Street
B2	Durham Hill	B1	Park Place	B2	Worthington Street
D2	East Cliff	B1	Park Street	B2	York Street
A1	East Street	B1	Pencester Road		
A1	Effingham Crescent	B2	Princes Street		
A2	Effingham Street	A2	Priory Gate Road		
A4	Elizabeth Street	A1	Priory Hill		

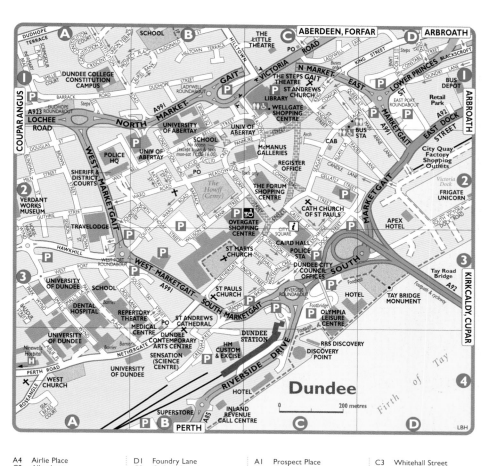

A4	Airlie Place
C2	Allan Lane
A3	Balfour Street
B2	Bank Street
A1	Barrack Road
B2	Barrack Street
B2	Bell Street
D1	Blackscroft
A2	Blinshall Street
A2	Brown Street
C2	Candle Lane
C2	Castle Street
C2	Commercial Street
D1	Constable Street
A1	Constitution Court
A1	Constitution Crescent
A1	Constitution Road
C1	Cowgate
C3	Crichton Street
A3	Cross Lane
D1	Dens Street
C3	Dock Street
A2	Douglas Street
B1	Dudhope Street
A1	Dudhope Terrace
D1	East Dock Street
D1	East Marketgait
B2	Euclid Crescent
B2	Euclid Street
C3	Exchange Street

D1	Foundry Lane
C2	Gellatly Street
B4	Greenmarket
A2	Guthrie Street
A3	Hawkhill
C3	High Street
B1	Hilltown
B1	Hilltown Terrace
A3	Horsewater Wynd
A1	Infirmary Brae
B1	Irvine's Square
A2	Johnston Street
C1	King Street
C1	Ladywell Avenue
B1	Laurel Bank
A1	Lochee Road
D1	Lower Princes Street
D1	Mary Anne Lane
B1	McDonald Street
B2	Meadowside
A2	Miln Street
A4	Nethergate
B2	Nicoll Street
B2	North Lindsay Street
B1	North Marketgait
C2	Panmure Street
A3	Park Place
A3	Park Wynd
A4	Perth Road

A1	Prospect Place
C1	Queen Street
B2	Rattray Street
B2	Reform Street
B4	Riverside Drive
A4	Roseangle
C1	St Andrews Street
D1	St Roques Lane
A1	Scrimgeour Place
A4	Seabraes Court
C1	Seagate
A3	Session Street
A3	Small's Lane
A3	Small's Wynd
A1	Smillie Court
B3	South Marketgait
B3	South Tay Street
D2	South Victoria Dock Road
B3	South Ward Road
C2	Trades Lane
C3	Union Street
A1	Union Terrace
C1	Victoria Road
B2	Ward Road
A2	West Bell Street
A2	West Marketgait
A3	West Port
C3	Whitehall Crescent

C3	Whitehall Street
B3	Willison Street
B3	Yeaman Shore

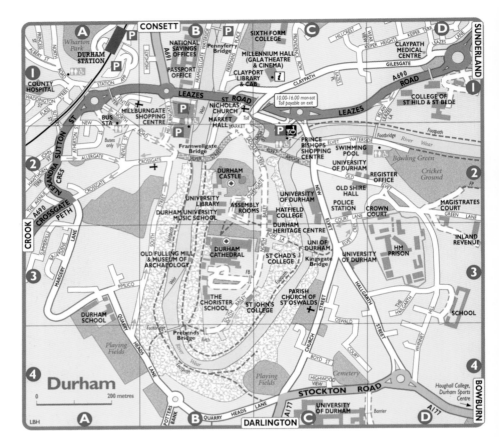

A1	Albert Street	D1	Leazes Lane	A2	The Avenue
A2	Alexandra Crescent	C1	Leazes Place	D3	The Hallgarth
A2	Allergate	B1	Leazes Road	A1	Waddington Street
A2	Atherton Street	A3	Margery Lane	D1	Wear View
C3	Bow Lane	B2	Market Place	D4	Whinney Hill
C4	Boyd Street	B1	Millburngate		
A3	Briardene	A2	Neville Street		
C4	Church Street	C2	New Elvet		
C1	Claypath	A1	New Street		
C2	Court Lane	C3	North Bailey		
A2	Crossgate	A1	North Road		
A2	Crossgate Peth	C2	Old Elvet		
C2	Elvet Bridge	C3	Oswald Court		
C3	Elvet Crescent	C2	Owengate		
C2	Elvet Waterside	D1	Pelaw Leazes Lane		
A1	Flass Street	A3	Pimlico		
B1	Framwellgate Waterside	B4	Potters Bank		
B1	Freemans Place	A1	Princess Street		
D1	Gilesgate	C1	Providence Row		
D2	Green Lane	A3	Quarry Heads Lane		
C3	Hallgarth Street	B2	Saddler Street		
A2	Hawthorn Terrace	B2	Silver Street		
B1	Highgate	B3	South Bailey		
C2	High Street	B3	South Street		
C4	Highwood View	A1	Station Approach		
C1	Hillcrest	C4	Stockton Road		
A2	John Street	A3	Summerville		
D1	Keiper Heights	A2	Sutton Street		
D1	Keiper Terrace	A1	Tenter Terrace		

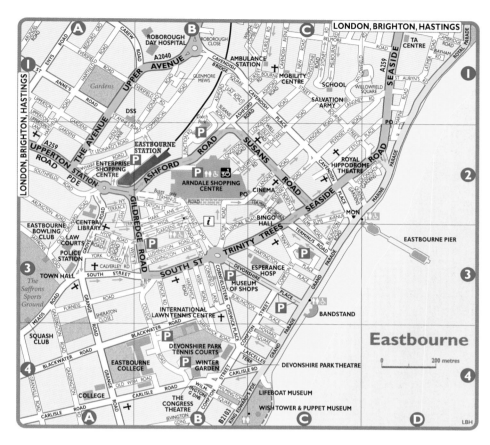

A3	Arlington Road	B3	Cornfield Terrace	B2	Longstone Road	B2	Terminus Road
A1	Arundel Road	B3	Devonshire Place	B3	Lushington Lane	A2	The Avenue
B2	Ashford Road	C1	Dursley Road	B3	Lushington Road	C2	Tideswell Road
B1	Ashford Square	C2	Elms Avenue	D2	Marine Parade	C3	Trinity Place
A2	Avenue Lane	C2	Elms Road	D1	Marine Road	B3	Trinity Trees
A3	Bath Road	A1	Enys Road	B2	Mark Lane	B1	Upper Avenue
D1	Bayham Road	A1	Eversfield Road	A3	Meads Road	A1	Upperton Gardens
A1	Bedford Grove	A3	Furness Road	C1	Melbourne Road	A2	Upperton Road
C1	Belmore Road	B3	Gildredge Road	C1	New Road	C2	Wellesley Road
A4	Blackwater Road	B1	Glenmore Mews	C2	North Street	A3	West Street
B3	Bolton Road	C4	Grand Parade	A3	Old Orchard Road	A2	West Terrace
C1	Bourne Street	A3	Grange Road	A4	Old Wish Road	A2	Wharf Road
B3	Burlington Place	A4	Granville Road	C2	Pevensey Road	C1	Willowfield Road
C3	Burlington Road	A4	Grassington Road	C2	Queens Gardens	D1	Willowfield Square
A3	Calverley Road	A3	Grove Road	B1	Roborough Close	B4	Wilmington Gardens
D1	Cambridge Road	B3	Hardwick Road	D1	Royal Parade	B4	Wilmington Square
A3	Camden Road	A2	Hartfield Road	A1	St Anne's Road	B1	Winchcombe Road
A1	Carew Road	C3	Hartington Place	D1	St Aubyn's Road	B3	Wish Road
A4	Carlisle Road	C4	Howard Square	A2	St Leonard's Road	A3	York Road
C1	Cavendish Avenue	B3	Hyde Gardens	A3	Saffrons Road		
B1	Cavendish Bridge	A3	Hyde Road	D1	Seaside		
C1	Cavendish Place	A2	Ivy Terrace	C2	Seaside Road		
C2	Ceylon Place	B4	Jevington Gardens	A3	Sheraton Close		
B3	Chiswick Place	B2	Junction Road	A3	South Street		
B3	College Road	B4	King Edward's Parade	A2	Southfields Road		
B1	Commercial Road	C2	Langney Road	B3	Spencer Road		
B4	Compton Street	C4	Lascelles Terrace	A2	Station Parade		
B3	Connaught Road	D1	Latimer Road	B2	Station Street		
B3	Cornfield Lane	B1	Leaf Road	B1	Susans Road		
B2	Cornfield Road	B3	Lismore Road	C1	Sydney Road		

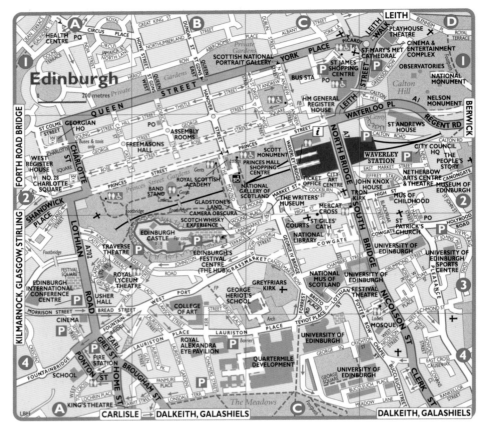

B1	Abercromby Place	D2	East Market Street	C1	Leith Street	D3	St Johns Hill
C1	Albany Street	A3	Festival Square	D1	Leith Walk	D2	St Mary's Street
D2	Blackfriar Street	C3	Forrest Road	A4	Lochrin Place	A1	Saunders Street
D1	Blenheim Place	A4	Fountainbridge	B4	Lonsdale Terrace	A4	Semple Street
A3	Bread Street	B1	Frederick Street	A3	Lothian Road	A2	Shandwick Place
C3	Bristo Place	A4	Gardener's Crescent	C3	Lothian Street	D3	South Bridge
A4	Brougham Street	C3	George IV Bridge	C2	Market Street	C1	South St Andrew Street
C4	Buccleuch Place	C4	George Square	D4	Meadow Lane	C1	South St David Street
D4	Buccleuch Street	B2	George Street	A3	Morrison Street	A3	Spital Street
D1	Calton Hill	B4	Glen Street	B3	Mound Place	A4	Tarvit Street
D2	Calton Road	B3	Grassmarket	D2	New Street	C4	Teviot Place
A3	Cambridge Street	B1	Great King Street	D3	Nicolson Street	B2	The Mound
C3	Candlemaker Row	D1	Greenside Row	A2	North Bridge	B1	Thistle Street
D2	Canongate	A3	Grindlay Street	C1	North Castle Street	C3	Victoria Street
A2	Castle Street	B1	Hanover Street	C1	North St Andrew Street	D3	Viewcraig Gardens
A3	Castle Terrace	B3	Heriot Place	C1	North St David Street	D1	Waterloo Place
B4	Chalmers Street	A1	Heriot Row	B1	Northumberland Street	C2	Waverley Bridge
C3	Chambers Street	D2	High Street	B4	Panmure Place	D3	West Adam Street
D4	Chapel Street	D3	Hill Place	C1	Picardy Place	C3	West Bow
A2	Charlotte Square	A2	Hill Street	D3	Pleasance	D4	West Nicholson Street
A2	Charlotte Street	D3	Holyrood Road	A4	Ponton Street	B3	West Port
A1	Circus Place	A4	Home Street	D3	Potter Row	D4	West Richmond Street
D4	Clerk Street	B1	Howe Street	B1	Princes Street	A4	West Tollcross
C2	Cockburn Street	A1	India Street	B1	Queen Street Gardens East	C1	York Lane
D4	Cowans Close	A1	Jamaica Street North Lane	B1	Queen Street Gardens West	C1	York Place
C3	Cowgate	D2	Jeffrey Street	D4	Rankeillor Street	A2	Young Street
D4	Crichton Street	B3	Johnston Terrace	D2	Regent Road		
D4	Davie Street	B4	Keir Street	B2	Rose Street		
A1	Dean Terrace	A3	King's Stables Road	D3	Roxburgh Place		
A1	Doune Terrace	B3	Lady Lawson Street	A1	Royal Circus		
D3	Drummond Street	B4	Lauriston Gardens	D1	Royal Terrace		
C1	Dublin Street	B4	Lauriston Park	A3	Rutland Street		
B1	Dundas Street	B4	Lauriston Place	C1	St Andrew Square		
A4	Earl Grey Street	B4	Lauriston Street	C2	St Colme Street		
D3	East Adam Street	C3	Lawnmarket	D2	St John Street		
D4	East Cross Causeway						

Exeter

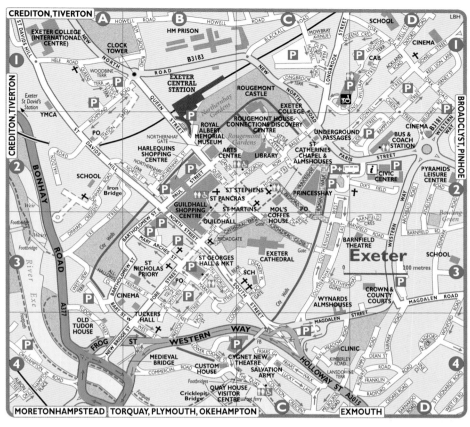

D1	Ackland Road	B4	Coombe Street	C1	Longbrook Terrace	B4	Rack Street
A4	Albion Street	D4	Dean Street	B4	Lower Coombe Street	D4	Radford Road
A3	Allhallows Close	C3	Deanery Place	B2	Lower North Street	D1	Red Lion Lane
D3	Archibald Road	D3	Denmark Road	C4	Lucky Lane	A2	Richmond Road
D2	Athelstan Road	A3	Dinham Crescent	D3	Magdalen Road	D4	Roberts Road
C2	Bailey Street	A2	Dinham Road	C4	Magdalen Street	C2	Roman Walk
D2	Bampfylde Street	D2	Dix's Field	B3	Market Street	A2	St Davids Hill
D4	Barnardo Road	B1	Elm Grove Road	B3	Mary Arches Street	D4	St Leonards Road
D3	Barnfield Crescent	A3	Exe Street	C4	Melbourne Road	D1	Sidwell Street
D3	Barnfield Road	D4	Fairpark Road	D4	Mount Radford Crescent	B3	Smythen Street
A3	Bartholomew Street	B3	Fore Street	C1	Mowbray Avenue	B3	South George Street
B3	Bartholomew Street East	D4	Franklin Street	C2	Musgrove Row	C3	South Street
A3	Bartholomew Street West	C4	Friars Gate	A4	New Bridge Street	C3	Southernhay East
B3	Bear Street	C4	Friars Walk	A1	New North Road	C3	Southernhay Gardens
C2	Bedford Street	B3	Frienhay Street	B3	North Street	C3	Southernhay West
D2	Belgrave Road	A4	Frog Street	B2	Northernhay Gate	A2	Station Yard
C1	Blackall Road	B2	Gandy Street	B2	Northernhay Square	D4	Temple Road
A2	Bonhay Road	A2	Haldon Road	B2	Northernhay Street	C4	The Quay
B3	Broadgate	A1	Hele Road	A4	Okehampton Place	A4	Tudor Street
D2	Bude Street	B3	High Street	A4	Okehampton Road	D1	Verney Street
C4	Bull Meadow Road	C4	Holloway Street	C1	Old Park Road	D4	Vine Close
A1	Bystock Terrace	B1	Howell Road	D1	Oxford Road	D1	Well Street
C2	Castle Street	B3	John Street	C3	Palace Gate	B4	West Street
C3	Cathedral Close	C4	Kimberley Road	C2	Paris Street	D4	West Grove Road
B3	Cathedral Yard	B3	King Street	B2	Paul Street	A3	West View Terrace
D4	Cedars Road	D1	King William Street	B4	Preston Street	B4	Western Way
C3	Chapel Street	C4	Lansdowne Terrace	C2	Princesshay	D3	Western Way
D1	Cheeke Street	D1	Leighton Terrace	B1	Queen Street	A1	Woodbine Terrace
C4	Colleton Crescent	C2	Little Castle Street	C1	Queens Crescent	D4	Wonford Road
B4	Commercial Road	C1	Longbrook Street	A1	Queens Terrace	D1	York Road

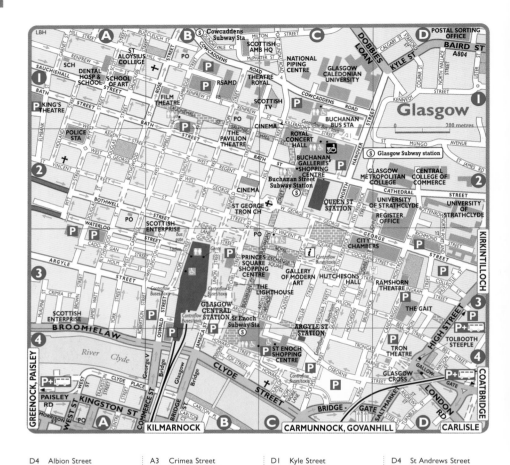

D4	Albion Street	A3	Crimea Street	D1	Kyle Street	D4	St Andrews Street
A3	Argyle Street	A1	Dalhousie Street	D1	Lister Street	D2	St James Road
C3	Argyll Arcade	B4	Dixon Street	D4	London Road	D2	St Mungo Avenue
D1	Baird Street	C1	Dobbies Loan	B1	McPhater Street	C3	St Vincent Place
A1	Bath Street	A2	Douglas Street	A3	McAlpine Street	B2	St Vincent Street
D4	Bell Street	B1	Dundasvale Court	C1	Milton Street	D4	Saltmarket
A3	Blythswood Street	C4	Dunlop Street	C3	Miller Street	B1	Sauchiehall Street
A2	Bothwell Street	A2	Elmbank Street	B3	Mitchell Street	A1	Scott Street
C4	Bridge Gate	B4	Fox Street	D3	Montrose Street	D3	Shuttle Street
B4	Bridge Street	D4	Gallowgate	A4	Morrison Street	C3	South Frederick Street
A3	Broomielaw	A1	Garnet Street	C2	North Frederick Street	D1	Stafford Street
A3	Brown Street	C2	George Square	C2	North Hanover Street	D4	Steel Street
C3	Brunswick Street	D3	George Street	D2	North Portland Street	C4	Stockwell Street
A1	Buccleuch Street	C3	Glassford Street	D1	North Wallace Street	A4	Tradeston Street
B3	Buchanan Street	B3	Gordon Street	C4	Osborne Street	C4	Trongate
A3	Cadogan Street	D4	High Street	B4	Oswald Street	D4	Turnbull Street
D1	Calgary Street	A1	Hill Street	A4	Paisley Road	B3	Union Street
B1	Cambridge Street	A2	Holland Street	C4	Parnie Street	C3	Viginia Street
D3	Candleriggs	A3	Holm Street	A2	Pitt Street	A2	Waterloo Street
B4	Carlton Court	B3	Hope Street	C1	Port Dundas Road	D4	Watson Street
B4	Carlton Place	B4	Howard Street	C3	Queen Street	B3	Wellington Street
D2	Cathedral Street	C3	Hutcheson Street	B2	Renfield Lane	B3	West Campbell Street
A4	Centre Street	C3	Ingram Street	B2	Renfield Street	B2	West George Street
A4	Clyde Place	B4	James Watt Street	B1	Renfrew Street	B2	West Nile Street
B4	Clyde Street	A3	James Watt Street	D3	Richmond Street	B2	West Regent Street
C3	Cochrane Street	C3	John Street	A3	Robertson Street	A4	West Street
D3	College Street	D1	Kennedy Street	C4	Ropework Lane	C3	Wilson Street
A4	Commerce Street	C1	Killermont Street	B1	Rose Street	A3	York Street
D1	Coupar Street	C4	King Street	D2	Rottenrow		
B1	Cowcaddens Road	A4	Kingston Street	C3	Royal Exchange Square		

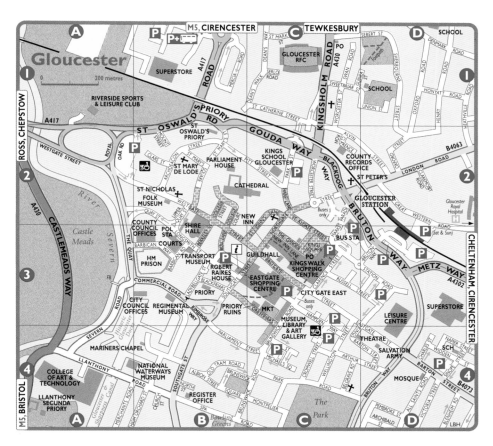

Gloucester

B4	Albion Street	C1	Dean's Way	C2	Northgate Street	C1	Sweetbriar Street
D4	All Saints Road	D1	Denmark Road	B4	Old Tram Road	C3	The Oxbode
C2	Alvin Street	C3	Eastgate Street	D1	Oxford Road	A2	The Quay
B2	Archdeacon Street	C2	Gouda Way	D2	Oxford Street	D1	Union Street
D4	Archibald Street	D2	Great Western Road	C4	Park Road	B2	Upper Quay Street
C4	Arthur Street	C3	Greyfriars	C2	Park Street	D4	Victoria Street
B3	Barbican Road	C1	Guinea Street	B4	Parliament Street	C4	Wellington Street
B3	Barbican Way	C3	Hampden Way	D4	Pembroke Street	B2	Westgate Street
D4	Barton Street	C2	Hare Lane	C2	Pitt Street	D4	Widden Street
C4	Belgrave Road	D1	Heathville Road	B1	Priory Road	C1	Worcester Street
B3	Berkeley Street	D1	Henry Road	B2	Quay Street		
C2	Blackdog Way	B4	High Orchard Street	A2	Royal Oak Road		
B3	Blackfriars	D1	Honyatt Road	C3	Russell Street		
D4	Blenheim Road	B3	Kimbrose Way	C2	St Aldate Street		
C4	Brunswick Road	C4	Kings Barton Street	C1	St Catherine Street		
B4	Brunswick Square	C3	Kings Square	C2	St John's Lane		
D3	Bruton Way	C1	Kingsholm Road	C1	St Mark Street		
B3	Bull Lane	B3	Ladybellgate Street	B2	St Mary's Square		
A2	Castlemeads Way	A4	Llanthony Road	B2	St Mary's Street		
D4	Charles Street	D2	London Road	C4	St Michael's Square		
B4	Church Street	B3	Longsmith Street	B2	St Oswald's Road		
B2	Clare Street	C2	Market Parade	D1	Sebert Street		
D2	Claremont Road	A4	Merchants Road	C1	Serlo Road		
C2	Clarence Row	B1	Mercia Road	A4	Severn Road		
C3	Clarence Street	D3	Metz Way	D1	Sherbourne Street		
B2	College Court	C4	Montpelier	D4	Sinope Street		
B2	College Street	B2	Mount Street	B3	Southgate Street		
B3	Commercial Road	D4	Napier Street	B4	Spa Road		
C4	Cromwell Street	C3	New Inn Lane	D3	Station Road		
C1	Dean's Walk	B4	North Street	C1	Swan Road		

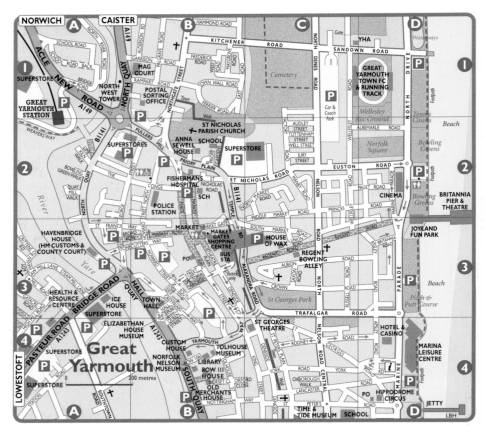

A1	Acle New Road	B3	Howard Street North	C2	Princes Road	B4	Tolhouse Street
D2	Albemarle Road	B3	Howard Street South	B2	Priory Gardens	C2	Tottenham Street
C3	Albion Road	C2	Jury Street	B2	Priory Plain	B1	Town Wall Road
B1	Alderson Road	B3	King Street	A2	Quay Mill Walk	C3	Trafalgar Road
C3	Alexandra Road	B1	Kitchener Road	B4	Queen Street	C3	Union Road
D3	Apsley Road	A3	Lady Haven Road	B1	Rampart Road	B3	Victoria Arcade
C2	Audley Street	C4	Lancaster Road	C3	Regent Road	A2	Weavers Way
A2	Bowling Green Walk	A2	Lime Kiln Walk	B3	Regent Street	C2	Well Street
A1	Bridge Road	C2	Manby Road	C4	Rodney Road	C2	Wellesley Road
A3	Bridge Road	D4	Marine Parade	B4	Row 106	B1	West Road
D3	Britannia Road	B3	Market Gates	C3	Russell Road	B4	Yarmouth Way
A3	Broad Row	B2	Market Place	A3	St Francis Way	C4	York Road
A3	Crittens Road	B3	Market Row	C4	St Georges Road		
C3	Crown Road	B1	Maygrove Road	B2	St Nicholas Road		
B3	Deneside	C2	Middle Market Road	C4	St Peter's Road		
B4	Dorset Close	A3	Mill Road	C4	St Peters Plain		
B1	East Road	C4	Nelson Road Central	C1	Sandown Road		
C2	Euston Road	C2	Nelson Road North	A3	Saw Mill Lane		
C2	Factory Road	C1	North Denes Road	C3	Saxon Road		
B1	Ferrier Road	D1	North Drive	A1	School Road		
B1	Frederick Road	C2	North Market Road	A1	School Road Back		
B2	Fullers Hill	A2	North Quay	C3	South Market Road		
B1	Garrison Road	A1	North River Road	B4	South Quay		
A3	Gatacre Road	B1	Northgate Street	A4	Southtown Road		
A2	George Street	B4	Nottingham Way	A4	Station Road		
B3	Greyfriars Way	B4	Orford Close	A3	Steam Mill Lane		
B3	Hall Plain	C4	Oxborough Walk	A3	Stonecutters Way		
B3	Hall Quay	D2	Paget Road	B2	Temple Road		
B1	Hammond Road	B1	Palgrave Road	B3	Theatre Plain		
A3	High Mill Road	A4	Pasteur Road				

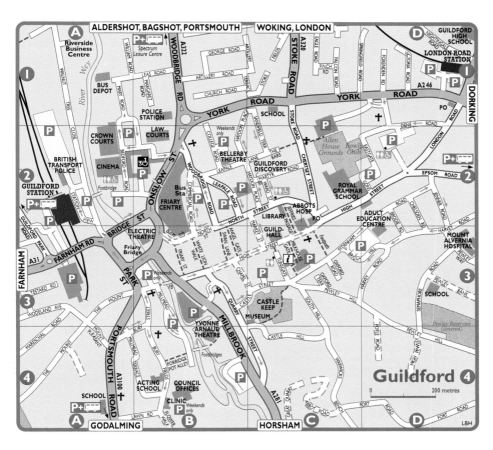

C4	Abbot Road	C4	Great Quarry	C3	Pewley Hill
B3	Angel Gate	A3	Guildford Park Road	D3	Pewley Way
B1	Artillery Road	D3	Harvey Road	B4	Porridge Pot Alley
B1	Artillery Terrace	B2	Haydon Place	A4	Portsmouth Road
A2	Bedford Road	D4	High Pewley	D4	Poyle Road
A3	Bridge Street	B3	High Street	B3	Quarry Street
C3	Bright Hill	C2	Jeffries Passage	C1	Sandfield Terrace
D2	Brodie Road	D2	Jenner Road	D3	Semaphore Road
B4	Bury Fields	B4	Lawn Road	C3	South Hill
B4	Bury Street	B2	Leapale Lane	D1	Springfield Road
C4	Castle Hill	B2	Leapale Road	A2	Station View
C3	Castle Street	B1	Leas Road	C1	Stoke Fields
B3	Chapel Street	D2	London Road	C1	Stoke Road
D2	Chelsden Road	A4	Mareschal Road	B3	Swan Lane
C2	Chertsey Street	B1	Margaret Road	C3	Sydenham Road
B1	Church Road	C2	Market Street	A3	Testard Road
B2	College Road	C2	Martyr Road	C2	The Bars
B2	Commercial Road	A1	Mary Road	A4	The Mount
D1	Dene Road	C3	Milkhouse Gate	C3	Tunsgate
C1	Eagle Road	B4	Millbrook	D1	Victoria Road
D2	Eastgate Gardens	B3	Millmead	A1	Walnut Tree Close
D2	Epsom Road	B4	Millmead Terrace	C2	Ward Street
C1	Falcon Road	A4	Mount Pleasant	C4	Warwicks Bench
A3	Farnham Road	D1	Nightingale Road	B3	White Lion Walk
C1	Finch Road	B3	North Street	A1	William Road
B4	Flower Walk	B2	Onslow Street	A3	Wodeland Avenue
D4	Fort Road	C3	Oxford Road	B1	Woodbridge Road
D1	Foxenden Road	C3	Oxford Terrace	B1	York Road
B3	Friary Street	A3	Park Street		
B1	George Road	D3	Pewley Bank		

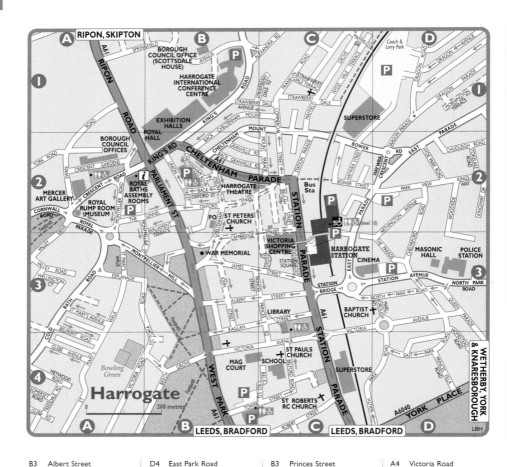

B3	Albert Street	D4	East Park Road	B3	Princes Street	A4	Victoria Road
C1	Alexandra Road	A3	Esplanade	D4	Princes Villa Road	A3	Wellington Court
D2	Arthington Avenue	C1	Franklin Road	D3	Queen Parade	B4	West Park
B1	Back Cheltenham	A4	Glebe Avenue	B3	Raglan Street	D2	Woodside
	Mount	A4	Glebe Road	A1	Ripon Road	D4	York Place
B2	Back Granville Road	B2	Granville Road	C4	Robert Street	A2	York Road
B2	Back Oxford Street	D2	Haywra Crescent	A2	Royal Parade		
B4	Beech Grove	C2	Haywra Street	A3	St Mary's Avenue		
C4	Belford Road	A4	Heywood Road	A4	St Mary's Walk		
C4	Belford Square	D4	Homestead Road	A4	Somerset Road		
A4	Belmont Road	D2	Hyde Park Road	D4	South Park Road		
C2	Beulah Street	B3	James Street	A1	Springfield Avenue		
C2	Bower Road	B3	John Street	D3	Station Avenue		
C2	Bower Street	B2	King's Road	C3	Station Bridge		
B3	Cambridge Street	D2	Kingsway	C2	Station Parade		
D3	Chelmsford Road	D2	Kingsway Drive	C3	Station Square		
B2	Cheltenham Crescent	D3	Marlborough Road	D2	Stokelake Road		
B2	Cheltenham Mount	C1	Mayfield Grove	C1	Strawberry Dale		
B2	Cheltenham Parade	A3	Montpellier Hill	B1	Strawberry Dale Avenue		
B2	Cheltenham Road	A2	Montpellier Road	C1	Strawberry Dale Square		
D2	Chudleigh Road	A2	Montpellier Street	C1	Strawberry Dale Terrace		
A3	Cold Bath Road	D1	Mornington Terrace	A2	Swan Road		
C1	Commercial Street	C2	Mount Parade	A2	The Ginnel		
A2	Cornwall Road	D3	North Park Road	D3	The Parade		
A2	Crescent Gardens	C1	Nydd Vale Terrace	B4	Tower Street		
A2	Crescent Road	B2	Oxford Street	A4	Treesdale Road		
D1	Dragon Avenue	D2	Park View	B2	Union Street		
D2	Dragon Parade	B2	Parliament Street	A3	Valley Drive		
D1	Dragon Road	B2	Parliament Terrace	A3	Valley Road		
C3	East Parade	C3	Princes Square	B4	Victoria Avenue		

Huddersfield

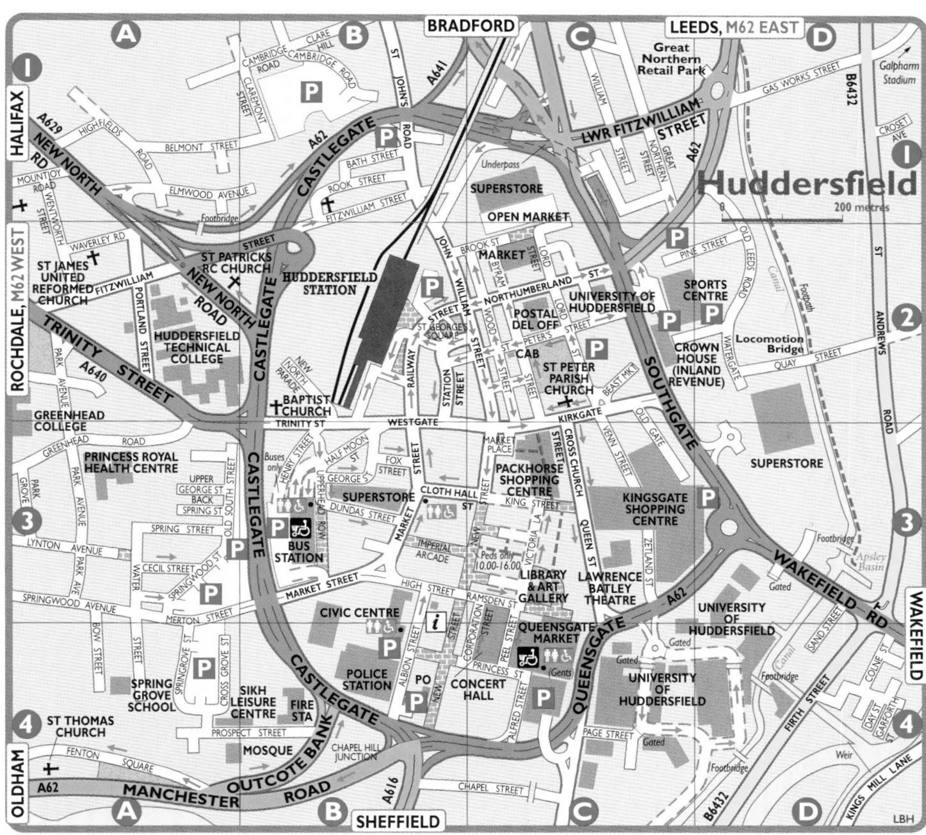

B4	Albion Street	B3	George Street	A3	Park Grove	D2	Watergate
C4	Alfred Street	C1	Great Northern Street	C4	Peel Street	A2	Waverley Road
A3	Back Spring Street	A3	Greenhead Road	C2	Pine Street	A1	Wentworth Street
B1	Bath Street	B3	Half Moon Street	A2	Portland Street	B3	Westgate
C2	Beast Market	B3	Henry Street	C4	Princess Street	C1	William Street
A1	Belmont Street	B3	High Street	A4	Prospect Street	C2	Wood Street
A4	Bow Street	A1	Highfields Road	D2	Quay Street	C3	Zetland Street
C2	Brook Street	B3	Imperial Arcade	C3	Queen Street		
C2	Byram Street	B2	John William Street	C4	Queensgate		
B1	Cambridge Road	C3	King Street	B2	Railway Street		
B1	Castlegate	D4	Kings Mill Lane	C3	Ramsden Street		
A3	Cecil Street	C2	Kirkgate	B1	Rook Street		
C4	Chapel Street	C1	Lower Fitzwilliam Street	D2	St Andrews Road		
B1	Clare Hill	A3	Lynton Avenue	B2	St George's Square		
B1	Claremont Street	A4	Manchester Road	B1	St John's Road		
B3	Cloth Hall Street	C3	Market Place	C2	St Peter's Street		
D4	Colne Street	B3	Market Street	D4	Sand Street		
C4	Corporation Street	A3	Merton Street	C2	Southgate		
D1	Croset Avenue	A1	Mountjoy Road	A4	Springrove Street		
C3	Cross Church Street	B2	New North Parade	A3	Spring Street		
A4	Cross Grove Street	A2	New North Road	A3	Springwood Avenue		
D4	Day Street	B4	New Street	A3	Springwood Street		
B3	Dundas Street	C2	Northumberland Street	B2	Station Street		
A1	Elmwood Avenue	D2	Old Leeds Road	A2	Trinity Street		
A4	Fenton Square	C3	Old Gate	A3	Upper George Street		
D4	Firth Street	A3	Old South Street	B3	Upperhead Row		
A2	Fitzwilliam Street	B4	Outcote Bank	C3	Venn Street		
B3	Fox Street	C4	Page Street	C3	Victoria Lane		
D4	Garforth Street	A2	Park Avenue	D3	Wakefield Road		
D1	Gas Works Street			A3	Water Street		

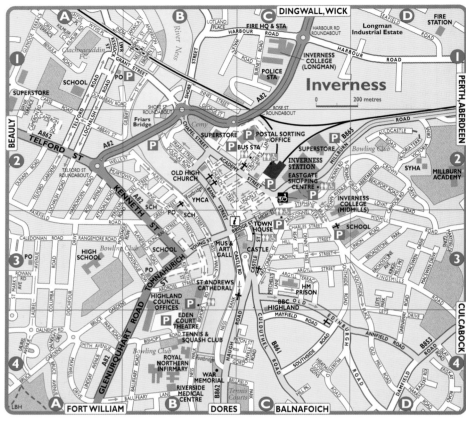

A2	Abban Street	A1	Carse Road	A1	Glendoe Terrace	D2	Lovat Road	D1	Seafield Road
D2	Abertarff Road	C3	Castle Road	A4	Glenurquhart Road	A1	Lower Kessock	B1	Shore Street
B2	Academy Street	C3	Castle Street	C4	Gordonville Road		Street	A4	Smith Avenue
B1	Anderson Street	D2	Cawdor Road	B1	Grant Street	D3	Macewen Drive	D3	Southside Place
D4	Annfield Road	B2	Celt Street	B3	Greig Street	B1	Madras Street	C4	Southside Road
C3	Ardconnel Street	B2	Chapel Street	C1	Harbour Road	D3	Maryfield Gardens	C2	Stephens Brae
C3	Ardconnel Terrace	C3	Charles Street	D4	Harris Road	A4	Maxwell Drive	C2	Strother's Lane
B3	Ardross Street	B2	Church Street	A2	Harrowden Road	C4	Mayfield Road	A2	Telford Gardens
C3	Argyll Street	A3	Columba Road	B4	Haugh Road	D3	Midmills Road	A2	Telford Road
C3	Argyll Terrace	C2	Crown Avenue	C4	Heathcote Gardens	C2	Millburn Road	A2	Telford Street
A2	Attadale Road	C2	Crown Circus	C3	High Street	C3	Mitchell's Lane	B3	Tomnahurich Street
D2	Auldcastle Road	D2	Crown Drive	C4	Hill Park	B3	Montague Row	D3	Union Road
B4	Ballifeary Lane	C2	Crown Road	C3	Hill Street	C4	Muirfield Road	C2	Union Street
B4	Ballifeary Road	C3	Crown Street	B2	Huntley Street	A2	Muirtown Street	D2	Victoria Drive
B2	Bank Street	C4	Culduthel Road	A1	India Street	B1	Nelson Street	D2	Victoria Terrace
D2	Beaufort Road	A4	Dalneigh Crescent	B1	Innes Street	B4	Ness Bank	B1	Walker Road
B4	Bellfield Park	A4	Dalneigh Road	D4	Islay Road	B4	Ness Walk	A2	Wells Street
A1	Benula Road	D4	Damfield Road	B1	Jamaica Street	C3	Old Edinburgh Road	A1	Wyvis Place
A1	Birnie Terrace	D4	Darnaway Road	A2	Kenneth Street	D4	Old Mill Road	B3	Young Street
B4	Bishop's Road	C3	Denny Street	A1	Kilmuir Court	A1	Ord Terrace		
C3	Bridge Street	A3	Dochfour Drive	A1	Kilmuir Road	A4	Park Road		
D3	Broadstone Avenue	B2	Douglas Row	B2	King Street	C4	Paton Street		
D3	Broadstone Park	A1	Dunabban Road	D3	Kingsmills Park	A3	Perceval Road		
B1	Brown Street	A2	Dunain Road	D3	Kingsmills Road	B3	Planefield Road		
A4	Bruce Avenue	B3	Duncraig Street	A3	Laurel Avenue	D4	Raasay Road		
A4	Bruce Gardens	D4	Eriskay Road	D4	Leys Drive	A3	Rangemore Road		
C1	Burnett Road	A3	Fairfield Road	D3	Leys Park	C3	Reay Street		
A3	Caledonian Road	B2	Friars Street	A4	Lindsay Avenue	A2	Ross Avenue		
A2	Cameron Road	B1	George Street	A2	Lochalsh Road	A3	Rowan Road		
A2	Cameron Square	B2	Gilbert Street	B1	Lotland Place	A3	St Mark's Avenue		

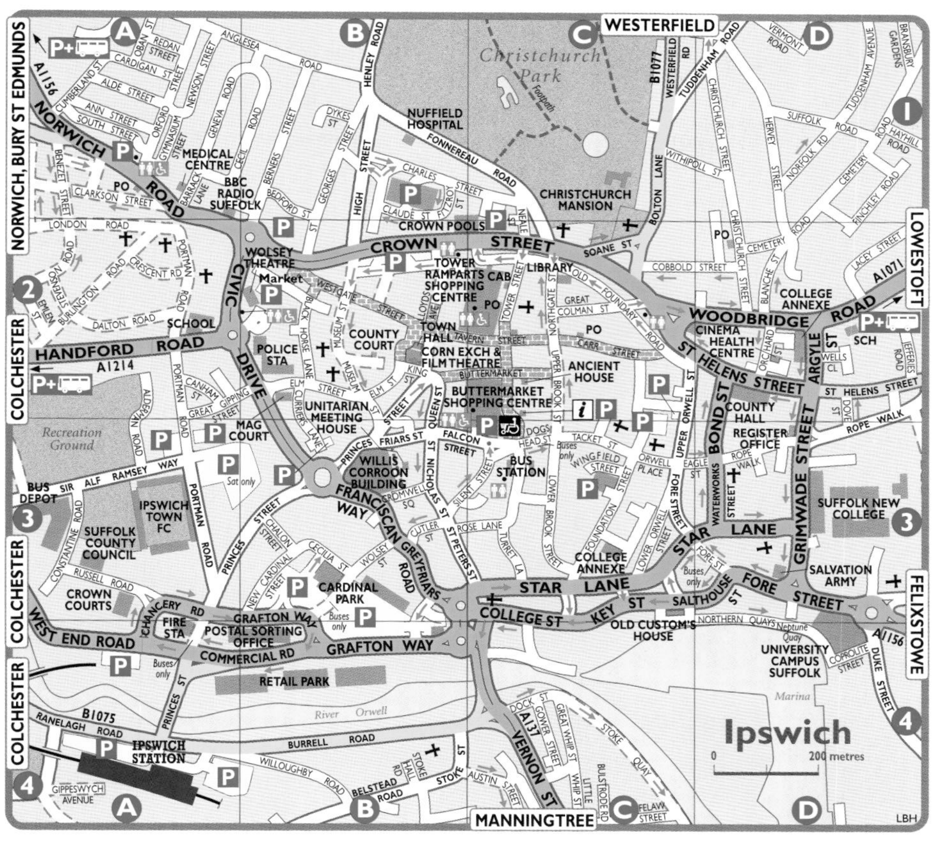

Ipswich

0   200 metres

A2	Alderman Road	A4	Commercial Road	A1	Gymnasium Street	B1	St Georges Street
A1	Anglesea Road	A3	Constantine Road	A2	Handford Road	D2	St Helens Street
A1	Ann Street	A2	Crescent Road	B1	Henley Road	B3	St Nicholas Street
D2	Argyle Street	B3	Cromwell Square	D1	Hervey Street	B3	St Peters Street
A1	Barrack Lane	B2	Crown Street	B1	High Street	C3	Salthouse Street
B1	Bedford Street	A1	Cumberland Street	C3	Key Street	B3	Silent Street
B4	Belstead Road	B2	Curriers Lane	B2	King Street	A3	Sir Alf Ramsey Way
B1	Berners Street	B3	Cutler Street	D2	Lacey Street	C2	Soane Street
B2	Black Horse Lane	A2	Dalton Road	B2	Lloyds Avenue	A1	South Street
D2	Blanche Street	C4	Dock Street	A2	London Road	C3	Star Lane
C1	Bolton Lane	C3	Dogs Head Street	C3	Lower Brook Street	A2	Stevenson Road
D3	Bond Street	D2	Dove Street	C3	Lower Orwell Street	C4	Stoke Quay
A2	Burlington Road	D4	Duke Street	B2	Museum Street	B4	Stoke Street
B4	Burrell Road	C3	Eagle Street	C1	Neale Street	D1	Suffolk Road
C2	Buttermarket	B2	Elm Street	B3	New Cardinal Street	C3	Tacket Street
A2	Canham Street	B3	Falcon Street	A1	Newson Street	C2	Tavern Street
A1	Cardigan Street	B1	Fitzroy Street	D3	Northern Quays	C2	Tower Street
C2	Carr Street	B1	Fonnereau Road	C2	Northgate Street	C1	Tuddenham Road
B1	Cecil Road	C3	Fore Street	A1	Norwich Road	C3	Turret Lane
B3	Cecilia Street	C3	Foundation Street	C2	Old Foundary Road	C2	Upper Brook Street
D2	Cemetery Road	B3	Franciscan Way	D2	Orchard Street	C3	Upper Orwell Street
B3	Chalon Street	B3	Friars Street	A1	Orford Street	C4	Vernon Street
A3	Chancery Road	A1	Geneva Road	C3	Orwell Place	D3	Waterworks Street
B1	Charles Street	C4	Gower Street	A2	Portman Road	A4	West End Road
D1	Christchurch Street	B3	Grafton Way	A4	Princes Street	C1	Westerfield Road
A2	Civic Drive	C2	Great Colman Street	B2	Queen Street	B2	Westgate Street
A1	Clarkson Street	A2	Great Gipping Street	A4	Ranelagh Road	B4	Willoughby Road
B1	Claude Street	C4	Great Whip Street	D3	Rope Walk	C1	Withipoll Street
C2	Cobbold Street	B3	Greyfriars Road	C3	Rose Lane	B3	Wolsey Street
C3	College Street	D3	Grimwade Street	A3	Russell Road	D2	Woodbridge Road

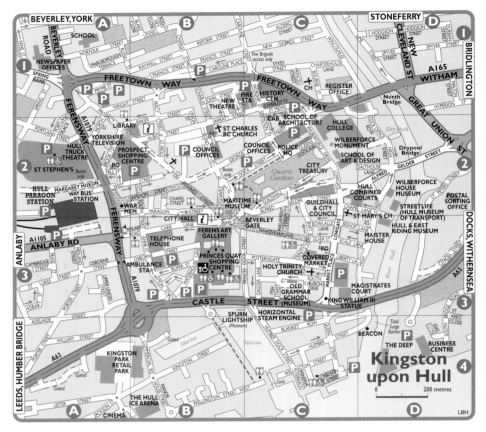

A4	Adelaide Street	D1	Durban Street	C3	Market Place
B2	Albion Street	A1	Ferensway	A1	Marlborough Terrace
C1	Aldbro Street	C3	Fish Street	A3	Midland Street
C2	Alfred Gelder Street	B1	Francis Street	A2	Mill Street
A3	Anlaby Road	A1	Freetown Way	C4	Minerva Terrace
B3	Anne Street	B2	George Street	B3	Myton Street
B2	Baker Street	D2	Great Union Street	C4	Nelson Street
A1	Beverley Road	C2	Grimston Street	D1	New Cleveland Street
C3	Bishop Lane	C2	Guildhall Road	C1	New George Street
B1	Blake Close	D2	High Street	A1	Norfolk Street
C4	Blanket Row	A3	Hobart Street	A2	North Street
B2	Bond Street	D1	Hodgson Street	A3	Osborne Street
C1	Bourne Street	C4	Humber Dock Street	B2	Paragon Street
C3	Bowlalley Lane	C4	Humber Street	C3	Parliament Street
A2	Brook Street	D1	Hyperion Street	A3	Pease Street
A3	Cambridge Street	D4	Idas Close	B1	Percy Street
B1	Caroline Place	A4	Jackson Street	A4	Porter Street
B1	Caroline Street	B2	Jameson Street	A2	Portland Place
B3	Carr Lane	B2	Jarratt Street	A2	Portland Street
B3	Castle Street	B1	John Street	C3	Posterngate
C2	Chapel Lane	B2	King Edward Street	C3	Princes Dock Street
B1	Charles Street	B4	Kingston Street	A1	Prospect Street
C1	Charlotte Street Mews	C3	Liberty Lane	A1	Pryme Street
C1	Charterhouse Lane	B1	Liddell Street	C4	Queen Street
D3	Citadel Street	D1	Lime Street	C2	Queens Dock Avenue
A2	Collier Street	A4	Lister Street	B1	Raywell Street
B4	Commercial Road	C3	Lowgate	B1	Reform Street
C3	Dagger Lane	D1	Malton Street	B1	Rodney Close
D2	Dock Office Row	B4	Manor House Street	B3	Roper Street
C2	Dock Street	A2	Margaret Moxon Way	A1	Russell Street
				D4	St Abbs Close
				A3	St Lukes Street
				D2	St Peters Street
				D2	Salthouse Lane
				B2	Savile Street
				C3	Scale Lane
				C3	Silver Street
				D4	South Bridge Road
				C3	South Churchside
				B2	South Street
				A1	Spring Bank
				A1	Spring Street
				D1	Spyvee Street
				B2	Story Street
				C1	Sykes Street
				C3	Trinity House Lane
				B1	Union Street
				A3	Upper Union Street
				A1	Vane Street
				B3	Waterhouse Lane
				C4	Wellington Street
				B4	Wellington Street West
				A2	West Street
				C3	Whitefriargate
				C2	Wilberforce Drive
				A4	William Street
				C1	Wincolmlee
				D1	Witham
				C1	Worship Street
				A1	Wright Street

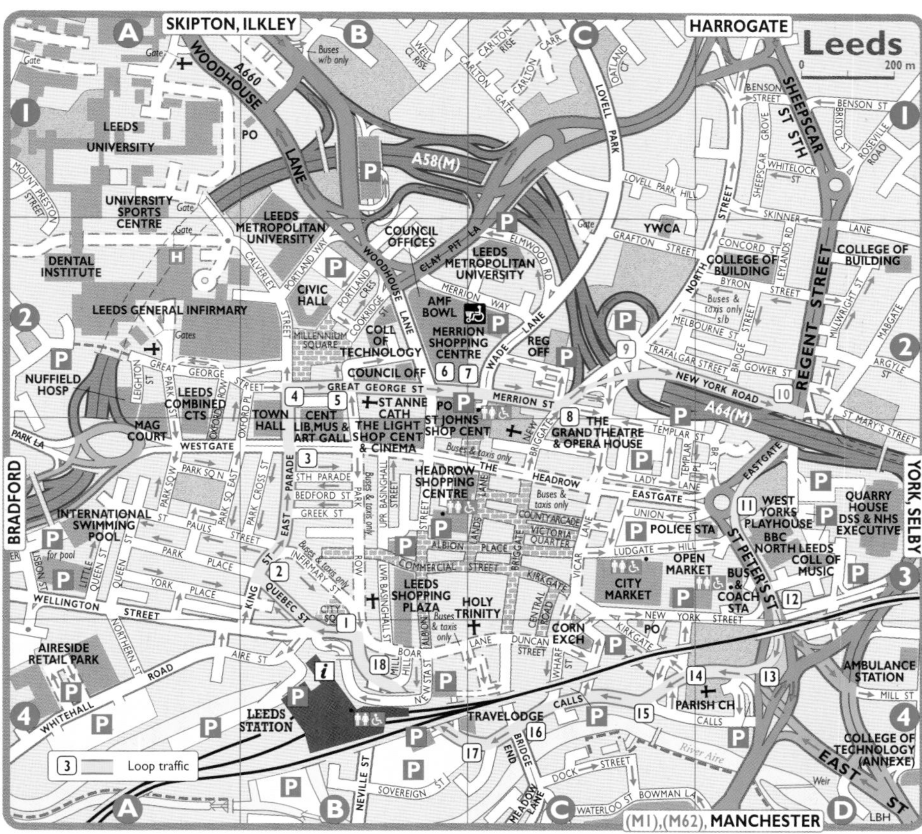

B4	Aire Street	C2	Elmwood Road	B4	New Station Street	C3	Templar Place
B3	Albion Place	D2	Gower Street	D2	New York Road	C3	Templar Street
B4	Albion Street	C2	Grafton Street	C3	New York Street	B3	The Headrow
D2	Argyle Street	B2	Great George Street	D2	North Street	C2	Trafalgar Street
B3	Bedford Street	B3	Greek Street	A4	Northern Street	C3	Union Street
D1	Benson Street	B3	Infirmary Street	C1	Oatland Court	B3	Upper Basinghall Street
B4	Boar Lane	B3	King Street	B3	Oxford Place	C3	Vicar Lane
C4	Bowman Lane	C3	Kirkgate	A3	Oxford Row	C3	Victoria Quarter
C4	Bridge End	C3	Lady Lane	B3	Park Cross Street	C2	Wade Lane
D2	Bridge Street	C3	Lands Lane	A3	Park Lane	C4	Waterloo Street
C3	Briggate	A2	Leighton Street	A3	Park Place	B1	Well Close Rise
D1	Bristol Street	D2	Leylands Road	B3	Park Row	A3	Wellington Street
D2	Byron Street	A3	Lisbon Street	A3	Park Square East	A3	Westgate
C4	Calls	A3	Little Queen Street	A3	Park Square North	C4	Wharf Street
B2	Calverley Street	C1	Lovell Park	A3	Park Square West	A4	Whitehall Road
C1	Carlton Carr	C1	Lovell Park Hill	A2	Park Street	D1	Whitelock Street
C1	Carlton Gate	B3	Lower Basinghall Street	B2	Portland Crescent	B1	Woodhouse Lane
C1	Carlton Rise	C3	Ludgate Hill	B2	Portland Way	A3	York Place
C3	Central Road	D2	Mabgate	B3	Quebec Street		
B3	City Square	C4	Meadows Lane	A3	Queen Street		
B2	Clay Pit Lane	C2	Melbourne Street	D2	Regent Street		
B3	Commercial Street	C2	Merrion Street	D1	Roseville Road		
D2	Concord Street	B2	Merrion Way	A3	St Pauls Street		
B2	Cookridge Street	B4	Mill Hill	D3	St Peter's Street		
C3	County Arcade	D4	Mill Street	D3	St Mary's Street		
C4	Dock Street	B2	Millennium Square	D1	Sheepscar Grove		
C4	Duncan Street	D2	Millwright Street	D1	Sheepscar Street South		
B3	East Parade	A1	Mount Preston Street	D1	Skinner Lane		
D4	East Street	B4	Neville Street	B3	South Parade		
C3	Eastgate	C3	New Briggate	B4	Sovereign Street		

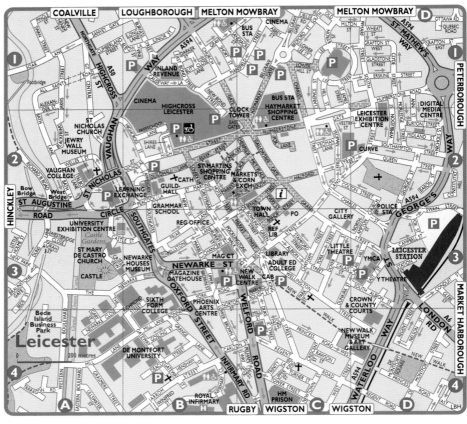

C1	Abbey Street	C2	Colton Street	B2	Guildhall Lane	A3	New Park Street	A1	Sanvey Gate
C3	Albion Street	D3	Conduit Street	C2	Halford Street	B2	New Street	B2	Shires Lane
A1	Alexander Street	D2	Constitution Hill	C1	Haymarket	C3	New Walk	B1	Short Street
A1	All Saints Road	C4	Crescent Street	B2	High Street	A4	Newarke Close	B2	Silver Street
D1	Ann Street	A1	Cumberland Street	A1	Highcross Street	B3	Newarke Street	A1	Soar Lane
B2	Applegate	B1	Darker Street	C1	Hill Street	C4	Newtown Street	D3	South Albion Street
A2	Bath Lane	D4	De Montfort Street	C2	Horsefair Street	D2	Nichols Street	D2	Southampton Street
A3	Bede Street	B4	Deacon Street	B2	Hotel Street	D3	Northampton Street	B3	Southgates
C1	Bedford Street South	C3	Dover Street	C2	Humberstone Gate	A1	Northgate	C3	Stamford Street
C1	Belgrave Gate	C4	Duke Street	D1	Humberstone Road	B3	Norton Street	D2	Swain Street
C3	Belvoir Street	C3	Dunkirk Street	B4	Infirmary Close	C1	Old Milton Street	A1	Swan Street
C3	Bishop Street	A3	Duns Lane	B4	Infirmary Road	D1	Ottawa Road	A2	Talbot Lane
A2	Blackfriars Street	D3	East Bond Street	B4	Jarrom Street	B3	Oxford Street	A4	Tarragon Road
B4	Bonners Road	B1	East Street	A1	Jarvis Street	C3	Park Street	B4	The Gateway
C3	Bowling Green Street	A4	Eastern Boulevard	C1	Jubilee Road	B2	Peacock Lane	A3	The Newarke
A3	Braunstone Gate	B1	Elbow Lane	B1	Junior Street	C4	Pelham Street	C4	Tower Street
B1	Burgess Street	D1	Erskine Street	C3	King Street	A1	Pingle Street	C4	Trinity Lane
D2	Burton Street	C2	Every Street	C1	Lee Street	B3	Pocklingtons Walk	C4	Turner Street
B1	Butt Close Lane	C2	Fox Lane	A3	Little Holme Street	D4	Princess Road East	A4	Ullswater Street
C1	Byron Street	D3	Fox Street	D4	London Road	C4	Princess Road West	B3	Upper Brown Street
D3	Calais Hill	B2	Freeschool Lane	B1	Long Lane	D1	Quebec Road	C4	Upper King Street
D3	Calais Street	B3	Friar Lane	B2	Loseby Lane	D2	Queen Street	A2	Vaughan Way
D3	Campbell Street	C2	Gallowtree Gate	B4	Lower Brown Street	C4	Rawson Street	B1	Vine Street
B2	Cank Street	A4	Gary Street	C1	Lower Hill Street	C4	Regent Road	D4	Waterloo Way
B4	Carlton Street	B4	Gateway Street	C1	Mansfield Street	D4	Regent Street	C3	Welford Road
A3	Castle Street	D1	Gladstone Street	B3	Marble Street	A2	Richard III Road	A2	Welles Street
A3	Castle View	D3	Glebe Street	B2	Market Place	C2	Rutland Street	C3	Wellington Street
B1	Causeway Lane	B4	Gosling Street	C2	Market Place South	A2	St Augustine Road	C4	West Street
B3	Chancery Street	D1	Grafton Street East	C3	Market Street	D2	St George's Road	A4	Western Boulevard
C1	Charles Street	D1	Grafton Street West	C3	Marlborough Street	D3	St George's Way	D1	Wharf Street South
C3	Chatham Street	C2	Granby Street	D2	Midland Street	C1	St James Street	D1	Wheat Street
C2	Cheapside	B4	Grange Lane	A4	Mill Lane	B2	St Martins	D2	Wimbledon Street
B1	Church Gate	A4	Grasmere Street	C4	Mill Street	D1	St Mathew's Way	C2	Yeoman Lane
D2	Church Street	B1	Gravel Street	B3	Millstone Lane	A2	St Nicholas Circle	C2	Yeoman Street
C1	Clarence Street	A1	Great Central Street	D1	Morledge Street	B2	St Nicholas Place	B3	York Road
D1	Clyde Street	B2	Greyfriars	D4	Nelson Street	C1	Sandiacre Street	C3	York Street

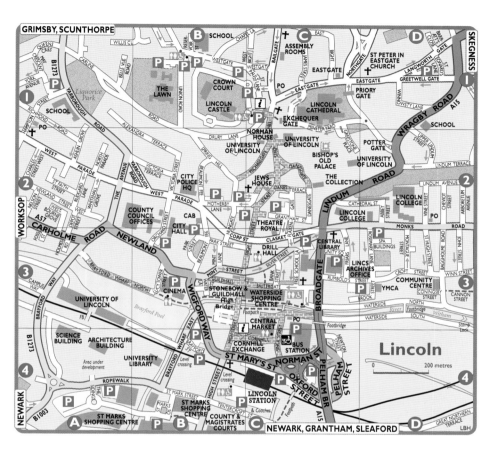

D2	Abbey Street	C2	Danesgate	D2	Monks Road	C3	Silver Street
B2	Alexandra Terrace	A2	Depot Street	D3	Montague Street	C4	Sincil Street
D2	Arboretum Avenue	B2	Drury Lane	B2	Motherby Lane	D3	Spa Buildings
A2	Ashlin Grove	C1	East Bight	A2	Nelson Street	B2	Spring Hill
D3	Baggholme Road	C1	Eastgate	A3	Newland	C2	Steep Hill
C1	Bailgate	C2	Flaxengate	A2	Newland Street West	C2	Strait
C3	Bank Street	A3	Foss Street	C4	Newton Street	B4	Tentercroft Street
D1	Barratt's Close	C3	Free School Lane	C4	Norman Street	A2	The Avenue
B2	Beaumont Fee	C3	Friars Lane	A2	North Parade	A4	The Sidings
A1	Belle Vue Road	C2	Grantham Street	C1	Northgate	B1	Union Road
B4	Brayford Street	D4	Great Northern Terrace	B3	Orchard Street	C3	Unity Square
A3	Brayford Way	C2	Greestone Place	C4	Oxford Street	D2	Upper Lindum Street
B4	Brayford Wharf East	D1	Greetwell Gate	B3	Park Street	B2	Victoria Street
A3	Brayford Wharf North	B3	Guildhall Street	C4	Pelham Bridge	B2	Victoria Terrace
C3	Broadgate	A1	Hampton Street	C4	Pelham Street	D2	Vine Street
D3	Brook Street	B4	High Street	A1	Queens Crescent	B3	Water Lane
A3	Campus Way	A3	Holmes Road	B1	Reservoir Street	D3	Waterside North
D3	Cannon Street	B2	Hungate	A1	Richmond Road	D3	Waterside South
A3	Carholme Road	C1	James Street	A4	Ropewalk	C1	West Bight
A1	Carline Road	D3	John Street	D3	Rosemary Lane	A2	West Parade
D2	Cathedral Street	D1	Langworth Gate	A2	Rudgard Lane	A2	Westbourne Grove
B1	Chapel Lane	D2	Lindum Avenue	C3	Rumbold's Street	B1	Westgate
A2	Charles Street West	C2	Lindum Road	A2	St Faith Street	A2	Whitehall Grove
D2	Cheviot Street	D2	Lindum Terrace	D3	St Hugh Street	B3	Wigford Way
C3	Clasket Gate	B3	Lucy Tower Street	D1	St Leonard's Lane	B1	Willis Close
D3	Coningsby Street	A1	May Crescent	B4	St Mark Street	D3	Winn Street
C4	Cornhill	C2	Michaelgate	B4	St Marks Square	D1	Winnowsty Lane
B3	Corporation Street	C1	Minster Yard	B4	St Mary's Street	D1	Wragby Road
D3	Croft Street	B3	Mint Lane	C1	St Paul's Lane	A1	Yarborough Road
C2	Danes Terrace	B3	Mint Street	C3	Saltergate	A1	York Avenue

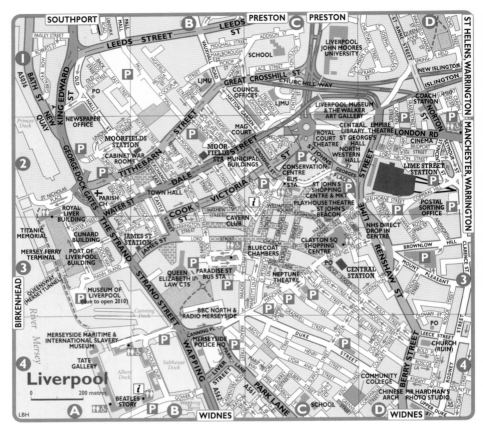

C1	Addison Street	B2	Cunliffe Street	C4	Kent Street	A1	Pall Mall	B2	Stanley Street
D3	Ainsworth Street	B2	Dale Street	A1	King Edward Street	B4	Paradise Street	B3	Strand Street
C4	Argyle Street	A2	Drury Lane	D4	Knight Street	B4	Park Lane	C4	Suffolk Street
D4	Back Colquitt Street	C4	Duke Street	C1	Lace Street	C3	Parker Street	C4	Surrey Street
A1	Back Leeds Street	A1	East Street	D1	Lambert Way	C3	Peters Lane	C4	Tabley Street
C3	Basnett Street	B2	Eberle Street	A1	Lanyork Road	B1	Pickop Street	C3	Tarleton Street
A1	Bath Street	A2	Edmund Street	D4	Leece Street	D4	Pilgrim Street	B2	Tempest Hey
D3	Benson Street	C2	Elliot Street	A1	Leeds Street	C2	Preston Street	B2	Temple Court
D4	Berry Street	B2	Exchange Street East	D2	Lime Street	B1	Prussia Street	B2	Temple Street
B2	Bixteth Street	B2	Fenwick Street	B4	Liver Street	D2	Pudsey Street	A3	The Strand
D4	Bold Place	C3	Fleet Street	D2	London Road	D1	Queen Anne Street	A2	Tithebarn Street
C3	Bold Street	C1	Fontenoy Street	D2	Lord Nelson Street	C3	Raneleigh Street	C1	Tom Mann Close
D2	Bolton Street	D1	Fraser Street	B3	Lord Street	D3	Renshaw Street	C1	Trueman Street
D2	Bridport Street	A2	George Dock Gates	C4	Lydia Ann Street	C2	Richmond Street	A2	Union Street
D3	Brownlow Hill	A3	George Dock Way	C2	Manchester Street	A1	Roberts Street	D4	Upper Duke Street
A3	Brunswick Street	D1	Gerard Street	C3	Manesty's Lane	D4	Rodney Street	C4	Upper Frederick Street
D1	Camden Street	A4	Gibraltar Row	A3	Mann Island	D4	Roscoe Lane	B1	Vauxhall Road
C3	Campbell Street	C4	Gilbert Street	C4	Maritime Way	D4	Roscoe Street	B2	Vernon Street
B4	Canning Place	B4	Gower Street	B1	Marlborough Street	D3	Royal Mail Street	B2	Victoria Street
B4	Carpenters Row	C3	Gradwell Street	B1	Marybone	A2	Rumford Street	C4	Vincent Court
B2	Castle Street	B4	Grayson Street	B2	Mathew Street			D1	Wakefield Street
B2	Cheapside	C3	Great Charlotte Street	B1	Midghall Street	D1	St Anne Street	B4	Wapping
D1	Christian Street	B1	Great Crosshill Street	B2	Moorfields	C2	St Georges Place	A2	Water Street
C3	Church Alley	C4	Grenville Street	D3	Mount Pleasant	C2	St Johns Lane	C2	Whitechapel
C3	Church Street	B2	Hackins Hey	D4	Mount Street	D1	St Josephs Crescent	C3	Williamson Street
C1	Churchill Way	C3	Hanover Street	D4	Nelson Street	D2	St Vincent Street	C3	Wood Street
D3	Clarence Street	D1	Harker Street	D1	New Islington	B4	Salthouse Quay	C4	York Street
B1	Cockspur Street	B3	Harrington Street	D3	Newington	C3	School Lane		
C3	College Lane	B1	Hatton Garden	A1	New Quay	D2	Seel Street		
D4	Colquitt Street	D2	Hawke Street	B2	North John Street	D2	Seymour Street		
B2	Cook Street	C4	Henry Street	C1	North Street	C2	Sir Thomas Street		
C4	Cornhill	B1	Highfield Street	D1	Norton Street	D2	Skelhorne Street		
D4	Cornwallis Street	D2	Hotham Street	D4	Old Hall Street	C4	Slater Street		
A2	Covent Garden	D1	Islington	A1	Old Leeds Street	B1	Smithfield Street		
D1	Craven Street	B3	James Street	D3	Oldham Street	D1	Soho Street		
C2	Crosshill Street	C1	Johnson Street	A1	Paisley Street	B3	South John Street		
								D1	Springfield

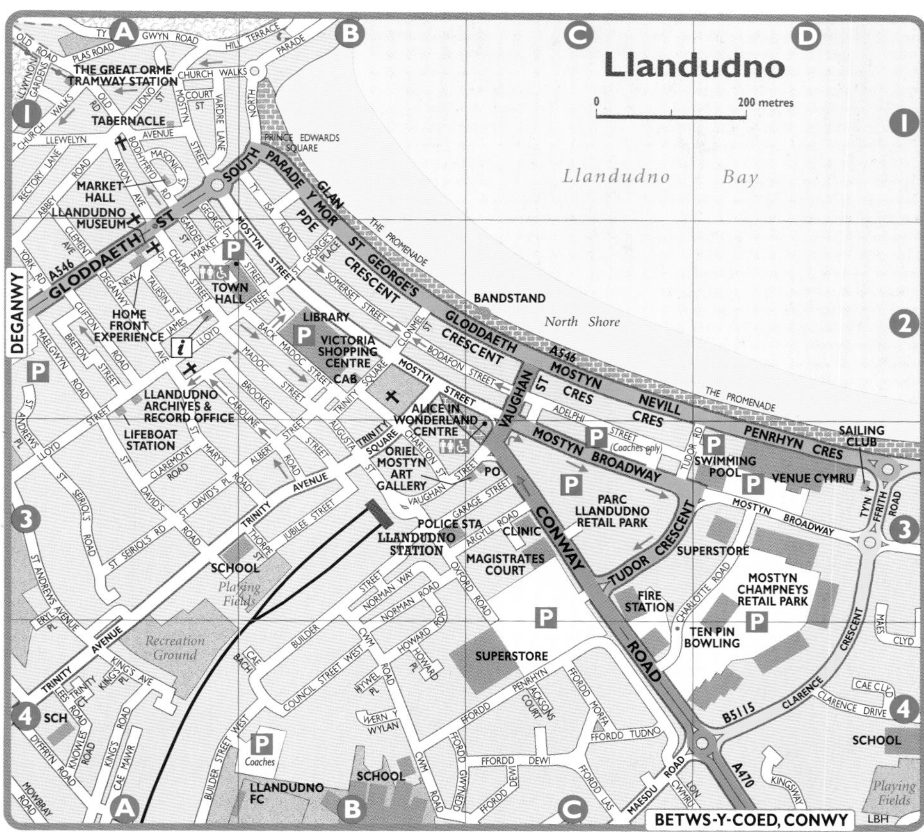

A1	Abbey Road	A2	Deganwy Avenue	B2	Madoc Street
C2	Adelphi Street	A4	Dyffryn Road	A2	Maelgwyn Road
B3	Albert Street	A3	Eryl Place	D4	Maes Clyd
C3	Argyll Road	C4	Ffordd Dewi	C4	Maesdu Road
A1	Arvon Avenue	B4	Ffordd Gwynedd	A2	Market Street
B3	Augusta Street	C4	Ffordd Las	A1	Masonic Street
B2	Back Madoc Street	C4	Ffordd Morfa	C3	Mostyn Broadway
B2	Bodafon Street	C4	Ffordd Penrhyn	C2	Mostyn Crescent
A1	Bodhyfryd Road	C4	Ffordd Tudno	A1	Mostyn Street
B2	Brookes Street	B3	Garage Street	A4	Mowbray Road
B4	Builder Street	A2	Garden Street	C2	Nevill Crescent
A4	Builder Street West	A2	George Street	A2	New Street
B4	Cae Bach	B1	Glan Y Mor Parade	B3	Norman Road
D4	Cae Clyd	B2	Gloddaeth Crescent	B1	North Parade
A4	Cae Mawr	A2	Gloddaeth Street	A1	Old Road
A2	Caroline Road	A1	Hill Terrace	B3	Oxford Road
A2	Chapel Street	B4	Howard Place	D3	Penrhyn Crescent
C3	Charlotte Road	B4	Howard Road	A1	Plas Road
B3	Charlton Street	B4	Hywel Place	B1	Prince Edwards Square
A1	Church Walks	C4	Jacksons Court	A1	Rectory Lane
A3	Claremont Road	A2	James Street	A3	St Andrews Avenue
D4	Clarence Crescent	B3	Jubilee Street	A2	St Andrews Place
D4	Clarence Drive	A4	King's Avenue	A3	St David's Place
A2	Clement Avenue	A4	King's Place	A3	St David's Road
A2	Clifton Road	A4	King's Road	B2	St George's Crescent
B2	Clonmell Street	D4	Kingsway	B2	St George's Place
C3	Conway Road	A1	Llewelyn Avenue	A2	St Mary's Road
B4	Council Street West	A3	Lloyd Street	A3	St Seiriol's Road
A1	Court Street	A1	Llwynon Gardens	B2	Somerset Street
B4	Cwm Road	C4	Lon Cwmru	B1	South Parade
				A2	Taliesin Street
				B3	Thorpe Street
				A4	Trinity Avenue
				B3	Trinity Square
				A1	Tudno Street
				C3	Tudor Crescent
				C3	Tudor Road
				A1	Ty Gwyn Road
				B1	Ty Isa Road
				D3	Ty'n Y Ffrith Road
				A1	Vardre Lane
				C2	Vaughan Street
				B4	Wern Y Wylan
				A2	York Road

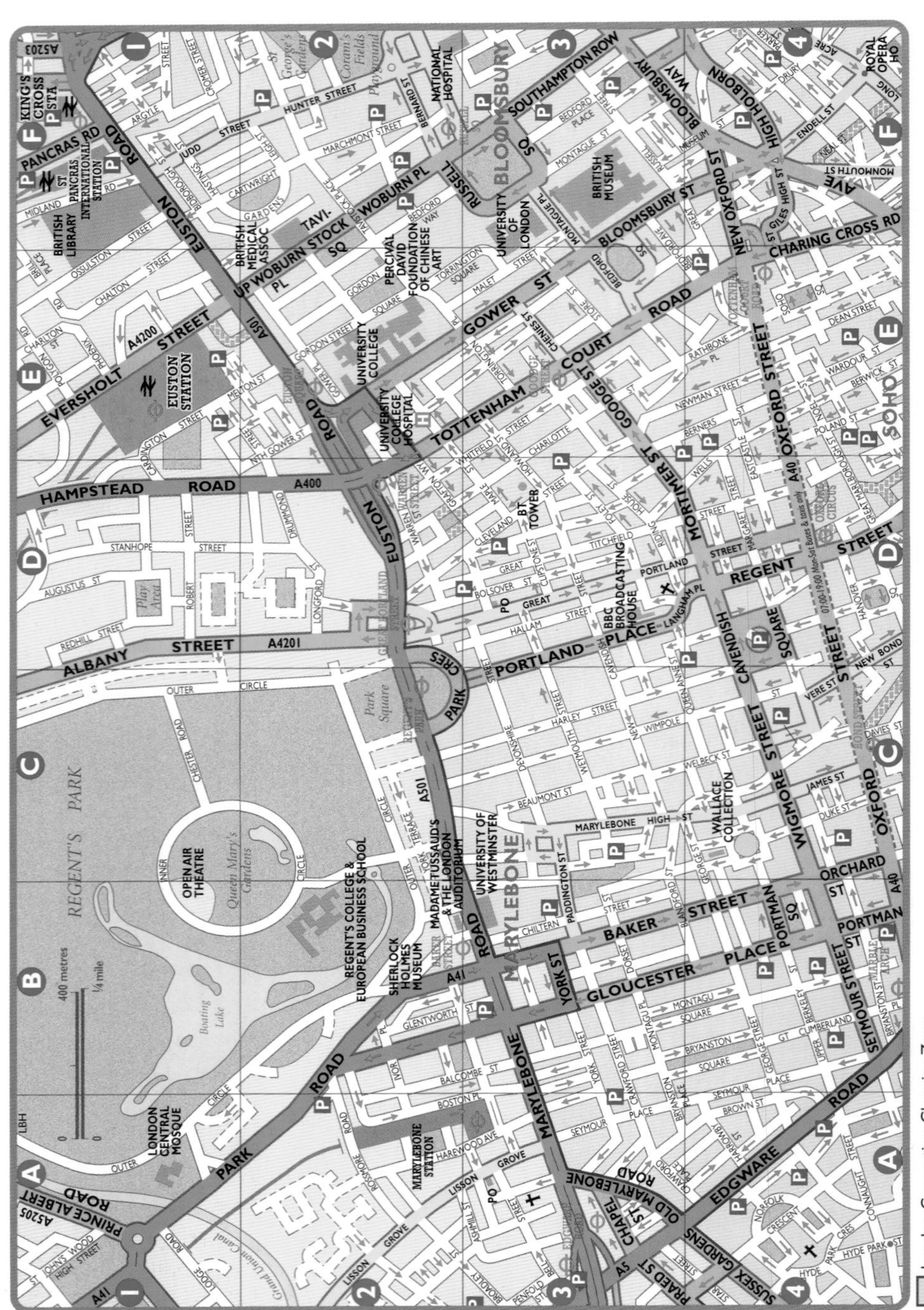

REGENT'S PARK
OPEN AIR THEATRE
Queen Mary's Gardens
Boating Lake
LONDON CENTRAL MOSQUE
REGENT'S COLLEGE & EUROPEAN BUSINESS SCHOOL
SHERLOCK HOLMES MUSEUM
MADAME TUSSAUD'S & THE LONDON AUDITORIUM
UNIVERSITY OF WESTMINSTER
MARYLEBONE STATION
MARYLEBONE
WALLACE COLLECTION
BBC BROADCASTING HOUSE
BT TOWER
UNIVERSITY COLLEGE HOSPITAL
UNIVERSITY COLLEGE
EUSTON STATION
BRITISH LIBRARY
ST PANCRAS INTERNATIONAL STATION
KING'S CROSS STA
BRITISH MEDICAL ASSOC
PERCIVAL DAVID FOUNDATION OF CHINESE ART
UNIVERSITY OF LONDON
BRITISH MUSEUM
BLOOMSBURY
NATIONAL HOSPITAL
SOHO
ROYAL OPERA HO
EUSTON ROAD
HAMPSTEAD ROAD
ALBANY STREET
EVERSHOLT STREET
TOTTENHAM COURT ROAD
GOWER ST
OXFORD STREET
REGENT STREET
PORTLAND PLACE
BAKER STREET
MARYLEBONE ROAD
EDGWARE ROAD
PARK ROAD
PRINCE ALBERT ROAD
GLOUCESTER PLACE
WIGMORE STREET
NEW OXFORD ST
CHARING CROSS RD
HIGH HOLBORN
SOUTHAMPTON ROW
400 metres
¼ mile
London Congestion Charging Zone

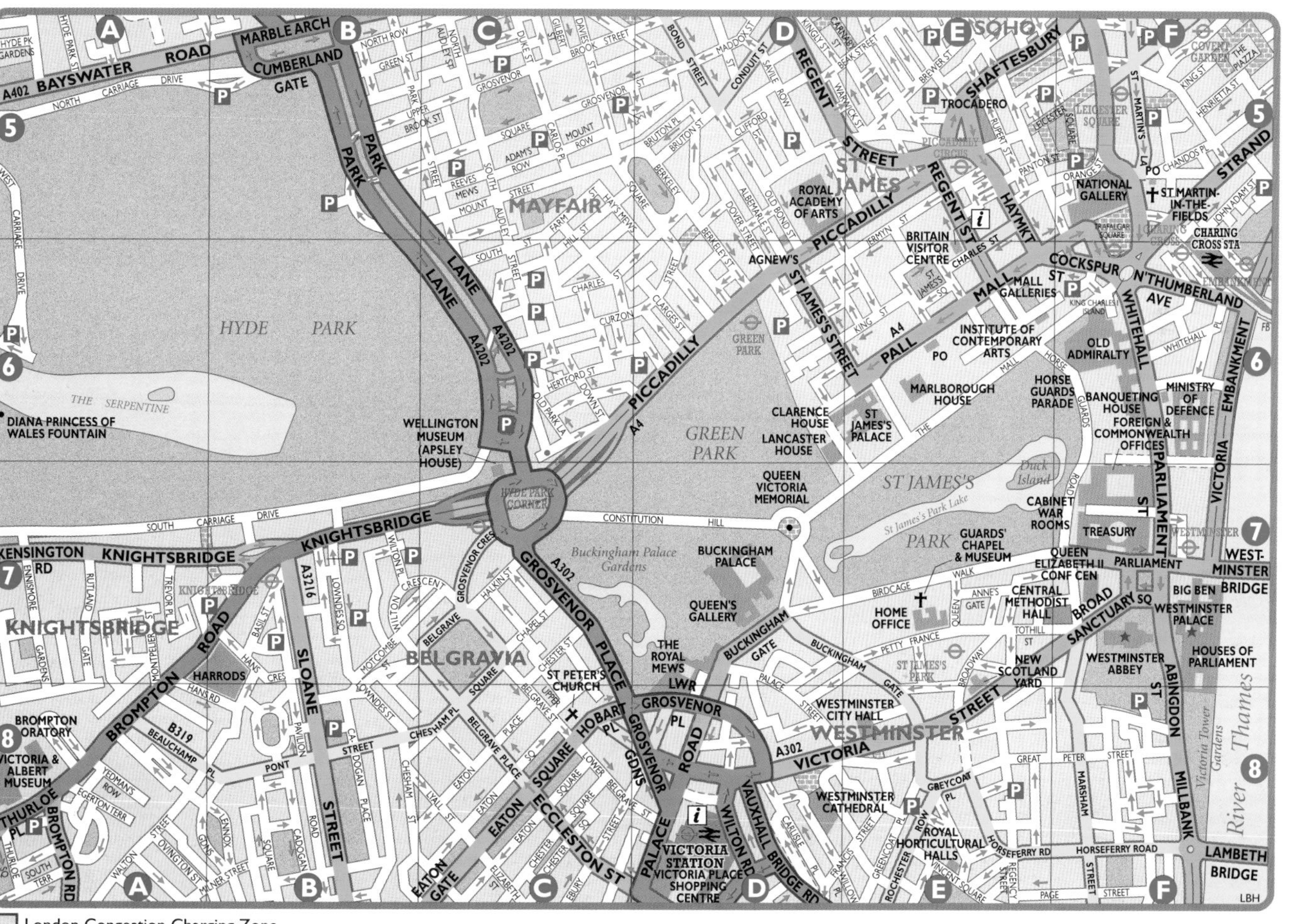
HYDE PARK
THE SERPENTINE
DIANA PRINCESS OF WALES FOUNTAIN
GREEN PARK
ST JAMES'S PARK
Buckingham Palace Gardens
BUCKINGHAM PALACE
QUEEN'S GALLERY
THE ROYAL MEWS
QUEEN VICTORIA MEMORIAL
CLARENCE HOUSE
LANCASTER HOUSE
ST JAMES'S PALACE
MARLBOROUGH HOUSE
INSTITUTE OF CONTEMPORARY ARTS
HORSE GUARDS PARADE
OLD ADMIRALTY
BANQUETING HOUSE
FOREIGN & COMMONWEALTH OFFICES
MINISTRY OF DEFENCE
TREASURY
CABINET WAR ROOMS
GUARDS' CHAPEL & MUSEUM
HOME OFFICE
CENTRAL METHODIST HALL
QUEEN ELIZABETH II CONF CEN
NEW SCOTLAND YARD
WESTMINSTER ABBEY
WESTMINSTER PALACE
HOUSES OF PARLIAMENT
BIG BEN
WESTMINSTER CITY HALL
WESTMINSTER CATHEDRAL
ROYAL HORTICULTURAL HALLS
VICTORIA STATION
VICTORIA PLACE SHOPPING CENTRE
ST PETER'S CHURCH
BELGRAVIA
MAYFAIR
SOHO
ST JAMES
WESTMINSTER
KNIGHTSBRIDGE
HARRODS
BROMPTON ORATORY
VICTORIA & ALBERT MUSEUM
WELLINGTON MUSEUM (APSLEY HOUSE)
HYDE PARK CORNER
ROYAL ACADEMY OF ARTS
BRITAIN VISITOR CENTRE
TROCADERO
NATIONAL GALLERY
ST MARTIN-IN-THE-FIELDS
CHARING CROSS STA
TRAFALGAR SQUARE
LEICESTER SQUARE
PICCADILLY CIRCUS
COVENT GARDEN
PARK LANE
PICCADILLY
REGENT STREET
PALL MALL
THE MALL
WHITEHALL
VICTORIA EMBANKMENT
MILLBANK
LAMBETH BRIDGE
WESTMINSTER BRIDGE
River Thames
Victoria Tower Gardens
VICTORIA STREET
GROSVENOR PLACE
BUCKINGHAM PALACE ROAD
VAUXHALL BRIDGE RD
SLOANE STREET
BROMPTON ROAD
KNIGHTSBRIDGE
BAYSWATER ROAD
MARBLE ARCH
London Congestion Charging Zone

London Congestion Charging Zone

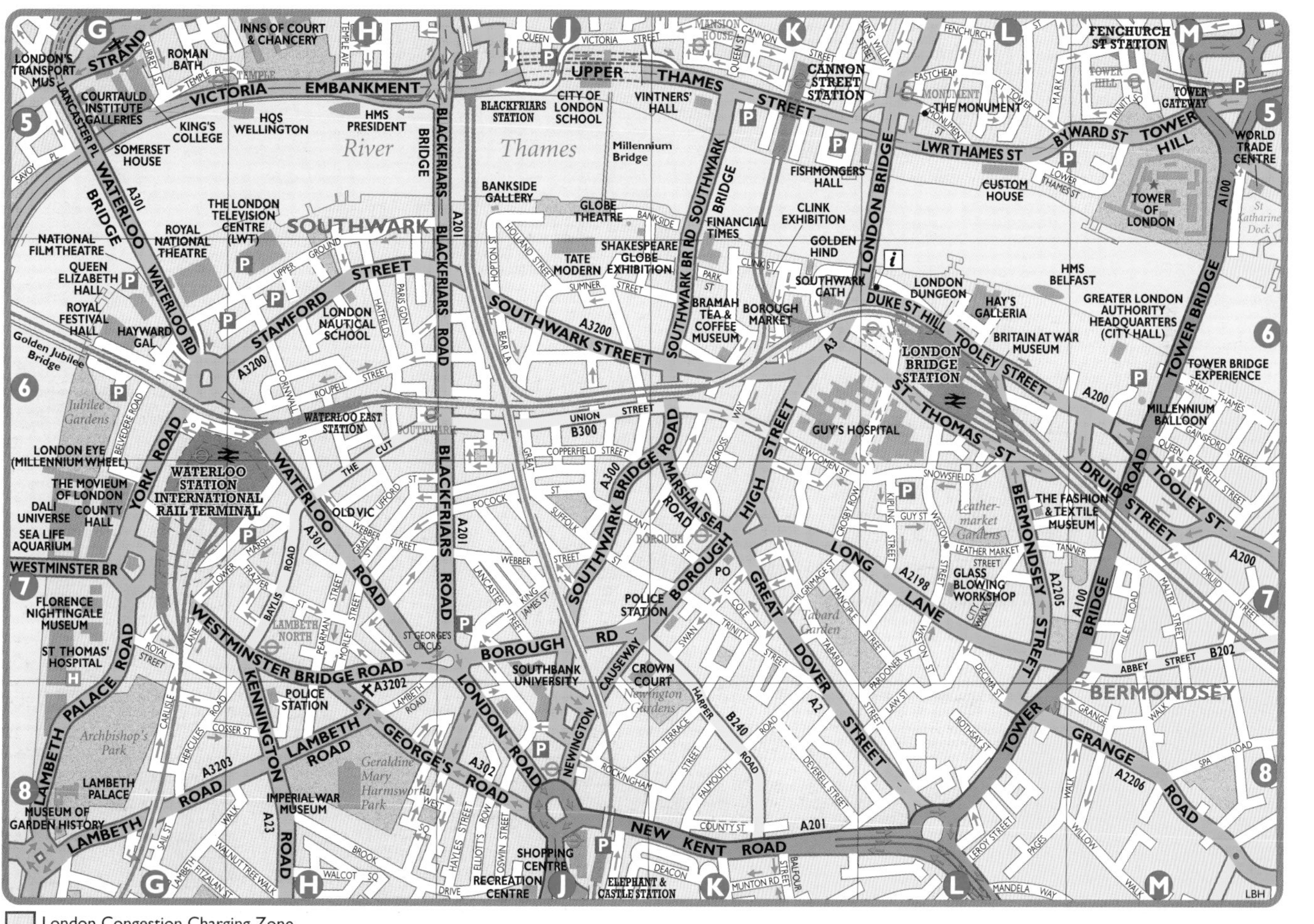

LONDON'S TRANSPORT MUS
STRAND
ROMAN BATH
INNS OF COURT & CHANCERY
TEMPLE AVE
VICTORIA EMBANKMENT
COURTAULD INSTITUTE GALLERIES
KING'S COLLEGE
HQS WELLINGTON
HMS PRESIDENT
SOMERSET HOUSE
River
Thames
LANCASTER PL
WATERLOO BRIDGE
A301
THE LONDON TELEVISION CENTRE (LWT)
ROYAL NATIONAL THEATRE
SOUTHWARK
NATIONAL FILM THEATRE
QUEEN ELIZABETH HALL
ROYAL FESTIVAL HALL
HAYWARD GAL
WATERLOO RD
STAMFORD STREET
A3200
LONDON NAUTICAL SCHOOL
Golden Jubilee Bridge
Jubilee Gardens
BELVEDERE ROAD
LONDON EYE (MILLENNIUM WHEEL)
THE MOVIEUM OF LONDON
DALI UNIVERSE
COUNTY HALL
SEA LIFE AQUARIUM
WESTMINSTER BR
YORK ROAD
WATERLOO STATION INTERNATIONAL RAIL TERMINAL
WATERLOO EAST STATION
THE CUT
OLD VIC
WATERLOO ROAD
FLORENCE NIGHTINGALE MUSEUM
ST THOMAS' HOSPITAL
LAMBETH PALACE ROAD
Archbishop's Park
LAMBETH PALACE
MUSEUM OF GARDEN HISTORY
LAMBETH ROAD
A3203
LAMBETH NORTH
WESTMINSTER BRIDGE ROAD
A3202
POLICE STATION
KENNINGTON ROAD
A23
IMPERIAL WAR MUSEUM
Geraldine Mary Harmsworth Park
ST GEORGE'S ROAD
A302
ST GEORGE'S CIRCUS
BLACKFRIARS BRIDGE
BLACKFRIARS ROAD
A201
BLACKFRIARS STATION
CITY OF LONDON SCHOOL
UPPER THAMES STREET
VINTNERS' HALL
Millennium Bridge
BANKSIDE GALLERY
GLOBE THEATRE
TATE MODERN
SHAKESPEARE GLOBE EXHIBITION
SOUTHWARK STREET
SOUTHWARK BR RD
SOUTHWARK BRIDGE
FINANCIAL TIMES
BRAMAH TEA & COFFEE MUSEUM
BOROUGH MARKET
SOUTHWARK CATH
CLINK EXHIBITION
GOLDEN HIND
FISHMONGERS' HALL
CANNON STREET STATION
LONDON BRIDGE
THE MONUMENT
LWR THAMES ST
CUSTOM HOUSE
BYWARD ST
TOWER HILL
FENCHURCH ST STATION
TOWER GATEWAY
WORLD TRADE CENTRE
TOWER OF LONDON
St Katharine Dock
A100
TOWER BRIDGE
HMS BELFAST
GREATER LONDON AUTHORITY HEADQUARTERS (CITY HALL)
TOWER BRIDGE EXPERIENCE
MILLENNIUM BALLOON
LONDON DUNGEON
HAY'S GALLERIA
BRITAIN AT WAR MUSEUM
DUKE ST HILL
TOOLEY STREET
LONDON BRIDGE STATION
A200
A3
ST THOMAS ST
GUY'S HOSPITAL
UNION STREET
B300
SOUTHWARK BRIDGE ROAD
A300
MARSHALSEA ROAD
HIGH STREET
BOROUGH HIGH STREET
PO
POLICE STATION
BOROUGH RD
SOUTHBANK UNIVERSITY
CAUSEWAY
CROWN COURT
Newington Gardens
NEWINGTON
LONDON ROAD
SHOPPING CENTRE
RECREATION CENTRE
ELEPHANT & CASTLE STATION
NEW KENT ROAD
GREAT DOVER STREET
A2
B240
Tabard Garden
LONG LANE
A2198
Leather-market Gardens
GLASS BLOWING WORKSHOP
BERMONDSEY STREET
A2205
THE FASHION & TEXTILE MUSEUM
DRUID STREET
TOOLEY ST
TOWER BRIDGE ROAD
ABBEY STREET
B202
BERMONDSEY
GRANGE ROAD
A2206
LBH

London Congestion Charging Zone

London

A
M7 Abbey Street
F7 Abingdon Street
G1 Acton Street
C5 Adam's Row
D1 Albany Street
D5 Albemarle Street
J2 Aldersgate Street
G4 Aldwych
M4 Alie Street
H1 Amwell Street
J4 Angel Street
L3 Appold Street
F1 Argyle Street
A3 Ashmill Street
D1 Augustus Street
H2 Aylesbury Street

B
B3 Baker Street
B2 Balcombe Street
H3 Baldwin's Gardens
K8 Balfour Street
J2 Baltic Street
J5 Bankside
K2 Banner Street
B7 Basil Street
K1 Bath Street
K8 Bath Terrace
H7 Baylis Road
A5 Bayswater Road
E5 Beak Street
J6 Bear Lane
A8 Beauchamp Place
C3 Beaumont Street
E4 Bedford Avenue
F3 Bedford Place
G3 Bedford Row
E3 Bedford Square
F2 Bedford Way
K3 Beech Street
C8 Belgrave Place
C7 Belgrave Square
M3 Bell Lane
A3 Bell Street
G6 Belvedere Road
D5 Berkeley Square
D5 Berkeley Street
L7 Bermondsey Street
F2 Bernard Street
E4 Berners Street
E4 Berwick Street
M2 Bethnal Green Road
F1 Bidborough Street
E7 Birdcage Walk
L3 Bishopsgate
J5 Blackfriars Bridge
J6 Blackfriars Road
B3 Blandford Street
F3 Bloomsbury Street
F3 Bloomsbury Way
D3 Bolsover Street
K7 Borough High Street
J7 Borough Road
A2 Boston Place
H2 Bowling Green Lane
M4 Braham Street
E5 Brewer Street
M2 Brick Lane
E1 Brill Place
F7 Broad Sanctuary
A3 Broadley Street
E7 Broadway
A8 Brompton Road
H8 Brook Drive
C5 Brook Street
A4 Brown Street
M3 Brushfield Street
D5 Bruton Place
D5 Bruton Street
A3 Bryanston Place
B4 Bryanston Square
B4 Bryanston Street
D7 Buckingham Gate
D8 Buckingham Palace Road
K2 Bunhill Row
L5 Byward Street

C
B8 Cadogan Place
B8 Cadogan Square
G2 Calthorpe Street
M2 Calvert Avenue
K5 Cannon Street
D1 Cardington Street
G4 Carey Street
G8 Carlisle Lane
D8 Carlisle Place
C5 Carlos Place
D5 Carnaby Street
J4 Carter Lane
F2 Cartwright Gardens
C4 Cavendish Square
J1 Central Street
G4 Chancery Lane
F5 Chandos Place
A3 Chapel Street
C7 Chapel Street
F4 Charing Cross Road
C6 Charles Street
E6 Charles Street
E3 Charlotte Street
E1 Chalton Street
L1 Chart Street
J3 Charterhouse Street
K4 Cheapside
E3 Chenies Street
C8 Chesham Place
B8 Chesham Street
C1 Chester Road
C8 Chester Square
C7 Chester Street
B3 Chiltern Street
K3 Chiswell Street
A2 Church Street
J1 City Garden Row
J1 City Road
L7 City Walk
D6 Clarges Street
H3 Clerkenwell Road
D3 Cleveland Street
D5 Clifford Street
L3 Clifton Street
K6 Clink Street
D3 Clipstone Street
M2 Club Row
F6 Cockspur Street
K7 Cole Street
K4 Coleman Street
M1 Columbia Road
M3 Commercial Street
J2 Compton Street
D5 Conduit Street
C7 Constitution Hill
A4 Connaught Street
J6 Copperfield Street
L4 Cornhill
H6 Cornwall Road
K8 County Street
H3 Cowcross Street
A3 Crawford Place
B3 Crawford Street
M1 Cremer Street
F1 Cromer Street
L1 Crondall Street
K7 Crosby Row
G1 Cubitt Street
B5 Cumberland Gate
L2 Curtain Road
C6 Curzon Street

D
C5 Davies Street
K8 Deacon Way
E4 Dean Street
L7 Decima Street
K8 Deverell Street
C3 Devonshire Street
J1 Dingley Road
M1 Diss Street
B3 Dorset Street
D5 Dover Street
C6 Down Street
M7 Druid Street
D2 Drummond Street
F4 Drury Lane
K2 Dufferin Street
L6 Duke St Hill
C4 Duke Street
M8 Dunton Road

E
K1 East Road
D4 Eastcastle Street
L5 Eastcheap
C8 Eaton Gate
C8 Eaton Place
C8 Eaton Square
C8 Ebury Street
C8 Eccleston Street
A4 Edgware Road
A8 Egerton Terrace
L3 Eldon Street
C8 Elizabeth Street
J8 Elliott's Row
F4 Endell Street
A7 Ennismore Gardens
L2 Epworth Street
D2 Euston Road
E1 Eversholt Street
L3 Exchange Square
H2 Exmouth Market

F
K8 Falmouth Road
L1 Fanshaw Street
C5 Farm Street
H2 Farringdon Road
H4 Farringdon Street
M3 Fashion Street
L5 Fenchurch Street
H4 Fetter Lane
L3 Finsbury Circus
L3 Finsbury Square
G8 Fitzalan Street
H4 Fleet Street
D3 Foley Street
M3 Folgate Street
K3 Fore Street
M3 Fournier Street
E8 Francis Street
H7 Frazier Street
G1 Frederick Street

G
M6 Gainsford Street
J1 Garden Row
J2 Gee Street
B4 George Street
C5 Gilbert Street
J4 Giltspur Street
B2 Glentworth Street
B3 Gloucester Place
K2 Golden Lane
E3 Goodge Street
E2 Gordon Square
E2 Gordon Street
H1 Goswell Road
G2 Gough Street
M4 Goulston Street
E2 Gower Place
E3 Gower Street
D2 Grafton Way
J1 Graham Street
M8 Grange Road
M8 Grange Walk
H7 Gray Street
G1 Gray's Inn Road
B4 Great Cumberland Place
K7 Great Dover Street
L2 Great Eastern Street
D4 Great Marlborough Street
G3 Great Ormond Street
E8 Great Peter Street
D3 Great Portland Street
G4 Great Queen Street
F4 Great Russell Street
J7 Great Suffolk Street
D3 Great Titchfield Street
L5 Great Tower Street
B5 Green Street
E8 Greencoat Place
K4 Gresham Street
E8 Greycoat Place
C7 Grosvenor Crescent
D8 Grosvenor Gardens
C7 Grosvenor Place
C5 Grosvenor Square
C5 Grosvenor Street
G2 Guilford Street
L7 Guy Street

H
M1 Hackney Road
C7 Halkin Street
D3 Hallam Street
D1 Hampstead Road
D4 Hanover Square
B7 Hans Crescent
A8 Hans Road
A2 Harewood Avenue
C3 Harley Street
K8 Harper Road
A4 Harrowby Street
F1 Hastings Street
H6 Hatfields
H3 Hatton Garden
C5 Hay's Mews
J8 Hayles Street
E5 Haymarket
F5 Henrietta Street
G8 Hercules Road
C6 Hertford Street
F4 High Holborn
M2 High Street
C6 Hill Street
C8 Hobart Place
H3 Holborn
H3 Holborn Viaduct
J5 Holland Street
J6 Hopton Street
F6 Horse Guards Road
E8 Horseferry Road
M4 Houndsditch
D3 Howland Street
L1 Hoxton Street
F2 Hunter Street
A4 Hyde Park Crescent
A5 Hyde Park Gardens
A4 Hyde Park Street

I
C1 Inner Circle
B2 Ivor Place

J
C4 James Street
E5 Jermyn Street
G3 Jockey's Fields
F5 John Adam Street
F1 Judd Street

K
H8 Kennington Road
A7 Kensington Road
J7 King James Street
E6 King Street
F5 King Street
L5 King William Street
G1 King's Cross Road
D5 Kingly Street
M1 Kingsland Road
G4 Kingsway
L7 Kipling Street
A7 Knightsbridge

L
M3 Lamb Street
G3 Lamb's Conduit Street
F8 Lambeth Bridge
G8 Lambeth Palace Road
G8 Lambeth Road
G8 Lambeth Walk
G5 Lancaster Place
J7 Lancaster Street
D3 Langham Place
J7 Lant Street
L8 Law Street
L4 Leadenhall Street
H3 Leather Lane
L7 Leather Market Street
E5 Leicester Square
F2 Leigh Street
B8 Lennox Gardens
L2 Leonard Street
L8 Leroy Street
J1 Lever Street
L4 Lime Street
G4 Lincoln's Inn Fields
A2 Lisson Grove
L3 Liverpool Street
G1 Lloyd Baker Street
A1 Lodge Road
L4 Lombard Street
L6 London Bridge
J8 London Road
K3 London Wall
F4 Long Acre
J3 Long Lane
L7 Long Lane
D2 Longford Street
C8 Lower Belgrave Street
D8 Lower Grosvenor Place
G7 Lower Marsh
L5 Lower Thames Street
B7 Lowndes Square
B8 Lowndes Street
J4 Ludgate Hill
L2 Luke Street
C8 Lyall Street

M
D5 Maddox Street
E3 Malet Street
M7 Maltby Street
K7 Manciple Street
L8 Mandela Way
M4 Mansell Street
D3 Maple Street
B5 Marble Arch
F2 Marchmont Street
D4 Margaret Street
H1 Margery Street
L5 Mark Lane
K7 Marshalsea Road
F8 Marsham Street
C3 Marylebone High Street
A3 Marylebone Road
E2 Melton Street
K1 Micawber Street
M4 Middlesex Street
F1 Midland Road
F8 Millbank
B8 Milner Street
M4 Minories
F4 Monmouth Street
B3 Montagu Place
B4 Montagu Square
F3 Montague Place
F3 Montague Street
A7 Montpelier Street
L5 Monument Street
K3 Moor Lane
K3 Moorgate
J1 Moreland Street
H7 Morley Street
D4 Mortimer Street
B7 Motcombe Street
C5 Mount Row
C5 Mount Street
K8 Munton Road
K1 Murray Grove
F4 Museum Street
H1 Myddleton Street

N
F4 Neal Street
D4 New Bond Street
J4 New Bridge Street
C3 New Cavendish Street
J4 New Change
H4 New Fetter Lane
J8 New Kent Road
L1 New North Road
F4 New Oxford Street
K6 Newcomen Street
J4 Newgate Street
J8 Newington Causeway
E4 Newman Street
K1 Nile Street
E4 Noel Street
A4 Norfolk Crescent
C5 North Audley Street
A5 North Carriage Drive
E2 North Gower Street
B5 North Row
G3 Northington Street
F6 Northumberland Avenue

O
J4 Old Bailey
D5 Old Bond Street
L4 Old Broad Street
E4 Old Compton Street
A3 Old Marylebone Road
C6 Old Park Lane
J2 Old Street
F5 Orange Street
C4 Orchard Street
E1 Ossulston Street
J8 Oswin Street
C2 Outer Circle
A8 Ovington Street
C4 Oxford Street

P
B3 Paddington Street
E8 Page Street
L8 Pages Walk
D7 Palace Street
E6 Pall Mall
F1 Pancras Road
E5 Panton Street
L7 Pardoner Street
H6 Paris Garden
C2 Park Crescent
B5 Park Lane
A1 Park Road
B5 Park Street
K6 Park Street
F4 Parker Street
F7 Parliament Square
F6 Parliament Street
B8 Pavilion Road
H7 Pearman Street
M1 Pelter Street
A3 Penfold Street
G1 Penton Rise
G1 Pentonville Road
J2 Percival Street
G1 Percy Circus
G1 Percy Street
M3 Petticoat Lane
E7 Petty France
E1 Phoenix Road
D6 Piccadilly
K7 Pilgrimage Street
L1 Pitfield Street
J7 Pocock Street
E4 Poland Street
E1 Polygon Road
B8 Pont Street
D3 Portland Place
B4 Portman Square
B4 Portman Street
G4 Portugal Street
K4 Poultry
A3 Praed Street
L3 Primrose Street
A1 Prince Albert Road
M3 Princelet Street
K4 Princes Street
K1 Provost Street

Q
M2 Quaker Street
C4 Queen Anne Street
E7 Queen Anne's Gate
M6 Queen Elizabeth Street
K5 Queen Street
J5 Queen Victoria Street

R
K2 Radnor Street
E4 Rathbone Place
G3 Red Lion Street
M2 Redchurch Street
K7 Redcross Way
D1 Redhill Street
C5 Reeves Mews
E8 Regency Street
D4 Regent Street
D3 Riding House Street
M7 Riley Road
H1 River Street
L2 Rivington Street
D1 Robert Street
E8 Rochester Row
J8 Rockingham Street
H2 Rosebery Avenue
A2 Rossmore Road
L8 Rothsay Street
H6 Roupell Street
G7 Royal Street
E5 Rupert Street
F3 Russell Square
A7 Rutland Gate

S
H3 Saffron Hill
G8 Sail Street
H8 St George's Road
F4 St Giles High Street
E6 St James's Square
D6 St James's Street
H1 St John Street
A1 St John's Wood High Street
F5 St Martin's Lane
L6 St Thomas Street
D5 Savile Row
G5 Savoy Place
M2 Sclater Street
L2 Scrutton Street
A3 Seymour Place
B4 Seymour Street
M6 Shad Thames
E5 Shaftesbury Avenue
K1 Shepherdess Walk
H4 Shoe Lane
K3 Silk Street
H2 Skinner Street
B7 Sloane Street
L7 Snowsfields
E4 Soho Square
C5 South Audley Street
A7 South Carriage Drive
C6 South Street
A8 South Terrace
F3 Southampton Row
K5 Southwark Bridge
J7 Southwark Bridge Road
J6 Southwark Street
M8 Spa Road
J1 Spencer Street
M3 Spital Square
H6 Stamford Street
D1 Stanhope Street
A4 Star Street
E3 Store Street
F5 Strand
J6 Sumner Street
L3 Sun Street
G5 Surrey Street
A4 Sussex Gardens
K7 Swan Street
M1 Swanfield Street
G1 Swinton Street

T
K7 Tabard Street
L2 Tabernacle Street
L7 Tanner Street
F2 Tavistock Place
F2 Tavistock Square
H5 Temple Avenue
G5 Temple Place
H7 The Cut
E6 The Mall
F5 The Piazza
G3 Theobald's Road
L4 Threadneedle Street
L4 Throgmorton Street
A8 Thurloe Place
A8 Thurlow Square
L6 Tooley Street
E3 Torrington Place
E7 Tothill Street
E2 Tottenham Court Road
M6 Tower Bridge
L8 Tower Bridge Road
M5 Tower Hill
F5 Trafalgar Square
A7 Trevor Place
M5 Trinity Square
K7 Trinity Street
H3 Turnmill Street

U
H7 Ufford Street
J6 Union Street
C8 Upper Belgrave Street
B4 Upper Berkeley Street
B5 Upper Brook Street
H6 Upper Ground
J5 Upper Thames Street
E2 Upper Woburn Place

V
D8 Vauxhall Bridge Road
C4 Vere Street
F7 Victoria Embankment
D8 Victoria Street
E8 Vincent Square
M1 Virginia Road

W
H8 Walcot Square
H8 Walnut Tree Walk
A8 Walton Street
E4 Wardour Street
D2 Warren Street
D5 Warwick Street
G5 Waterloo Bridge
G6 Waterloo Road
K4 Watling Street
H7 Webber Street
C4 Welbeck Street
D4 Wells Street
K1 Wenlock Road
M4 Wentworth Street
A5 West Carriage Drive
H8 West Square
F7 Westminster Bridge
G7 Westminster Bridge Road
L7 Weston Street
C3 Weymouth Street
J1 Wharf Road
G1 Wharton Street
K2 Whitecross Street
F6 Whitehall
F6 Whitehall Place
E3 Whitfield Street
G1 Wicklow Street
C4 Wigmore Street
G4 Wild Street
E8 Willow Place
M8 Willow Walk
L3 Wilson Street
B7 Wilton Crescent
B7 Wilton Place
D8 Wilton Road
C3 Wimpole Street
F2 Woburn Place
K4 Wood Street
L2 Worship Street

Y
A8 Yeoman's Row
G7 York Road
B3 York Street
C2 York Terrace

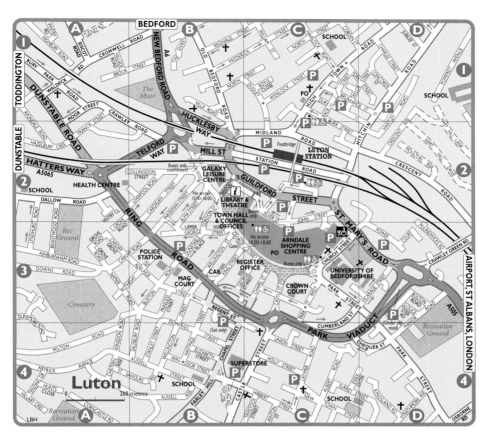

B3	Adelaide Street	D2	Crescent Rise	A1	Hillside Road	B1	Reginald Street
C4	Albert Road	D2	Crescent Road	D2	Hitchin Road	B2	Ring Road
B2	Alma Street	A1	Cromwell Road	C4	Holly Street	A3	Rothesay Road
A3	Ashburnham Road	C4	Cumberland Street	B1	Hucklesby Way	B4	Russell Rise
C4	Ashton Street	A2	Dallow Road	B2	Inkerman Street	B4	Russell Street
A1	Avondale Road	A3	Downs Road	C2	John Street	C2	St Mary's Road
C1	Back Street	C1	Dudley Street	B3	King Street	A4	St Saviours Crescent
A1	Biscot Road	C1	Duke Street	D4	Kingsland Road	B4	Salisbury Road
D3	Bolton Road	B4	Dumfries Street	C4	Latimer Road	C2	Silver Street
C1	Boyle Close	B3	Dunstable Place	B2	Liverpool Road	B4	South Road
A3	Brantwood Road	A1	Dunstable Road	A3	Lyndhurst Road	B4	Stanley Street
B2	Bridge Street	B4	Elizabeth Street	D4	Manor Road	C2	Station Road
A1	Brook Street	C4	Essex Close	A4	Meyrick Avenue	D4	Strathmore Avenue
C1	Brunswick Street	B4	Farley Hill	C2	Midland Road	C4	Surrey Street
C2	Burr Street	A2	Francis Street	B2	Mill Street	C4	Tavistock Street
A1	Bury Park Road	B1	Frederick Street	A1	Moor Street	C1	Taylor Street
B3	Buxton Road	B3	George Street	D2	Moulton Rise	B2	Telford Way
A3	Cardiff Grove	B3	George Street West	A3	Napier Road	A4	Tenzing Grove
A3	Cardiff Road	D3	Gloucester Road	B1	New Bedford Road	B1	The Shires
B2	Cardigan Street	B3	Gordon Street	C4	New Town Street	C4	Union Street
B4	Castle Street	A3	Grove Road	B1	North Street	B3	Upper George Street
B4	Chapel Street	C2	Guildford Street	B1	Old Bedford Road	A2	Vestry Close
D1	Charles Street	D2	Hart Hill Drive	D4	Osborne Road	D3	Vicarage Street
D4	Chequer Street	D2	Hartley Road	C3	Park Street	B1	Villa Road
A4	Chiltern Rise	B4	Hastings Street	C3	Park Street West	A1	Waldeck Road
C3	Church Street	A2	Hatters Way	C4	Park Viaduct	B4	Wellington Street
B2	Collingdon Street	C1	Havelock Road	D3	Poundwicks Road	C1	Wenlock Street
D1	Concorde Street	A2	Hazelbury Crescent	D3	Power Court	B4	Windsor Street
D3	Crawley Green Road	C4	Hibbert Street	B3	Princess Street	A4	Winsdon Road
A1	Crawley Road	C1	High Town Road	B3	Regent Street	C1	York Street

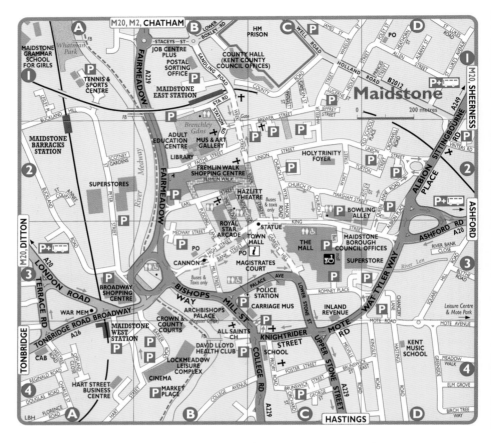

D1	Albany Street	C4	Foster Street	B2	Museum Street	D3	Wat Tyler Way
D2	Albion Place	B2	Fremlin Walk	D2	Old School Place	B2	Waterside
D1	Allen Street	C3	Gabriel's Hill	C4	Orchard Street	B1	Week Street
D3	Ashford Road	C4	George Street	C3	Palace Avenue	C1	Well Road
D2	Astley Street	D4	Greenside	D1	Princes Street	A4	Westree Road
B3	Bank Street	A4	Hart Street	C4	Priory Road	C1	Wheeler Street
B4	Barker Road	D4	Hastings Road	B2	Pudding Lane	C1	Wollett Street
D4	Birch Tree Way	D1	Heathorn Street	D2	Queen Anne Road	C2	Wyatt Street
B3	Bishops Way	C1	Hedley Street	A4	Reginald Road	C2	Wyke Manor Road
D3	Blythe Road	B3	High Street	D3	River Bank Close		
C1	Brewer Street	D1	Holland Road	C3	Romney Place		
A3	Broadway	C1	James Street	B2	Rose Yard		
C4	Brunswick Street	C1	Jeffrey Street	A4	Rowland Close		
C4	Brunswick Street East	C3	King Street	A2	St Annes Court		
A1	Buckland Hill	D4	Kingsley Road	B2	St Faiths Street		
A2	Buckland Road	C4	Knightrider Street	D1	St Luke's Avenue		
C1	Camden Street	A1	Lesley Place	D1	St Lukes Road		
D3	Chancery Lane	A3	London Road	A2	St Peter Street		
A4	Charles Street	B1	Lower Boxley Road	B1	Sandling Road		
C2	Church Street	C3	Lower Stone Street	A2	Scotney Gardens		
B4	College Avenue	C1	Lucerne Street	D2	Sittingbourne Road		
C4	College Road	B2	Market Buildings	D3	Square Hill Road		
C1	County Road	B2	Market Street	B1	Staceys Street		
D2	Cromwell Road	C2	Marsham Street	B1	Station Road		
A4	Douglas Road	D4	Meadow Walk	A3	Terrace Road		
B2	Earl Street	B3	Medway Street	A4	Tonbridge Road		
D4	Elm Grove	C4	Melville Road	D2	Tufton Street		
B1	Fairmeadow	B3	Mill Street	C2	Union Street		
A4	Florence Road	D4	Mote Avenue	C4	Upper Stone Street		
D1	Foley Street	C4	Mote Road	D2	Vinters Road		

Manchester

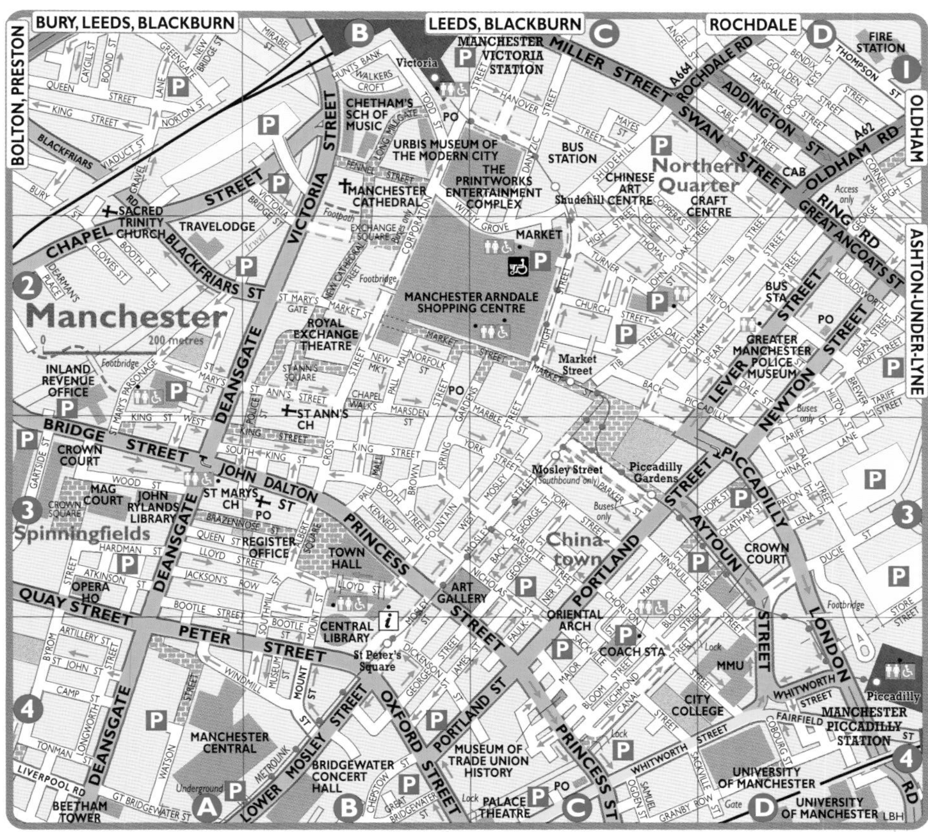

D1 Addington Street	C1 Copperas Street	A3 Jackson's Row	B4 Oxford Street	A4 Tonman Street
B3 Albert Square	D1 Cornell Street	A3 John Dalton Street	B3 Pall Mall	C1 Trinity Way
C1 Angel Street	B2 Corporation Street	C2 John Street	C3 Parker Street	C2 Turner Street
A4 Artillery Street	D1 Cross Keys Street	B3 Kennedy Street	D3 Paton Street	A1 Viaduct Street
A3 Atkinson Street	B3 Cross Street	B3 King Street	A4 Peter Street	B1 Victoria Bridge Street
D4 Aytoun Street	A3 Crown Square	A1 King Street	B3 Piccadilly	B2 Victoria Street
C3 Back George Street	D2 Dale Street	A2 King Street West	B2 Police Street	B1 Walkers Croft
C2 Back Piccadilly	C1 Dantzic Street	D3 Lena Street	D2 Port Street	A4 Watson Street
D1 Bendix Street	D2 Dean Street	D2 Lever Street	C3 Portland Street	B3 West Mosley Street
A1 Blackfriars Road	A3 Dearman's Place	A4 Liverpool Road	B3 Princess Street	C4 Whitworth Street
A2 Blackfriars Street	A2 Deansgate	A3 Lloyd Street	A3 Quay Street	A4 Windmill Street
C4 Bloom Street	B4 Dickenson Street	D3 London Road	A1 Queen Street	B1 Withy Grove
A1 Boond Street	D3 Ducie Street	B1 Long Millgate	A3 Queen Street	A3 Wood Street
A2 Booth Street	C2 Edge Street	A4 Longworth Street	C4 Richmond Street	C3 York Street
B3 Booth Street	B2 Exchange Square	A4 Lower Mosley Street	C1 Rochdale Road	
A3 Bootle Street	D4 Fairfield Street	C4 Major Street	C1 Sackville Street	
A3 Brazennose Street	C4 Faulkner Street	C2 Marble Street	B2 St Ann's Street	
D2 Brewer Street	B1 Fennel Street	B2 Market Street	B2 St Ann's Square	
A3 Bridge Street	B3 Fountain Street	B2 Marsden Street	B4 St James Street	
B3 Brown Street	A3 Gartside Street	D1 Marshall Street	A4 St John Street	
A1 Bury Street	D1 George Leigh Street	C1 Mayes Street	B2 St Mary's Gate	
A4 Byrom Street	B4 George Street	C1 Miller Street	A3 St Mary's Parsonage	
D1 Cable Street	D1 Golden Street	C3 Minshull Street	A2 St Mary's Street	
A4 Camp Street	C4 Granby Row	B1 Mirabel Street	C4 Samuel Ogden Street	
C4 Canal Street	A1 Gravel Lane	C3 Nicholas Street	C1 Shudehill	
A1 Caygill Street	D1 Great Ancoats Street	B2 Norfolk Street	A3 South King Street	
A2 Chapel Street	A4 Great Bridgewater	A1 Norton Street	B4 Southmill Street	
B2 Chapel Walks	Street	C2 Oak Street	D2 Spear Street	
C3 Charlotte Street	A1 Greengate	A1 Oldham Road	B3 Spring Gardens	
D3 Chatham Street	C1 Hanover Street	C3 Oldham Street	D3 Store Street	
B4 Chepstow Street	A3 Hardman Street		C1 Swan Street	
D3 China Lane	C2 High Street		D3 Tariff Street	
C3 Chorlton Street	D2 Hilton Street		C2 Thomas Street	
C2 Church Street	D3 Hope Street		D1 Thompson Street	
C2 Clowes Street	D2 Houldsworth Street		C2 Tib Street	
D4 Cobourg Street	B1 Hunts Bank		B1 Todd Street	

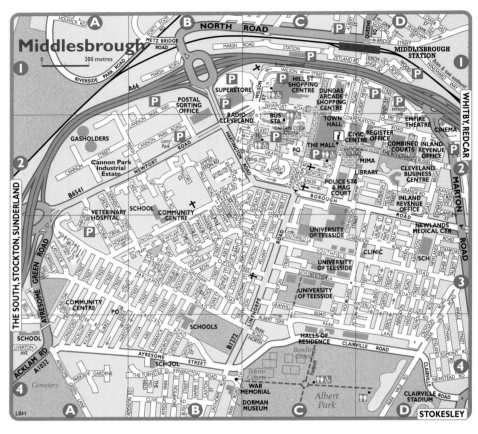

D4	Abingdon Road	A2	Cannon Street	C2	Gilkes Street	D3	Maple Street	C2	St Aidens Drive
A4	Acklam Road	C2	Captain Cook Square	B3	Glebe Road	B1	Marsh Road	B2	St Pauls Road
C4	Acton Street	A2	Carey Close	C2	Grange Road	A2	Marsh Street	D1	School Croft
B4	Addison Road	A3	Carlow Street	C3	Granville Road	D2	Marton Road	D2	Somerset Street
B4	Aire Street	B4	Caxton Street	B3	Gresham Road	A3	Meath Street	C3	Southfield Lane
B3	Albany Street	B4	Chester Street	A2	Greta Street	D2	Melrose Street	C3	Southfield Road
D1	Albert Mews	D4	Clairville Road	D1	Grey Street	B1	Metz Bridge Road	D3	Stamford Street
C2	Albert Road	C3	Clarendon Road	D2	Gurney Street	A3	Mills Street	C3	Stephenson Street
C1	Albert Street	B3	Clifton Street	D4	Haddon Street	D3	Myrtle Street	B3	Stowe Street
C4	Albert Terrace	B4	Clive Road	A4	Harford Street	B4	Napier Street	A4	Surrey Street
B2	Alwent Road	B3	Colville Street	B2	Hartington Road	D3	Newlands Road	D3	Talbot Street
C2	Amber Street	C2	Corporation Road	A1	Holwick Road	A2	Newport Road	C3	Tennyson Street
B2	Ammerston Road	B4	Costa Street	A3	Howard Street	D4	Newstead Road	D2	The Boulevard
D3	Angle Street	B3	Craven Street	B3	Howe Street	B1	North Road	B4	The Midfield
B3	Aske Road	A3	Crescent Road	D2	Jedbergh Street	A3	Orwell Street	B4	The Turnstile
B3	Athol Street	D4	Croydon Road	B4	Kensington Road	B3	Outram Street	B3	Union Street
D3	Aubrey Street	A2	Derwent Street	A4	Kildare Street	B4	Oxford Street	C3	Victoria Road
A4	Ayresome Green Lane	B3	Diamond Road	B2	Kingston Street	D3	Palm Street	C2	Victoria Square
A3	Ayresome Green Road	D3	Egerton Street	A3	Lamport Street	C4	Park Lane	A3	Victoria Street
B4	Ayresome Park Road	D4	Egmont Street	C4	Laura Street	C4	Park Road North	B2	Walpole Street
A4	Ayresome Street	C2	Emerald Street	D3	Laurel Street	B4	Park Road South	B3	Warren Street
C2	Baker Street	D2	Emily Street	A3	Laycock Street	D4	Park Vale Road	B4	Warwick Street
C2	Bedford Street	B3	Enfield Street	B2	Lees Road	A4	Parkside Gardens	D3	Waterloo Road
A3	Bell Street	D4	Errol Street	A4	Leinster Road	A3	Parliament Road	B3	Waverley Street
C2	Borough Road	D3	Esher Street	A3	Leven Street	C2	Pearl Street	B3	Wentworth Street
B3	Bow Street	B2	Eshwood Square	B4	Linthorpe Road	C3	Pelham Street	A4	Wicklow Street
C2	Brentnall Street	A4	Essex Street	A4	Liverton Avenue	C3	Percy Street	C1	Wilson Street
D1	Bridge Street	C2	Exchange Square	A4	Longford Street	C3	Portman Street	C3	Wilton Street
D2	Bright Street	D1	Fairbridge Street	B3	Lonsdale Street	B3	Princes Road	B2	Windsor Street
B4	Brompton Street	B3	Falkland Street	A3	Lorne Street	D1	Queens Square	D1	Windward Way
B4	Bush Street	D4	Falmouth Street	D4	Lothian Road	A1	Riverside Park Road	D1	Wood Street
D4	Byelands Street	D2	Fife Street	D1	Lower East Street	B3	Romney Street	C3	Woodlands Road
B3	Cadogan Street	B3	Finsbury Street	D1	Lower Feversham Street	D3	Roscoe Street	B4	Worcester Street
D2	Camden Street	B2	Fleetham Street	D1	Lower Gosford Street	B3	Ross Street	B3	Wylam Street
B2	Cannon Park Road	B1	Forty Foot Road	B3	Mallory Close	C2	Ruby Street	C1	Zetland Road
B2	Cannon Park Way	C2	Garnet Street	B3	Manor Street	D2	Russell Street		

Milton Keynes

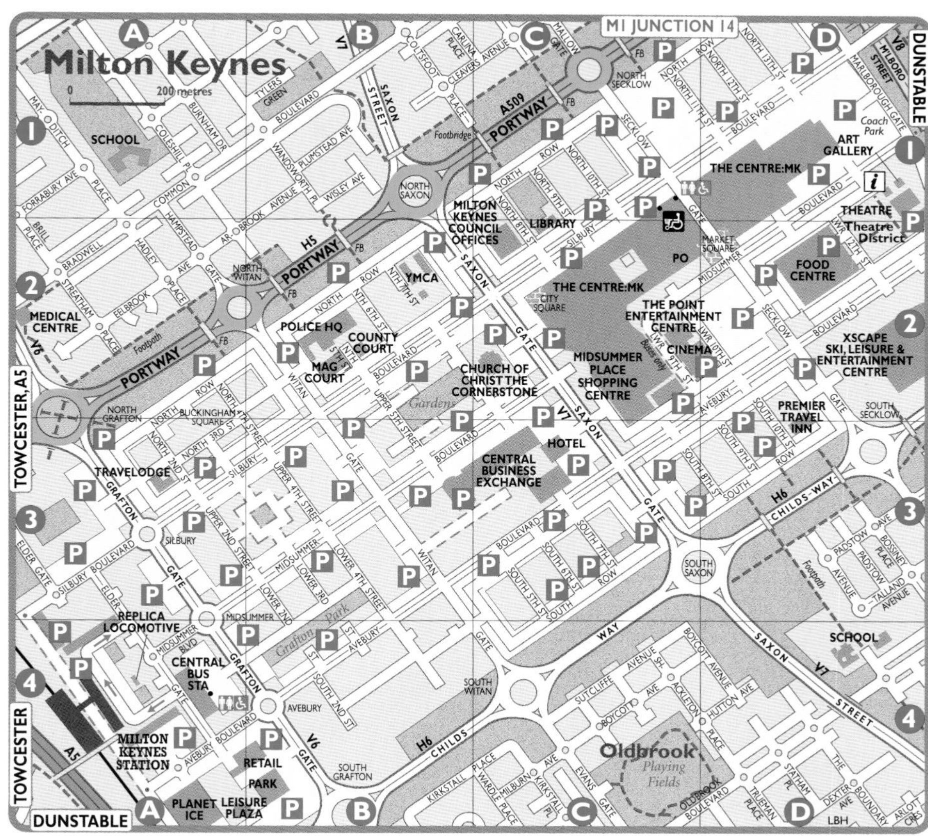

|---|---|---|---|
A2 Arbrook Avenue	C2 Lower 9th Street	B1 Plumstead Avenue	B1 Wandsworth Place
D4 Arlott Crescent	D2 Lower 10th Street	A2 Portway	C4 Wardle Place
B4 Avebury	D2 Lower 12th Street	C2 Saxon Gate	B1 Wisley Avenue
A4 Avebury Boulevard	C1 Mallow Gate	B1 Saxon Street	B2 Witan Gate
D3 Bossiney Place	D2 Market Square	D4 Saxon Street	
C4 Boycott Avenue	D1 Marlborough Gate	C1 Secklow Gate	
A2 Bradwell Common	D1 Marlborough Street	C4 Shackleton Place	
Boulevard	A1 Mayditch Place	A3 Silbury	
A2 Brill Place	A3 Midsummer	A3 Silbury Boulevard	
A2 Buckingham Square	A4 Midsummer Boulevard	C3 South 5th Street	
A1 Burnham Drive	C4 Milburn Avenue	C3 South 6th Street	
B1 Carlina Place	A3 North 2nd Street	C3 South 7th Street	
B4 Childs Way	A3 North 3rd Street	C3 South 8th Street	
C2 City Square	A2 North 4th Street	D3 South 9th Street	
B1 Cleavers Avenue	B2 North 5th Street	D2 South 10th Street	
A1 Coleshill Place	B2 North 5th Street	B4 South Grafton	
B1 Coltsfoot Place	B2 North 7th Street	C3 South Row	
D4 Dexter Avenue	C1 North 8th Street	C3 South Saxon	
A2 Eelbrook Avenue	C1 North 9th Street	D2 South Secklow	
A3 Elder Gate	C1 North 10th Street	C4 South Witan	
C4 Evans Gate	C1 North 11th Street	D4 Statham Place	
A1 Forrabury Avenue	D1 North 12th Street	A2 Streatham Place	
A3 Grafton Gate	D1 North 13th Street	C4 Sutcliffe Avenue	
A2 Hadley Place	A2 North Grafton	D3 Talland Avenue	
A2 Hampstead Gate	A2 North Row	D4 The Boundary	
D4 Hutton Avenue	B1 North Saxon	D4 Trueman Place	
B4 Kirkstall Place	C1 North Secklow	B1 Tylers Green	
B3 Lower 2nd Street	A2 North Witan	A3 Upper 2nd Street	
B3 Lower 3rd Street	D4 Oldbrook Boulevard	B3 Upper 4th Street	
B3 Lower 4th Street	D3 Padstow Avenue	B2 Upper 5th Street	

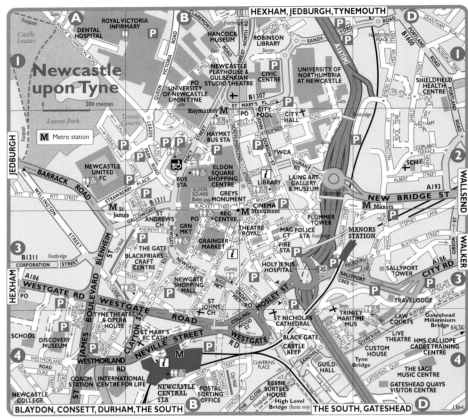

C4	Akenside Hill	D2	Falcaner Street	C3	Market Street East	C3	Sallyport Crescent
D2	Albert Street	B3	Fenkle Street	C3	Melbourne Street	D3	Sandgate
D3	Argyle Street	B4	Forth Street	D1	Milton Place	C4	Sandhill
A2	Barrack Road	B3	Friars Street	C3	Mosley Street	C1	Sandyford Road
A3	Bath Lane	B3	Gallowgate	B3	Nelson Street	D2	Shield Street
B3	Bigg Market	D4	Gateshead Quay	B4	Neville Street	B4	South Street
B2	Blackett Street	A4	George Street	C2	New Bridge Street	D3	Stepney Lane
A4	Blandford Square	D3	Gibson Street	D2	New Bridge Street	A3	Stowell Street
A4	Blandford Street	B3	Grainger Street	B3	Newgate	B2	Strawberry Lane
D3	Broad Chare	B4	Grainger Street West	C2	Northumberland Road	A2	Strawberry Place
A1	Burnside	D1	Grantham Road	B2	Northumberland Street	A4	Sunderland Street
D4	Buryside	C1	Great North Road	B3	Nun Street	A4	Temple Street
D3	Buxton Street	C3	Grey Street	B4	Orchard Street	C4	The Close
D1	Byron Street	B3	Groat Market	D3	Pandon Bank	D3	Tower Street
D1	Chester Street	B4	Hanover Street	A4	Peel Lane	C3	Trafalgar Street
D3	City Road	D1	Harrison Place	B2	Percy Street	A4	Waterloo Street
B1	Claremont Road	D2	Henry Square	C3	Pilgrim Street	A2	Wellington Street
C4	Clavering Place	C3	High Bridge	A2	Pitt Street	A3	Westgate Road
B4	Clayton Street	C3	Hood Street	D1	Portland Road	A4	Westmorland Road
C3	Cloth Market	C1	Jesmond Road West	B4	Pudding Chare	D2	Wretham Place
C2	College Street	C2	John Dobson Street	D4	Quayside		
B4	Collingwood Street	B1	King's Road	B1	Queen Victoria Road		
D2	Copland Terrace	C4	King Street	A1	Richardson Road		
D1	Coppice Way	B2	Leazes Lane	C2	Ridley Place		
A3	Corporation Street	B2	Leazes Park Road	D1	Rosedale Terrace		
C3	Dean Street	A2	Leazes Terrace	B3	St Andrews Street		
A4	Duke Street	C1	Link Road	A4	St James Boulevard		
C2	Durant Road	C4	Lombard Street	B2	St James Street		
B2	Eldon Square	B3	Low Friar Street	C1	St Mary's Place		
C2	Ellison Place	B3	Market Street	B2	St Thomas Street		

Newport (Wales)

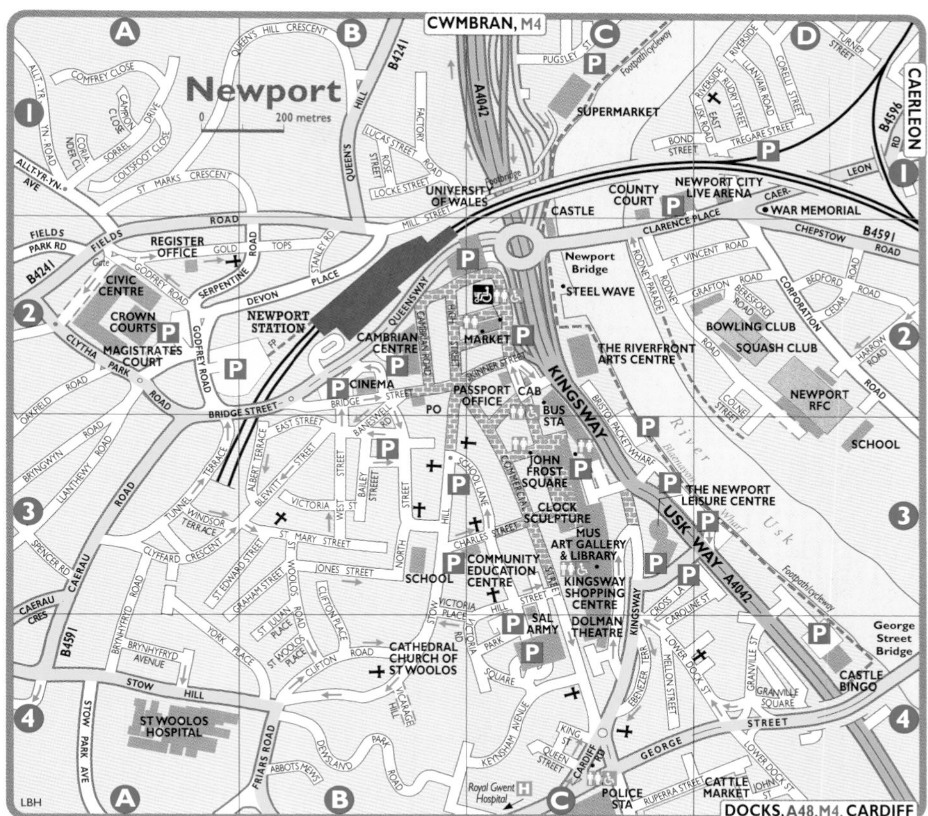

Map of Newport city centre, Wales. 200 metres scale. Surrounding references: CWMBRAN, M4; CAERLEON; SUPERMARKET; NEWPORT CITY LIVE ARENA; WAR MEMORIAL; DOCKS, A48, M4, CARDIFF.

Index

Ref	Name
B4	Abbots Mews
B3	Albert Terrace
A1	Allt Yr Yn Avenue
A1	Allt Yr Yn Road
B3	Bailey Street
B3	Baneswell Road
D2	Bedford Road
D2	Beresford Road
B3	Blewitt Street
C1	Bond Street
B2	Bridge Street
C2	Bristol Packet Wharf
A3	Bryngwyn Road
A4	Brynhyfryd Avenue
A4	Brynhyfryd Road
A3	Caerau Crescent
A3	Caerau Road
D1	Caerleon Road
B2	Cambrian Road
A1	Campion Close
C4	Cardiff Road
C4	Caroline Street
D2	Cedar Road
C3	Charles Street
D2	Chepstow Road
C2	Clarence Place
B3	Clifton Place
B4	Clifton Road
A3	Clyffard Crescent
A2	Clytha Park Road
D2	Colne Street
A1	Coltsfoot Close
A1	Comfrey Close
C3	Commercial Street
D1	Corelii Street
A1	Coriander Close
D2	Corporation Road
C3	Cross Lane
B2	Devon Place
B4	Dewsland Park Road
B3	East Street
D1	East Usk Road
C4	Ebenezer Terrace
B1	Factory Road
A2	Fields Park Road
A2	Fields Road
B4	Friars Road
C4	George Street
A2	Godfrey Road
A2	Gold Tops
D2	Grafton Road
B3	Graham Street
D4	Granville Square
D4	Granville Street
D2	Harrow Road
B2	High Street
C3	Hill Street
D4	John Street
B3	Jones Street
C4	Keynsham Avenue
C4	King Street
C2	Kingsway
A3	Llanthewy Road
D1	Llanvair Road
B1	Locke Street
C4	Lower Dock Street
B1	Lucas Street
C4	Mellon Street
B2	Mill Street
B3	North Street
A2	Oakfield Road
C4	Park Square
C1	Pugsley Street
C4	Queen Street
B1	Queen's Hill
B1	Queen's Hill Crescent
B2	Queensway
D1	Riverside
C2	Rodney Parade
C2	Rodney Road
B1	Rose Street
D1	Rudry Street
C4	Ruperra Street
A3	St Edward Street
B4	St Julian Place
A1	St Marks Crescent
B3	St Mary Street
C2	St Vincent Road
B4	St Woolos Place
B3	St Woolos Road
C3	School Lane
A2	Serpentine Road
C2	Skinner Street
A1	Sorrel Drive
A3	Spencer Road
B2	Stanley Road
A4	Stow Hill
A4	Stow Park Avenue
D1	Tregare Street
A3	Tunnel Terrace
D1	Turner Street
C3	Usk Way
B4	Vicarage Hill
B3	Victoria Place
C4	Victoria Road
B3	Victoria Street
B3	West Street
A3	Windsor Terrace
A4	York Place

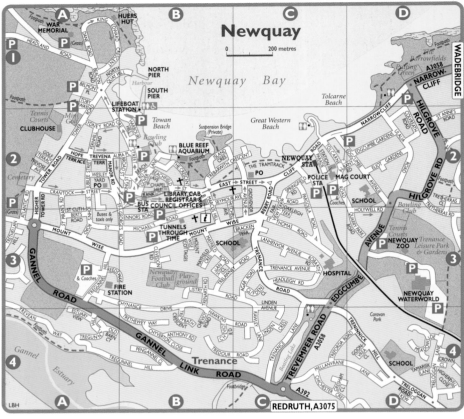

Newquay

Newquay Bay

0   200 metres

C3	Agar Road	A4	Estuary View	B2	Marcus Hill	B2	The Crescent
C2	Albany Road	C3	Fairview Terrace	B3	Mayfield Crescent	A1	Toby Way
B2	Alma Place	A2	Fernhill Road	B3	Mayfield Road	C2	Tolcarne Road
B4	Anthony Road	B2	Fore Street	D4	Meadowside	C2	Tor Road
A3	Atlantic Road	B4	Gannel Link Road	C4	Mellanvrane Lane	A2	Tower Road
B2	Bank Street	A3	Gannel Road	B2	Mitchell Avenue	B2	Trebarwith Crescent
B2	Beach Road	A2	Golf Terrace	A3	Mount Wise	B4	Tredour Road
B2	Beachfield Avenue	D4	Goonvrea Close	B3	Mount Wise Cottages	C4	Treforda Road
A1	Beacon Road	B2	Gover Lane	D2	Narrowcliff	A3	Tregunnel Hill
A1	Belmont Place	C4	Gresham Close	A1	North Quay Hill	B3	Trelawney Road
C2	Berry Road	C2	Grosvenor Avenue	C3	Oakleigh Terrace	D4	Treloggan Lane
C3	Bracken Terrace	B2	Harbour Hill	A4	Old Barn Court	D4	Treloggan Road
B2	Broad Street	B4	Hawkins Road	C2	Pargolla Road	B4	Trembath Crescent
B2	Chapel Hill	A1	Headland Road	B4	Pengannel Close	C3	Trenance Avenue
B4	Cheviot Road	C3	Headleigh Road	D3	Quarry Park Road	C4	Trenance Lane
C4	Chichester Crescent	A2	Higher Tower Road	C4	Rawley Lane	C3	Trenance Road
B3	Chynance Drive	D4	Higherwell Close	A3	Reeds Way	B3	Trenarth Road
B4	Chyverton Close	D2	Hilgrove Road	C3	Robartes Road	D4	Treninnick Hill
B3	Clevedon Road	D3	Holywell Road	D2	St Anne's Road	A3	Trethellan Hill
C3	Clifden Close	A2	Hope Terrace	A3	St Cuthberts Road	D2	Tretherras Close
C2	Cliff Road	B2	Island Crescent	B3	St George's Road	D3	Tretherras Road
D2	Colvreath Road	A2	Jubilee Street	A3	St John's Road	B4	Trethewey Way
A2	Crantock Street	D4	Kew Close	A3	St Michael's Road	A4	Trevean Way
D4	Crown Close	A1	King Edward Crescent	A3	St Piran's Road	C4	Trevemper Road
A1	Dane Road	B2	King Street	C3	St Thomas Road	A2	Trevena Terrace
B2	East Street	C3	Lanhenvor Avenue	B2	Seymour Avenue	A2	Trevose Avenue
C3	Edgcumbe Avenue	C3	Linden Avenue	C2	Springfield Road	D2	Ulalia Road
D2	Edgcumbe Gardens	C4	Linden Crescent	C2	Station Parade	B3	Vivian Close
D2	Eliot Gardens	B3	Listry Road	A2	Sydney Road	A2	Wesley Yard
B3	Ennors Road	A2	Manor Road	D4	Tamarisk Lane		

Northampton

151

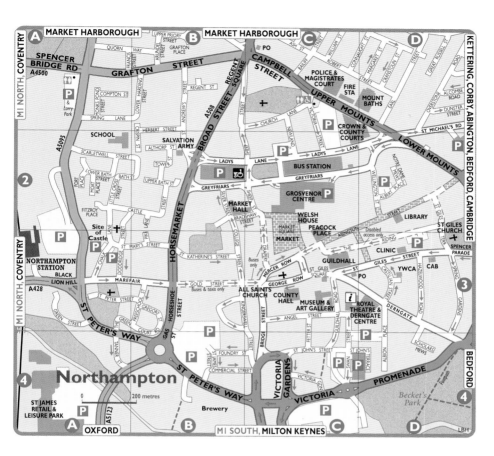

C3	Abington Street	C4	Fetter Street	A2	Moat Place	C4	Swan Street
D2	Albert Place	A2	Fitzroy Place	A1	Monks Pond Street	A4	Tanner Street
D4	Albion Place	A2	Fort Place	C2	Newland	C2	The Drapery
D1	Alcombe Road	B4	Foundry Street	D2	Notre Dame Mews	A3	The Green
B2	Althorp Street	A1	Francis Street	D1	Overstone Road	C3	The Riding
C3	Angel Street	B3	Freeschool Street	B3	Pike Lane	B2	Tower Street
B1	Arundel Street	B4	Gas Street	A1	Quorn Way	B2	Upper Bath Street
C1	Ash Street	C3	George Row	B1	Regent Square	C1	Upper Mounts
C1	Bailiff Street	B3	Gold Street	B1	Regent Street	B1	Upper Priory Street
A2	Bath Street	B1	Grafton Place	C1	Robert Street	C4	Victoria Gardens
A3	Black Lion Hill	A1	Grafton Street	B1	St Andrews Street	C4	Victoria Promenade
B2	Bradshaw Street	D1	Great Russell Street	C3	St Giles Square	C1	Victoria Street
C4	Bridge Street	A3	Green Street	D3	St Giles Street	D2	Wellington Street
B2	Broad Street	B3	Gregory Street	D2	St Giles Terrace	C1	William Street
C1	Campbell Street	B2	Greyfriars	B4	St James Street		
D3	Castilian Street	C3	Guildhall Road	C4	St John's Street		
B2	Castle Street	D3	Hazelwood Road	D4	St John's Terrace		
A3	Chalk Lane	B1	Herbert Street	B3	St Katherine's Street		
C1	Church Lane	B3	Horsemarket	A3	St Mary's Street		
B3	College Street	B3	Horseshoe Street	D1	St Michael's Road		
B4	Commercial Street	B3	Kingerswell Street	A3	St Peter Street		
A1	Compton Street	B2	Lady's Lane	B4	St Peter's Way		
C1	Connaught Street	A2	Little Cross Street	A2	Scarletwell Street		
B3	Court Road	A2	Lower Bath Street	D4	Scholars Mews		
D1	Cranstoun Street	B1	Lower Harding Street	C2	Sheep Street		
B2	Crispin Street	D2	Lower Mounts	B2	Silver Street		
D3	Derngate	A3	Marefair	A1	Spencer Bridge Road		
A3	Doddridge Street	D1	Margaret Street	D3	Spencer Parade		
D1	Dunster Street	C2	Market Square	D3	Spring Gardens		
D1	Earl Street	C3	Mercer Row	A1	Spring Lane		

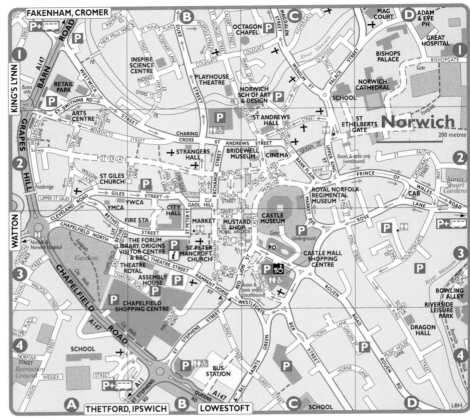

C4	All Saints Green
C2	Bank Plain
C2	Bank Street
A1	Barn Road
B2	Bedford Street
C4	Ber Street
A3	Bethel Street
D1	Bishopgate
B3	Brigg Street
B1	Calvert Street
C3	Castle Meadow
C2	Castle Street
D2	Cathedral Street
B3	Chantry Road
A3	Chapelfield East
A3	Chapelfield North
A3	Chapelfield Road
B2	Charing Cross
A3	Cleveland Road
B1	Colegate
B1	Coslany Street
A2	Cow Hill
B3	Davey Place
B2	Dove Street
B1	Duke Street
B1	Dyers Yard
C1	Elm Hill
A1	Ely Street
B2	Exchange Street
C1	Fishergate

B2	Fishers Lane
C1	Friars Quay
B2	Gaol Hill
C4	Garden Street
A2	Giles Street
A4	Globe Place
A2	Grapes Hill
B3	Haymarket
C4	Horns Lane
B1	Indigo Yard
A3	Johnson Place
C2	King Street
A3	Little Bethel Street
B2	London Street
B2	Lower Goat Lane
C1	Magdalen Street
B4	Malthouse Road
A1	Mandela Close
C2	Market Avenue
D3	Mountergate
D4	Music House Lane
B1	Muspole Street
A1	New Mills Yard
A4	Norfolk Street
B1	Oak Street
C2	Opie Street
B3	Orford Place
C1	Palace Street
C1	Pigg Lane
A2	Pottergate

D2	Prince of Wales Road
C2	Princes Street
C1	Quayside
C2	Queen Street
B4	Queens Road
B3	Rampant Horse Street
B3	Red Lion Street
C2	Redwell Street
D3	Rose Lane
B1	Rosemary Lane
C3	Rouen Road
B3	Royal Arcade
B2	St Andrews Street
D3	St Ann Lane
A2	St Benedicts Street
D2	St Faiths Lane
B1	St Georges Street
D3	St John Street
A2	St Margarets Street
B1	St Marys Plain
B3	St Peter Street
B4	St Stephens Road
B4	St Stephens Street
A1	St Swithins Road
B4	Surrey Street
A2	Ten Bell Lane
B3	Theatre Street
C4	Thorn Lane
C3	Timberhill
A4	Union Street

A3	Unthank Street
B2	Upper Goat Lane
C2	Upper King Street
A2	Upper St Giles Street
A3	Vauxhall Street
A3	Walpole Street
A2	Wellington Lane
C1	Wensum Street
A4	Wessex Street
C3	Westlegate
A1	Westwick Street
B3	White Lion Street
A2	Willow Lane

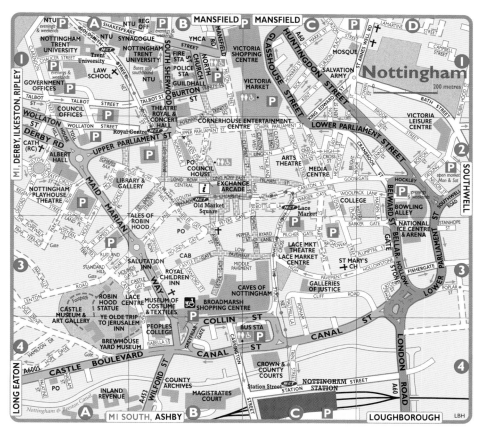

B3	Albert Street	D2	Cranbrook Street	C2	Lincoln Street	C1	Rick Street
B2	Angel Row	A2	Cumberland Place	B3	Lister Gate	C2	Risters Place
C3	Barker Gate	C1	Curzon Place	D4	London Road	D1	Robin Hood Street
D1	Bath Street	C1	Curzon Street	B2	Long Row Central	A3	Rutland Street
B2	Beastmarket Hill	A2	Derby Road	B2	Long Row East	D1	St Annes Well Road
C1	Beck Street	A2	East Circus Street	B3	Low Pavement	A3	St James's Street
D3	Bellargate	C2	East Street	C2	Lower Parliament Street	A3	St James's Terrace
D2	Belward Street	D3	Fishergate	A2	Maid Marion Way	C1	St Marks Street
D2	Boston Street	C3	Fletcher Gate	D2	Maiden Lane	C2	St Mary's Gate
C2	Bottle Lane	B2	Forman Street	C3	Maltmill Lane	B3	St Peters Gate
C2	Bridlesmith Gate	A3	Friar Lane	B1	Mansfield Road	A1	Shakespeare Street
D2	Brightmoor Street	D2	Gedling Street	B2	Market Street	B2	South Parade
C2	Broad Street	C2	George Street	C3	Middle Hill	B1	South Sherwood Street
C3	Broadway	C1	Glasshouse Street	C3	Middle Pavement	D2	Southwell Road
A2	Bromley Place	A1	Goldsmith Street	B1	Milton Street	B3	Spaniel Row
D1	Brook Street	C2	Goosegate	A3	Mount Street	A3	Standard Hill
B1	Burton Street	B4	Greyfriar Gate	D2	Nelson Street	B3	Stanford Street
C3	Byard Lane	A4	Hamilton Drive	D2	Nile Street	D3	Stanhope Street
D1	Campbell Street	A4	Haslam Street	B2	Norfolk Place	C4	Station Street
B4	Canal Street	C2	Heathcote Street	A3	Ogle Drive	C2	Stoney Street
C2	Carlton Street	C2	High Cross Street	C2	Old Lenton Street	A1	Talbot Street
B4	Carrington Street	C3	High Pavement	A2	Oxford Street	A3	The Ropewalk
A4	Castle Boulevard	C2	High Street	A4	Palatine Street	C2	Thurland Street
B3	Castle Gate	D2	Hockley	A3	Park Row	A2	Toll House Hill
A3	Castle Road	D3	Hollowstone	A3	Park Terrace	C4	Trent Street
A2	Chapel Bar	A4	Hope Drive	A3	Park Valley	B1	Trinity Square
A1	Chaucer Street	A3	Hounds Gate	C2	Pelham Street	A2	Upper Parliament Street
B2	Cheapside	C1	Howard Street	D3	Pemberton Street	C2	Victoria Street
C3	Cliff Road	C1	Huntingdon Street	C3	Pepper Street	C2	Warser Gate
C2	Clinton Street East	B4	Isabella Street	C3	Pilcher Gate	C3	Weekday Cross
C2	Clinton Street West	C1	Kent Street	D3	Plumptre Street	A2	Wellington Circus
A1	Clarendon Street	C1	King Edward Street	C3	Popham Street	B2	Wheeler Gate
C2	Clumber Street	B2	King Street	D3	Poplar Street	B4	Wilford Street
B4	Collin Street	D1	Lamartine Street	A3	Postern Street	A2	Wollaton Street
C1	Conuent Street	D2	Lennox Street	B2	Queen Street	C2	Woolpack Lane
D1	Cowan Street	A3	Lenton Road	A2	Regent Street		

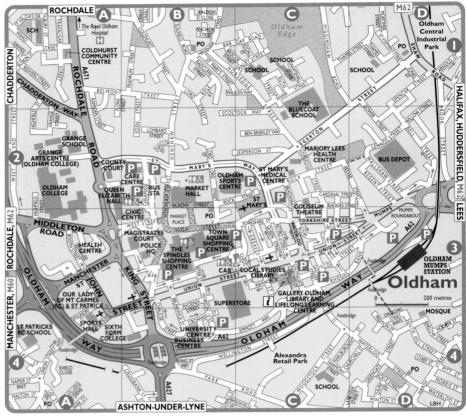

B2	Albion Street	A4	Foundry Street	D4	Minton Street	B2	St Mary's Way
B1	Anchor Street	B1	Franklin Street	D4	Morris Street	D1	St Stephen's Street
D1	Arnold Street	D2	Gower Street	D1	Mortimer Street	B2	Scoltock Way
B1	Bar Gap Road	A2	Grange Street	D3	Mumps	D1	Shaw Road
D4	Barlow Street	C3	Greaves Street	A4	Napier Street East	C1	Shaw Street
D2	Beever Street	D4	Greengate Street	B2	Naylor Street	A4	Shield Close
D2	Bell Street	D4	Hardy Street	A3	Oldham Way	D4	Sickle Street
A1	Belmont Street	C4	Harmony Street	D4	Orme Street	C1	Siddall Street
C2	Ben Brierley Way	B2	Henshaw Street	B4	Park Road	D4	South Hill Street
A3	Booth Street	C1	Higginshaw Road	A4	Park Street	D1	Spencer Street
C3	Bow Street	B3	High Street	B3	Peter Street	B1	Sunfield Road
C2	Bradshaw Street	A2	Highfield Street	D4	Pitt Street	C1	Thames Street
B1	Briscoe Street	B3	Hobson Street	D2	Preston Street	A1	Tilbury Street
D2	Brook Street	D4	Hooper Street	C3	Queen Street	A1	Trafalgar Street
B4	Brookfield Street	C1	Horsedge Street	B1	Radcliffe Street	B1	Trinity Street
B4	Brunswick Street	C2	Jesperson Street	B1	Raleigh Close	B3	Union Street
C2	Cardinal Street	A3	John Street	A1	Ramsden Street	A4	Union Street West
A1	Chadderton Way	D1	Jones Street	A1	Redvers Street	A4	Villiers Drive
B4	Chaucer Street	B3	King Street	D2	Regent Street	B4	Wall Street
B2	Cheapside	C4	Landseer Street	C3	Retiro Street	D2	Wallshaw Street
D4	Chief Street	A4	Lee Street	B1	Rhodes Bank	A1	Ward Street
C4	Churchill Street	D2	Lemnos Street	C2	Rhodes Street	C3	Waterloo Street
B1	Coldhurst Street	B2	Lombard Street	B1	Rifle Street	B4	Wellington Street
B4	Cromwell Street	B1	Lord Street	A1	Rochdale Road	A2	West End Street
B4	Crossbank Street	C1	Malby Street	B2	Rock Street	B3	West Street
A1	Davies Street	A4	Malton Street	C3	Roscoe Street	C1	Whitehall Street
B2	Eden Street	A3	Manchester Street	A1	Ruskin Street	D2	Willow Street
C2	Egerton Street	B3	Market Place	C1	Ruth Street	B1	Wilson Way
C4	Emmott Way	C4	Marlborough Street	A1	St Hilda's Drive	C4	Woodstock Street
A1	Flora Street	A3	Middleton Road	B1	St Mary's Street	C3	Yorkshire Street

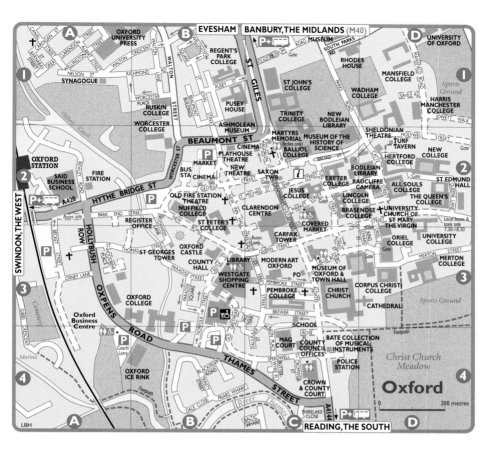

A1 Albert Street
C4 Albion Place
C3 Alfred Street
C4 Baltic Wharf
B1 Beaumont Buildings
B2 Beaumont Street
A3 Becket Street
B4 Blackfriars Road
C3 Blue Boar Street
C3 Brewer Street
C2 Broad Street
C4 Butterwyke Place
A1 Canal Street
A1 Cardigan Street
B3 Castle Street
D2 Catte Street
C2 Cornmarket Street
C4 Cromwell Street
B4 Dale Close
C4 Faulkner Street
B4 Friars Wharf
B2 George Street
A3 Gibbs Crescent
A1 Great Clarendon Street
C2 High Street
A3 Hollybush Row
D2 Holywell Street
A2 Hythe Bridge Street
D1 Jowett Walk
D3 King Edward Street

C2 Magdalen Street
D1 Mansfield Road
C2 Market Street
D3 Merton Street
C1 Museum Road
A1 Nelson Street
B2 New Inn Hall Street
B2 New Road
B4 Norfolk Street
B4 Old Greyfriars Street
D3 Oriel Street
A3 Osney Lane
A3 Oxpens Road
B3 Paradise Square
B3 Paradise Street
A2 Park End Street
C1 Parks Road
C3 Pembroke Street
C3 Pike Terrace
B1 Pusey Street
C3 Queen Street
D2 Queens Lane
A2 Rewley Road
B1 Richmond Road
C4 Rose Place
C3 St Aldates
A1 St Barnabas Street
C3 St Ebbe's Street
C1 St Giles
B1 St John Street

B2 St Michael Street
A3 St Thomas Street
D1 Savile Road
C2 Ship Street
C4 Shirelake Close
C1 South Parks Road
C4 Speedwell Street
B4 Thames Street
B2 Tidmarsh Lane
B4 Trinity Street
C2 Turl Street
A1 Walton Crescent
B1 Walton Lane
B1 Walton Street
B1 Wellington Square
A1 Wellington Street
A3 Woodbine Place
B1 Worcester Place
B2 Worcester Street

University Colleges
D2 All Souls College
C2 Balliol College
D2 Brasenose College
C3 Christ Church College
D3 Corpus Christi College
C2 Exeter College
D2 Hertford College
C2 Jesus College
C2 Lincoln College
D1 Manchester College
D1 Mansfield College
D3 Merton College
D2 New College
B2 Nuffield College
D3 Oriel College
C3 Pembroke College
D2 Queen's College
B1 Regent's Park College
B1 Ruskin College
D2 St Edmund Hall
C1 St John's College
B2 St Peter's College
C1 Trinity College
D3 University College
D1 Wadham College
B2 Worcester College

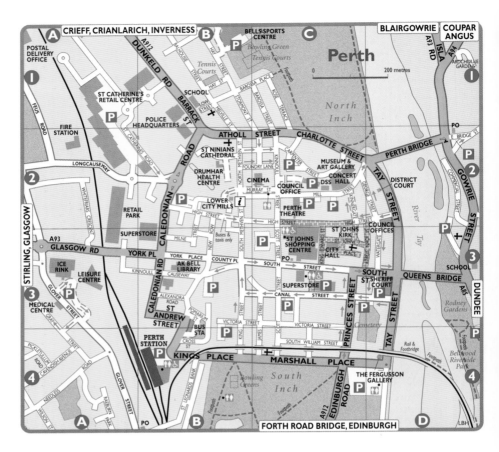

B3	Alexandra Road	B4	King Street	C4	South William Street
D1	Ardchoillie Gardens	B4	Kings Place	B1	Stormont Street
B2	Atholl Street	B3	Kinnoull Causeway	D2	Tay Street
B1	Balhousie Street	C2	Kinnoull Street	B3	Victoria Street
B1	Barossa Place	A2	Longcauseway	D3	Watergate
C1	Barossa Street	B1	Low Street	A2	Whitefriars Crescent
B1	Barrack Street	C4	Marshall Place	A4	Wilson Street
B3	Caledonian Road	B1	Melville Street	B3	York Place
C3	Canal Street	C2	Mill Street		
C2	Carpenter Street	B3	Milne Street		
A4	Cavendish Avenue	C2	Murray Street		
C2	Charlotte Street	A4	Needless Road		
D2	Commercial Street	B3	New Row		
B3	County Place	B2	North Methven Street		
B4	Cross Street	D2	Perth Bridge		
B1	Dunkeld Road	A4	Pickletullum Road		
D2	East Bridge Street	B3	Pomarium Street		
C4	Edinburgh Road	C4	Princes Street		
A1	Feus Road	D3	Queens Bridge		
C2	Foundry Lane	A4	Raeburn Park		
D2	George Street	C1	Rose Terrace		
A3	Glasgow Road	B3	St Andrew Street		
A3	Glover Street	A2	St Catherines Road		
D2	Gowrie Street	D3	St John Street		
A3	Gray Street	C3	St Johns Place		
B2	Hay Street	B4	St Leonards Bank		
B2	High Street	C3	Scott Street		
D1	Isla Road	C2	Skinnergate		
C4	James Street	B3	South Methven Street		
C3	King Edward Street	C3	South Street		

Peterborough

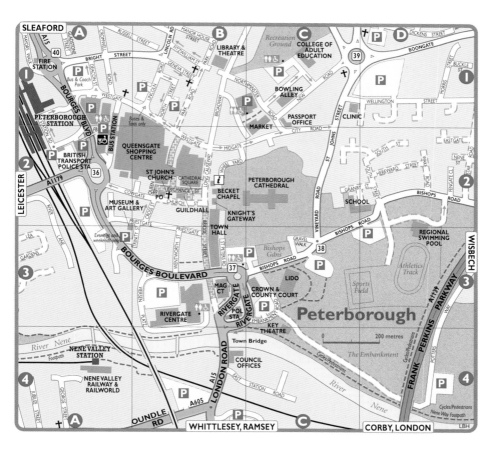

C3	Bishops Road	A3	Lea Gardens	B3	Wentworth Street	
D1	Boongate	B1	Lincoln Road	A1	Westgate	
A1	Bourges Boulevard	B4	London Road	B2	Wheel Yard	
B3	Bridge Street	B2	Long Causeway			
A1	Bright Street	B1	Manor House Street			
B1	Broadway	A1	Mayors Walk			
D1	Buckle Street	B2	Midgate			
B2	Cathedral Square	D1	Morris Street			
B2	Church Street	D2	Nene Street			
C2	City Road	C1	New Road			
A2	Cowgate	B1	North Street			
A1	Cromwell Road	B1	Northminster Road			
B2	Cross Street	B4	Oundle Road			
A1	Deacon Street	B1	Park Road			
D1	Dickens Street	D4	Potters Way			
B4	East Station Road	B2	Priestgate			
D2	Eastgate	B2	Queen Street			
C3	Embankment Road	A2	River Lane			
B2	Exchange Street	B3	Rivergate			
D2	Fengate Close	A1	Russell Street			
B1	Fitzwilliam Street	C2	St Johns Street			
D4	Frank Perkins	B3	St Peters Road			
	Parkway	D2	South Street			
B1	Geneva Street	D2	Star Road			
A4	George Street	A2	Station Road			
A1	Gladstone Street	B3	Trinity Street			
C2	Granby Street	B3	Versen Platz			
C3	Gravel Walk	C2	Vineyard Road			
D2	Hereward Street	D2	Wake Road			
A4	Jubilee Street	D1	Wellington Street			

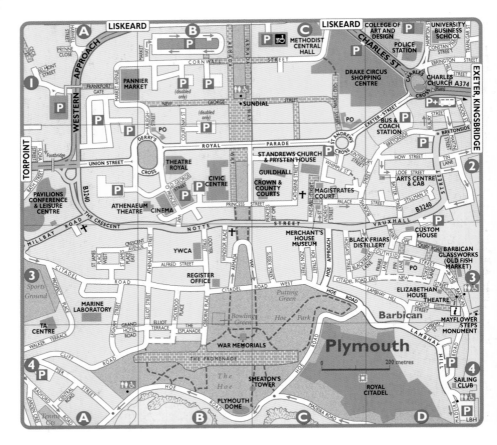

B3	Alfred Street	C2	Fineswell Street	B3	Notte Street	A2	Union Street
B1	Armada Way	A2	Flora Street	B2	Old George Street	D3	Vauxhall Street
B3	Athenaeum Street	A1	Frankfort Gate	C1	Old Town Street	A4	Walker Terrace
D3	Basket Opie	D3	Friars Lane	B3	Osborne Place	A2	Western Approach
A2	Bath Street	A4	Garden Crescent	C2	Palace Street	C2	Whimple Street
D2	Batter Street	A4	Grand Hotel Road	A4	Pier Street	B3	Windsor Place
A1	Belmont Street	D1	Hampton Street	D3	Pin Lane	C3	Zion Street
D2	Bilbury Street	A1	Harwell Street	B2	Princess Street		
C3	Blackfriars Lane	D1	Hill Street	C2	Princess Street Ope		
D2	Breton Side	C3	Hoe Approach	B2	Princess Way		
D2	Buckwell Street	B4	Hoe Road	A3	Prospect Place		
D3	Castle Street	C3	Hoe Street	A1	Prynne Close		
C2	Catherine Street	C3	Hoegate Street	D3	Quay Road		
A1	Cecil Street	B3	Holyrood Place	A4	Radford Road		
A4	Central Road	D2	How Street	B2	Raleigh Street		
D1	Charles Cross	A1	King Street	B2	Royal Parade		
C1	Charles Street	C2	Kinterbury Street	C2	St Andrew Street		
A3	Citadel Road	D3	Lambhay Hill	C2	St Andrews Cross		
C3	Citadel Road East	D4	Lambhay Street	A3	St James Place East		
B3	Citadel Road West	A4	Leigham Street	A3	St James Place West		
A4	Cliff Road	B3	Lockyer Street	D3	Southside Street		
D1	Constantine Street	D2	Looe Street	D2	Stillman Street		
B1	Cornwall Street	C4	Madeira Road	D3	Stokes Lane		
B2	Courtenay Street	A1	Market Avenue	C3	Sussex Street		
A3	Crescent Avenue	B1	Market Way	D3	The Barbican		
B2	Derry's Cross	D2	Martin Street	A2	The Crescent		
D1	Ebrington Street	A3	Millbay Road	B4	The Esplanade		
B3	Elliot Street	D1	Moon Street	B4	The Promenade		
B4	Elliot Terrace	B1	New George Street	D2	Tin Lane		
D1	Exeter Street	D3	New Street	D1	Trafalgar Street		

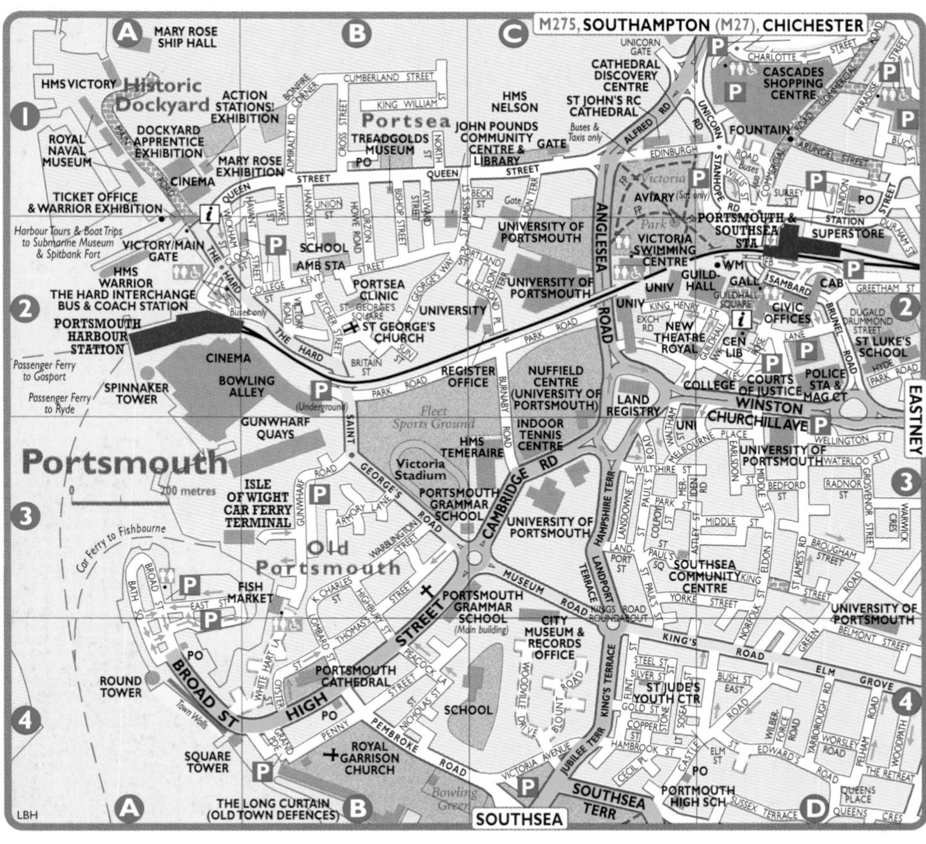

LBH

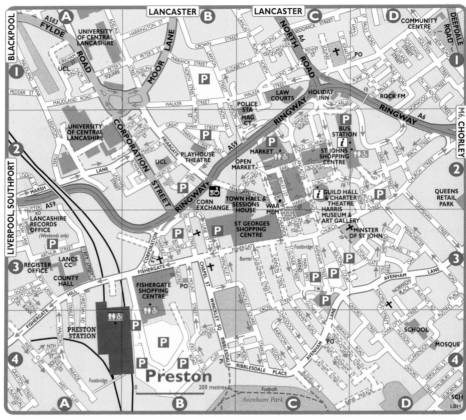

B1	Adelphi Place	D1	East View Road	C1	Lancaster Road North	A1	Radnor Street
A1	Adelphi Street	B2	Edward Street	C4	Latham Street	C4	Regent Street
A3	Arthur Street	D1	Egan Street	A4	Lauderdale Street	C4	Ribblesdale Place
C4	Avenham Lane	B1	Elizabeth Street	D3	Laurel Street	B2	Ringway
C4	Avenham Road	B3	Fishergate	B1	Lawson Street	D4	St Austin's Place
C3	Avenham Street	A4	Fishergate Hill	A2	Leighton Street	D3	St Austin's Road
C4	Bairstow Street	B3	Fleet Street	C2	Lodge Street	C1	St Ignatius Square
C4	Bank Terrace	B3	Fox Street	C2	Lord Street	D1	St Pauls Road
C4	Berwick Road	C4	Frenchwood Street	C1	Lund Street	D1	St Pauls Square
C2	Birley Street	B2	Friargate	B3	Lune Street	A1	St Peter's Square
C3	Boltons Court	A1	Fylde Road	C3	Main Sprit Wynd	B1	St Peter's Street
A3	Bow Lane	B4	Garden Street	D3	Manchester Road	B3	St Wilfred's Street
B2	Bowran Street	C1	Gardner Street	B2	Market Street West	D1	Schleswig Street
C4	Bushell Place	C3	Glover Street	A2	Marsh Lane	C1	Sedgwick Street
C4	Camden Place	A4	Good Street	A1	Maudland Bank	B2	Seed Street
C3	Cannon Street	A4	Grafton Street	A1	Maudland Road	D4	Selborne Street
C1	Carlisle Street	C4	Great Avenham Street	C1	Melling Street	D1	Shaw Street
C4	Chaddock Street	B2	Great Shaw Street	B1	Moor Lane	D3	Shepherd Street
B3	Chapel Street	D3	Grimshaw Street	B3	Mount Street	B2	Snow Hill
D4	Charlotte Street	C3	Guildhall Street	A4	North Cliffe Street	A1	South Cliffe Street
B3	Charnley Street	D4	Halsbury Street	C1	North Road	D1	South Meadow Street
C3	Cheapside	B1	Harrington Street	B1	North Street	A3	Spring Bank
A3	Christchurch Street	C2	Harris Street	D3	Norwich Place	A3	Stanley Place
A3	Christian Road	B2	Heatley Street	A2	Nutter Road	C4	Starkie Street
D2	Church Row	D4	Herschell Street	D3	Oak Street	D3	Skye Hill
C3	Church Street	D1	Holstein Street	C2	Old Vicarage Street	C3	Syke Street
D4	Clarendon Street	B2	Hope Street	C2	Orchard Street	B3	Theatre Street
B2	Corporation Street	D1	Hopwood Street	C2	Ormskirk Road	B1	Walker Street
C2	Crooked Lane	C3	Jacson Street	D4	Oxford Street	A4	Walton's Parade
C3	Cross Street	D1	Jutland Street	B2	Patton Street	B1	Warwick Street
B1	Crown Street	A1	Kirkham Street	A1	Pedder Street	A4	West Cliff
D1	Deepdale Road	D3	Knowsley Street	C1	Penny Street	B3	Winckley Square
D2	Derby Street	C1	Lady Street	D2	Percy Street	B3	Winckley Street
C2	Earl Street	A2	Ladywell Street	A3	Pitt Street		
B4	East Cliff	C2	Lancaster Road	D2	Pole Street		
B4	East Cliff Road			D1	Pump Street		

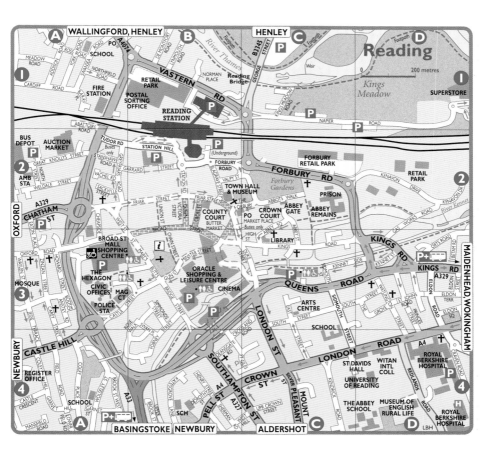

A1	Abattoirs Road	C3	East Street	A4	Lower Field Road	B2	Station Road
C2	Abbey Square	A2	Eaton Place	B1	Lynmouth Road	B3	Swan Place
C2	Abbey Street	D3	Eldon Road	A4	Mansfield Road	A1	Swansea Road
C2	Abbots Walk	D3	Eldon Square	A1	Meadow Road	D3	The Grove
A1	Addison Road	D3	Eldon Street	B3	Minster Street	A2	Tudor Road
A3	Anstey Road	D3	Eldon Terrace	C4	Mount Pleasant	B2	Union Street
A1	Barry Place	A4	Field Road	C1	Napier Road	B4	Upper Brook Street
D3	Betam Road	B4	Fobney Street	B1	Norman Place	C4	Upper Crown Street
B2	Blagrave Street	B2	Forbury Road	A2	North Street	A2	Vachel Road
A3	Body Road	B2	Friar Street	A1	Northfield Road	B2	Valpy Street
B3	Bridge Street	A4	Garnet Hill	D3	Orts Road	B1	Vastern Road
B3	Broad Street	A4	Garnet Street	A3	Oxford Road	D3	Watlington Street
A4	Brook Street West	B2	Garrard Street	B4	Pell Street	A3	Waylen Street
A1	Cardiff Road	D2	Gas Works Road	B2	Queen Victoria Street	A2	Weldale Street
A3	Carey Street	C1	George Street	C3	Queens Road	C4	West Hill
A4	Castle Crescent	A2	Great Knollys Street	D4	Redlands Road	A2	West Street
A4	Castle Hill	A2	Greyfriars Road	B3	Rose Walk	A4	Wolseley Street
A3	Castle Street	B3	Gun Street	A1	Ross Road	A1	York Road
B3	Chain Street	B4	Henry Street	A2	Sackville Street	A3	Zinzan Street
A2	Cheapside	A3	Howard Street	C4	St Giles Close		
A4	Coley Hill	A3	Jesse Terrace	D3	St Johns Road		
A4	Coley Place	B4	Katesgrove Lane	B3	St Mary's Butts		
D4	Craven Road	D2	Kenavon Drive	B4	Sherman Road		
B2	Cross Street	C4	Kendrick Road	C3	Sidmouth Street		
B4	Crossland Road	C3	Kennet Side	C4	Silver Street		
C4	Crown Street	D3	Kennet Street	B3	Simmonds Street		
B4	Deansgate Road	C1	Kings Meadow Road	C3	South Street		
B1	Demontfort Road	D3	Kings Road	B4	Southampton Street		
B4	Dorothy Street	C4	London Road	A2	Stanshawe Road		
C3	Duke Street	C3	London Street	B2	Station Hill		

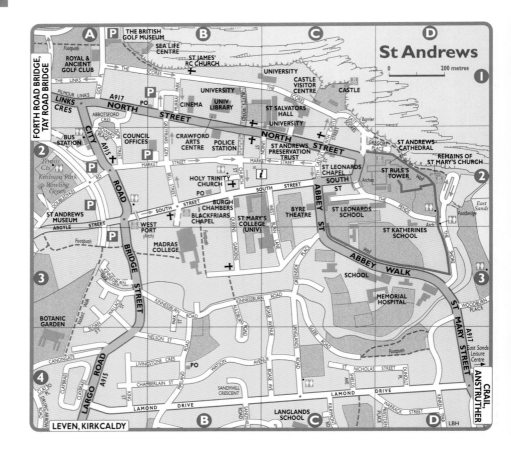

St Andrews

C2	Abbey Street	B3	Kinnessburn Road	A3	Wallace Street
C3	Abbey Walk	A3	Kinnessburn Terrace	D4	Warrack Street
A1	Abbotsford Crescent	A4	Lamond Drive	B4	Watson Avenue
A2	Argyle Street	C4	Langlands Road	C2	West Burn Lane
B3	Auldburn Road	A4	Largo Road	D3	Woodburn Place
B2	Bell Street	A1	Links Crescent	D3	Woodburn Terrace
C4	Boase Avenue	A4	Livingstone Crescent		
A3	Bridge Street	B2	Market Street		
B1	Butts Wynd	B1	Murray Park		
A4	Canongate	B4	Nelson Street		
A4	Chamberlain Street	C2	North Castle Street		
B2	Church Street	A1	North Street		
A2	City Road	B3	Park Street		
A4	Clatto Place	A1	Pilmour Links		
A4	Claybraes	B4	Pipeland Road		
A2	Doubledykes Road	D4	Priestden Place		
A4	Drumcarrow Road	B2	Queens Gardens		
D4	Dunolly Place	D3	St Mary Street		
C1	East Scores	C4	St Nicholas Street		
C4	Glebe Road	B4	Sandyhill Crescent		
A1	Golf Place	B4	Sandyhill Road		
C3	Greenside Place	C4	Shields Avenue		
C2	Gregory Place	A3	Sloan Street		
B2	Greyfriars Garden	C2	South Castle Street		
A2	Hope Street	B2	South Street		
A2	Howard Place	A1	The Links		
A3	James Street	D2	The Pends		
C4	Kilrymont Road	A1	The Scores		
A4	King Street	D3	The Shore		
D4	Kinkell Terrace	C2	Union Street		

Salisbury

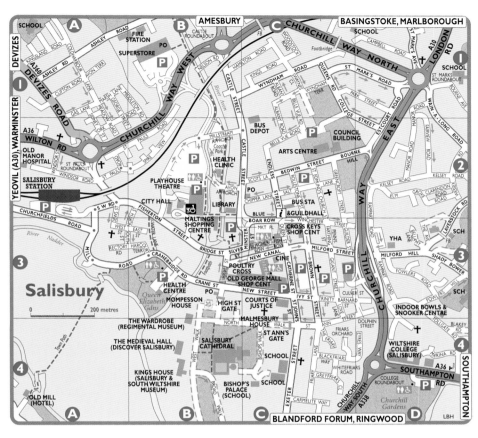

C1	Albany Road	A1	Coldharbour Lane	D2	Kelsey Road	C3	St John's Street
A1	Ashley Road	C1	College Street	C1	Kings Road	D1	St Mark's Avenue
B2	Avon Approach	B3	Crane Street	A1	Kingsland Road	C1	St Mark's Road
A1	Avon Terrace	B3	Cranebridge Road	D3	Laverstock Road	A2	St Pauls Road
C3	Barnard Street	C3	Culver Street	D1	London Road	C2	Salt Lane
C2	Bedwin Street	A1	Devizes Road	C3	Love Lane	C2	Scots Lane
D3	Bellamy Lane	A3	Dews Street	D2	Manor Road	D3	Shady Bower
C2	Belle Vue Road	D3	Dolphin Street	D4	Marina Road	A1	Sidney Street
C4	Bishops Walk	B3	East Street	C3	Market Place	B3	Silver Street
C4	Blackfriars Way	D2	Elm Grove Road	A1	Marsh Lane	B3	South Street
D4	Blakey Road	C2	Endless Street	A1	Meadow Road	A2	South Western Road
C3	Blue Boar Row	D2	Estcourt Road	A1	Middleton Road	D4	Southampton Road
D1	Bourne Avenue	C4	Exeter Street	D3	Milford Hill	C1	Swaynes Close
C2	Bourne Hill	D4	Eyres Way	C3	Milford Street	D3	The Avenue
B3	Bridge Street	D2	Fairview Road	A3	Mill Road	C4	The Friary
B4	Broad Walk	B2	Fisherton Street	B2	Millstream Approach	D4	Tollgate Road
C3	Brown Street	D3	Fowlers Hill	C3	Minster Street	C3	Trinity Street
C3	Butchers Row	D3	Fowlers Road	B1	Nelson Road	D1	Wain-A-Long Road
D1	Campbell Road	C4	Friars Orchard	C3	New Canal	D2	Wessex Road
C4	Carmelite Way	C4	Friary Lane	C3	New Street	A3	West Street
B1	Castle Street	A1	Gas Lane	B3	North Street	B4	West Walk
C3	Catherine Street	A1	George Street	B4	North Walk	C4	Whitefriars Road
C2	Chipper Lane	C3	Gigant Street	C1	Park Street	A2	Wilton Road
A2	Churchfields Road	C2	Greencroft Street	C3	Pennyfarthing Street	C3	Winchester Street
D3	Churchill Way East	C4	Greyfriars Close	C1	Queens Road	A2	Windsor Road
C1	Churchill Way North	C3	Guilder Street	D2	Rampart Road	A2	Windsor Road
C4	Churchill Way South	B1	Hamilton Road	A3	Rectory Road	C1	Woodstock Road
B2	Churchill Way West	B3	Harcourt Terrace	C2	Rollestone Street	C1	Wyndham Road
D2	Clarendon Road	B3	High Street	C4	St Ann Street	C1	Wyndham Terrace
A1	Clifton Road	C3	Ivy Street	C2	St Edmunds Church Street	A2	York Road

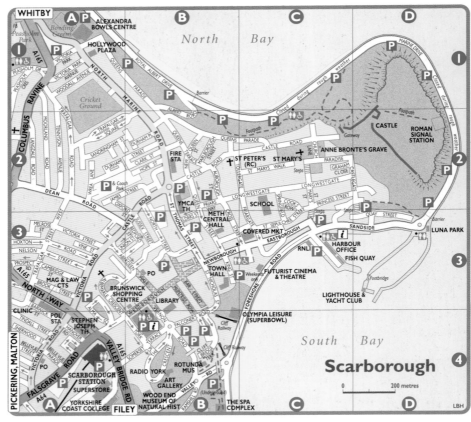

B3	Aberdeen Walk	A4	Hanover Road	B1	Royal Albert Drive	A2	Wrea Lane
A3	Albermarle Crescent	B2	Hope Street	C2	St Mary's Street	B4	York Place
B2	Albert Road	A3	Hoxton Road	C2	St Marys Walk		
A4	Alma Square	B3	Huntriss Row	B3	St Nicholas Street		
B2	Auborough Street	A2	James Street	C3	St Sepulchre Street		
B3	Bar Street	B3	King Street	B3	St Thomas Street		
A3	Barwick Street	A2	Langdale Road	A2	Sandringham Street		
B3	Bedford Street	C2	Longwestgate	D3	Sandside		
A4	Bellevue Parade	D1	Marine Drive	A4	Sherwood Street		
A4	Bellevue Street	B2	Marlborough Street	B4	Somerset Terrace		
A3	Brook Street	A3	Melrose Street	C2	Springfield		
A3	Cambridge Street	A2	Moorland Road	B3	Sussex Street		
B3	Castle Road	A3	Nelson Street	A2	Tennyson Avenue		
C2	Castlegate	B2	New Queen Street	B4	The Crescent		
C2	Church Lane	B3	Newborough	A4	Tindall Street		
B2	Clark Street	A1	North Marine Road	B2	Tollergate		
B4	Cliff Bridge Terrace	B3	North Street	A2	Trafalgar Road		
A2	Columbus Ravine	A3	North Way	A2	Trafalgar Square		
C2	Cooks Row	A2	Oxford Street	A3	Trafalgar Street West		
B3	Cross Street	C2	Paradise	A3	Union Street		
A2	Dean Road	A1	Peasholm Crescent	A4	Valley Bridge Road		
A2	Durham Street	A1	Peasholm Drive	B4	Valley Road		
C3	Eastborough	C2	Princess Street	B4	Vernon Road		
B3	Elders Street	A3	Prospect Road	A1	Victoria Park		
B4	Falconer's Road	D3	Quay Street	A1	Victoria Park Avenue		
A4	Falsgrave Road	B2	Queen Street	A4	Victoria Road		
C3	Foreshore Road	A1	Queens Parade	A3	Victoria Street		
C3	Friargate	B2	Queens Parade	A3	Vine Street		
B2	Friars Way	B2	Queens Terrace	B3	Westborough		
C2	Graham Close	B4	Ramshill Road	A1	Woodall Avenue		

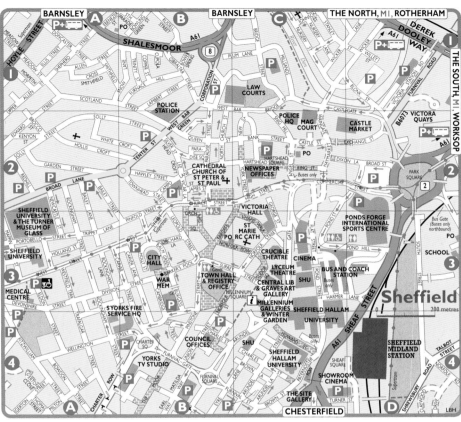

A1	Allen Street	B1	Cupola	B2	Lee Croft	A1	Shepherd Street
C2	Angel Street	A3	Devonshire Street	B3	Leopold Street	D4	Shrewsbury Road
C4	Arundel Gate	A3	Division Street	A3	Mappin Street	B2	Silver Street Head
C4	Arundel Lane	C2	Dixon Lane	B4	Matilda Way	A1	Smithfield
C4	Arundel Street	A1	Doncaster Street	A1	Meadow Street	C2	Snig Hill
A2	Bailey Lane	B4	Earl Way	A4	Milton Street	B1	Snow Lane
A2	Bailey Street	A1	Ebenezer Street	A1	Morpeth Street	A2	Solly Street
B3	Balm Green	A2	Edward Street	C2	New Street	B1	South Parade
C2	Bank Street	A4	Egerton Street	A2	Newcastle Street	D3	South Street
B3	Barker's Pool	A3	Eldon Street	D4	Norfolk Road	B1	Spring Street
D1	Blonk Street	A1	Ellis Street	B3	Norfolk Row	C1	Stanley Street
A4	Bowdon Street	D2	Exchange Street	C3	Norfolk Street	B3	Surrey Street
B1	Bowling Green Street	B4	Eyre Lane	B2	North Church Street	D4	Talbot Street
C1	Bridge Street	B3	Fargate	C1	Nursery Lane	B2	Tenter Street
A2	Broad Lane	A4	Fitzwilliam Street	C1	Nursery Street	B4	The Moor
D2	Broad Street	C3	Flat Street	B3	Orchard Lane	A4	Thomas Street
A2	Brocco Street	B1	Furnace Hill	B3	Orchard Square	B2	Townhead Street
C4	Brown Lane	B4	Furnival Gate	B2	Paradise Square	A4	Trafalgar Street
C4	Brown Street	D1	Furnival Road	B2	Paradise Street	B1	Trinity Street
B3	Burgess Street	B4	Furnival Street	D2	Park Square	A3	Trippet Lane
B3	Cambridge Street	A2	Garden Street	C4	Paternoster Row	C3	Tudor Square
B2	Campo Lane	C2	George Street	B3	Pinfold Street	B4	Union Street
B3	Carver Lane	B1	Gibraltar Street	B4	Pinstone Street	A1	Upper Allen Street
B3	Carver Street	C3	Harmer Lane	B1	Plum Lane	C2	Vicar Lane
C2	Castle Street	C2	Hartshead	D3	Pond Hill	D1	Victoria Station Road
C1	Castlegate	B2	Hawley Street	C3	Pond Street	C2	Waingate
C3	Chapel Walk	C2	Haymarket	A3	Portobello Street	A4	Wellington Street
B4	Charles Street	C2	High Street	B2	Queen Street	B1	West Bar
A4	Charter Row	A3	Holland Street	A3	Rockingham Lane	B2	West Bar Green
B4	Charter Square	A2	Hollis Croft	A2	Rockingham Street	A3	West Street
B2	Church Street	B3	Holly Street	B1	Russell Street	A3	Westfield Terrace
D4	Claywood Drive	A1	Hoyle Street	B2	St James Street	A2	White Croft
C2	Commercial Street	C1	Johnson Street	A1	Scotland Street	D1	Wicker
B1	Copper Street	A2	Kenyon Street	B1	Shalesmoor	C1	Wicker Lane
B1	Corporation Street	C2	King Street	C4	Sheaf Square	D1	Willey Street
A1	Cross Smithfield	B1	Lambert Street	D4	Sheaf Street	C2	York Street

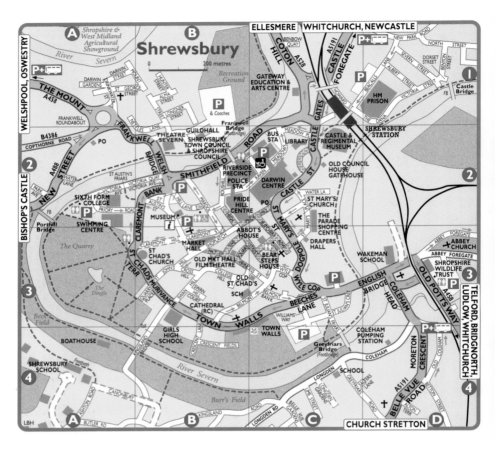

D3	Abbey Foregate	A1	Darwin Gardens	D3	Old Potts Way	A2	Water Lane
D1	Albert Street	A1	Darwin Street	A2	Park Avenue	C2	Water Lane
B1	Alma Street	C3	Dogpole	C2	Pride Hill	B2	Welsh Bridge
D4	Alton Terrace	D1	Dorset Street	B3	Princess Street	C3	William's Way
A4	Ashton Road	A1	Drinkwater Street	A2	Priory Road	C3	Wyle Cop
D1	Beacalls Lane	D3	English Bridge	B3	Quarry Place		
C3	Beeches Lane	A2	Frankwell	C2	Raven Meadows		
C4	Belle Vue Gardens	C4	Greyfriars Road	B2	Roushill		
D4	Belle Vue Road	B2	High Street	A2	St Austin's Friars		
B3	Belmont	B2	Hill Lane	B2	St Austin's Street		
C3	Belmont Bank	C1	Howard Street	B3	St Chads Terrace		
C1	Benbow Quay	B1	Hunter Street	A1	St George Street		
D1	Benyon Street	B4	Kingsland Bridge	B3	St John's Hill		
D4	Betton Street	B4	Kingsland Road	C3	St Julian's Crescent		
C3	Butchers Row	C4	Lime Street	C3	St Julian's Friars		
A4	Butler Road	C4	Longden Coleham	C2	St Mary's Place		
A4	Canonbury	C4	Longden Gardens	C2	St Mary's Street		
C1	Castle Foregate	C4	Longden Road	C4	Salters Lane		
C2	Castle Gates	B1	Longner Street	D1	Severn Street		
C2	Castle Street	B2	Mardol	B3	Shoplatch		
B2	Claremont Bank	B3	Market Street	B2	Smithfield Road		
B3	Claremont Hill	C2	Meadow Place	B3	Swan Hill		
B3	Claremont Street	D4	Moreton Crescent	B3	Swan Hill Court		
D3	Coleham Head	B1	Mount Street	D1	The Dana		
B3	College Hill	B3	Murivance	A1	The Mount		
A2	Copthorne Road	A1	Nettles Lane	B3	The Square		
C1	Coton Hill	D1	New Park Road	B3	Town Walls		
B4	Crescent Fields	A2	New Street	A2	Victoria Avenue		
B4	Crescent Lane	D1	North Street	B2	Victoria Quay		
B3	Cross Hill	D4	Old Coleham	D1	Victoria Street		

Southampton

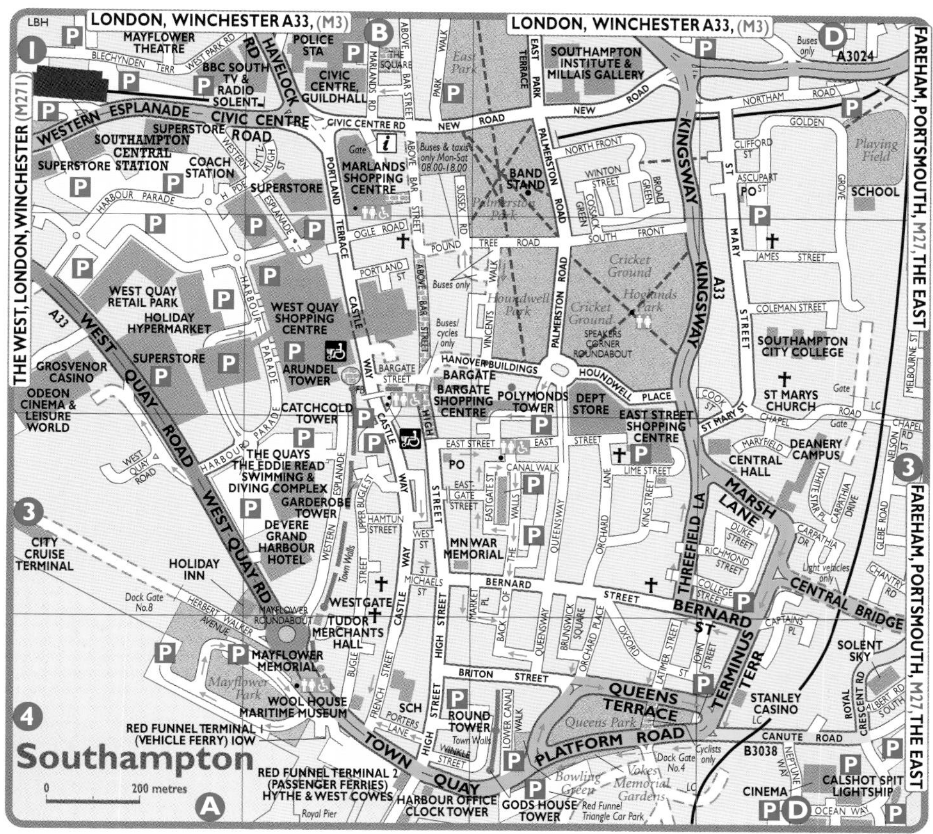

B1	Above Bar Street	B4	French Street	C4	Oxford Street
D4	Albert Road South	D3	Glebe Road	C1	Palmerston Road
D1	Ascupart Street	D1	Golden Grove	B1	Park Walk
C4	Back of the Walls	B3	Hamtun Street	C4	Platform Road
B2	Bargate Street	B2	Hanover Buildings	B4	Porters Lane
C3	Bernard Street	A1	Harbour Parade	B2	Portland Street
A1	Blechynden Terrace	B1	Havelock Road	B1	Portland Terrace
C4	Briton Street	A3	Herbert Walker Avenue	B2	Pound Tree Road
C1	Broad Green	B4	High Street	C4	Queens Terrace
C4	Brunswick Square	C2	Houndwell Place	C4	Queensway
B4	Bugle Street	D2	James Street	D3	Richmond Street
C3	Canal Walk	D4	John Street	D4	Royal Crescent Road
D4	Canute Road	C3	King Street	D1	St Mary Street
D4	Captains Place	C1	Kingsway	B3	St Michaels Street
D3	Carpathia Drive	C4	Latimer Street	A1	Southbrook Road
B2	Castle Way	C3	Lime Street	C2	South Front
D3	Central Bridge	C4	Lower Canal Walk	B1	Sussex Road
D3	Chantry Road	C3	Market Place	D4	Terminus Terrace
D3	Chapel Road	D3	Marsh Lane	B1	The Square
A1	Civic Centre Road	D3	Maryfield	C3	Threefield Lane
D1	Clifford Street	D2	Melbourne Street	B4	Town Quay
D2	Coleman Street	D3	Nelson Street	B3	Upper Bugle Street
D3	College Street	D4	Neptune Way	C2	Vincents Walk
D2	Cook Street	B1	New Road	B1	West Marlands Road
C1	Cossack Green	C1	North Front	A1	West Park Road
D3	Duke Street	D1	Northam Road	A2	West Quay Road
C1	East Park Terrace	D4	Ocean Way	B3	West Street
B3	East Street	B2	Ogle Road	A1	Western Esplanade
B3	Eastgate Street	C3	Orchard Lane	B4	Winkle Street
B1	Fitzhugh Street	C4	Orchard Place	C1	Winton Street
				D3	White Star Place

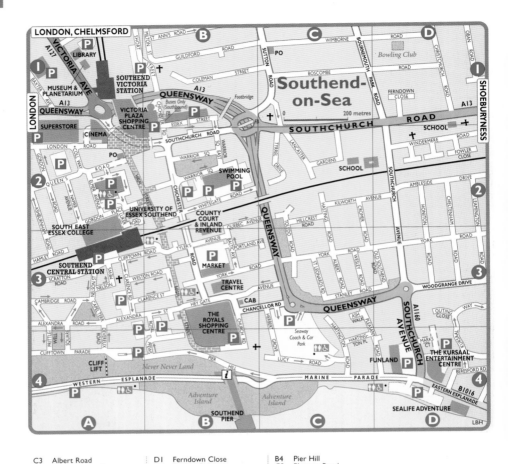

C3	Albert Road
A3	Alexandra Road
A3	Alexandra Street
D2	Ambleside Drive
C3	Ash Walk
A2	Ashburnham Road
B3	Baltic Avenue
A1	Baxter Avenue
D4	Beresford Road
C1	Boscombe Road
C1	Bournemouth Park Road
A3	Cambridge Road
A3	Capel Terrace
B3	Chancellor Road
D2	Cheltenham Road
B1	Chichester Road
D1	Christchurch Road
B3	Church Road
A3	Clarence Road
B3	Clarence Street
A4	Clifftown Parade
A3	Clifftown Road
B1	Coleman Street
A2	College Way
C2	Cromer Road
A4	Devereux Road
A2	Elmer Avenue
D4	Eastern Esplanade
B1	Essex Street
D1	Ferndown Close
D2	Fowler Close
A2	Gordon Place
A2	Gordon Road
B1	Guildford Road
A3	Hamlet Road
C4	Hartington Place
C4	Hartington Road
C2	Hastings Road
C3	Herbert Grove
B3	Heygate Avenue
B3	High Street
C2	Hillcrest Road
D2	Honiton Road
C2	Kilworth Avenue
D4	Kursaal Way
C2	Lancaster Gardens
D2	Leamington Road
A2	London Road
C4	Lucy Road
A2	Luker Road
C4	Marine Parade
D4	Marks Court
B1	Milton Street
A2	Napier Avenue
A3	Nelson Mews
A3	Nelson Street
D1	Oban Road
D3	Old Southend Road
D3	Outing Close
B4	Pier Hill
C3	Pleasant Road
B3	Portland Avenue
A4	Prittlewell Square
B2	Quebec Avenue
A2	Queen's Road
A1	Queensway
B4	Royal Mews
B1	St Ann's Road
C3	St Leonards Road
A3	Scratton Road
A1	Short Street
D2	Southchurch Avenue
B2	Southchurch Road
C3	Stanley Road
C1	Sutton Road
C2	Toledo Road
B3	Tylers Avenue
C2	Tyrrel Drive
A1	Victoria Avenue
B2	Warrior Square East
B2	Warrior Square
C3	Wesley Road
A4	Western Esplanade
A3	Weston Road
B2	Whitegate Road
C1	Wimborne Road
D2	Windermere Road
D3	Woodgrange Drive
B3	York Road

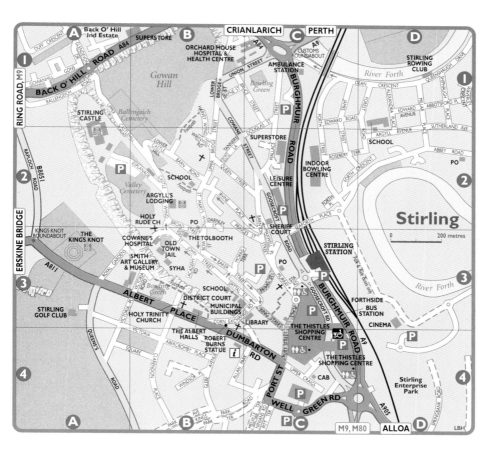

D2	Abbey Road
D1	Abbotsford Place
B4	Abercromby Place
B3	Academy Road
B3	Albert Place
D1	Alexandra Place
B4	Allan Park
D2	Argyll Avenue
A1	Back O' Hill Road
B3	Baker Street
A1	Ballengeich Road
B2	Barn Road
C2	Barnton Street
B1	Bayne Street
B3	Bow Street
B2	Broad Street
C1	Bruce Street
C1	Burghmuir Road
B2	Castle Wynd
B4	Clarendon Place
B3	Corn Exchange Road
B1	Cowane Street
B2	Darnley Street
D1	Dean Crescent
C2	Douglas Street
A1	Duff Crescent
C4	Dumbarton Road
D1	Edward Avenue
C1	Edward Road
B2	Esplanade

D1	Forest Road
C2	Forth Crescent
C2	Forth Place
C1	Forth Street
C3	Friars Street
B4	Glebe Avenue
A1	Glendevon Drive
C2	Goosecroft Road
A1	Gowanhill Gardens
B1	Harvey Wynd
B2	Irvine Place
C1	James Street
C3	King Street
B4	Kings Park Road
B1	Lower Bridge Street
B2	Lower Castle Hill
C3	Maxwell Place
C4	Melville Terrace
D1	Millar Place
B3	Morris Terrace
C3	Murray Place
C4	Ninians Road
B4	Park Avenue
B4	Park Terrace
C4	Pitt Terrace
C4	Port Street
B3	Princes Street
B2	Queen Street
D1	Queenshaugh Drive
A4	Queen's Road

A2	Raploch Road
C2	Rosebery Terrace
A3	Royal Gardens
B3	St John Street
B2	St Mary's Wynd
C2	Seaforth Place
D1	Shiphaugh Place
B3	Spittal Street
D4	Springbank Road
C3	Station Road
D1	Sutherland Avenue
B2	Tannery Lane
B1	Union Street
B2	Upper Bridge Street
A1	Upper Castlehill
C4	Upper Craigs
A3	Victoria Place
B3	Victoria Road
B4	Victoria Square
C2	Wallace Street
D1	Waverley Crescent
C4	Well Green Road
B2	Whinwell Road
B4	Windsor Place

Stockton-on-Tees

200 metres

B3	Albion Street	A4	Eleanor Place	A1	Phoenix Sidings	A1	Vicarage Street
B1	Allison Street	A4	Edward Street	C1	Portrack Lane	C1	Wade Avenue
B1	Alma Street	A3	Ewbank Drive	B3	Prince Regent Street	A3	Webster Close
D3	Anchorage Mews	B3	Finkle Street	C1	Princess Avenue	B2	Wellington Square
C1	Bath Lane	B1	Frederick Street	D4	Princess Street	A2	Wellington Street
A1	Bedford Street	D3	Fudan Way	D4	Princeton Drive	B3	West Row
B2	Bishop Street	B1	Garbutt Street	D3	Radcliffe Crescent	A4	Westbourne Street
A1	Bishopton Lane	A4	Grove Street	C3	Riverside	B4	Westcott Street
A1	Bishopton Road	A3	Hartington Road	D4	Robert Street	C3	Westpoint Road
C4	Boathouse Lane	D3	Harvard Avenue	B2	Russell Street	A4	Whitwell Close
A4	Bowesfield Lane	B2	High Street	C1	Ryan Avenue	B3	William Street
B3	Bridge Road	B1	Hume Street	A3	St Bernard Road	A4	Woodland Street
B2	Bright Street	A2	Hutchison Street	B1	St Johns Close	A3	Worthing Street
B3	Brunswick Street	A4	Lawrence Street	C3	St Marks Court	D3	Yale Crescent
A3	Buchanan Street	B2	Leeds Street	A1	Samuel Street	A4	Yarm Lane
A2	Burgess Street	A4	Lightfoot Grove	A2	Scarth Walk	A4	Yarm Road
A2	California Close	D1	Limeoak Way	A4	Shaftesbury Street		
B2	Carlton Close	D4	Mandale Road	B2	Silver Street		
C1	Cedar Street	A3	Manfield Street	B3	Skinner Street		
B4	Chalk Close	C1	Maritime Road	B2	Smith Street		
D4	Chapel Street	D3	Massey Road	C4	Sorbonne Close		
B2	Church Road	A2	Melbourne Street	A1	Stamp Street		
D4	Claremont Court	A2	Mill Street West	C3	Stanford Close		
C1	Clarence Row	C1	Neasham Close	D4	Station Street		
C3	Columbia Drive	A4	Northcote Street	D4	Stephenson Street		
C2	Commercial Street	B1	Norton Road	A2	Sydney Street		
A2	Corporation Street	A4	Outram Street	A3	Tarring Street		
C2	Council of Europe	A4	Oxbridge Lane	B2	The Square		
	Boulevard	A2	Palmerston Street	C2	Thistle Green		
B1	Cromwell Avenue	A4	Park Road	B3	Tower Street		
A2	Derby Street	B3	Park Terrace	D3	Trinity Mews		
A2	Dixon Street	B4	Parkfield Road	B4	Trinity Street		
A3	Dovecot Street	B4	Parkfield Way	C1	Union Street East		
A1	Dunmail Road	B4	Parliament Street	D3	University Boulevard		
A1	Durham Road	B4	Pearson Walk	C3	Vasser Way		
A1	Durham Street	A2	Petch Street	A1	Vicarage Avenue		

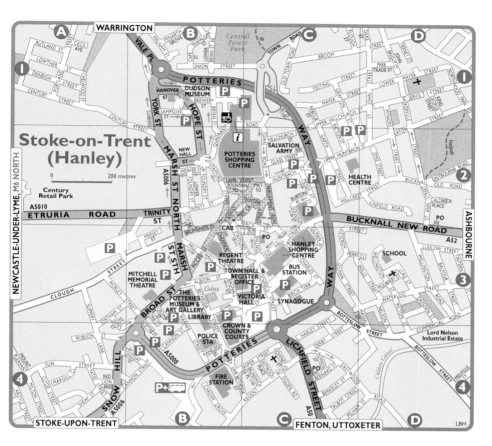

B3	Albion Street
C1	Arbour Street
A4	Argyle Street
B3	Bagnall Street
D3	Balfour Street
D1	Baskerville Street
C4	Berkeley Street
C4	Bernard Street
B3	Bethesda Street
C3	Birch Terrace
C3	Botteslow Street
B1	Brewery Street
B3	Broad Street
C1	Broom Street
C4	Brunswick Place
B3	Brunswick Street
B1	Bryan Street
D2	Bucknall New Road
D2	Bucknall Old Road
C2	Burton Place
D2	Caldbeck Place
B4	Cannon Street
B1	Cape Street
B4	Cardiff Grove
A1	Cecil Avenue
A1	Century Street
C3	Charles Street
B3	Cheapside
A1	Chelwood Street
A3	Clough Street
A4	Clyde Street
D4	Commercial Road
B3	Crown Street
A1	Denbigh Street
C4	Derby Street
D1	Dilke Street

C4	Downey Street
D3	Dresden Street
D2	Dyke Street
D2	Eastbourne Road
C4	Eastwood Place
C4	Eastwood Road
D2	Eaton Street
A2	Etruria Road
C1	Festing Street
B2	Foundry Street
B2	Fountain Square
C2	Free Trade Street
C2	Garth Street
C3	Gilman Street
B2	Gitana Street
C2	Glass Street
C2	Goodson Street
C1	Grafton Street
B1	Hanover Street
C4	Harley Street
D3	Hassall Street
C2	Hillchurch Street
C2	Hillcrest Street
B1	Hope Street
C3	Hordley Street
C4	Howson Street
C2	Huntbach Street
C4	Jasper Street
D1	Jervis Street
D1	John Bright Street
B3	John Street
D1	King George Street
B2	Lamb Street
C3	Lichfield Street
B4	Lindsay Street
D2	Linfield Road

B4	Lower Bethesda Street
B1	Lower Bryan Street
B2	Lower Foundry Street
D1	Lower Mayer Street
A1	Lowther Street
D3	Ludlow Street
D3	Luke Street
B1	Malnam Street
A4	Margill Close
C2	Market Lane
C2	Market Square
B2	Marsh Street North
B3	Marsh Street South
C1	Mayer Street
C2	Meigh Street
D4	Melville Street
B3	Mersey Street
A4	Milton Street
A3	Morley Street
A4	Mount Pleasant
D3	Mulberry Street
D1	Mynors Street
D3	Nelson Place
B2	New Hall Street
C4	Ogden Road
C3	Old Hall Street
C1	Old Town Road
B3	Orb Street
B3	Pall Mall
C2	Parliament Row
C4	Pelham Street
B1	Penarth Grove
C2	Percy Street
C3	Perry Close
B3	Piccadilly

D3	Picton Street
C1	Plough Street
A1	Portland Street
B1	Potteries Way
B2	Quadrant Road
B4	Raneleigh Street
C2	Ratton Street
A4	Red Lion Pass
C4	Regent Road
A4	Robson Street
A1	Rutland Street
D2	St Ann Street
A3	St James Street
D1	St John Street
B1	Sampson Street
B4	Sceptre Street
A4	Sheaf Street
A3	Slippery Lane
A4	Snow Hill
B3	Stafford Street
A3	Statham Street
A4	Sun Street
C4	Talbot Street
D1	Tierney Street
D3	Tintern Street
C3	Tontine Square
C3	Tontine Street
C2	Town Road
B1	Trafalgar Street
B2	Trinity Street
B1	Union Street
C1	Upper Hillchurch Street
C2	Upper Huntbach Street
B1	Vale Place

B3	Warner Street
D3	Waterloo Street
B2	Weaver Street
D3	Wellington Road
D3	Wells Street
A4	Yates Street
B1	York Street

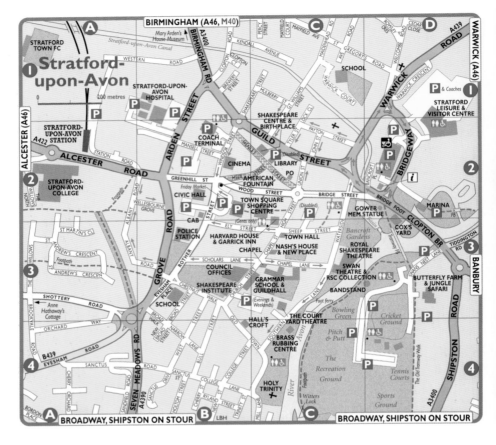

Stratford-upon-Avon

A3 Albany Road
A2 Alcester Road
B2 Arden Street
C1 Avenue Road
D2 Bancroft Place
B1 Birmingham Road
A4 Bordon Place
B1 Brewery Street
D2 Bridge Foot
C2 Bridge Street
D2 Bridgeway
B3 Broad Street
B3 Broad Walk
A3 Brookvale Road
B4 Bull Street
D1 Cedar Close
C3 Chapel Lane
C3 Chapel Street
A4 Cherry Orchard
B4 Cherry Street
B3 Chestnut Walk
B3 Church Street
D3 Clopton Bridge
B1 Clopton Court
B1 Clopton Road
B4 College Lane
B4 College Street
B3 Ely Street
B3 Evesham Place
A4 Evesham Road
C1 Great Williams Street
B2 Greenhill Street
B3 Grove Road
C2 Guild Street
B2 Henley Street
C2 High Street
B4 Holtom Street
C2 John Street
B1 Kendall Avenue
C1 Lock Close
C1 Maidenhead Road
B2 Mansell Street
C1 Mayfield Avenue
C1 Mayfield Court
B2 Meer Street
C4 Mill Lane
C1 Mulberry Street
B4 Narrow Lane
B4 New Broad Street
B4 New Street
B3 Old Town
A4 Orchard Way
C2 Payton Street
C1 Percy Street
B3 Rother Street
D1 Rowley Crescent
B4 Ryland Street
A3 St Andrew's Crescent
C1 St Gregory's Road
A3 St Martin's Close
B4 Sanctus Drive
A4 Sanctus Road
B4 Sanctus Street
A4 Sandfield Road
B3 Scholars Lane
A4 Seven Meadows Road
B1 Shakespeare Street
C3 Sheep Street
D4 Shipston Road
A3 Shottery Road
C4 Southern Lane
A2 Station Road
D3 Swans Nest Lane
A3 The Willows
A2 The Willows North
D3 Tiddington Road
B4 Trinity Street
C2 Tyler Street
C2 Union Street
C1 Warwick Court
D1 Warwick Crescent
D1 Warwick Road
C3 Waterside
D1 Welcombe Road
B2 Wellesbourne Grove
B4 West Street
A1 Western Road
B2 Windsor Street
B2 Wood Street

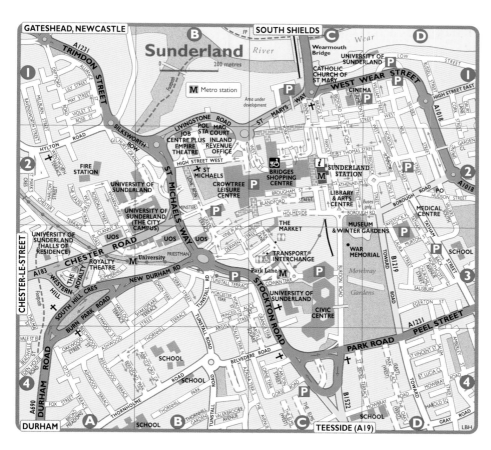

B4	Abbotsford Grove	D3	Egerton Street	A4	Oakwood Street	A4	Thornholme Road
B3	Alice Street	A3	Elmwood Street	A4	Otto Terrace	D3	Toward Road
C4	Argyle Square	C2	Fawcett Street	C1	Pann Lane	A1	Trimdon Street
B3	Argyle Street	A4	Fox Street	C3	Park Lane	B3	Tunstall Road
A4	Ashwood Street	D2	Foyle Street	D4	Park Place East	B3	Tunstall Terrace
A4	Ashwood Terrace	D2	Frederick Street	D4	Park Place West	A4	Vale Street East
C2	Athenaeum Street	A2	Gilhurst Grange	C4	Park Road	B4	Valerbrooke Avenue
B4	Azalea Terrace North	C4	Gorse Road	D3	Peel Street	B3	Vine Place
B4	Azalea Terrace South	C3	Grange Terrace	B3	Princess Street	A1	Violet Street
A4	Beachville Street	D4	Gray Road	A1	Ravensworth Street	A2	Wentworth Terrace
C1	Bedford Street	B2	Green Terrace	A1	Rose Street	C2	West Street
A4	Beechwood Street	A2	Harlow Street	A2	Rosedale Street	C1	West Wear Street
A4	Beechwood Terrace	D4	Harold Square	D1	Russell Street	A2	Westbourne Road
B4	Belvedere Road	A3	Havelock Terrace	C4	St Bedes Terrace	A3	Western Hill
A4	Beresford Park	D1	High Street East	D4	St Lucia Close	A2	Wharncliffe Street
C2	Blandford Street	B2	High Street West	A2	St Mark's Crescent	D1	William Street
C2	Borough Road	C1	High Street West	C1	St Marys Way	B3	Worcester Street
C1	Bridge Street	C2	Holmeside	B2	St Michaels Way	B3	Worcester Terrace
A4	Broad Meadows	D2	Hudson Street	C2	St Thomas Street	C2	York Street
C2	Brougham Street	A2	Hylton Road	D4	St Vincent Street		
C3	Burdon Road	C2	John Street	D4	Salem Street		
A4	Burn Park Road	C1	Lambton Street	B3	Shakespeare Terrace		
C4	Carlton Street	D3	Laura Street	A2	Silksworth Row		
A3	Chester Road	A1	Lily Street	A3	South Hill Crescent		
A2	Chester Terrace	B1	Livingstone Road	D2	Spring Garden Close		
D3	Churchill Street	C4	Lorne Terrace	C3	Stockton Road		
A3	Clanny Street	B2	Low Row	A3	Summerhill		
D1	Cork Street	D1	Low Street	D2	Tavistock Place		
C3	Cowan Terrace	A1	May Street	C4	The Avenue		
A1	Deptford Road	A1	Millburn Street	C4	The Elms		
B3	Derby Street	D4	Mowbray Road	C4	The Elms West		
B3	Derwent Street	D3	Murton Street	A2	The Leazes		
D1	Drury Lane	B3	New Durham Road	D4	The Oaks West		
A4	Durham Road	D2	Nile Street	A3	The Royalty		
A4	Eden House Road	D2	Norfolk Street	A3	Thelma Street		
B3	Edwin Terrace	D3	Northcote Avenue	B4	Thornhill Gardens		

Swansea

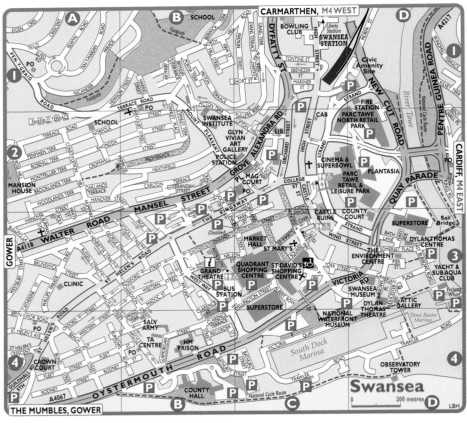

C3 Albert Row
C2 Alexandra Road
A3 Argyle Street
D3 Bath Lane
B4 Bathurst Street
A4 Beach Street
C2 Belle Vue Way
D2 Benthall Place
B1 Berwick Terrace
A4 Bond Street
A2 Brooklands Terrace
A3 Brunswick Street
B1 Brynsifi Terrace
A3 Burman Street
D3 Burrows Place
A4 Burrows Road
C3 Caer Street
D3 Cambrian Place
B2 Carlton Terrace
C3 Castle Square
C2 Castle Street
A3 Catherine Street
B3 Clarence Street
B4 Clarence Terrace
C2 Clifton Hill
C2 College Street
A2 Constitution Hill
B2 Craddock Street
A3 Crole Street
A2 Cromwell Street
B2 Dock Union Street
A3 Duke Street
C1 Dyfatty Street
D3 East Burrows Road
C1 Ebenezer Street
A1 Eigen Crescent
A1 Elfed Road
C1 Evans Terrace
A2 Fairfield Terrace
D3 Ferry Side
B1 Firm Street
A4 Fleet Street
C2 Fullers Row
A3 George Street
B4 Glamorgan Street
D3 Gloucester Place
C1 Graig Terrace
C2 Grove Place
A4 Guildhall Road South
A3 Hanover Street
B2 Harcourt Street
B2 Heathfield
A3 Henrietta Street
A1 Hewson Street
C1 High Street
B1 Hill Street
A2 Humphrey Street
A1 Islwyn Road
D1 Kilvey Terrace
B3 Madoc Street
B2 Mansel Street
C1 Mariner Street
B1 Milton Terrace
A2 Montpellier Terrace
D1 Morfa Street
B2 Mount Pleasant
B3 Nelson Street
D1 New Cut Road
A1 Nicander Parade
B3 Nicholl Street
A2 Norfolk Street
B1 North Hill
A2 Oaklands Terrace
C2 Orchard Street
A4 Oxford Street
A4 Oystermouth Road
B3 Page Street
C3 Park Street
A1 Pen-y-Graig Road
A2 Penmaen Terrace
D2 Pentre Guinea Road
A3 Phillips Parade
B1 Picton Terrace
D3 Pier Street
B3 Plymouth Street
C2 Portland Street
B1 Portia Terrace
B2 Primrose Hill
C3 Princess Way
B2 Promenade
D2 Quay Parade
B4 Recorder Street
A2 Rhondda Street
B3 Richardson Street
A4 Rodney Street
A2 Rose Hill
A2 Rosehill Terrace
A3 Russell Street
A4 St Helen's Avenue
A4 St Helen's Crescent
A3 St Helen's Road
C3 St Mary Street
C3 St Mary's Square
C1 Short Street
D3 Somerset Place
B4 Spring Terrace
B2 Stanley Place
C2 Strand
A1 Tan-y-Marian Road
A1 Teilo Crescent
A2 Terrace Road
B3 The Kingsway
C1 Tontine Street
C4 Trawler Road
B3 Union Street
B2 Verandah Street
C4 Victoria Quay
C3 Victoria Road
A4 Vincent Street
A3 Walter Road
C1 Watkin Street
C3 Wellington Street
A3 Westbury Street
A4 Western Street
B3 West Way
A2 White Street
B3 William Street
C3 Wind Street
D1 Windmill Terrace
A2 Woodlands Terrace
C3 York Street

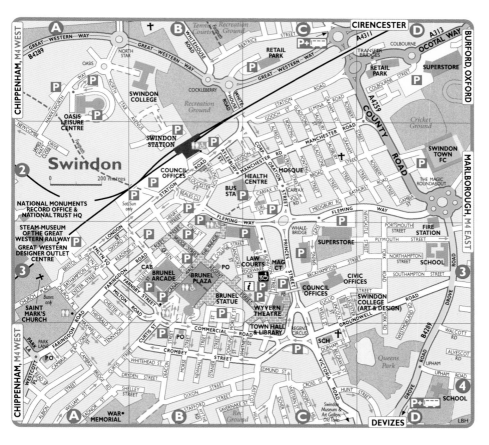

A4	Albion Street	B4	Dowling Street	B3	King Street	C1	Salisbury Street
C2	Alfred Street	D4	Drove Road	C3	Leicester Street	B3	Sandford Street
D4	Alvescot Road	B4	Dryden Street	C3	Lincoln Street	B4	Savernake Street
B2	Aylesbury Street	C4	Durham Street	A3	London Street	A4	Shelley Street
A3	Bathampton Street	C4	Eastcott Hill	A4	Lorne Street	D3	Southampton Street
C2	Bathurst Road	C3	Edgeware Road	C2	Manchester Road	B4	Stafford Street
B2	Beales Close	C4	Edmund Street	A4	Maxwell Street	B4	Stanier Street
C1	Beatrice Street	C1	Elmina Road	C2	Medgbury Road	B2	Station Road
C3	Beckhampton Street	A3	Emlyn Square	A3	Milton Road	A4	Tennyson Street
C4	Belgrave Street	C3	Euclid Street	B3	Morley Street	B3	The Parade
B2	Bridge Street	A3	Exeter Street	B4	Morse Street	A3	Theobald Street
A3	Bristol Street	A4	Faringdon Road	D3	Newcastle Street	C2	Turl Street
C2	Broad Street	A3	Farnsby Street	A2	Newcombe Drive	D4	Upham Road
A4	Cambria Bridge Road	B3	Fleet Street	B4	Newhall Street	C4	Victoria Road
A4	Cambria Place	B2	Fleming Way	A1	North Star Avenue	B3	Villett Street
B3	Canal Walk	D2	Gambia Street	D3	Northampton Street	C2	Volta Road
C2	Carfax Street	C1	Gladstone Street	D1	Ocotal Way	D4	Walcott Road
A3	Chester Street	B2	Gloucester Street	A3	Oxford Street	B2	Wellington Street
A3	Church Place	C1	Gooch Street	A4	Park Lane	C3	Wells Street
D1	Colbourne Street	C1	Graham Street	D3	Plymouth Street	A4	Westcott Place
B3	College Street	A1	Great Western Way	C2	Ponting Street	C4	Western Street
B4	Commercial Road	C3	Groundwell Road	D3	Portsmouth Street	D4	Westmorland Road
C2	Corporation Street	B3	Havelock Street	C3	Princes Street	B4	Whitehead Street
D1	County Road	A1	Hawksworth Way	C4	Prospect Hill	B1	Whitehouse Road
B4	Crombey Street	C2	Haydon Street	B3	Queen Street	C4	Whitney Street
C4	Cross Street	B2	Henry Street	A4	Radnor Street	A4	William Street
A4	Curtis Street	C4	Hunt Street	A4	Read Street	D3	York Road
B4	Deacon Street	B4	Hythe Road	A3	Reading Street		
B4	Dixon Street	C3	Islington Street	B3	Regent Street		
C4	Dover Street	A2	James Watt Close	C1	Rosebery Street		

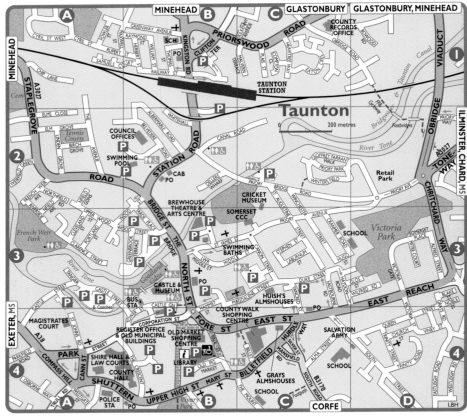

B2	Albermarle Road	B4	Fore Street	C1	Plas Street	B4	Upper High Street
D3	Alfred Street	A1	Fowler Street	A3	Portland Street	A3	Upper Wood Street
C4	Alma Street	A2	French Weir Avenue	B1	Priorswood Road	D3	Victoria Gate
B2	Belvedere Road	C2	Geoffrey Farrant Walk	C3	Priory Avenue	D4	Victoria Street
C4	Billet Street	D3	Gloucester Street	C2	Priory Bridge Road	D4	Viney Street
C4	Billetfield	D4	Grays Road	C2	Priory Park	A2	Weirfield Green
A2	Birch Grove	B3	Greenbrook Terrace	D2	Priory Way	A4	Westgate Street
D3	Blake Street	B1	Greenway Avenue	D4	Queen Street	D4	Westleigh Road
D1	Bowood Road	B3	Hammet Street	B1	Railway Street	B2	Whitehall
B3	Bridge Street	C3	Haydon Road	B1	Raymond Street	D3	Wilfred Road
B2	Canal Road	C1	Heavitree Way	A2	Riverside	B1	William Street
A4	Cann Street	B1	Herbert Street	A1	Rupert Street	C3	Winchester Street
C3	Canon Street	C3	Hugo Street	C3	St Augustine Street	C2	Winters Field
B3	Castle Green	C4	Hurdle Way	B3	St James Street	B3	Wood Street
A3	Castle Street	B1	Kingston Road	A4	St Johns Road	B3	Yarde Place
A1	Chip Lane	C3	Laburnum Street	A1	Samuels Court		
D4	Church Street	A2	Linden Grove	A4	Shuttern		
A3	Clarence Street	B3	Lower Middle Street	C4	Silver Street		
A3	Cleveland Street	C3	Magdalene Street	D3	Somerset Place		
B1	Clifton Terrace	C4	Malvern Terrace	C4	South Road		
A4	Compass Hill	C4	Mansfield Road	D4	South Street		
C1	Compton Close	B4	Mary Street	A1	Staplegrove Road		
B4	Corporation Street	A1	Maxwell Street	B2	Station Road		
C3	Cranmer Road	B3	Middle Street	C3	Stephen Street		
D2	Critchard Way	D3	Noble Street	C3	Tancred Street		
A1	Cyril Street	B3	North Street	A3	Tangier		
A1	Cyril Street West	A2	Northfield Avenue	A2	The Avenue		
B2	Dellers Wharf	A2	Northfield Gardens	B3	The Bridge		
C3	Duke Street	A2	Northfield Road	B4	The Crescent		
D3	East Reach	C1	Obridge Road	C4	The Mount		
C4	East Street	D2	Obridge Viaduct	B1	Thomas Street		
C3	Eastbourne Road	B4	Old Pig Market	D2	Toneway		
D4	Eastleigh Road	A4	Osborne Way	B4	Tower Street		
C1	Eaton Crescent	A4	Park Street	D4	Trinity Road		
A2	Elm Grove	A4	Parkfield Road	D4	Trinity Street		
A2	Elms Close	B4	Paul Street	A4	Trull Road		

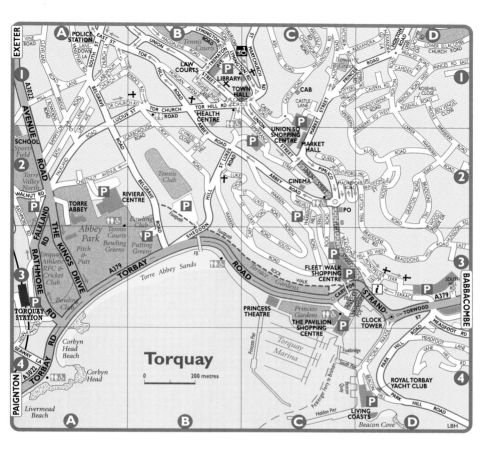

Torquay

0   200 metres

B2	Abbey Road	B2	Croft Hill
D1	Alexandra Lane	B2	Croft Road
D1	Alexandra Road	B2	Cypress Close
D2	Alpine Road	A1	East Street
C1	Ash Hill Road	C1	Ellacombe Road
A1	Avenue Road	A3	Falkland Road
A2	Bampfylde Road	C3	Fleet Street
A2	Bath Lane	D2	Grafton Road
D4	Beacon Hill	A4	Hennapyn Road
A1	Belgrave Road	B1	Higher Union Lane
D1	Ben Venge Close	D2	Hillesdon Road
D3	Braddons Hill Road	D1	Hoxton Road
D3	Braddons Hill Road East	D3	Hunsdon Road
D3	Braddons Hill Road West	A1	Laburnum Street
		A1	Lansdown Lane
D2	Braddons Street	A2	Lime Avenue
A1	Bridge Road	D1	Lower Ellacombe
D1	Camden Road		Church Road
C3	Cary Parade	D2	Lower Warberry Road
C2	Cary Road	A1	Lucius Street
B1	Castle Circus	B1	Lymington Road
C1	Castle Lane	C2	Madrepore Road
C1	Castle Road	B1	Magdalene Road
D1	Cavern Road	C1	Market Street
C1	Chatsworth Road	D4	Meadfoot Lane
A2	Chestnut Avenue	D3	Meadfoot Road
A1	Church Lane	C2	Melville Street
A1	Church Street	D1	Middle Warberry Road
A1	Cleveland Road	A1	Mill Lane
D2	Clifton Terrace	D3	Montpelier Terrace
B1	Morgan Avenue	B1	Thurlow Road
C3	Palk Street	A1	Tor Church Road
D4	Park Hill Road	B1	Tor Hill Road
D1	Pennsylvania Road	A4	Torbay Road
C2	Pimlico	D3	Torwood Street
C1	Potters Hill	B1	Trematon Avenue
C1	Princes Road	B1	Union Street
D1	Princes Road East	D3	Upper Braddons Hill
D1	Princes Road West		Road
C2	Queen Street	D4	Vane Hill Road
A3	Rathmore Road	A1	Vansittart Road
C3	Rock Road	D3	Vaughan Parade
D1	Rosehill Close	D4	Victoria Parade
D1	Rosehill Road	C1	Victoria Road
A1	Rowdens Road	A1	Vine Road
B1	St Efride's Road	A2	Walnut Road
B2	St Lukes Road	C1	Warberry Road West
C2	St Lukes Road North	C2	Warren Hill
C2	St Lukes Road South	C2	Warren Road
C1	St Marychurch Road	C1	Wellesley Road
B2	Scarborough Road	C1	Wellington Road
A4	Seaway Lane	D2	Woodside Drive
B2	Sheddon Hill		
D3	South Hill Road		
A1	South Street		
C2	Stentiford Hill Road		
D3	Strand		
C2	Temperance Street		
A3	The Kings Drive		
D3	The Terrace		

Tunbridge Wells

TONBRIDGE, LONDON
KENT & SUSSEX HOSPITAL
ROYAL VICTORIA PLACE SHOPPING CENTRE
CAMDEN CENTRE
ST JAMES
SANDROCK RD
SCHOOL
TUNBRIDGE WELLS GATEWAY
ST JAMES MEDICAL CENTRE
TUNBRIDGE WELLS MUSEUM & ART GALLERY
LIBRARY
TRINITY THEATRE & ARTS CENTRE
TOWN HALL
POLICE STA
CALVERLEY COURT
EAST GRINSTEAD
CHURCH ROAD
HOMEOPATHIC HOSPITAL
CRESCENT
ASSEMBLY HALL THEATRE
SALVATION ARMY
PEMBURY
TUNBRIDGE WELLS STATION
DSS
COUNTY COURT
BANDSTAND
Calverley Grounds
Tennis Courts
GT HALL ARCADE
FIRE STATION
Tunbridge Wells
200 metres
CHRIST CHURCH CENTRE
The Grove
GROVE BOWLS CLUB
SCHOOL
The Common
KING CHARLES THE MARTYR CHURCH HALL
Playing Field
LEWES
EASTBOURNE
THE PANTILES SHOPPING ARCADE
MAJOR YORK'S RD
Playing Field
LBH

C4 Arundel Road	B4 Cumberland Yard	A2 Mount Ephraim	A4 The Pantiles
D4 Banner Farm Road	C1 Dale Street	B1 Mount Ephraim Road	B3 Vale Avenue
D2 Bayhall Road	B1 Dudley Road	B2 Mount Pleasant Road	B3 Vale Road
B1 Belgrave Road	C4 Farmcombe Road	B4 Mount Sion	C1 Victoria Road
B4 Berkeley Road	B4 Frog Lane	C3 Mountfield Gardens	B4 Warwick Road
A1 Boyne Park	C1 Garden Road	C3 Mountfield Road	B2 York Road
C4 Buckingham Road	C1 Garden Street	A4 Nevill Street	
C2 Calverley Park	B1 Goods Station Road	B1 Newton Road	
D2 Calverley Park Gardens	C4 Grecian Road	C4 Norfolk Road	
B1 Calverley Road	B1 Grosvenor Road	D2 North Street	
C1 Calverley Street	B3 Grove Avenue	D3 Oakfield Court Road	
D3 Cambridge Street	C3 Grove Hill Gardens	D3 Park Street	
D3 Camden Gardens	C3 Grove Hill Road	D2 Pembury Road	
D3 Camden Hill	C1 Grover Street	C4 Poona Road	
D4 Camden Park	C3 Guildford Road	D3 Princes Street	
C1 Camden Road	B1 Hanover Road	D3 Prospect Road	
D2 Carlton Crescent	B4 High Street	B1 Rock Villa Road	
D1 Carlton Road	C1 Lansdowne Road	B4 Rodmell Road	
A4 Castle Road	C2 Lansdowne Square	B2 Rosehill Walk	
B3 Castle Street	B1 Lime Hill Road	A1 Royal Chase	
B4 Chapel Place	B4 Little Mount Sion	D1 St James's Road	
A2 Church Road	A2 London Road	D1 Sandrock Road	
B2 Clanricarde Gardens	B2 Lonsdale Gardens	A1 Somerville Gardens	
B2 Clanricarde Road	B4 Madeira Park	B3 South Grove	
C4 Claremont Gardens	A4 Major York's Road	B4 Spencer Mews	
B4 Claremont Road	C3 Meadow Hill Road	B3 Station Approach	
B2 Clarence Road	B1 Meadow Road	D1 Stone Street	
C2 Crescent Road	A2 Molyneux Park Road	B3 Sutherland Road	
B1 Culverden Street	B2 Monson Road	D1 The Ferns	
B4 Cumberland Gardens	A3 Mount Edgcumbe Road	A4 The Pantiles Lower Walk	

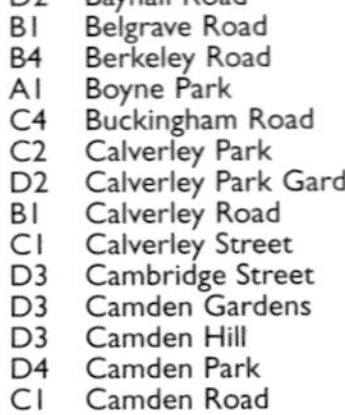

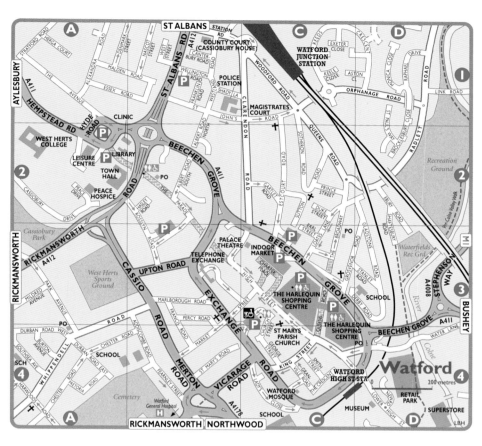

B4	Addiscombe Road	C4	George Street	C3	Queens Road	A4	Whippendell Road
B2	Albert Road North	D3	Gladstone Road	C2	Queens Road	C1	Woodford Road
B2	Albert Road South	C4	Granville Road	D2	Radlett Road		
A1	Alexandra Road	C3	Grosvenor Road	D1	Raphael Drive		
D1	Aston Close	A4	Harwoods Road	C1	Reeds Crescent		
C3	Beechen Grove	B2	Hasley Road	A3	Rickmansworth Road		
D2	Brocklesbury Close	A1	Hempstead Road	B2	Rosslyn Road		
A4	Burton Avenue	A1	Herga Court	B1	St Albans Road		
B1	Canterbury Road	C3	High Street	B1	St John's Road		
B3	Cassio Road	A2	Hyde Road	B4	St Mary's Road		
A2	Cassiobury Drive	C1	Keele Close	D1	St Paul's Way		
C3	Charter Place	C4	King Street	B1	Shady Lane		
A4	Chester Road	C4	Lady's Close	D2	Shaftesbury Road		
C4	Church Street	D1	Link Road	C4	Smith Street		
C1	Clarendon Road	C3	Loates Lane	C2	Sotheron Road		
A1	Denmark Street	D4	Lower High Street	A4	Southsea Avenue		
D3	Derby Road	A1	Malden Road	D3	Stanley Road		
C2	Duke Street	B4	Market Street	B1	Station Road		
A4	Durban Road East	B3	Marlborough Road	A1	Stratford Road		
A4	Durban Road West	B4	Merton Road	C2	Sutton Road		
C3	Earl Street	A3	Mildred Avenue	A1	The Avenue		
D2	Ebury Road	D1	Monica Close	C3	The Broadway		
A1	Essex Road	B1	Nascot Street	C4	The Crescent		
C2	Estcourt Road	D4	New Road	B2	The Parade		
B3	Exchange Road	C1	Orphanage Road	B3	Upton Road		
C1	Exeter Close	A3	Park Avenue	B4	Vicarage Road		
B4	Fearnley Street	A2	Peace Drive	D4	Water Lane		
B3	Francis Road	B3	Percy Road	B1	Wellington Road		
B1	Franklin Road	A4	Pretoria Road	B1	West Street		
C2	Gartlet Road	C2	Prince Street	B1	Westland Road		

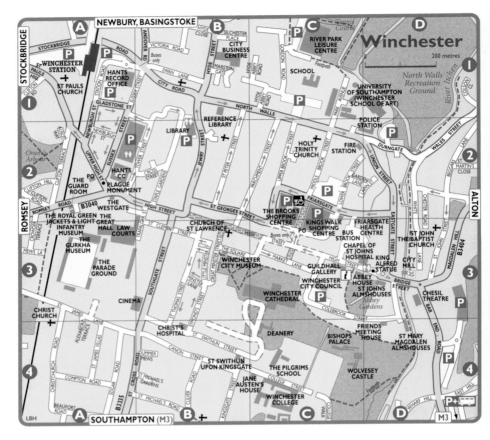

A4	Alexandra Terrace	A1	Gladstone Street	B4	St Michael's Gardens
A2	Alison Way	C1	Gordon Road	B4	St Michael's Road
B1	Andover Road	B3	Great Minster Street	A1	St Pauls Hill
D3	Bar End Road	B2	High Street	B2	St Peter Street
A4	Beaufort Road	C1	Hyde Abbey Road	B4	St Swithun Street
D2	Beggars Lane	B1	Hyde Close	B3	St Thomas Street
D3	Bridge Street	B1	Hyde Street	B3	Southgate Street
B4	Canon Street	B2	Jewry Street	B2	Staple Gardens
D2	Chester Road	B4	Kingsgate Street	A1	Station Road
A4	Christchurch Road	D2	Lawn Street	A1	Stockbridge Road
B1	City Road	B3	Little Minster Street	A2	Sussex Street
A2	Clifton Hill	C2	Lower Brook Street	B1	Swan Lane
A2	Clifton Road	D3	Magdalen Hill	B3	Symond's Street
A1	Clifton Road	C3	Market Lane	B3	The Square
A2	Clifton Terrace	B1	Marston Gate	B2	Tower Street
C3	Colebrook Street	A3	Mews Lane	B3	Trafalgar Street
C4	College Street	C2	Middle Brook Street	D2	Union Street
C4	College Walk	B3	Minster Lane	C2	Upper Brook Street
D1	Colson Close	A2	Newburgh Street	A2	Upper High Street
A4	Compton Road	B1	North Walls	B1	Victoria Road
B2	Cross Street	C2	Parchment Street	D2	Wales Street
A3	Crowder Terrace	C1	Park Avenue	D4	Wharf Hill
B4	Culver Road	A2	Romsey Road	D2	White Lane
B4	Dummer Mews	B3	St Clement Street		
D2	Durngate	A4	St Cross Road		
D4	East Hill	B2	St Georges Street		
D3	Eastgate Street	A3	St James Lane		
A4	Edgar Road	A4	St James Villas		
C2	Friarsgate	D3	St John Street		
C2	Garden Lane	D2	St Martin's Close		

Wolverhampton

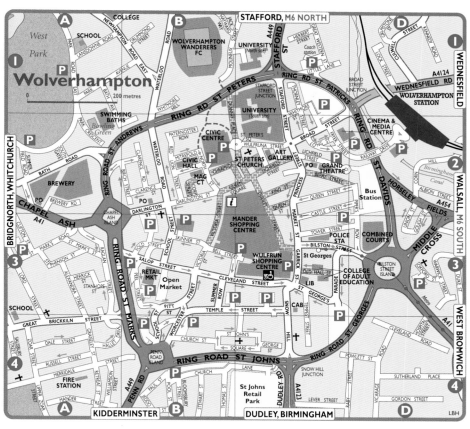

D2	Albion Street
A3	Alexandra Street
A1	Bath Avenue
A2	Bath Road
B3	Bell Street
C2	Berry Street
C3	Bilston Street
B2	Birch Street
B4	Bloomsbury Street
C2	Broad Street
C2	Castle Street
A2	Chapel Ash
B2	Cheapside
B4	Church Lane
B4	Church Street
B2	Clarence Road
B2	Clarence Street
D4	Cleveland Road
B3	Cleveland Street
A3	Clifton Street
D2	Corn Hill
B2	Corporation Street
D1	Culwell Street
A4	Dale Street
B2	Darlington Street
B1	Drummond Street
C4	Dudley Road
C2	Dudley Street
D3	Duke Street
B3	Fold Street
C2	Fryer Street
C3	Garrick Street
C4	George Street
D4	Gordon Street
D3	Gough Street
A4	Graiseley Street

A4	Great Brickkiln Street
C1	Great Western Street
D1	Grimstone Way
A4	Hallet Drive
C1	Herbert Street
A3	Herrick Street
D2	Horseley Fields
D4	Hospital Street
B4	Jeddo Street
D1	Kennedy Road
C2	King Street
A1	Lansdowne Road
C4	Lever Street
C2	Lichfield Street
C1	Littles Lane
D1	Lock Street
C2	Long Street
A3	Lord Street
A4	Mander Street
C4	Market Street
C4	Melbourne Street
A4	Merridale Street
D3	Middle Cross
B2	Mitrefold
B1	Molineux Street
B1	Molineux Way
A1	New Hampton East
B2	North Street
C3	Old Hall Street
D3	Oxford Street
A1	Park Avenue
A2	Park Crescent
A1	Park Road East
B2	Paternoster Row
B4	Paul Street
B3	Peel Street

B4	Penn Road
D2	Piper's Row
B3	Pitt Street
B4	Pool Street
D4	Powlett Street
C2	Princess Street
C2	Queen Square
C2	Queen Street
C4	Raby Street
A3	Raglan Street
D2	Railway Drive
B2	Red Lion Street
A4	Retreat Street
A2	Ring Road St Andrews
D2	Ring Road St Davids
C4	Ring Road St Georges
B4	Ring Road St Johns
A3	Ring Road St Marks
C1	Ring Road St Patricks
B1	Ring Road St Peters
C3	Russell Street
C3	St George's Parade
D3	St James Street
C4	St John's Square
A3	St Mark's Road
A3	St Mark's Street
B1	St Peter's Square
A4	Salisbury Street
B3	Salop Street
B4	School Street
B3	Skinner Street
C3	Snow Hill
C1	Stafford Street
A3	Stanhope Street
A3	Stephenson Street
B4	Stewart Street

A2	Summer Field Road
B3	Summer Row
D4	Sutherland Place
C3	Tempest Street
B3	Temple Street
B4	Thomas Street
C1	Thornley Street
C3	Tower Street
D3	Union Street
A4	Upper Zoar Street
D4	Vicarage Road
B3	Victoria Street
D3	Warwick Street
B1	Waterloo Road
D1	Wednesfield Road
B1	Whitmore Hill
C1	Whitmore Street
A4	Williamson Street
B4	Worcester Street
A4	Wulfruna Street
A4	Zoar Street

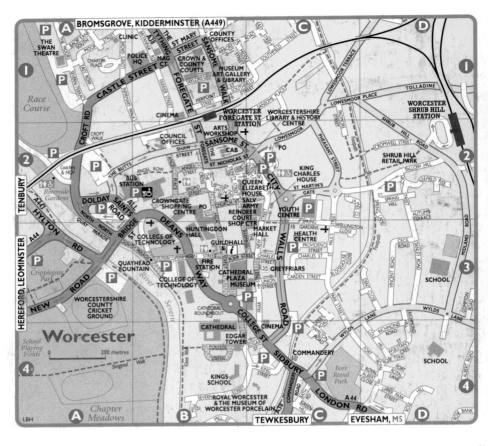

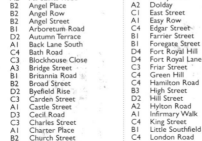

D4	Albert Road	D3	Dent Close	A3	North Parade	A3	South Parade
A2	All Saints Road	C4	Derby Road	A2	North Quay	C1	Southfield Street
B2	Angel Place	A2	Dolday	C1	Padmore Street	C3	Spring Gardens
B2	Angel Row	C1	East Street	C3	Park Street	D2	Spring Hill
B2	Angel Street	A1	Easy Row	C2	Pheasant Street	D2	Spring Lane
B1	Arboretum Road	C4	Edgar Street	B1	Pierpoint Street	D3	Stanley Road
D2	Autumn Terrace	B1	Farrier Street	C3	Providence Street	D2	Tallow Hill
A1	Back Lane South	B1	Foregate Street	B3	Pump Street	B1	Taylors Lane
C4	Bath Road	D4	Fort Royal Hill	C2	Queen Street	A2	The Butts
C3	Blockhouse Close	D4	Fort Royal Lane	D4	Richmond Hill	B2	The Cross
A3	Bridge Street	C3	Friar Street	D4	Richmond Road	B2	The Foregate
B1	Britannia Road	C4	Green Hill	D4	Rose Bank	A1	The Moors
B2	Broad Street	C4	Hamilton Road	D4	Rose Hill	C3	The Shambles
D2	Byefield Rise	B3	High Street	D4	Rose Terrace	B1	The Tything
C3	Carden Street	D2	Hill Street	D4	Royal Albert Close	D1	Tolladine
A1	Castle Street	A2	Hylton Road	C2	St James Close	B2	Trinity Street
D3	Cecil Road	A1	Infirmary Walk	C2	St Martin's Gate	C3	Union Street
C3	Charles Street	C4	King Street	B1	St Mary Street	D4	Upper Park Street
A1	Charter Place	B1	Little Southfield Street	B2	St Nicholas Street	D3	Vincent Road
B2	Church Street	C4	London Road	C3	St Paul's Street	C3	Wellington Close
C2	City Walls Road	A1	Love's Grove	B2	St Swithuns Street	C4	Wylds Lane
D4	Cole Hill	C2	Lowesmoor	D4	St Wulstan's Crescent		
B4	College Green	C1	Lowesmoor Place	C1	Sansome Place		
B3	College Street	C1	Lowesmoor Terrace	B2	Sansome Street		
C4	Commandery Road	B1	Middle Street	B1	Sansome Walk		
D3	Compton Road	D3	Midland Road	B4	Severn Street		
B3	Copenhagen Street	B4	Mill Street	A1	Severn Terrace		
A2	Croft Road	A1	Moor Street	B2	Shaw Street		
D2	Cromwell Street	A3	New Road	D2	Shrub Hill Road		
B3	Deans Way	C3	New Street	C4	Sidbury		

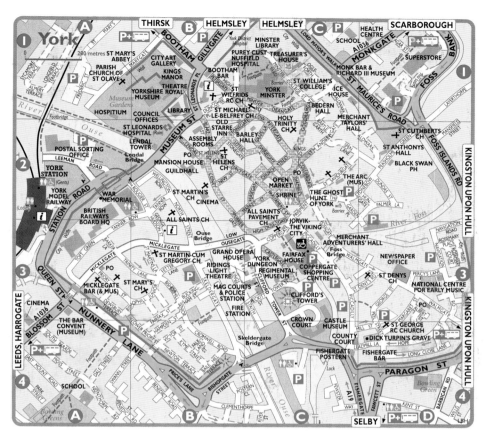

D1	Agar Street
D3	Albert Street
C1	Aldwark
A1	Almery Terrace
B4	Baile Hill Terrace
D4	Barbican Road
A3	Barker Lane
C2	Bartle Garth
B4	Bishopgate Street
A3	Bishophill Junior
B3	Bishophill Senior
B2	Blake Street
A4	Blossom Street
B1	Bootham
B1	Bootham Row
B3	Buckingham Street
C3	Castlegate
C2	Church Street
B4	Clementhorpe
C3	Clifford Street
C1	College Street
C2	Colliergate
B2	Coney Street
C3	Coppergate
B4	Cromwell Road
A4	Dale Street
B2	Davygate
C1	Deangate
A3	Dewsbury Terrace
B1	Duncombe Place
D2	Dundas Street
A4	East Mount Road
B3	Fairfax Street
B4	Falkland Street
D4	Fawcett Street
C2	Feasegate
B3	Fetter Lane
C4	Fewster Way
D4	Fishergate
D1	Foss Bank
D2	Foss Islands Road
C3	Fossgate
A1	Frederic Street
C2	Garden Place
D3	George Hudson Street
D3	George Street
B1	Gillygate
C2	Goodramgate
C2	Grape Lane
B4	Hampden Street
C3	High Ousegate
B1	High Petergate
D4	Hope Street
D2	Hungate
D4	Kent Street
C2	Kings Square
B3	Kings Staith
B4	Kyme Street
D1	Layerthorpe
D4	Leadmill Lane
A2	Leeman Road
B2	Lendal
B2	Little Stonegate
D4	Long Close Lane
A1	Longfield Terrace
C1	Lord Mayor's Walk
B3	Low Ousegate
C1	Low Petergate
B4	Lower Priory Street
D2	Mansfield Street
D2	Margaret Street
C2	Market Street
B1	Marygate
A3	Micklegate
D4	Mill Street
C1	Minster Yard
C1	Monkgate
A4	Moss Street
B2	Museum Street
C3	Navigation Road
B2	New Street
B4	Newton Terrace
B2	North Street
A3	Nunnery Lane
A4	Nunthorpe Road
C1	Ogleforth
D2	Palmer Lane
D4	Paragon Street
A4	Park Street
C2	Parliament Street
C2	Pavement
D2	Peasholme Green
C3	Peckitt Street
D3	Peel Street
D3	Percy's Lane
C3	Piccadilly
B4	Postern Close
B4	Price's Lane
A3	Priory Street
A3	Queen Street
C4	River Street
D3	Rosemary Court
D3	Rosemary Place
B2	Rougier Street
C2	St Andrewgate
A4	St Benedict Road
C3	St Denys Road
B2	St Helens Square
B1	St Leonards Place
B3	St Martins Lane
A1	St Mary's
C1	St Maurice's Road
C2	St Saviourgate
C2	Shambles
B3	Skeldergate
A4	South Parade
C2	Spen Lane
B2	Spurrier Gate
A3	Station Road
B2	Stonegate
A4	Swann Street
C2	Swinegate
A1	Sycamore Terrace
A3	Tanner Row
C2	The Stonebow
A3	Toft Green
C3	Tower Street
A3	Trinity Lane
B4	Victor Street
C3	Walmgate
B2	Wellington Row
D4	Willis Street

Major airports

London Heathrow Airport

16 miles west of London

Telephone: 0870 000 0123 or visit *www.heathrowairport.com*
Parking: short-stay, long-stay and business parking is available. For charge details tel: 0870 000 1000
Public Transport: coach, bus, rail and London Underground.

There are several 4-star and 3-star hotels within easy reach of the airport.
Car hire facilities are available.

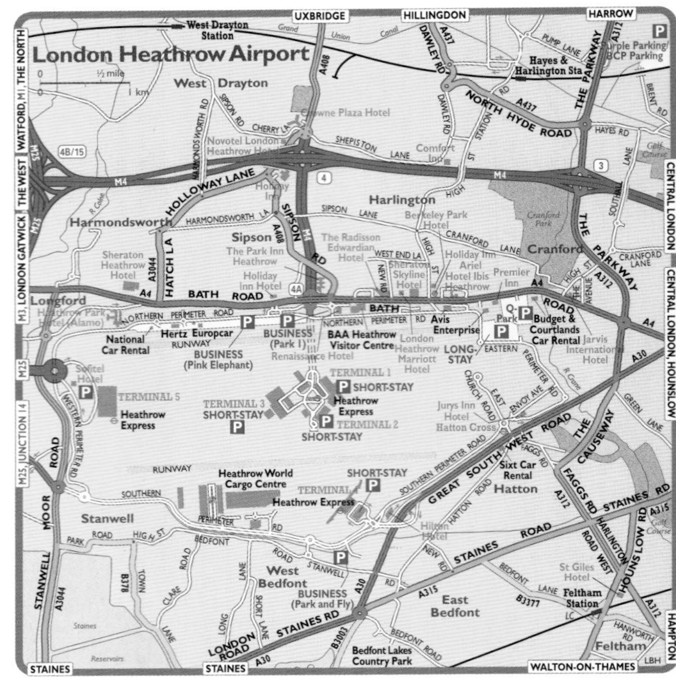

London Gatwick Airport

35 miles south of London

Telephone: 0870 000 2468 or visit *www.gatwickairport.com*
Parking: short and long-stay parking is available at both the North and South terminals. For charge details tel: 0870 000 1000
Public Transport: coach, bus and rail.
There are several 4-star and 3-star hotels within easy reach of the airport.
Car hire facilities are available.

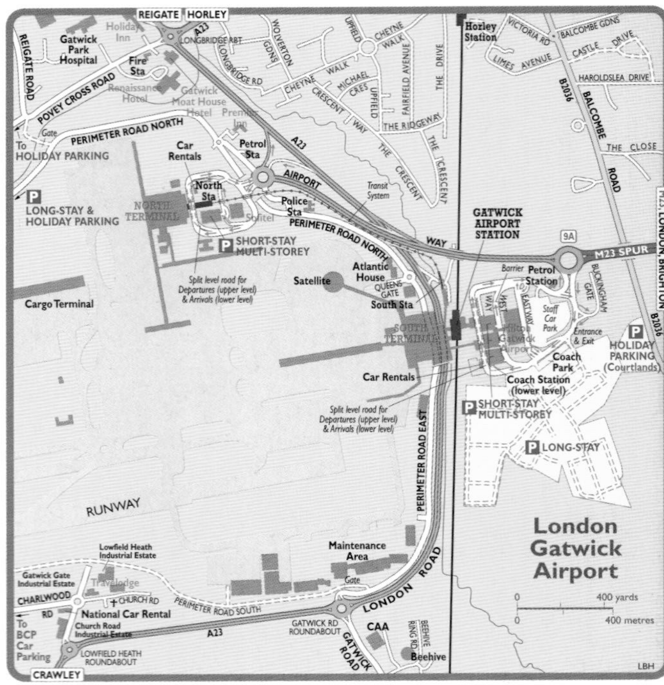

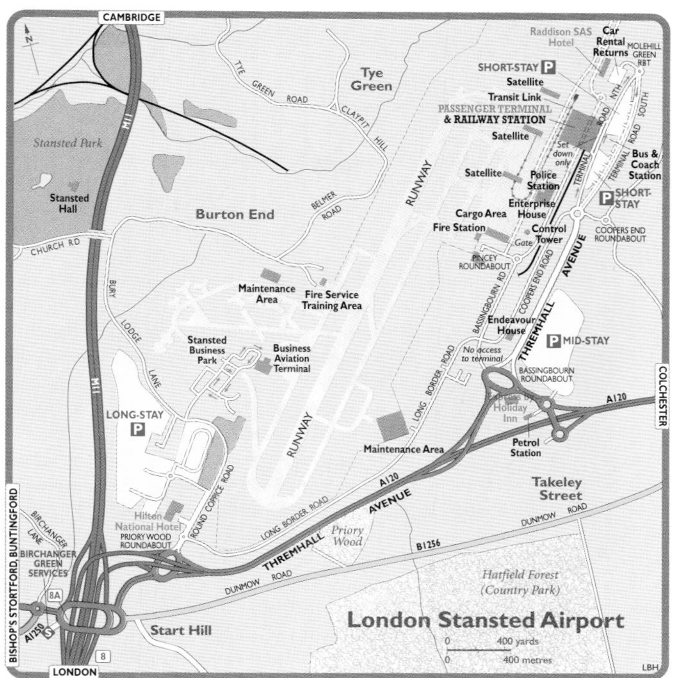

London Stansted Airport

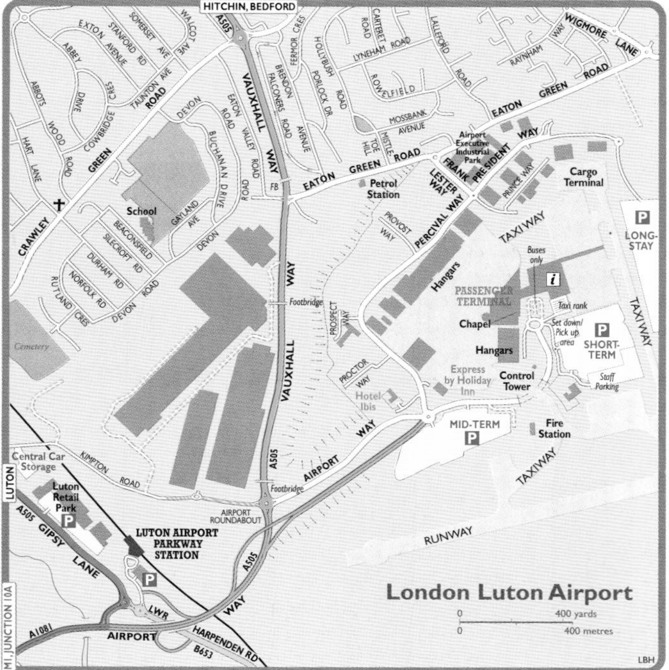

London Luton Airport

London Stansted Airport

36 miles north east of London

Telephone: 0870 000 0303 or visit *www.stanstedairport.com*
Parking: short, mid and long-stay open-air parking is available. For charge details tel: 0870 000 1000
Public Transport: coach, bus and direct rail link to London on the Stansted Express.
There are several hotels within easy reach of the airport.
Car hire facilities are available.

London Luton Airport

33 miles north of London

Telephone: 01582 405100 or visit *www.london-luton.co.uk*
Parking: short-term, mid-term and long-stay parking is available.
For charge details tel: 01582 395 484
Public Transport: coach, bus and rail.
There are several hotels within easy reach of the airport.
Car hire facilities are available.

Major airports

London City Airport

7 miles east of London

Telephone: 020 7646 0088 or visit *www.londoncityairport.com*
Parking: short and long-stay open-air parking is available. For charge details tel: 020 7646 0088
Public Transport: easy access to the rail network, Docklands Light Railway and the London Underground.
There are 5-star, 4-star and 3-star hotels within easy reach of the airport.
Car hire facilities are available.

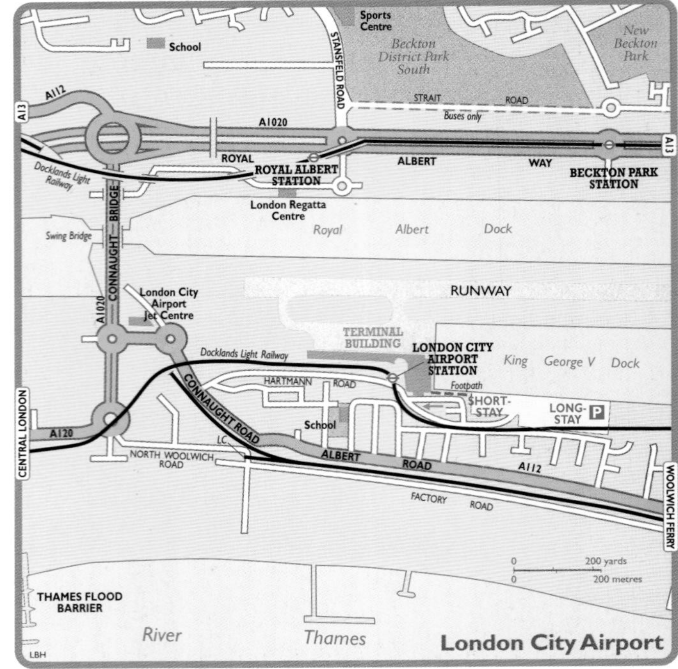

London City Airport

Birmingham International Airport

8 miles east of Birmingham

Telephone: 0844 576 6000 or visit *www.bhx.co.uk*
Parking: short and long-stay parking is available. For charge details tel: 0844 576 6000
Public Transport: Air-Rail Link service operates every 2 minutes to and from Birmingham International Railway Station & Interchange.
There is one 3-star hotel adjacent to the airport and several 4-star and 3-star hotels within easy reach of the airport.
Car hire facilities are available.

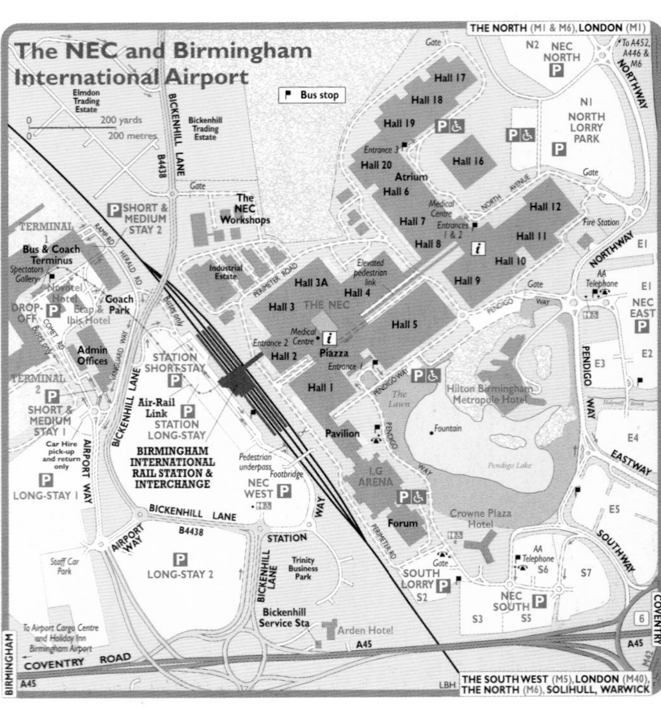

The NEC and Birmingham International Airport

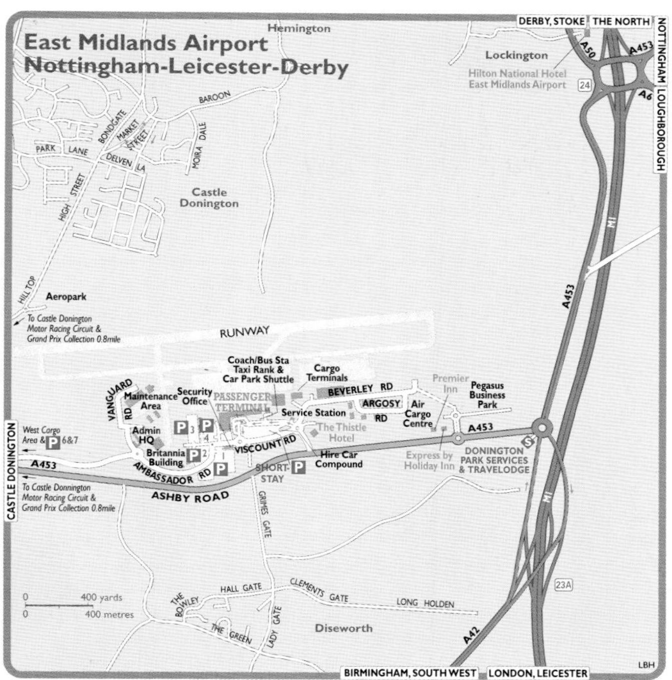

East Midlands Airport

15 miles south west of Nottingham, next to the M1 at junctions 23A and 24

Telephone: 0871 919 9000 or visit

www.eastmidlandsairport.com

Parking: short and long-stay parking is available. For charge details tel: 0871 310 3300

Public Transport: bus and coach services to major towns and cities in the East Midlands. Call 0870 608 2608 for information.

There are several 3-star hotels within easy reach of the airport. Car hire facilities are available.

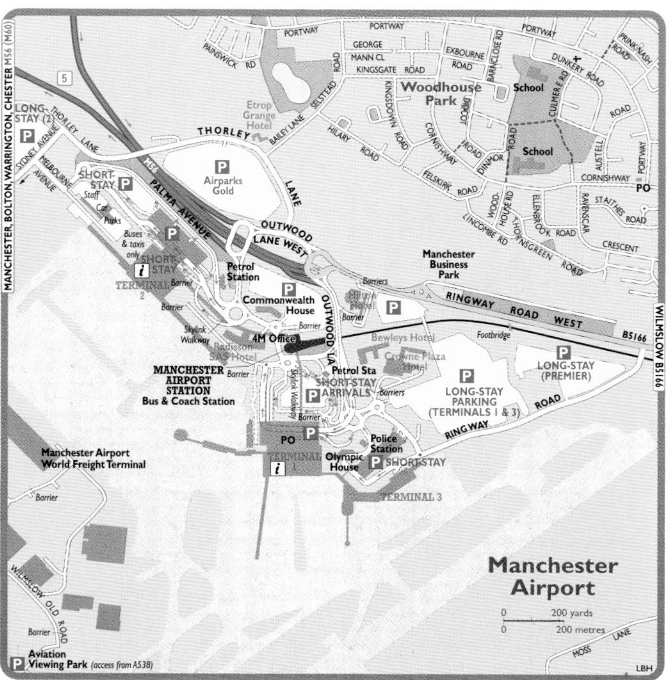

Manchester Airport

10 miles south of Manchester

Telephone: 0871 2710 711 or visit

www.manchesterairport.co.uk

Parking: short and long-stay parking is available. For charge details tel: 0871 310 2200

Public Transport: bus, coach and rail.

There are several 4-star and 3-star hotels within easy reach of the airport. Car hire facilities are available.

Major airports

Leeds Bradford International Airport

7 miles north east of Bradford and 9 miles north west of Leeds

Telephone: 0113 250 9696 or visit *www.leedsbradfordairport.co.uk*
Parking: short and long-stay parking is available. For charge details
tel: 0113 250 9696
Public Transport: bus service operates every 30 minutes from Bradford, Leeds and Otley. There are several 4-star and 3-star hotels within easy reach of the airport.
Car hire facilities are available.

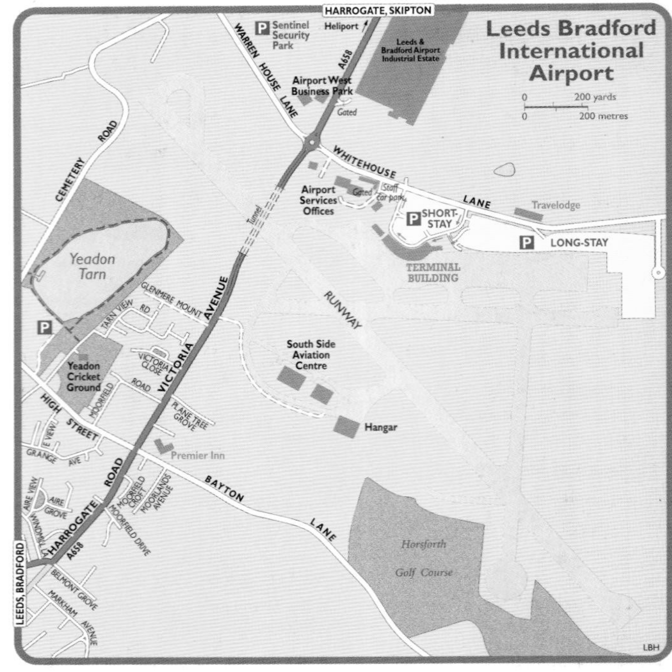

Aberdeen Airport

7 miles north west of Aberdeen

Telephone: 0870 040 0006 or visit *www.aberdeenairport.com*
Parking: short and long-stay parking is available.
For charge details
tel: 0870 000 1000
Public Transport: regular bus service to central Aberdeen. There are several 4-star and 3-star hotels within easy reach of the airport.
Car hire facilities are available.

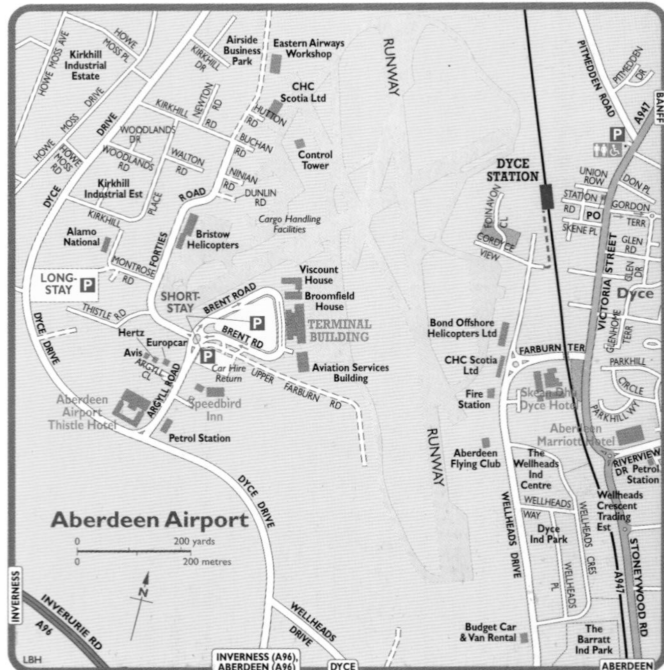

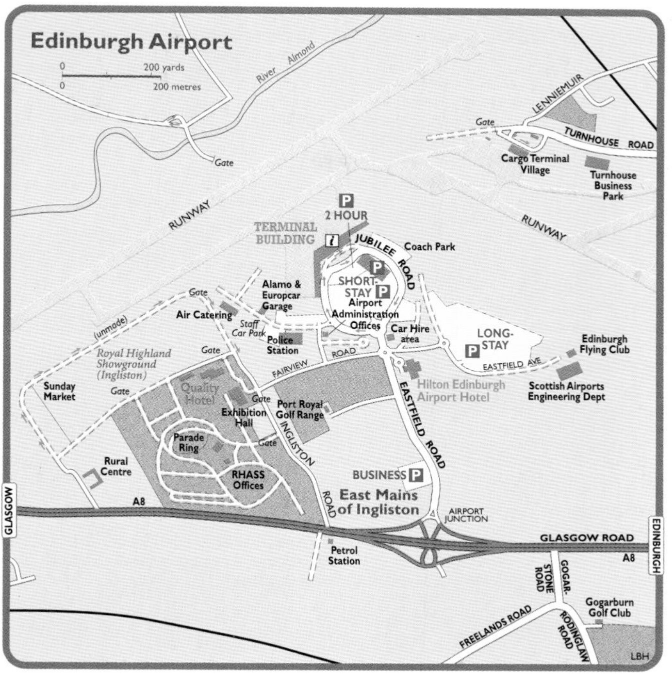

Edinburgh Airport
7 miles west of Edinburgh

Telephone: 0870 040 0007 or visit *www.edinburghairport.com*
Parking: short and long-stay parking is available.
For charge details
tel: 0870 000 1000
Public Transport: regular bus services to central Edinburgh. There are several 4-star and 3-star hotels within easy reach of the airport.
Car hire facilities are available.

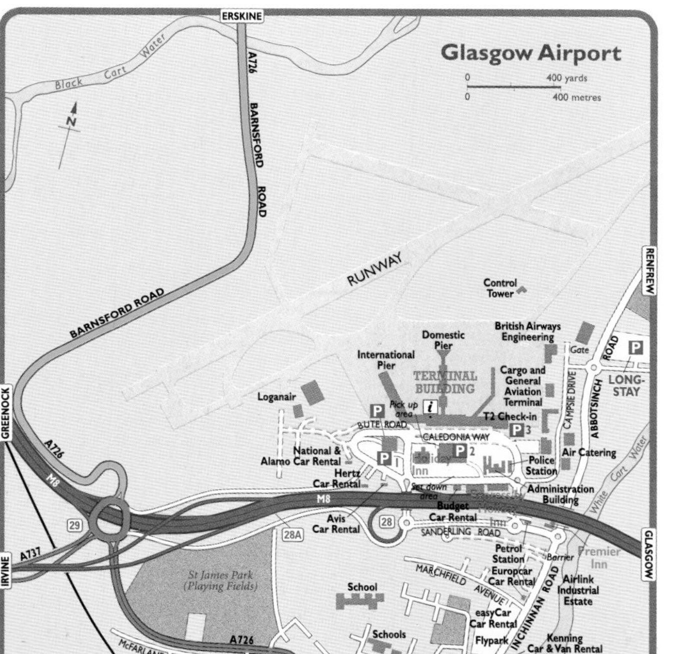

Glasgow Airport
8 miles west of Glasgow

Telephone: 0870 040 0008 or visit *www.glasgowairport.com*
Parking: short and long-stay parking is available.
For charge details
tel: 0870 000 1000
Public Transport: regular coach services operate direct to central Glasgow and Edinburgh. There are several 3-star hotels within easy reach of the airport.
Car hire facilities are available.

Folkestone Terminal

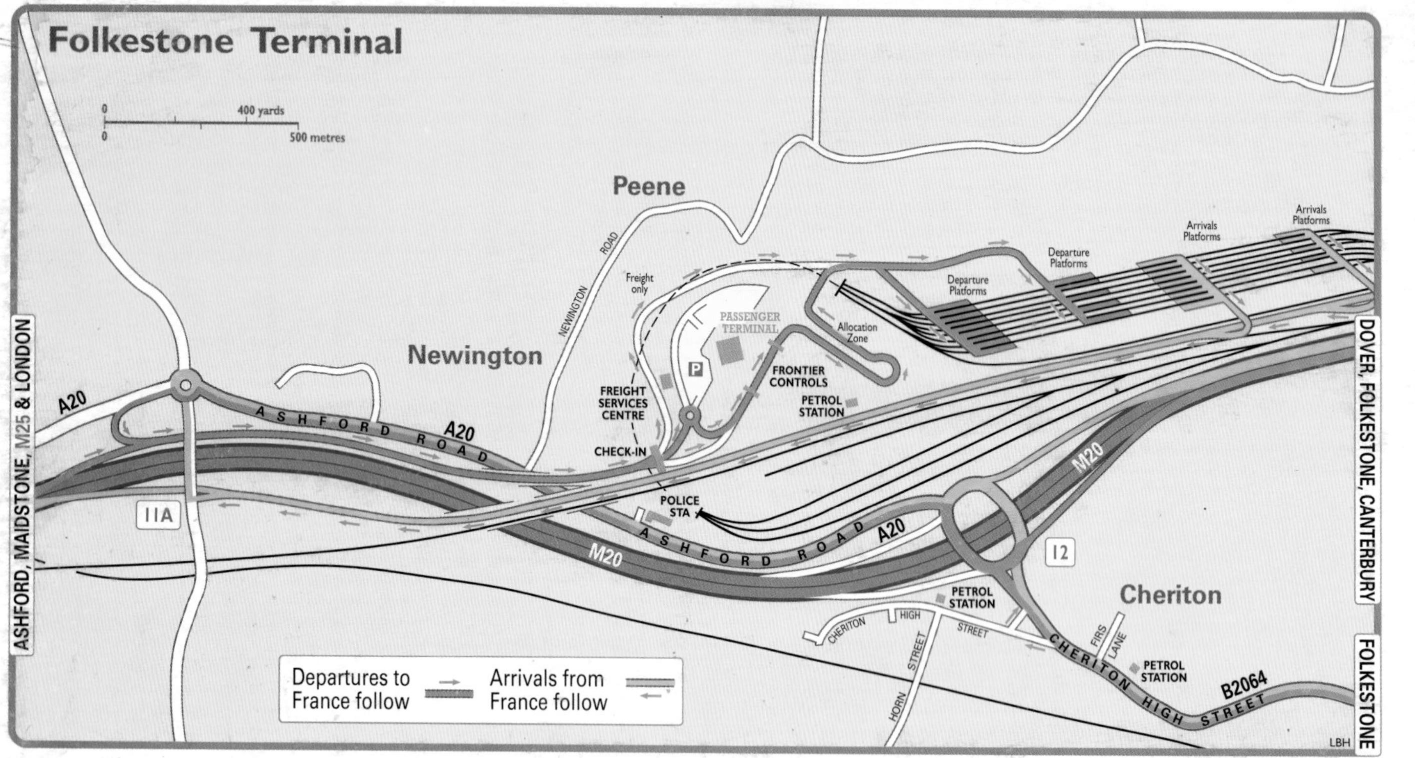

DOVER, FOLKESTONE, CANTERBURY

FOLKESTONE

Cheriton

B2064

CHERITON HIGH STREET

PETROL STATION

FIRS LANE

I2

M20

PETROL STATION

HIGH STREET

HORN STREET

CHERITON

Arrivals Platforms

Arrivals Platforms

Departure Platforms

Departure Platforms

Allocation Zone

FRONTIER CONTROLS

PETROL STATION

ASHFORD ROAD A20

M20

PASSENGER TERMINAL

P

Peene

Freight only

FREIGHT SERVICES CENTRE

CHECK-IN

POLICE STA

NEWINGTON ROAD

Newington

A20

ASHFORD ROAD

A20

ASHFORD ROAD

M20

11A

500 metres

400 yards

Departures to France follow

Arrivals from France follow

ASHFORD, MAIDSTONE, M25 & LONDON

LBH